HOTELS
IN EUROPE

RAC
Publishing

Published by RAC Publishing, RAC House,
PO Box 100, South Croydon CR2 6XW.
© RAC Enterprises Ltd 1993

ISBN 0 86211-256 7

A CIP catalogue record for this book is available from the British Library.

Compilation:	Lawrie Hammond, Millrace Books
Design:	Douglas Whitworth
Editorial:	Steve Parker; Aardvark Editorial; Zibba George
Cartography:	RAC Publishing.
Cover Design:	Chuck Goodwin
Cover Picture:	Hotel Aigua Blava, Bagur, Spain
Advertisement Managers:	Mongoose Communications Ltd
	55 Greek Street
	London W1V 5LR
	Tel: 071 306 0300
Printed and bound in Spain by:	Grafo SA, Bilbao

CONTENTS

UP POPS
ANOTHER BRIGHT IDEA
FROM CANON.

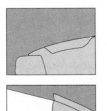

Once you see it, it becomes glaringly obvious.

Now you can carry your lighting with you, without spoiling your good looks.

Because the Canon E300 is the world's first camcorder with a built-in pop-up light.

Like the world's most streamlined cars the light is there when you need it and retracts out of sight when you don't.

You'll find the 10x Zoom is equally refined, offering a choice of two zoom speeds with a shutter boasting exposures as fast as 1/10,000th a second.

Other bright ideas include multi-program AE, (for optimum exposure settings), full Wireless Remote Control, Sports Finder, Flexi-Grip for easy handling from any angle and Age Insert.

What a brilliant idea.

WE TAKE THE MOST MOVING PICTURES

For further details on these cameras phone 0800 616417

INTRODUCTION

Welcome to *RAC Hotels in Europe*, fully revised for 1994. We have details of more than 1,200 hotels across the continent, from Norway to Greece, Portugal to Turkey. They range from huge, luxury hotels offering every facility you can imagine, to small, informal, family-run establishments.

RAC Hotels in Europe is one of the few truly pan-European guides available. We endeavour to include the widest selection of hotels, to cover most tastes and budgets. But as you read through the directory pages, wondering which establishment to choose, you may wonder: "So what's new?". The answer is: Plenty. For the situation has changed dramatically in recent years.

With new rules (or lack of them) governing passports and visas, and the growing influence of the European Community, it has never been easier to pass from one European nation to another. Travel is also becoming quicker and simpler. There are new motorway systems, a wide choice of ferry services, the EuroTunnel under the Channel, and a selection of motorail and fly-drive packages.

Map locations

These refer to the series of maps near the end of the book. The hotel may not be in the town itself, but nearby. Refer to the hotel entry in the hotel directory for the full address and precise location.

Value for money?

These changes have had a number of effects on European hotels. One is the hotel client's ever-widening appreciation of value for money. As people travel farther, and more often, they experience the costs of accommodation in a broader selection of countries. People also compare notes with their friends and colleagues, who have been to other countries. As a result, the "word" gets around. More people are knowledgeable about the places which offer good value – whatever the price band.

5D	map location	m	metres (1 m is 39 in, about 1 yard)
★	star rating of country	TARIFF	guide prices in local currency for a typical single or double room, usually with en suite facilities
☎	telephone number		
♿	some facilities for disabled people	Bk	breakfast
km	kilometres (1 km is 0.62 miles)	CC	credit cards

Such increasingly international discrimination can only work towards widening the competitive field, and improving the lot of hotel customers.

The "EuroHotel"

A second aspect of the recent changes is that some hoteliers, especially those running large groups of establishments, have tended to standardise their perceptions of what customers want. As a result, we have seen the rise of the "EuroHotel". It has the same facilities, decor, furnishings and menus – whether it is in Sweden or Italy.

This may not suit some travellers. But it is ideal for people who like to be sure of what they will find, when they arrive in a strange place for the first time. The standardised approach is also suitable for those who like the comfort and confidence of familiar surroundings, where they know their way around.

Maintaining diversity

Other hoteliers are realising that certain types of travellers do not want the familiar and well-known. They wish to sample something new and different – the traditions, culture, food, drink and ambience of the region. To cater for such wishes, these hoteliers are retaining the distinctive regional character of their hotels from the decor to the cuisine.

At the same time, both sets of hoteliers are maintaining and improving the "nuts and bolts" of hotel-keeping, such as standards of hygiene, price displays, and safety precautions. Many of these basic features are controlled by Euro-wide regulations.

How the guide is organised

The whole directory is arranged on the A-Z basis. Countries are arranged in alphabetical order, according to the Contents list on page 3. The country is indicated by the coloured band and title letter in the margin of each page.

Within each country, the hotels are grouped under the name of their city, town, resort or nearest centre. These names are posted at the top of each page as a handy guide when flicking through the pages. If there are several hotels in one town, the hotels are listed in alphabetical order (ignoring the word "Hotel"). Should you have trouble locating a particular town, consult the index at the back of the book.

Notes on the hotel entries

The main abbreviations used in the hotel entries are explained on page 5. In addition, please note these points.

When you telephone, do not forget to add the international code. You may have to omit the first 0 or 9 when dialling from the UK. Many hotels now have fax numbers. Enquiring or booking by fax has certain advantages. It helps to overcome translation problems and provides a written record of what has been agreed. If you write to the hotel, use the full postal address and code, as shown in the entry. "English spoken" usually means that the staff speak enough English to understand basic requests, such as booking a room, or being asked for the bill.

Opening times may vary at short notice, especially if there are local religious or other events, or during the low season. Where facilities for disabled people are indicated, this is in the opinion of the hotel management. Hotels with noted restaurants are classified as "good", "very good" or "excellent". However many other hotels offer good-value meals. We especially welcome comments on menus and the quality of cuisine (see below).

Guide prices

Prices are in the local currency, unless stated. They are the hotel management's predicted mid-season prices for 1994, again unless stated. So they may vary according to the time of year, and local taxes may be due. The prices are given for a single or double room, usually including en suite facilities, but not food. Separate sample prices are provided for a range of set menus, and for breakfast (Bk). (Unlike hotels in the UK, many continental hotels do not include breakfast in the room price.)

Currency exchange rates fluctuate daily, so check in newspapers or at banks. Credit cards indicated are: Amex (American Express), Diners (Diners Club), Euro/Access (Eurocard/Access), Visa (Visa/Barclaycard).

We hope that you find the information easy to use and helpful. Remember that details may change through the year, so it is always wise to check ahead by telephone, to confirm facilities and prices. If you have comments on a hotel, or on the guide generally, write to the address on the hotel report page after the maps. Please also let us know about your travel and holiday experiences, with a view to sharing them with other readers in next year's edition. And above all – have a great time!

Star ratings

The star rating for each hotel is derived from the national star-rating system of its country. This is generally organised by the country's own tourist board, and you can usually rely on the number of stars as an indicator of quality. However there may not be a direct comparison between star ratings in different countries. Also, some private châteaux do not subscribe to any star scheme.

If you like St. Michael

sing our praises to your friends

FREE SHOPPING AT MARKS & SPENCER EVERY TIME YOU INTRODUCE A FRIEND

"Quality, value & service." It's the hallmark of Marks & Spencer. It's also what we stand for here at the RAC. As an RAC Member you can get even more for your money because every time you introduce a friend to the RAC you'll both receive a Marks & Spencer Voucher worth up to £10.

THE REWARDS ARE UNLIMITED

The more friends you introduce, the more you get to spend at Marks & Spencer. You can build up your Vouchers to obtain a substantial item such as a new suit, or you could even put it towards the cost of your weekly shopping excursion to the food hall.

HOW TO CLAIM YOUR VOUCHERS

Just pass the telephone number and code below on to a friend who you feel might be interested in RAC membership. If they choose New Rescue or New Recovery, you'll each receive a £5 Voucher, and if they opt for Reflex or Reflex Europe, we'll send you both a Voucher worth £10.

What's more, your friend gets up to £25 off the RAC membership fee if they pay by a continuous payment method.

PHONE
0800
550
550
AND QUOTE
M K 0 0 5 2
H W 0 3 0 3
N A 0 0 0 1

ANDORRA

One of Europe's smallest independent states, Andorra is a tiny principality in the eastern Pyrénées. It is set into the border between France and Spain, and so is surrounded by both. The land area is 453 sq km, only 0.2 per cent that of the UK. The population is about 45,000, with some 60 per cent being of Spanish origin, and only 5 per cent of French origin. The official language is Catalan.

Andorra's landscape is a contrast of deep valleys and high, rocky peaks. There is no airport. The single major highway runs from Spain in the south-east to France in the north-west. It is designated the N145 in Spain, becoming the N1 to the capital Andorra-la-Vella, then the N2 to the mountainous eastern border, and the N22/N20 in France, heading north towards Toulouse. Only a fraction of Andorra's land is arable. There are fields of cereals and potatoes in the sheltered lower valleys, a few vineyards and odd tiny corners growing tobacco. Sheep graze on the higher pastures in summer and share them with small groups of wild horses.

Andorra's main businesses are connected with tourism, especially the excellent skiing in winter, also fishing, hunting, mountain-climbing, hill-walking, and the mineral spa baths. Photographers and artists are drawn by the spectacular mountain scenery, with peaks rising to almost 3,000 metres. In addition, bargain-hunters are drawn by low prices. Andorra is a duty-free zone, with attractive prices on many taxable goods, and both French and Spanish currencies are legal tender.

ANDORRA LA VELLA   9D

Hotel Altea Panorama ★★★★ Ctra de l'Obac, Andorra la Vella.
☎ 61861, Fax 61742. English spoken.
Open all year. 177 bedrooms (all en suite with telephone). Indoor swimming pool, garage, parking, restaurant. &

Large modern hotel on hillside. Ideal conference centre. Integral health/spa club.

TARIFF: Single 6,700–10,000,
Double 7,000–12,000, Bk 1,200,
Set menu 2,500.
CC: Amex, Diners, Euro/Access, Visa.

Hotel Cassany ★★★ 28 Avda
Meritxell, Andorra la Vella.
☎ 20636, Fax 63609. English spoken.
Open all year. 54 bedrooms (all en suite with telephone). &

Situated in the commercial centre of town.

TARIFF: Single 5,850–6,500,
Double 6,800–8,000, Bk .
CC: Euro/Access, Visa.

Hotel Xalet Sasplugas ★★★ La Creu Grossa
15, Andorra la Vella.
☎ 20331, Fax 28698. English spoken.

Open all year. 26 bedrooms (all en suite with telephone). Garage.
RESTAURANT: Closed Sun eve & Mon lunch.

A small hotel overlooking the city, only 5 minutes' walk to the centre and 20 minutes' drive to ski areas.

TARIFF: Single 5,500–6,800,
Double 8,500–10,500, Set menu 2,500–3,000.
CC: Amex, Euro/Access, Visa.

Hotel Eden Roc ★★★★ Avda Dr
Mitjavila, Andorra la Vella.
☎ 21000, Fax 60319. English spoken.

Open all year. 56 bedrooms (all en suite with telephone). Garage.

Very good, modernised hotel in the town centre. Adjoining garden.

TARIFF: Single 7,500–10,400, Double 10,400–13,800, Bk 850.
CC: Amex, Diners, Euro/Access, Visa.

ARINSAL 9D

Hotel St Gothard ★★★★ Ctra d'Arinsal, Erts, Arinsal.
☎ 36005, Fax 37051. English spoken.

Open all year. 170 bedrooms (all en suite with telephone). Outdoor swimming pool, tennis, garage, parking, restaurant. &

Splendid situation in the Arinsal valley. Convention room, children's play area and gardens.

TARIFF: Single 4,900–5,675, Double 6,800–8,350, Set menu 1,950.
CC: Amex, Euro/Access, Visa.

CANILLO 9D

Hotel Bonavida ★★★ Plaça Major, Canillo.
☎ 51300, Fax 51722.
Open 04/12 to 12/10. 43 bedrooms (all en suite with telephone). Garage. &
RESTAURANT: Closed May & June.

A quiet, comfortable hotel. All rooms with balcony overlooking the mountains.

TARIFF: Single 4,800–7,250, Double 6,600–9,600, Set menu 1,900.
CC: Amex, Diners, Euro/Access, Visa.

ENCAMP 9D

Hotel Coray ★★★ Ctra de los Caballers 38, Encamp.
☎ 31513, Fax 31806. English spoken.
Open 01/12 to 15/11. 85 bedrooms

(all en suite with telephone). Garage, restaurant. &

A comfortable, modern hotel with a private garden and garage.

TARIFF: (1993) Single 3,200–3,750, Double 4,400–5,000, Set menu 1,000–1,250.
CC: Euro/Access, Visa.

LES ESCALDES 9D

Hotel Comtes d'Urgell ★★★ 29 Avda de les Escoles, Les Escaldes.
☎ 20621, Fax 20465. English spoken.
Open all year. 200 bedrooms (all en suite with telephone). Garage, restaurant.

Modern, fully-equipped hotel. From behind the church of Les Escaldes, take first turn on left and hotel is 100 m.

TARIFF: Single 5,050, Double 7,500, Set menu 2,300.
CC: Amex, Diners, Euro/Access, Visa.

Hotel Delfos ★★★★ Avda del Fener 17, Les Escaldes.
☎ 24642, Fax 61642. English spoken.
Open all year. 200 bedrooms (all en suite with telephone). Garage, parking, restaurant.

Located in the commercial centre, this modern hotel has very good facilities and is ideal for conferences.

TARIFF: Single 5,475–7,475, Double 9,150–9,600.
CC: Amex, Diners, Euro/Access, Visa.

Hotel Roc Blanc ★★★★ 5 Place Coprinces, Les Escaldes.
☎ 21486, Fax 60244. English spoken.
Open all year. 240 bedrooms (all en suite with telephone). Indoor swimming pool, outdoor swimming pool, garage, parking, restaurant.

Surrounded by private gardens and waterfalls and overlooking the most beautiful square in the Principality, this luxury hotel offers excellent cuisine with international specialities.

TARIFF: Single 11,000–12,650, Double 16,000–18,400, Set menu 1,300–4,600.
CC: Amex, Diners, Euro/Access, Visa.

ORDINO 9D

Hotel Coma ★★★ Ordino.
☎ 35116, Fax 37909. English spoken.
Open all year. 48 bedrooms (all en suite with telephone). Outdoor swimming pool, tennis, garage, parking, restaurant.

Ordino is a mountain village, close to ski slopes and ideal for hiking or for just enjoying the peaceful atmosphere. Comfortable hotel with good facilities. 8 km from Andorra la Vella.

TARIFF: Single 5,250–7,250, Double 11,000–13,000, Set menu 2,750–5,800. CC: Amex, Euro/Access, Visa.

ST JULIA DE LORIA 9D

Hotel Coma Bella ★★ Santa Julia de Loria.
✆ 41220, Fax 41460. English spoken.
Open all year. 28 bedrooms (all en suite with telephone). Parking, restaurant. ♿

A comfortable hotel offering panoramic views from restaurant and terraces. Large gardens. Health-and-beauty treatments. From Santa Julia, 6 km on Rabassa road.

TARIFF: Single 4,400–6,800, Double 5,500–7,800, Bk 500, Set menu 1,650. CC: Amex, Euro/Access, Visa.

SOLDEU 9D

Hotel Del Tarter ★★★ Ctra General, El Tarter, Soldeu.
✆ 51165, Fax 51474. English spoken.

Open 01/12 to 15/10. 37 bedrooms (all en suite with telephone). Garage, parking, restaurant.

Chalet-style hotel, completely renovated and family run. Near the sports centre, 3 km outside Soldeu on the main road.

TARIFF: Single 3,000–4,000, Double 5,500–7,150, Bk 850, Set menu 1,500–2,000. CC: Amex, Diners, Euro/Access, Visa.

AUSTRIA

If you are looking for sandy beaches and ocean breakers, it is best to avoid Austria. However this landlocked mid-European country has a wealth of beautiful mountain scenery, specialising in wonderful views and sparkling clean air. With an area of 83,835 sq km, Austria is about one-third the size of the UK. It has borders with Lichtenstein and Switzerland to the west, Hungary to the east, Germany and Czechoslovakia to the north, and Italy and Yugoslavia to the south. The landscape is dominated by the Alps, which stretch across three-quarters of the country from the west. The highest peak is the Grossglockner, at 3,797 m. The other major geographical feature is the Danube, Europe's largest river, which flows across the north of the country through Linz and Vienna.

Austria's climate is similar to the UK, though it is slightly colder in winter and warmer in summer. Of course, temperatures drop with altitude, by about 6°C per 1,000 m (3.5°F per 1,000 ft). The countryside is composed of mixed woodlands and farmlands in the north, conifers on the mountain slopes, and grassy alpine pastures above. The wildlife includes many alpine flowers, red deer, chamois, marmot, grouse, gray goose, white-tailed and spotted eagles, great white herons and white storks.

The country's population is about 7.6 million, with 1.5 million living in the historic capital, Vienna. Local currency is the Austrian schilling, made up of 100 groschen. There are about 11,000 km of motorways and 97,000 km of other roads, making a road density (km per sq km) of 1.3 compared to the UK's 1.5.

ALPBACH   19C

Hotel Boglerhof ★★★★ 6236 Alpbach.
☎ 05336 5227, Fax 05336 5227402.
Open 01/05 to 31/10 & 01/12 to 30/04.
48 bedrooms (all en suite).
TARIFF: (1993) Single 850–1600,
Double 1300–2500.
CC: Euro/Access, Visa.

ATTERSEE   19B

Hotel Seegasthof Oberndorfer ★★★★
Hauptstrasse 18, 4864 Attersee.
☎ 07666 364, Fax 07666 36491.
Open 01/03 to 30/11. 26 bedrooms
(all en suite).
TARIFF: (1993) Single 570–620,
Double 1180–1800.
CC: Amex, Diners, Euro/Access, Visa.

BAD GASTEIN   19C

Hotel Grüner Baum ★★★★ Kotschachtal 25,
5640 Bad Gastein.
☎ 06434 25160, Fax 06434 251625.
Open 20/12 to 06/04 & 08/05 to 20/10.
90 bedrooms (all en suite).
TARIFF: (1993) Single 950–1650,

Double 1700–3100.
CC: Amex, Diners, Euro/Access, Visa.

BAD HOFGASTEIN   19C

Hotel Karnten ★★★★ Dr Zimmermannstr,
5630 Bad Hofgastein.
☎ 06432 67110, Fax 06432 67118.
Open 19/12 to 31/10. 70 bedrooms
(all en suite).
TARIFF: (1993) Single 780–1155,
Double 1520–2740.
CC: Amex, Diners, Euro/Access, Visa.

BAD ISCHL   19B

Kurhotel Bad Ischl Voglhuberstrasse,
4820 Bad Ischl.
☎ 06132 4271, Fax 06132 7682. English spoken.
Open all year. 115 bedrooms (all en suite
with telephone). Indoor swimming pool,
golf 6 km, garage, parking, restaurant.
*The hotel is in a quiet, central position,
surrounded by parkland. Railway station
nearby.*
TARIFF: (1993) Single 880–980,
Double 1460–1660, Set menu 140–190.
CC: Amex, Diners, Euro/Access, Visa.

BAD KLEINKIRCHEIM 19D

Hotel Ronacher ★★★★★ 9546 Bad
Kleinkircheim.
☎ 04240 282, Fax 04240 282606.
Open all year. 92 bedrooms (all en suite).
TARIFF: (1993) Single 990–1350,
Double 1700–3200.
CC: Amex, Diners, Euro/Access, Visa.

BADEN 19B

Hotel Kranerhütte ★★★★★ Helental,
2500 Baden.
☎ 02252 44511, Fax 02252 4451499.
Open all year. 60 bedrooms (all en suite).
TARIFF: (1993) Single 930–1220,
Double 1480–1740.
CC: Amex, Diners, Euro/Access, Visa.

BERWANG 19C

Hotel Blitz ★★★ 6622 Berwang.
☎ 05674 8272, Fax 05674 827225.
English spoken.
Open all year. 24 bedrooms (all en suite
with telephone). Garage, parking,
restaurant. ♿

*Comfortable hotel with modern facilities
including sauna.*
TARIFF: Single 250–475, Double 720–1620.
CC: Amex, Diners, Euro/Access, Visa.

BEZAU 19C

Ferienhotel Gasthof Gams 6870 Bezau.
☎ 05514 2220, Fax 05514 2220 24.
English spoken.
Open 19/12 to 01/11. 38 bedrooms
(all en suite with telephone). Outdoor
swimming pool, tennis, parking, restaurant.

*Converted 17th-century coaching inn,
renovated in local style. On the edge of the
town with fine views. Family run but offers
modern-day comforts with friendly
atmosphere and very good local cuisine.
Bezau is the capital of the Vorarlberg region,
30 km from Bregenz.*
TARIFF: (1993) Single 570–690,
Double 840–1620, Set menu 220–460.
CC: Amex, Diners, Euro/Access, Visa.

BLUDENZ 19C

Schlosshotel ★★★★ Schlossplatz 5,
6700 Bludenz.
☎ 05552 63016, Fax 05552 630168.
Open all year. 42 bedrooms (all en suite).

TARIFF: (1993) Single 580–680,
Double 800–1120.
CC: Amex, Diners, Euro/Access, Visa.

BRAND 19C

Hotel Scesaplana ★★★★ Vorarlberg,
6708 Brand.
☎ 05559 221, Fax 05559 445.
Open all year. 72 bedrooms (all en suite).
TARIFF: (1993) Single 550–1300,
Double 900–2400.
CC: Amex, Diners, Euro/Access, Visa.

BREGENZ 19C

Hotel Weisses Kreuz ★★★★ Romerstrasse 5,
6900 Bregenz.
☎ 05574 49880, Fax 05574 498867.
Open all year. 44 bedrooms (all en suite).
TARIFF: (1993) Single 760–1100,
Double 1250–1650.
CC: Amex, Diners, Euro/Access, Visa.

DURNSTEIN 19B

Hotel Schloss Dürnstein ★★★★★ Wachau
Gorge, 3601 Dürnstein.
☎ 02711 212, Fax 02711 351.
Open all year. 37 bedrooms (all en suite).
TARIFF: (1993) Single 1200–1400,
Double 1650–3400.
CC: Amex, Diners, Euro/Access, Visa.

EISENSTADT 19B

Hotel Burgenland ★★★★ Schubertplatz 1,
7000 Eisenstadt.
☎ 02682 5521, Fax 02682 5531.
Open all year. 88 bedrooms (all en suite).
TARIFF: (1993) Single 790, Double 1090.
CC: Amex, Diners, Euro/Access, Visa.

FELDKIRCH 19C

Hotel Illpark ★★★★ Leonhardsplatz 2,
6800 Feldkirch.
☎ 05522 24600, Fax 05522 28646.
Open all year. 92 bedrooms (all en suite).
TARIFF: (1993) Single 900–1050,
Double 1400–1600.
CC: Amex, Diners, Euro/Access, Visa.

FREISTADT 19B

Hotel Zum Goldenen Hirschen ★★★
Böhmergasse 8, 4240 Freistadt.
☎ 07942 22580, Fax 07942 225840.
Open all year. 23 bedrooms (all en suite).
TARIFF: (1993) Single 400–420,

Double 680–760.
cc: Amex, Diners, Euro/Access, Visa.

FUSCHL-AM-SEE   19B

Parkhotel Waldhof ★★★★ Seepromenade,
5330 Fuschl-am-See.
☎ 06226 264, Fax 06226 644. English spoken.

Open 20/12 to 31/10. 70 bedrooms
(all en suite with telephone). Indoor
swimming pool, outdoor swimming pool,
tennis, golf 4 km, parking, restaurant. &
Very pretty chalet-style hotel, right on the lake.
TARIFF: Single 730–920, Double 1300–2160,
Set menu 180–410.
cc: none.

GALTUR   19C

Hotel Fluchthorn ★★★★ 6563 Galtür.
☎ 05443 202, Fax 05443 3005. English spoken.
Open 01/06 to 30/09 & 15/12 to 30/04.
67 bedrooms (all en suite with telephone).
Garage, restaurant.
*A refined, comfortable hotel which prides itself
on the personal touch. Set in the high alpine
Silvretta mountains. Sauna, solarium and
disco.*
TARIFF: Single 610–1380, Double 760–1700,
Set menu 120–190.
cc: none.

GARGELLEN   19C

Hotel Madrisa ★★★★ Vorarlberg,
6787 Gargellen.
☎ 0557 6331, Fax 0557 633182. English spoken.
Open 18/12 to 20/04 & 27/06 to 29/09.
65 bedrooms (55 en suite, 55 telephone).
Indoor swimming pool, tennis, golf 1 km,
parking, restaurant.
Near the church in Gargellen centre.

*Traditional ski-hotel on the slopes. Close to
Madrisa drag-lift and Schafberg chair-lift.*
TARIFF: Double 760–1300.
cc: Amex, Diners, Euro/Access, Visa.

GMUNDEN   19B

Parkhotel Am See ★★★★ Schiffslande 17,
4810 Gmunden.
☎ 07612 4230, Fax 07612 423066.
English spoken.
Open 20/05 to 25/09. 48 bedrooms
(all en suite with telephone). Tennis, garage,
parking, restaurant.
*Beautiful situation on the lakeside where you
can swim from bathing piers! Five minutes'
walk to town centre. Bistro restaurant.*
TARIFF: Single 740–910, Double 1080–1420.
cc: Euro/Access, Visa.

GRAZ   19D

Hotel Daniel ★★★★ Europaplatz 1,
8021 Graz.
☎ 0316 911080, Fax 0316 911085.
English spoken.
Open 10/01 to 23/12. 100 bedrooms
(all en suite with telephone). Garage, parking,
restaurant. &
*Modern hotel in the heart of the new
commercial centre. Near station and
motorway. Air terminal in the hotel.*
TARIFF: Single 1030–1530, Double 1550–2000,
Set menu 200.
cc: Amex, Diners, Euro/Access, Visa.

Hotel Schlossberg ★★★★ Kaiser Franz-Josef
Kai 30, 8020 Graz.
☎ 0316 80700, Fax 0316 8070160.
Open all year. 55 bedrooms (all en suite).
TARIFF: (1993) Single 1250–1500,
Double 1700–2000.
cc: Amex, Diners, Euro/Access, Visa.

The Weitzer ★★★★ Grieskai 12-14,
8011 Graz.
☎ 0316 9030, Fax 0316 90388.
English spoken.
Open all year. 200 bedrooms (all en suite
with telephone). Golf 15 km, garage, parking,
restaurant. &
*A traditional town centre hotel. On the banks
of the Mur with a marvellous view of the old
city.*
TARIFF: Single 1215–1650, Double 1770–2780,
Set menu 200.
cc: Amex, Diners, Euro/Access, Visa.

HEILIGENBLUT 19C

Hotel Glocknerhof ★★★★ Grossglockner, 9844 Heiligenblut.
☎ 04824 2244, Fax 04824 225658.
Open all year. 52 bedrooms (50 en suite).
TARIFF: (1993) Single 750–1200,
Double 1220–2200.
CC: Amex, Diners, Euro/Access, Visa.

INNSBRUCK 19C

Hotel Goldener Adler ★★★★ Herzog-Friedrichstr 6, 6020 Innsbruck.
☎ 0512 586334, Fax 0512 584409.
Open all year. 35 bedrooms (all en suite with telephone).
TARIFF: (1993) Single 800–1100,
Double 1200–2400.
CC: Amex, Diners, Euro/Access, Visa.

Hotel Schwarzer Adler ★★★★
Kaiserjagerstrasse, 6020 Innsbruck.
☎ 0512 587109, Fax 0512 561697.
Open all year. 26 bedrooms (all en suite).
TARIFF: (1993) Single 800–1050,
Double 1400–1800.
CC: Amex, Diners, Euro/Access, Visa.

Gasthof Traube Isserwirt ★★★ 6072 Lans.
☎ 0512 377261, Fax 0512 37726129.
English spoken.
Open 10/11 to 18/10. 24 bedrooms (all en suite with telephone). Golf 1 km, garage, parking, restaurant.

A warm welcome in this Tyrolean hotel overlooking Innsbruck. Superb mountain scenery and good traditional cooking. Close to tennis courts in summer and ski slopes in winter. From München/Kufstein motorway, take Innsbruck Ost exit to Olympic Stadium, then left via Aldrans-Lans.
TARIFF: Single 390–560, Double 780–920,
Set menu 150–240.
CC: Euro/Access, Visa.

KITZBUHEL 19C

Hotel Klausner ★★★ 6370 Kitzbühel.
☎ 05356 2136, Fax 05356 73925.
English spoken.
Open 01/06 to 15/10 & 15/12 to 01/04.
80 bedrooms (45 en suite, 45 telephone).
Golf 1 km, garage, parking, restaurant.
TARIFF: Single 470–830, Double 1440–1800.
CC: Amex, Diners, Euro/Access.

Hotel Zur Tenne ★★★★ 6370 Kitzbühel.
☎ 05356 4444, Fax 05356 480356.
English spoken.

Open all year. 51 bedrooms (all en suite with telephone). Golf 1 km, parking.
Tyrolean-style apartments with open fireplace and balcony (some with jacuzzi and steam-bath). At the very centre of Kitzbühel, close to cable-cars, ski-lifts and the spa. Access to hotel is through the pedestrian area.
TARIFF: Single 900–1500, Double 1500–2600.
CC: Amex, Diners, Euro/Access, Visa.

KLAGENFURT 19D

Hotel Bad Heilbrunn ★★★★ Neuhofen, 8983 Bad Mittendorf.
☎ 06153 2486, Fax 06453 248633.
Open all year. 100 bedrooms (all en suite).
TARIFF: (1993) Single 655–865,
Double 1210–1470.
CC: Amex, Diners, Euro/Access, Visa.

KREMS 19B

Hotel Park ★★★★ Edmund Hofbauerstr 19, 3500 Krems.
☎ 02732 875650, Fax 02732 8756652.
Open all year. 72 bedrooms (all en suite).
TARIFF: (1993) Single 520–540,
Double 780–820.
CC: Amex, Diners, Euro/Access, Visa.

KUFSTEIN 19A

Hotel Alpenrose ★★★★ Weissachstr 47, 6330 Kufstein.
☎ 05372 62122, Fax 05372 621227.
Open all year. 19 bedrooms (all en suite).
TARIFF: (1993) Single 540–680,
Double 1980–1150.
CC: Amex, Diners, Euro/Access, Visa.

LANDECK 19C

Hotel Schrofenstein ★★★★ 6500 Landeck, Tyrol.
☎ 05442 62395, Fax 05442 6495455.
English spoken.
Open all year. 100 bedrooms (54 en suite, 54 telephone). Parking, restaurant.
Family-run hotel in the centre of town. Good Austrian cuisine. Summer-centre for sightseeing tours, hiking, rafting and paragliding. Ski trips in winter (25 km).
TARIFF: Single 500–600, Double 800–1200.
CC: Amex, Diners, Euro/Access, Visa.

LERMOOS 19C

Sporthotel Loisach ★★★★ Unterdorf 6, 6631 Lermoos.

Austria

☎ 05673 2394, Fax 05673 3540.
Open all year. 46 bedrooms (all en suite).
TARIFF: (1993) Single 565–765,
Double 990–1900.
CC: Amex, Diners, Euro/Access, Visa.

LIENZ 19C

Hotel Traube ★★★★★ Hauptplatz 14,
9900 Lienz.
☎ 04852 64444, Fax 04852 64184.
Open all year. 51 bedrooms (all en suite
with telephone).
TARIFF: (1993) Single 780–1100,
Double 1560–2600.
CC: Amex, Diners, Euro/Access, Visa.

LIEZEN 19B

Hotel Karow ★★★ Bahnhofstr 3,
8940 Liezen.
☎ 03612 22381, Fax 03612 22381.
English spoken.
Open all year. 30 bedrooms (14 en suite,
1 bath/shower only, 1 telephone). Golf 3 km,
garage, parking, restaurant.

*The hotel is situated on the Graz to Salzburg
road.*

TARIFF: Single 350–400, Double 680–800,
Set menu 120–170.
CC: none.

LINZ 19B

Hotel Spitz ★★★★ Karl Fiedlerstrasse 6,
4020 Linz.
☎ 0732 2364410, Fax 0732 230841.
Open all year. 56 bedrooms (all en suite).
TARIFF: (1993) Single 1070–1410,
Double 1410–1750.
CC: Amex, Diners, Euro/Access, Visa.

MALLNITZ 19C

Alpenhotel Albert Tauern, 9822 Mallnitz.
☎ 04784 525, Fax 04784 527.
Open all year. 56 bedrooms (49 en suite).
TARIFF: (1993) Single 420–630,
Double 740–1160.
CC: Amex, Diners, Euro/Access, Visa.

MAYRHOFEN 19C

Elisbeth Hotel ★★★★★ 6290 Mayrhofen.
☎ 05285 2929, Fax 05285 2929222.
Open all year. 36 bedrooms (all en suite).
TARIFF: (1993) Single 1350–1395,
Double 2500–3790.
CC: Amex, Diners, Euro/Access, Visa.

MILLSTATT 19D

Hotel Die Forelle ★★★★ Carinthia,
9872 Millstatt.
☎ 04766 2050, Fax 04766 205011.
Open all year. 68 bedrooms (all en suite
with telephone).
TARIFF: (1993) Single 700–850,
Double 1300–2300.
CC: Amex, Diners, Euro/Access, Visa.

MONDSEE 19B

Hotel Leitnerbrau ★★★ Marktplatz 9,
5310 Mondsee.
☎ 06232 2219, Fax 06232 2219 22.
English spoken.
Open all year. 9 bedrooms (all en suite
with telephone). Golf 3 km, parking,
restaurant.

*A comfortable hotel, situated in the centre of
town and opposite the church made famous in
"The Sound of Music".*

TARIFF: Single 420–500, Double 740–1000,
Set menu 110–200.
CC: Amex, Diners, Euro/Access, Visa.

OBERGURGL 19C

Pension Alpengluhn Untergurgl 97,
6456 Obergurgl.
☎ 05256 301, Fax 05256 48150. English spoken.
Open 27/06 to 19/09. 23 bedrooms
(all en suite with telephone). Parking,
restaurant.

*A cosy Tyrolean hotel with sun-terrace and
solarium. From Innsbruck, take motorway to
Arlberg then turn off at Otztal.*

TARIFF: (1993) Single 500–550,
Double 840–960.
CC: Amex, Diners, Euro/Access, Visa.

OBERTRAUN 19D

Berghotel Krippenstein ★★★
4831 Obertraun.
☎ 06131 527, Fax 06131 52841.
Open all year. 41 bedrooms (all en suite).
TARIFF: (1993) Single 660, Double 1080–1160.
CC: Amex, Diners, Euro/Access, Visa.

OTZ 19C

Hotel Drei Mohren Haupstr 54, 6433 Otz.
☎ 05252 6301, Fax 05252 6301. English spoken.
Open all year. 23 bedrooms (all en suite
with telephone). Tennis, garage, parking,
restaurant.

A typically Tyrolean-style hotel with rustic

wood-panelled rooms and good local cuisine.
TARIFF: Single 320–360, Double 600–660,
Set menu 90–200.
CC: Amex, Diners, Euro/Access, Visa.

PERTISAU-AM-ACHENSEE 19C

Strandhotel Entner ★★★★
6213 Pertisau-am-Achensee.
✆ 05243 5259, Fax 05243 5985113.
English spoken.
Open 18/12 to 31/03 & 04/05 to 31/10.
80 bedrooms (all en suite with telephone).
Indoor swimming pool, outdoor swimming
pool, golf 1 km, parking, restaurant. &
*Very comfortable lakeside hotel, not far from
the centre.*
TARIFF: Single 800–1200, Double 1300–2100.
CC: Amex, Diners, Euro/Access, Visa.

PORTSCACH-AM-WORTHERSEE 19D

Hotel Schloss Seefels ★★★★★ Toschling 1,
9210 Pörtscach-am-Wörthersee.
✆ 04272 2377, Fax 04272 3704.
Open all year. 73 bedrooms (all en suite).
TARIFF: (1993) Single 1040–3990,
Double 1360–4300.
CC: Amex, Diners, Euro/Access, Visa.

ST ANTON-AM-ARLBERG 19C

Hotel Schwarzer Adler ★★★★★
6580 St Anton-am-Arlberg.
✆ 05446 22440, Fax 05446 224462.
Open all year. 50 bedrooms (all en suite).
TARIFF: (1993) Double 2400–3400.
CC: Amex, Diners, Euro/Access, Visa.

ST WOLFGANG 19B

Hotel Appesbach ★★★★ 5360 St Wolfgang.
✆ 06138 2209, Fax 06138 220914.
English spoken.
Open 15/04 to 30/10 & 20/12 to 15/01.
25 bedrooms (all en suite with telephone).
Tennis, golf 4 km, garage, parking.
RESTAURANT: Closed 20/12-15/01.

*Formerly a private mansion and once host to
the Duke of Windsor, this elegant hotel is right
on the lake shore with lovely gardens. Ideal
location for enjoying the surrounding
countryside, water sports and fishing.*
TARIFF: Single 800–1100, Double 1300–2800,
Set menu 260–500.
CC: Amex, Diners, Euro/Access, Visa.

Hotel Im Weissen Rossl ★★★★ Markt 74,
5360 St Wolfgang.

✆ 06138 2306, Fax 06138 230641.
English spoken.
Open 20/12 to 31/10. 72 bedrooms
(all en suite with telephone). Indoor
swimming pool, outdoor swimming pool,
tennis, golf 8 km, garage, parking. &
RESTAURANT: Closed 01/11-19/12.

*A first-class hotel on the shores of the
Wolfgangsee which was the inspiration for the
operetta "The White Horse Inn". Combines the
atmosphere of the past with up-to-date
comforts.*
TARIFF: Single 850–1250, Double 1100–2400,
Set menu 290.
CC: Amex, Diners, Euro/Access, Visa.

Hotel Tirol ★★★ Robert Stolz Str 111,
5360 St Wolfgang.
✆ 06138 23250, Fax 06138 25099.
English spoken.
Open 01/04 to 31/10. 13 bedrooms
(all en suite with telephone). Outdoor
swimming pool, golf 10 km, garage, parking,
restaurant.

*A charming lakeside hotel, offering the
personal touch. Suites and apartments
available with traditional farmhouse
furniture. From the village, it is the first hotel
at the end of the lake promenade.*
TARIFF: Single 560–760, Double 1000–1900,
Set menu 170–280.
CC: Amex, Diners, Euro/Access, Visa.

SALZBURG 19A

Austrotel Salzburg ★★★★ Mirabellplatz 8,
5020 Salzburg.
✆ 0662 881688, Fax 0662 881687.
English spoken.
Open all year. 74 bedrooms (all en suite

with telephone). Garage, restaurant. &

In the city centre opposite the Schloss Mirabell.
TARIFF: Single 1330–1680, Double 1880–2580.
CC: Amex, Diners, Euro/Access, Visa.

Hotel Bristol ★★★★★ Masktplatz 4,
5020 Salzburg.
☎ 0662 873557, Fax 0662 8735576.
English spoken.
Open 15/03 to 04/01. 70 bedrooms
(all en suite with telephone). Golf 20 km,
garage, parking, restaurant. &

Traditional 5-star hotel in centre of town.
TARIFF: Single 1950–2810, Double 2300–5600,
Set menu 350–700.
CC: Amex, Diners, Euro/Access, Visa.

Hotel Kobenzl ★★★★★ Am Gaisburg 11,
5020 Salzburg.
☎ 0662 64510, Fax 0662 642238.
Open all year. 36 bedrooms (all en suite).
TARIFF: (1993) Single 1050–2850,
Double 1850–4200.
CC: Amex, Diners, Euro/Access, Visa.

SEEFELD 19C

Hotel Larchenhof ★★★★ 6100 Mösern.
☎ 05212 8167, Fax 05212 81684.
English spoken.
Open 01/05 to 31/10 & 01/12 to 01/04.
45 bedrooms (all en suite with telephone).
Golf 4 km, garage. &

*Set high in the mountains, this luxury hotel in
its own grounds offers a solarium, sauna and
putting green. 50% reduction on green fees at
the Seefeld Golf Academy.*
TARIFF: Single 330–350, Double 620–660.
CC: Visa.

Hotel Tummlerhof ★★★★★ Münchnerstr
215, 6100 Seefeld.
☎ 05212 25710, Fax 05212 2571104.
English spoken.
Open 18/12 to 05/04 & 01/06 to 22/10.
135 bedrooms (77 en suite, 77 telephone).
Indoor swimming pool, outdoor swimming
pool, golf 4 km, garage, parking. &
RESTAURANT: good. Closed Wed.

*Comfortable, family-run hotel. Set on a sunny
plateau at 1200 m and offering the very best to
the mountain holidaymaker. From Inn Valley
motorway, take Zirl exit. From München-
Garmisch motorway, exit Seefeld Nord.*
TARIFF: Single 940–1750, Double 940–2450,
Set menu 300–400.
CC: Amex, Diners, Euro/Access, Visa.

SPITTAL AN DER DRAU 19D

Hotel Ertl ★★★ Bahnhofstr 26,
9802 Spittal an der Drau.
☎ 04762 20480, Fax 04762 20485.
Open all year. 40 bedrooms (all en suite).
CC: Amex, Diners, Euro/Access, Visa.

STEYR 19B

Hotel Minichmayr ★★★★ Haratzmüllerstr 3,
4400 Steyr.
☎ 07252 53410, Fax 07252 4820255.
Open all year. 50 bedrooms (all en suite).
TARIFF: (1993) Single 605–1110,
Double 870–1460.
CC: Amex, Diners, Euro/Access, Visa.

STUBEN-AM-ARLBERG 19C

Hotel Gasthof Post ★★★★★ Vorarlberg,
6764 Lech-am-Arlberg.
☎ 05583 22060, Fax 05583 220623.
Open all year. 40 bedrooms (all en suite).
TARIFF: (1993) Single 2400–2980,
Double 4200–5200.
CC: Amex, Diners, Euro/Access, Visa.

VELDEN-AM-WORTHERSEE 19D

Hotel Europa ★★★★ Wrannpark 3,
9220 Velden-am-Wörthersee.
☎ 04274 2770, Fax 04274 51120. English spoken.
Open 10/05 to 20/10. 153 bedrooms
(82 en suite, 82 telephone). Outdoor
swimming pool, tennis, golf 10 km, parking.
RESTAURANT: Closed 20/10-10/05.

*On the banks of the Wörthersee and set in its
own grounds, the hotel is perfectly situated for
all water sports. Three 18-hole golf courses
within a few minutes' drive. From Salzburg to
Villach (220 km) then from Villach 15 km on
highway to Velden.*
TARIFF: Single 920–1450, Double 1780–3900.
CC: Amex, Diners, Euro/Access, Visa.

VILLACH 19D

Austrotel Villach Ossiacher Zeile 39,
9500 Villach.
☎ 04242 2002, Fax 04242 2390. English spoken.
Open all year. 96 bedrooms (all en suite
with telephone). Garage, restaurant. &

*Modern, well-equipped hotel, ideal for
conferences. Take motorway A2 or A10, exit
Faaker See and follow hotel sign at second
crossing.*
TARIFF: (1993) Single 880, Double 1430.
CC: Amex, Diners, Euro/Access, Visa.

Kurhotel Warmbaderhof ★★★★★ Warmbad Villach, 9500 Villach.
☎ 04242 30010, Fax 04242 3001309.
English spoken.
Open all year. 186 bedrooms (128 en suite, 128 telephone). Indoor swimming pool, outdoor swimming pool, tennis, golf 17 km, parking, restaurant.
TARIFF: Single 1050–1580, Double 1560–3600, Set menu 145–890.
CC: Amex, Diners, Euro/Access.

WEIZ   19D

Hotel Modernshof ★★★★ Buchl 32, 8160 Weiz.
☎ 03172 3747, Fax 03172 37472.
Open all year. 7 bedrooms (all en suite).
CC: Amex, Diners, Euro/Access, Visa.

WELS   19B

Austrotel Wels ★★★★ Kaiser Joseph Platz 50, 4600 Wels.
☎ 07242 45361, Fax 07242 44629.
English spoken.
Open all year. 82 bedrooms (61 en suite, 61 telephone). Golf 10 km, garage, parking, restaurant.
Renovated in 1992 and conveniently situated in town centre. In-house theatre, close to fair.
TARIFF: Single 990, Double 1390, Set menu 150–210.
CC: Amex, Diners, Euro/Access, Visa.

WIEN (VIENNA)   19B

Hotel Atlanta ★★★★ Währingerstrasse 33, 1090 Wien.
☎ 0222 424234, Fax 0222 425375.
English spoken.

Open all year. 57 bedrooms (all en suite with telephone). Garage.
RESTAURANT: Closed Sun & Mon.

A completely renovated 19th-century hotel with every modern facility. Centrally located between Volksoper and Votivkirche with good public transport.
TARIFF: Single 780–980, Double 950–1600, Set menu 80–250.
CC: Amex, Diners, Euro/Access, Visa.

Hotel Austria ★★★ Wolfengasse 3, Am Fleischmarkt 20, 1011 Wien.
☎ 0222 51523, Fax 0222 51523506.
English spoken.
Open all year. 51 bedrooms (42 en suite, 46 telephone). Garage, parking.
A comfortable Bed and Breakfast hotel with good facilities. Quiet situation in the old city.
TARIFF: Single 560–1080, Double 1035–1590.
CC: Amex, Diners, Euro/Access, Visa.

Austrotel ★★★★ Felberstrasse 4, 1150 Wien.
☎ 01 98111 0, Fax·01 98111 930.
English spoken.
Open all year. 253 bedrooms (all en suite with telephone). Garage, restaurant. &
Modern hotel with all amenities. Opposite the western railway station and city air terminal. The city centre can be reached by public transport in five minutes.
TARIFF: Single 1700, Double 2250.
CC: Amex, Diners, Euro/Access, Visa.

Hotel Beethoven ★★★★ Millöckergasse 6, 1010 Wien.
☎ 0222 58744820, Fax 0222 5874442.
Open all year. 37 bedrooms (all en suite).
TARIFF: (1993) Single 1150–1200, Double 1650–1700.
CC: Amex, Diners, Euro/Access, Visa.

Hotel Erzherzog Rainer ★★★★ Wiedner Hauptstrasse 27-29, 1010 Wien.
☎ 01 50111, Fax 01 50111350.
Open all year. 84 bedrooms (all en suite with telephone).
TARIFF: Single 1100–1690, Double 1850–2280.
CC: Amex, Diners, Euro/Access, Visa.

Hotel Fürst Metternich ★★★ Esterhazy Gasse 33, 1060 Wien.
☎ 0222 58870, Fax 0222 5875268.
English spoken.
Open all year. 120 bedrooms (54 en suite, 54 telephone). Parking.
A typically Viennese turn-of-the-century hotel which has been recently renovated to provide every modern convenience.
TARIFF: Single 800–1100, Double 1100–1620.
CC: Amex, Diners, Euro/Access, Visa.

Austria

Hotel Kaiserhof ★★★★ Frankenberggasse, 1010 Wien.
☎ 0222 5051701, Fax 0222 5058875.
English spoken.
Open all year. 85 bedrooms (all en suite with telephone).
TARIFF: Single 1100–1360, Double 1400–2200.
CC: Amex, Diners, Euro/Access, Visa.

Hotel Römischer Kaiser ★★★★
Annagasse 16, 1010 Wien.
☎ 0222 5127751, Fax 0222 512775113.
Open all year. 24 bedrooms (all en suite).
TARIFF: (1993) Single 1650–1800,
Double 1800–2600.
CC: Amex, Diners, Euro/Access, Visa.

ZELL-AM-SEE 19C

Hotel Berner ★★★★ Nikolaus Gassner Promenade 1, 5700 Zell-am-See.
☎ 06542 2557, Fax 06542 25577.
English spoken.

Open 01/06 to 31/10 & 01/12 to 31/03.
35 bedrooms (all en suite with telephone).
Outdoor swimming pool, golf 4 km, garage, parking, restaurant.
Quietly situated, comfortable, family-run hotel with beautiful views. Excellent cuisine,

including vegetarian. Centrally located 150 m from the tourist office.
TARIFF: Single 650–880, Double 1000–1360, Set menu 180–250.
CC: Visa.

ZIRL 19C

Hotel Goldener Löwe ★★★★ Kirchstrasse 2, 6170 Zirl.
☎ 05238 2313, Fax 05238 231317.
Open all year. 36 bedrooms (19 en suite).
TARIFF: (1993) Single 509–649,
Double 918–1196.
CC: Amex, Diners, Euro/Access, Visa.

BELGIUM

One of Western Europe's 'Low Countries', Belgium is also one of the most industrialised countries in the world – and one of the most densely populated. Its 10 million inhabitants live in an area of 30,519 sq km (about one-eighth that of the UK). However more than nine-tenths of the people dwell in large towns and cities, so there is some unspoilt countryside, especially along the coast. Belgium has borders to the north with the Netherlands, to the east with Germany, and to the south with Luxembourg and France.

Most of the countryside is low-lying, with coastal areas reclaimed from the North Sea. The land rises south of the River Meuse towards the south-east and the highest peak, Botrange, at 694 m high. Winters are generally cool or cold and summers are usually warm, though westerly storms can occur at any time of the year. Most of the fertile land is farmed, but there are natural areas of sand dunes, marshes, heaths, fens, swamps and mixed woodlands, which are home to deer, wildcats and martens.

Belgium's capital is Brussels. Its population of just less than 1 million is usually swollen by Eurocrats, since the city is also the headquarters of the European Community. The second city is Antwerp, on the River Schelde. Local currency is the Belgian franc, made up of 100 centimes. Belgium's 128,000 km of roads form one of the densest networks in Europe, with seven international highways. The road density (km per sq km) is 4.2, compared to the UK's 1.5. There are no tolls, except for Antwerp's Liefenhoek Tunnel.

ANTWERPEN (ANTWERP) 7A

Hôtel Arcade ★★★ Meistraat 39,
2000 Antwerpen.
☎ 032 318830, Fax 032 342921. English spoken.
Open all year. 150 bedrooms
(all bath/shower only with telephone). &
Modern hotel in city centre, close to the famous Vogelenmarkt. Business facilities. Buffet breakfast.
TARIFF: Single 2850, Double 3450.
CC: Amex, Euro/Access, Visa.

Hôtel Firean ★★★★ Karel Oomsstraat 6,
2018 Antwerpen.
☎ 032 370260, Fax 032 381168. English spoken.
Open 21/08 to 31/07. 17 bedrooms
(all en suite with telephone). Golf 8 km, garage.
Elegant and very comfortable hotel near the city centre and old Antwerp. Good access to ports and airport. Peaceful location.
TARIFF: Single 3400–6400, Double 4500–7400.
CC: Amex, Diners, Euro/Access, Visa.

Hôtel de Rosier Rosier 23, 2000 Antwerpen.
☎ 032 250140, Fax 032 314111. English spoken.
Open all year. 12 bedrooms (all en suite with telephone). Indoor swimming pool, tennis, golf 5 km, garage, parking. &
Lovely 17th-century hotel with gardens, in city centre.
TARIFF: (1993) Double 6500–30,000, Bk 600.
CC: Amex, Diners, Euro/Access, Visa.

Hôtel Scandic Crown ★★★★ Lippenslaan 66,
2000 Antwerpen.
☎ 032 2359191, Fax 032 2350896.
English spoken.
Open all year. 204 bedrooms (all en suite with telephone). Indoor swimming pool, golf 8 km, parking, restaurant. &
From motorway, take exit Borgerhout/Deurne.
TARIFF: Single 4750, Double 4750–5200,
Bk 500, Set menu 900.
CC: Amex, Diners, Euro/Access, Visa.

BOUILLON 7D

Hôtel Panorama rue au-dessus de la Ville 25,
6830 Bouillon.
☎ 061 466138, Fax 061 468122. English spoken.
Open 15/03 to 30/10. 45 bedrooms
(42 en suite). Garage, parking, restaurant.
Situated above the town, with superb

views of the château, town and river.

TARIFF: Single 850–1050, Double 1700–2100, Bk .

CC: Amex, Diners, Euro/Access, Visa.

Hôtel Le Feuillantin ★★★★ 23 rue de la Ville, 6830 Bouillon.

✆ 061 466293, Fax 061 468074. English spoken.

Open 11/02 to 09/01. 11 bedrooms (all en suite with telephone). Garage, parking, restaurant.

Overlooking Bouillon and the castle, hotel is quietly situated with an exceptional panoramic view. Excellent cuisine which is served on the terrace in good weather. Comfortably furnished with small lounges and open fireplaces. Off the E411.

TARIFF: (1993) Single 1400–1600, Double 2200–2400.

CC: Amex, Diners, Euro/Access, Visa.

Hôtel Poste ★★★ pl St Arnauld 1, 6830 Bouillon.

✆ 061 466506, Fax 061 467202. English spoken.

Open all year. 80 bedrooms (57 en suite, 22 telephone). Garage, restaurant. &

TARIFF: Single 1000–1950, Double 2000–2700, Set menu 895–2750.

CC: Amex, Diners, Euro/Access, Visa.

Hôtel Adornes ★★★ St-Annarei 26, 8000 Brugge.

✆ 050 341336, Fax 050 342085. English spoken.

Open 12/02 to 31/12. 20 bedrooms (all en suite with telephone). Garage, parking.

Small cosy hotel, full of character. In the city centre overlooking canals.

TARIFF: Single 2350–3100, Double 2550–3300.

CC: Amex, Euro/Access, Visa.

Hôtel Aragon ★★★★ Naaldenstraat 24, 8000 Brugge.

✆ 050 333533, Fax 050 342805. English spoken.

Open 01/02 to 31/12. 18 bedrooms (all en suite with telephone). Golf 6 km, garage, parking.

Once a stately mansion, now a family-run hotel. Quiet location in the city centre.

TARIFF: Single 2250–3500, Double 2950–3950.

CC: Amex, Diners, Euro/Access, Visa.

Hôtel Bryghia ★★★★ Oosterlingenplein 4, 8000 Brugge.

✆ 050 338059, Fax 050 341430. English spoken.

Open all year. 18 bedrooms (all en suite with telephone). Golf 10 km, garage, parking.

Belgium

A handsomely restored 15th-century hotel in the heart of Brugge with good views across the city. Family run and an ideal base for exploring this medieval city.
TARIFF: Single 2950–3500, Double 3200–4200.
CC: Amex, Diners, Euro/Access, Visa.

Flanders Hôtel ★★★★ Langestraat 38, 8000 Brugge.
☎ 050 338889, Fax 050 339345. English spoken.
Open all year. 16 bedrooms (all en suite with telephone). Indoor swimming pool, golf 10 km, garage, parking.
Small hotel on east side of city, taking pride in offering personal service. Exit ringroad N30 at Kruisport. Turn left into Langestraat.
TARIFF: Single 2500–2950, Double 2950–3950.
CC: Amex, Diners, Euro/Access, Visa.

Hôtel Févery ★★★ Collaert Mansionstraat 3, 8000 Brugge.
☎ 050 331269, Fax 050 331791. English spoken.

Open all year. 11 bedrooms (all en suite with telephone). Garage, parking.
Small Bed and Breakfast hotel, quietly situated near St Giles Church and offering free transport to and from the station.
TARIFF: Single 1650–1750, Double 2050–2200.
CC: Amex, Diners, Euro/Access, Visa.

Mirabel Hôtel ★★ J Wauterstraat 61, 8200 Brugge.
☎ 050 380988, Fax 050 382310.
English spoken.
Open all year. 48 bedrooms (all en suite with telephone). Parking, restaurant. &
Modern hotel on the outskirts, close to the A17 and E40 motorways but still within walking distance of the old city centre.
TARIFF: Single 2450, Double 3100,
Set menu 590–975.
CC: Amex, Diners, Euro/Access, Visa.

Hôtel Jacobs ★★★ Baliestraat 1, 8000 Brugge.
☎ 050 339831, Fax 050 335694. English spoken.

Open 04/02 to 31/12. 26 bedrooms (24 en suite, 26 telephone). Golf 6 km, garage.
Typical Brugge-style hotel. Quiet situation close to market square.
TARIFF: Single 1300–1950, Double 1500–2300.
CC: Amex, Euro/Access, Visa.

Hôtel Navarra ★★★ 41 St Jacobsstraat, 8000 Brugge.
☎ 050 340561, Fax 050 336790. English spoken.
Open all year. 83 bedrooms (all en suite with telephone). Indoor swimming pool, golf 12 km, parking, restaurant.
Located in the city centre a few minutes' drive from the central market square.
TARIFF: Single 2700–3700, Double 3300–4700.
CC: Amex, Diners, Euro/Access, Visa.

Hôtel de Orangerie ★★★★
Karluizerinnestraat 10, 8000 Brugge.
☎ 050 341649, Fax 050 333016.
Open all year. 19 bedrooms (all en suite with telephone).
Situated in a beautifully landscaped garden and next to the most picturesque canal in Brugge. Close to famous museums and shops, in the heart of the city.
TARIFF: Single 4950, Double 5500–7950.
CC: Amex, Diners, Euro/Access, Visa.

Pandhotel ★★★★ Pandreitje 16, 8000 Brugge.
☎ 050 340666, Fax 050 340556. English spoken.
Open all year. 24 bedrooms (all en suite with telephone). Golf 8 km.
This elegantly furnished hotel is situated in a very quiet area, close to the canals, the market square and the museums. 1 km from the station.
TARIFF: Single 3600–4990, Double 4490–5990.
CC: Amex, Diners, Euro/Access, Visa.

Belgium

Hôtel de Pauw ★★ St Gilliskerkhof 8,
8000 Brugge.
📞 050 337118, Fax 050 345140. English spoken.
Open all year. 8 bedrooms (6 en suite).
Garage.
TARIFF: Single 1650, Double 2250.
CC: none.

Hôtel Portinari ★★★★ 't Zand 15,
8000 Brugge.
📞 050 341034, Fax 050 344180. English spoken.
Open all year. 40 bedrooms (all en suite
with telephone). Golf 6 km, parking. &
*Comfortable hotel with pavement café on tree-
lined square. Convenient for all city amenities.*
TARIFF: Single 2500–3000, Double 3500–4500.
CC: Amex, Diners, Euro/Access, Visa.

Hôtel Prinsenhof ★★★★ Ontvangersstraat 9,
8000 Brugge.
📞 050 342690, Fax 050 342321. English spoken.
Open all year. 16 bedrooms (all en suite
with telephone). Golf 5 km, garage,
parking. &
*Very comfortable and elegant hotel in central
location.*
TARIFF: Single 2800–3200, Double 3500–6000.
CC: Amex, Diners, Euro/Access, Visa.

Hôtel Pullman ★★★★ Boeveriestraat,
8000 Brugge.
📞 050 340971, Fax 050 344053. English spoken.
Open all year. 155 bedrooms (all en suite
with telephone). Indoor swimming pool,
parking, restaurant. &
*The hotel is built behind the walls of a 17th-
century monastery, in the centre of town on
the 't Zand Square.*
TARIFF: Single 4950, Double 5400.
CC: Amex, Diners, Euro/Access, Visa.

Hôtel die Swaene Steenhouwersdijk,
8000 Brugge.
📞 050 342798, Fax 050 336674.
Open all year. 24 bedrooms (all en suite).
TARIFF: (1993) Single 3300–8800,
Double 3850–8800.
CC: none.

Hôtel de Tuilerieen ★★★★ Dyver 7,
8000 Brugge.
📞 050 343691, Fax 050 340400.
English spoken.
Open all year. 26 bedrooms (all en suite
with telephone). Indoor swimming pool,
garage, parking. &
*Former 15th-century mansion, now a
luxurious hotel. Stands beside a picturesque*

*canal in the enchanting atmosphere of the old
city.*
TARIFF: Single 5500, Double 6950–9950.
CC: Amex, Diners, Euro/Access, Visa.

Hôtel Ter Duinen ★★★ Langerei 52,
8000 Brugge.
📞 050 330437, Fax 050 344216.
English spoken.

Open 01/02 to 31/12. 18 bedrooms
(all en suite with telephone). Golf 10 km,
garage, parking.
*An excellent hotel beside a very beautiful
canal. Lavish breakfasts!*
TARIFF: Single 2300–3500, Double 2800–3500.
CC: Amex, Diners, Euro/Access, Visa.

Hôtel Wilgenhof ★★★ Polderstraat 151,
Sint Kruis, 8310 Brugge.
📞 050 362744, Fax 050 362821.
English spoken.

Open all year. 6 bedrooms (all en suite
with telephone). Golf, garage, parking.
*Small country hotel on the banks of the canal,
2 km north of Brugge.*
TARIFF: Single 2500–3600, Double 3000–4100.
CC: Amex, Diners, Euro/Access, Visa.

BRUXELLES (BRUSSELS) 7A

Hôtel Amigo ★★★★★ rue de l'Amigo,
1000 Bruxelles.
☎ 02 5474747, Fax 02 5135277. English spoken.

Open all year. 186 bedrooms (all en suite
with telephone). Garage, restaurant.
*Large, luxurious and elegant hotel on La
Grand'Place.*
TARIFF: Single 5950–6950, Double 6750–8550.
CC: Amex, Diners, Euro/Access, Visa.

Hôtel Arcade Ste Catherine ★★★ 2 rue
Joseph Plateau, 1000 Bruxelles.
☎ 02 5137620, Fax 02 5142214. English spoken.
Open all year. 235 bedrooms (1 en suite,
all bath/shower only with telephone).
Golf 15 km. &
*Modern hotel with business facilities in centre
of city. Buffet breakfast.*
TARIFF: (1993) Double 3900.
CC: Amex, Euro/Access, Visa.

Hôtel Mayfair ★★★★★ 381 av Louise,
1000 Bruxelles.
☎ 02 6499800, Fax 02 6492249.
Open all year. 99 bedrooms (all en suite).
TARIFF: (1993) Double 8200.
CC: none.

Hôtel New Continental Flathotel rue
Defacqz, 33, 1050 Bruxelles.
☎ 02 5361077, Fax 20 5361015. English spoken.
Open all year. 43 bedrooms (all en suite
with telephone). Garage, parking.
*Hotel apartments with cleaning service.
Weekly and monthly rates. Close to business
centre.*
TARIFF: Double 3000–4000, Bk .
CC: Amex, Diners, Euro/Access, Visa.

Novotel Brussels ★★★ rue Marché aux
Herbes 120, 1000 Bruxelles.
☎ 02 5143333, Fax 02 5117723. English spoken.

Open all year. 136 bedrooms (all en suite
with telephone). Parking, restaurant. &
*Modern hotel in the heart of old Bruxelles, 100
m from La Grand'Place.*
TARIFF: (1993) Double 4860–4970, Bk 460,
Set menu 700–1350.
CC: Amex, Diners, Euro/Access, Visa.

Hôtel Palace ★★★★ rue Gineste 3,
1210 Bruxelles.
☎ 02 2176200, Fax 02 2181651. English spoken.
Open all year. 360 bedrooms (all en suite).
Parking, restaurant. &
*Spacious, elegant hotel with good facilities.
Centrally situated, facing the Botanical
Gardens and within easy reach of the
Grand'Place, Opera and shops. 5 minutes'
walk from La Gare du Nord.*
TARIFF: Single 4500–6000, Double 5200–6000,
Set menu 900–2500.
CC: Amex, Diners, Visa.

Hôtel Pullman Astoria ★★★★ 103 rue
Royale, 1000 Bruxelles.
☎ 02 2176290, Fax 02 2171150.
Open all year. 125 bedrooms (all en suite).
TARIFF: (1993) Single 5400–6500,
Double 7500–8300.
CC: none.

Hôtel Rembrandt rue de la Concorde 42,
1050 Bruxelles.
☎ 02 5127139.
Open all year. 15 bedrooms (7 en suite,
8 bath/shower only).
TARIFF: (1993) Single 1350–2050,
Double 1850–2550.
CC: none.

Hôtel Rogier ★★★★ rue du Brabant 80,
1210 Bruxelles.
☎ 02 2230707, Fax 02 2230324. English spoken.
Open all year. 73 bedrooms (all en suite
with telephone). Parking.
*Comfortable hotel, close to the city centre and
the famous Grand'Place. Five minutes' walk
from La Gare du Nord and just a ten minute
train ride from the airport.*
TARIFF: Single 3000–3600, Double 3500–4000.
CC: Amex, Diners, Euro/Access, Visa.

Hôtel Royal Windsor ★★★★ 7 rue
Duquesnoy, 1000 Bruxelles.
☎ 02 5114215, Fax 02 5116004. English spoken.
Open all year. 275 bedrooms (all en suite).
Parking, restaurant.
*The hotel is ideally located in the historic heart
of the city, only minutes away from the*

Belgium

medieval grandeur of La Grand'Place and the central railway station air terminal, with its direct link to Bruxelles airport.
TARIFF: Single 10,300–12,300, Double 11,300–13,300.
CC: Amex, Diners, Euro/Access, Visa.

CHARLEROI 7C

Holiday Inn Garden Court ★★★ rue du Poirier 1, 6000 Charleroi.
☎ 071 302424, Fax 071 304949. English spoken.
Open all year. 57 bedrooms (all en suite with telephone). Parking.
RESTAURANT: good. Closed Sun eve.
Modern hotel close to city centre on the ring road. (Exit 29 Est.)
TARIFF: Double 2950, Bk 400, Set menu 695–1950.
CC: Amex, Diners, Euro/Access, Visa.

DE HAAN 7A

Auberge des Rois/Beach Hotel ★★★★
Zeedyk, 8420 De Haan aan Zee.
☎ 059 233018, Fax 059 236078. English spoken.

Open 05/03 to 25/10 & 20/12 to 05/01.
30 bedrooms (all en suite with telephone).
Golf 1 km, garage, parking.
RESTAURANT: Closed Tues LS.
Modern hotel with sea view, only 10 km from Oostende. Excellent location on the beach in De Haan.
TARIFF: Single 2650–3950, Double 2550–5000.
CC: Euro/Access, Visa.
SEE ADJACENT ADVERTISEMENT

DINANT 7D

Hôtel du Moulin de Lisogne ★★★ 60 rue de la Lisonette, Lisogne, 5500 Dinant.
☎ 082 226380, Fax 082 222147. English spoken.

Open 15/02 to 15/12. 9 bedrooms (all en suite with telephone). Tennis, golf 15 km, garage, parking.
RESTAURANT: good. Closed Sun eve & Mon.
Comfortable hotel/restaurant built over a 17th-century watermill. Located in Lisogne, 3 km north-east of Dinant. Very quiet and peaceful countryside.
TARIFF: Double 3000–3200, Set menu 1250–1900.
CC: Amex, Diners, Euro/Access, Visa.

DURBUY 7D

Hostellerie Le Sanglier ★★★★ rue Comte d'Ursel 99, 5480 Durbuy.
✆ 086 213262, Fax 086 212465. English spoken. Open all year. 45 bedrooms (all en suite with telephone). Golf 2 km, parking. &
RESTAURANT: Closed Thurs.

Quiet and elegant hotel with good restaurant.

TARIFF: Double 3000–3800, Bk 450.
CC: Amex, Diners, Euro/Access, Visa.

EUPEN 7B

Hôtel Rathaus ★★★ Rathausplatz 13, 4700 Eupen.
✆ 087 742812, Fax 087 744664. English spoken. Open all year. 20 bedrooms (all en suite with telephone). Golf 10 km, parking. &
RESTAURANT: Closed Wed.

Family-owned hotel in centre of town, opposite town hall.

TARIFF: Single 2200, Double 2750.
CC: Amex, Diners, Euro/Access, Visa.

FLORENVILLE 7D

Auberge de la Vallée ★★★★ 7 rue du Fond des Naux, 6821 Lacuisine-sur-Semois.
✆ 061 311140, Fax 061 312661. English spoken. Open 15/02 to 02/01. 10 bedrooms (all en suite with telephone). Outdoor swimming pool, golf 15 km, parking.
RESTAURANT: Closed Sun eve & Mon LS.

Country hotel in parkland 2 km north of Florenville. Excellent restaurant.

TARIFF: Single 2025–2225, Double 2000–2200, Bk 325.
CC: Amex, Diners, Euro/Access, Visa.

FRANCORCHAMPS 7B

Hôtel Moderne ★★★ rue de Spa, 4970 Francorchamps.
✆ 087 275026, Fax 087 275527. English spoken. Open all year. 14 bedrooms (all en suite with telephone). Golf 8 km, garage, parking.
RESTAURANT: Closed Wed LS.

Francorchamps is between Spa and Malmédy on N621.

TARIFF: Single 1500–1700, Double 2300–2700, Set menu 800–1500.
CC: Amex, Diners, Euro/Access, Visa.

Hôtel Le Roannay ★★★★ rue de Spa 155, 4970 Francorchamps.
✆ 087 275311, Fax 087 275547. English spoken. Open all year. 18 bedrooms (all en suite with telephone). Outdoor swimming pool, golf 8 km, garage, parking. &
RESTAURANT: excellent. Closed Tues.

Very comfortable hotel, 1 km from famous car and motorbike circuit of Francorchamps. Excellent cuisine. Private heliport. Sauna, swimming pool.

TARIFF: Double 3200–4450, Bk 400, Set menu 1490–2150.
CC: Amex, Diners, Euro/Access, Visa.

GENT 7A

Hôtel Arcade ★★★ Nederkouter 26, 9000 Gent.
✆ 092 250707, Fax 092 235907. English spoken. Open all year. 134 bedrooms (all en suite with telephone). Golf 5 km, garage, restaurant. &

Modern, comfortable hotel in centre of town. Good access to motorway (E17).

TARIFF: Single 2950, Double 3500.
CC: Amex, Euro/Access, Visa.

Hôtel Condor ★ Ottergemsesteenweg 703, 9000 Gent.
✆ 091 218041, Fax 091 204084. Open all year. 48 bedrooms (all en suite). TARIFF: (1993) Single 2450, Double 3100. CC: none.

Hôtel Cours St Georges ★★★ Botermarkt 2, 9000 Gent.
✆ 09 2242424, Fax 09 2242640. English spoken.

Open all year. 28 bedrooms (all en suite with telephone). Garage, restaurant.

Built in 1228, the oldest hotel in Europe, but with all modern comforts. In centre of town opposite town hall.

TARIFF: Single 2600–3900, Double 3300–5500, Set menu 920.
CC: Amex, Diners, Euro/Access, Visa.

HAMOIS EN CONDROZ 7D

Château de Pickeim ★★★★ 136 rte Ciney Liège, 5360 Hamois en Condroz.
☎ 083 611274, Fax 083 611351.

Open 01/02 to 31/12. 20 bedrooms (all en suite). Golf 8 km, parking. &
RESTAURANT: Closed Tues.
Pretty château set in parkland, 8 km north-east of Ciney.
TARIFF: Single 1250–1500, Double 1250–1750, Bk 200, Set menu 675–1475.
CC: Amex, Euro/Access, Visa.

IEPER (YPRES) 7A

Hostellerie Kemmelberg ★★★★ Berg 4, 8956 Heuvelland-Kemmel.
☎ 057 444145, Fax 057 444089.
English spoken.

Open 16/03 to 14/01. 16 bedrooms (all en suite with telephone). Tennis, golf 10 km, parking.
RESTAURANT: very good. Closed Sun eve & Mon.
South-west of Ieper (Ypres), with panoramic views and excellent cuisine.
TARIFF: Single 1500–2400, Double 2500–4000.
CC: Amex, Diners, Euro/Access, Visa.

Hôtel Ariane ★★★★ Slachthuisstraat 58, 8900 Ieper.
☎ 057 218218, Fax 057 218799. English spoken.
Open all year. 36 bedrooms (all en suite with telephone). Golf 3 km, parking. &
RESTAURANT: Closed Sat lunch.
New hotel 200 m from the main square. Restaurant specialises in fish and game. Meals can be taken outside in the garden when weather permits.
TARIFF: Single 2600, Double 3300, Set menu 570–2000.
CC: Amex, Diners, Euro/Access, Visa.

KNOKKE-HEIST 7A

Hôtel Memlinc Palace ★★★★ Albert Plein 23, Knokke Zoute, 8300 Knokke-Heist.
☎ 050 601134, Fax 050 615743. English spoken.
Open all year. 73 bedrooms (all en suite with telephone). Tennis, golf 2 km, parking, restaurant. &
From Knokke take the road towards Het Zoute. Hotel is opposite the main beach of Zoute. Very comfortable accommodation.
TARIFF: Single 2600–3000, Double 3600–4700, Set menu 775–950.
CC: Amex, Euro/Access, Visa.

LIEGE 7B

Hostellerie Lafarque chemin des Douys 20, 4860 Pepinster.
☎ 087 460651, Fax 087 469728.

Open all year. 6 bedrooms (all en suite with telephone). Golf 15 km, parking, restaurant.
Small, elegant hotel set in parkland, 20 km south-east of Liège.
TARIFF: Single 3000, Double 3750–4750, Bk 355.
CC: Amex, Diners, Euro/Access, Visa.

Post House ★★★★ rue Hurbise, Herstal, 4400 Liège.
☎ 041 646400, Fax 041 480690. English spoken.
Open all year. 93 bedrooms (all en suite with telephone). Outdoor swimming pool, garage, parking, restaurant. &
Modern hotel in parkland grounds, north of Liège. Excellent facilities.
TARIFF: Single 2575–4125, Double 3200–5370.
CC: Amex, Diners, Euro/Access, Visa.

NAMUR 7B

Château de Namur ★★★ 1 Av de l'Ermitage, 5000 Namur.
☎ 081 742630, Fax 081 742392.
English spoken.

Open 28/12 to 24/12. 29 bedrooms (all en suite with telephone). Tennis, golf 15 km, parking, restaurant. &
Charming 19th-century château with splendid views. Good restaurant. 10 minutes from town centre and station.
TARIFF: Single 1700–4200, Double 2200–4200, Bk 400.
CC: Amex, Diners, Euro/Access, Visa.

Novotel Namur ★★★ 1149 chausée du Dinant, 5100 Namur.
☎ 081 460811, Fax 081 461990. English spoken.
Open all year. 110 bedrooms (all en suite with telephone). Indoor swimming pool, outdoor swimming pool, golf 3 km, garage, parking, restaurant.
Motorway E411 Bruxelles to Luxembourg, exit 14, then head towards Dinant. The hotel is 7 km from town centre.
TARIFF: Single 2900, Double 2900–3400, Bk 400.
CC: Amex, Diners, Euro/Access, Visa.

OOSTENDE (OSTEND) 7A

Hôtel Altea Accès ★★★★ Van Iseghemlaan 21-25, 8400 Oostende.
☎ 059 804082, Fax 059 808839. English spoken.

Open all year. 63 bedrooms (all en suite with telephone). Golf 8 km, restaurant. &
Modern hotel, 50 m from the sea in city centre. 250 m from casino.
TARIFF: Single 2200–2900, Double 2400–3600.
CC: Amex, Diners, Euro/Access, Visa.

Hôtel Ambassadeur ★★★★ Wapenplein 8A, 8400 Oostende.
☎ 059 700941, Fax 059 801878. English spoken.
Open all year. 24 bedrooms (all en suite with telephone). Tennis, golf 5 km, garage, parking, restaurant. &
Comfortable hotel situated in the shopping centre in the heart of Oostende, near the casino and the beach.
TARIFF: Single 2000–2400, Double 2500–3600.
CC: Amex, Diners, Euro/Access, Visa.

Hôtel New Astoria ★★ Van Iseghemlaan 38A, 8400 Oostende.
☎ 059 709961. English spoken.
Open all year. 60 bedrooms (all en suite with telephone). Restaurant. &
19th-century hotel with modern style and comfort in city centre, close to beach and casino. Good access to motorway (E40).
TARIFF: (1993) Single 1450, Double 2000.
CC: Amex, Diners, Euro/Access, Visa.

Hôtel Bellevue Brittania ★★★ 55/56 Albert 1 Promenade, 8400 Oostende.
☎ 059 706373, Fax 059 503258.
English spoken.
Open 20/12 to 11/11. 61 bedrooms (52 en suite, 61 telephone). Golf 8 km, parking. &
Modern hotel on the sea front next to the

Casino-Kursaal. Good access to motorway to Brussels (E40).

TARIFF: Single 1700–2400, Double 2505–3450.
CC: Amex, Diners, Euro/Access, Visa.

Hôtel Bero Hofstraat 1A, 8400 Oostende.
☎ 059 702335, Fax 059 702591. English spoken.

Open all year. 85 bedrooms (all en suite with telephone). Indoor swimming pool, tennis, golf 4 km, garage, parking.

Modern hotel with pool, sauna etc. Follow road to railway station, continue along quayside to monument and turn left. Signposted.

TARIFF: Single 2200–3200, Double 2800–3800.
CC: Amex, Diners, Euro/Access, Visa.

Hôtel Glenmore ★★★ Hofstraat 25, 8400 Oostende.
☎ 059 702022, Fax 059 704708. English spoken.

Open 11/02 to 01/01. 40 bedrooms (all en suite with telephone). Garage.
RESTAURANT: Closed Feb, Mar & Nov.

A family hotel 20 m from the sea front and near to the town centre. From the railway station go towards the promenade and take first street on left to the monument..

TARIFF: Single 1600–1700, Double 2400–2600.
CC: Amex, Diners, Euro/Access, Visa.

Hôtel Ostend ★★★ Londenstraat 6, 8400 Oostende.
☎ 059 704625, Fax 059 804622.
English spoken.

Open all year. 164 bedrooms (all en suite with telephone). Golf 8 km, parking, restaurant.

Pleasant hotel 50 m from the sea. Facilities include whirlpool, sauna and solarium, English pub.

TARIFF: Single 1400–1800, Double 1700–2500.
CC: Amex, Diners, Euro/Access, Visa.

Hôtel Pacific ★★★ Hofstraat 11, 8400 Oostende.
☎ 059 701507, Fax 059 803566.
Open all year. 50 bedrooms (40 en suite).
TARIFF: (1993) Single 1700, Double 3000.
CC: none.

Hôtel die Prince 41 Albert 1 Promenade, 8400 Oostende.
☎ 059 706507, Fax 059 807851.
English spoken.
Open all year. 46 bedrooms (40 en suite, 46 telephone). Golf 5 km.

Modern-style hotel on sea front. 100 m from market, casino and harbour.

TARIFF: Single 1150–2100, Double 1700–2900.
CC: Amex, Diners, Euro/Access, Visa.

Hôtel Strand ★★★ Visserskaai 1, 8400 Oostende.
☎ 059 703383, Fax 059 803678.
English spoken.
Open 31/01 to 01/12. 21 bedrooms (all en suite with telephone). Parking.
RESTAURANT: Closed Dec and Jan.

Opposite station and ferry/jet-foil terminals. One of Oostende's few hotels with an à la carte restaurant.

TARIFF: Single 2750–3300, Double 3300–4000.
CC: Amex, Diners, Euro/Access, Visa.

LA ROCHE-EN-ARDENNE 7D

Hôtel Claire Fontaine ★★★★ rte de Hotton,
6980 La Roche-en-Ardenne.
☎ 084 412470, Fax 084 412472.
English spoken.
Open all year. 25 bedrooms (all en suite
with telephone). Parking, restaurant.

*Traditional hotel set in parkland by the River
Ourthe just to the north of La Roche-en-
Ardenne.*

TARIFF: Single 2200–3000, Double 3000–3800.
CC: Amex, Euro/Access, Visa.

Hostellerie Linchet ★★★★ 11 route de
Houffalize, 6980 La Roche-en-Ardenne.
☎ 084 411327, Fax 084 411098.
English spoken.

Open all year. 11 bedrooms (all en suite
with telephone). Golf 20 km, garage, parking.
RESTAURANT: good. Closed Tues & Wed.

*Very comfortable hotel, 1.5 km from town
centre, surrounded by woods with lovely views
of river and hills. Within one and a half hours
of Luxembourg, Germany and France.*

TARIFF: Single 1750–3000, Double 2500–4200,
Set menu 1000–2250.
CC: Amex, Diners, Euro/Access, Visa.

ROCHEFORT 7D

Hôtel La Malle Poste ★★★ 46 rue de
Behogne, 5580 Rochefort.
☎ 084 210986, Fax 084 221113. English spoken.
Open all year. 11 bedrooms (all en suite
with telephone). Tennis, golf 20 km, garage,
restaurant.

*Dating from the 18th century, traditional-style
hotel with gardens. Opposite the church.*

TARIFF: (1993) Single 1950, Double 2250,
Set menu 975–1875.
CC: Amex, Diners, Euro/Access, Visa.

TOURNAI 7A

Hôtel Cathédrale ★★★ place St Pierre,
7500 Tournai.
☎ 069 215077, Fax 069 215078. English spoken.
Open all year. 45 bedrooms (38 en suite,
38 telephone). Parking, restaurant.

*Comfortable hotel located in the centre of
historic city, 300 m from the cathedral. Good
restaurant.*

TARIFF: (1993) Single 2450, Double 3100.
CC: Amex, Diners, Euro/Access, Visa.

VERVIERS-EN-ARDENNE 7B

Hôtel Amigo ★★★★ rue Herla 1,
4800 Verviers.
☎ 087 221121, Fax 087 230369. English spoken.
Open all year. 50 bedrooms (all en suite
with telephone). Indoor swimming pool,
golf 6 km, parking, restaurant. ⅖

*Very comfortable hotel with solarium, sauna
and heated swimming pool. Golf, riding and
many other indoor and outdoor activities at
nearby hotel. Take motorway E42, exit 6 to
Verviers-Sud.*

TARIFF: Single 2600–3900, Double 3900–6200.
CC: Amex, Diners, Euro/Access, Visa.

WAVRE 7B

Novotel Wavre ★★★★ rue de la Wastinne,
1300 Wavre.
☎ 010 411363, Fax 010 411922. English spoken.

Open all year. 102 bedrooms (all en suite
with telephone). Outdoor swimming pool,
golf 7 km, parking, restaurant. ⅖

*From motorway E411, exit 6 to Wavre. Hotel is
5 minutes from town centre. Walibi
amusement park is opposite.*

TARIFF: Single 3200, Double 3600, Bk 400.
CC: Amex, Diners, Euro/Access, Visa.

CZECH & SLOVAK REPUBLICS

This landlocked, mid-European 'dual country' has a varied history, with its emergence from communism and the establishment of two republics in the past few years. The main languages are, as you might expect, Czech in the west and Slovak in the east. There are also many ethnic groups from neighbouring countries, with their own languages and customs. The capital of the Czech Republic is Prague, with a population of 1.2 million and many beautiful buildings, including Hradcany Castle. The capital and largest city of Slovakia is Bratislava, in the far south, only 40 miles (65 km) from Vienna in Austria.

The climate in the region is warm and humid in summer, and very cold in winter. To the west, in the Czech highlands, are the mountains and forests of Bohemia and Moravia, drained by the River Elbe. To the east, in Slovakia, are the Carpathian Mountains with Gerlach Peak, at 2,663 m the highest point in the country. Since much of the land is unsuitable for farming, wildlife abounds. There are bears, wild boars and lynx in the nature reserves.

The total land area of the two republics is 127,896 sq km (about half that of the UK). There are borders with Poland to the north, Germany to the west, Russia to the east, and Hungary and Austria to the south. The total population of both republics approaches 16 million, with about three-quarters of people living in towns and cities. Local currency is the koruna, made up of 100 haleru. The 74,000 km of roads give a road density (km per sq km) of 0.6, compared to the UK's 1.5. Some of the mountain roads are of variable quality.

BRNO   22C

Austrotel-Grand ★★★★ Benesova 18/20, 65783 Brno.
☎ 05 42321287, Fax 05 42210345.
English spoken.
Open all year. 113 bedrooms (all en suite with telephone). Golf 10 km, parking, restaurant.
Built in 1870 and renovated in 1988, this luxury hotel is opposite the station in the city centre. Three restaurants, night-club and casino.
TARIFF: Single 1800–2700, Double 2700–4000.
CC: Amex, Diners, Euro/Access, Visa.

KARLOVY VARY   22C

Grandhotel Pupp ★★★★ Mirove namesti 2, 36091 Karlovy Vary.
☎ 017 209111, Fax 017 24032. English spoken.
Open all year. 270 bedrooms (all en suite with telephone). Outdoor swimming pool, tennis, golf 3 km, parking, restaurant. ఈ
One of the oldest in Europe, this excellent hotel has a superb setting. Spacious and elegant with friendly service and modern-day comforts. One of the previous Pupp proprietors
was the first to use sugar in the preparation of sweets. (Prices in DMs.)
TARIFF: Single 100–135, Double 165–219, Set menu 25–100.
CC: Amex, Diners, Euro/Access, Visa.

PRAHA (PRAGUE)   22C

Club Hotel Praha ★★★★
25243 Pruhonice 400.
☎ 02 6436501, Fax 02 6436773. English spoken.
Open all year. 100 bedrooms (all en suite with telephone). Indoor swimming pool, tennis, parking, restaurant. ఈ
Modern, friendly hotel with excellent sporting and fitness facilities. Pretty gardens and very attractive restaurant.
TARIFF: Single 2109–2685, Double 2630–3576, Set menu 160–350.
CC: Amex, Diners, Euro/Access, Visa.

Jalta Hotel Vaclavske namesti 45, 11000 Praha 1.
☎ 02 265541, Fax 02 226390.
Open all year. 88 bedrooms (all en suite with telephone). Golf 10 km, garage, parking, restaurant. ఈ
This fine hotel is in Wenceslas Square in centre

of city and can be easily reached by underground train (Muzeum station).

TARIFF: (1993) Single 3800–5650, Double 5100–6380, Set menu 400–1000.
CC: Amex, Diners, Euro/Access, Visa.

Hotel Ambassador ★★★★ Vaclavske namesti 5, 11124 Praha 1.
☎ 02 24193111, Fax 02 24230620.
English spoken.

Open all year. 172 bedrooms (all en suite with telephone). Golf 10 km, parking, restaurant.

Famous, traditional hotel in the town centre with excellent facilities. Very good restaurant, casino and night-club. (Prices in $US.)

TARIFF: Single 140–180, Double 180–220, Set menu 15–100.
CC: Amex, Diners, Euro/Access, Visa.

Palace Hotel ★★★★★ Panska 12, 11000 Praha 1.
☎ 02 24220834, Fax 02 24221240.
English spoken.

Open all year. 125 bedrooms (all en suite with telephone). Golf 12 km, garage, parking, restaurant. ♿

Luxurious hotel in Art Nouveau style, centrally located near Wenceslas Square.

TARIFF: Single 7540, Double 8900.
CC: Amex, Diners, Euro/Access, Visa.

Czech & Slovak Republics

DENMARK

Denmark is the lowest country in Europe. Its highest point, Yding Skovhoj, is only 173 m above sea level. The country consists of a peninsula, Jutland, that borders Denmark's only land neighbour, Germany, to the south, and more than 500 islands. These stretch west almost to Sweden, dividing the North and Baltic Seas. The total land area is 43,069 sq km (about one-fifth that of the UK), making Denmark one of Europe's smaller countries. However, the population is only 5 million, so the density of population is only half that of the UK. More than four-fifths of the inhabitants live in towns and cities. The currency is the krone (krona), made up of 100 ore.

Denmark's climate is generally mild, with cool winters, dry springs and moist summers. Most of the country is either farmed or forested. The woods are both deciduous and coniferous; a few areas are natural, but many are managed for timber such as spruce and pine.

The capital is Copenhagen, on the east side of the largest island, Zealand. It is little more than 12 miles (20 km) from the Swedish coast, a lovely city of waterways and open spaces, and home to 470,000 inhabitants. Other major cities are Ålborg and Århus on the peninsula of Jutland, and Odense on the island of Fyn. Denmark has 70,000 km of roads, and the road density (km per sq km) is 1.5, about the same as the UK. Much travel is over water, by bridges or ferry services between the islands. Note that the resorts for Danish islands, such as Bornholm, are listed under their island names in the A–Z directory.

ÅLBORG 12A

Hotel Scandic Ålborg Hadsundvej 200, 9220 Ålborg.
✆ 98 15 45 00, Fax 98 15 55 88. English spoken.

Open all year. 101 bedrooms (all en suite with telephone). Golf 5 km, parking, restaurant. &

Comfortable, modern hotel in large, unspoilt grounds. Sports/fitness room with solarium. Conference facilities. Off E45 highway, 10 km from airport, 6 km from town centre.

TARIFF: Double 595–845, Set menu 98–195.
CC: Amex, Diners, Euro/Access, Visa.

ÅRHUS 12A

Ansgar Missions Hotel Banegårdsplads 14, Box 34, 8100 Århus.
✆ 86 12 41 22, Fax 86 20 29 04.
English spoken.
Open all year. 170 bedrooms (157 en suite, 170 telephone). Golf 5 km, parking, restaurant.

Modern hotel in the heart of Århus, close to town hall and the famous concert hall.

TARIFF: Single 410–465, Double 530–470.
CC: Diners, Euro/Access, Visa.

BORNHOLM

RONNE, BORNHOLM ISLAND 12D

Hotel Fredensborg Strandvejen 116, 3700 Ronne, Bornholm Island.
✆ 56 95 44 44, Fax 56 95 03 14.
English spoken.
Open all year. 75 bedrooms (all en suite).
Tennis, parking, restaurant. &
TARIFF: (1993) Single 720, Double 860.
CC: Amex, Diners, Euro/Access, Visa.

END OF BORNHOLM RESORTS

ESBJERG 12C

Hotel Scandic Olympic Strandbygade 3,
6700 Esbjerg.
☎ 75 18 11 88, Fax 75 18 11 08. English spoken.
Open all year. 86 bedrooms (all en suite
with telephone). Golf 10 km, garage, parking,
restaurant.
Recently refurbished, city centre hotel.
TARIFF: (1993) Double 715.
CC: Amex, Diners, Euro/Access, Visa.

FREDRICKSHAVN 12B

Hotel Mariehonen Skolegade 2,
9900 Fredrickshavn.
☎ 98 42 01 22. English spoken.
Open 02/01 to 23/12. 31 bedrooms
(11 en suite). Parking, restaurant.
TARIFF: (1993) Single 250–340,
Double 350–590.
CC: Amex, Diners, Euro/Access, Visa.

HADERSLEV 12C

Hotel Haderslev Damparken,
6100 Haderslev.
☎ 74 52 60 10, Fax 74 52 65 42. English spoken.
Open all year. 70 bedrooms (all en suite).
Garage, parking, restaurant.
TARIFF: (1993) Single 500, Double 725.
CC: Amex, Diners, Euro/Access, Visa.

HELSINGØR 12B

Hotel Hamlet Bramstraede 5, 3000 Helsingør.
☎ 49 21 05 91. English spoken.
Open 02/01 to 23/12. 36 bedrooms
(all en suite). Restaurant.
CC: Amex, Diners, Euro/Access, Visa.

KØBENHAVN (COPENHAGEN) 12D

Hotel D'Angleterre ★★★★★ Kongens Nytorv,
1000 København.
☎ 33 12 00 95, Fax 33 12 11 18. English spoken.
Open all year. 130 bedrooms (all en suite
with telephone). Garage, parking, restaurant.
*De luxe hotel located on Kings New Square
and overlooking the Royal Theatre. Nyhavn,
with its waterfront cafés is just across the
square. Two restaurants. Parking nearby.*
TARIFF: Single 1850–2700, Double 2050–2900,
Bk 120.
CC: Amex, Diners, Euro/Access, Visa.

Hotel Mercur Vester Farimagsgade,
1000 København.
☎ 33 12 57 11, Fax 33 12 57 17. English spoken.

Open all year. 109 bedrooms (all en suite
with telephone). Tennis, parking, restaurant.
TARIFF: (1993) Single 995, Double 1200–1600.
CC: Amex, Diners, Euro/Access, Visa.

Nyhavn Hotel Nyhavn 71, 1051 København.
☎ 33 11 85 85, Fax 33 93 15 85. English spoken.
Open all year. 82 bedrooms (all en suite
with telephone). Golf 10 km, parking.
RESTAURANT: Closed 24-26/12.
*200 year-old warehouse converted to a
modern hotel in 1971. Most of the rooms with
a view of the harbour or the Nyhavn Channel.*
TARIFF: (1993) Single 950–1250,
Double 1350–1550, Bk 88, Set menu 295.
CC: Amex, Diners, Euro/Access, Visa.

Hotel Richmond Vester Farimagsgade,
1000 København.
☎ 33 12 33 66, Fax 33 12 97 17. English spoken.
Open 02/01 to 23/12. 132 bedrooms (all en suite
with telephone). Tennis, parking, restaurant.
TARIFF: (1993) Single 995, Double 1200–1600.
CC: Amex, Diners, Euro/Access, Visa.

Savoy Hotel ★★ 34 Vesterbrogade,
1620 København.
☎ 31 41 40 73, Fax 31 31 31 37. English spoken.
Open all year. 66 bedrooms (all en suite
with telephone). Golf 15 km.
RESTAURANT: Closed Sat & Sun.
*In city centre within walking distance of all
major attractions. Rooms free from traffic
noise. No parking at hotel (Reception will
advise nearest garage).*
TARIFF: Single 770–870, Double 870–990.
CC: Amex, Diners, Euro/Access, Visa.

Hotel Scandic Kettevej 4, 1000 København.
☎ 31 49 82 22, Fax 31 49 81 70. English spoken.
Open all year. 207 bedrooms (all en suite
with telephone). Indoor swimming pool,
parking, restaurant. &
TARIFF: (1993) Double 895.
CC: Amex, Diners, Euro/Access, Visa.

Hotel Sheraton Vester Soegadeb 1601,
1000 København.
☎ 33 14 35 35, Fax 33 32 12 23. English spoken.
Open all year. 471 bedrooms (all en suite
with telephone). Garage, parking, restaurant.
TARIFF: (1993) Single 1100–2100,
Double 1650–2400.
CC: Amex, Diners, Euro/Access, Visa.

KOLDING 12C

Hotel Saxildhus Banegaardspladsen,
6000 Kolding.

(sidebar) **Denmark**

☎ 75 52 12 00, Fax 75 53 53 10. English spoken. Open all year. 95 bedrooms (all en suite with telephone). Golf 2 km, restaurant.
Charming old hotel dating from 1905, located in the centre of Kolding by the railway station.
TARIFF: Single 345–645, Double 445–745, Set menu 18–22.
CC: Amex, Diners, Euro/Access, Visa.

NAESTVED 12D

Hotel Menstrup Kro Menstrup Bygade 29, 4700 Menstrup.
☎ 53 74 30 03, Fax 53 74 33 63. English spoken. Open all year. 80 bedrooms (all en suite with telephone). Indoor swimming pool, tennis, parking, restaurant. &
This 200 year-old hotel is conveniently situated for both sightseeing and sporting activities. A one hour drive from København, between Naestved and Skaelskør.
TARIFF: Single 488–518, Double 648–678.
CC: Amex, Diners, Euro/Access, Visa.

NYBORG 12D

Hotel Hesselet ★★★★★ Christianslundsvej 119, 5800 Nyborg.
☎ 65 31 30 29, Fax 65 31 29 58. English spoken.

Open 05/01 to 20/12. 46 bedrooms (all en suite with telephone). Indoor swimming pool, golf 3 km, parking, restaurant.
Luxurious and elegant in beautiful surroundings near woods and sea. Views to the new great belt bridge. Tennis court opens summer 1994.
TARIFF: Single 690–890, Double 1080–1280, Set menu 245–415.
CC: Amex, Diners, Euro/Access, Visa.

ODENSE 12D

Hotel Motel Brasilia Middelfartvej 420, 5491 Blommenslyst.
☎ 65 96 70 12, Fax 65 96 79 37. English spoken. Open 02/01 to 22/12. 52 bedrooms (all en suite with telephone). Tennis, golf 2 km, parking.
RESTAURANT: Closed 22/12 to 02/01.
Renowned hotel set in peaceful, park-like gardens. 8 km from the centre of Odense and its many attractions. Leave the motorway at exit 53 and go towards Blommenslyst on the 161.
TARIFF: Single 420–560, Double 595–695, Set menu 90–160.
CC: Amex, Diners, Euro/Access, Visa.

Hotel Windsor Vindegade 45, 5000 Odense.
☎ 66 12 06 52, Fax 65 91 00 23. English spoken. Open all year. 62 bedrooms (all en suite). Garage, parking, restaurant.
TARIFF: (1993) Single 450–800, Double 650–990.
CC: Amex, Diners, Euro/Access, Visa.

SVENDBORG 12D

Hotel Tre Roser Faborgvej 90, 5700 Svendborg.
☎ 62 21 64 26, Fax 62 21 15 26. English spoken. Open all year. 70 bedrooms (all en suite with telephone). Outdoor swimming pool, golf 2 km, parking, restaurant. &
Modern, comfortable hotel approximately 2 km from the idyllic port of Svendborg and 5 km from the nearest beach. Attractive gardens. Conference facilities.
TARIFF: Single 365–375, Double 495–515, Bk 52, Set menu 95.
CC: Amex, Diners, Euro/Access, Visa.

VIBORG 12A

Palads Hotel Sanct Mathiasgade 5, 8800 Viborg.
☎ 86 62 37 00, Fax 86 62 40 46. English spoken. Open all year. 72 bedrooms (52 en suite, 20 bath/shower only, 72 telephone). Golf 3 km, garage, parking. &
RESTAURANT: Closed lunch.
Luxury hotel, with suites and apartments, in centre of town near main shopping area.
TARIFF: Single 495–995, Double 595–1495, Set menu 95–125.
CC: Amex, Diners, Euro/Access, Visa.

FINLAND

Suomi in Finnish, this is Europe's fifth-largest country, and the most northerly apart from Norway. Indeed, one-third of Finland is inside the Arctic Circle. The mainland and some 30,000 islands in the Baltic Sea cover an area of 338,145 sq km. This is one-third as large again as the UK, whereas Finland's population is about 5 million, less than one-tenth that of the UK. Finland has borders with Norway in the north, Sweden to the west, and Russia in the east.

Contrary to the ideas of some people, most of Finland is low-lying. There are mountains only in the north-west tip, where Haltia rises to 1,328 m. The central regions of the country are mostly lakes – over 60,000 of them – and the conifer forests that represent Finland's main industry, timber products. The climate varies between warm and moist in the south, to arctic conditions in the north, only a few miles from the Arctic Ocean. In the far north the land is frozen, treeless tundra. Bears, wolves, elk and reindeer still roam wild.

Most Finns live in the warmer south of the country. One-tenth dwell in the capital city, Helsinki, which is the most northerly capital city in the world after Reykjavik, Iceland. Finland has many ethnic groups, including the Lapps and various gypsies. Most people speak Finnish, but the numbers who also speak Swedish, Russian, English or German are on the increase. The local currency is the markaa, made up of 100 pennia. There are 46,000 km of surfaced roads and about 31,000 km of unmade roads, giving a road density (km per sq km) of only 0.2, compared to the UK's 1.5.

Finland

ESPOO 11B

Hotel Tapiola Garden ★★★ Tapiontori, 02100 Espoo.
☎ 90 461 711, Fax 90 462 332. English spoken. Open all year. 82 bedrooms (all en suite). Outdoor swimming pool, parking, restaurant.
CC: Amex, Diners, Euro/Access, Visa.

HELSINKI 11B

Hotel Anna ★★★ Annankatu 1, 00120 Helsinki.
☎ 90 648 011, Fax 90 602 664. English spoken. Open all year. 60 bedrooms (all en suite with telephone).

Modern, cosy hotel with lots of charm. Located in the city centre, close to the only pedestrianised street in Helsinki.

TARIFF: Single 290–420, Double 390–520.
CC: Amex, Diners, Euro/Access, Visa.

Hotel Helka ★★★ Pohoinen Rautatieaktu 23, 00100 Helsinki.
☎ 90 440 581, Fax 90 441 087. English spoken. Open 02/01 to 22/12. 161 bedrooms (all en suite with telephone). Garage, parking. &
RESTAURANT: Closed Christmas.

Best Western Hotel Helka is a moderately

priced, comfortable business hotel within the heart of Helsinki.

CC: Amex, Diners, Euro/Access, Visa.

Hotel Kalastajatorppa ★★★★★
Kalastajatorpantie 1, 00330 Helsinki.
☎ 90 045 811, Fax 90 458 1668. English spoken. Open all year. 235 bedrooms (all en suite with telephone). Indoor swimming pool, tennis, golf 3 km, garage, parking, restaurant. &

Business hotel by the sea with a private park. From down-town Helsinki head west towards Munkkiniemi suburb. At Munkkiniemi turn towards Otaniemi along Ramsaynranta and hotel is signposted.

TARIFF: (1993) Single 400–770, Double 480–890, Bk 26, Set menu 90–200.
CC: Amex, Diners, Euro/Access, Visa.

JYVASKYLA 11B

Hotel Alexandra Hannikaisenkatu 35, 40100 Jyvaskyla.
☎ 941 651 211, Fax 941 651 200. English spoken. Open all year. 133 bedrooms (all en suite). Garage, parking, restaurant.
CC: Amex, Diners, Euro/Access, Visa.

Finland

KUOPIO 10D

Hotel Rivoli ★★★★★ Satamakatu 1,
70100 Kuopio.
📞 971 195 111, Fax 971 195 170.
English spoken.
Open all year. 141 bedrooms (all en suite).
Indoor swimming pool, outdoor swimming
pool, parking, restaurant.
cc: Amex, Diners, Euro/Access, Visa.

OULU 10D

Hotel Vaakuna Oulu ★★★★ Hallituskatu 1,
90100 Oulu.
📞 981 374 666, Fax 981 374 682.
English spoken.
Open all year. 216 bedrooms (all en suite).
Indoor swimming pool, parking, restaurant.
cc: Amex, Diners, Euro/Access, Visa.

PORI 11B

Hotel Vaakuna Gallen-Kallelankatu 7,
28100 Pori.
📞 939 820 100, Fax 939 820 182.
Open all year. 205 bedrooms (all en suite).
cc: Amex, Diners, Euro/Access, Visa.

RIIHIMAKI 11B

Hotel Seurahuone Hameenkatu 29,
11100 Riihimaki.
📞 914 32 914, Fax 914 722 350. English spoken.
Open all year. 64 bedrooms (all en suite).
Parking, restaurant.
cc: Amex, Diners, Euro/Access, Visa.

TAMPERE 11B

Hotel Ilves ★★★★★ Hatanpaanvaltatie 1,
33100 Tampere.
📞 931 121 212, Fax 931 132 565.
English spoken.
Open all year. 336 bedrooms (all en suite).
Indoor swimming pool, parking, restaurant. ♿
cc: Amex, Diners, Euro/Access, Visa.

TURKU 11B

Hotel City Bors Eerikinkatu 11, 20100 Turku.
📞 921 637 381, Fax 921 311 010. English
spoken.
Open all year. 60 bedrooms (all en suite).
Parking. ♿
cc: Amex, Diners, Euro/Access, Visa.

FRANCE

Europe's largest country, and favourite holiday destination, France draws people for its beautiful and varied scenery, marvellous beaches and coastlines and, of course, the finest of food and drink, art and architecture. France is at the 'crossroads' of Europe, having borders with Belgium, Luxembourg, Germany, Switzerland, Italy, Spain, Andorra and Monaco. With an area of 543,965 sq km, more than twice that of the UK, the population is almost the same as the UK, at 56 million. French is the international language of travellers and diplomats, and many French people now speak English and German, too. The currency is the French franc, made up of 100 centimes.

The north is mainly low-lying plains, rising to the wooded Massif Central in the south, the Alps in the south-east, and the Pyrenees in the south-west. Mont Blanc in the Alps is the highest peak in Europe, at 4,807 m. Climate varies from mild winters and warm summers with plenty of rain in the north-west, to the famously hot, dry summers of the south. The major rivers are the Seine flowing north through Paris, the Loire going west through Nantes, the Garonne flowing north-east to Bordeaux, and the Rhone heading south through Lyon. Nearly all fertile land is farmed; forests are restricted mainly to mountains and national parks.

There are more than 1,500,000 km of roads, giving a road density (km per sq km) of 2.7, compared to the UK's 1.5. Many are quiet country lanes; much of the motorway system is toll-paying autoroute. Note that resorts for French islands, such as Corsica, are listed under their island names in the A–Z directory.

France

ABBEVILLE Somme   1A

Hôtel Conde ★ 14 pl Libération,
80100 Abbeville.
☎ 22 24 06 33.
Open all year. 5 bedrooms. Parking.
RESTAURANT: Closed Mon & Sun eve.
Small modern hotel and restaurant situated in the centre of town behind the Hôtel de Ville on the main road.
TARIFF: Single 140, Double 140, Bk 30,
Set menu 85–200.
CC: Euro/Access, Visa.

AGDE Hérault   5C

Hôtel Azur ★★ 18 av Illes d'Amérique,
34300 Agde.
☎ 67 26 98 22, Fax 67 26 48 14.
English spoken.
Open all year. 34 bedrooms (all en suite with telephone). Outdoor swimming pool, golf 1 km, parking. ﹠
The hotel is at Cap d'Agde just 400 m from the beach – Plage Richelieu. The restaurant is 30 m from hotel. Sauna. Special group discounts. English satellite television in all rooms.

TARIFF: Single 200–330, Double 250–380, Bk 30.
CC: Amex, Euro/Access, Visa.

Hôtel La Tamarissière ★★★ lieu-dit
La Tamarissière, 34300 Agde.
☎ 67 94 20 87. Fax 67 21 38 40. English spoken.
Open 01/04 to 31/10. 27 bedrooms (all en suite with telephone). Outdoor swimming pool, golf 8 km, parking.
RESTAURANT: very good. Closed Sun eve & Mon.
Overlooking the Hérault estuary and tiny

---

fishing port. Pretty bedrooms with balconies. Tempting Languedoc cuisine.

TARIFF: (1993) Single 400−620, Double 440−620, Bk 60, Set menu 140−315.
CC: Amex, Euro/Access, Visa.

Hôtel Capao ★★★ Plage Richelieu, 34300 Cap d'Agde.
✆ 67 26 99 44, Fax 67 26 67 72. English spoken.

Open 01/04 to 01/11. 55 bedrooms (all en suite with telephone). Outdoor swimming pool, golf 1 km, parking, restaurant. &

The hotel stands on a private sandy beach with two swimming pools, a sauna and jacuzzi on site. All rooms fully equipped including air conditioning.

TARIFF: Single 370−655, Double 390−695, Bk 45, Set menu 90−145.
CC: Amex, Diners, Euro/Access, Visa.

AGEN Lot/Garonne 4D

Château des Jacobins ★★★★ place des Jacobins, 47000 Agen.
✆ 53 47 03 31, Fax 53 47 02 80. English spoken.
Open all year. 15 bedrooms (all en suite with telephone). Golf 4 km, garage, parking. &

18th-century hotel in centre of town, 100 m from the River Garonne. Close to airport and A62.

TARIFF: Single 280−400, Double 500−600, Bk 60.
CC: Amex, Euro/Access, Visa.

L'AIGLE Orne 2C

Hôtel du Dauphin ★★★ 4 place de la Halle, 61300 L'Aigle.
✆ 33 24 42 12, Fax 33 34 09 28. English spoken.
Open all year. 30 bedrooms (28 en suite, 2 bath/shower only, 30 telephone). Parking.
RESTAURANT: very good. Closed 24/12 eve & 01/01 eve.

Built before 1618 this fine hotel maintains many of the old French traditions. On the N26 in the centre of Aigle.

TARIFF: Single 349−412, Double 349−508, Bk 40, Set menu 128−410.
CC: Amex, Diners, Euro/Access, Visa.

AIGUILLON Lot/Garonne 4D

Hôtel Le Jardin des Cygnes ★★ route de Villeneuve, 47190 Aiguillon.
✆ 53 79 60 02, Fax 53 88 10 22. English spoken.
Open 10/01 to 20/12. 26 bedrooms (24 en suite, 26 telephone). Outdoor swimming pool, golf 25 km, parking, restaurant. &

In a small and quiet town by the River Lot. By the motorway A61, exit for Aiguillon. (Half-board from 180 F to 272 F.)

TARIFF: Single 160−245, Double 180−270, Bk 32, Set menu 76−148.
CC: Amex, Diners, Euro/Access, Visa.

Hôtel La Terrasse de l'Etoile ★★ cours A Lorraine, 47190 Aiguillon.
✆ 53 79 64 64. English spoken.

Open all year. 18 bedrooms (all en suite with telephone). Outdoor swimming pool, golf 4 km, garage, parking, restaurant. &

An 18th-century building, with exposed stone walls but decorated in 1930s style with antique furniture. Family atmosphere. In town centre.

TARIFF: Single 190, Double 240, Bk 28.
CC: Amex, Euro/Access, Visa.

AIGUINES Var 6C

Hôtel Grand Canyon ★★ Falaie des Cavaliers, 83630 Aiguines.
✆ 94 76 91 31, Fax 94 76 92 29. English spoken.
Open 01/05 to 17/10. 16 bedrooms (all en suite with telephone). Parking. &
RESTAURANT: Closed Sun eve & Mon.

Situated 300 m above the river with an exceptional view of the Gorges-du-Verdon. 15 km from Aiguines on the D71.
TARIFF: Single 300–360, Double 380–450, Bk 40.
CC: Amex, Diners, Euro/Access, Visa.

AINHOA Pyrénées-Atlan 4C

Hôtel Argi-Eder ★★★ rte Notre Dame de l'Atlbepine, 64250 Aïnhoa.
℡ 59 29 91 04, Fax 59 29 74 33. English spoken.
Open 01/04 to 15/11. 36 bedrooms (all en suite with telephone). Outdoor swimming pool, tennis, golf 10 km, parking, restaurant.
Very comfortable chalet-style hotel in large grounds. 200 m from village centre. From A63 at Bayonne, exit for Esplette and Cambo-les-Bains on D932. Turn right on D20 for Aïnhoa.
TARIFF: Single 580–680, Double 680–780, Bk 50, Set menu 135–240.
CC: Amex, Diners, Euro/Access, Visa.

Hôtel Oppoca ★★ rue Principale, 64250 Aïnhoa.
℡ 59 29 90 72. English spoken.
Open 15/03 to 15/11. 12 bedrooms (11 en suite, 1 bath/shower only, 12 telephone). Parking.
RESTAURANT: good. Closed Mon in LS.
In the heart of beautiful Basque country, this hotel combines all modern comforts in a charming 17th-century post house. Warm welcome and good food.
TARIFF: Single 190–300, Double 190–420, Bk 42, Set menu 125–200.
CC: Amex, Euro/Access, Visa.

AIRE-SUR-L'ADOUR Landes 4D

Hôtel Chez l'Ahumat rue des Ecoles, 40800 Aire-sur-l'Adour.
℡ 58 71 82 61.
Open all year. 13 bedrooms (11 en suite, 2 bath/shower only). Parking.
RESTAURANT: good. Closed Wed.
Small, family-run hotel with gourmet restaurant.
TARIFF: (1993) Single 102–130, Double 110–165, Bk 20.
CC: Euro/Access, Visa.

AIRE-SUR-LA-LYS Pas-de-Calais 2B

Hostellerie des Trois Mousquetaires ★★★★
Château du Fort de la Redoute, 62120 Aire-sur-la-Lys.

℡ 21 39 01 11, Fax 21 39 50 10. English spoken.
Open 20/01 to 20/12. 33 bedrooms (all en suite with telephone). Golf 20 km, parking.
RESTAURANT: good. Closed Sun eve & Mon.
19th-century château in gardens, parkland and lakes, with restaurant overlooking Lys valley. N43.
TARIFF: Single 250–525, Double 250–840, Bk 44.
CC: Amex, Diners, Euro/Access, Visa.

Hôtel du Lion d'Or 5 avenue Carnot, 62120 Aire-sur-la-Lys.
℡ 93 61 38 66, Fax 93 67 39 22. English spoken.
Open all year. 7 bedrooms (4 en suite, 3 bath/shower only, 7 telephone). Parking. ⅋
RESTAURANT: Closed Sun eve.
Near the junction of D157 (Boulogne) and N43 (Calais), south of Argues.
TARIFF: Single 150, Double 180–200, Bk 25, Set menu 60–200.
CC: Euro/Access, Visa.

AIX-EN-PROVENCE B-du-Rhône 5D

Hôtel La Caravelle ★★★ 29-31 bd Roi René, 13100 Aix-en-Provence.
℡ 42 21 53 05, Fax 42 96 55 46. English spoken.
Open all year. 32 bedrooms (28 en suite, 4 bath/shower only, 32 telephone). Golf 7 km, parking. ⅋
Town centre hotel 300 m from Cours-Mirabeau and 800 m from railway station.
TARIFF: Single 185–390, Double 250–390, Bk 32.
CC: Amex, Diners, Euro/Access, Visa.

Hôtel de France ★★ 63 rue Espariat, 13100 Aix-en-Provence.
℡ 42 27 90 15, Fax 42 26 11 47. English spoken.
Open all year. 27 bedrooms (all en suite with telephone). Golf 10 km. ⅋
Charming former mansion situated in town

France

centre. 350 m from station and buses.
TARIFF: Single 200–300, Double 250–350, Bk 35.
CC: Amex, Euro/Access, Visa.

Domaine de Châteauneuf ★★★★ Au Logis
de Nans, 83860 Nans-les-Pins.
☎ 94 78 90 06, Fax 94 78 63 30. English spoken.

Open 01/03 to 30/11. 30 bedrooms
(all en suite with telephone). Outdoor
swimming pool, tennis, parking.
RESTAURANT: Closed Mon LS.

*19th-century country house set on a golf
course with its own helicopter pad. A8/E80
motorway exit St-Maximin, N560, D80 south.*
TARIFF: Single 560–650, Double 600–1160,
Bk 70, Set menu 230–410.
CC: Amex, Diners, Euro/Access, Visa.

Hôtel Mas d'Entremont ★★★★ Montée
d'Avignon, 13090 Aix-en-Provence.
☎ 42 23 45 32, Fax 42 21 15 83.
English spoken.
Open 15/03 to 01/11. 18 bedrooms
(17 en suite, 18 telephone). Outdoor
swimming pool, tennis, golf, parking. &
RESTAURANT: Closed Sun eve & Mon lunch.

*In parkland, comfortable, air-conditioned and
full of antiques. 4 km north of Aix on the N7
towards Avignon.*
TARIFF: Single 550–700, Double 600–900,
Bk 55, Set menu 190–230.
CC: Euro/Access, Visa.

Hôtel Le Mas des Ecureuils ★★★ chemin de
Castel Blanc, petite route des Milles,
13009 Aix-en-Provence.
☎ 42 24 40 48, Fax 42 39 24 57.
English spoken.
Open all year. 23 bedrooms (all en suite
with telephone). Outdoor swimming pool,
golf 2 km, parking, restaurant. &

*In a wooded setting yet close to motorway, exit
Les Milles or Aix-Pont-de-l'Arc.*

TARIFF: Single 380–660, Double 480–760,
Bk 50, Set menu 125–250.
CC: Amex, Diners, Euro/Access, Visa.

Hôtel Le Moulin ★★ 1 av R Schumann,
13090 Aix-en-Provence.
☎ 42 59 41 68, Fax 42 20 44 28.
English spoken.
Open all year. 37 bedrooms (32 en suite,
37 telephone). Tennis, garage, parking.

*The hotel is near the university in a quiet area.
12 of the rooms have their own kitchenettes for
stays of 5 days or longer.*
TARIFF: Single 210–290, Double 205–365,
Bk 37.
CC: Amex, Diners, Euro/Access, Visa.

Hôtel Le Pigonnet ★★★★ 5 av Pigonnet,
13090 Aix-en-Provence.
☎ 42 59 02 90, Fax 42 59 47 77. English spoken.
Open 01/01 to 30/12. 52 bedrooms
(all en suite with telephone). Outdoor
swimming pool, golf 8 km, parking, restaurant.

*Beautiful old hotel once cherished by
Cézanne. Family-run, with sun terrace,
gardens and fountains, close to centre of Aix
but in a peaceful location. From Aix follow the
road to Marseille (1 km).*
TARIFF: Single 500–800, Double 600–1200,
Bk 85.
CC: Amex, Diners, Euro/Access, Visa.

AIX-LES-BAINS Savoie   6A

Chambaix Hôtel ★★ Viviers-du-Lac,
73420 Aix-les-Bains.
☎ 79 61 31 11, Fax 79 88 43 69. English spoken.
Open all year. 29 bedrooms (all en suite
with telephone). Outdoor swimming pool,
tennis, golf 2 km, garage, parking, restaurant.

*Surrounded by mountains and overlooking
Lac Bourget, this modern hotel has a terrace
and large garden with swings and a tennis
court. 4 km from Aix-les-Bains on the D991,
follow directions for Viviers-du-Lac.*
TARIFF: Single 240–280, Double 260–300,
Bk 35.
CC: Amex, Diners, Euro/Access, Visa.

ALBI Tarn   5C

Hôtel Altea ★★★ 41 bis rue Porta, 81000 Albi.
☎ 63 47 66 66, Fax 63 46 18 40. English spoken.
Open all year. 56 bedrooms (all en suite
with telephone). Golf 2 km, parking. &
RESTAURANT: Closed Sat.

*Former mill on the River Tarn, facing the
cathedral.*

TARIFF: Double 320–500, Bk 55.
CC: Amex, Diners, Euro/Access, Visa.

Hôtel St Clair ★★★★ rue St-Clair, 81000 Albi.
☎ 63 54 04 04, Fax 63 47 10 47.
English spoken.
Open all year. 50 bedrooms (all en suite with telephone). Garage, parking, restaurant. ⚫

Comfortable and quiet 18th-century hotel, run by the same family for five generations. Full of antiques with garden. Close to tennis and swimming pool. Near the cathedral and Toulouse-Lautrec museum.

TARIFF: Single 360–550, Double 400–850, Bk 60, Set menu 150–290.
CC: Amex, Diners, Euro/Access, Visa.

Hôtel Le Vieil Alby ★★ 25 rue Toulouse-Lautrec, 81000 Albi.
☎ 63 54 14 69, Fax 63 54 96 75. English spoken.
Open all year. 9 bedrooms (all en suite with telephone). Golf 2 km, garage, restaurant.
TARIFF: Single 220, Double 220–260, Bk 28, Set menu 80–250.
CC: Amex, Euro/Access, Visa.

ALENCON Orne 2C

Hôtel du Grand Cerf ★★★ 21 rue St-Blaise, 61000 Alençon.
☎ 33 26 00 51, Fax 33 26 63 07.
English spoken.

Open all year. 32 bedrooms (25 en suite, 32 telephone). Garage, restaurant.
Historic building in centre of town, high quality cuisine, seafood and local specialities. Warm atmosphere and character.
TARIFF: Single 280–350, Double 320–400, Bk 35, Set menu 80–160.
CC: Euro/Access, Visa.

Hôtel Touring-Best Western ★★★
72590 St-Leonard-des-Bois.
☎ 43 97 28 03, Fax 43 97 07 72. English spoken.

Open 15/02 to 15/11. 35 bedrooms (all en suite with telephone). Indoor swimming pool, garage, parking, restaurant. ⚫
Modern hotel in gardens on the River Sarthe in the Mancelles Alps. The village lies south-west of Alençon. Drive south on N138, turn west to Fresnay, on the D130, then north-west on the D15.
TARIFF: Single 228–370, Double 305–460, Bk 45, Set menu 105–240.
CC: Amex, Diners, Euro/Access, Visa.

L'ALPE-D'HUEZ Isère 6A

Hôtel au Chamois d'Or ★★★
38750 L'Alpe-d'Huez.
☎ 76 80 31 32, Fax 76 80 34 90. English spoken.
Open 15/12 to 25/04. 45 bedrooms (all en suite with telephone). Indoor swimming pool, tennis, garage, parking, restaurant.

Situated on the ski slopes at the highest point of the resort with views of mountain peaks. Superb south-facing terrace and sports facilities. North of N91.

TARIFF: Double 750–1100, Bk 70, Set menu 130–260.
CC: Visa.

Hôtel Petit Prince ★★★ rte de la Poste, 38750 L'Alpe-d'Huez.
☎ 76 80 33 51, Fax 76 80 41 45. English spoken.
Open 20/12 to 15/04. 40 bedrooms (all en suite with telephone). Parking, restaurant.

The hotel is near La Grande Sure chairlift, with direct access to the slopes. Bedrooms are south facing and each has a balcony. There is a cosy lounge with open fire, and elegant dining-room with panoramic views. Turn off the N91 to L'Alpe-d'Huez.

TARIFF: Single 420–550, Double 480–720, Set menu 220.
CC: Amex, Diners, Euro/Access, Visa.

France

ALTKIRCH Haut-Rhin   3D

Hôtel La Terrasse ★★ 44-46 rue du 3ème Zouave, 68130 Altkirch.
☎ 89 40 98 02, Fax 89 08 82 92. English spoken.
Open all year. 19 bedrooms (4 en suite, 9 bath/shower only, 19 telephone).
Golf 15 km, garage, parking. &

Delightful overnight accommodation, with parking, in quiet country area outside town, near St-Morand Hospital. Ideal for touring, 30 km from Basle.

TARIFF: Single 140–230, Double 140–250, Bk 25.
CC: Amex, Diners, Euro/Access, Visa.

AMBOISE Indre/Loire   2C

Hôtel La Brèche ★★ 26 rue J Ferry, 37400 Amboise.
☎ 47 57 00 79. English spoken.
Open 10/01 to 24/12. 13 bedrooms (10 en suite, 1 bath/shower only, 13 telephone). Golf 10 km, garage, parking.

Small, comfortable hotel on the north side of the river towards railway station.

TARIFF: Single 175–290, Double 220–360.
CC: Euro/Access, Visa.

Château de la Huberdière ★★★★ Vallée de Vaugadeland, 37530 Nazelles.
☎ 47 57 39 32, Fax 47 23 15 79. English spoken.

Open all year. 6 bedrooms (all en suite).
Golf 11 km, parking, restaurant.

Private château, catering for just a few guests. Situated in the heart off the Loire valley, 7 km north of Amboise. Just off N152, 25 km east of Tours.

TARIFF: Single 340, Double 390–560, Set menu 160–220.
CC: none.

Hôtel du Parc ★★ 8 av L de Vinci, 37400 Amboise.
☎ 47 57 06 93, Fax 47 30 52 06. English spoken.

Open 15/01 to 15/12. 19 bedrooms (14 en suite, 4 bath/shower only, 19 telephone). Golf 15 km, parking.
RESTAURANT: Closed 01/11 to 01/03.

A French mansion dating from the turn of the century, and in a park. From the city centre follow signs to Hôtel du Parc.

TARIFF: Double 230–425, Bk 35.
CC: Amex, Euro/Access, Visa.

AMELIE-LES-BAINS Pyrénées Orient   5C

Hôtel Catalogne ★★ 67 rte Vieux Pont, 66110 Amélie-les-Bains.
☎ 68 39 80 31, Fax 69 39 20 23. English spoken.
Open 01/02 to 15/12. 38 bedrooms (all en suite with telephone). Garage, restaurant. &

A hotel with unusually large rooms and located by the river in charming Amélie-les-Bains. On D115 south of Céret. Beside the Office du Tourisme.

TARIFF: (1993) Single 250–300, Double 280–340, Bk 37.
CC: Visa.

AMIENS Somme   2B

Hôtel de l'Univers ★★★ 2 rue de Noyon, 80000 Amiens.
☎ 22 91 52 51, Fax 22 92 81 66. English spoken.
Open all year. 41 bedrooms (40 en suite, 1 bath/shower only, 41 telephone). Golf 5 km.

Traditional hotel close to cathedral and 200 m from station.

TARIFF: Single 250–490, Double 345–550, Bk 50.
CC: Amex, Diners, Euro/Access, Visa.

Hôtel Postillon ★★★ 19 pl au Feurre, 80000 Amiens.
☎ 22 91 46 17, Fax 22 91 86 57.
English spoken.
Open 02/01 to 24/12. 48 bedrooms (all en suite with telephone). Golf 10 km, garage, parking. &

Traditional-style hotel in a quiet area of Amiens, 500 m from the main shopping centre and 300 m from the cathedral and old quarter.

TARIFF: Single 310–520, Double 340–520, Bk 41.
CC: Amex, Diners, Euro/Access, Visa.

ANDUZE Gard   5D

Hôtel Demeures du Ranquet ★★★★ Tornac, 30140 Anduze.
☎ 66 77 51 63, Fax 66 77 55 62.
English spoken.

Open 01/03 to 30/11. 10 bedrooms (all en suite with telephone). Outdoor swimming pool, parking. &
RESTAURANT: good. Closed Tue eve & Wed LS.

A converted stone farmhouse at the foot of the Cevennes. The restaurant specialises in traditional dishes and offers cookery courses. In Tornac, just south of Anduze.

TARIFF: Single 500–640, Double 600–800, Bk 65.
CC: Euro/Access, Visa.

ANGERS Maine/Loire 2C

Hôtel de France ★★★ 8 place de la Gare, 49100 Angers.
℡ 41 88 49 42, Fax 41 86 76 70.

Open all year. 56 bedrooms (all en suite with telephone). Golf 5 km, restaurant. &
The Bouyer family has run the hotel since 1893, offering traditional hospitality and gourmet restaurant. In centre of Angers.

TARIFF: Single 330–480, Double 480–600, Bk 50, Set menu 95–150.
CC: Amex, Diners, Euro/Access, Visa.

Hôtel du Mail ★★ 8 rue des Ursules, 49100 Angers.
℡ 41 88 56 22, Fax 41 86 91 20.
English spoken.

Open all year. 28 bedrooms (25 en suite, 3 bath/shower only, 28 telephone). Golf 6 km, parking.

Easy access from A11 (exit Angers-Centre) and TGV. Pretty 17th-century hotel in heart of the city, offering warm atmosphere and quality service.

TARIFF: Single 145–235, Double 165–280, Bk 30.
CC: Diners, Euro/Access, Visa.

Hôtel Climat de France ★★ rue du Château-d'Orgemont, 49100 Angers.
℡ 41 66 30 45, Fax 41 66 76 08. English spoken.
Open all year. 42 bedrooms (all en suite with telephone). Golf 5 km, parking, restaurant. &

Enjoy the friendly atmosphere of the Climat de France and discover the regional cooking and wines in the restaurant. 5 minutes from the city centre.

TARIFF: Double 275, Bk 30, Set menu 85–120.
CC: Amex, Euro/Access, Visa.

ANGLET Pyrénées-Atlan 4C

Hôtel de Chiberta et du Golf ★★★★ 104 bd des Plages, 64600 Anglet.
℡ 59 52 15 16, Fax 59 52 11 23. English spoken.
Open all year. 45 bedrooms (all en suite with telephone). Outdoor swimming pool, tennis, golf on site, parking. &

Quiet and peaceful rooms in the heart of Chiberta's forest and golfcourse, just 300 m from the beach.

TARIFF: (1993) Single 370–716, Double 395–892, Bk 56.
CC: Amex, Diners, Euro/Access, Visa.

ANGOULEME Charente 4B

Motel PM 16 ★★ rte de Poitiers, 16430 Angoulême.
℡ 45 68 03 22, Fax 45 69 07 67. English spoken.
Open all year. 41 bedrooms (all en suite with telephone). Parking. &
RESTAURANT: Closed Mon.

The motel has a pleasant patio and garden, with parking in front of each room. On N10 between Poitiers and Angoulême, 7 km north.

TARIFF: Single 225–280, Double 255–320, Bk 32, Set menu 72–200.
CC: Amex, Diners, Euro/Access, Visa.

ANNECY Haute-Savoie 6A

Hôtel Ibis ★★ 12 rue de la Gare, 74000 Annecy.
℡ 50 45 43 21, Fax 50 52 81 08. English spoken.

France

Open all year. 85 bedrooms (all en suite with telephone). Golf 15 km, parking, restaurant. &

In the old town by the River Thiou which is overlooked by some of the bedrooms' balconies. Take Annecy-Sud exit from A41 follow signs for the station, then park at the Marie-Claire municipal car park as the Ibis is in a pedestrianised area.

TARIFF: Single 305–310, Double 340–350, Bk 33.
CC: Amex, Euro/Access, Visa.

Hôtel du Lac ★★ 74410 Duingt.
☏ 50 68 90 90, Fax 50 68 50 18. English spoken.
Open 12/02 to 31/10. 23 bedrooms (all en suite with telephone). Golf 10 km, parking.
RESTAURANT: good. Closed 31/10 to 30/04.

The hotel has recently been fully renovated. Beautiful views of the surrounding lake and countryside. Meals served outside on the terrace in summer. 12 km from Annecy in the towards Albertville.

TARIFF: Double 280–370, Bk 39,
Set menu 130–250.
CC: Euro/Access, Visa.

Hôtel La Reserve ★★★ 21 av Albigny,
74000 Annecy.
☏ 50 23 50 24, Fax 50 23 51 17. English spoken.
Open all year. 12 bedrooms (all en suite).
Golf 10 km, parking, restaurant.

Stunning position overlooking Lake Annecy and near beach, just a ten-minute stroll through the park to town centre. Sympathetically renovated.

TARIFF: Single 300–350, Double 370–430, Bk 38.
CC: Diners, Euro/Access, Visa.

ANTIBES Alpes-Marit 6C

Hôtel Don César ★★★★ 46 bd de la Garoupe,
06160 Cap d'Antibes.
☏ 93 67 15 30, Fax 93 67 18 25. English spoken.

Open 22/03 to 31/12. 19 bedrooms (all en suite with telephone). Outdoor swimming pool, golf 15 km, garage, parking. &
RESTAURANT: Closed Sun eve & Mon LS.

On the east side of Cap d'Antibes overlooking the sea. All rooms have sea views, air conditioning and are fully equipped. Meals served beside the heated pool.

TARIFF: Double 600–1050, Bk 75,
Set menu 195.
CC: Amex, Diners, Euro/Access, Visa.

Château Fleuri ★★ 15 bd du Cap,
06600 Cap d'Antibes.
☏ 93 61 38 66, Fax 93 67 39 22.
English spoken.
Open 01/04 to 01/11. 19 bedrooms
(all en suite with telephone). Parking.

Small hotel in a garden, five minutes from sandy beach and fifteen minutes from old town. Enclosed parking. In direction of Cap d'Antibes.

TARIFF: Single 200–300, Double 250–400, Bk 30.
CC: Amex, Euro/Access, Visa.

APT Vaucluse 5D

Auberge du Lubéron ★★★ 17 quai Léon
Sagy, 84400 Apt.
☏ 90 74 12 50, Fax 90 04 79 49.
English spoken.
Open 19/01 to 01/07 & 08/07 to 20/12.
15 bedrooms (all en suite with telephone).
Garage, parking.
RESTAURANT: Closed Sun eve & Mon.

Quiet hotel close to town centre of Apt in the Lubéron Regional park, 50 km from Avignon. Good cuisine. Meals can be taken on the flowered terrace with fine views across the town and River Calavon.

TARIFF: Single 235–390, Double 235–490,
Bk 45, Set menu 125–220.
CC: Amex, Diners, Euro/Access, Visa.

ARDRES Pas-de-Calais 2B

Hôtel La Chaumière ★★ 67 av Rouville,
62610 Ardres.
☏ 21 35 41 24. English spoken.
Open all year. 12 bedrooms (10 en suite,
2 bath/shower only, 12 telephone). Golf 5 km,
parking, restaurant. &

17 km from Calais (N43). The hotel is located in the middle of the town. Terrace and garden.

TARIFF: Single 160–270, Double 160–310,
Bk 27.
CC: Euro/Access, Visa.

France

ARGELES-SUR-MER Pyrénées Orient   5C

Grand Hôtel le Commerce ★★ 14 rte
Nationale, 66700 Argelès-sur-Mer.
✆ 68 81 00 33, Fax 68 81 69 49.
English spoken.
Open all year. 38 bedrooms (31 en suite,
4 bath/shower only, 38 telephone). Outdoor
swimming pool, golf 15 km, garage, parking,
restaurant.

*Recently restored, right in the centre of town
near the post office. Restaurant specialises in
Catalan cuisine.*

TARIFF: (1993) Single 160–210,
Double 168–276, Bk 31.
CC: Amex, Diners, Euro/Access, Visa.

ARGENTAN Orne   2C

Hôtel Faisan Dore ★★ Fontenai-sur-Orne,
61200 Argentan.
✆ 33 67 18 11, Fax 33 35 82 15.
English spoken.
Open 01/01 to 15/02 & 01/03 to 31/12.
15 bedrooms (all en suite with telephone).
Golf 10 km, parking.
RESTAURANT: Closed Sun eve.

*The hotel is a pretty, half-timbered inn with
landscaped gardens, on the road to Flers.*

TARIFF: Single 245, Double 290, Bk 35,
Set menu 90–280.
CC: Euro/Access, Visa.

Hôtel France ★★ 8 bd Carnot,
61200 Argentan.
✆ 33 67 03 65, Fax 33 36 62 24. English spoken.

Open all year. 13 bedrooms (11 en suite,
2 bath/shower only, 13 telephone). Garage,
parking. &
RESTAURANT: Closed Sun eve & Mon.

*Good value for money is keyword at this
traditional hotel/restaurant set in a pretty
garden with terrace. Lots to do and see in town.*

TARIFF: Single 125–240, Double 145–270,
Bk 26, Set menu 68–178.
CC: none.

ARGENTEUIL Val-d'Oise   2B

Hôtel Climat de France ★★ 35 bd Lénine,
Val-Notre-Dame, 95100 Argenteuil.
✆ 39 61 98 05, Fax 39 61 99 15. English spoken.
Open all year. 44 bedrooms (all en suite
with telephone). Parking, restaurant. &

*From Paris, use A86 and take exit for Colombes-
Centre. Follow signs to Val-Notre-Dame.*

TARIFF: Double 250–310, Bk 32.
CC: Amex, Euro/Access, Visa.

ARGENTON-SUR-CREUSE Indre   4B

Manoir de Boisvillers ★★ 11 rue Moulin de
Bord, 36200 Argenton-sur-Creuse.
✆ 54 24 13 88.
Open 10/01 to 20/12. 14 bedrooms
(13 en suite, 1 bath/shower only,
14 telephone). Outdoor swimming pool,
golf 20 km, garage, parking.

*In the heart of Argenton, an 18th-century
manor situated on the river in an area noted
for its Roman history.*

TARIFF: Single 180–260, Double 220–340, Bk 35.
CC: Euro/Access, Visa.

ARLES Bouches-du-Rhône   5D

Hôtel d'Arlatan ★★★ 26 rue Sauvage,
13200 Arles.
✆ 90 93 56 66, Fax 90 49 68 45. English spoken.
Open all year. 40 bedrooms (all en suite
with telephone). Golf 15 km, garage.

*15th-century mansion house with Roman
relics, courtyard and garden. On the east bank
of the Rhône. Leave N113 at Nouveau-Pont.*

TARIFF: Single 385–560, Double 465–695, Bk 55.
CC: Amex, Diners, Euro/Access, Visa.

Auberge La Fenière ★★★
13280 Raphèle-lès-Arles.
✆ 90 98 47 44, Fax 90 98 48 39. English spoken.
Open all year. 25 bedrooms (all en suite with
telephone). Golf 15 km, garage, parking. &
RESTAURANT: Closed 10/11 to 20/12.

*Overlooking the grasslands of La Crau, ideally
located for scenic trips around the region.
Traditional refined cooking. From Arles centre,
go towards Raphèle for 5 km on the N453.*

TARIFF: Single 307–363, Double 363–640,
Bk 47, Set menu 170–250.
CC: Euro/Access, Visa.

France

Hôtel Jules Cesar ★★★★ 9 bd des Lices,
BP 116, 13631 Arles.
☎ 90 93 43 20, Fax 90 93 33 47. English spoken.
Open 23/12 to 02/11. 55 bedrooms (all en suite
with telephone). Outdoor swimming pool,
golf 18 km, garage, parking. ⅃
RESTAURANT: very good. Closed 02/11 to 23/12.
*An old Carmelite convent and now an
excellent hotel. In the heart of Provence in a
town rich in history, archaeology and culture.*
TARIFF: Single 500–950, Double 600–950, Bk 65.
CC: Amex, Diners, Euro/Access, Visa.

Hôtel Rodin ★★★ 84 av de Stalingrad,
13200 Arles-sur-Rhône.
☎ 90 49 69 10, Fax 90 93 53 12. English spoken.
Open 01/01 to 15/01 & 15/02 to 31/12.
30 bedrooms (all en suite with telephone).
Outdoor swimming pool, garage, parking.
RESTAURANT: Closed Sun lunch.
*Ideal base for exploring Provence and The
Camargue, Pont du Gard etc. Well equipped
rooms with balconies overlooking gardens and
pool. Quiet situation 800 m from town centre.*
TARIFF: Single 365–375, Double 375, Bk 47,
Set menu 55–210.
CC: Amex, Diners, Euro/Access, Visa.

ARRAS Pas-de-Calais   2B

Hôtel Les 3 Luppars ★★ 49 Grand'Place,
62000 Arras.
☎ 21 07 41 41, Fax 21 24 24 80. English spoken.

Open all year. 42 bedrooms (all en suite
with telephone). Golf 2 km, parking. ⅃
*15th-century house in the centre of town. Arras
is a city of history and fine arts. From Lille south
on the D925 to Lens, then N17 south to Arras.*
CC: Amex, Diners, Euro/Access, Visa.

Hôtel Le Manoir ★★ 35 route Nationale,
62580 Gavrelle.
☎ 21 58 68 58, Fax 21 55 37 87. English spoken.

Open 01/01 to 24/07 & 23/08 to 25/12.
20 bedrooms (all en suite with telephone).
Golf 3 km, garage, parking. ⅃
RESTAURANT: Closed Sat lunch & Sun eve.
*Situated between Arras and Douai. Meals
eaten around log fire in winter and on the
terrace during summer. Take N50
Arras/Douai, then exit to Fresnes.*
TARIFF: Single 210–240, Double 240–260,
Bk 30, Set menu 68–168.
CC: Amex, Euro/Access, Visa.

Hôtel Moderne ★★★ 1 bd Faidherbe,
62000 Arras.
☎ 21 23 39 57, Fax 21 71 55 42.
English spoken.

Open all year. 55 bedrooms (all en suite
with telephone). Golf 6 km, parking,
restaurant. ⅃
*A pleasant hotel on the station square in
town centre.*
TARIFF: Single 200–320, Double 250–350,
Bk 35, Set menu 90–180.
CC: Amex, Diners, Euro/Access, Visa.

ARVERT Charente-Marit   4A

Hôtel Villa Fantaisie ★★★ rue du Moulin,
La Palmyre, 17530 Arvert.
☎ 46 36 40 09. English spoken.
Open all year. 23 bedrooms (17 en suite,
6 bath/shower only, 23 telephone). Garage,
parking. ⅃
RESTAURANT: Closed Sun eve & Mon LS.
*In a tranquil setting enjoying the gentle
climate of the Arvert peninsula.*
TARIFF: (1993) Single 310–380,
Double 348–456, Bk 35, Set menu 140–270.
CC: Amex, Euro/Access, Visa.

France

AUCH Gers 4D

Hôtel de France ★★★★ pl de la Libération, 32000 Auch.
☎ 62 61 71 71, Fax 62 61 71 81. English spoken.
Open all year. 29 bedrooms (all en suite with telephone). Golf 2 km, garage, parking.
RESTAURANT: very good. Closed Sun eve & Mon.

Well-appointed hotel. The chef, André Daguin, is renowned for his Gascon cuisine in this region of France known for its foie gras.

TARIFF: (1993) Single 280–950, Double 350–1500, Bk 80.
CC: none.

AURILLAC Cantal 5A

Auberge de la Tomette ★★ 15220 Vitrac.
☎ 71 64 70 94, Fax 71 64 77 11. English spoken.

Open 01/04 to 31/12. 21 bedrooms (all en suite with telephone). Outdoor swimming pool, golf 14 km, restaurant. ♿

25 km south of Aurillac, Vitrac is a small village amongst the hills. Regional meals can be taken on the terrace. Cycling, walking in the woods, canoeing. From Aurillac N122 south then left on to D66 to Vitrac.

TARIFF: Single 250–270, Double 250–300, Bk 40, Set menu 70–175.
CC: Amex, Euro/Access, Visa.

AUTUN Saône/Loire 3C

Hôtel St-Louis ★★ 6 rue de l'Arbalète, 71400 Autun.
☎ 85 52 21 03, Fax 85 86 32 54. English spoken.
Open 01/02 to 20/12. 52 bedrooms (38 en suite, 52 telephone). Golf 2 km, parking.
RESTAURANT: Closed 21/12 to 31/01.

A comfortable establishment in the charming environment of a former 17th-century post house. Situated close to the old city in the heart of the commercial centre.

TARIFF: Single 125–300, Double 125–335, Bk 40, Set menu 80–150.
CC: Amex, Diners, Euro/Access, Visa.

AUXERRE Yonne 2D

Hôtel Normandie ★★ 41 bd Vauban, 89000 Auxerre.
☎ 86 52 57 80, Fax 86 51 54 33. English spoken.
Open all year. 47 bedrooms (all en suite with telephone). Garage, parking. ♿

The hotel is in the centre of town and provides a good base for sightseeing. The rooms are quiet and have views of the garden. A gym, sauna and billiards are available, and the proprietors offer traditional French hospitality. Good conference facilities.

TARIFF: Single 230–260, Double 260–350, Bk 32.
CC: Amex, Diners, Euro/Access, Visa.

AVALLON Yonne 3C

Hôtel Alt'H ★★ La Tuilerie, 89200 Magny.
☎ 86 33 01 33, Fax 86 33 00 66. English spoken.

Open all year. 42 bedrooms (all en suite with telephone). Indoor swimming pool, tennis, golf 5 km, parking, restaurant. ♿

In a small, quiet hamlet surrounded by the Morvandelle countryside, the hotel is at the entrance to the Morvan Regional Nature Park, at the foot of Veselay in Burgundy. From the A6 take the Avallon exit.

TARIFF: Double 280, Bk 33, Set menu 85–135.
CC: Amex, Diners, Euro/Access, Visa.

AVENE-LES-BAINS Hérault 5C

SNC Hôtel ★★★ 34260 Avène-lès-Bains.
☎ 67 23 44 45, Fax 67 23 44 03. English spoken.
Open 01/04 to 31/10. 59 bedrooms (all en suite with telephone). Outdoor swimming pool, tennis, golf 30 km, parking, restaurant. ♿

In a wooded area with thermal spa nearby.

Accessed from Lodève on N9 via D35 and D8 going westwards.
TARIFF: Double 350–410, Bk 47, Set menu 85.
CC: Amex, Diners, Euro/Access, Visa.

AVIGNON Gard 5D

Hôtel Les Cèdres ★★ 39 bd Pasteur, 30400 Villeneuve-lès-Avignon.
℡ 90 25 43 92, Fax 90 25 14 66. English spoken.
Open 01/03 to 30/11. 24 bedrooms (all en suite with telephone). Outdoor swimming pool, golf 10 km, parking.
RESTAURANT: Closed lunch.

A Louis XIV-style building set in shady grounds not far from Avignon.
TARIFF: Double 290–360, Bk 38, Set menu 124.
CC: Euro/Access, Visa.

Hôtel La Magnaneraie ★★★ 37 rue Camp de Bataille, 30400 Villeneuve-lès-Avignon.
℡ 90 25 11 11, Fax 90 25 46 37. English spoken.
Open all year. 27 bedrooms (all en suite with telephone). Outdoor swimming pool, tennis, golf 4 km, garage, parking, restaurant. &

A former cardinal's house, transformed into a luxury hotel, on a hill, in a large garden with pine trees, overlooking the historic village of Villeneuve-lès-Avignon. Opposite the Pope's Palace, across the River Rhône.
TARIFF: Single 300–800, Double 400–1000, Bk 65, Set menu 170–350.
CC: Amex, Diners, Euro/Access, Visa.

AVRANCHES Manche 1D

Hôtel Les Abricantes ★★ 37 bd du Luxembourg, 50300 Avranches.
℡ 33 58 66 64, Fax 33 58 40 11. English spoken.
Open 10/01 to 20/12. 29 bedrooms (all en suite with telephone). Garage. &
RESTAURANT: Closed 27/12 to 08/01.

Located above the bay of Mont St-Michel (20 km away) with superb views. The hotel is in the centre of Avranches and the restaurant offers traditional cuisine with fish specialities.
TARIFF: (1993) Single 260–290, Double 270–320, Bk 30.
CC: Euro/Access, Visa.

AZAY-LE-RIDEAU Indre/Loire 2C

Le Grand Monarque ★★ 3 place de la République, 37190 Azay-le-Rideau.
℡ 47 45 40 08, Fax 47 45 46 25.
English spoken.
Open 01/02 to 15/12. 27 bedrooms (26 en suite, 1 bath/shower only,

27 telephone). Golf 12 km, garage, parking.
RESTAURANT: good. Closed 15/11 to 15/03.
Delightful old, very cosy hotel in the town centre, with luxurious rooms, and grassy courtyard. Take the St-Avertin exit from the A10 (towards Chinon).
TARIFF: (1993) Single 235–500, Double 280–600, Bk 45, Set menu 90–395.
CC: Amex, Diners, Euro/Access, Visa.

BAGNOLES-DE-L'ORNE Orne 2C

Hôtel Le Cheval Blanc ★★ place de l'Eglise, 61140 La Chapelle-d'Andaine.
℡ 33 38 11 88.
Open all year. 12 bedrooms (7 en suite, 12 telephone). Golf 5 km, parking. &
RESTAURANT: Closed Sun eve.

One of the Logis de France hotels offering traditional regional cuisine. La Chapelle-d'Andaine lies 5 km south-west of Bagnoles on the Domfront to Alençon road (D176).
TARIFF: Double 120–200, Bk 26, Set menu 55–198.
CC: Amex, Euro/Access, Visa.

Hôtel Le Diamant Bleu ★★★ rue Casinos, 61140 Bagnoles-de-l'Orne.
℡ 33 38 44 44, Fax 33 38 46 23. English spoken.

Open all year. 75 bedrooms (all en suite with telephone). Indoor swimming pool, golf 1 km, parking, restaurant. &
Modern hotel with fitness room, jacuzzi, satellite TV. In the centre of Bagnoles, overlooking the lake. Special rates on ample sports facilities nearby.
TARIFF: Double 320–410, Bk 45.
CC: Amex, Diners, Euro/Access, Visa.

Hôtel Lutetia-Reine Astrid ★★★ bd Paul Chalvet, 61140 Bagnoles-de-l'Orne.
℡ 33 37 94 77, Fax 33 30 09 87. English spoken.
Open 01/04 to 01/11. 33 bedrooms

France

(27 en suite, 33 telephone). Tennis, golf 2 km, parking, restaurant. &

Situated in the heart of the Andaine forest, the hotel has a large garden with sun terrace and flowerbeds, and offers Normandy cuisine.

TARIFF: Single 190–430, Double 270–430, Bk 45, Set menu 120–340.
CC: Amex, Diners, Euro/Access, Visa.

Manoir du Lys ★★★
61140 Bagnoles-de-l'Orne.
📞 33 37 80 69, Fax 33 30 05 80.
English spoken.
Open 01/03 to 31/12. 23 bedrooms (all en suite with telephone). Tennis, golf 1 km, garage, parking, restaurant.
The hotel is in the heart of Normandy, on the edge of the forest and only 300 m from Bagnoles golf course. Hotel closes Sunday evening and Mondays in low season. The spa town of Bagnoles-de-l'Orne is 2 km away.
TARIFF: Single 300–650, Double 360–800, Bk 50.
CC: Amex, Diners, Euro/Access, Visa.

BAPAUME Pas-de-Calais 2B

Hôtel Paix ★★ av A Guidet, 62450 Bapaume.
📞 21 07 11 03, Fax 21 07 43 66. English spoken.
Open all year. 13 bedrooms (all en suite with telephone). Garage, parking, restaurant.
Small, friendly hotel offering regional cuisine in its recently opened restaurant.
TARIFF: Double 220–320, Bk 25, Set menu 65–250.
CC: Euro/Access, Visa.

BAR-SUR-SEINE Aube 3C

Hôtel Barsequanais ★ av Gén Leclerc, 10110 Bar-sur-Seine.
📞 25 29 82 75, Fax 25 29 70 01.
Open all year. 24 bedrooms (18 en suite, 24 telephone). Golf 14 km, parking.
RESTAURANT: Closed Sun eve.
TARIFF: Double 100–190, Bk 25, Set menu 65–170.
CC: Euro/Access, Visa.

BARBIZON Seine/Marne 2D

Hôtel Bas-Breau ★★★★ 22 rue Grande, 77630 Barbizon.
📞 1 60 66 40 05, Fax 1 60 69 22 89. English spoken.
Open all year. 12 bedrooms (all en suite with telephone). Outdoor swimming pool, tennis, golf 3 km, garage, parking, restaurant. &
A luxurious hotel with a large garden and

furnished to a very high standard. It is situated in the centre of Barbizon.
TARIFF: (1993) Single 800, Double 1300–1500, Bk 90, Set menu 320–380.
CC: Amex, Euro/Access, Visa.

BARBOTAN-LES-THERMES Gers 4D

Château Bellevue ★★★ 19 rue Joseph Cappin, 32150 Cazaubon.
📞 62 09 51 95, Fax 62 09 54 57. English spoken.
Open 01/03 to 01/01. 25 bedrooms (all en suite with telephone). Outdoor swimming pool, golf 20 km, parking, restaurant.
Stylish château in quiet and relaxing countryside, but close to all watersports (lac de l'Uby) and horse riding. From Barbotan, south past lake, turn right through Cazaubon and château is on left.
TARIFF: Single 215–475, Double 310–475, Bk 47.
CC: Amex, Diners, Euro/Access, Visa.

Hôtel Paix ★★ 32150 Barbotan-les-Thermes.
📞 62 69 52 06, Fax 62 09 55 73. English spoken.
Open 01/04 to 20/11. 32 bedrooms (all en suite with telephone). Outdoor swimming pool, golf 25 km, parking, restaurant.
Modern hotel with a covered terrace in a pedestrianised area with a swimming pool. From Condom, turn off D931 at Eauze following D626 until Cazaubon, then take the D656 towards Cabarret.
TARIFF: Double 250–350, Bk 30.
CC: Euro/Access, Visa.

BAREGES Htes-Pyrénées 4D

Hôtel Richelieu ★★ rue Ramond, 65120 Barèges.
📞 62 92 68 11, Fax 62 92 66 00. English spoken.
Open 19/12 to 04/04 & 01/06 to 04/10. 34 bedrooms (all en suite with telephone). Parking, restaurant.
The hotel is in the centre of Barèges, a ski resort, but also an ideal base for summer visitors with mountain, valley and woodland walks.
TARIFF: (1993) Double 250, Bk 35, Set menu 70–150.
CC: Amex, Euro/Access, Visa.

LA BAULE Loire-Atlan 1D

Hôtel Bellevue Plage ★★★ 27 bd Océan, 44500 La Baule.
📞 40 60 28 55, Fax 40 60 10 18. English spoken.

Open 15/02 to 15/11. 34 bedrooms (all en suite with telephone). Golf 5 km, parking. RESTAURANT: good. Closed Tues LS.

Ideally situated facing the sea, in the centre of the La Baule bay. The hotel provides lounge and terrace, restaurant, bar, fitness room, sunbed and private car park. A warm welcome awaits.

TARIFF: Single 390–480, Double 490–780, Bk 50, Set menu 165–200.
CC: Amex, Diners, Euro/Access, Visa.

Hôtel La Concorde ★★★ 1 av de la Concorde, 44500 La Baule.
☎ 40 60 23 09, Fax 40 42 72 14. English spoken.
Open 01/04 to 31/10. 47 bedrooms (all en suite with telephone). Garage, parking.

A pleasant, family-run hotel, facing the sea and the beach.

TARIFF: Double 400–530, Bk 42.
CC: Amex, Euro/Access, Visa.

Hôtel Hermitage ★★★★★ 5 esplanade Lucien Barrière, 44504 La Baule.
☎ 40 11 46 46, Fax 40 11 46 45. English spoken.

Open 01/04 to 31/10. 222 bedrooms (all en suite with telephone). Outdoor swimming pool, tennis, golf 7 km, garage, parking, restaurant. ᕕ

Set on a 10 km stretch of sandy beach. Built in 1926 in French château style with direct access to the sea. At no extra cost one sport activity per person per day, is included. For example, a green fee for the golf course, one hour of tennis, horse-riding or windsurfing (in season).

TARIFF: Single 800–2050, Double 900–2250, Bk 85.
CC: Amex, Diners, Euro/Access, Visa.

Castel Marie-Louise ★★★★ 1 av Andrieu, BP 409, 44504 La Baule.
☎ 40 11 48 38, Fax 40 11 48 35. English spoken.

Open 11/02 to 02/01. 31 bedrooms (all en suite with telephone). Tennis, golf 6 km, parking, restaurant. ᕕ

A charming Belle Epoque manor set in attractive shaded lawns overlooking the bay. Following the esplanade, the hotel is just after the Grand Casino.

TARIFF: Single 700–1540, Double 850–2200, Bk 80.
CC: Amex, Diners, Euro/Access, Visa.

Hôtel Welcome ★★ 7 av des Impairs, 44504 La Baule.
☎ 40 60 30 25. English spoken.
Open 11/04 to 15/10. 18 bedrooms (all en suite with telephone). Golf 5 km.

Well-appointed hotel with pleasant atmosphere. Situated between the Casino and shopping centre, and 30 m from the sea.

TARIFF: Single 340–365, Double 340–385, Bk 35.
CC: Euro/Access, Visa.

BAYEUX Calvados   1B

Hôtel Lion d'Or ★★★ 71 rue St-Jean, 14400 Bayeux.
☎ 31 92 06 90, Fax 31 22 15 64. English spoken.
Open 20/01 to 20/12. 27 bedrooms (all bath/shower only with telephone). Golf 9 km, garage, parking, restaurant.

A former 17th-century coaching inn, full of character. Heading for the town centre, turn into rue de Crèmel by the railway station. Keep on this road towards the town centre and hotel is on the right.

TARIFF: Single 300–450, Double 420–900, Bk 55.
CC: Amex, Diners, Euro/Access, Visa.

Manoir du Carel 14400 Bayeux.
☎ 31 22 37 00, Fax 31 21 57 00. English spoken.
Open all year. 4 bedrooms (all en suite with telephone). Tennis, golf 2 km, garage, parking.
Ideal base for D-Day beaches and Bayeux

tapestry. Elegantly furnished manor house. From Bayeux D6 towards Port-en-Bessin. 4.5 km after traffic lights turn left. Entry marked after 1 km.
TARIFF: Single 350, Double 450–550, Bk 45.
CC: Euro/Access, Visa.

Hôtel d'Argouges ★★ 21 rue St-Patrice, 14400 Bayeux.
☏ 31 92 88 86, Fax 31 92 69 16. English spoken.

Open all year. 25 bedrooms (all en suite with telephone). Golf 10 km, garage, parking.
In the heart of the historic and artistic city of Bayeux (world famous 11th-century tapestry, museums, cathedral). Rooms overlooking courtyard, with small park and flower garden.
TARIFF: Double 190–390, Bk 38.
CC: Amex, Diners, Euro/Access, Visa.

Hôtel Churchill ★★★ 14 rue St-Jean, 14404 Bayeux.
☏ 31 21 31 80, Fax 31 21 41 66. English spoken.

Open 01/03 to 15/11. 32 bedrooms (all en suite with telephone). Golf 7 km, parking, restaurant. ♿
This highly recommended hotel is situated in the centre of Bayeux, near the tapestry museum and cathedral but in a quiet street.

TARIFF: Single 260–350, Double 280–480, Bk 38.
CC: Amex, Diners, Euro/Access, Visa.

Château de Goville ★★★ Littry, 14330 Le Breuil-en-Bessin.
☏ 31 22 19 28, Fax 31 22 68 74. English spoken.

Open all year. 10 bedrooms (all en suite with telephone). Golf 12 km, parking, restaurant.
18th-century hotel set in a 12-acre park, with warm atmosphere, original furnishings and beautiful décor. 10 km from Bayeux, close to D-Day beaches. From Caen north-west on N13 towards coast to Bayeux. Then D5 to Château.
TARIFF: Single 425–495, Double 425–695, Bk 50, Set menu 140–245.
CC: Amex, Diners, Euro/Access, Visa.

Hôtel La Ranconniere ★★ route d'Arromanches, 14480 Crépon.
☏ 31 22 21 73, Fax 31 22 98 39. English spoken.
Open all year. 33 bedrooms (all en suite with telephone). Golf 20 km, parking, restaurant. ♿

Converted 14th-century manor house with period furniture and seasonal menus. From Bayeux take D12 direction Ouistreham, then from Sommervieu D112 to Crépon 7 km.
TARIFF: Double 180–350, Bk 40, Set menu 50–240.
CC: Amex, Diners, Euro/Access, Visa.

BEAUGENCY Loiret   2D

Hôtel L'Abbaye ★★★ 2 quai de l'Abbaye, 45190 Beaugency.
☏ 38 44 67 35, Fax 38 44 87 92. English spoken.
Open all year. 18 bedrooms (all en suite with telephone). Golf 6 km, parking, restaurant.

An old 17th-century abbey in the town of Beaugency on the River Loire. There are tennis courts and a swimming pool close by.

France

TARIFF: Single 420–480, Double 500–560, Bk 42, Set menu 185.
CC: Amex, Diners, Euro/Access, Visa.

Hôtel La Tonnellerie ★★★★ 12 rue des Eaux-Bleues, Tavers, 45190 Beaugency.
☎ 38 44 68 15, Fax 38 44 10 01. English spoken.

Open 15/04 to 15/10. 20 bedrooms (all en suite with telephone). Outdoor swimming pool, golf 9 km, parking, restaurant.

In the Châteaux de la Loire region. Discreet charm of an old manor in a quiet location with up-to-date local cuisine. 3 km east of Beaugency (towards Blois).

TARIFF: Double 705–880, Bk 55, Set menu 125–417.
CC: Euro/Access, Visa.

BEAUJEU Rhône   5B

Hôtel Anne de Beaujeu ★ 28 rue de la République, 69430 Beaujeu.
☎ 74 04 87 58, Fax 74 69 22 13. English spoken.
Open 20/01 to·20/12. 7 bedrooms (all en suite with telephone). Parking.
RESTAURANT: Closed Sun eve & Mon.

Old house in old village with beautiful country around. 13 km from the Paris-Lyon motorway. Exit Belleville-sur-Saône, then west on the D37 to Beaujeu.

TARIFF: Double 250–350, Bk 35, Set menu 110–310.
CC: Euro/Access, Visa.

Hôtel Mont-Brouilly ★★ 69430 Quincie-en-Beaujolais.
☎ 74 04 33 73, Fax 74 69 00 72. English spoken.
Open 01/03 to 01/02. 29 bedrooms (all en suite with telephone). Outdoor swimming pool, garage, parking, restaurant. &

In the heart of the Beaujolais region. West of Belleville and A6 on the D37, towards Beaujeu. Hotel is 1 km from the village of Cercié.

TARIFF: Single 220–300, Double 270–320, Bk 34, Set menu 90–250.
CC: Amex, Euro/Access, Visa.

BEAULIEU-SUR-MER Alpes-Marit   6C

Hôtel Frisia ★★★ bd Mar Leclerc, 06310 Beaulieu-sur-Mer.
☎ 93 01 01 04, Fax 93 01 31 92. English spoken.

Open 22/12 to 31/10. 35 bedrooms (28 en suite, 35 telephone).

Beside the marina and with splendid views of the sea, hotel the also has a pretty garden overlooking the hills. From Nice follow the coast road to Beaulieu towards Monaco.

TARIFF: Single 200–520, Double 220–560, Bk 30.
CC: Amex, Euro/Access, Visa.

Hôtel Metropole ★★★★ bd Mar Lerclerc, 06310 Beaulieu-sur-Mer.
☎ 93 01 00 08, Fax 93 01 18 51. English spoken.
Open 20/12 to 20/10. 50 bedrooms (all en suite with telephone). Outdoor swimming pool, golf 15 km, parking, restaurant.

Prices quoted are for half board. Beaulieu-sur-Mer is between Nice and Monaco.

TARIFF: Single 1060–2040, Double 1760–3700, Set menu 400–490.
CC: Amex, Euro/Access, Visa.

BEAUNE Côte-d'Or   3C

Beaun Hôtel ★★ 55 bis fg Bretonnière, 21200 Beaune.
☎ 80 22 11 01. English spoken.

Open 15/02 to 15/01. 16 bedrooms (14 en suite, 16 telephone). Golf 2 km, parking.

A new hotel in a quiet location, just 10 minutes from the centre of this old town. Going towards Lyon, the hotel is opposite the Fiat garage.

TARIFF: Single 150–264, Double 150–287, Bk 26.
CC: Euro/Access, Visa.

Hôtel Belle Epoque ★★★ 15 fg Bretonnière, 21200 Beaune.
☎ 80 24 66 15, Fax 80 24 17 49. English spoken.
Open all year. 16 bedrooms (all en suite with telephone). Golf 5 km, garage.

A medieval yet modernised local-style house close to the famous Hospices de Beaune. On the N74 from the town centre towards Autun.

TARIFF: Double 315–610, Bk 40.
CC: Amex, Visa.

Hôtel Climat de France ★★ av Charles de Gaulle, Parc Hôtelier, 21200 Beaune.
☎ 80 22 74 10, Fax 80 22 40 45. English spoken.

Open all year. 50 bedrooms (all en suite with telephone). Golf 2 km, parking, restaurant. &

A modern hotel, all rooms having English channel colour television. Facilities include several family rooms, a sauna and garden with playground. There is a wine bar, and the restaurant serves regional cuisine. Friendly, efficient service. 500 m from A6 exit towards Beaune, and 500 m from town centre.

TARIFF: Single 285–295, Double 285–315, Bk 35, Set menu 60–120.
CC: Amex, Euro/Access, Visa.

Hôtel Le Cep ★★★★ 27 rue Maufoux, 21200 Beaune.
☎ 80 22 35 48, Fax 80 22 76 80. English spoken.
Open all year. 52 bedrooms (all en suite with telephone). Golf 4 km, garage, parking, restaurant. &

A 16th-century private residence in the centre of Beaune. Stunning décor in traditional French style.

TARIFF: Single 500–700, Double 600–1200, Bk 65.
CC: Amex, Diners, Euro/Access, Visa.

Hôtel Le Chalet d'Ivry ★★
21340 Ivry-en-Montagne.
☎ 80 20 21 18, Fax 80 20 24 70.
English spoken.
Open all year. 10 bedrooms (all en suite with telephone). Tennis, parking, restaurant.

Good regional food and a family atmosphere. On N6 north of Nolay, west of Beaune.

TARIFF: Double 165–190, Bk 28, Set menu 65–145.
CC: Amex, Euro/Access, Visa.

Hôtel La Closerie ★★★ 61 route de Pommard, 21200 Beaune.
☎ 80 22 15 07, Fax 80 24 16 22. English spoken.
Open 15/01 to 23/12. 47 bedrooms (all en suite with telephone). Outdoor swimming pool, golf 4 km, garage, parking. &

Charming and peaceful hotel with large garden and heated pool.

TARIFF: Single 300–495, Double 320–520, Bk 39.
CC: Amex, Diners, Euro/Access, Visa.

Hôtel Mercure ★★★ Beane Centre, avenue Charles de Gaulle, 21200 Beaune.
☎ 80 22 22 00, Fax 80 22 91 74.
English spoken.

Open all year. 120 bedrooms (all en suite with telephone). Outdoor swimming pool, golf 3 km, parking, restaurant. &

In the town centre near the famous Hospices de Beaune. Swimming pool with terrace and garden.

TARIFF: Single 350–400, Double 350–430, Bk 50, Set menu 98–165.
CC: Amex, Diners, Euro/Access, Visa.

France

Hôtel Les Paulands ★★★ Ladoix-Serrigny,
21550 Beaune.
📞 80 26 41 05, Fax 80 26 47 56. English spoken.
Open all year. 20 bedrooms (all en suite
with telephone). Outdoor swimming pool,
golf 6 km, parking. ♿
*Burgundian house standing in its own
vineyards. From A6, Nuits-St-George exit, take
the N74 towards Aloxe-Corton/Ladoix-Serrigny.*
TARIFF: Double 240–380, Bk 42.
CC: Euro/Access, Visa.
SEE ADVERTISEMENT

BEAUVAIS Oise   2B

Hôtel Palais ★★ 9 rue St-Nicholas,
60000 Beauvais.
📞 44 45 12 58, Fax 44 45 66 23. English spoken.
Open all year. 15 bedrooms (10 en suite,
5 bath/shower only, 15 telephone). ♿
Two minutes' walk from cathedral.
TARIFF: Single 105–235, Double 115–250, Bk 24.
CC: Amex, Euro/Access, Visa.

BENODET Finistère   1C

Hôtel Armoric ★★ 3 rue Penfoul,
29950 Bénodet.

📞 98 57 04 03, Fax 98 57 21 28. English spoken.
Open 01/03 to 15/11. 40 bedrooms
(22 en suite, 18 bath/shower only,

40 telephone). Tennis, golf 3 km, garage,
parking, restaurant.
*A pleasant family hotel close to beaches and
marina. From Quimper go to Fouesnant and
then Bénodet.*
TARIFF: Single 200–450, Double 295–550, Bk 45.
CC: Euro/Access, Visa.

Hôtel L'Ancre de Marine ★★ 5 av de l'Odet,
29950 Bénodet.
📞 98 57 05 29.

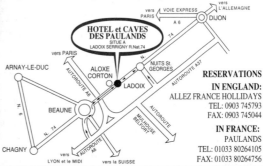

Open all year. 12 bedrooms (10 en suite, 12 telephone). Golf 4 km.

Small hotel near coast, west of Fouesnant and south of Quimper on D34.

TARIFF: Single 200–310, Double 280–320, Bk 38.
CC: Amex, Euro/Access, Visa.

Hôtel de la Poste ★★ 17 rue de l'Eglise, 29950 Bénodet.
℡ 98 57 01 09, Fax 98 57 27 48. English spoken.
Open all year. 36 bedrooms (34 en suite, 36 telephone). Golf 5 km, garage, parking, restaurant. &

Comfortable hotel with restaurant serving local and traditional cuisine. Situated 150 m from the port and south-facing beaches. Off D44 coast road east of Fouesnant.

TARIFF: Single 170–400, Double 200–400, Bk 40.
CC: Amex, Diners, Euro/Access, Visa.

BERGERAC Dordogne 4B

Hôtel Bordeaux ★★★ 38 pl Gambetta, 24100 Bergerac.
℡ 53 57 12 83, Fax 53 57 72 14. English spoken.

Open 01/02 to 20/12. 40 bedrooms (all en suite with telephone). Outdoor swimming pool, garage, parking, restaurant. &

The Maury family has been welcoming guests to the hotel since 1855. All modern facilities are offered including colour TV and lifts. Activities include riding, parachuting and cycling.

TARIFF: Single 280–350, Double 320–420, Bk 45, Set menu 95–210.
CC: Amex, Diners, Euro/Access, Visa.

Auberge de la Devinière ★★★ rte de Mussidan, 24130 Bergerac.
℡ 53 81 66 43, Fax 53 81 54 44. English spoken.
Open all year. 7 bedrooms (all en suite with telephone). Outdoor swimming pool, golf 15 km, parking, restaurant.

Lovely old Périgord inn with individually decorated rooms, amid meadows, forest and litle lake. Mushroom-picking in hotel grounds! Regional cuisine and warm welcome. North of Bergerac D709, D15.

TARIFF: Double 350–650, Bk 55.
CC: Euro/Access, Visa.

BERNAY Eure 2A

Hôtel Acropole ★★ 27300 Bernay.
℡ 32 46 06 06, Fax 32 44 01 04. English spoken.
Open all year. 51 bedrooms (all en suite with telephone). Parking. &

A modern hotel 4 km from Bernay, on the N138 towards Alençon.

TARIFF: (1993) Double 220–270, Bk 30.
CC: Amex, Euro/Access, Visa.

BESANCON Doubs 3D

Hôtel 3 Iles ★★ Chalezeule, 25220 Besançon.
℡ 81 61 00 66, Fax 81 61 73 09. English spoken.

Open all year. 16 bedrooms (all en suite with telephone). Parking.

Pleasant hotel, 5 minutes from Besançon centre, in Chalezeule, on the banks of the River Doubs. From Besançon take N83 towards

France

Belfort (north-east) then right for Carrefour supermarket, SNCF and Chalezeule.
TARIFF: Single 240–250, Double 260–280, Bk 28.
CC: Euro/Access, Visa.

Hôtel Climat de France ★★ CD 108 Ecole Valentin, Miserey Salines, 25000 Besançon.
℡ 81 88 04 11, Fax 81 80 31 22. English spoken.
Open all year. 43 bedrooms (all en suite with telephone). Golf 1 km, parking, restaurant. ⅃
Leave Besançon centre via rue de Versoul, after about 5 km take right turn towards Gray. Hotel is about 500 m on the left.
TARIFF: Double 270, Bk 32.
CC: Euro/Access, Visa.

BETHUNE Pas-de-Calais   2B

Hôtel La Chartreuse du Val ★★★ 1 rue de Fouquières, 62199 Gosnay.
℡ 21 62 80 00, Fax 21 62 42 50. English spoken.

Open all year. 58 bedrooms (all en suite with telephone). Tennis, parking, restaurant. ⅃
Château built in 1792 on a 14th-century monastery site. Restored in 1986 as a luxurious hotel with two restaurants. Hotel is located south-west of Béthune. Leave A26 at junction 6 towards Labuissière and follow signs to Les Chartreuses.
TARIFF: Single 390–500, Double 450–800, Bk 50, Set menu 110–375.
CC: Amex, Euro/Access, Visa.

Hôtel du Vieux Beffroi ★★ 48 Grand'Place, 62400 Béthune.
℡ 21 68 15 00, Fax 21 56 66 32. English spoken.
Open all year. 65 bedrooms (55 en suite, 65 telephone). Parking, restaurant. ⅃
In the centre of town, facing the 600 year-old belfry.
TARIFF: Single 150–300, Double 230–350, Bk 30, Set menu 89–185.
CC: Amex, Diners, Euro/Access, Visa.

BEYNAC Dordogne   4B

Hôtel Bonnet ★★ 24220 Beynac.
℡ 53 29 50 01. English spoken.
Open 01/04 to 15/10. 22 bedrooms (20 en suite, 22 telephone). Garage, parking, restaurant.
Traditional Périgord hotel, good food and lovely views on to river and garden. From Sarlat (10 km), first hotel on right as you enter Beynac.
TARIFF: Single 175–260, Double 240–310, Bk 32, Set menu 120–280.
CC: Euro/Access, Visa.

BEZIERS Hérault   5C

Hôtel Splendid ★★ 24 av du 22-Août, 34500 Béziers.
℡ 67 28 23 82. English spoken.
Open all year. 24 bedrooms (16 en suite, 24 telephone). Golf 6 km, garage.
This hotel is in the centre of the town, near the theatre in a quiet location.
TARIFF: Single 130–220, Double 140–250, Bk 27.
CC: Euro/Access, Visa.

BIARRITZ Pyrénées-Atlan   4C

Hôtel Palais ★★★★ 1 av Impératrice, 64200 Biarritz.
℡ 59 41 64 00, Fax 59 41 67 99. English spoken.

Open all year. 155 bedrooms (all en suite with telephone). Outdoor swimming pool, golf 1 km, parking, restaurant. ⅃
In the heart of the city, and formerly an imperial palace, the hotel looks out on the fine beaches of Biarritz. It has been recently renovated and has a world-wide reputation for luxury.
TARIFF: Single 1100–1950, Double 1400–2650, Bk 100, Set menu 300.
CC: Amex, Diners, Euro/Access, Visa.

BILLIERS Morbihan   1D

Domaine de Rochevilaine ★★★★ Pointe de
Pen Lan, 56190 Billiers.
☎ 97 41 61 61, Fax 97 41 44 85. English spoken.

Open 01/01 to 18/01 & 05/03 to 31/12.
25 bedrooms (all en suite with telephone).
Outdoor swimming pool, parking,
restaurant. ♿

*Dramatic setting, standing right on the edge of
the rocky point in about an acre, with
stunning views. Individual annexes available.*
TARIFF: Double 420–1600, Bk 60,
Set menu 250–400.
CC: Amex, Diners, Euro/Access, Visa.

LE BLANC Indre   4B

Domaine de l'Etape ★★★ route de Bélâbre,
36300 Le Blanc.
☎ 54 37 18 02, Fax 54 37 75 59.
English spoken.

Open all year. 35 bedrooms (all en suite
with telephone). Golf 6 km, parking,
restaurant. ♿

*Delightful 19th-century building in 380-acre
park, with 45-acre boating and fishing lake.
Horse-riding, flying, gliding and parachuting*

*nearby. From Le Blanc head south-east on
D10 for 6 km towards Bélâbre.*
TARIFF: Single 210–370, Double 210–430,
Bk 42, Set menu 115–130.
CC: Amex, Diners, Euro/Access, Visa.

Hôtel Villa Varsovie 73 rue de la République,
36300 Le Blanc.
☎ 54 37 29 03, Fax 54 37 42 48. English spoken.
Open all year. 8 bedrooms (all en suite with
telephone). Golf 10 km, parking, restaurant.
*Hotel is close to the Gendarmerie in the village
of Le Blanc.*
TARIFF: Double 250–350, Bk 40,
Set menu 98–198.
CC: Euro/Access, Visa.

BLOIS Loir-et-Cher   3D

Hôtel La Clé des Champs ★★
41120 Chitenay.
☎ 54 70 42 03. English spoken.
Open 01/02 to 30/12. 8 bedrooms (3 en suite).
Parking, restaurant.

*Traditional restaurant with rooms,
concentrates on good food using fresh local
produce. Large terrace for open-air eating.
Surrounded by the Loire châteaux. From Blois,
south on the D936 towards Contres. Turn right
after 10 km.*
TARIFF: Single 130–150, Double 150, Bk 30,
Set menu 130–175.
CC: Euro/Access, Visa.

BLOTZHEIM Ht-Rhin   3D

Captain Hôtel ★★ rue du 19 novembre,
68730 Blotzheim.
☎ 89 68 82 82, Fax 89 68 86 43. English spoken.

Open all year. 63 bedrooms (all en suite
with telephone). Parking, restaurant. ♿
*This pleasant Alsace-style hotel is 3 km from
Basle-Mulhouse Airport and 5 minutes from*

France

the Swiss and German borders. The rooms are quiet and fully equipped. Restaurant serves regional specialities. Shuttle to airport. Special weekend and family rates. Leave the A35 at airport exit, then follow signs to Blotzheim.

TARIFF: Double 260–260, Bk 32,
Set menu 40–110.
CC: none.

BOLBEC Seine Marit 2A

Hôtel Promotour ★★ av du Marechal-Joffre, 76210 Bolbec.
✆ 35 31 88 89, Fax 35 31 94 26. English spoken.

Open all year. 42 bedrooms (all en suite with telephone). Parking, restaurant. &

Pleasant 2-star hotel with fully equipped bedrooms. The restaurant specialises in regional food. Special rates for weekends and families. On the N15 between Le Havre and Rouen.

TARIFF: Single 210, Double 240, Bk 32,
Set menu 69–120.
CC: Amex, Euro/Access, Visa.

BONLIEU Jura 6A

Hôtel L'Alpage ★★ 39130 Bonlieu.
✆ 84 25 57 53, Fax 84 25 50 74. English spoken.

Open all year. 10 bedrooms (all en suite with telephone). Parking. &
RESTAURANT: Closed Mon lunch.

The hotel is deep in the heart of the Jura region, with lakes and pine forests. It is situated on the N78, at an altitude of 850 m.

TARIFF: Double 225–250, Bk 35,
Set menu 100–180.
CC: Amex, Euro/Access, Visa.

BORDEAUX Gironde 4B

Hôtel Résidence Corus ★★★ 42 rue Peyronnet, 33800 Bordeaux.
✆ 56 33 82 00, Fax 56 31 46 77. English spoken.
Open all year. 50 bedrooms (all en suite with telephone). Golf 10 km, parking. &

In the centre of Bordeaux, studios with car park, telephone and satellite TV, for the independent traveller.

TARIFF: Double 260–350, Bk 40.
CC: Amex, Euro/Access, Visa.

Hôtel Sainte-Catherine ★★★ 27 rue Parlement Ste-Catherine, 33000 Bordeaux.
✆ 56 81 95 12, Fax 56 44 50 51. English spoken.

Open all year. 85 bedrooms (all en suite with telephone). Garage. &

A beautifully renovated, 18th-century building in the heart of the city, close to the theatre, museum, pedestrian streets and restaurants. Comfortable rooms with all modern facilities, piano bar, conference hall.

TARIFF: Single 530–830, Double 600–900, Bk 70.
CC: Amex, Diners, Euro/Access, Visa.

BORMES-LES-MIMOSAS Var 6C

Hôtel Le Mirage ★★★★ 38 rue de la vue des Iles, 83230 Bormes-les-Mimosas.
✆ 94 71 09 83, Fax 94 64 93 03. English spoken.
Open 13/03 to 31/10. 35 bedrooms

(all en suite with telephone). Outdoor swimming pool, tennis, golf 10 km, parking, restaurant.

Victorian-style hotel with typical Provence decoration. Panoramic view of "Golden Islands" and the Mediterranean Sea. Hotel is situated below the medieval village of Bormes-les-Mimosas on the N98.

TARIFF: (1993) Double 585–890, Bk 65.
CC: Amex, Diners, Euro/Access, Visa.

LA BOUILLE Seine Marit   2A

Hôtel St-Pierre ★★ 76530 La Bouille.
✆ 35 18 01 01, Fax 35 18 12 76. English spoken.
Open all year. 7 bedrooms (all en suite with telephone). Parking, restaurant.
Not far from Rouen, in the centre of a typical village. Restaurant and some rooms with views over River Seine. From the Le Havre to Paris autoroute, take exit 24 From Rouen to Caen for 26 km, exit 24.

TARIFF: Single 280–320, Double 320–350, Bk 40, Set menu 140–240.
CC: Amex, Diners, Euro/Access, Visa.

BOULOGNE-SUR-MER Pas-de-Calais   2B

Hôtel Arcade ★★ bd Eurvin,
62200 Boulogne-sur-Mer.
✆ 31 31 21 01, Fax 21 31 48 25. English spoken.
Open all year. 50 bedrooms (all en suite with telephone). Golf 7 km, garage, parking. &
Highly recommended, near the old town and a few minutes from the ferry boat terminal. Soundproofed rooms, friendly atmosphere.

TARIFF: Single 275, Double 315, Bk 38.
CC: Amex, Euro/Access, Visa.

Hôtel Clery ★★★ Hésdin-l'Abbé,
62360 Boulogne-sur-Mer.
✆ 21 83 19 83, Fax 21 87 52 59. English spoken.
Open 15/01 to 20/12. 19 bedrooms (all en suite with telephone). Tennis, golf 9 km, parking.
The hotel is in a 12-acre park very close to the port of Boulogne. Take N1 from Boulogne for 10 km. In Hésdin-l'Abbé, turn left at traffic lights.

TARIFF: Single 325–400, Double 350–560, Bk 50.
CC: Amex, Diners, Euro/Access, Visa.

Hôtel Metropole ★★★ 51 rue Thiers,
62200 Boulogne-sur-Mer.
✆ 21 31 54 30, Fax 21 30 45 72. English spoken.
Open 05/01 to 20/12. 25 bedrooms (all en suite with telephone). Golf 6 km.

Located in the town centre, the hotel has just been completely redecorated. Rooms have luxury bathrooms. There is a pleasant lounge and pretty garden.

TARIFF: Single 325–370, Double 360–410, Bk 42.
CC: Amex, Diners, Euro/Access, Visa.

BOURG-EN-BRESSE Ain   5B

Hôtel Mercure-Chantecler ★★★ 10 av Bad-Kreuznach, 01000 Bourg-en-Bresse.
✆ 74 22 44 88, Fax 74 23 43 57. English spoken.
Open all year. 60 bedrooms (all en suite with telephone). Golf 10 km, garage, parking, restaurant. &
In a quiet location at the entrance of the town, heading towards Strasbourg. Restaurant offers regional specialities.

TARIFF: Single 325, Double 350–450, Bk 47, Set menu 115–240.
CC: Amex, Diners, Euro/Access, Visa.

Hôtel du Prieure ★★★ 49 bd de Brou,
01000 Bourg-en-Bresse.
✆ 74 22 44 60, Fax 74 22 71 07. English spoken.
Open all year. 14 bedrooms (all en suite with telephone). Golf 10 km, garage, parking. &
Sited in a quiet position in a park, 200 m from the church of Brou. The rooms are spacious and stylish.

TARIFF: Single 380–460, Double 400–550, Bk 46.
CC: Amex, Diners, Euro/Access, Visa.

BOURGES Cher   2D

Hôtel d'Angleterre ★★★ 1 pl des Quatre Piliers, 18000 Bourges.
✆ 48 24 68 51, Fax 48 65 21 41. English spoken.
Open all year. 31 bedrooms (all en suite with telephone). Golf 2 km, garage.
RESTAURANT: Closed 15/12 to 15/01.

Quiet, comfortable and fully restored hotel not far from the cathedral, in old Bourges. Le

France

Windsor restaurant decorated in Louis XVI style.
TARIFF: Single 382, Double 420, Bk 37,
Set menu 88–139.
CC: Amex, Diners, Euro/Access, Visa.

Hôtel Bourbon ★★★ bd République,
18000 Bourges.
☏ 48 70 70 00, Fax 48 70 21 22. English spoken.
Open all year. 60 bedrooms (all en suite
with telephone). Golf 3 km, parking. &
RESTAURANT: Closed Sat lunch.

Opened in the spring of 1991, restored historic abbey, situated in wooded grounds. Motorway from Paris A71.
TARIFF: Single 400–525, Double 485–610, Bk 65.
CC: Amex, Diners, Euro/Access, Visa.

LE BOURGET-DU-LAC Savoie 6A

Hôtel Orée du Lac ★★★★
73370 Le Bourget-du-Lac.
☏ 79 25 24 19, Fax 79 25 08 51. English spoken.
Open 01/03 to 30/11. 12 bedrooms
(all en suite with telephone). Outdoor
swimming pool, tennis, golf 8 km, parking,
restaurant. &

Imposing stylish château, in a dominant position above Lac Bourget across from Aix-le-Bains. Surrounded by 5 acres of grounds. From Aix, drive around the south end of the lake to Le Bourget.
TARIFF: Single 590–720, Double 650–870,
Bk 60, Set menu 130–160.
CC: Amex, Diners, Euro/Access, Visa.

BRANTOME Dordogne 4B

Hôtel le Châtenet ★★★ 24310 Brantôme.
☏ 53 05 81 08, Fax 53 05 85 52. English spoken.
Open all year. 8 bedrooms (all en suite
with telephone). Outdoor swimming pool,
garage, parking. &

A small comfortable manor built at the end of the 17th century. On D78 1.5 km west of Brantôme.
TARIFF: Double 480–780, Bk 55.
CC: Euro/Access, Visa.

BREST Finistère 1C

Hôtel de la Paix ★★★ 32 rue Algésiras,
29200 Brest.
☏ 98 80 12 97, Fax 98 43 40 95. English spoken.
Open all year. 25 bedrooms (all en suite
with telephone). Golf 15 km, parking.
Located in the heart of Brest, a few steps away

from the St-Louis covered market, near the post office, town hall, conference centre and famous rue de Siam. Take N12 towards the coast to Brest.
TARIFF: Single 245–275, Double 270–300, Bk 30.
CC: Amex, Diners, Euro/Access, Visa.

BRIANCON Htes-Alpes 6A

Hôtel Paris ★★ 41 av Gén de Gaulle,
05100 Briançon.
☏ 92 20 15 30, Fax 92 20 30 82.
English spoken.
Open all year. 22 bedrooms (15 en suite,
7 bath/shower only, 22 telephone).
Golf 14 km, garage, parking, restaurant. &

Near the centre of the town and the railway station. 300 m from the sports centre and the ski-lifts. On the N94 close to the Italian border.
TARIFF: Double 145–265, Bk 30,
Set menu 75–148.
CC: Amex, Diners, Visa.

BRIOUDE Haute-Loire 5A

Hôtel Le Brivas avenue du Velay,
43100 Brioude.
☏ 71 50 10 49, Fax 71 74 90 69. English spoken.
Open 01/01 to 15/12. 30 bedrooms
(all en suite with telephone). Outdoor
swimming pool, parking, restaurant. &

Modern hotel on the main road to Le Puy, on the town's edge. Garden terrace. Large comfortable bedrooms and well furnished.
TARIFF: Single 220–260, Double 280–300, Bk 34.
CC: Amex, Diners, Euro/Access, Visa.

BRIVE Corrèze 4B

Soph'Motel ★★★ Saint Pardoux l'Artigier,
19270 Brive.
☏ 55 84 51 02, Fax 55 84 50 14. English spoken.

Open 01/02 to 31/12. 25 bedrooms
(all en suite with telephone). Outdoor
swimming pool, tennis, parking, restaurant. &

*25 independent luxury flats and motel in
peaceful surroundings. On the N20, north of
Donzenac, between Brive (15 km) and
Uzerche (18 km).*

TARIFF: Double 270–320, Bk 35,
Set menu 69–200.
CC: Diners, Euro/Access, Visa.

BUSSANG Vosges   3D

Hôtel du Tremplin ★★ 8 rue du 3ème RTA,
88540 Bussang.
☎ 29 61 50 30, Fax 29 61 50 89.
English spoken.
Open 01/11 to 30/09. 19 bedrooms
(13 en suite, 19 telephone). Garage, parking.
RESTAURANT: Closed Sun eve & Mon.

*Small, family-run hotel in the centre of
Bussang which is in the heart of the Hautes-
Vosges and the source of the Moselle River. Ski
centre in winter.*

TARIFF: Single 130–250, Double 140–300,
Bk 30, Set menu 70–300.
CC: Amex, Diners, Euro/Access, Visa.

BUZANCAIS Indre   4B

Hôtel L'Hermitage ★★ rte d'Argy,
36500 Buzançais.
☎ 54 84 03 90, Fax 54 02 13 19.
English spoken.
Open 01/01 to 18/09 & 25/09 to 31/12.
14 bedrooms (11 en suite, 3 bath/shower only,
14 telephone). Golf 7 km, garage, parking.
RESTAURANT: Closed Sun eve & Mon.

*A manor house in its own grounds, offering
excellent cuisine. Fishing nearby in the Indre
river. 600 m from the town centre.*

TARIFF: Single 115–255, Double 140–300,
Bk 26, Set menu 78–265.
CC: Euro/Access, Visa.

CABRERETS Lot   5C

Hôtel Les Falaises ★★ Bouziès,
46330 Cabrerets.
☎ 65 31 26 83, Fax 65 30 23 87.
English spoken.
Open 02/02 to 30/11. 39 bedrooms
(all en suite with telephone). Outdoor
swimming pool, tennis, parking, restaurant. &

*Regional food and good wine, on the banks of
the River Lot in a small village. 27 km from
historic Cahors.*

TARIFF: Double 222–273, Bk 33.
CC: Amex, Euro/Access, Visa.

CADENET Vaucluse   5D

Hôtel Le Moulin de Lourmarin ★★★★
84160 Lourmarin.
☎ 90 68 06 69, Fax 90 68 31 76. English spoken.
Open all year. 20 bedrooms (all en suite
with telephone). Outdoor swimming pool,
golf 9 km, parking. &
RESTAURANT: good. Closed Wed LS.

*A former silkworm-rearing house totally
restored in 1988 to provide a small,
atmospheric hotel in beautiful surroundings.
On D943 north of Cadenet.*

TARIFF: Single 500–1200, Double 500–1800,
Bk 70, Set menu 160–260.
CC: Amex, Diners, Euro/Access, Visa.

LA CADIERE-D'AZUR Var   6C

Hostellerie Berard ★★★ rue Gabriel Peri,
83740 La Cadière-d'Azur.
☎ 94 90 11 43, Fax 94 90 11 71. English spoken.
Open 20/03 to 15/01. 40 bedrooms
(all en suite with telephone). Outdoor
swimming pool, garage, restaurant.

*The hotel is in the heart of an old Provençal
town, about 7 km west of Toulon on the A50.*

TARIFF: (1993) Single 390–500,
Double 500–750, Bk 60.
CC: Amex, Euro/Access, Visa.

CAEN Calvados   2A

Hôtel Campanile ★★ bd du Bois,
14200 Hérouville-St-Clair.
☎ 31 95 29 24, Fax 31 95 74 87. English spoken.
Open all year. 70 bedrooms (all en suite
with telephone). Tennis, golf 2 km, parking,
restaurant. &

Between Ouistreham car ferry and Caen, on

France

the main road. A pleasant situation in quiet countryside.

TARIFF: Double 270, Bk 30, Set menu 80−100.
CC: Amex, Euro/Access, Visa.

Friendly Hôtel ★★★ 2 pl de Boston Citis, à Hérouville-St-Clair, 14200 Caen.
☎ 31 44 05 05, Fax 31 44 95 94. English spoken.
Open all year. 90 bedrooms (all en suite with telephone). Indoor swimming pool, golf 4 km, parking, restaurant. ♿

Comfortable hotel with excellent service and facilities including a gym, sauna, spa, children's play area and a traditional restaurant. Follow the directions for Côte de Nacre, Douvres.

TARIFF: Single 380−410, Double 420−450, Bk 46, Set menu 115−150.
CC: Amex, Diners, Euro/Access, Visa.

CAHORS Lot   4D

Hôtel Terminus ★★★ 5 av Charles de Freycinet, 46000 Cahors.
☎ 65 35 24 50. English spoken.
Open all year. 31 bedrooms (all en suite with telephone). Garage, parking. ♿
RESTAURANT: very good. Closed Mon LS.

Elegant traditional hotel offering comfortable accommodation near town centre, and station.

TARIFF: (1993) Single 230−390, Double 260−415, Bk 35, Set menu 120−300.
CC: Euro/Access, Visa.

CALAIS Pas-de-Calais   2B

Hôtel Climat de France ★★ digue Gaston Berthe, 62100 Calais.
☎ 21 34 64 64, Fax 21 34 35 39. English spoken.
Open all year. 44 bedrooms (all en suite with telephone). Parking. ♿
RESTAURANT: Closed Sun eve Oct to Mar.

The restaurant/bar overlooks the seafront in this modern hotel. Try the mussels, the speciality of the hotel's La Soupière restaurant. Private parking.

TARIFF: Double.270−295, Bk 38.
CC: Amex, Diners, Euro/Access, Visa.

Hôtel George V ★★★ 36 rue Royale, 62100 Calais.
☎ 21 97 68 00, Fax 21 97 34 73. English spoken.
Open all year. 45 bedrooms (all en suite with telephone). Golf 15 km, parking. ♿
RESTAURANT: good. Closed Sat lunch & Sun eve.

Comfortable and quiet, in the centre of Calais.

Follow Calais Nord signs from the car ferry terminal and the brown arrow marked George V.

TARIFF: Single 210−290, Double 290−450, Bk 40, Set menu 80−250.
CC: Amex, Diners, Euro/Access, Visa.

Hôtel du Golf ★★ digue Gaston Berthe, 62100 Calais.
☎ 21 96 88 99, Fax 21 34 35 39. English spoken.
Open all year. 31 bedrooms (all en suite with telephone). Parking, restaurant. ♿

Hôtel du Golf has been open since 1989. From the centre of the town take the road La Plage. The hotel is overlooking the sea. Self-catering facilities available.

TARIFF: Double 270−295, Bk 38.
CC: Amex, Euro/Access, Visa.

Holiday Inn Garden Court ★★★ bd Alliés, 62100 Calais.
☎ 21 34 69 69, Fax 21 97 09 15.
English spoken.

Open all year. 65 bedrooms (all en suite with telephone). Golf 15 km, garage, parking. ♿
RESTAURANT: Closed Sat lunch.

In the town centre overlooking the harbour and the sea. 5 minutes from the ferry terminal and channel tunnel.

TARIFF: Double 500−600, Bk 55.
CC: Amex, Diners, Euro/Access, Visa.

Metropol Hotel ★★★ 45 quai du Rhin, 62100 Calais.
☎ 21 97 54 00, Fax 21 96 69 70.
English spoken.
Open 03/01 to 23/12. 40 bedrooms (all en suite with telephone). Garage, parking. ♿

A quiet hotel in the town centre, behind the railway station.

TARIFF: Single 200−280, Double 300−380, Bk 46.
CC: Amex, Diners, Euro/Access, Visa.

Hôtel Meurice ★★★ 5 rue Edmond Roche, 62100 Calais.
☎ 21 34 57 03, Fax 21 34 14 71. English spoken. Open all year. 39 bedrooms (all en suite with telephone). Golf 20 km, garage, parking, restaurant. **&**

In the centre of Calais, but in a particularly quiet, residential quarter, by the Richelieu Park. The hotel has a long tradition of quality and service.

TARIFF: Double 325–475, Bk 35, Set menu 100–280.
CC: Amex, Diners, Euro/Access, Visa.

CALVINET Cantal   5A

Hôtel Beauséjour ★★ route de Maurs, 15340 Calvinet.
☎ 71 49 91 68, Fax 71 49 98 63. English spoken. Open 01/03 to 30/11. 12 bedrooms (all en suite with telephone). Tennis, garage, parking. **&**
RESTAURANT: very good. Closed Sun eve.

Small hotel with gourmet restaurant. Close to the Gorges du Lot and Conques.

TARIFF: (1993) Single 200–250, Double 240–300, Bk 30, Set menu 85–220.
CC: Euro/Access, Visa.

CANNES Alpes-Marit   6C

Hôtel de l'Olivier ★★★ 5 rue Tambourinaires, 06400 Cannes.
☎ 93 39 53 28, Fax 93 39 55 85. English spoken.

Open all year. 24 bedrooms (all en suite with telephone). Outdoor swimming pool, golf 3 km, parking.
Luxuriously furnished hotel with a covered terrace by a swimming pool. Located looking down on the old town in Le Suquet. Only 3 minutes from beaches and old port. From A8 turn right from Pont Carnot heading along voie rapide, turning right off the rue Clemenceau.

TARIFF: Single 285–475, Double 365–585, Bk 40.
CC: Amex, Diners, Euro/Access, Visa.

Le Grand Hôtel ★★★★ 45 bd Croisette, 06400 Cannes.
☎ 93 38 15 45, Fax 93 68 97 45.
Open 01/01 to 01/11 & 10/12 to 31/12. 76 bedrooms (all en suite with telephone). Restaurant. **&**

Luxury hotel on La Croisette, set in a park with private beach. Air-conditioned rooms with terraces. Approach from La Croisette via rue de CDT André or rue Amoretti.

TARIFF: Single 550–1110, Double 660–1460, Bk 60, Set menu 120–190.
CC: Amex, Diners, Euro/Access, Visa.

Hôtel de Paris ★★★ 34 bd d'Alsace, 06400 Cannes.
☎ 93 38 30 89, Fax 93 39 04 61. English spoken.

Open 01/01 to 15/11 & 17/12 to 31/12. 50 bedrooms (all en suite with telephone). Outdoor swimming pool, golf 3 km, garage, parking, restaurant.

Comfortable hotel, with old fashioned charm in the centre of Cannes just 300 m from the private beach. Rooms are air conditioned and sound proofed. Sauna and jacuzzi. Eat on the terraces, surrounded by palm trees. Bd d'Alsace runs parallel to the beach close to the Palais des Festivals.

TARIFF: Single 450–650, Double 500–700, Bk 50.
CC: Amex, Diners, Euro/Access, Visa.

CARCASSONNE Aude   5C

Hôtel Donjon ★★★ 2 rue Comte Roger, Cité Medievale, 11000 Carcassonne.
☎ 68 71 08 80, Fax 68 25 06 60. English spoken.

France

Open all year. 38 bedrooms (all en suite with telephone). Golf 3 km, garage, parking. &
RESTAURANT: Closed Sunday 01/11 to 31/03.

In the middle of the medieval city, the hotel dates back to the middle ages and provides modern comforts, tranquillity and a warm welcome. By the motorway A61, exit at Carcassonne-Est towards Cité.

TARIFF: Single 290–600, Double 360–750, Bk 50, Set menu 70–120.
CC: Amex, Diners, Euro/Access, Visa.

Hôtel La Gentilhommière ★★
11800 Carcassonne.
℡ 68 88 14 14, Fax 68 78 65 80. English spoken.

Open all year. 31 bedrooms (all en suite with telephone). Outdoor swimming pool, golf 5 km, parking, restaurant. &

2 km from the old city of Carcassonne. Motorway A61, exit Carcassonne-Est.

TARIFF: Single 220, Double 270–290, Bk 35, Set menu 80–180.
CC: Amex, Euro/Access, Visa.

Hôtel Montsegur ★★★ 27 allée Léna, 11000 Carcassonne.
℡ 68 25 31 41, Fax 68 47 13 22. English spoken.
Open all year. 21 bedrooms (all en suite with telephone). Golf 2 km, parking.
RESTAURANT: good. Closed Sun & Mon eve LS.

Spacious and elegant 19th-century manor in centre of town. The restaurant is actually opposite but run by the same family. Good regional food.

TARIFF: Single 290–390, Double 390–490, Bk 49, Set menu 135–250.
CC: Amex, Diners, Euro/Access, Visa.

CARENTAN Manche   1B

Hôtel Aire de la Baie ★★ 50500 Carentan.
℡ 33 42 20 99, Fax 33 71 06 94. English spoken.
Open 10/01 to 23/12. 40 bedrooms (all en suite

with telephone). Parking, restaurant.

Not far from World War Two landing beaches and the junctions of N13 and N174. 50 km south-east of Cherbourg.

TARIFF: Single 240–250, Double 240–280, Bk 35, Set menu 70–140.
CC: Amex, Diners, Euro/Access, Visa.

CARNAC Morbihan   1C

Hôtel Celtique ★★★ 17 av de Kermario, 56340 Carnac.
℡ 97 52 11 49, Fax 97 52 71 10. English spoken.

Open all year. 49 bedrooms (all en suite with telephone). Golf 7 km, parking, restaurant. &

A recently renovated hotel, quietly situated amongst pine trees. Just a stone's throw from the beach and next to the tourist office in Carnac.

TARIFF: Single 410–530, Double 420–640, Bk 45, Set menu 95–265.
CC: Amex, Diners, Euro/Access, Visa.

Hôtel Plancton ★★★ 12 bd Plage, 56340 Carnac.
℡ 97 52 13 65, Fax 97 52 87 63. English spoken.
Open 30/03 to 15/10. 23 bedrooms (all en suite with telephone). Golf 8 km, parking, restaurant. &

Luxury holiday hotel overlooking fine sandy beach. Sailing club and sea-water hydrotherapy centre nearby. Access via D781 coastal road running south-west from L'Orient.

TARIFF: Single 395–510, Double 510–580, Bk 48, Set menu 90–180.
CC: Euro/Access, Visa.

CARPENTRAS Vaucluse   5D

Hôtel de Crillon-le-Brave ★★★★ pl Eglise, 84410 Crillon-le-Brave.
℡ 90 65 61 61, Fax 90 65 62 86. English spoken.
Open 01/04 to 01/01. 21 bedrooms (all en suite

with telephone). Outdoor swimming pool, garage, parking.
RESTAURANT: good. Closed Lunch Mon to Fri.

A charming country-house hotel perched above a tiny Provençal village with spectacular gardens and views; countryside, tranquillity. From Carpentras, direction Mont Ventaux Sud.
TARIFF: Single 750–950, Double 750–1450, Bk 75.
CC: Amex, Euro/Access, Visa.

Hôtel Les Trois Colombes ★★★
148 av des Garrigues, 84210 St-Didier.
☎ 90 66 07 01, Fax 90 66 11 54.
English spoken.
Open 01/03 to 31/12. 30 bedrooms (all en suite with telephone). Outdoor swimming pool, tennis, golf 6 km, parking, restaurant. &

Charming Provençal country residence with shady grounds covering 800 sq metres. From the A7 take the Avignon-Nord exit and go through Carpentras towards St-Didier, following signposts to the hotel.
TARIFF: Single 300, Double 320–400, Bk 45, Set menu 105–190.
CC: Amex, Diners, Euro/Access, Visa.

CASTELJALOUX Lot/Garonne   4D

Château de Ruffiac ★★★ Ruffiac,
47700 Casteljaloux.
☎ 53 93 18 63, Fax 53 89 67 93.
English spoken.
Open 01/03 to 31/01. 10 bedrooms (all en suite with telephone). Outdoor swimming pool, golf 8 km, parking.
RESTAURANT: Closed Feb.

Vast 14th-century vicarage, next to church, with views of both mountains and valleys. Water sports nearby. From Casteljaloux, north-west on D655 for 8 km.
TARIFF: Single 320–420, Double 380–480, Bk 40, Set menu 150–290.
CC: Euro/Access, Visa.

CASTERA-VERDUZAN Gers   4D

Hôtel Thermes ★★ 32410 Castéra-Verduzan.
☎ 62 68 13 07, Fax 62 68 10 49.
English spoken.
Open 01/02 to 01/01. 47 bedrooms (37 en suite, 37 telephone). Parking, restaurant. &

In the village centre of Castéra-Verduzan and on the D930 north west of Auch.
TARIFF: Single 175–198, Double 228–260, Bk 30.
CC: Amex, Diners, Euro/Access, Visa.

CASTRES Tarn   5C

Hôtel Café du Pont Les Salvages,
81100 Castres.
☎ 63 35 08 21, Fax 63 51 09 82.
Open all year. 6 bedrooms (1 en suite, 4 bath/shower only). Golf 2 km, parking.
RESTAURANT: Closed Feb.

A small hotel with a good restaurant. 5 km from Castres on the D89.
TARIFF: Single 170–190, Double 190–240, Bk 35, Set menu 90–250.
CC: Amex, Diners, Euro/Access, Visa.

CAUDEBEC-EN-CAUX Seine Marit   2A

Normotel La Marine ★★ 18 quai Guilbaud, 76490 Caudebec-en-Caux.
☎ 35 96 20 11, Fax 35 56 54 40. English spoken.
Open 01/02 to 11/01. 29 bedrooms (all en suite with telephone). Parking.
RESTAURANT: good. Closed Sun eve 15/11 to 15/03.

The hotel overlooks the River Seine, in the town centre.
TARIFF: Double 250–420, Bk 35, Set menu 78–230.
CC: Amex, Euro/Access, Visa.

CAUTERETS Htes-Pyrénées   4D

Hôtel Aladin ★★★ Gén Leclerc, 65110 Cauterets.
☎ 62 92 60 00, Fax 62 92 63 30.
English spoken.
Open 01/06 to 30/09 & 01/12 to 30/04. 70 bedrooms (all en suite with telephone). Indoor swimming pool, golf 20 km, garage, restaurant. &

Cosy, comfortable, quality hotel with friendly atmosphere and excellent food. Squash court and fitness room. From Lourdes, follow signs to Les Pyrénées and go through Argelès-Gazost and Pierrefitte. After Pierrefitte, turn right to Cauterets (10 km).
TARIFF: Single 430, Double 610, Bk 52, Set menu 150.
CC: Euro/Access, Visa.

Hôtel Etche Ona ★★ 20 rue Richelieu, 65110 Cauterets.
☎ 62 92 51 43, Fax 62 92 54 99.
English spoken.
Open 01/12 to 31/12 & 01/06 to 10/10. 32 bedrooms (27 en suite, 32 telephone). Golf 20 km, parking, restaurant.

In the centre of Cauterets, opposite the spa and close to the cable-car and ice rink. Friendly

*hotel in comfortable, modern surroundings.
Good restaurant serving local produce.*
TARIFF: Single 190–260, Double 260–320,
Bk 30, Set menu 65–160.
CC: Amex, Euro/Access, Visa.

CHABLIS Yonne 3C

Hôtel des Clos ★★★ rue Jules Rathier,
89800 Chablis.
📞 86 42 10 63, Fax 86 42 17 11. English spoken.

Open 10/01 to 10/12. 26 bedrooms
(all en suite with telephone). Golf 25 km,
garage, parking. &
RESTAURANT: very good. Closed Wed & Thurs
lunch LS.

*Elegant hotel from which to enjoy the Chablis
region. Tranquil garden setting encompassing
12th-century chapel.*
TARIFF: Single 240–495, Double 268–530,
Bk 50, Set menu 160–400.
CC: Euro/Access, Visa.

CHALONS-SUR-MARNE Marne 3A

Hôtel aux Armes de Champagne ★★★
31 av du Luxembourg, 51460 L'Epine.
📞 26 69 30 30, Fax 26 66 92 31. English spoken.
Open 16/02 to 07/01. 37 bedrooms (all en suite
with telephone). Tennis, garage, parking.
RESTAURANT: very good. Closed Sun eve &
Mon LS.

*Traditional French hostelry in the shadow of
the basilica of Notre Dame in pretty L'Epine.
8 km from Châlons-sur-Marne on N3 to Metz,
Verdun.*
TARIFF: Single 320–780, Double 400–780,
Bk 55, Set menu 205–480.
CC: Euro/Access, Visa.

Hôtel Bristol ★★ 77 av P Sémard,
51510 Fagnières.
📞 26 68 24 63, Fax 26 68 22 16. English spoken.

Open 02/01 to 23/12. 24 bedrooms
(23 en suite, 1 bath/shower only,
24 telephone). Golf 10 km, garage, parking.
*A comfortable hotel with spacious rooms that
can accommodate extra beds for children.*
TARIFF: Single 150–210, Double 195–230, Bk 28.
CC: Euro/Access, Visa.

Hôtel Moritz ★ 16 rue Lochet,
51000 Châlons-sur-Marne.
📞 26 68 09 27, Fax 26 21 37 98. English spoken.
Open all year. 25 bedrooms (9 en suite,
9 bath/shower only, 25 telephone).
Golf 10 km, garage, parking. &

*Close to the junction of the A4 and A26, south-
east of Reims.*
TARIFF: Single 105–185, Double 125–230, Bk 20.
CC: Amex, Diners, Euro/Access, Visa.

CHAMONIX Haute-Savoie 6A

Hôtel des Aiglons ★★★ 270 av de
Courmayeur, 74400 Chamonix.
📞 50 55 90 93, Fax 50 53 51 08. English spoken.
Open 19/12 to 15/10. 54 bedrooms
(all en suite with telephone). Golf 2 km,
garage, parking. &
RESTAURANT: good. Closed lunch.

*Brand new, state of the art hotel with superb
views from most rooms and offering excellent
service. 50 m from cable car. Conference
room, fitness room, terrace bar. From
autoroute exit Chamonix-Sud and hotel is
immediately on left.*
TARIFF: Single 300–620, Double 460–800, Bk 40.
CC: Amex, Diners, Euro/Access, Visa.

Hôtel Albert 1er ★★★★ 119 impasse du
Montenvers, 74400 Chamonix-Mont-Blanc.
📞 50 53 05 09, Fax 50 55 35 48.
English spoken.
Open 01/12 to 02/05 & 10/05 to 24/10.
32 bedrooms (all en suite with telephone).

Outdoor swimming pool, tennis, golf 2 km, garage, parking. &
RESTAURANT: very good. Closed Wed lunch.

Beautiful hotel with a backdrop of mountains and only a stone's throw from the centre of town. Traditional Savoie welcome. Fine restaurant. Just to the south of the N506.

TARIFF: Single 450–900, Double 590–1150, Bk 68, Set menu 175–410.
CC: Amex, Diners, Euro/Access, Visa.

Hôtel Richemond ★★ 228 rue Dr Paccord, 74400 Chamonix.
℡ 50 53 08 85, Fax 50 55 91 69. English spoken. Open 01/01 to 20/04 & 13/06 to 15/09. 53 bedrooms (all en suite with telephone). Golf 2 km, parking, restaurant.

A traditional hotel in town centre close to cable car and bus stations. Rear entrance on allée Recteur Poyot.

TARIFF: Single 290, Double 470.
CC: Amex, Diners, Euro/Access, Visa.

CHAMPAGNAC Cantal   5A

Château de Lavendes ★★★ route de Neuvic, 15350 Champagnac.
℡ 71 69 62 79, Fax 71 69 65 33. English spoken. Open 01/03 to 30/11. 8 bedrooms (all en suite with telephone). Outdoor swimming pool, golf 10 km, parking.
RESTAURANT: good. Closed Mon LS.

10 km from Bort-les-Orgues. Elegant château set in parkland, on D15 to Neuvic. Good regional food.

TARIFF: Double 400–540, Bk 52, Set menu 150–260.
CC: Euro/Access, Visa.

CHAMROUSSE Isère   6A

Hôtel Hermitage ★★★ Le Recoin, 38410 Chamrousse.
℡ 76 89 93 21, Fax 76 89 95 30. English spoken. Open 15/12 to 15/04. 50 bedrooms (all en suite with telephone). Garage, restaurant.

Chamrousse is 32 km east of Grenoble in the hills via Uriage.

TARIFF: Single 300–350, Double 350–440, Bk 36, Set menu 120–170.
CC: Amex, Euro/Access, Visa.

CHANTILLY Oise   2B

Hostellerie du Lys ★★★ 63 7ème av, rond point de la Reine, 60260 Lamorlaye.
℡ 44 21 26 19, Fax 44 21 28 19. English spoken.

Open all year. 35 bedrooms (all en suite with telephone). Golf 1 km, parking.
RESTAURANT: Closed 21/12 to 02/01.

Swiss-style building set in large wooded estate. The Hostellerie offers all the facilities of an exclusive country club. From Chantilly take the N16 towards Lamorlaye.

TARIFF: Single 180–515, Double 320–515, Bk 42, Set menu 150–180.
CC: Amex, Diners, Euro/Access, Visa.

CHANTONNAY Vendée   4A

Manoir de Ponsay St-Mars-des-Prés, 85110 Chantonnay.
℡ 51 46 96 71, Fax 51 46 80 07. English spoken. Open all year. 8 bedrooms (all en suite). Parking, restaurant.

A private château where you are welcomed as friends. Comfortable and quiet, situated in a park between Nantes and La Rochelle.

TARIFF: Double 350–560, Bk 40, Set menu 170.
CC: Amex, Diners, Euro/Access, Visa.

LA CHAPELLE-EN-VECORS Drôme   5B

Hôtel Le Veymont ★★
26420 St-Agnan-en-Vercors.
℡ 75 48 20 19, Fax 75 48 10 34. English spoken. Open 20/12 to 01/11. 20 bedrooms (all en suite with telephone). Parking, restaurant.

Le Veymont is situated in a small village in the National Park of the Vercors, with excellent views of the surrounding mountains. (English owned.) St-Agnan-en-Vercors is 4 km south of La Chapelle-en-Vercors.

TARIFF: (1993) Single 150–220, Double 185–225, Bk 35, Set menu 95–150.
CC: Amex, Diners, Euro/Access, Visa.

LA CHARITE-SUR-LOIRE Nièvre   2D

Hôtel Grand Monarque ★★ 33 quai Clémenceau, 58400 La Charité-sur-Loire.
℡ 86 70 21 73, Fax 86 69 62 32. English spoken. Open all year. 9 bedrooms (all en suite with telephone). Golf 20 km, garage, restaurant.

This hotel and restaurant have delightful views over a sweep of the River Loire, crossed by a 16th-century hump-backed, stone bridge. The comfortable bedrooms are in a 17th-century house. The restaurant is a new addition and most tables have good river views. Imaginative, regional cuisine. On the N151.

TARIFF: (1993) Single 160–240, Double 180–320, Bk 33, Set menu 98–230.
CC: Amex, Diners, Euro/Access, Visa.

France

CHARLEVILLE-MEZIERES Ardennes 3A

Hôtel Mercure ★★★ Villers-Semeuse,
08340 Charleville-Mézières.
☎ 24 37 55 29, Fax 24 57 39 43. English spoken.
Open all year. 68 bedrooms (all en suite with
telephone). Golf 15 km, parking, restaurant. &
*Rimbaud's native town and the 'marionette
capital of the world'. From Charleville-
Mézières go towards Sedan on A203, exit 7
Villers-Semeuse.*
TARIFF: Single 370, Double 400, Bk 46.
CC: Amex, Diners, Euro/Access, Visa.

LA CHARTRE-SUR-LE-LOIR Sarthe 2C

Hôtel France ★★ 20 place de la République,
72340 La Chartre-sur-le-Loir.
☎ 43 44 40 16, Fax 43 79 62 20. English spoken.
Open 15/12 to 15/11. 29 bedrooms (all en suite
with telephone). Garage, restaurant.
*Very French hotel in central position, with
pavement café in front and large garden
behind. Good local fishing.*
TARIFF: Double 215–275, Bk 38,
Set menu 69–260.
CC: Euro/Access, Visa.

CHARTRES Eure/Loir 2D

Hôtel Ibis ★★ 14 pl Drouaise, 28000 Chartres.
☎ 37 36 06 36, Fax 37 36 17 20. English spoken.
Open all year. 79 bedrooms (all en suite with
telephone). Golf 15 km, garage, restaurant. &
*From Paris take the A11 and exit at Chartres.
Ten minutes' walk from the cathedral and
railway station.*
TARIFF: Single 285–295, Double 320–340,
Bk 32, Set menu 73–95.
CC: Amex, Euro/Access, Visa.

CHATEAU-THIERRY Aisne 2B

Hôtel Ile de France ★★★ rte de Soissons,
02400 Château-Thierry.
☎ 23 69 10 12, Fax 23 83 49 70. English spoken.
Open all year. 50 bedrooms (all en suite
with telephone). Golf 2 km, parking,
restaurant.
*Imposing, modern hotel set in extensive
grounds overlooking the Marne Valley.
Gourmet restaurant. Three conference rooms
cater for up to 40 guests. 30 minutes from
Euro Disney.*
TARIFF: Single 200–280, Double 250–330,
Bk 38, Set menu 98–180.
CC: Amex, Diners, Euro/Access, Visa.

CHATEAUBOURG Ille/Vilaine 1D

Hôtel Pen'Roc ★★★ La Peinière, 35220 St-
Didier.
☎ 99 00 33 02, Fax 99 62 30 89. English spoken.
Open all year. 33 bedrooms (all en suite
with telephone). Outdoor swimming pool,
golf 15 km, garage, parking. &
RESTAURANT: good. Closed Sun eve.
*Situated between Rennes and Paris in a quiet
rural setting, this attractive modern hotel, built
in local style, has a swimming pool, sauna
and fitness room. The restaurant serves refined
cuisine using local ingredients (with the fish
being especially delicious). Take the motorway
Paris to Rennes A81/N157 then exit
Châteaubourg D857 and go 7.5 km to St-
Didier (D33).*
TARIFF: Single 320–360, Double 360–410,
Bk 44, Set menu 145–250.
CC: Amex, Diners, Euro/Access, Visa.

CHATEAUBRIANT Loire-Atlan 1D

Hôtel La Ferrière ★★★ route de Nantes,
44110 Châteaubriant.
☎ 40 28 00 28, Fax 40 28 29 21. English spoken.
Open all year. 25 bedrooms (all en suite
with telephone). Golf 10 km, parking,
restaurant. &
*Charming, small 18th-century manor house,
set in superb landscaped gardens situated on
the outskirts of Châteaubriant on the D178
towards Nantes.*
TARIFF: Single 270–330, Double 330–600,
Bk 39, Set menu 120–220.
CC: Amex, Diners, Euro/Access, Visa.

CHATEAUNEUF-LES-BAINS P-de-D 5A

Hôtel du Château ★★ Le Bordan,
63390 Châteauneuf-les-Bains.
☎ 73 86 67 01. English spoken.
Open 30/04 to 30/09. 36 bedrooms (all en suite
with telephone). Garage, parking, restaurant.
*A country hotel close to the River Sioule, with
large gardens in a quiet location.*
TARIFF: (1993) Single 200–220,
Double 200–240, Bk 26.
CC: Euro/Access, Visa.

CHATEAUROUX Indre 5A

Auberge Arc en Ciel ★★ La Forge-de-l'Ile,
36330 Châteauroux.
☎ 54 34 09 83, Fax 54 34 46 74. English spoken.
Open all year. 24 bedrooms (18 en suite,
6 bath/shower only, 24 telephone). Parking.

Attractive setting for this hotel with comfortable rooms beside the Indre River and near oak wood forest. Ten minutes from the town centre on the D943 leading to Châtre.

TARIFF: Single 150–195, Double 180–230, Bk 22.
CC: Diners, Euro/Access, Visa.

Hôtel Boischaut ★★ 135 av La Châtre, 36000 Châteauroux.
\ 54 22 22 34, Fax 54 22 64 89. English spoken.
Open all year. 27 bedrooms (all en suite with telephone). Garage, parking.

Comfortable hotel next to railway station with family rooms available (3 or 4 people) located on the D943 La Châtre road.

TARIFF: Double 195–235, Bk 24.
CC: Euro/Access, Visa.

CHATELAILLON-PLAGE Char-Marit   4A

Majestic Hotel ★★ bd de la Libération, 17340 Châtelaillon-Plage.
\ 46 56 20 53, Fax 46 56 29 24. English spoken.
Open 10/01 to 15/12. 30 bedrooms (26 en suite, 30 telephone). Golf 15 km, garage.
RESTAURANT: Closed Sat & Sun LS.

Built in 1927 and decorated in 20s style, this hotel is only 100 m from the beach and 500 m from indoor/outdoor swimming pools and tennis courts. Follow Centre-Ville and Mairie signs in Châtelaillon-Plage.

TARIFF: Single 200–260, Double 200–300, Bk 32, Set menu 100–145.
CC: Amex, Diners, Euro/Access, Visa.

CHATELGUYON Puy-de-Dôme   5A

Hôtel Régence 31 av Etats-Unis, 63140 Châtelguyon.
\ 73 86 02 60. English spoken.
Open 10/04 to 24/10. 27 bedrooms (24 en suite, 27 telephone). Golf 7 km, garage, restaurant.

Traditional French hotel in a thermal spa town with 18th-century antique furniture.

TARIFF: Single 170–220, Double 190–230, Bk 35, Set menu 80–95.
CC: Euro/Access, Visa.

CHATILLON-SUR-SEINE Côte-d'Or   3C

Hôtel de la Côte d'Or ★★★ rue Charles Ronot, 21400 Châtillon-sur-Seine.
\ 80 91 13 29, Fax 80 91 29 15. English spoken.
Open 01/03 to 31/12. 10 bedrooms (all en suite with telephone). Golf 20 km, garage, parking, restaurant.

Built in 1738, this old coach house, now a

small hotel and restaurant, still gives a warm welcome to weary travellers. In summer meals served outside.

TARIFF: Double 300–560, Bk 35, Set menu 95–185.
CC: Amex, Diners, Euro/Access, Visa.

LA CHATRE Indre   2D

Hôtel Les Dryades ★★★★ Pouligny-Notre-Dame, 36160 La Châtre.
\ 54 30 28 00, Fax 54 30 10 24. English spoken.
Open all year. 85 bedrooms (all en suite with telephone). Indoor swimming pool, outdoor swimming pool, tennis, golf on site, parking, restaurant. &

A first-class hotel, situated in the grounds of an international 18-hole golf course. There are aquatic and fitness centres and three gourmet restaurants. 10 km from La Châtre in the direction of Guerat, on the D940.

TARIFF: Single 650, Double 700, Bk 50, Set menu 180–350.
CC: Amex, Diners, Euro/Access, Visa.

Château de la Vallée Bleue ★★★ route de Verneuil, 36400 St-Chartier.
\ 54 31 01 91, Fax 54 31 04 48. English spoken.
Open 01/03 to 31/01. 13 bedrooms (all en suite with telephone). Outdoor swimming pool, golf 15 km, parking, restaurant. &

In the heart of George Sand's country. A romantic spot. Regional cooking with chef specialities and exhaustive wine list. From La Châtre D943 then D69 in St-Chartier.

TARIFF: Single 200–395, Double 320–550, Bk 50, Set menu 130–350.
CC: Euro/Access, Visa.

CHAUMONT Haute-Marne   3C

Hôtel La Chaumière ★ Condes, 52000 Chaumont.
\ 25 03 03 84.
Open all year. 11 bedrooms (3 en suite, 5 bath/shower only, 11 telephone).
Golf 20 km, parking, restaurant.

Set in the Haute-Marne area. North of the A5 on the D10 from junction 18 towards Chaumont.

TARIFF: Double 145–215, Bk 27, Set menu 62–150.
CC: Visa.

CHENONCEAUX Indre/Loire   2C

Hôtel du Roy ★★ rue du Dr Bretonneau, 37150 Chenonceaux.
\ 47 23 90 17, Fax 47 23 89 81. English spoken.

France

Open 15/02 to 15/11. 41 bedrooms
(24 en suite, 39 telephone). Tennis,
golf 20 km, parking, restaurant. &
*Situated in the village centre, near the castle
and with a garden. Access: A10, exit at
Amboise or Blois.*
TARIFF: Single 100–220, Double 140–260, Bk 30.
CC: Amex, Euro/Access, Visa.

CHERBOURG Manche 1B

Hôtel Louvre ★★ 2 rue H Dunant,
50100 Cherbourg.
☎ 33 53 02 28, Fax 33 53 43 88. English spoken.
Open 01/01 to 24/12. 42 bedrooms (37 en suite,
42 telephone). Golf 2 km, garage. &
*A cheerful, friendly hotel close to town centre.
Facilities include a lift and covered, secure
parking. From the town centre, turn right after
the bridge and then left after statue of
Napoleon and traffic lights.*
TARIFF: Single 210–310, Double 270–340, Bk 32.
CC: Amex, Diners, Euro/Access, Visa.

CHINON Indre/Loire 2C

Chris'Hôtel ★★ 12 pl Jeanne d'Arc,
37500 Chinon.
☎ 47 93 36 92, Fax 47 98 48 92. English spoken.
Open all year. 40 bedrooms (all en suite
with telephone). Golf 15 km, garage, parking.
*Situated in a quiet square, near the ancient
part of Chinon. Finely decorated in Louis XV
style. Friendly atmosphere.*
TARIFF: Single 220–300, Double 240–400, Bk 40.
CC: Amex, Diners, Euro/Access, Visa.

Hôtel Diderot ★★ 4 rue Buffon,
37500 Chinon.
☎ 47 93 18 87, Fax 47 93 37 10. English spoken.
Open 10/01 to 20/12. 28 bedrooms
(all en suite with telephone). Parking. &
*A few yards from place Jeanne d'Arc, this
interesting 18th-century building features
half-timbered walls and an especially fine
staircase. Family atmosphere, home-made
jams for breakfast.*
TARIFF: Single 200–300, Double 280–380, Bk 36.
CC: Amex, Diners, Euro/Access, Visa.

Château de Marcay ★★★★ Marcay,
37500 Chinon.
☎ 47 93 03 47, Fax 47 93 45 33. English spoken.
Open 15/03 to 15/01. 38 bedrooms (all en suite
with telephone). Outdoor swimming pool,
tennis, golf 20 km, parking, restaurant.
The hotel is a 15th-century fortress surrounded

*by its own vineyards, in Rabelais country. It is
6 km south of Chinon, on the D116.*
TARIFF: Double 495–1500, Bk 85,
Set menu 145–350.
CC: Amex, Visa.

LA CIOTAT Bouches-du-Rhône 6C

Hôtel Plage ★★★ plage du Bestouan,
13260 Cassis.
☎ 42 01 05 70, Fax 42 01 34 82. English spoken.
Open 15/03 to 15/10. 30 bedrooms (all en suite
with telephone). Golf 10 km, restaurant.
*North-west of La Ciotat. Join D559 from A50
towards Cassis.*
TARIFF: Single 300–400, Double 400–600, Bk 40.
CC: Amex, Diners, Euro/Access, Visa.

CLECY Calvados 2A

Hôtel Moulin du Vey ★★★ 14570 Clécy.
☎ 31 69 71 08, Fax 31 69 14 14. English spoken.
Open 28/12 to 30/11. 25 bedrooms (all en suite
with telephone). Golf 3 km, parking.
RESTAURANT: Closed 30/11 to 28/12.
*An old mill near the River l'Orne, with 2
annexes. The restaurant is a gastronomic
delight. Take the D133A, over Le Pont du Vey
bridge.*
TARIFF: (1993) Single 370–450,
Double 370–500, Bk 48, Set menu 137–370.
CC: Amex, Diners, Euro/Access, Visa.

CLERMONT-FERRAND Puy-de-Dôme 5A

Hôtel Lafayette ★★★ 53 av Union Soviétique,
63000 Clermont-Ferrand.
☎ 73 91 82 27, Fax 73 91 17 26. English spoken.
Open all year. 50 bedrooms (all en suite
with telephone). Golf 10 km, parking. &
*Modern hotel with friendly atmosphere in front
of the railway station, near to the beautiful
Auvergne region with its lakes and volcanoes.*
TARIFF: Single 245–300, Double 300–330, Bk 35.
CC: Amex, Euro/Access, Visa.

Hôtel Metropole ★★★ 2 bd Vaquez,
63130 Royat.
☎ 73 35 80 18, Fax 73 35 66 67. English spoken.
Open 01/05 to 30/09. 71 bedrooms (58 en suite,
71 telephone). Golf 2 km, garage, restaurant. &
*Large hotel surrounded by parkland, 2 km
from town centre and close to casino, near
"Puy-de-Dôme".*
TARIFF: Single 210–480, Double 280–540,
Bk 40, Set menu 160–190.
CC: Amex, Euro/Access, Visa.

COGNAC Charente 4B

Hôtel L'Echassier ★★★ 72 rue Bellerue, Châteaubernard, 16100 Cognac.
☎ 45 35 01 09, Fax 45 32 22 43. English spoken.
Open all year. 22 bedrooms (all en suite with telephone). Outdoor swimming pool, golf 1 km, parking. ♿
RESTAURANT: very good. Closed Sun.

Quiet, comfortable hotel enjoying good reputation for its food. From motorway, take Cognac exit, towards Angoulême and Rouillac.

TARIFF: Single 370–450, Double 420–830, Bk 55, Set menu 138–320.
CC: Amex, Diners, Euro/Access, Visa.

COLLIOURE Pyrénées Orient 5C

Hôtel Relais des Trois Mas ★★★★ rte Port-Vendres, 66190 Collioure.
☎ 68 82 05 07, Fax 68 82 38 08. English spoken.

Open 16/12 to 15/11. 23 bedrooms (all en suite with telephone). Outdoor swimming pool, golf 18 km, parking, restaurant.

All rooms are fully equipped including air conditioning and satellite TV. Heated swimming pool, with whirlpool. The hotel is south of Collioure (road to Port-Vendres), with direct access to the beach.

TARIFF: Single 395–660, Double 395–1650, Bk 68, Set menu 165–345.
CC: Euro/Access, Visa.

COLMAR Haut-Rhin 3D

Hôtel Husseren-les-Châteaux ★★★ rue Schlossberg, 68420 Husseren-les-Châteaux.
☎ 89 49 22 93, Fax 89 49 24 84.
English spoken.
Open all year. 38 bedrooms (all en suite with telephone). Indoor swimming pool, tennis, golf 22 km, garage, parking, restaurant. ♿

Modern, interesting hotel with bedrooms on two levels. Views over vineyards and the Rhine Valley. 6 km south of Colmar on the N83.

TARIFF: Single 390–490, Double 490–690, Bk 54, Set menu 115–320.
CC: Amex, Diners, Euro/Access, Visa.

Hostellerie Le Maréchal ★★★★
4 pl des 6 Montaignes Noire, Petite-Venise, 68000 Colmar.
☎ 89 41 60 32, Fax 89 24 59 40.
English spoken.

Open all year. 30 bedrooms (all en suite with telephone). Golf 10 km, parking, restaurant.

Beautiful, old, heavily-timbered building dating back to 1565, Le Maréchal is situated in the old quarter known as Little Venice. Dining-rooms overlooking the river. Elegantly furnished.

TARIFF: Single 450, Double 550–700, Bk 60.
CC: Amex, Euro/Access, Visa.

Hôtel Altea Champ de Mars ★★★ 2 av de la Marne, 68000 Colmar.
☎ 89 41 54 54, Fax 89 23 13 76. English spoken.
Open all year. 75 bedrooms (all en suite with telephone). Golf 10 km, garage.
Hotel is situated in the middle of the Park

Champ de Mars, 5 km from the centre of town. Quiet and very comfortable rooms.

TARIFF: Single 330–490, Double 330–560, Bk 52.
CC: Amex, Diners, Euro/Access, Visa.

Hôtel St-Martin ★★★ 38 Grand'rue, 68000 Colmar.
☏ 89 24 11 51, Fax 89 23 47 78. English spoken.

Open 01/03 to 31/12. 24 bedrooms (all en suite with telephone). Golf 10 km.
Near the cathedral in the centre of the old town, a nicely renovated and quiet hotel.
TARIFF: Single 350–450, Double 350–650, Bk 48.
CC: Amex, Diners, Euro/Access, Visa.

COLOMBEY-LES-DEUX-EGLISES 3C

Hôtel Les Dhuits ★★★
52330 Colombey-Les-Deux-Eglises.
☏ 25 01 50 10, Fax 25 01 56 22.
English spoken.

Open 05/01 to 20/12. 42 bedrooms (all en suite with telephone). Tennis, golf 25 km, garage, parking. &
RESTAURANT: Closed 05/01 to 20/01.
Quietly situated modern hotel and restaurant in this historic town on the champagne route. On N19.

TARIFF: Single 250–280, Double 280–350, Bk 35, Set menu 80–160.
CC: Amex, Diners, Euro/Access, Visa.

COMBEAUFONTAINE Haute-Saône 3C

Hôtel Balcon ★★ 70120 Combeaufontaine.
☏ 84 92 11 13, Fax 84 92 15 89.
Open 12/01 to 26/12. 18 bedrooms (16 en suite, 2 bath/shower only, 18 telephone). Garage, parking, restaurant.

Pretty, flower-bedecked, hotel in a quiet part of France. Comfortable, with a heavy emphasis on the kitchen. Specialises in regional Franche-Comté meals. You can walk, fish and get lost here. Combeaufontaine lies on the N19 between Langres and Vesoul.

TARIFF: Single 140–300, Double 140–360, Bk 40, Set menu 140–360.
CC: Amex, Diners, Euro/Access, Visa.

COMBLOUX Haute-Savoie 6A

Hôtel Feug ★★★ route de Megève, 74920 Combloux.
☏ 50 93 00 50, Fax 50 21 21 44. English spoken.
Open all year. 28 bedrooms (all en suite with telephone). Indoor swimming pool, outdoor swimming pool, tennis, golf 2 km, garage, parking, restaurant. &
Facing Mont Blanc, the hotel offers many facilities and has a good restaurant.
TARIFF: Double 290–550, Bk 45, Set menu 105–195.
CC: Amex, Diners, Euro/Access, Visa.

COMBOURG Ille/Vilaine 1D

Hôtel Château et Voyageurs ★★ pl Châteaubriand, 35270 Combourg.
☏ 99 73 00 38, Fax 99 73 25 79. English spoken.
Open 20/01 to 15/12. 33 bedrooms (all en suite with telephone). Golf 10 km, garage, parking, restaurant.

Charming hotel situated near the lake and château on the edge of town. Located between the roads to Dinan and Rennes.
TARIFF: Double 260–450, Bk 42.
CC: Amex, Diners, Euro/Access, Visa.

COMPIEGNE Oise 2B

Hôtel à la Bonne Idée ★★★ St-Jean-aux-Bois, 60350 Compiègne.
☏ 44 42 84 09, Fax 44 42 80 45. English spoken.
Open all year. 24 bedrooms (all en suite with telephone). Parking, restaurant. &
In the heart of the Forêt de Compiègne, this

France

hotel specialises in regional cooking. Located in the centre of St-Jean-aux-Bois on the D85, just 10 minutes' drive from the A1.

TARIFF: Double 395–440, Bk 58, Set menu 190–430.
CC: Amex, Euro/Access, Visa.

CONCARNEAU Finistère   1C

Hôtel Le Galion ★★★ 15 rue St-Guénoléne Ville Clos, 29110 Concarneau.
☎ 98 97 30 16, Fax 98 50 67 88. English spoken.
Open 01/01 to 31/10 & 01/03 to 31/12.
5 bedrooms (all en suite with telephone).
Golf 12 km.
RESTAURANT: very good. Closed Sun eve and Mon LS.

Traditional old hotel within the walled town. Daytime motorised traffic restrictions.

TARIFF: Single 320–400, Double 380–400, Bk 40, Set menu 150–370.
CC: Amex, Diners, Euro/Access, Visa.

LE CONQUET Finistère   1C

Hôtel Pointe Ste-Barbe ★★
29217 Le Conquet.
☎ 98 89 00 26, Fax 98 89 14 81. English spoken.
Open 18/12 to 12/11. 49 bedrooms
(37 en suite, 12 bath/shower only,
49 telephone). Golf 8 km, parking. &
RESTAURANT: good. Closed Mon LS.

Exceptional situation by the seaside and harbour. 25 km west of Brest on the D789.

TARIFF: Double 182–613, Bk 33, Set menu 19–425.
CC: Amex, Diners, Euro/Access, Visa.

CORSE (CORSICA)

AJACCIO Corse-du-Sud   6D

Hôtel Les Mouettes ★★★★ 9 cours L Bonaparte, 20000 Ajaccio, Corse.
☎ 95 21 44 38, Fax 95 21 71 80. English spoken.

Open 01/05 to 30/10. 19 bedrooms
(all en suite with telephone). Outdoor swimming pool, parking. &
RESTAURANT: Closed Mon.

1.5 km from centre of town (8 km from airport, by the coast road to Iles Sanguinaires) in quiet surroundings close to the sea with direct access to the beach. The hotel is a comfortable family residence. Prices shown are for half-board.

TARIFF: Double 1560–2820, Set menu 240.
CC: Amex, Diners, Euro/Access, Visa.

PIOGGIOLA Corse-du-Sud   6D

Auberge Aghjola ★★ 20259 Pioggiola, Corse.
☎ 95 61 90 48, Fax 95 61 92 99.
Open 01/04 to 30/10. 10 bedrooms (all en suite).
Outdoor swimming pool, parking, restaurant.

Set in the heart of this rugged island. Clean and simple rooms with perfectly adequate facilities. Restaurant serves unusual local dishes at very reasonable prices.

TARIFF: (1993) Single 250–320, Double 320–350, Set menu 150–180.
CC: Amex, Diners, Euro/Access, Visa.

PORTO-POLLO Corse-du-Sud   6D

Hôtel Les Eucalyptus ★★
20140 Petreto-Bicchisano, Corse.
☎ 95 74 01 52, Fax 95 74 06 56. English spoken.
Open 22/05 to 02/10. 27 bedrooms (all en suite with telephone). Tennis, parking, restaurant.

Les Eucalyptus is set in a green and pleasant position, overlooking the Gulf of Valinco. Sports and sandy beaches 50 m away.

TARIFF: Double 260–320, Bk 35, Set menu 98–150.
CC: Amex, Diners, Euro/Access, Visa.

PROPRIANO Corse-du-Sud   6D

Hôtel Roc e Mare ★★★
20110 Propriano, Corse.
☎ 95 76 04 85, Fax 95 76 17 55. English spoken.
Open 01/05 to 31/10. 62 bedrooms
(all en suite with telephone). Parking.

Located in the Gulf of Valinco, overlooking the sea and 1 km from Propriano. The hotel has a bar and lounge with panoramic views, a private beach with snack bar and all aquatic sports are available.

TARIFF: (1993) Single 325–585, Double 345–995, Bk 45.
CC: Amex, Diners, Euro/Access, Visa.

END OF CORSE (CORSICA) RESORTS

France

France

COSNE-COURS-SUR-LOIRE Nièvre 2D

Hôtel Gd Monarque ★★ près Église,
58220 Donzy.
☎ 86 39 35 44, Fax 86 39 37 09. English spoken.
Open all year. 14 bedrooms (8 en suite,
14 telephone). Garage, parking.
RESTAURANT: Closed Sun eve and Mon.

Small hotel with old-world charm and fine cuisine. Donzy is south-east of Cosne-Cours-sur-Loire on D33.

TARIFF: Single 170–270, Double 170–310,
Bk 40, Set menu 98–200.
CC: Euro/Access, Visa.

COURCHEVEL Savoie 6A

Hôtel Byblos des Neiges ★★★★ BP 98,
73122 Courchevel.
☎ 79 08 12 12, Fax 79 08 19 38. English spoken.
Open 18/12 to 16/04. 77 bedrooms
(all en suite with telephone). Indoor
swimming pool, garage, parking, restaurant. ᵴ

Located in the forest, as luxurious as a palace and as warm as a chalet. 15 minutes from the centre of the town. Only open during skiing season.

TARIFF: Single 1500–2050, Double 2500–3400,
Bk 110, Set menu 300–340.
CC: Amex, Diners, Euro/Access, Visa.

COUTANCES Manche 1B

Hôtel Cositel ★★ route de Coutainville,
50200 Coutances.
☎ 33 07 51 64, Fax 33 07 06 23. English spoken.
Open all year. 55 bedrooms (all en suite
with telephone). Golf 10 km, garage, parking,
restaurant. ᵴ

From Coutances, head towards Coutainville. You will find the hotel on your left.

TARIFF: (1993) Single 275–295,
Double 320–340, Bk 37, Set menu 95.
CC: Amex, Diners, Euro/Access, Visa.

CROZON Finistère 1C

Hôtel Moderne ★★ 61 rue Alsace Lorraine,
29160 Crozon.
☎ 98 27 00 10, Fax 98 26 19 21. English spoken.
Open all year. 37 bedrooms (22 en suite,
37 telephone). Parking, restaurant.

In Crozon, with rustic furniture and a well-known restaurant and wine cellar.

TARIFF: Single 147–250, Double 170–324,
Bk 32, Set menu 78–198.
CC: Euro/Access, Visa.

DEAUVILLE Calvados 2A

Hôtel de l'Amiraute ★★★ Touques,
14800 Deauville.
☎ 31 81 82 83, Fax 31 81 82 93. English spoken.

Open all year. 121 bedrooms (all en suite
with telephone). Outdoor swimming pool,
tennis, golf 3 km, parking, restaurant. ᵴ

A hotel for those wishing to keep fit, with sauna, jacuzzi, and squash courts, as well as exercise classes!

TARIFF: Double 710–760, Bk 45.
CC: Amex, Diners, Euro/Access, Visa.

Hôtel du Golf ★★★★ New Golf,
14800 Deauville.
☎ 31 88 19 01, Fax 31 88 75 99. English spoken.

Open 01/03 to 30/11. 179 bedrooms
(all en suite with telephone). Outdoor
swimming pool, tennis, parking, restaurant.

Overlooking the sea, near the top of Mount Canisy and surrounded by 175 acres of golf course, surely Hotel du Golf is perfectly situated! Excellent facilities; just 3 km from Deauville town and within easy reach of the pretty port of Honfleur.

TARIFF: Double 600–1500, Bk 90.
CC: Amex, Diners, Euro/Access, Visa.

Hôtel Normandy ★★★★ 38 rue J Mermoz, 14800 Deauville.
☎ 31 98 66 22, Fax 31 98 66 23.
English spoken.

Open all year. 300 bedrooms (all en suite with telephone). Indoor swimming pool, tennis, golf 3 km, garage, parking, restaurant. ⅙

Stunningly picturesque hotel, inside and out. Every possible comfort, including a swimming pool with sliding roof, as well as gourmet restaurants and even direct access to the casino next door! Good conference facilities.

TARIFF: Double 980–2000, Bk 90.
CC: Amex, Diners, Euro/Access, Visa.

LES DEUX-ALPES Isère 6A

Hôtel Aalborg ★★★ 38860 Les Deux-Alpes.
☎ 76 80 54 11, Fax 76 79 07 02.
English spoken.

Open 05/12 to 30/03 & 16/07 to 05/09.
25 bedrooms (all en suite with telephone).
Golf 1 km, parking, restaurant.

Modern hotel, right on the slopes. Good for summer and winter breaks.

TARIFF: Single 300–600, Double 450–600.
CC: Amex, Visa.

DIEPPE Seine Marit 2A

Hôtel La Présidence ★★★ 2 bd Verdun, 76200 Dieppe.
☎ 35 84 31 31, Fax 35 84 86 70. English spoken.

Open all year. 89 bedrooms (all en suite with telephone). Golf 4 km, garage, restaurant. ⅙

Situated on the seafront and at the foot of an old château. Two and three-day mid-week golfing breaks available, including accommodation with breakfast and green fees.

TARIFF: Single 350–550, Double 400–590, Bk 50.
CC: Amex, Diners, Euro/Access, Visa.

Hôtel Windsor ★★ 18 bd de Verdun, 76200 Dieppe.
☎ 35 84 15 23, Fax 35 84 74 52. English spoken.
Open all year. 48 bedrooms (42 en suite, 48 telephone). Golf 1 km, parking, restaurant. ⅙

Comfortable hotel situated on the seafront, between the harbour and the casino.

TARIFF: Double 145–345, Bk 45,
Set menu 80–250.
CC: Amex, Diners, Euro/Access, Visa.

DIJON Côte-d'Or 3C

Hôtel du Nord ★★★ pl Darcy, 21000 Dijon.
☎ 80 30 58 58, Fax 80 30 61 26. English spoken.
Open 01/01 to 15/12. 28 bedrooms (24 en suite, 28 telephone). Golf 20 km, parking.
RESTAURANT: Closed 15/12 to 01/01.

The hotel is situated in the centre of Dijon, 5 minutes' walk from the station. Near information point.

TARIFF: Single 310–360, Double 360–400,
Bk 50, Set menu 100–190.
CC: Amex, Diners, Euro/Access, Visa.

Hôtel St-Georges carrefour de l'Europe, 21700 Nuits-St-Georges.
☎ 80 61 15 00, Fax 80 61 23 80.

France

Open all year. 47 bedrooms (all en suite with telephone). Outdoor swimming pool, tennis, garage, parking, restaurant. &

Just off the Nuits-St-Georges A31 motorway exit. Drive towards the town centre.

TARIFF: Single 264–300, Double 275–336, Bk 39, Set menu 90–252.
CC: Amex, Diners, Euro/Access, Visa.

Hôtel Wilson ★★★ place Wilson, 21000 Dijon.
✆ 80 66 82 50, Fax 80 36 41 54. English spoken.

Open all year. 27 bedrooms (all en suite with telephone). Golf 10 km, garage, parking. &
RESTAURANT: excellent. Closed Sun & Mon lunch.

17th-century hotel situated south of Dijon just 5 minutes' walk from the town centre, towards the airport.

TARIFF: Single 330–450, Double 370–450, Bk 50.
CC: Euro/Access, Visa.

DINARD Ille/Vilaine   1D

Hôtel Altair ★★ 18 bd Féart, 35800 Dinard.
✆ 99 46 13 58, Fax 99 88 20 49. English spoken.
Open all year. 21 bedrooms (all en suite with telephone). Golf 6 km.
RESTAURANT: very good. Closed Sun eve & Mon LS.

Modern-day cuisine in an old-fashioned atmosphere. The hotel is in the centre of Dinard, has gardens and a patio and is just 30 m or so from the beach.

TARIFF: Single 200–280, Double 250–380, Bk 33, Set menu 88–190.
CC: Amex, Diners, Euro/Access, Visa.

Grand Hôtel ★★★★ 46 ave George V, BP 53, 35801 Dinard.
✆ 99 88 26 26, Fax 99 88 26 27. English spoken.
Open 01/04 to 31/10. 66 bedrooms

(all en suite with telephone). Outdoor swimming pool, tennis, golf 5 km, parking, restaurant.

Dating from the second Empire, this grand hotel offers fine views across the Vicomte Bay and to St-Malo. An ideal place for discovering the Emerald Coast and enjoying the wide range of local leisure and sports.

TARIFF: Double 480–1200, Bk 60, Set menu 180.
CC: Amex, Diners, Euro/Access, Visa.

Manoir de la Rance ★★★ Château de Jouvente, 35730 Pleurtuit.
✆ 99 88 53 76, Fax 99 88 63 03.
English spoken.
Open 10/03 to 06/01. 10 bedrooms (all en suite with telephone). Golf 6 km, parking.

19th-century manor at Jouvente. Stands right on the rocky coast with views across the La Rance estuary. Converted into a hotel from a private house in 1983. South of Dinard.

TARIFF: Single 340–400, Double 450–700, Bk 45.
CC: Euro/Access, Visa.

DOMPIERRE-SUR-BESBRE Allier   5A

Hôtel du Commerce ★★ 167 Grande rue, 03290 Dompierre-sur-Besbre.
✆ 70 34 67 85, Fax 70 34 50 03.
English spoken.
Open 04/02 to 04/01. 12 bedrooms (8 en suite, 2 bath/shower only, 12 telephone). Garage, parking.
RESTAURANT: good. Closed Wed.

Close to River Besbre. Restaurant serves regional cuisine and can seat 80. N7 from Paris, turn left at La Palisse. D480 to Dompierre 30 km.

TARIFF: (1993) Single 90–185, Double 185–245, Bk 25.
CC: Amex, Diners, Euro/Access, Visa.

France

DOUAI Nord   2B

Manoir de Fourcy ★★★★ 48 rue de la Gare,
59500 Corbehem.
✆ 27 96 44 90, Fax 27 91 84 49. English spoken.
Open all year. 8 bedrooms (all en suite
with telephone). Golf 15 km, parking. ♿
RESTAURANT: good. Closed Sun eve.

*An early 19th-century manor house set in a
park, close to the village of Corbehem. Good
restaurant. Just south of Douai.*

TARIFF: Double 380, Bk 40, Set menu 145–340.
CC: Amex, Diners, Euro/Access, Visa.

DRAGUIGNAN Var   6C

Hôtel du Moulin de la Foux ★★ ch St-Jean,
83300 Draguignan.
✆ 94 68 55 33, Fax 94 68 70 10. English spoken.

Open all year. 29 bedrooms (all en suite
with telephone). Golf 10 km, parking,
restaurant. ♿

*The hotel/restaurant is a renovated, stone-built
former mill, in quiet surroundings by a
stream. Garden and private fossil collection on
site. Situated at the southern edge of
Draguignan and 30 km from the sea (Ste-
Maxime/St-Tropez).*

TARIFF: (1993) Double 270–280, Bk 35,
Set menu 80–300.
CC: Amex, Euro/Access, Visa.

Hôtel Victoria ★★★ 54 av Carnot,
83300 Draguignan.
✆ 94 47 24 12, Fax 94 68 31 69.
English spoken.
Open all year. 22 bedrooms (all en suite
with telephone). Golf 10 km, garage, parking.
RESTAURANT: good. Closed Jan lunch.

*Traditional Victorian hotel in centre of town,
recently renovated and now air conditioned.
Pleasant little terrace garden with massive
cedar.*

TARIFF: Single 260–380, Double 280–480, Bk 38.
CC: Amex, Euro/Access, Visa.

DRAVEIL Essonne   2D

Hôtel Le Relais des Bergeries ★★
35 rue de l'Industrie, 91210 Draveil.
✆ 1 69 42 88 88. English spoken.
Open all year. 44 bedrooms (all en suite
with telephone). Parking, restaurant. ♿

*Situated on the edge of the Forêt de Sénart.
Canoeing and fishing nearby. On the N448,
south of Paris.*

TARIFF: (1993) Single 220–280, Double 280–300.
CC: Euro/Access, Visa.

DUCEY Manche   1D

Auberge de la Selune ★★ 2 rue St-Germain,
50220 Ducey.
✆ 33 48 53 62, Fax 33 48 90 30. English spoken.
Open all year. 19 bedrooms (all en suite
with telephone). Parking. ♿
RESTAURANT: Closed Mon LS.

*In a quiet, green setting by the River Selune,
reputed for its salmon fishing. Located south of
Avranches and only 15 km from Mont-St-
Michel.*

TARIFF: Double 255–275, Bk 38,
Set menu 75–190.
CC: Diners, Euro/Access, Visa.

DUNKERQUE Nord   2B

Hôtel Climat de France ★★
59279 Loon-Plage.
✆ 28 27 32 88, Fax 28 21 36 11. English spoken.
Open all year. 53 bedrooms (all en suite
with telephone). Parking, restaurant. ♿

*Close to business centre and only 12 km south-
west of Dunkerque, on N1.*

TARIFF: Double 294, Bk 30, Set menu 84–145.
CC: Amex, Diners, Euro/Access, Visa.

France

Welcome Hôtel ★★★ 37 rue Poincaré, 59140 Dunkerque.
☎ 28 59 20 70, Fax 28 21 03 49. English spoken.
Open all year. 40 bedrooms (all en suite with telephone). Golf 10 km, garage, restaurant. ᕗ

Right in the centre of town with a large restaurant and only 20 minutes from the sea.
TARIFF: Single 330, Double 380, Bk 46, Set menu 65–200.
CC: Amex, Euro/Access, Visa.

ELINCOURT-STE-MARGUERITE Oise   2B

Château de Bellinglise ★★★★
route de Lassigny, 60157 Elincourt.
☎ 44 76 04 76, Fax 44 76 54 75. English spoken.

Open all year. 53 bedrooms (all en suite with telephone). Tennis, golf 5 km, parking, restaurant. ᕗ

The château is a 16th-century manor, totally refurbished in 1987. It is set in 640 acres of wooded parkland. Gourmet restaurant with silk and wood panelling. Coming from Paris (1 hour's drive) on the A1, take exit 11 at Ressone and go eastwards through Margny on the D15 to Elincourt.
TARIFF: Single 680–1250, Double 770–1370, Bk 72, Set menu 215–295.
CC: Amex, Diners, Euro/Access, Visa.

ENGHIEN-LES-BAINS Val-d'Oise   3B

Grand Hôtel ★★★★ 85 rue Gén de Gaulle, 95880 Enghien-les-Bains.
☎ 1 34 12 80 00, Fax 1 34 12 73 81.
English spoken.
Open all year. 51 bedrooms (all en suite with telephone). Golf 10 km, parking, restaurant. ᕗ

Traditional, discreet white building surrounded by verdant lawns and situated near a lake. From the Paris ringroad to Port Maillot then take La Defense and follow Cergy Pontoise and leave the road at Enghien.
TARIFF: (1993) Single 980–1100, Double 980–1400, Bk 70, Set menu 80–165.
CC: Amex, Diners, Euro/Access, Visa.

EPERNAY Marne   3A

Château d'Etoges ★★★ 51270 Etoges.
☎ 26 59 30 08, Fax 26 59 35 57. English spoken.

Open 31/01 to 15/01. 20 bedrooms (19 en suite, 1 bath/shower only, 20 telephone). Golf 15 km, parking.
RESTAURANT: Closed Wed.

Renovated 17th-century château in the heart of champagne region. Etoges is 20 km south of Epernay on D33.
TARIFF: Single 300–400, Double 480–950, Bk 45, Set menu 160–280.
CC: Amex, Euro/Access, Visa.

ERDEVEN Morbihan   1C

Auberge du Sous Bois ★★ route de Pont Lorois, 56410 Erdeven.
☎ 97 55 66 10, Fax 97 55 68 82. English spoken.
Open 01/04 to 30/09. 22 bedrooms (all en suite with telephone). Golf 5 km, parking.
RESTAURANT: Closed lunch ex Sun Jul/Aug.

Typical Breton hotel set amid pines, modern and comfortable.
TARIFF: Double 330–365, Bk 40.
CC: Amex, Diners, Euro/Access, Visa.

ERNEE Mayenne   1D

Hôtel Grand Cerf ★★ 19 rue A Briand, 53500 Ernée.
☎ 43 05 13 09, Fax 43 05 02 90. English spoken.
Open all year. 8 bedrooms (all en suite with telephone). Golf 30 km, garage, parking.
RESTAURANT: very good. Closed 15/01-30/01.

France

Quiet and comfortable. Excellent cuisine with an amazing selection of exquisite wines. Facilities for receptions. On the N12.
TARIFF: Single 195, Double 230, Bk 30, Set menu 108–148.
CC: none.

EVIAN-LES-BAINS Haute-Savoie 6A

Hôtel Ermitage ★★★★ Rive Sud du Lac de Genève, 74500 Evian.
℡ 50 26 85 00, Fax 50 75 61 00.
English spoken.

Open 12/02 to 30/11. 91 bedrooms (all en suite with telephone). Indoor swimming pool, tennis, parking, restaurant. &

Located in a 40-acre park, with views towards Switzerland. Hôtel Ermitage is a fully restored, charming, turn-of-the-century country residence, with a warm and relaxed atmosphere. Fitness and sports programs at special package rates. Children's Club and Casino/night-Club.
TARIFF: Single 490–1410, Double 780–2200, Bk 85, Set menu 190–310.
CC: Amex, Diners, Euro/Access, Visa.

Hôtel Renardière ★★ La Beunaz, St-Paul-en-Chablais, 74500 Evian.
℡ 50 73 60 02, Fax 50 73 69 29.
English spoken.
Open all year. 17 bedrooms (all en suite with telephone). Indoor swimming pool, golf 12 km, parking.
RESTAURANT: good. Closed Wed & Thur HS.

Not far from Lac Léman, in an exceptional situation. From Evian via Publier take the D21 towards Bernex.
TARIFF: Single 170–320, Double 220–440, Bk 35, Set menu 120–195.
CC: Amex, Euro/Access, Visa.

EVREUX Eure 2A

Hôtel de France ★★ 29 rue St-Thomas, 27000 Evreux.
℡ 32 39 09 25. English spoken.
Open all year. 16 bedrooms (all en suite with telephone). Golf 20 km, garage, parking.
RESTAURANT: very good. Closed Sun eve & Mon.

The hotel is an elegant provincial building in a quiet location off the main street. Traditional service and a very fine restaurant.
TARIFF: Single 245–330, Double 260–330, Bk 32, Set menu 160–270.
CC: Diners, Euro/Access, Visa.

EYGALIERES Bouches-du-Rhône 5D

Hôtel Mas de la Brune 13810 Eygalières.
℡ 90 95 90 77, Fax 90 95 99 21. English spoken.
Open all year. 10 bedrooms (all en suite with telephone). Outdoor swimming pool, golf 10 km, parking, restaurant.

Beautiful, 16th-century château listed as an historical monument. Large sun terrace overlooking pool and parkland. Antique furniture and some four-poster beds. Dinner is included in the room rate. Situated 27 km south-east of Avignon on D74A at Eygalières.
TARIFF: Single 1280–1460, Double 1640–2370.
CC: Euro/Access, Visa.

LES EYZIES-DE-TAYAC Dordogne 4B

Manoir de Bellerive ★★★ route de Siorac, 24480 Le Buisson-de-Cadouin.
℡ 53 27 16 19, Fax 53 22 09 05. English spoken.

Open 15/04 to 31/10. 16 bedrooms (all en suite with telephone). Outdoor swimming pool, tennis, golf 10 km, garage, restaurant. &

Small château in an 8-acre park on the edge of the Dordogne. Peaceful setting near Lascaux and Les Eyzies.
TARIFF: Single 400–550, Double 400–680, Bk 60, Set menu 150–220.
CC: Amex, Diners, Euro/Access, Visa.

FERNEY-VOLTAIRE Ain 6A

Hôtel France ★★ 1 rue Genève,
01210 Ferney-Voltaire.
☎ 50 40 63 87, Fax 50 40 47 27.
English spoken.
Open all year. 14 bedrooms (all en suite
with telephone). Golf 5 km, garage, parking.
RESTAURANT: Closed Sun & Mon lunch.
*Small, comfortable hotel just 1 km from
Geneva Airport.*
TARIFF: Single 270, Double 330, Bk 35,
Set menu 115–165.
CC: Amex, Euro/Access, Visa.

FONTAINEBLEAU Seine/Marne 2D

Hôtel de l'Aigle Noir ★★★★ 27 pl Napoléon
Bonaparte, 77300 Fontainebleau.
☎ 1 64 22 32 65, Fax 1 64 22 17 33.
English spoken.
Open all year. 57 bedrooms (all en suite
with telephone). Indoor swimming pool,
golf 1 km, garage, parking, restaurant. ⅙
*Opposite the prestigious Château de
Fontainebleau, this elegant, luxury hotel
upholds the great traditions of French
hospitality. Price for weekend: 650F and one
week 950F. As well as the indoor pool there is
sauna and gymnasium.*
CC: Amex, Diners, Euro/Access, Visa.

Hôtel Grand Monarque ★★★ route de
Fontainebleau, 77000 Melun-la-Rochette.
☎ 1 64 39 04 40, Fax 1 64 39 94 10.
English spoken.

Open all year. 50 bedrooms (all en suite
with telephone). Outdoor swimming pool,
tennis, golf 10 km, parking.
RESTAURANT: good. Closed 24/12 eve.
*On the edge of Fontainebleau forest,
45 minutes' drive from Paris. The Grand*

*Monarque is in a quiet 7-acre private park, an
ideal spot for relaxation. Restaurant with
terrace. From Fontainebleau, follow signs for
Melun and on entering Melun, the hotel is on
the left.*
TARIFF: Single 500–550, Double 550–600,
Bk 48, Set menu 190.
CC: Amex, Diners, Euro/Access, Visa.

Manoir de St-Herem ★★ Parc John François
Millet, 77630 Fontainebleau/Barbizon.
☎ 1 60 66 42 42, Fax 1 60 69 20 98.
English spoken.
Open all year. 14 bedrooms (13 en suite,
1 bath/shower only, 14 telephone).
Golf 10 km, parking, restaurant. ⅙
*An old manor house, situated behind the artist
Millet's house in a large park. Refurbished in
1985. Gourmet cuisine. Access by the A6
motorway (Paris to Lyon, Fontainebleau exit)
and N7. In the middle of Barbizon.*
TARIFF: Double 320–370, Bk 42, Set menu 150.
CC: Amex, Diners, Euro/Access, Visa.

Hôtel Le Vieux Logis ★★★ 5 rue Sado Carnot,
Thomery, 77810 Fontainebleau.
☎ 1 60 96 44 77, Fax 1 60 96 42 71.
English spoken.

Open all year. 14 bedrooms (all en suite
with telephone). Outdoor swimming pool,
tennis, golf 7 km, parking, restaurant.
*Until recently, a private mansion situated in
the heart of the small historic village of
Thomery. Elegant gourmet restaurant with
bright warm atmosphere, flowered verandah.
Cosy and finely decorated bedrooms. New
heated pool. From the obelisk in Fontainebleau,
take N5 to Sens and bear left at the 4th exit to
Thomery.*
TARIFF: Double   –400, Bk 50,
Set menu 145–240.
CC: Amex, Euro/Access, Visa.

FONTVIEILLE Bouches-du-Rhône 5D

Auberge La Regalido ★★★★ rue Frédéric Mistral, 13990 Fontvieille.
☎ 90 54 60 22, Fax 90 54 64 29. English spoken. Open 01/02 to 30/11. 14 bedrooms (all en suite with telephone). Golf 10 km, parking. ♿
RESTAURANT: very good. Closed Tues lunch & Mon.

An old oil-mill, beautifully restored, right in the heart of Provence. Situated in the village of Fontvieille, on D17, about 10 km east of Arles.

TARIFF: Single 410–950, Double 600–1350, Bk 78.
CC: Amex, Diners, Euro/Access, Visa.

FORGES-LES-EAUX Seine Marit 2B

Auberge du Beau Lieu Le Fossé, 76440 Forges-les-Eaux.
☎ 35 90 50 36, Fax 35 90 35 98. English spoken. Open 01/01 to 24/01 & 07/02 to 31/12. 3 bedrooms (all en suite with telephone). Parking.
RESTAURANT: very good. Closed 25/01 to 06/02.

Comfortable auberge with rooms, terrace and parking. The highly-rated restaurant offers excellent cuisine using local produce. On D915.

TARIFF: Single 250, Double 345, Bk 38, Set menu 140–350.
CC: Amex, Diners, Euro/Access, Visa.

FOUESNANT Finistère 1C

Hôtel Pointe Mousterlin ★★ Pointe de Mousterlin, 29170 Fouesnant.
☎ 98 56 04 12, Fax 98 56 61 02. English spoken. Open 02/04 to 30/09. 52 bedrooms (all en suite with telephone). Tennis, golf 6 km, parking, restaurant. ♿

6 km from the village of Fouesnant, the hôtel is only 30 m from a long sandy beach. Comfortable rooms. Some rooms are interconnecting. The restaurant offers family cooking with seafood and a special menu for children.

TARIFF: Single 262–290, Double 290–425, Bk 34.
CC: Amex, Euro/Access, Visa.

FUMEL Lot/Garonne 4D

Hôtel Climat de France ★★ 47500 Fumel.
☎ 53 40 93 93, Fax 53 71 27 94. English spoken. Open all year. 32 bedrooms (all en suite with telephone). Outdoor swimming pool, garage, restaurant. ♿

A warm welcome is guaranteed at this new family hotel. Quietly situated in Fumel, overlooking the Lot valley. Traditional and regional cuisine in the restaurant or on the terrace. The hotel is next to the park.

TARIFF: Double 270–275, Bk 34, Set menu 75–125.
CC: Amex, Euro/Access, Visa.

GAP Hautes-Alpes 6C

Hôtel Le Clos ★★ route de Grenoble, 05000 Gap.
☎ 92 51 37 04, Fax 92 52 41 06. English spoken.
Open all year. 39 bedrooms (30 en suite, 9 bath/shower only, 39 telephone). Tennis, golf 15 km, parking, restaurant.

A traditional family hotel, close to the town centre.

TARIFF: Double 160–240, Bk 33.
CC: Euro/Access, Visa.

LA GAUDE Alpes-Marit 6C

Hôtel Alliance Nice ★★★ Le Plan du Bois, Les Nertières, 06610 La Gaude.
☎ 93 24 47 77, Fax 93 24 85 84. English spoken.
Open all year. 52 bedrooms (all en suite with telephone). Outdoor swimming pool, parking.
RESTAURANT: Closed Sat lunch & Sun eve.

Hotel located in the hinterland of Nice, a few minutes' drive from the airport and Nice centre. From St-Laurent-du-Var to the hotel, drive towards St Jeannet/La Gaude for 10 km. The hotel is just in front of the IBM Centre.

TARIFF: (1993) Single 380–430, Double 440–500, Bk 60.
CC: Amex, Euro/Access, Visa.

GEMENOS Bouches-du-Rhône 5D

Hôtel Relais de la Magdeleine ★★★★ N396, 13420 Gémenos.
☎ 42 32 30 16, Fax 42 32 02 26. English spoken.
Open 15/03 to 15/01. 24 bedrooms (all en suite with telephone). Outdoor swimming pool, golf 12 km, parking, restaurant.

Built in the 18th century, this charming hotel is set in the quiet, Provençal countryside. When driving from Marseille towards Toulon, take the Aubagne-Sud/Commercial Centre exit from the motorway and then at the second roundabout turn right to Gémenos.

TARIFF: (1993) Single 420–550, Double 530–750, Bk 65.
CC: Euro/Access, Visa.

France

GENLIS Côte-d'Or   3C

Hôtel de la Place-Rey ★★ Echigey,
21110 Genlis.
☎ 80 29 74 00, Fax 80 29 79 55. English spoken.

Open all year. 13 bedrooms (9 en suite,
9 telephone). Parking.
RESTAURANT: Closed Jan.
*Set in pleasant grounds, with a gourmet
restaurant and specialising in regional
cheeses. From Genlis follow signs to Echigey,
cross country to the south.*
TARIFF: Double 110–190, Bk 25,
Set menu 65–205.
CC: Diners, Euro/Access, Visa.

GIEN Loiret   2D

Hôtel Rivage ★★★ 1 quai Nice, 45500 Gien.
☎ 38 37 79 00, Fax 38 38 10 21. English spoken.
Open all year. 19 bedrooms (all en suite
with telephone). Golf 20 km, parking.
RESTAURANT: very good. Closed 10/02 to 8/03 &
30/05 to 08/06.
Family hotel on the banks of the Loire.
TARIFF: Single 295–500, Double 360–500,
Bk 45, Set menu 155–320.
CC: Amex, Diners, Euro/Access, Visa.

GORDES Vaucluse   5D

Hôtel Les Bories ★★★★ route de l'Abbaye de
Senanque, 84220 Gordes.
☎ 90 72 00 51, Fax 90 72 01 22. English spoken.
Open all year. 18 bedrooms (all en suite with
telephone). Indoor swimming pool, outdoor
swimming pool, tennis, golf 12 km, parking,
restaurant.
*In countryside overlooking Gordes and Lubéron
mountains, amidst lavender fields. 2 km from
village on road to the abbey of Senanque.*
TARIFF: (1993) Double 550–1450, Bk 70.
CC: Amex, Diners, Euro/Access, Visa.

GOURDON Lot   4B

Hôtel de la Bouriane ★★★ pl Foirail,
46300 Gourdon.
☎ 65 41 16 37, Fax 65 41 04 92. English spoken.
Open 08/03 to 15/01. 20 bedrooms (all en suite
with telephone). Golf 20 km, parking. &
RESTAURANT: Closed Mon.
*A country inn, just five minutes' walk from the
centre of Gourdon, with its Gothic cathedral.
The hotel has a terrace overlooking the garden,
in this lush, wooded region.*
TARIFF: Single 260–280, Double 280–340,
Bk 40, Set menu 80–275.
CC: Amex, Euro/Access, Visa.

Hôtel Le Terminus ★★ 7 av de la Gare,
46300 Gourdon.
☎ 65 41 03 29, Fax 65 41 29 49. English spoken.
Open all year. 23 bedrooms (all en suite
with telephone). Outdoor swimming pool,
golf 15 km, parking, restaurant.
*Hotel has all comforts plus garden and play
area for children. Excellent cuisine; near
station.*
TARIFF: Single 200–300, Double 230–300,
Bk 38, Set menu 135–300.
CC: Amex, Diners, Euro/Access, Visa.

LA GRAND-MOTTE Hérault   5D

Hôtel Mercure ★★★ 140 rue du Port,
34280 La Grand-Motte.
☎ 67 56 90 81, Fax 67 56 92 29. English spoken.
Open 01/03 to 30/11. 135 bedrooms (all
en suite with telephone). Outdoor swimming
pool, golf 2 km, garage, parking, restaurant. &
*Air-conditioned rooms with most having
private balconies overlooking the sea. Access
from the A9 motorway.*
TARIFF: Single 380–595, Double 650–735,
Bk 58, Set menu 120–145.
CC: Amex, Diners, Euro/Access, Visa.

GRANVILLE Manche   1B

Hôtel des Bains ★★★ 19 rue G Clemenceau,
50400 Granville.
☎ 33 50 17 31, Fax 33 50 89 22. English spoken.
Open all year. 49 bedrooms (all en suite
with telephone). Golf 6 km, parking. &
RESTAURANT: Closed Sun eve & Mon LS.
*Large hotel facing the sea with car parking
adjacent.*
TARIFF: Single 300–900, Double 350–1200,
Bk 45, Set menu 80–140.
CC: Amex, Euro/Access, Visa.

GRASSE Alpes-Marit　　　　　　6C

Hôtel Panorama ★★ 2 pl Cours,
06130 Grasse.
☎ 93 36 80 80, Fax 93 36 92 04. English spoken.
Open all year. 36 bedrooms (all en suite
with telephone). Golf 5 km, parking. ♿

*Conveniently situated near the town centre, 2
minutes from the Palais du Congrès and with
a fine view over the countryside. A perfect
location for exploring the surrounding area
and visiting perfume factories.*
TARIFF: Single 265–295, Double 295–480, Bk 40.
cc: Amex, Euro/Access, Visa.

Auberge de la Vignette Haute ★★★★ rte du
Village, 06810 Auribeau-sur-Siagne.
☎ 93 42 20 01, Fax 93 42 31 16. English spoken.
Open 05/12 to 15/11. 11 bedrooms
(all en suite with telephone). Outdoor
swimming pool, tennis, golf 5 km, garage,
parking. ♿
RESTAURANT: Closed Mon & Tues lunch LS.

*Romantic 17th-century auberge, high above
the city. Offers modern-day comfort in
medieval surroundings. Garden and terrace
with farm beyond. From A8 exit Mandelieu-la-
Napoule, towards Grasse.*
TARIFF: Single 500–1120, Double 500–1400,
Bk 70, Set menu 250–490.
cc: Amex, Euro/Access, Visa.

LE GRAU-DU-ROI Gard　　　　　5D

Relais de l'Oustau Camarguen ★★★ 3 rte
Marines, Port Camargue,
30240 Le Grau-du-Roi.
☎ 66 51 51 65, Fax 66 53 01 65. English spoken.

Open 25/03 to 11/10. 39 bedrooms
(all en suite with telephone). Indoor
swimming pool, outdoor swimming pool,
golf 5 km, garage, parking. ♿
RESTAURANT: Closed Tues eve & Wed.

*An old farmhouse which has been turned into
a very comfortable hotel. Local cuisine is
served. From Port Camargue follow signs to
Plage Sud.*
TARIFF: Double 380–485, Bk 45.
cc: Amex, Diners, Euro/Access, Visa.

GRENOBLE Isère　　　　　　　6A

Hôtel Alpha ★★★ 34 av Verdun, Meylan,
38240 Grenoble.
☎ 76 90 63 09, Fax 76 90 28 27. English spoken.
Open all year. 86 bedrooms (all en suite
with telephone). Outdoor swimming pool,
golf 10 km, garage, parking, restaurant. ♿

*5 minutes from the city centre towards
Chambéry, the Alpha is a Best Western Hotel
set in a one-acre park with mountain views.
Blues bar, banqueting and conference facilities.*
TARIFF: Single 395–465, Double 395–485, Bk 49.
cc: Amex, Diners, Euro/Access, Visa.

Château de la Commanderie ★★★ 17 av
Echirolles, Eybens, 38320 Eybens.
☎ 76 25 34 58, Fax 76 24 07 31. English spoken.

Open all year. 25 bedrooms (all en suite
with telephone). Outdoor swimming pool,
golf 3 km, parking.
RESTAURANT: Closed Sat & Sun.

*An old 18th-century house, with comfortable
rooms and set in a park. From Grenoble,
follow Rocade Sud signs, then take exit 6
Eybens-Bresson and follow the signs.*
TARIFF: Single 380–590, Double 420–630,
Bk 50, Set menu 139–160.
cc: Amex, Diners, Euro/Access, Visa.

Hôtel Porte de France ★★★ 27 quai C
Bernard, 38000 Grenoble.
☎ 76 47 39 73, Fax 76 50 95 03.
English spoken.
Open all year. 40 bedrooms (all en suite
with telephone). Garage, parking.

Near the town centre, the hotel is five minutes' walk from the bus and train stations.
TARIFF: Single 200–305, Double 260–330, Bk 35.
CC: Euro/Access, Visa.

GREOUX-LES-BAINS Alpes/Hte-Prov 6C

Hôtel Villa Borghese ★★★ av des Thermes, 04800 Gréoux-les-Bains.
☎ 92 78 00 91, Fax 92 78 09 55. English spoken.

Open 08/03 to 27/11. 70 bedrooms (all en suite with telephone). Outdoor swimming pool, tennis, golf 18 km, garage, parking, restaurant.
Facing the Thermal Park, a charming hotel with garden. Large lounges, beauty and health centre and bridge club.
TARIFF: Single 330, Double 440–600, Bk 50, Set menu 150–250.
CC: Amex, Diners, Euro/Access, Visa.

GRIMAUD Var 6C

Hôtel La Boulangerie ★★★ route de Collobrières, 83310 Grimaud.
☎ 94 43 23 16, Fax 94 43 38 27. English spoken.
Open 01/04 to 10/10. 11 bedrooms (all en suite with telephone). Outdoor swimming pool, tennis, golf 5 km, parking. ♿
RESTAURANT: Closed lunch.
A small and charming hotel offering a wonderful view over the Chain des Maures. 2 km from Grimaud village on the D14 towards Collobrières.
TARIFF: (1993) Single 560–660, Double 660–780, Bk 50.
CC: Amex, Diners, Euro/Access, Visa.

LE HAVRE Seine Marit 2A

Hôtel d'Angleterre ★★ 1 rue Louis-Philippe, 76600 Le Havre.
☎ 35 42 48 42, Fax 35 22 70 69.

Open all year. 27 bedrooms (19 en suite, 6 bath/shower only, 27 telephone). Garage.
Small quiet hotel close to the beach.
TARIFF: Single 200–250, Double 220–280, Bk 30.
CC: Euro/Access, Visa.

Hôtel Astoria ★★ 13 cours de la République, 76600 Le Havre.
☎ 35 25 00 03, Fax 35 26 48 34. English spoken.
Open all year. 37 bedrooms (all en suite with telephone). Indoor swimming pool, golf 5 km, garage, parking, restaurant. ♿
Large fully-equipped hotel located in the town centre, opposite the station near the harbour.
TARIFF: Single 200–300, Double 240–330, Bk 25, Set menu 56–129.
CC: Amex, Diners, Euro/Access, Visa.

HONFLEUR Calvados 2A

Hôtel Castel Albertine ★★★
19 cours Albert-Manuel, 14600 Honfleur.
☎ 31 98 85 56, Fax 31 98 83 18. English spoken.
Open all year. 26 bedrooms (all en suite with telephone). Golf 3 km, parking. ♿
Charming 18th-century hotel set amid ancient trees yet only 500 m from the old port and town centre.
TARIFF: Double 350–600, Bk 50.
CC: Amex, Diners, Euro/Access, Visa.

Auberge de la Source ★★
Barneville-la-Bertran, 14600 Honfleur.
☎ 31 89 25 02, Fax 31 89 44 40. English spoken.
Open 15/02 to 15/11. 14 bedrooms (all en suite with telephone). Golf 4 km, parking. ♿
RESTAURANT: Closed Wed.
Beautiful house set in quiet gardens with trout ponds, this hotel is a real Normandy auberge, by the forest just outside Honfleur on the D279. Prices are for half-board.
TARIFF: Single 400–560, Double 580–800, Set menu 145–170.
CC: Euro/Access, Visa.

ISIGNY-SUR-MER Calvados 2A

Hôtel de France ★★ 15 rue Emile Demagny, 14230 Isigny-sur-Mer.
☎ 31 22 00 33, Fax 31 22 79 19. English spoken.
Open 15/01 to 15/12. 19 bedrooms (14 en suite, 19 telephone). Outdoor swimming pool, parking. ♿
On the wartime landing beaches circuit, this is a comfortable hotel with a brand new restaurant.
TARIFF: Single 160–220, Double 180–280, Bk 32.
CC: Euro/Access, Visa.

LES ISSAMBRES Var   5C

Hôtel Villa Tricoli Impasse du Temps Perdu,
San-Peire, 83380 Les Issambres.
☎ 94 49 65 32, Fax 94 49 68 20. English spoken.
Open all year. 10 bedrooms (all en suite
with telephone). Golf 6 km, parking. ⚥
Small privately owned hotel in quiet street.
Stylish, even romantic! 600 m from beach. In
Les Issambres, turn after the port entrance and
look for hotel signpost.
TARIFF: (1993) Single 180–325,
Double 220–390, Bk 45.
CC: none.

ISSOIRE Puy-de-Dôme   5A

Hôtel Le Relais 1 av Gare, 63500 Issoire.
☎ 73 89 16 61, Fax 73 89 55 62. English spoken.
Open all year. 6 bedrooms (3 en suite,
3 bath/shower only, 6 telephone). Garage,
restaurant.
In town centre, close to church and railway
station. From Issoire, north on N9 towards
Clermont-Ferrand.
TARIFF: Single 170–200, Double 170–230, Bk 25.
CC: Euro/Access, Visa.

ISSOUDUN Indre   2D

Hôtel La Cognette ★★★ rue des Minimes,
36100 Issoudun.
☎ 54 21 21 83, Fax 54 03 13 03. English spoken.
Open all year. 14 bedrooms (all en suite
with telephone). Golf 8 km, garage. ⚥
RESTAURANT: very good. Closed Sun & Mon
eves LS.
A very attractive and individual hotel with a
garden. Described by Balzac. Exceptional
cuisine.
TARIFF: (1993) Double 350–950, Bk 50,
Set menu 210–500.
CC: Amex, Diners, Euro/Access, Visa.

JOINVILLE Haute-Marne   3C

Hôtel Poste pl Grève, 52300 Joinville.
☎ 25 94 12 63, Fax 25 94 36 23.
English spoken.
Open 10/02 to 10/01. 10 bedrooms (all en suite
with telephone). Garage, parking, restaurant.
Traditional hotel enjoying a good cuisine.
Joinville is on the N67, between St-Dizier and
Chaumont.
TARIFF: Single 180–250, Double 180–280,
Bk 26, Set menu 80–200.
CC: Amex, Diners, Euro/Access, Visa.

JUAN-LES-PINS Alpes-Marit   6C

Beachôtel ★★★ av Alexandre III,
06160 Juan-les-Pins.
☎ 93 61 81 85, Fax 93 61 51 97. English spoken.
Open 15/03 to 15/10 & 20/12 to 05/01.
43 bedrooms (all en suite with telephone).
Garage, parking, restaurant.
Modern hotel situated a few metres away from
the beach. West side of Juan.
TARIFF: Single 335–550, Double 410–650, Bk 45.
CC: Amex, Diners, Euro/Access, Visa.

Garden Beach Hôtel ★★★★
15-17 bd Baudoin, 06160 Juan-les-Pins.
☎ 93 67 25 25, Fax 93 61 16 65. English spoken.

Open all year. 175 bedrooms (all en suite
with telephone). Golf 7 km, garage, parking,
restaurant. ⚥
Very modern hotel on private sandy beach,
close to town centre and modern art collection
of the Maeght Foundation. 25 km from Nice on
the N98 and south of Antibes, on coast road.
TARIFF: Double 600–1800, Bk 90.
CC: Amex, Diners, Euro/Access, Visa.

KAYSERSBERG Ht-Rhin   3D

Hôtel Château ★ 38 rue du C de Gaulle,
68240 Kaysersberg.
☎ 89 78 24 33. English spoken.
Open 15/03 to 20/01. 11 bedrooms
(5 bath/shower only). Golf 4 km, parking.
RESTAURANT: Closed Thurs.
TARIFF: (1993) Double 120–260, Bk 30,
Set menu 70–180.
CC: Euro/Access, Visa.

LABASTIDE-MURAT Lot   4D

Hôtel Climat de France ★★ place de la
Mairie, 46240 Labastide-Murat.
☎ 65 21 18 80, Fax 65 21 10 97. English spoken.

France

Open 15/01 to 15/12. 20 bedrooms (all en suite with telephone). Golf 3 km, restaurant. &

An old castle built in 1261, now completely up-to-date but with a special charm. From the N20 take the D667 to Labastide-Murat.

TARIFF: Double 270, Bk 30.
CC: Amex, Diners, Euro/Access, Visa.

LABOUHEYRE Landes 4C

Hôtel Unic ★★ rte Bordeaux, 40210 Labouheyre.
℡ 58 07 00 55, Fax 58 04 50 59. English spoken.
Open 15/04 to 15/11. 8 bedrooms (all en suite with telephone). Parking, restaurant.

Small hotel south of Bordeaux on N10 towards Castets.

TARIFF: Single 200–250, Double 250–300, Bk 30, Set menu 85–150.
CC: Amex, Diners, Euro/Access, Visa.

LAMASTRE Ardèche 5B

Château d'Urbilhac ★★★ route de Vernoux, 07270 Lamastre.
℡ 75 06 42 11, Fax 75 06 52 75. English spoken.
Open 01/05 to 05/10. 13 bedrooms (all en suite with telephone). Outdoor swimming pool, tennis, garage, parking. &
RESTAURANT: good. Closed Mon to Fri lunch.

A château in exceptionally beautiful, forested countryside. Elegant and comfortable rooms with panoramic views across 162-acre park. Sun-terrace above pool on the château ramparts. Quiet and very relaxing.

TARIFF: Single 450–600, Double 500–650, Bk 65.
CC: Amex, Diners, Euro/Access, Visa.

LAMBALLE Côtes-du-Nord 1D

Hôtel Angleterre ★★★ 29 bd Jobert, 22400 Lamballe.
℡ 96 31 00 16, Fax 96 31 91 54. English spoken.
Open all year. 20 bedrooms (19 en suite, 1 bath/shower only, 20 telephone). Golf 8 km, garage.
RESTAURANT: Closed 01/03 to 15/03.

A modern hotel situated in the town centre. Rooms have colour TV.

TARIFF: Single 200–290, Double 220–320, Bk 38, Set menu 82–250.
CC: Amex, Diners, Euro/Access, Visa.

LANDIVISIAU Finistère 1C

Hôtel L'Enclos ★★ Lampaul Guimiliau, 29400 Landivisiau.
℡ 98 68 77 08, Fax 98 68 61 06. English spoken.

Open all year. 36 bedrooms (all en suite with telephone). Parking, restaurant. &

Quiet hotel in country surroundings situated in heart of Brittany.

TARIFF: Single 220–230, Double 255, Bk 30.
CC: Amex, Diners, Euro/Access, Visa.

Hôtel au Relais du Vern ★★
ZA du Vern BP 26, 29400 Landivisiau.
℡ 98 24 42 42, Fax 98 24 42 00. English spoken.
Open all year. 52 bedrooms (all en suite with telephone). Tennis, golf 14 km, garage, parking, restaurant. &

On the crossroads N12 (Rennes/Brest) and C69 (Roscoff/Quimper). A modern hotel with comfortable and sound-proofed rooms, in a garden of 1.5 acres.

TARIFF: Single 284, Double 330, Bk 34, Set menu 68–147.
CC: Amex, Diners, Euro/Access, Visa.

LANGEAIS Indre/Loire 2C

Auberge de la Bonde ★★ St-Michel-sur-Loire, 37130 Langeais.
℡ 47 96 83 13, Fax 47 96 85 72.
English spoken.

Open 23/01 to 23/12. 13 bedrooms (8 en suite, 4 bath/shower only, 13 telephone).
Golf 20 km, parking.
RESTAURANT: Closed Sat.

On château and vineyards circuit, close to banks of Loire. 30 km from Tours going towards Saumur on the N152.

TARIFF: Double 160–270, Bk 32, Set menu 80–185.
CC: none.

LANGRES Haute-Marne 3C

Grand Hôtel Europe ★★ 23 rue Diderot, 52200 Langres.
℡ 25 87 10 65, Fax 25 87 60 65. English spoken.
Open 25/10 to 08/05 & 23/05 to 01/10.

France

28 bedrooms (26 en suite, 28 telephone). Garage, parking.
RESTAURANT: Closed Sun eve & Mon lunch.

A 17th-century hotel in centre of town just a stone's throw from the city walls and the countryside beyond.

TARIFF: Single 150–240, Double 220–280, Bk 32, Set menu 68–190.
CC: Amex, Diners, Euro/Access, Visa.

LAON Aisne 2B

Hôtel Mercure Holigolf ★★★ Golf de l'Ailette, 02860 Chamouille.
☎ 23 24 84 85, Fax 23 24 81 20.
English spoken.

Open 15/03 to 15/11. 60 bedrooms (all en suite with telephone). Outdoor swimming pool, golf on site, parking, restaurant. &

Comfortable hotel in a peaceful, lakeside setting. Many leisure and sporting facilities available. South of Laon and accessed via N44 and Corbeny.

TARIFF: Single 390–400, Double 430–490, Bk 45, Set menu 110.
CC: Amex, Diners, Euro/Access, Visa.

LAVAL Mayenne 2C

Hôtel Climat de France ★★
bd des Trappistines, 53000 Laval.
☎ 43 02 88 88, Fax 43 02 87 00.
English spoken.
Open all year. 44 bedrooms (all en suite with telephone). Golf 5 km, parking, restaurant. &

Near an abbey with woodland surroundings, this recently built hotel provides a quiet and cosy atmosphere with good food. South of Laval off the N157.

TARIFF: Double 268, Bk 30, Set menu 60–120.
CC: Amex, Euro/Access, Visa.

LENS Pas-de-Calais 2B

Novotel Henin-Douai-Lens ★★★
62950 Noyelles-Godault.
☎ 21 75 16 01, Fax 21 75 88 59. English spoken.
Open all year. 81 bedrooms (all en suite with telephone). Outdoor swimming pool, parking, restaurant. &

Close to A1 Lille/Paris, exit 17 next to Auchan shopping centre. From Lens, A21 east.

CC: Amex, Diners, Euro/Access, Visa.

LILLE Nord 2B

Hôtel Carlton ★★★★ 3 rue de Paris, 59800 Lille.
☎ 20 13 33 13, Fax 20 51 48 17.
English spoken.
Open all year. 60 bedrooms (all en suite with telephone). Golf 7 km, garage, parking, restaurant. &

Completely renovated, the Carlton Hotel has the class of a de-luxe hotel. Situated in the centre of Lille, facing the Opera.

TARIFF: Single 690–750, Double 720–790, Bk 65, Set menu 130.
CC: Amex, Diners, Euro/Access, Visa.

Hôtel La Howarderie 1 rue des Fusillés, 59320 Emmerin.
☎ 20 44 83 52, Fax 20 50 18 42.
English spoken.
Open 02/01 to 23/12. 6 bedrooms (all en suite with telephone). Golf 10 km, parking.

17th-century, Flemish farmhouse with barn and cobbled courtyard. South-west of Lille off D549/D147.

TARIFF: Double 600–700.
CC: Amex, Euro/Access, Visa.

LIMOGES Haute-Vienne 4B

Hôtel Climat de France ★★
Le Ponteix - Secteur Laugerie, 87220 Feytiat.
☎ 55 06 14 60, Fax 55 06 38 93.
English spoken.
Open all year. 50 bedrooms (all en suite with telephone). Golf 3 km, parking, restaurant. &

This recently-built hotel has a cosy atmosphere and all rooms are well furnished and equipped. Most rooms have a colour TV and all have direct dial telephone and radio alarm clock.

TARIFF: Double 260–270, Bk 32, Set menu 80–110.
CC: Amex, Euro/Access, Visa.

Hôtel La Chapelle St-Martin ★★★
St-Martin-du-Fault, 87510 Limoges.
☎ 55 75 80 17, Fax 55 75 89 50. English spoken.

Open 01/03 to 31/12. 12 bedrooms (all en suite with telephone). Outdoor swimming pool, tennis, golf 10 km, garage, parking. ᴕ
RESTAURANT: very good. Closed Mon.
Elegant country house in large park with landscaped ornamental lakes. North-west of Limoges on D35.
TARIFF: Single 590–1100, Double 690–1500, Bk 75, Set menu 180–380.
CC: Amex, Euro/Access, Visa.

LOCHES Indre/Loire   2C

Grill Motel ★ rue des Lézards, 37600 Loches.
☎ 47 91 50 04, Fax 47 91 53 80.
English spoken.
Open 03/01 to 18/12. 27 bedrooms (all en suite with telephone). Parking. ᴕ
RESTAURANT: Closed Sun.
Modern hotel set in 2 acres of grounds overlooking Loches and castle. Restaurant serves traditional dishes. Access via N143 south-east of Tours.
TARIFF: Double 170, Bk 25, Set menu 35–90.
CC: Euro/Access, Visa.

Hôtel Lucotel ★★ rue Lézards, 37600 Loches.
☎ 47 91 50 50, Fax 47 94 01 18.
English spoken.
Open 15/01 to 18/12. 42 bedrooms (all en suite with telephone). Indoor swimming pool, tennis, golf 20 km, parking. ᴕ
RESTAURANT: Closed Sat lunch.
A quiet and comfortable hotel set in parkland overlooking Loches.
TARIFF: Single 250–330, Double 330–380, Bk 35, Set menu 90–200.
CC: Euro/Access, Visa.

LODEVE Hérault   5C

Hôtel Paix ★★ 11 bd Montalangue, 34700 Lodève.
☎ 67 44 07 46. English spoken.
Open all year. 21 bedrooms (all en suite with telephone). Garage, parking, restaurant.
The hotel is 100 years old, completely renovated and quiet. Situated by a river in the centre of the town. Motorway N9 north from Béziers. N109/E11 west from Montpellier.
TARIFF: Single 200, Double 220, Bk 25, Set menu 65–160.
CC: Euro/Access, Visa.

LONS-LE-SAUNIER Jura   5B

Hôtel Genève ★★ 39 rue J Moulin, 39000 Lons-le-Saunier.
☎ 84 24 19 11, Fax 84 24 81 42.
English spoken.
Open all year. 35 bedrooms (all en suite with telephone). Golf 5 km, garage, parking, restaurant. ᴕ
Small, 19th-century hotel in town centre with own garden. Quiet and charming.
TARIFF: Single 240–380, Double 280–420, Bk 35.
CC: Amex, Diners, Euro/Access, Visa.

LORIENT Morbihan   1C

Hôtel Ibis ★★ centre hôtelier, Kerpont-Bellevue, Lanester, 56600 Lorient.
☎ 97 76 40 22, Fax 97 76 00 24.
English spoken.
Open all year. 41 bedrooms (all en suite). Outdoor swimming pool, golf 10 km, parking, restaurant. ᴕ
TARIFF: Single 265, Double 295, Bk 33, Set menu 69.
CC: Amex, Diners, Euro/Access.

LOUDEAC Côtes-du-Nord   1D

Hôtel des Voyageurs ★★ 10 rue de Cadélac, 22600 Loudéac.
☎ 96 28 00 47, Fax 96 28 22 30.
English spoken.
Open all year. 25 bedrooms (all en suite with telephone). Garage.
RESTAURANT: good. Closed Sat.
In the town centre, about 100 m from the church. A very comfortable hotel with a good restaurant.
TARIFF: Single 160–250, Double 186–300, Bk 30, Set menu 70–245.
CC: Amex, Diners, Euro/Access, Visa.

LOURDES Htes-Pyrénées 4D

Hôtel Le Miramont ★★ route de Lourdes, 65380 Orincles.

☎ 62 45 41 02. English spoken.
Open all year. 10 bedrooms (9 en suite, 10 telephone). Outdoor swimming pool, golf 8 km, parking.

Small hotel set in attractive grounds, fishing, cycling, tennis, lake nearby. 8 km from Lourdes D937 going east, then left onto D7 to Orincles.

TARIFF: Double 200–230, Bk 25.
CC: Euro/Access, Visa.

LOUVIERS Eure 2A

Hôtel La Haye-le-Comte ★★★ 4 route de la Haye-le-Comte, 27400 Louviers.

☎ 32 40 00 40, Fax 32 25 03 85. English spoken.

Open 15/03 to 01/01. 16 bedrooms (all en suite with telephone). Tennis, golf 9 km, garage, parking. &
RESTAURANT: Closed lunch.

16th-century manor house set in a 12-acre park mid-way between Paris and Deauville. Take the D133 from Louviers towards Neubourg and on the outskirts of Louviers turn left, the hotel is 700 m on the right. Follow the blue signs 'La Haye-le-Compte' from town centre.

TARIFF: Single 180–450, Double 250–450, Bk 45, Set menu 110–160.
CC: Amex, Euro/Access, Visa.

LUCON Vendée 4A

Grand Hotel du Croissant ★ place des Acacias, 85400 Luçon.

☎ 51 56 11 15. English spoken.
Open 01/11 to 30/09. 40 bedrooms (20 en suite, 10 bath/shower only, 20 telephone). Garage, parking.
RESTAURANT: Closed Sun LS.

In the centre of Luçon, the Croissant Hotel offers a warm, family-style welcome with traditional cooking, at reasonable prices.
TARIFF: Single 105–195, Double 128–250, Bk 30, Set menu 60–110.
CC: Euro/Access, Visa.

LYON Rhône 5B

Hôtel Climat de France ★★ 11 chemin de Gargantua, Porte de Lyon Norde, 69570 Dardilly.

☎ 78 35 98 47, Fax 78 66 08 18. English spoken.
Open all year. 50 bedrooms (all en suite with telephone). Outdoor swimming pool, golf 3 km, parking, restaurant. &

Comfortable hotel with restaurant offering traditional cuisine. North-west of Lyon off A6 towards Dardilly.
TARIFF: Double 280, Bk 34, Set menu 85–125.
CC: none.

Grand Hôtel Concorde ★★★★ 11 rue Grolée, 69002 Lyon.

☎ 72 40 45 45, Fax 78 37 52 55. English spoken.
Open all year. 140 bedrooms (all en suite with telephone). Garage.
RESTAURANT: Closed Sun lunch.

In the centre of Lyon on the banks of the Rhône. This 19th-century hotel has been completely redecorated to combine old world elegance with traditional charm and contemporary comfort. Follow the River Rhône up to the Wilson Bridge.
TARIFF: Single 595–890, Double 640–890, Bk 60.
CC: Amex, Diners, Euro/Access, Visa.

Hôtel Les Provinces ★★ 10 place St-Lus, 69110 Ste-Foy-les-Lyon.

☎ 78 25 01 55. English spoken.
Open all year. 14 bedrooms (all en suite with telephone). Garage, parking.

Good quality, simply furnished hotel giving very good value. Travelling south from Paris, go through the tunnel and turn immediately right towards Vieux Lyon.
TARIFF: Single 145–220, Double 155–220, Bk 20.
CC: Amex, Euro/Access, Visa.

Hôtel Pullman Perrache ★★★★ 12 cours Verdun, Perrache, 69000 Lyon.

☎ 78 37 58 11, Fax 78 37 06 56. English spoken.
Open all year. 121 bedrooms (all en suite, all bath/shower only with telephone). Garage, parking, restaurant. &

Traditional-style hotel built in 1906 and

France

tastefully redecorated. Centrally located in Lyon.
TARIFF: Double 490–790, Bk 62,
Set menu 135–250.
CC: Amex, Diners, Euro/Access, Visa.

MAGNAC-BOURG Haute-Vienne 4B

Hôtel Midi ★★ N 20, 87380 Magnac-Bourg.
☎ 55 00 80 13, Fax 55 48 70 96. English spoken.
Open 15/02 to 15/01. 13 bedrooms (all en suite
with telephone). Tennis, garage, parking.
RESTAURANT: Closed Mon.

*Very pretty, small hotel with beautiful garden
behind. Good cuisine serving traditional
regional food.*
TARIFF: (1993) Double 210–250, Bk 30.
CC: Amex, Diners, Euro/Access, Visa.

MANCIET Gers 4D

Hôtel Le Moulin du Comte ★★ D109
Bourrouillan, 32370 Manciet.
☎ 62 09 06 72.
Open 01/03 to 31/12. 10 bedrooms (all en suite
with telephone). Outdoor swimming pool,
golf 20 km, parking, restaurant. &

*Tucked away in the heart of the Gers
countryside, in a tree and flower-filled park is
Le Moulin du Comte, a former 18th-century
mill now restored. Local specialities in the
restaurant. 5 km north-west of Manciet on the
D153 to Bourrouillan.*
TARIFF: (1993) Double 250–300, Bk 30,
Set menu 100–200.
CC: Amex, Euro/Access, Visa.

LE MANS Sarthe 2C

Hôtel Maine Atlantique ★★ 24 rue Emile
Chesne, 72100 Le Mans.
☎ 43 84 35 11, Fax 43 85 75 41.
English spoken.
Open all year. 29 bedrooms (14 en suite,
12 bath/shower only, 29 telephone).
Golf 5 km, parking.

*Newly renovated. Tranquil family atmosphere.
Take the A11 from Paris to Le Mans, and then
follow the signs to Le Mans-Pontlieue.*
TARIFF: Single 155–230, Double 155–270, Bk 28.
CC: Amex, Euro/Access, Visa.

MARSEILLE Bouches-du-Rhône 5D

Hôtel Arcade ★★ sq Narvik, 13001 Marseille.
☎ 91 95 62 09, Fax 91 50 68 42. English spoken.
Open all year. 172 bedrooms (all en suite
with telephone). Parking. &
RESTAURANT: Closed Sat & Sun.

*Located right in the centre of the city, the hotel
offers a haven of peace and greenery, near the
Gare St-Charles.*
TARIFF: Single 295–395, Double 325–400,
Bk 35, Set menu 65–88.
CC: Amex, Visa.

MELUN Seine/Marne 2D

Hôtel Le Flamboyant 98 rue Paris,
77127 Lieusaint.
☎ 1 60 60 05 50, Fax 1 60 60 05 32.
English spoken.

Open all year. 72 bedrooms (all en suite
with telephone). Outdoor swimming pool,
tennis, golf 3 km, parking, restaurant. &

*Comfortable hotel just 27 km from Paris. From
périphérique take Porte d'Orléans exit on to
A6. Leave A6 at Melun-Senant then 'la
Francilienne' to Lieusaint.*
TARIFF: Single 280, Double 310, Bk 33,
Set menu 90–220.
CC: Amex, Diners, Euro/Access, Visa.

MENTON Alpes-Marit 6C

Hôtel Méditerranée ★★★ 5 rue République,
06500 Menton.
☎ 93 28 25 25, Fax 93 57 88 38.
English spoken.
Open all year. 90 bedrooms (all en suite
with telephone). Golf 18 km, garage,
restaurant. &

*A quiet and comfortable hotel, 30 minutes
from Nice airport.*
TARIFF: Single 350–460, Double 380–500,
Bk 35, Set menu 110–120.
CC: Amex, Diners, Euro/Access, Visa.

Hôtel Prince de Galles ★★★ 4 av Gén de
Gaulle, BP 21, 06500 Menton.
☎ 93 28 21 21, Fax 93 35 92 91.
English spoken.

Open all year. 68 bedrooms (all en suite with telephone). Golf 13 km, parking. &
RESTAURANT: Closed 18/11 to 24/12.

Carefully restored, overlooking beach. Tropical garden, with terrace. From Menton Casino follow promenade road towards Monaco for 2 km.

TARIFF: Single 235–305, Double 298–510, Bk 42, Set menu 88–180.
cc: Amex, Diners, Euro/Access, Visa.

METZ Moselle   3B

Hôtel Cecil ★★ 14 rue Pasteur, 57000 Metz.
✆ 87 66 66 13, Fax 87 56 96 02.
English spoken.
Open all year. 39 bedrooms (35 en suite, 4 bath/shower only, 39 telephone). Golf 8 km, garage.

Hotel in the town centre. Quiet and comfortable, room service, personal attention, near the station.

TARIFF: Single 185–270, Double 185–270, Bk 26.
cc: Euro/Access, Visa.

Hôtel du Théâtre ★★★ Port St-Marcel, 57000 Metz.
✆ 87 31 10 10, Fax 87 30 04 66. English spoken.

Open all year. 36 bedrooms (all en suite with telephone). Outdoor swimming pool, golf 3 km, garage, parking, restaurant. &

In one of the oldest parts of Metz, this hotel is part of a redevelopment plan for the old port of St-Marcel. Rooms with views of river or docks and waterside terraces. Fitness room with sauna, UVA solarium, spa, swimming pool. Next to the cathedral. Follow directions to 'Parking Port St-Marcel' (direct access to the reception).

TARIFF: Single 425–550, Double 490–590, Bk 50, Set menu 98–165.
cc: Amex, Diners, Euro/Access, Visa.

MODANE Savoie   6A

Hôtel Bellevue ★ 15 rue de Replat, Fourneaux, 73500 Modane.
✆ 79 05 20 64, Fax 79 05 37 42.
English spoken.
Open all year. 14 bedrooms (2 en suite, 10 bath/shower only, 11 telephone). Parking, restaurant.

A small hotel with good cuisine and relaxed atmosphere. South of the N6 in the Vallée de la Maurienne. 3 km from the tunnel du Fréjus leading to Italy.

TARIFF: Single 160–200, Double 190–250, Bk 28, Set menu 70–140.
cc: Euro/Access, Visa.

MONTE-CARLO   6C

Hôtel Paris ★★★★ pl Casino, 98000 Monte-Carlo, Monaco.
✆ 92 16 30 00, Fax 93 25 59 17.
English spoken.
Open all year. 210 bedrooms (all en suite with telephone). Indoor swimming pool, outdoor swimming pool, golf 10 km, garage, parking, restaurant.

A traditional 'Grand Hotel' with panoramic views and offering excellent cuisine.

TARIFF: Single 1900–2600, Double 2100–2900, Bk 140.
cc: Amex, Diners, Euro/Access, Visa.

MONT-DE-MARSAN Landes   4C

Hôtel Richelieu ★★ rue Wlérick, BP224, 40004 Mont-de-Marsan.
✆ 58 06 10 20, Fax 58 06 00 68.
English spoken.
Open all year. 49 bedrooms (all en suite with telephone). Golf 3 km, garage restaurant. &
The hotel is in centre of the town near the

France

museum and monuments. Take directions to the Préfecture.
TARIFF: (1993) Single 225–280, Double 240–300, Bk 30.
CC: Amex, Diners, Euro/Access, Visa.

LE MONT-ST-MICHEL Manche   1D

Hôtel Altea K Motel ★★★ BP 8,
50116 Le Mont-St-Michel.
✆ 33 60 14 18, Fax 33 60 39 28. English spoken.
Open 05/02 to 13/11. 100 bedrooms
(all en suite with telephone). Parking,
restaurant. ⅋

In the countryside on the banks of a river, at the end of the Mont-St-Michel dyke. A modern, recently-built hotel blending in with its surroundings. Large well shaded grounds. D976 Pontorson 1.5 km, D275 Avranches 20 km.
TARIFF: Single 350–460, Double 390–530, Bk 48.
CC: Amex, Euro/Access, Visa.

Hôtel de la Digue ★★★
50116 Le Mont-St-Michel.
✆ 33 60 14 02, Fax 33 60 37 59. English spoken.
Open 01/04 to 15/11. 35 bedrooms (all en suite with telephone). Parking, restaurant.

Seafood specialities in panoramic restaurant with views of Mont-St-Michel, brightly illuminated at night. Located 2 km from Mont-St-Michel at the start of the famous dyke on the D976.
TARIFF: Single 320–380, Double 350–450, Bk 48, Set menu 85–220.
CC: Amex, Diners, Euro/Access, Visa.

MONTAUBAN Tarn/Garonne   4D

Hôtel du Commerce ★ 9 pl Franklin
Roosevelt, 82000 Montauban.
✆ 63 66 31 32, Fax 63 03 18 46.
English spoken.

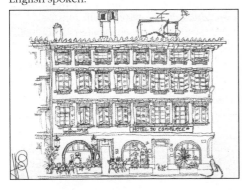

Open all year. 28 bedrooms (14 en suite, 2 bath/shower only, 28 telephone).
Golf 10 km, garage, parking, restaurant. ⅋
Good value in this town centre hotel, directly opposite cathedral.
TARIFF: Single 90–180, Double 115–250, Bk 22, Set menu 65–200.
CC: Euro/Access, Visa.

MONTAUBAN-DE-BRETAGNE   1D

Hôtel de France 34 rue de Gén de Gaulle,
35360 Montauban-de-Bretagne.
✆ 99 06 40 19. English spoken.
Open 01/02 to 20/12. 12 bedrooms (9 en suite, 3 bath/shower only, 12 telephone). Parking, restaurant.

Hotel/restaurant set in the centre of the village. One hour from St-Malo, 2 hrs from Roscoff. N12, 30 km from Rennes.
TARIFF: Single 110–220, Double 220, Bk 28, Set menu 62–150.
CC: Euro/Access, Visa.

MONTBARD Côte-d'Or   3C

Hôtel Ecu ★★★ 7 rue A Carré,
21500 Montbard.
✆ 80 92 11 66, Fax 80 92 14 13. English spoken.
Open all year. 25 bedrooms (all en suite with telephone). Garage, parking, restaurant.

An old family house with delightful interior and restaurant serving regional specialities. North of A6 or D980 towards Montbard.
TARIFF: Single 250–290, Double 330–400, Bk 38.
CC: Amex, Diners, Euro/Access, Visa.

MONTELIMAR Drôme   5D

Hôtel Cremaillère ★★★ 138 av Jean-Jaurès,
26200 Montélimar.
✆ 75 01 87 46, Fax 75 52 36 87. English spoken.
Open 01/01 to 18/12. 20 bedrooms
(all en suite with telephone). Outdoor swimming pool, golf 5 km, garage, parking. ⅋
RESTAURANT: Closed Jan.

Situated 1.5 km from the city centre.
TARIFF: Single 240–310, Double 270–310, Bk 30.
CC: Amex, Euro/Access, Visa.

MONTOIRE-SUR-LE-LOIR Loir-et-Cher 2C

Hôtel Cheval Blanc ★★ place de la
Libération, 41800 Trôo.
✆ 54 72 58 22, Fax 54 72 55 44.
Open all year. 9 bedrooms (all en suite with telephone). Parking.

France

RESTAURANT: Closed Mon/Tues lunch.

From Vendôme west on the D917 to Montoire-s-le-Loir then Trôo.

TARIFF: Double 270–290, Bk 30,
Set menu 100–250.
CC: Euro/Access, Visa.

MONTPELLIER Hérault 5C

Hôtel Altea Antigone ★★★ 218 rue du
Bastion Ventadour, 34000 Montpellier.
☎ 67 64 65 66, Fax 67 22 22 21. English spoken.
Open all year. 116 bedrooms (all en suite
with telephone). Garage, restaurant. &
*Large modern hotel in heart of business
district.*

TARIFF: Single 340–520, Double 340–570,
Bk 55, Set menu 85–175.
CC: Amex, Diners, Euro/Access, Visa.

MONTREUIL Pas-de-Calais 2B

Hôtel Le Shakespeare ★★ 7 rue de Change,
62170 Montreuil-sur-Mer.
☎ 21 86 16 04. English spoken.
Open all year. 14 bedrooms (4 en suite,
1 bath/shower only). Golf 15 km, restaurant.
*Warm welcome to families from the English
owners of this town-centre hotel.*

TARIFF: Single 120–205, Double 220–280,
Bk 30, Set menu 68.
CC: Euro/Access, Visa.

Hôtel Le Val de Canche ★ 2 Grand rue,
62990 Beaurainville.
☎ 21 90 32 22. English spoken.

Open 01/01 to 25/12. 10 bedrooms (1 en suite,
3 bath/shower only). Parking.
RESTAURANT: Closed Sun eve & Mon LS.

*Family-run, British-owned hotel in village
centre. Just off N39 between Montreuil and
Hesdin.*

TARIFF: Double 140–225, Bk 27.
CC: Euro/Access, Visa.

MONTRICHARD Loir-et-Cher 2D

Hôtel de la Tête Noire ★★★
24 rue de Tours, BP3, 41401 Montrichard.
☎ 54 32 05 55, Fax 54 32 78 37.
English spoken.
Open 01/02 to 31/12. 38 bedrooms
(31 en suite, 38 telephone). Golf 17 km,
parking.
RESTAURANT: Closed 04/01 to 02/02.

*The hotel is in a small friendly town on the
River Cher, ideal for visiting nearby Loire
Valley châteaux.*

TARIFF: Single 195–275, Double 195–315,
Bk 34, Set menu 95–250.
CC: Euro/Access, Visa.

MORTAGNE-AU-PERCHE Orne 2C

Hôtel Le Tribune ★★ 4 place du Palais,
61400 Mortagne-au-Perche.
☎ 33 25 04 77, Fax 33 83 60 83.
English spoken.

Open all year. 10 bedrooms (all en suite
with telephone). Golf 15 km, garage, parking,
restaurant.

*Very old building dating back to the 13th
century with lots of beams, studs and local
stone. Flower-covered terrace and bedrooms
have a garden view. Mortagne-au-Perche lies
in the 'Vieux Mortagne' region and is
renowned for its black puddings! From
Alençon east on N12.*

TARIFF: Double 220–320, Bk 40,
Set menu 80–160.
CC: Euro/Access, Visa.

France

MOUGINS Alpes-Marit   6C

Hôtel Le Mas Candille ★★★★ bd Rebuffel, 06250 Mougins.
☎ 93 90 00 85, Fax 92 92 85 56. English spoken.

Open 01/03 to 31/10. 23 bedrooms (all en suite with telephone). Outdoor swimming pool, tennis, golf 2 km, parking.
RESTAURANT: very good. Closed Nov to Jan.

Situated in the old village, five minute's walk from the centre, with beautiful views of the surrounding hillside. Terrace restaurant.
TARIFF: Double 650–950, Bk 75, Set menu 125–165.
CC: Amex, Diners, Euro/Access, Visa.

MOULINS Allier   5A

Hôtel Paris Jacquemart ★★★ 21 rue Paris, 03000 Moulins.
☎ 70 44 00 58, Fax 70 34 05 39. English spoken.
Open all year. 28 bedrooms (all en suite with telephone). Outdoor swimming pool, golf 5 km, garage, parking.
RESTAURANT: very good. Closed Sun & Mon eve.

Situated in the centre of the town, near the Préfecture, offering a high standard of service and a well-known restaurant.
TARIFF: Single 330–480, Double 330–980, Bk 50, Set menu 160–440.
CC: Amex, Diners, Euro/Access, Visa.

MULHOUSE Haut-Rhin   3D

Hôtel Inter Salvator ★★ 29 passage Centrale, BP 1354, 68100 Mulhouse.
☎ 89 45 28 32, Fax 89 56 49 59. English spoken.
Open all year. 54 bedrooms (all en suite with telephone). Golf 15 km, garage, parking.

Quiet hotel with a warm welcome, situated jclose to the motorway exit (Mulhouse-Centre).
TARIFF: Single 260–275, Double 275–300, Bk 35.
CC: Amex, Diners, Euro/Access, Visa.

MUS Gard   5D

Aub de la Paillère ★★★ av de Puits Vieux, 30121 Mus.
☎ 66 23 78 79, Fax 66 73 79 28. English spoken.
Open 10/02 to 01/01. 7 bedrooms (all en suite with telephone). Golf 15 km, parking.
RESTAURANT: Closed Mon.

A charming 17th-century house in a small village. Between N113 and A9, exit A9 towards Gallargues.
TARIFF: Single 350–480, Double 380–480, Set menu 110–230.
CC: Amex, Euro/Access, Visa.

NAJAC Aveyron   5C

Hôtel Le Belle Rive ★★ Le Roc du Pont, 12270 Najac-en-Rouergue.
☎ 65 29 73 90. English spoken.
Open 04/04 to 01/11. 35 bedrooms (all en suite with telephone). Outdoor swimming pool, tennis, garage, parking. ♿
RESTAURANT: Closed 02/11 to 03/04.

Rouergue is a pretty town on the River Aveyron and overlooked by a castle with fishing, canoeing, horseriding and pot-holing all available. The hotel offers local cuisine and country wines. 2 km from Najac on the D139.
TARIFF: Double 240–280, Bk 40, Set menu 80–250.
CC: Diners, Euro/Access, Visa.

NANCY Meurthe/Moselle   3D

Hôtel Altea Thiers ★★★ 11 rue Raymond Poincaré, 54000 Nancy.
☎ 83 39 75 75, Fax 83 32 78 17. English spoken.
Open all year. 192 bedrooms (all en suite with telephone). Golf 10 km, parking, restaurant.

Town centre hotel opposite the railway station, sound-proofed and air-conditioned rooms.

France

A31 exit Nancy-Centre-Ville, follow signs to Gare SNCF.
TARIFF: Double 360–625, Bk 52.
CC: Amex, Diners, Euro/Access, Visa.

NANTES Loire-Atlan 1D

Hôtel Astoria ★★★ 11 rue Richebourg, 44000 Nantes.
☎ 40 74 39 90, Fax 40 14 05 49. English spoken.
Open all year. 45 bedrooms (42 en suite, 45 telephone). Garage, parking. ♿
In the centre of Nantes, near the cathedral, Musée Beaux Arts and the railway station. Quiet street close to public gardens.
TARIFF: Single 280–300, Double 290–320, Bk 35.
CC: Euro/Access, Visa.

Holiday Inn Garden Court ★★★ 1 bd
Martyrs Nantais, 44200 Nantes.
☎ 40 47 77 77, Fax 40 47 36 52.
English spoken.

Open all year. 108 bedrooms (all en suite with telephone). Golf 6 km, garage, parking. ♿
RESTAURANT: Closed Sat lunch and Sun.
On the River Loire near the old quarter. Motorway A11 south-west of Angers, towards city centre and Ile-Beaulieu.
TARIFF: Single 380–490, Double 390–490, Bk 55, Set menu 89–120.
CC: Amex, Diners, Euro/Access, Visa.

NANTUA Ain 6A

Hôtel Embarcadère ★★ av Lac, 01130 Nantua.
☎ 74 75 22 88, Fax 74 75 22 25.
English spoken.
Open 20/01 to 30/04 & 08/05 to 20/12.
50 bedrooms (all en suite with telephone).
Parking, restaurant.
Peaceful lake and forest setting with good restaurant. From Paris, exit 8 off A40.

TARIFF: Double 240, Bk 30, Set menu 105–280.
CC: Euro/Access, Visa.

Hôtel de France ★★★ 44 rue du Docteur Mercier, 01130 Nantua.
☎ 74 75 00 55, Fax 74 75 26 22. English spoken.
Open 20/12 to 01/11. 17 bedrooms (all en suite with telephone). Garage, parking.
RESTAURANT: Closed 01/11 to 20/12.
Old coaching inn offering good food and a warm welcome. On A40 from Paris, take exit 8, from Genève, exit 9.
TARIFF: Single 200–260, Double 275–400, Bk 33, Set menu 125–195.
CC: Euro/Access, Visa.

NARBONNE Aude 5C

Hôtel Relais du Val d'Orbieu ★★★
11200 Ornaisons.
☎ 68 27 10 27, Fax 68 27 52 44. English spoken.

Open all year. 20 bedrooms (all en suite with telephone). Outdoor swimming pool, tennis, golf 15 km, parking, restaurant. ♿
Within 15 minutes of the centre of Narbonne, in 2 acres of wooded garden. The hotel is an old mill which has been renovated and combines luxury and comfort together with charm. Take the A9 and exit Narbonne-Sud.
TARIFF: Single 350–570, Double 450–650, Bk 65, Set menu 165–295.
CC: Amex, Diners, Euro/Access, Visa.

NEMOURS Seine/Marne 2D

Hôtel L'Ecu de France ★★ 3 rue de Paris, 77140 Nemours.
☎ 1 64 28 11 54, Fax 1 64 45 03 65.
English spoken.
Open all year. 28 bedrooms (25 en suite, 25 bath/shower only, 25 telephone). Garage, parking, restaurant.
An inviting hotel dating from the 14th century.

France

France

Exit A6 or N7 towards Nemours.
TARIFF: Single 140–250, Double 140–300,
Bk 28, Set menu 69–260.
CC: Amex, Diners, Euro/Access, Visa.

NEUF-BRISACH Haut-Rhin 3D

Hôtel de France ★★ 17 rue de Bâle,
68600 Neuf-Brisach.
☎ 89 72 56 06, Fax 89 72 99 26. English spoken.
Open all year. 22 bedrooms (18 en suite,
22 telephone). Restaurant.

*Pleasant hotel in small town close to Swiss
border.*
TARIFF: (1993) Single 140–220,
Double 180–240, Bk 30, Set menu 60–95.
CC: Amex, Euro/Access, Visa.

NEVERS Nièvre 2D

Hôtel de Diane ★★★★ 38 rue du Midi,
58000 Nevers.
☎ 86 57 28 10, Fax 86 59 45 08. English spoken.
Open 10/01 to 22/12. 30 bedrooms
(all en suite with telephone). Garage.
RESTAURANT: Closed Sun & Mon lunch.

*In the centre of town near the station and
Loire. Cable TV. From the station, take av de
Gaulle, opposite main gate, and then second
right.*
TARIFF: Single 380–440, Double 450–490, Bk 40.
CC: Amex, Diners, Euro/Access, Visa.

Hôtel Loire ★★★★ quai de Médine,
58000 Nevers.
☎ 86 61 50 92. English spoken.
Open all year. 58 bedrooms (all en suite
with telephone). Golf 9 km, parking. ♿
RESTAURANT: Closed 15/12 to 10/01.

*The hotel stands at the edge of the River Loire.
The restaurant and most of the rooms overlook
the river and old bridge. A quiet hotel, about
200 m from town centre and shopping
facilities. 5 minutes drive from town railway
station. Near N7.*
TARIFF: Single 320–335, Double 390–420, Bk 37.
CC: Amex, Diners, Euro/Access, Visa.

NICE Alpes-Marit 6C

Hôtel Agata ★★★ 46 bd Carnot, 06300 Nice.
☎ 93 55 97 13, Fax 93 55 67 38. English spoken.
Open all year. 45 bedrooms (all en suite
with telephone). Garage, parking.
Set in a residential area close to the port of Nice.
TARIFF: Single 400–480, Double 420–550.
CC: Amex, Euro/Access, Visa.

Occidental Nice Hôtel ★★★★ 179 bd René-
Cassin, 06200 Nice.
☎ 93 83 91 92, Fax 93 21 69 57. English spoken.

Open all year. 150 bedrooms (all en suite
with telephone). Outdoor swimming pool,
garage, restaurant. ♿
*Modern high-rise hotel with all amenities close
to town centre, near Nice airport on the French
Riviera. Also surprisingly close to the ski resorts
of southern Alps.*
TARIFF: Single 680–850, Double 760–950,
Bk 78, Set menu 95.
CC: Amex, Diners, Euro/Access, Visa.

Hôtel Pullman ★★★ 28 av Notre Dame,
06000 Nice.
☎ 93 13 36 36, Fax 93 62 61 69. English spoken.

Open all year. 201 bedrooms (all en suite
with telephone). Outdoor swimming pool,
golf 15 km, garage.

*Large, air-conditioned modern hotel set in
gardens, in the heart of Nice. Rooms fully
equipped. Five minutes from the beach and the
promenade des Anglais. 7 km from
international airport, railway station 300 m.*

TARIFF: Single 495–830, Double 550–930, Bk 70.
CC: Amex, Diners, Euro/Access, Visa.

Hôtel Splendid ★★★★ 50 bd Victor Hugo,
06048 Nice.
☎ 93 16 41 00, Fax 93 87 02 46. English spoken.
Open all year. 127 bedrooms (all en suite
with telephone). Outdoor swimming pool,
golf 20 km, garage, restaurant. &

*Family-run, air-conditioned hotel in the
centre of town. 300 m from beach.*

TARIFF: Single 650–800, Double 690–900,
Bk 75, Set menu 135–221.
CC: Amex, Diners, Euro/Access, Visa.

Hôtel Westminster Concorde ★★★★ 27
promenade des Anglaises, 06000 Nice.
☎ 93 88 29 44, Fax 93 82 45 35. English spoken.
Open all year. 102 bedrooms (all en suite
with telephone). Golf 15 km, parking,
restaurant.

*On the famous promenade des Anglais in the
heart of Nice, walking distance from the beach
and the shops.*

TARIFF: Double 700–1000, Bk 100.
CC: Amex, Diners, Euro/Access, Visa.

Hôtel Windsor ★★★ 11 rue Dalpozzo,
06000 Nice.
☎ 93 88 59 35, Fax 93 88 94 57. English spoken.
Open all year. 60 bedrooms (all en suite
with telephone). Outdoor swimming pool,
golf 10 km, parking.
RESTAURANT: Closed Sun.

*In the heart of Nice. From the promenade des
Anglais, close to Westminster Hotel, turn
into Meyerbeer Street, take first right, then
second left.*

TARIFF: Single 350–525, Double 460–670, Bk 40.
CC: Amex, Diners, Euro/Access, Visa.

NIMES Gard 5D

Hôtel Majestic ★★ 10 rue Pradier,
30000 Nîmes.
☎ 66 29 24 14, Fax 66 29 77 33. English spoken.
Open all year. 26 bedrooms (24 en suite,
2 bath/shower only, 26 telephone). Outdoor
swimming pool, tennis, golf 2 km, garage. &
Next to the train and bus stations in town centre.

TARIFF: Single 190–230, Double 220–250, Bk 35.
CC: Euro/Access, Visa.

NIORT Deux-Sèvres 4B

Hôtel Moulin 27 rue Espingole, 79000 Niort.
☎ 49 09 07 07.
Open all year. 34 bedrooms (all en suite).

Modern hotel in town centre beside the river.
TARIFF: Single 240–250, Double 240–280, Bk 25.
CC: Amex, Visa.

NOIRMOUTIER-EN-L'ILE Vendée 1D

Hôtel Fleur de Sel ★★★
85330 Noirmoutier-en-l'Ile.
☎ 51 39 21 59, Fax 51 39 75 66.
English spoken.

Open 19/02 to 01/11. 35 bedrooms
(all en suite with telephone). Outdoor
swimming pool, tennis, parking, restaurant. &

*In a quiet island location between the port and
beaches. Excellent restaurant with seafood
specialities, overlooking gardens. Approach
island on D948.*

TARIFF: Double 325–595, Bk 47,
Set menu 155–245.
CC: Euro/Access, Visa.

ONZAIN Loir-et-Cher 2C

Château des Tertres ★★★ route de
Monteaux, 41150 Onzain.
☎ 54 20 83 88, Fax 54 20 89 21. English spoken.
Open 26/03 to 14/11. 19 bedrooms
(all en suite with telephone). Golf 5 km,
parking.

*19th-century château near some of France's
most sumptuous royal residences. The village
of Onzain is halfway between Blois and
Amboise (17km) on N152.*

TARIFF: (1993) Double 320–460, Bk 37.
CC: Amex, Euro/Access, Visa.

ORBEY Haut-Rhin 3D

Hôtel au Bois Le Sire ★★★ 20 rue Charles de
Gaulle, 68370 Orbey.
☎ 89 71 25 25, Fax 89 71 30 75. English spoken.
Open 15/02 to 03/01. 36 bedrooms
(all en suite with telephone). Indoor

swimming pool, golf 10 km, parking. &
RESTAURANT: Closed Mon.
From Kaysersberg take N415 towards St-Die, then left to Orbey. Family-run hotel at foot of Vosges.
TARIFF: Single 230–330, Double 250–350, Bk 48, Set menu 78–320.
CC: Amex, Euro/Access, Visa.

ORGEVAL Yvelines   2B

Hôtel Moulin d'Orgeval ★★★★ rue de l'Abbaye, 78630 Orgeval.
☎ 1 39 75 85 74, Fax 1 39 75 48 52.
English spoken.
Open all year. 14 bedrooms (all en suite with telephone). Outdoor swimming pool, golf 15 km, parking, restaurant.
This luxurious former abbey stands in beautiful grounds. From A13, exit at Poissy-Villennes. Turn right towards Orgeval, and look for signs.
TARIFF: Single 550, Double 720, Bk 50.
CC: Amex, Diners, Euro/Access, Visa.

ORLEANS Loiret   2D

Orléans Parc Hôtel ★★★ 55 rte d'Orléans, 45380 La Chapelle-St-Mesmin.
☎ 38 43 26 26, Fax 38 72 00 99. English spoken.

Open all year. 32 bedrooms (all en suite with telephone). Garage, parking. &
19th-century house in 8 acres, on the Loire. A71, exit Orléans-Centre. N152 to La Chapelle-St-Mesmin.
TARIFF: Single 300–320, Double 390–450, Bk 35.
CC: Amex, Euro/Access, Visa.

OUISTREHAM Calvados   2A

Hôtel Normandie ★★ 71 av M Cabieu, 14150 Ouistreham.
☎ 31 97 19 57, Fax 31 97 20 07. English spoken.

Open all year. 24 bedrooms (all en suite with telephone). Golf 10 km, parking, restaurant.
Classic, comfortable hotel near the port and 400 m from the ferry. 12 km from Caen.
TARIFF: Double 230–320, Bk 35, Set menu 98–325.
CC: Amex, Diners, Euro/Access, Visa.

PAIMPOL Côtes-du-Nord   1A

Hôtel Le Repaire de Kerroc'h ★★★ 29 quai Morand, Port de Plaisance, 22500 Paimpol.
☎ 96 20 50 13, Fax 96 22 07 46. English spoken.
Open 16/02 to 31/05 & 08/06 to 14/11.
13 bedrooms (all en suite with telephone). Golf 10 km, parking.
RESTAURANT: good. Closed Tues & Wed lunch.
Small hotel in historic house, built by Privateer Kersanx in 1793. Rooms have views of bay and harbour. Take D786 from St-Brieuc.
TARIFF: Single 250, Double 390–580, Bk 45.
CC: Euro/Access, Visa.

Motoring in France – Vehicle Lights
Vehicles on French roads no longer need to have yellow light beams. However, for a right-hand-drive car, you should change the direction of the headlamp beams so that they angle to the right nearside, not to the left. This may be done with clip-on, re-useable headlamp covers, or stick-on beam convertors that are suitable for once-only use.

PARIS

CENTRAL PARIS

PARIS I Paris 3B

Hôtel Britannique ★★★ 20 av Victoria, 75001 Paris.
📞 1 42 33 74 59, Fax 1 42 33 82 65.
English spoken.

Open all year. 40 bedrooms (all en suite with telephone).

Located in a quiet avenue, 40 individualized guest rooms complete with sound proofing and colour TV with 10 channels (CNN, Sky News, etc), personal safe box. (Place du Châtelet.)

TARIFF: Single 530–640, Double 640–740, Bk 45.
CC: Amex, Diners, Euro/Access, Visa.

Novotel Paris Halles ★★★ 8 place Marguerite de Navarre, 75001 Paris.
📞 1 42 21 31 31, Fax 1 40 26 05 79.
English spoken.
Open all year. 285 bedrooms (all en suite with telephone). Parking, restaurant. ♿

Modern hotel, located in the heart of old Paris, near the Forum des Halles and the Seine.

CC: Amex, Diners, Euro/Access, Visa.

Hôtel Le Relais du Louvre ★★★ 19 rue des Prêtres-St-Germain, L'Auxerrois, 75001 Paris.
📞 1 40 41 96 42, Fax 1 40 41 96 44.
English spoken.
Open all year. 20 bedrooms (all en suite with telephone). Parking.

A tastefully decorated, modern hotel situated in the centre of Paris.

TARIFF: Single 570–750, Double 750–1400, Bk 50.
CC: Amex, Diners, Euro/Access, Visa.

PARIS IV Paris 3B

Hôtel du Jeu de Paume ★★★★
54 rue St-Louis-en-l'Ile, 75004 Paris.
📞 1 43 26 14 18, Fax 1 40 46 02 76.
English spoken.
Open all year. 32 bedrooms (all en suite with telephone).

Small, comfortable hotel on Ile-St-Louis in the middle of the Seine. Close to Notre Dame.

TARIFF: Single 795–895, Double 795–1190, Bk 75.
CC: Amex, Diners, Euro/Access, Visa.

PARIS V Paris 3B

Hôtel Carofftel Gobelins ★★ 18 av des Gobelins, 75005 Paris.
📞 1 45 35 80 12, Fax 1 45 35 00 57.
English spoken.
Open all year. 23 bedrooms (all en suite with telephone).

Close to the Latin quarter and Montparnasse. Nearest métro is Les Gobelins.

TARIFF: Single 330–390, Double 370–480, Bk 30.
CC: Amex, Diners, Euro/Access, Visa.

PARIS VI Paris 3B

Hôtel Latitudes St-Germain ★★★
7-11 rue St-Benoît, 75006 Paris.
📞 1 42 61 53 53, Fax 1 49 27 09 33.
English spoken.

Open all year. 117 bedrooms (all en suite with telephone). &

In the heart of St-Germain-des-Prés, next to Café Flore and Les Deux Magots. Near to Rue Bonaparte. Parking on nearby Boulevard St-Germain.

TARIFF: Single 640–930, Double 640–930, Bk 60.
CC: Amex, Diners, Euro/Access, Visa.

Hôtel Vieux Paris ★★ 9 rue Gît-le-Coeur, 75006 Paris.
☎ 1 39 61 98 05, Fax 1 33 61 99 15.
English spoken.
Open all year. 44 bedrooms (all en suite with telephone). Parking, restaurant. &

In north-west Paris; from A86 take 'Colombes Centre' exit then follow signs to Val Notre Dame.

TARIFF: Double 250–310, Bk 32.
CC: Amex, Euro/Access, Visa.

PARIS VII Paris   3B

Hôtel Les Jardins d'Eiffel ★★★ 8 rue Amélie, 75007 Paris.
☎ 1 47 05 46 21, Fax 1 45 55 28 08.
English spoken.

Open all year. 44 bedrooms (all en suite with telephone). Garage, parking. &

Completely renovated hotel in a residential area close to the Eiffel Tower and Invalides.

TARIFF: Single 550–690, Double 650–810.
CC: Amex, Diners, Euro/Access, Visa.

PARIS VIII Paris   3B

Hôtel Napoléon ★★★★ 40 av de Friedland, 75008 Paris.
☎ 1 47 66 02 02, Fax 1 47 66 82 33.
English spoken.
Open all year. 102 bedrooms (all en suite with telephone).
RESTAURANT: very good. Closed Sat & Sun.

Empire-style hotel offering friendly and efficient service. Close to l'Arc de Triomphe and Champs-Elysées.

TARIFF: Single 800–1150, Double 1150–1650, Bk 195, Set menu 170.
CC: Amex, Diners, Euro/Access, Visa.

L'Ouest-Hotel 3 rue de Rocher, 75008 Paris.
☎ 1 43 87 57 49, Fax 1 43 87 90 27.
English spoken.
Open all year. 53 bedrooms (all en suite with telephone).

Next to Saint-Lazare station, in the heart of the business centre, between Montmartre and the Champs-Elysées.

TARIFF: Single 360–480, Double 430–510, Bk 30.
CC: Amex, Diners, Euro/Access, Visa.

Hôtel Résidence Monceau ★★★ 85 rue du Rocher, 75008 Paris.
☎ 1 45 22 75 11, Fax 1 45 22 30 88.
English spoken.
Open all year. 51 bedrooms (all en suite with telephone). &

Comfortable hotel with spacious accommodation and gardens. Breakfast served outside when weather permits.

TARIFF: Double 650, Bk 46.
CC: Amex, Diners, Euro/Access, Visa.

PARIS IX Paris   3B

Les Hôtels du Pré ★★★ 10 rue du P Sémard, 75009 Paris.
☎ 1 42 81 37 11. English spoken.

Open all year. 115 bedrooms (all en suite with telephone). Parking.

Renovated throughout, central Paris location between Opéra, Gare du Nord and Sacré Coeur. From autoroute du Nord, exit via Porte de la Chapelle along Gare du Nord to hotel.

TARIFF: Single 395, Double 435–510, Bk 50.
CC: Amex, Diners, Euro/Access, Visa.

PARIS X Paris 3B

Hôtel Ibis Jemmapes ★★ 12 rue Louis-Blanc, 75010 Paris.
☎ 1 42 01 21 21, Fax 1 42 08 21 40.
English spoken.
Open all year. 49 bedrooms (all en suite with telephone). Parking. &

Conveniently situated only 5 minutes' walk from Gare du Nord station with its direct RER access to Roissy/Charles de Gaulle airport.

TARIFF: Single 410, Double 430, Bk 36.
CC: Amex, Euro/Access, Visa.

PARIS XII Paris 3B

Hôtel Belle Epoque ★★★ 66 rue de Charenton, 75012 Paris.
☎ 1 43 44 06 66, Fax 1 43 44 10 25.
English spoken.

Open all year. 29 bedrooms (all en suite with telephone). Parking.

Built around a patio to ensure privacy and quiet, the hotel is decorated in the Art Deco style and is near to the new Bastille Opera House and the Gare de Lyon.

TARIFF: Single 530, Double 670–950, Bk 50.
CC: Amex, Diners, Euro/Access, Visa.

Nouvel Hôtel ★★ 9 rue d'Austerlitz, 75012 Paris.
☎ 1 43 42 15 79, Fax 1 43 42 31 11.
English spoken.
Open all year. 24 bedrooms (all en suite with telephone). Parking. &

Ideally situated between Gare de Lyon and Gare d'Austerlitz. 10 mins to Omnisport de Bercy and place de Bastille. Three stops to Etoile and two stops to Opéra on the métro. All rooms are comfortable, fully equipped and have sound-proofing.

TARIFF: Single 300–360, Double 350–380, Bk 25.
CC: Amex, Diners, Euro/Access, Visa.

Hôtel Le Relais de Lyon ★★★
64 rue Crozatier, 75012 Paris.
☎ 1 43 44 22 50, Fax 1 43 41 55 12.
English spoken.

Open all year. 34 bedrooms (27 en suite, 7 bath/shower only, 34 telephone). Garage, parking.

Located in eastern central Paris, this hotel is conveniently close to both the Bastille and the Gare de Lyon. It is a modern 5-floor property, built in 1984. Period furnishing, quiet location.

TARIFF: Single 415, Double 530, Bk 40.
CC: Amex, Diners, Euro/Access, Visa.

PARIS XIII Paris 3B

Hôtel Arts ★★ 8 rue Coypel, 75013 Paris.
☎ 1 47 07 76 32, Fax 1 43 31 18 09.
English spoken.
Open all year. 37 bedrooms (29 en suite, 8 bath/shower only, 37 telephone).

Comfortable hotel in a quiet residential street. Close to the d'Italie-Gobelins métro station.

TARIFF: Single 287–307, Double 314–394.
CC: Amex, Euro/Access, Visa.

PARIS XIV Paris 3B

Hôtel Mercure Paris Montparnasse ★★★
20 rue de La Gaité, 75014 Paris.
☎ 1 43 35 28 28, Fax 1 43 27 98 64.
English spoken.
Open all year. 185 bedrooms (all en suite with telephone). Garage, restaurant. &

A modern hotel located on the left bank in the heart of the city's entertainment area, close to St-Germain.

TARIFF: Double 790–930, Bk 68,
Set menu 120–170.
CC: Amex, Diners, Euro/Access, Visa.

France

Hôtel Istria ★★ 29 rue Campagne Première, 75014 Paris.
☎ 1 43 20 91 82, Fax 1 43 22 48 45.
English spoken.

Open all year. 26 bedrooms (all en suite with telephone).

Hotel is situated in a very quiet street in artists' Montparnasse area, close to Luxembourg gardens. All rooms have a hair-dryer, direct telephone, colour TV and safe box.
TARIFF: Single 460–510, Double 510–560, Bk 40.
CC: Amex, Euro/Access, Visa.

Hôtel Sophie Germain ★★★ 12 rue Sophie Germain, 75014 Paris.
☎ 1 43 21 43 75, Fax 1 43 20 82 89.
English spoken.
Open all year. 33 bedrooms (all en suite with telephone).

Close to Montparnasse, St-Germain-des-Prés and Latin quarter. RER train to Denfert. Easy access to Orly Airport.
TARIFF: Single 490, Double 560, Bk 35.
CC: Amex, Diners, Euro/Access, Visa.

PARIS XV Paris   3B

Abaca Messidor Hôtel ★★★
330 rue de Vaugirard, 75015 Paris.
☎ 1 48 28 03 74, Fax 1 48 28 75 17.
English spoken.
Open all year. 72 bedrooms (all en suite with telephone). Parking.

Rooms with character and garden views in the centre of Paris, between métro stations Porte de Versailles and Convention.
TARIFF: Single 405–720, Double 545–900, Bk 50.
CC: Amex, Diners, Euro/Access, Visa.

Hôtel Adagio ★★★ 253 rue de Vaugirard, 75015 Paris.
☎ 1 40 45 11 50, Fax 1 40 45 10 10.
English spoken.

Open all year. 187 bedrooms (all en suite with telephone). Garage, restaurant. &
Situated close to Porte de Versailles with easy access from Vaugirard métro station and 5 minutes by car from Montparnasse train station.
TARIFF: Single 780–890, Double 840–950, Bk 65, Set menu 145.
CC: Amex, Diners, Euro/Access, Visa.

Hôtel Arcade Cambronne ★★
2 rue Cambronne, 75015 Paris.
☎ 1 45 67 35 20, Fax 1 45 66 49 58.
English spoken.
Open all year. 523 bedrooms (all en suite with telephone). Parking, restaurant.

10 mins walk from the Eiffel Tower. 10 minutes on the métro from the Parc des Expositions, Porte de Versailles and from the Montparnasse Tower, close to UNESCO.
TARIFF: Single 410–450, Double 440–450, Bk 42.
CC: Amex, Euro/Access, Visa.

Hôtel Ares ★★★ 7 rue du Général de Larminat, 75015 Paris.
☎ 1 47 34 74 04, Fax 1 47 34 48 56.
English spoken.

Open all year. 43 bedrooms (all en suite with telephone).

Situated close to the Eiffel Tower and the Champ de Mars, the hotel boasts a very quiet city location.
TARIFF: Single 490, Double 580, Bk 38.
CC: Amex, Euro/Access, Visa.

Hôtel Bailli de Suffren ★★★
149 av Suffren, 75015 Paris.
☎ 1 47 34 58 61, Fax 1 45 67 75 82.
English spoken.
Open all year. 25 bedrooms (all en suite with telephone). Parking.

Furnished with antiques and all rooms

France

individually styled. Close to Eiffel Tower, Champs de Mars and Invalides. From métro, travel from the centre out on Boulogne-Pont de St-Cloud Line (10) and exit at Ségur station.

TARIFF: Single 580, Double 620–650, Bk 40.
CC: Amex, Diners, Euro/Access, Visa.

Hôtel Lilas Blanc Grenelle ★★
5 rue de l'Avre, 75015 Paris.
☏ 1 45 75 30 07, Fax 1 45 78 66 65.
English spoken.

Open all year. 32 bedrooms (all en suite with telephone). Restaurant.

In the centre of the 15th district. Quiet and comfortable, with well-equipped rooms. From the Seine take Boulevard de Grenelle then a right turn on to rue de l'Avre.

TARIFF: Single 345–405, Double 395–445, Bk 32.
CC: Amex, Diners, Euro/Access, Visa.

PARIS XVI Paris 3B

Hôtel Baltimore ★★★★ 88 bis av Kléber, 75116 Paris.
☏ 1 44 34 54 54, Fax 1 44 34 54 44.
English spoken.
Open all year. 105 bedrooms (all en suite with telephone). Garage.
RESTAURANT: Closed Sat and Sun.

Open all year with elegant décor enhanced by the work of contemporary artists. Located near to the place Charles de Gaulle between place de L'Etoile and the Trocadero.

TARIFF: Single 1300–2500, Double 1600–2500, Bk 115.
CC: Amex, Diners, Euro/Access, Visa.

Hôtel Etoile Maillot ★★★
10 rue Bois de Boulogne, 75116 Paris.
☏ 1 45 00 42 60, Fax 1 45 00 55 89.
English spoken.
Open all year. 28 bedrooms (all en suite with telephone).

Small traditional hotel combining charm and modern facilities. Close to the Arc de Triomphe and business centre of Paris. Métro: Line 1 Argentine station, RER Line A Etoile station.

TARIFF: Single 560–690, Double 600–730.
CC: Amex, Diners, Euro/Access, Visa.

Hôtel Hameau de Passy ★★ 48 rue de Passy, 75016 Paris.
☏ 1 42 88 47 55, Fax 1 42 30 83 72. English spoken.
Open all year. 32 bedrooms (all en suite with telephone). ♿

Recently renovated hotel with small garden. In a residential area between Muette and Passy métro stations and close to the Eiffel Tower.

TARIFF: Single 450–495, Double 500–560.
CC: Amex, Diners, Euro/Access, Visa.

Hôtel Le Parc Victor Hugo ★★★★
55 ave Raymond Poincaré, 75016 Paris.
☏ 1 44 05 66 66, Fax 1 44 05 66 00.
English spoken.

Open all year. 115 bedrooms (all en suite with telephone). Restaurant. ♿

Elegantly renovated throughout, this hotel is situated between L'Etoile and the Trocadero in the heart of the 16th arrondissement.

TARIFF: Single 1600–1900, Double 1900–2200, Bk 115.
CC: Amex, Diners, Euro/Access, Visa.

France

Hôtel Pergolèse ★★★★ 3 rue Pergolèse,
75116 Paris.
☎ 1 40 67 96 77, Fax 1 45 00 12 11.
English spoken.

Open all year. 40 bedrooms (all en suite
with telephone).

*Near Champs Elysées, between Arc de
Triomphe and Palais de Congrès. Direct line to
business area La Défense. Decorated by the
famous designer Rena Dumas.*
TARIFF: Single 850–1200, Double 950–1500,
Bk 70.
CC: Amex, Diners, Euro/Access, Visa.

Queen's Hôtel ★★ 4 rue Bastien Lepage,
75016 Paris.
☎ 1 42 88 89 85, Fax 1 40 50 67 52.
English spoken.
Open all year. 22 bedrooms (all en suite
with telephone).

*In the 16th district, very near the Périphérique.
Direct métro line to the Champs Elysées and
St-Germain-des-Prés.*
TARIFF: Single 235–400, Double 400–510, Bk 35.
CC: Amex, Diners, Euro/Access, Visa.

Hôtel Rond Point de Longchamp ★★★
86 rue Longchamp, 75116 Paris.
☎ 1 45 05 13 63, Fax 1 47 55 12 80.
English spoken.

Open all year. 57 bedrooms (all en suite
with telephone). Restaurant.
TARIFF: Single 640–790, Double 730–910, Bk 65.
CC: Amex, Diners, Euro/Access, Visa.

PARIS XVII Paris   3B

Hôtel Abrial ★★★ 176 rue Cardinet,
75017 Paris.
☎ 1 42 63 50 00, Fax 1 42 63 50 03.
English spoken.
Open all year. 80 bedrooms (all en suite
with telephone). Garage. ♿

*A new hotel with a garden terrace, between the
Champs-Elysées and Montmartre.*
TARIFF: Single 490–590, Double 550–650, Bk 39.
CC: Amex, Euro/Access, Visa.

Hôtel Acacias Etoile ★★★ 11 rue Acacias,
75017 Paris.
☎ 1 43 80 60 22, Fax 1 48 88 96 40.
English spoken.

Open all year. 37 bedrooms (all en suite
with telephone). Garage.

*Charming hotel located in a quiet position
near the Arc de Triomphe. Private garden.*
TARIFF: Single 400–500, Double 590–630, Bk 37.
CC: Amex, Diners, Euro/Access, Visa.

Hôtel Ouest ★★ 165 rue de Rome,
75017 Paris.
☎ 1 42 27 50 29, Fax 1 42 27 27 40.
English spoken.
Open all year. 48 bedrooms (all en suite
with telephone). Parking.

*All rooms ahve colour TV. Close to Porte
Maillot conference centre, l'Opera and the
Parc Monceau. Métro: Rome, Villiers,
Brochant. Easy access from RER. From the
Péripherique via Porte Clichy.*
TARIFF: Single 315–415, Double 365–415,
Bk 30.
CC: Diners, Euro/Access, Visa.

France

PARIS XVIII Paris   3B

Hôtel Mercure Paris Monmartre ★★★
1 rue Caulaincourt, 75018 Paris.
☎ 1 42 94 17 17, Fax 1 42 93 66 14.
English spoken.
Open all year. 308 bedrooms (all en suite
with telephone). Parking. ♿

*Modern décor and efficient service from one of
the largest hotels in the Mercure Group. Close
to the artistic Monmartre area of Paris, down
the hill from the Sacré-Coeur. Métro station
Clichy.*

TARIFF: Double 680–900, Bk 68.
CC: Amex, Diners, Euro/Access, Visa.

Hôtel Utrillo ★★ 7 rue A Bruant,
75018 Paris.
☎ 1 42 58 13 44, Fax 1 42 23 93 88.
English spoken.

Open all year. 30 bedrooms (all en suite
with telephone).
*In the heart of the celebrated artists' centre of
Montmartre near the métro stations, Abbesses
and Blanche.*
TARIFF: Single 310–360, Double 370–440, Bk 40.
CC: Amex, Diners, Euro/Access, Visa.

PARIS XX Paris   3B

Hôtel Climat de France ★★ 2 av Prof A
Lemière, 75020 Paris.
☎ 1 43 63 16 16, Fax 1 43 63 31 32.
English spoken.
Open all year. 325 bedrooms (all en suite
with telephone). Golf 2 km, garage, parking,
restaurant. ♿

*A modern hotel next to the Périphérique at
Porte de Montreuill exit. Close to the A3 and
A4 exits, with easy access to airports and Euro
Disney. Métro station at 100 m with direct link
to centre.*

TARIFF: Double 440–445, Bk 38.
CC: Amex, Diners, Euro/Access, Visa.

PARIS WEST

BOULOGNE-BILLANCOURT   3B

Hôtel Acanthe ★★★ 9 rondpoint Rhin et
Danube, 92100 Boulogne-Billancourt.
☎ 1 46 99 10 40, Fax 1 46 99 00 05.
English spoken.
Open all year. 34 bedrooms (all en suite
with telephone). ♿

*South-west of Paris. Hotel is 20 m from métro
Boulogne, Pont de St Cloud.*

TARIFF: Single 580–670, Double 580–760, Bk 55.
CC: Amex, Diners, Euro/Access, Visa.

COURBEVOIE Hts de Seine   3B

Hôtel Blois ★★ 85 bd St-Denis,
92400 Courbevoie.
☎ 1 47 88 28 58, Fax 1 47 88 24 80.
English spoken.
Open all year. 33 bedrooms (all en suite
with telephone). Parking.

*Completely modernised hotel with fully
equipped rooms. Close to the Etoile and La
Défense. Cross the Seine at the Courbevoie*

Bridge and hotel is visible on the opposite side.
TARIFF: Double 390–450, Bk 40.
CC: Amex, Diners, Euro/Access, Visa.

PUTEAUX Hts de Seine 3B

Hôtel Syjac ★★★ 20 quai de Dion Bouton,
La Défense, 92800 Puteaux.
☎ 1 42 04 03 04, Fax 1 45 06 78 69.
English spoken.
Open all year. 36 bedrooms (all en suite
with telephone). Golf 5 km, parking.
*Comfort and old-world elegance in new-world
setting, just below La Défense. RER to La
Défense or métro to Pont-de-Neuilly.*
TARIFF: Single 550–650, Double 650–730, Bk 55.
CC: Amex, Diners, Euro/Access, Visa.

RUEIL-MALMAISON Hts de Seine 3B

Atria Novotel Rueil ★★★ av Edouard Belin,
92501 Rueil-Malmaison.
☎ 1 47 51 41 33, Fax 1 47 51 09 29.
English spoken.
Open all year. 118 bedrooms (all en suite with
telephone). Golf 1 km, parking, restaurant. &
*From the ring road (towards La Défense), exit
Rueil-Malmaison. 8 km from the centre of
Paris, and 6 km from Versailles.*
TARIFF: (1993) Single 530–550,
Double 560–620, Bk 50.
CC: Amex, Diners, Euro/Access, Visa.

ST-CLOUD Hts de Seine 3B

Hôtel Quorum ★★★ 2 bd République,
92210 St-Cloud.
☎ 1 47 71 22 33, Fax 1 46 02 75 64.
English spoken.
Open all year. 58 bedrooms (all en suite
with telephone). Golf 1 km, garage, parking,
restaurant. &
*Modern hotel with traditional charms close
to the gardens of St-Cloud. To the south-west
of Paris.*
TARIFF: (1993) Single 460–520,
Double 520–580, Bk 55.
CC: Amex, Diners, Euro/Access, Visa.

PARIS NORTH-EAST

AULNAY-SOUS-BOIS Seine-St-Denis 3B

Hôtel de Strasbourg ★★ 43 bd de Strasbourg,
93600 Aulnay-sous-Bois.
☎ 1 48 66 60 38, Fax 1 48 66 15 71.
English spoken.

Open all year. 24 bedrooms (all en suite
with telephone). Parking.
*10 minutes from Roissy/Charles de Gaulle
airport and Villepinte exhibition centre.
Comfortable hotel with TV lounge and bar.*
TARIFF: Single 225–280, Double 225–305, Bk 33.
CC: Amex, Diners, Euro/Access, Visa.

BAGNOLET Seine-St-Denis 3B

Novotel Paris Bagnolet ★★★ 1 av de la
République, 93177 Bagnolet.
☎ 1 49 93 63 00, Fax 1 43 60 83 95.
English spoken.
Open all year. 611 bedrooms (all en suite
with telephone). Outdoor swimming pool,
parking, restaurant.
*Modern hotel on eastern edge of Paris, near
the Hallieni métro station. Five minutes from
the Cité des Sciences at La Vellette Park and
ten minutes from the centre of Paris.*
TARIFF: (1993) Single 615–630,
Double 660–670, Bk 55.
CC: Amex, Diners, Euro/Access, Visa.

LE BLANC-MESNIL Seine-St-Denis 3B

Novotel ★★★ ZI Pont Y Blon,
93153 Le Blanc-Mesnil.
☎ 1 48 67 48 88, Fax 1 45 91 08 27.
English spoken.
Open all year. 143 bedrooms (all en suite
with telephone). Outdoor swimming pool,
golf 5 km, parking, restaurant. &
*Located 8 km from Porte de la Chapelle. From
A3 motorway, exit Le Blanc-Mesnil or from A1
exit 5, Le Bourget. Hotel is 30 km from
Euro Disney.*
TARIFF: (1993) Single 470, Double 490, Bk 50.
CC: Amex, Diners, Euro/Access, Visa.

LE BOURGET Seine-St-Denis 3B

Hôtel Bleu Marine ★★★ Aéroport du
Bourget, Zone Aviation d'Affaires,
93350 Le Bourget.
☎ 1 49 34 10 38, Fax 1 49 34 10 35.
English spoken.
Open all year. 86 bedrooms (all en suite
with telephone). Golf 5 km, parking,
restaurant. &
*Soundproofed and air-conditioned, smoking
and non-smoking rooms with every facility to
make your stay a pleasant one. From
Paris/Lille A1 take Bourget/Blanc Mesnil exit,
then follow signs for airport and 'Zone
d'Aviation d'Affaires'.*

France

TARIFF: Double 510, Bk 48.
CC: Amex, Diners, Euro/Access, Visa.

NOISY-LE-GRAND Seine-St-Denis   3B

Novotel Marne-La-Vallée ★★★
Porte de Paris, 2 allée Bienvenue,
93885 Noisy-le-Grand.
℡ 1 48 15 60 60, Fax 1 43 04 78 83.
English spoken.
Open all year. 142 bedrooms (all en suite
with telephone). Outdoor swimming pool,
golf 15 km, parking, restaurant. &

From Paris, Reims, EuroDisney: A4 exit Noisy-le-Grand then Noisy-Horizon.
TARIFF: (1993) Single 470–500,
Double 550–590, Bk 51.
CC: Amex, Diners, Euro/Access, Visa.

PARIS SOUTH-EAST

CHARENTON Val-de-Marne   3B

Atria Paris Charenton ★★★
5 place des Marseillais, 94227 Charenton.
℡ 1 46 76 60 60, Fax 1 49 77 68 00.
English spoken.
Open all year. 132 bedrooms (all en suite
with telephone). Parking, restaurant. &

*Situated close to the Bois de Vincennes. From
the Paris ring road (Périphérique) go to
Charenton-Centre. Métro station Liberté
20 m away.*
TARIFF: (1993) Single 590–620,
Double 640–690, Bk 51.
CC: Amex, Diners, Euro/Access, Visa.

CHOISY-LE-ROI Val-de-Marne   3B

Hôtel Climat de France ★★ 12 rue du Dr
Roux, 94600 Choisy-le-Roi.
℡ 1 46 82 43 43, Fax 1 45 73 21 91.
English spoken.

Open all year. 58 bedrooms (all en suite
with telephone). Parking, restaurant. &
*7 km from the centre of Paris, exit 11 for
Coudray, Monceaux, Auvernaux.*
TARIFF: (1993) Double 315, Bk 33,
Set menu 88–125.
CC: Amex, Euro/Access, Visa.

CRETEIL Val-de-Marne   3B

Novotel Creteil Le Lac ★★★ rue Jean Gabin,
94034 Créteil.
℡ 1 42 07 91 02, Fax 1 48 99 03 48.
English spoken.
Open all year. 110 bedrooms (all en suite
with telephone). Outdoor swimming pool,
parking, restaurant.

*Situated facing the lake in the entertainment
area, near the centre of Créteil. N19 south-east
of Paris, then N186.*
TARIFF: (1993) Single 470, Double 510, Bk 50.
CC: Amex, Diners, Euro/Access, Visa.

ST-MAURICE Val-de-Marne   3B

Hôtel Mercure ★★★ 12 rue Mar Leclerc,
94410 St-Maurice.
℡ 43 75 94 94, Fax 48 93 21 14. English spoken.
Open all year. 99 bedrooms (all en suite
with telephone). Garage, parking, restaurant.

*Modern, fully-equipped rooms, all with air
conditioning in a recently renovated castle by
the Marne river. 3 km from Paris. From the
ring road, take the Porte de Bercy exit.
30 minutes from Euro Disney on the A4,
Val d'Europe exit.*
TARIFF: Single 470–640, Double 470–690,
Bk 52, Set menu 75–95.
CC: Amex, Diners, Euro/Access, Visa.

END OF PARIS HOTELS

PAU Pyrénées-Atlan   4D

Hôtel Béarn ★★ 14 rue Las Bordes,
64420 Soumoulou.
℡ 59 04 60 09, Fax 59 04 63 33.
English spoken.
Open 05/02 to 05/01. 14 bedrooms
(all en suite with telephone). Golf 15 km,
garage, parking.
RESTAURANT: Closed Sun eve & Mon LS.

*Country hotel within reach of the Pyrénées.
N117 east of Pau, towards Lourdes and Tarbes.*
TARIFF: Single 200–280, Double 220–310,
Bk 35, Set menu 70–195.
CC: Amex, Diners, Euro/Access, Visa.

France

PAUILLAC Gironde   4A

Hôtel de France et d'Angleterre ★★
3 quai A Pichon, 33250 Pauillac.
☏ 56 59 01 20, Fax 56 59 02 31. English spoken.

Open 10/01 to 20/12. 29 bedrooms
(all en suite with telephone). Parking. ᵫ
RESTAURANT: Closed Sun eve & Mon LS.
*In the heart of the Médoc region, Pauillac is
45 km from Bordeaux. The hotel has terraces
and a garden, and the Château Mouton
Rothschild is just a few minutes' drive away.
Pauillac is on the D2, on the edge of the
Gironde.*
TARIFF: Double 300–350, Bk 33,
Set menu 90–290.
CC: Amex, Euro/Access, Visa.

PAYRAC Lot   4B

Hôtel de la Paix ★★ N20, 46350 Payrac.
☏ 65 37 95 15, Fax 65 37 90 37. English spoken.
Open 20/02 to 31/12. 50 bedrooms
(all en suite with telephone). Outdoor
swimming pool, parking, restaurant. ᵫ
*An old building in the centre of the village, full
of character, a former staging post totally
renovated and comfortably furnished. Almost
all rooms are at the rear of the building, and
quiet.*
TARIFF: Single 205–265, Double 225–310,
Bk 27.
CC: Amex, Euro/Access, Visa.

PERIGUEUX Dordogne   4B

Hôtel Chandelles ★★★ Antonne-et-
Trigonant, 24420 Périgueux.
☏ 53 06 05 10, Fax 53 06 07 33. English spoken.
Open 01/02 to 01/01. 7 bedrooms (all en suite
with telephone). Outdoor swimming pool,
tennis, golf 9 km, parking.
RESTAURANT: Closed Mon ex Jul/Aug.

*9 km from Périgueux on the way to Limoges.
This is an old farm building now turned into a
small hotel. Very good restaurant.*
TARIFF: Single 200–350, Double 280–350,
Bk 40, Set menu 145–395.
CC: Amex, Diners, Euro/Access, Visa.

Château de Rognac ★★ 24330 Bassillac.
☏ 53 54 40 78. English spoken.
Open 25/03 to 30/09. 12 bedrooms
(all en suite with telephone). Golf 12 km,
parking, restaurant.
*Listed château with 16th-century mill, on an
'island', 9 km north-east of Périgueux on the
N21 near Périgueux/Bassillac airfield.*
TARIFF: Single 252–384, Double 252–498,
Bk 37, Set menu 130–285.
CC: Euro/Access, Visa.

PERONNE Somme   2B

Hôtel des Remparts ★★ 21 rue Beaubois,
80200 Peronne.
☏ 22 84 01 22, Fax 22 84 31 96.
Open all year. 16 bedrooms (12 en suite,
4 bath/shower only, 16 telephone). Garage,
parking, restaurant.
*East of the A1 or N17. Leave A1 at junction
14 for Bapaune.*
TARIFF: Double 180–450, Bk 30,
Set menu 85–240.
CC: Amex, Diners, Euro/Access, Visa.

PERPIGNAN Pyrénées Orient   5C

Hôtel de la Loge ★★★ pl Loge,
66000 Perpignan.
☏ 68 34 41 02, Fax 68 34 25 13. English spoken.
Open all year. 22 bedrooms (all en suite
with telephone). Golf 20 km, parking.
*An old Catalan-style hotel in the pedestrian
district of Perpignan town centre. It is
3 minutes' walk from the République car park,
which the hotel will pay for.*
TARIFF: Single 230–320, Double 320–380, Bk 35.
CC: Amex, Diners, Euro/Access, Visa.

PLANCOET Côtes-du-Nord   1D

Hôtel Chez Crouzil ★★★ 20 Les Quais,
22130 Plancoët.
☏ 96 84 10 24, Fax 96 84 01 93. English spoken.
Open all year. 7 bedrooms (all en suite
with telephone). Golf 8 km, garage, parking.
RESTAURANT: very good. Closed Mon.
*More a restaurant with rooms, but exquisitely
decorated and furnished. There are plenty of*

other activities in the region to prolong your stay if you can drag yourself away from Mr Crouzil's dining-room.
TARIFF: Single 350–500, Double 350–700, Bk 65, Set menu 120–480.
CC: Amex, Euro/Access, Visa.

PLOERMEL Morbihan 1D

Hôtel Le Cobh ★★★ 10 rue des Forges, 56800 Ploërmel.
☎ 97 74 00 49. English spoken.
Open all year. 13 bedrooms (all en suite with telephone). Golf 2 km, garage, parking, restaurant. ♿

An old Breton house in the centre of Ploërmel, near the magnificent church. Traditional local cuisine in quality restaurant.
TARIFF: Single 200–300, Double 200–330, Bk 38, Set menu 69–210.
CC: Euro/Access, Visa.

POITIERS Vienne 4B

Château Clos Ribaudière ★★★ 10 place de Champ de Foire, 86360 Chasseneuil-du-Poitou.
☎ 49 52 86 66, Fax 49 52 86 32. English spoken.
Open all year. 19 bedrooms (all en suite with telephone). Golf 8 km, parking, restaurant. ♿

A 19th-century château in a riverside park, boasting exceptional décor and creative cuisine. Take Futuroscope exit, towards Chasseneuil-Centre Village.
TARIFF: Single 300–580, Double 360–600, Bk 50.
CC: Amex, Diners, Euro/Access, Visa.

POIX-DE-PICARDIE Somme 2B

Hôtel Le Cardinal ★★ place de la République, 80290 Poix-de-Picardie.
☎ 22 90 08 23, Fax 22 90 18 61. English spoken.
Open all year. 35 bedrooms (all en suite with telephone). Parking, restaurant.

A 16th-century hotel situated in the centre of the town. Warm atmosphere.
TARIFF: Single 230, Double 255, Bk 32, Set menu 85–160.
CC: Amex, Diners, Euro/Access, Visa.

POMPADOUR Corrèze 4B

Auberge de la Mandrie ★★ route de la Périgueux, 19230 Pompadour.
☎ 55 73 37 14, Fax 55 73 67 13. English spoken.
Open 28/11 to 15/11. 22 bedrooms (all en suite with telephone). Outdoor swimming pool, garage, parking. ♿

RESTAURANT: Closed 15/11 to 28/11.

Five km from Pompadour going towards Payzac and Ségur-le-Château (D7). Comfortable hotel/restaurant in the country. Traditional cooking.
TARIFF: Double 210–235, Bk 29, Set menu 72–202.
CC: Diners, Euro/Access, Visa.

PONT-AUDEMER Eure 2A

Hôtel Belle Isle-sur-Risle ★★★★ 112 rte Rouen, 27500 Pont-Audemer.
☎ 32 56 96 22, Fax 32 42 88 96. English spoken.
Open all year. 18 bedrooms (all en suite with telephone). Indoor swimming pool, outdoor swimming pool, tennis, parking, restaurant.

Charming mansion on a river island. 20 km from Honfleur and 39 km from Deauville. Prices are for half board. From Le Havre via Pont-Detanlarville, then Pont-Audemer.
TARIFF: Single 575–790, Double 650–1250, Bk 68.
CC: Amex, Diners, Euro/Access, Visa.

Hôtel Les Cloches de Corneville ★★★ 27500 Pont-Audemer.
☎ 32 57 01 04, Fax 32 57 10 96. English spoken.
Open 15/03 to 15/11. 13 bedrooms (12 en suite, 1 bath/shower only, 13 telephone). Parking.
RESTAURANT: good. Closed Mon.

Comfortable, country inn, where you may visit the bells of Corneville inside the property. On the N715 on the Rouen side of Pont-Audemer.
TARIFF: Single 260–300, Double 240–420, Bk 40.
CC: Euro/Access, Visa.

PONT-L'ABBE Finistère 1C

Hôtel de Bretagne ★★ 24 place de la République, 29120 Pont-l'Abbé.
☎ 98 87 17 22, Fax 98 82 89 34. English spoken.
Open all year. 18 bedrooms (all en suite with telephone). Golf 18 km, parking.
RESTAURANT: Closed Mon LS.

A charming family hotel quietly situated and just a few minutes from the Bay of Audierne. The restaurant specialises in seafood.
TARIFF: Single 230–290, Double 270–360, Bk 36, Set menu 110–380.
CC: Amex, Euro/Access, Visa.

PONT-SUR-YONNE Yonne 2D

Hôtel L'Ecu ★ 3 rue Carnot, 89140 Pont-sur-Yonne.
☎ 86 67 01 00. English spoken.

Open 01/01 to 21/01 & 24/02 to 31/12.
8 bedrooms (3 en suite, 5 bath/shower only).
Golf 7 km, parking, restaurant.
Old coaching inn 12 km north of Sens.
TARIFF: Single 90–160, Double 160–210, Bk 35.
cc: Amex, Diners, Euro/Access, Visa.

PORNIC Loire-Atlan 1D

Hôtel La Flotille ★★ pointe St-Gildas,
44770 Préfailles.
☎ 40 21 61 18, Fax 40 64 51 72. English spoken.

Open all year. 26 bedrooms (all en suite
with telephone). Indoor swimming pool,
golf 8 km, garage, parking, restaurant. ⅃
*Pretty, friendly hotel with sea view. North of
Pornic on D13 towards Préfailles.*
TARIFF: Set menu 95–270.
cc: Amex, Diners, Euro/Access, Visa.

PORT-LA-NOUVELLE Aude 5C

Hôtel Méditerranée ★★★ BP 92,
11210 Port-la-Nouvelle.
☎ 68 48 03 08, Fax 68 48 53 81. English spoken.

Open all year. 31 bedrooms (all en suite
with telephone). Garage, parking, restaurant.
A fine modern building which is ideally

*situated on the seafront, facing the beach. In
the centre of town.*
TARIFF: Single 180–390, Double 200–490,
Bk 35, Set menu 60–290.
cc: Amex, Diners, Euro/Access, Visa.

POUILLY-SUR-LOIRE Nièvre 2D

Hôtel Le Relais Fleuri ★★★ 2 av de la
Tuileric, 58150 Pouilly-sur-Loire.
☎ 86 39 12 99, Fax 86 39 14 15. English spoken.
Open 15/02 to 15/01. 9 bedrooms (all en suite
with telephone). Golf 4 km, garage, parking,
restaurant. ⅃
*Traditional hotel, overlooking the Loire with
sun terrace and gardens. Quality cuisine in
the Coq Hardi restaurant. Situated in the
village.*
TARIFF: Double 250–300, Bk 35,
Set menu 99–250.
cc: Amex, Diners, Euro/Access, Visa.

PRIVAS Ardèche 5B

Hôtel Le Panoramic Escrinet ★★
07000 Privas.
☎ 75 87 10 11, Fax 75 87 10 34. English spoken.
Open 15/03 to 15/11. 20 bedrooms
(all en suite with telephone). Outdoor
swimming pool, garage, parking. ⅃
RESTAURANT: Closed 15/11 to 15/03.
*Small hotel/restaurant with wonderful views,
on N104 west of Privas.*
TARIFF: Double 270–330, Bk 35.
cc: Amex, Diners, Euro/Access, Visa.

LE PUY-EN-VELAY Haute-Loire 5A

Hôtel Brivas ★★ av Charles Massot,
43750 Vals-près-le-Puy.
☎ 71 05 68 66, Fax 71 05 65 88. English spoken.
Open all year. 60 bedrooms (all en suite
with telephone). Tennis, golf 5 km, parking,
restaurant. ⅃
*Two minutes from centre of Le Puy-en-Velay,
in a pleasant and tranquil quarter, with
ample parking.*
TARIFF: Single 250, Double 280, Bk 32,
Set menu 90–160.
cc: Amex, Diners, Euro/Access, Visa.

QUINEVILLE Manche 1B

Château de Quineville ★★★
50310 Quinéville.
☎ 33 21 42 67, Fax 33 21 05 79. English spoken.
Open 15/03 to 05/01. 20 bedrooms (all en suite
with telephone). Tennis, golf 2 km, parking. ⅃

RESTAURANT: good. Closed Wed LS.

Bask in the extraordinary splendour of this 18th-century mansion, lying in 25 acres of parkland. There are delights here for the history buff and closeby, everything for the more sporty. From Cherbourg on the N13 to Montebourg and turn left.

TARIFF: (1993) Double 390–440, Bk 42, Set menu 68–180.

CC: Amex, Euro/Access, Visa.

RAMBOUILLET Yvelines   2D

Hôtel Abbaye les Vaux de Cernay ★★★★
78720 Cernay-la-Ville.
☎ 1 34 85 23 00, Fax 1 34 85 20 95.
English spoken.

Open all year. 58 bedrooms (all en suite with telephone). Outdoor swimming pool, tennis, golf 15 km, parking, restaurant.

An 800-year-old abbey set in parkland. 12 km east of Rambouillet on N306 towards Paris. Just before Cernay-la-Ville fork left then turn left to Abbaye.

TARIFF: Single 390–850, Double 490–1050, Bk 75.

CC: Amex, Diners, Euro/Access, Visa.

REIMS Marne   3A

Hôtel Paix ★★★ 9 rue Buirette,
51100 Reims.
☎ 26 40 04 08, Fax 26 47 75 04.
English spoken.
Open all year. 105 bedrooms (all en suite with telephone). Outdoor swimming pool, golf 8 km, garage, restaurant.

Newly-built hotel with conference facilities in the centre of Reims. Pool garden and rustic tavern. Between railway station and cathedral.

CC: Amex, Diners, Euro/Access, Visa.

RENNES Ille/Vilaine   1D

Hôtel Garden ★★ 3 rue Duhamel,
35000 Rennes.
☎ 99 65 45 06, Fax 99 65 02 62. English spoken.
Open all year. 24 bedrooms (16 en suite, 6 bath/shower only, 24 telephone). Golf 8 km, parking.

Centrally placed for seeing Rennes and the surrounding countryside.

TARIFF: Single 140–260, Double 175–280, Bk 29.

CC: Amex, Euro/Access, Visa.

RIBEAUVILLE Haut-Rhin   3D

Hôtel Tour ★★ 1 rue Mairie,
68150 Ribeauvillé.
☎ 89 73 72 73, Fax 89 73 38 74. English spoken.
Open 01/03 to 01/01. 35 bedrooms (all en suite with telephone). Tennis, golf 12 km, garage, parking.

Attrative old hotel in centre of medieval village.

TARIFF: Single 255–340, Double 290–390, Bk 35.

CC: Diners, Euro/Access, Visa.

RIBERAC Dordogne   4B

Hôtel de France ★★ rue M Dufraisse,
24600 Ribérac.
☎ 53 90 00 61. English spoken.
Open all year. 20 bedrooms (16 en suite, 3 bath/shower only, 20 telephone). Parking, restaurant.

A comfortable hotel in the centre of Ribérac, it is near the place Général de Gaulle.

TARIFF: Single 160–200, Double 170–250, Bk 28, Set menu 68–270.

CC: Amex, Euro/Access, Visa.

ROANNE Loire   5B

Hôtel Ibis ★★ 53 bd Ch de Gaulle, au Coteau,
42120 Roanne.
☎ 77 68 36 22, Fax 77 71 24 99. English spoken.
Open all year. 67 bedrooms (all en suite with telephone). Outdoor swimming pool, golf 6 km, parking, restaurant. &

The hotel is south of Roanne, towards Lyon and St-Etienne.

TARIFF: Single 270–295, Double 290–300, Bk 34, Set menu 68–98.

CC: Amex, Euro/Access, Visa.

ROCAMADOUR Lot   5A

Hôtel Beau Site et Notre Dame ★★★
46500 Rocamadour.
☎ 65 33 63 08, Fax 65 33 65 23. English spoken.

France

Open 12/02 to 13/03 & 26/03 to 12/11.
44 bedrooms (all en suite with telephone).
Garage, parking, restaurant.

In the heart of the ancient medieval city of Rocamadour, two hundred-year-old hotel with exceptional views. Guests cars allowed in pedestrian area to reach hotel car park.

TARIFF: Single 200–440, Double 340–600,
Bk 45, Set menu 95–230.
CC: Amex, Diners, Euro/Access, Visa.

Hôtel Panoramic ★★ 46500 Rocamadour.
☎ 65 33 63 06, Fax 65 33 69 26. English spoken.

Open 15/02 to 05/11. 21 bedrooms (16 en suite,
5 bath/shower only, 21 telephone). Outdoor
swimming pool, parking.
RESTAURANT: Closed Fri ex school hols.

Traditional hotel with large, sunny terrace facing the Causses Mountains and overlooking historic Rocamadour. Quiet setting. Horse-riding and canoeing nearby.

TARIFF: Double 220–280, Bk 35.
CC: Amex, Diners, Euro/Access, Visa.

LA ROCHE-SUR-YON Vendée   4A

Hôtel Marie Stuart ★★ 86 rue Louis Blanc,
85000 La Roche-sur-Yon.
☎ 51 37 02 24, Fax 51 37 86 37.
Open all year. 14 bedrooms (all en suite
with telephone). Golf 4 km, restaurant.

Friendly, family-run 19th-century hotel in heart of picturesque Vendée. Comfortable rooms and superb cuisine. In town centre.

TARIFF: Single 229, Double 279, Bk 32,
Set menu 69–210.
CC: Amex, Euro/Access, Visa.

Hôtel Le Point du Jour ★★ 7 rue Gutenberg,
85000 La Roche-sur-Yon.
☎ 51 37 08 98, Fax 51 46 22 44. English spoken.
Open all year. 25 bedrooms (22 en suite,

3 bath/shower only, 25 telephone). Golf 3 km,
parking. &
RESTAURANT: Closed Sun eve LS.

Family hotel 1 km from town centre, with country and traditional cuisine. From Nantes, head for the town centre.

TARIFF: Single 190–230, Double 210–280,
Bk 28, Set menu 58–230.
CC: Amex, Euro/Access, Visa.

LA ROCHELLE Charente-Marit   4A

Hôtel du Commerce ★★ 6 place de Verdun,
17000 La Rochelle.
☎ 46 41 08 22, Fax 46 41 74 85. English spoken.
Open 20/01 to 23/12. 63 bedrooms
(49 en suite, 63 telephone). Golf 7 km.
RESTAURANT: Closed Fri lunch/Sat 01/10 to
28/02.

Located in the centre of old town, opposite cathedral and car park.

TARIFF: Double 120–300, Bk 30,
Set menu 70–150.
CC: Amex, Diners, Euro/Access, Visa.

Hôtel Le Relais de Benon ★★★
17170 Courçon.
☎ 46 01 61 63, Fax 46 01 70 89. English spoken.

Open all year. 30 bedrooms (all en suite
with telephone). Outdoor swimming pool,
tennis, parking, restaurant. &

Set in 5 acres of parkland in the middle of the Aunis forest and very peaceful. Situated between Niort and La Rochelle on the main N11 and 20 minutes' drive from the sea.

TARIFF: Single 330–360, Double 410–420,
Bk 45, Set menu 85–230.
CC: Amex, Diners, Euro/Access, Visa.

Hôtel St-Nicolas ★★ 13 rue Sardinerie,
17000 La Rochelle.
☎ 46 41 71 55, Fax 46 41 70 46. English spoken.

France

Open all year. 79 bedrooms (all en suite with telephone). Golf 5 km, garage. &

Charming, renovated mansion in the heart of the old town. Close to the pedestrian precinct and a few minute's walk from the ancient harbour. Indoor garden; locked, open or covered garage available.

TARIFF: Single 265–370, Double 300–405, Bk 35.
CC: Amex, Diners, Euro/Access, Visa.

ROCROI Ardennes 3A

Hôtel du Commerce ★★ pl A Briaud, 08230 Rocroi.
✆ 24 54 11 15.
Open all year. 9 bedrooms (7 en suite, 9 telephone). Parking, restaurant.

The hotel is situated in the main square of the town.

TARIFF: Single 140–160, Double 140–210, Bk 19.
CC: Euro/Access, Visa.

Hôtel Lenoir ★★★ 08260 Auvillers-les-Forges.
✆ 24 54 30 11, Fax 24 54 34 70. English spoken.
Open 01/03 to 01/01. 21 bedrooms (18 en suite, 21 telephone). Parking. &
RESTAURANT: very good. Closed Fri.

Tourist hotel with good cuisine, terraces and attractive garden. From Rocroi south-west on D877 over N43 to Auvillers.

TARIFF: Single 150–420, Double 150–420, Bk 35.
CC: Amex, Diners, Euro/Access, Visa.

RODEZ Aveyron 5C

Hôtel Eldorado ★★ rte d'Espalion, 12740 Sébazac.
✆ 65 46 99 77, Fax 65 46 99 80. English spoken.
Open all year. 22 bedrooms (all en suite with telephone). Parking. &
RESTAURANT: Closed Sun eve.

A new hotel, 5 km north of Rodez on the D904 (off the D988).

TARIFF: Single 250, Double 280, Bk 35, Set menu 90–180.
CC: Amex, Diners, Euro/Access, Visa.

ROISSY Val-d'Oise 2B

Hôtel de Louvres ★★ 94 rue de Paris, Louvres, 95380 Roissy.
✆ 1 34 72 44 44, Fax 1 34 72 42 42.
English spoken.
Open all year. 40 bedrooms (all en suite with telephone). Golf 10 km, parking. &

Near Charles de Gaulle airport. From Paris take the A1 and exit Louvres. There is a direct métro line to the centre of Paris.

TARIFF: (1993) Single 200–320, Double 215–340, Bk 32.
CC: Amex, Diners, Euro/Access, Visa.

ROUEN Seine Marit 2A

Hôtel Dieppe ★★★ pl Bernerd Tissot, 76000 Rouen.
✆ 35 71 96 00, Fax 35 89 65 21. English spoken.
Open all year. 41 bedrooms (all en suite with telephone). Golf 5 km, restaurant.

Typical traditional hotel, fully renovated, founded and managed by the Guerer family since 1880. Excellent town-centre location in a district noted for art and painting. Good restaurant, well-known for its roast duck.

TARIFF: Single 435–510, Double 495–610, Bk 40, Set menu 135–195.
CC: Amex, Diners, Euro/Access, Visa.

ROYAN Charente-Marit 4A

Family Golf Hôtel ★★★ 28 bd Garnier, 17200 Royan.
✆ 46 05 14 66, Fax 46 06 52 56. English spoken.
Open 09/04 to 30/09. 33 bedrooms (all en suite with telephone). Golf 5 km, parking.

In the middle of the long beach of Royan, near the yachting harbour and fishing harbour.

TARIFF: Single 350–380, Double 390–450, Bk 40.
CC: Euro/Access, Visa.

Grand Hotel de Pontaillac ★★★ 195 av Pontaillac, 17200 Royan.
✆ 46 39 00 44, Fax 46 39 04 05.
English spoken.
Open 01/05 to 30/09. 40 bedrooms (all en suite with telephone). Golf 4 km, garage.

Sea-front hotel, halfway along Pontillac beach, with pleasant shady garden. Follow the coast road from the centre of Royan.

CC: Euro/Access, Visa.

France

Hôtel Résidence de Rohan ★★★ Parc des Feés, route de St-Palais, 17640 Royan.
☎ 46 39 00 75, Fax 46 38 29 99. English spoken. Open 01/04 to 15/11. 41 bedrooms (all en suite with telephone). Tennis, golf 4 km, parking.
Old house opening on to the beach of Vaux-Nauzan, just at the end of the garden. From the centre of Royan go towards the beach at Pontaillac and St-Palais-sur-Mer (D25).
TARIFF: Single 300–600, Double 300–650, Bk 45.
CC: Amex, Euro/Access, Visa.

SABLES-D'OR-LES-PINS Côtes-du-N   1D

Hôtel Le Manoir St-Michel ★★ La Carquois, Les Sables-d'Or-les-Pins, 22240 Fréhel.
☎ 96 41 48 87, Fax 96 41 41 55. English spoken. Open 01/04 to 02/11. 20 bedrooms (all en suite with telephone). Golf 1 km, parking. &
16th-century manor house in extensive grounds with lake and views to the sea. Tranquil and charming. Satellite TV. North of Sables-d'Or towards Cap-Fréhel.
TARIFF: Single 250–380, Double 280–550, Bk 40.
CC: Euro/Access, Visa.

ST-BRIEUC Côtes-du-Nord   1D

Hôtel du Champ de Mars ★★ 13 rue du champs de Mars, 22000 St-Brieuc.
☎ 96 33 60 99, Fax 96 33 60 05. English spoken. Open 03/01 to 26/12. 21 bedrooms (all en suite with telephone). Golf 10 km. &
The hotel has been completely refurbished, both inside and out. Situated in the centre of town, opposite a park.
TARIFF: Single 220–250, Double 240–280, Bk 30.
CC: Amex, Euro/Access, Visa.

ST-DIZIER Haute-Marne   3C

Hôtel Le Gambetta 62 rue Gambetta, 52100 St-Dizier.
☎ 25 56 52 10, Fax 25 56 39 47. English spoken. Open all year. 63 bedrooms (all en suite with telephone). Golf 15 km, garage, parking. &
RESTAURANT: Closed Sun eve.
TARIFF: Single 180–290, Double 240–390, Bk 30.
CC: Amex, Diners, Euro/Access, Visa.

ST-ETIENNE Loire   5B

Hôtel Midi ★★★ 19 bd Pasteur, 42000 St-Etienne.
☎ 77 57 32 55, Fax 77 59 11 43. English spoken. Open 01/09 to 31/07. 33 bedrooms (all en suite with telephone). Garage, parking. &

A comfortable business hotel near the Bellevue Hospital south of St-Etienne.
TARIFF: Single 275–310, Double 310–380, Bk 36.
CC: Amex, Diners, Euro/Access, Visa.

ST-GENIEZ-D'OLT Aveyron   5C

Hôtel Poste ★★ 3 pl Charles de Gaulle, 12130 St-Geniez-d'Olt.
☎ 65 47 43 30, Fax 65 47 42 75. English spoken. Open 09/04 to 15/11. 50 bedrooms (all en suite with telephone). Outdoor swimming pool, tennis, golf 25 km, garage, parking, restaurant.
In the Lot Valley, a quiet hotel set in attractive garden. From Rodez take D988 north-east to St-Geniez-d'Olt.
TARIFF: Single 195–250, Double 250–290, Bk 38, Set menu 83–120.
CC: Euro/Access, Visa.

ST-GERMAIN-EN-LAYE Yvelines   2B

Hôtel La Cazaudehore et La Forest ★★★★ 1 av Prés Kénnédy, 78100 St-Germain-en-Laye.
☎ 1 34 51 93 80, Fax 1 39 73 73 88. English spoken.
Open all year. 30 bedrooms (all en suite with telephone). Golf 1 km, parking.
RESTAURANT: Closed Mon.
Stylish hotel located in the heart of the Saint-Germain Forest. 1.5 km from the town (towards Pontoise) and 20 km from Paris.
TARIFF: Single 700, Double 860, Bk 68.
CC: Euro/Access, Visa.

ST-GOBAIN Aisne   2B

Hôtel Les Roses de Picardie ★★ 11 rue Clémenceau, 02410 St-Gobain.
☎ 23 52 88 74. English spoken.
Open all year. 13 bedrooms (9 en suite, 13 telephone). Parking, restaurant. &
St-Gobain is a small town in the heart of the magnificent forest where you can take long, quiet walks and may even discover deer. Situated between St-Quentin and Laon, 5 km from N44.
TARIFF: Single 130–230, Double 180–230, Bk 25.
CC: Euro/Access, Visa.

ST-HILAIRE-ST-MESMIN Loiret   2D

Hôtel L'Escale du Port-Arthur ★★ 205 rue de l'Eglise, 45160 Orléans.
☎ 38 76 30 36, Fax 38 76 37 67. English spoken. Open all year. 20 bedrooms (all en suite with telephone). Golf 10 km, parking, restaurant. &

Charming hotel on the banks of the River Loire. On the D951 7 km south of Orléans.
TARIFF: Single 130–150, Double 260–300, Bk 30, Set menu 102–190.
CC: Amex, Diners, Euro/Access, Visa.

ST-HIPPOLYTE Haut-Rhin   3D

Hôtel aux Ducs de Lorraine ★★★ 16 route du Vin, 68590 St-Hippolyte.
☏ 89 73 00 09, Fax 89 73 05 46. English spoken.
Open 01/03 to 30/11 & 15/12 to 10/01.
40 bedrooms (all en suite with telephone).
Golf 20 km, garage, parking.
RESTAURANT: Closed Sun eve & Mon.

Elegant hotel with period atmosphere on outskirts of the village. Wonderful views of mountains and vineyards.
TARIFF: Single 290–460, Double 400–700, Bk 60, Set menu 110–310.
CC: Euro/Access, Visa.

ST-JEAN-DE-LUZ Pyrénées-Atlan   4C

Hôtel de Chantaco ★★★★ Golf de Chantaco, route d'Ascain, 64500 St-Jean-de-Luz.
☏ 59 26 14 76, Fax 59 26 35 97.
English spoken.
Open 01/04 to 30/11. 24 bedrooms
(all en suite with telephone). Outdoor swimming pool, tennis, golf on site, parking, restaurant. &

In the heart of the lush green Basque countryside, just opposite Chantaco golf course. A century-old wisteria hugs the patio archways, stately trees shade the terraces with flower-fragrant gardens. Warm atmosphere with refined cuisine. South of St-Jean on the D918 towards Ascain.
TARIFF: Single 600–1100, Double 800–1500, Bk 75, Set menu 160–290.
CC: Amex, Diners, Euro/Access, Visa.

Hôtel Chez Antoinette ★★ Hendaye village, 64700 Hendaye.
☏ 59 20 08 47, Fax 59 48 11 64.
English spoken.
Open 01/04 to 31/10. 20 bedrooms
(12 en suite, 4 bath/shower only, 20 telephone). Golf 10 km, restaurant.

Small hotel offering a warm welcome and simple but good cuisine. South-west of St-Jean-de-Luz, off the N10, and close to sea, mountains and Spanish border.
TARIFF: Double 180–250, Bk 30, Set menu 125–165.
CC: Euro/Access, Visa.

ST-JEAN-DE-MONTS Vendée   4A

Hôtel Altea Le Sloi ★★★ av des Pays de Monts, 85160 St-Jean-de-Monts.
☏ 51 59 15 15, Fax 51 59 91 03. English spoken.

Open 06/03 to 06/11. 44 bedrooms (all en suite with telephone). Outdoor swimming pool, golf 1 km, garage, parking, restaurant. &

Located outside the hustle-bustle of the resort, between the golf course and the spa, 300 m from the beach in a pine forest.
TARIFF: Single 390–620, Double 410–660, Bk 50.
CC: Amex, Diners, Euro/Access, Visa.

Hôtel Robinson ★★ 28 bd Gén Leclerc, 65160 St-Jean-de-Monts.
☏ 51 58 21 01, Fax 51 58 88 03. English spoken.
Open all year. 66 bedrooms (54 en suite, 12 bath/shower only, 66 telephone).
Indoor swimming pool, golf 1 km, parking, restaurant. &

Comfortable hotel with garden and terrace. Close to town centre and 900 m from beach.
TARIFF: Double 180–350, Bk 31, Set menu 70–220.
CC: Amex, Diners, Euro/Access, Visa.

Hôtel Tante Paulette 32 rue Neuve, 65160 St-Jean-de-Monts.
☏ 51 58 01 12. English spoken.
Open 01/03 to 04/11. 32 bedrooms (all en suite with telephone). Parking, restaurant.

In the coastal town of St-Jean-de-Monts. South-west of Nantes, take D753 west from A83.
TARIFF: Single 210–280, Double 230–300, Bk 27, Set menu 65–290.
CC: Amex, Diners, Euro/Access, Visa.

ST-JEAN-PIED-DE-PORT Pyr-Atlan   4C

Hôtel Central ★★ ch de Gaulle, 64220 St-Jean-Pied-de-Port.
☏ 59 37 00 22, Fax 59 37 27 79. English spoken.

France

Open 01/02 to 31/12. 14 bedrooms (all en suite with telephone). Parking, restaurant.

A building of character beside the river, nestling in a valley. Last stopover before Spain. Family-run hotel with regional cuisine. Located where D918 crosses D933.

TARIFF: Single 300–380, Double 320–480, Bk 40, Set menu 98–220.
CC: Amex, Diners, Euro/Access, Visa.

Hôtel Continental ★★★ 3 av Renaud, 64220 St-Jean-Pied-de-Port.
☎ 59 37 00 25, Fax 59 37 27 81. English spoken.
Open 01/04 to 15/11. 18 bedrooms (all en suite with telephone). Parking.

Peaceful and very comfortable hotel in Basque country. From Bayonne go south-east on D918.

TARIFF: Single 350–400, Double 380–480, Bk 45.
CC: Amex, Euro/Access, Visa.

ST-LAURENT-EN-GRANDVAUX Jura   6A

Hôtel Moulin des Truites Bleues ★★★★
39150 St-Laurent-en-Grandvaux.
☎ 84 60 83 03, Fax 84 60 87 23. English spoken.

Open all year. 20 bedrooms (all en suite with telephone). Golf 25 km, parking, restaurant.

This extraordinary collection of buildings, dating from the 2nd century with a 17th-century mill, now provides the setting for a spectacular hotel. Built on a wooded hillside beside a waterfall, you will find high quality cuisine and service. North of St-Laurent on the N5 towards Champagnole.

TARIFF: Double 450–725, Bk 58, Set menu 140–380.
CC: Amex, Diners, Euro/Access, Visa.

ST-LO Manche   2A

Château d'Agneaux ★★★ av Ste-Marie a Agneaux, 50180 Agneaux.
☎ 33 57 65 88, Fax 33 56 59 21.

Open all year. 12 bedrooms (all en suite with telephone). Tennis, garage, parking. &
RESTAURANT: Closed 02/01 to 30/03.

Agneaux is 2 km west of St-Lo.

TARIFF: (1993) Double 360–880, Set menu 180–260.
CC: Amex, Euro/Access, Visa.

ST-MALO Ille/Vilaine   1D

Hôtel La Cité 26 rue Ste-Barbe, BP77, 35412 St-Malo.
☎ 99 56 66 52, Fax 99 40 10 04. English spoken.
Open all year. 41 bedrooms (all en suite with telephone). Golf 10 km, garage, parking. &

Inside the town wall. Enter by the main gate Porte St Vincent, turn right, near the ramparts. The hotel was built in 1990 in an 18th-century architectural style. Quiet and very comfortable, many rooms with a sea view.

TARIFF: Single 350–500, Double 450–520, Bk 40.
CC: Amex, Diners, Euro/Access, Visa.

Hôtel Digue ★★★ 35400 St-Malo.
☎ 99 56 09 26, Fax 99 56 41 65. English spoken.
Open 04/02 to 02/01. 53 bedrooms (all en suite with telephone). Golf 15 km, garage, parking. &

Comfortable hotel just a short walk from town and situated on the seafront.

TARIFF: Single 280–420, Double 280–550, Bk 44.
CC: Amex, Diners, Euro/Access, Visa.

ST-MARTIN-EN-BRESSE Saône/Loire   3C

Hôtel au Puits Enchante ★★
71620 St-Martin-en-Bresse.
☎ 85 47 71 96, Fax 85 47 74 58. English spoken.
Open all year. 14 bedrooms (12 en suite, 2 bath/shower only, 14 telephone). Golf 5 km, parking.
RESTAURANT: Closed Sun eve & Tues.

Surrounded by pretty countryside, this family-run hotel is in the centre of the little village of St-Martin-en-Bresse. Traditional dishes of Burgundy, including freshwater fish specialities, served in the restaurant. Take the D35 from the N73 to St-Martin.

TARIFF: Double 150–260, Bk 35, Set menu 90–198.
CC: Euro/Access, Visa.

ST-NAZAIRE Loire-Atlan   1D

Hôtel La Boissière ★★ 70 avenue de Mindin, 44250 St-Brévin-les-Pins.
☎ 40 27 21 79, Fax 40 39 11 88. English spoken.

France

Open 01/04 to 10/10. 23 bedrooms (21 en suite, 2 bath/shower only, 23 telephone).
Golf 16 km, garage, parking, restaurant.
More in the style of a large residential house than a hotel, in architecture and atmosphere. From St-Nazaire go south over the bridge. Turn immediately right to St-Brévin-les-Pins.
TARIFF: Single 220–280, Double 235–395, Bk 30.
CC: Euro/Access, Visa.

ST-PAUL-DE-VENCE Alpes-Marit   6C

Hôtel Climat de France ★★★ quartier les Fumérates, 940 route de la Colle, 06570 St-Paul.
☎ 93 32 94 24, Fax 93 32 91 07. English spoken.

Open all year. 19 bedrooms (all en suite with telephone). Outdoor swimming pool, golf 15 km, parking.
RESTAURANT: Closed eves 24/12 to 31/12.
This family hotel, set in the beautiful countryside surrounding St-Paul, is a haven if you hate the noise and bustle of the coast. The hotel can be found just after the village La Colle-sur-Loup, 900 m before St-Paul-de-Vence. Motorway exit for Cagnes-sur-Mer.
TARIFF: Single 380–600, Double 460–650, Bk 50, Set menu 100–180.
CC: Amex, Euro/Access, Visa.

ST-RAPHAEL Var   6C

Hôtel Sol e Mar ★★★ rte Corniche d'Or, 83700 St-Raphaël.
☎ 94 95 25 60, Fax 94 83 83 61. English spoken.
Open 01/04 to 15/10. 47 bedrooms (all en suite with telephone). Outdoor swimming pool, golf 3 km, parking, restaurant.
Adjacent to sea and beach, with exceptional views. On the N98, between St-Raphaël and Cannes.

TARIFF: Double 470–640, Bk 50,
Set menu 145–210.
CC: Euro/Access, Visa.

ST-REMY-DE-PROVENCE B-du-Rhône   5D

Hôtel Castelet des Alpilles ★★★
pl Mireille, 13210 St-Rémy-de-Provence.
☎ 90 92 07 21, Fax 90 92 52 03. English spoken.

Open 01/04 to 31/10. 18 bedrooms (17 en suite, 18 telephone). Golf 8 km, parking.
RESTAURANT: Closed Mon/Tues lunch.
In a restful garden, with the shade of a century-old cedar tree. The rooms face south towards the Alpilles range, some with terrace. The hotel is 300 m from the centre of St-Rémy towards 'Les Antiques les Baux'.
TARIFF: Single 220–370, Double 335–460, Bk 42, Set menu 125–185.
CC: Amex, Diners, Visa.

Sunshine
In Marseille, the main city on France's south coast, the sun shines for about 3,000 hours each year. This gives an average of more than eight hours of sunshine each day.

France

Château de Roussan rte Tarascon par, 13210 St-Rémy-de-Provence.
☎ 90 92 11 63, Fax 90 92 37 32. English spoken.

Open all year. 21 bedrooms (18 en suite, 3 bath/shower only, 20 telephone).
Golf 12 km, parking. ♿
RESTAURANT: Closed Wed.

Early 18th-century château, set in a beautiful garden. Historically linked with the family of Nostradamus. On the N99 road to Arles. 2 km from St-Rémy.

TARIFF: Single 380–780, Double 380–1000, Bk 50, Set menu 135.
CC: Amex, Diners, Euro/Access, Visa.

Host. du Vallon de Valruge ★★★★
13210 St-Rémy-de-Provence.
☎ 90 92 04 40, Fax 90 92 44 01. English spoken.

Open all year. 53 bedrooms (all en suite with telephone). Indoor swimming pool, outdoor swimming pool, tennis, golf 8 km, garage, parking, restaurant. ♿

Luxurious hotel with a restful atmosphere set in the enchanting landscape of the Alpilles. Excellent cuisine, good sporting facilities. Apartments also available.

TARIFF: Single 600–700, Double 760–960, Bk 90, Set menu 220–430.
CC: Amex, Diners, Euro/Access, Visa.

Domaine de Valmouriane ★★★★ petite route des Baux, 13210 St-Rémy-de-Provence.
☎ 90 92 44 62, Fax 90 92 37 32. English spoken.

Open all year. 14 bedrooms (all en suite with telephone). Outdoor swimming pool, tennis, golf 10 km, parking, restaurant. ♿

Small, comfortable, quiet and exclusive hotel, 5 km from the centre of St-Rémy in the middle of the Alpilles. On leaving St-Rémy take D99 towards Arles. Turn left 4 km after St-Rémy on to D27 towards Les Baux.

TARIFF: Double 940–1140, Bk 60, Set menu 150–220.
CC: Amex, Euro/Access, Visa.

ST-SYMPHORIEN-LE-CHATEAU   2D

Château d'Esclimont ★★★★
28700 St-Symphorien-le-Château.
☎ 37 31 15 15, Fax 37 31 57 91. English spoken.

Open all year. 53 bedrooms (all en suite with telephone). Outdoor swimming pool, tennis, golf 17 km, parking, restaurant.

A superb 16th-century château with its moat, lake, landscaped gardens and 150 acres of woodland park. From Paris take A11 and exit at Ablis, 6 km after on N10 turn right.

TARIFF: Single 685–1165, Double 820–2020.
CC: Visa.

ST-TROPEZ Var   6C

Hôtel Byblos ★★★★ av P Signac,
83991 St-Tropez.
☎ 94 97 00 04, Fax 94 97 40 52. English spoken.

Open 01/03 to 31/10. 107 bedrooms
(all en suite with telephone). Outdoor
swimming pool, golf 9 km, garage, parking,
restaurant.

*Just a few steps away from the place des Lices,
in the shadow of the Citadel. Each room has its
own personal character, all have satellite
television and some a jaccuzzi.*

TARIFF: Single 700–2260, Double 1030–2260,
Bk 100.
CC: Amex, Diners, Euro/Access, Visa.

Hôtel Lou Troupelen ★★★ chemin des
Vendanges, 83990 St-Tropez.
☎ 94 97 44 88, Fax 94 97 41 76. English spoken.
Open 25/03 to 01/11. 45 bedrooms (all en suite
with telephone). Golf 15 km, parking.

*Excellent location, 400 m walk from the town
centre. Quick and easy access to the beaches.
Quiet garden.*

TARIFF: Single 320, Double 380–490, Bk 45.
CC: Amex, Diners, Euro/Access, Visa.

STE-FOY-LA-GRANDE Gironde   4B

Hôtel Domaine de Loselly ★★★
38 av G Clemenceau, Pineuilh,
33220 Ste-Foy-la-Grande.
☎ 57 46 10 59, Fax 57 46 05 01. English spoken.
Open all year. 10 bedrooms (all en suite with
telephone). Golf 8 km, parking, restaurant.

*Country house with grounds giving on to the
Dordogne, just east of Ste-Foy-la-Grande.
From town centre follow signs from Fleix-
Mussidan road.*

TARIFF: (1993) Single 185–230,
Double 260–300, Bk 30, Set menu 95.
CC: Euro/Access, Visa.

STE-MAXIME Var   6C

Hôtel de la Poste ★★★ 7 bd F Mistral,
83120 Ste-Maxime.
☎ 94 96 18 33, Fax 94 96 41 68. English spoken.
Open 20/05 to 20/10. 24 bedrooms
(all en suite with telephone). Outdoor
swimming pool, golf 2 km, restaurant.

*The hotel is located in the middle of Ste-Maxime,
opposite the post office. Only 100 m from a fine
sandy beach and the port. Breakfast is served
on a terrace overlooking the swimming pool
and solarium, surrounded by a small garden.*

TARIFF: Single 300–500, Double 400–580, Bk 45.
CC: Amex, Diners, Euro/Access, Visa.

STES-MARIES-DE-LA-MER   5D

Hôtel L'Etrier Camarguais ★★★
13460 Stes-Maries-de-la-Mer.
☎ 90 97 81 14, Fax 90 97 88 11. English spoken.
Open 01/04 to 30/11. 27 bedrooms
(all en suite with telephone). Outdoor
swimming pool, tennis, parking, restaurant.

*Comfortable rooms in the garden or near the
pool. Attractive restaurant and bar. 2 km
before Stes-Maries-de-la-Mer, by the route d'Arles.*

TARIFF: Single 540, Double 540–980, Bk 50.
CC: Amex, Diners, Euro/Access, Visa.

SALAUNES Gironde   4A

Hôtel Les Ardillières ★★★ rte de la Lacanau,
33160 Salaunes.
☎ 56 58 58 08, Fax 56 58 51 01. English spoken.
Open all year. 40 bedrooms (all en suite
with telephone). Outdoor swimming pool,
tennis, golf 5 km, parking, restaurant. &

*In beautiful grounds with outdoor health
facilities, swimming pool, tennis, bicycle track
and lake. On the N215 towards Lacanau.*

TARIFF: (1993) Single 300–385,
Double 350–385, Bk 35, Set menu 110–350.
CC: Amex, Visa.

SALIES-DE-BEARN Pyrénées-Atlan   4C

Hôtel du Golf ★★ 64270 Salies-de-Béarn.
☎ 59 65 02 10, Fax 59 38 05 84. English spoken.
Open all year. 33 bedrooms (all en suite
with telephone). Outdoor swimming pool,
tennis, golf on site, parking, restaurant. &

*Hotel can be accessed via D30 running south
from junction 3 of the A64 towards Salies.*

TARIFF: Single 175–250, Double 210–300,
Bk 25, Set menu 70–150.
CC: Euro/Access, Visa.

France

SALON-DE-PROVENCE B-du-Rhône 5D

Domaine de Roquerousse ★★ rte d'Avignon,
13300 Salon-de-Provence.
✆ 90 59 50 11, Fax 90 59 53 75. English spoken.
Open all year. 30 bedrooms (all en suite
with telephone). Outdoor swimming pool,
tennis, golf 7 km, parking.
RESTAURANT: Closed 24/12 eve & 25/12.

*Peacefully set in 1000 acres in the heart of
Provence, offering facilities for walking and
relaxing. 4 km from Salon, towards Avignon.*
TARIFF: Single 230–420, Double 260–480,
Bk 45, Set menu 75–150.
CC: Amex, Diners, Euro/Access, Visa.

SARLAT-LA-CANEDA Dordogne 4B

Hôtel Relais du Touron ★★ Le Touron,
24200 Carsac-Aillac.
✆ 53 28 16 70. English spoken.
Open 01/04 to 14/11. 12 bedrooms
(all en suite with telephone). Outdoor
swimming pool, golf 3 km, parking. &
RESTAURANT: Closed Tues lunch & Wed, all
lunch LS.

*In a large park, on the outskirts of Sarlat.
Friendly atmosphere, good regional and
traditional cooking. Fishing and canoeing on
the Dordogne. From Sarlat go south on the
D704 to Carsac-Aillac.*
TARIFF: Single 235–295, Double 260–370,
Bk 33, Set menu 90–240.
CC: Euro/Access, Visa.

SAUMUR Maine/Loire 2C

Hôtel Anne d'Anjou ★★★ 32 quai Mayaud,
49400 Saumur.
✆ 41 67 30 30, Fax 41 67 51 00. English spoken.
Open all year. 50 bedrooms (all en suite
with telephone). Tennis, golf 15 km, garage,
parking, restaurant. &
*Between the River Loire and the Château of
Saumur, this 18th-century building overlooks
the river. Charming illuminated interior
courtyard.*
TARIFF: Single 270–640, Double 350–640, Bk 48.
CC: Amex, Diners, Euro/Access, Visa.

Relais Château Le Prieure ★★★★
Chênehutte-les-Tuffeaux, 49350 Chênehutte.
✆ 41 67 90 14, Fax 41 67 92 24. English spoken.
Open 06/03 to 03/01. 34 bedrooms
(all en suite with telephone). Outdoor
swimming pool, tennis, parking, restaurant.

*On a site chosen by the Benedictine monks,
this beautiful Renaissance manor is built on a*
*hill overlooking the River Loire. 6 km from
Saumur.*
TARIFF: Single 600–1200, Double 700–1500,
Bk 70.
CC: Amex, Euro/Access, Visa.

SENS Yonne 2D

Hôtel Pavillon Bleu ★★ 89330 Villevallier.
✆ 86 91 12 17, Fax 86 91 17 74.

Open 01/02 to 31/12. 18 bedrooms
(13 en suite, 5 bath/shower only,
18 telephone). Parking, restaurant.

*Pleasantly located back from the N6 and close
to the river. From Sens, south on the N6.*
TARIFF: Single 150–195, Double 150–195,
Bk 30, Set menu 78–195.
CC: Amex, Diners, Euro/Access, Visa.

SERRE-CHEVALIER Hautes-Alpes 6A

Hôtel Plein Sud ★★★ 05330 Serre-Chevalier.
✆ 92 24 17 01, Fax 92 24 10 21. English spoken.
Open 19/12 to 19/04 & 19/06 to 19/09.
42 bedrooms (all en suite with telephone).
Indoor swimming pool, outdoor swimming
pool, golf 18 km, garage, parking.

*Every modern comfort in a relaxing,
harmonious atmosphere with efficient service.
Buffet breakfast. There are a number of
restaurants very close by.*
TARIFF: Single 300–410, Double 360–510, Bk 45.
CC: Euro/Access, Visa.

SEE ADVERTISEMENT

SEURRE Côte-d'Or 3C

Hôtel Le Castel ★★ av Gare, 21250 Seurre.
✆ 80 20 45 07.
Open all year. 22 bedrooms (18 en suite,
4 bath/shower only, 22 telephone). Restaurant.

Small, family-run hotel with comfortable

France

rooms and offering a warm welcome. Good food, pretty garden terrace.

TARIFF: Double 150–280, Bk 35, Set menu 95–270.

CC: Euro/Access, Visa.

SIGEAN Aude 5C

Château de Villefalse ★★★★ Le Lac, 11130 Sigean.

☎ 68 48 54 29, Fax 68 48 34 37. English spoken. Open 01/02 to 31/12. 25 bedrooms (all en suite with telephone). Indoor swimming pool, outdoor swimming pool, tennis, parking.

RESTAURANT: Closed Sun eve & Mon LS.

Superb château 5 km from the sea and set in 400 acres. Very good health and sports facilities. Excellent cuisine. 15 km south of Narbonne via Sigean. Exit from A9 towards Portel-des-Corbières.

TARIFF: Double 650–1800, Bk 85.

CC: Amex, Diners, Euro/Access, Visa.

SOUILLAC Lot 4B

Hôtel La Vieille Auberge ★★ 1 rue de la Recège, 46200 Souillac.

☎ 65 32 79 43, Fax 65 32 65 19. English spoken. Open all year. 20 bedrooms (all en suite with telephone). Indoor swimming pool, outdoor swimming pool, garage, parking. RESTAURANT: Closed Sun eve & Mon 01/11 to 01/04.

A comfortable, well-equipped hotel including fitness room and solarium. All rooms have video. N20, D703.

TARIFF: Single 200–265, Double 220–330, Bk 35.

CC: Amex, Diners, Euro/Access, Visa.

STRASBOURG Bas-Rhin 3D

Hôtel Altea pont de L'Europe ★★★ Par du Rhin, 67000 Strasbourg.

☎ 88 61 03 23, Fax 88 60 43 05. English spoken. Open all year. 93 bedrooms (all en suite with telephone). Indoor swimming pool, outdoor swimming pool, parking, restaurant. &

In Strasbourg follow directions to Offenburg. Just before the bridge, near the border, turn right into a large park.

TARIFF: Single 380–450, Double 380–480, Bk 50, Set menu 75–150.

CC: Amex, Diners, Euro/Access, Visa.

Hôtel Arcade ★★ 7 rue de Molsheim, 67000 Strasbourg.

☎ 88 22 30 00, Fax 88 75 65 31. English spoken.

Open all year. 244 bedrooms (all en suite with telephone). Parking, restaurant. &

Situated in the centre of Strasbourg, the hotel has a restaurant with terrace in summer. From motorway exit 3, towards Porte Blanche and Petite France.

TARIFF: Single 320–330, Double 340–350, Bk 42.
CC: Amex, Euro/Access, Visa.

Bonôtel de France ★★ 59 rte de Rhin, 67000 Strasbourg.
☎ 88 60 10 52, Fax 88 60 22 77. English spoken.

Open all year. 70 bedrooms (all en suite with telephone). Indoor swimming pool, outdoor swimming pool, tennis, parking. &

Prominent hotel close to the Rhine. From the centre of Strasbourg follow signs to Germany and Kehl. The hotel stands on the left, directly opposite the Office du Tourisme, just before the frontier (the Pont du Europe over the Rhine).

CC: Euro/Access, Visa.

Hôtel du Dragon ★★★ 2 rue de l'Ecarlate, 67000 Strasbourg.
☎ 88 35 79 80, Fax 88 25 78 95. English spoken.
Open all year. 32 bedrooms (all en suite with telephone). Golf 6 km. &

In a quiet street of the old city near La Petite France, 17th-century house converted into a stylish hotel. Some rooms with view of the cathedral. Small garden. Many restaurants within walking distance. Approach the hotel via quai St-Nicolas.

TARIFF: Single 435–565, Double 475–610, Bk 54.
CC: Euro/Access, Visa.

Hôtel des Rohan ★★★ 17 rue du Maroquin, 67000 Strasbourg.
☎ 88 32 85 11, Fax 88 75 65 37. English spoken.
Open all year. 36 bedrooms (all en suite with telephone). Golf 15 km, garage, parking.

From the ring road take the exit place de

L'Etoile and follow Centre-Ville and parking-Gutenberg signs. Porters are available at the hotel from 7 am to 8 pm.

TARIFF: Single 350–540, Double 350–595, Bk 50.
CC: Amex, Euro/Access, Visa.

TALLOIRES Haute-Savoie 6A

Hôtel Beau Site ★★★ 74290 Talloires.
☎ 50 60 71 04, Fax 50 60 79 22. English spoken.
Open 11/05 to 12/10. 29 bedrooms (all en suite with telephone). Tennis, golf 3 km, parking.

Excellent location in a park, directly adjoining the east shores of Lake Annecy. Very quiet. Superb views of the lake and mountains. On D509A.

TARIFF: Single 280–300, Double 400–720, Bk 50.
CC: Amex, Diners, Euro/Access, Visa.

TARASCON Bouches-du-Rhône 5D

Hôtel Les Mazets des Roches ★★★ rte de Fontvieille, 13150 Tarascon.
☎ 90 91 34 89, Fax 90 43 53 29. English spoken.
Open 01/04 to 31/10. 24 bedrooms (all en suite with telephone). Outdoor swimming pool, tennis, golf 12 km, parking, restaurant.

A country house in the heart of Provence, at the foot of the unspoilt Alpilles hills, close to the spectacular village of Les Baux. On the D33 just north of Fontvieille.

TARIFF: (1993) Single 340–430, Double 380–650, Bk 45, Set menu 130
CC: Amex, Diners, Euro/Access, Visa.

THURY-HARCOURT Calvados 2A

Relais de la Poste ★★★ 2 route de Caen, 14220 Thury-Harcourt.
☎ 31 79 72 12, Fax 31 39 53 55.
English spoken.
Open all year. 11 bedrooms (8 en suite, 3 bath/shower only, 11 telephone). Indoor swimming pool, tennis, golf 7 km, garage, parking.
RESTAURANT: Closed Sun eve & Mon LS.

Very French hotel with creepers covering the walls around shuttered windows. Pleasant rooms and apartments. On the river. Good for fishing and walking. Restaurant specialises in local shellfish. South from Caen on D562 to Thury-Harcourt.

TARIFF: Single 250–400, Double 250–600, Bk 40, Set menu 135–400.
CC: Amex, Euro/Access, Visa.

France

TOULON Var 6C

Hôtel La Corniche ★★★ 17 Littoral Frédéric Mistral, 83000 Toulon.
☎ 94 41 35 12, Fax 94 41 24 58.
English spoken.
Open all year. 22 bedrooms (all en suite with telephone). Garage, parking. ᕁ
RESTAURANT: very good. Closed Sun eve & Mon lunch.

Simple stylish décor, recently renovated, each room now air conditioned. From Toulon, head for Le Mourillon and Les Plages, hotel overlooks the Port Saint-Louis.
TARIFF: Single 320–440, Double 320–580, Bk 40.
CC: Amex, Diners, Euro/Access, Visa.

New Hôtel Tour Blanche ★★★
83000 Toulon.
☎ 94 24 41 57, Fax 94 22 42 25.
English spoken.
Open all year. 92 bedrooms (all en suite with telephone). Outdoor swimming pool, golf 15 km, parking, restaurant. ᕁ

Just below Mt Faron, only a few minutes from the harbour and town centre. Large swimming pool in lovely gardens. Conference facilities, spectacular views over bay.
TARIFF: Single 410, Double 460, Bk 50.
CC: Amex, Diners, Euro/Access, Visa.

Hôtel Promotour ★★ Les Espaluns, 83160 La Valette.
☎ 94 08 38 08, Fax 94 08 48 60.
English spoken.

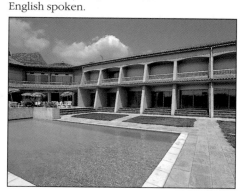

Open all year. 42 bedrooms (all en suite with telephone). Outdoor swimming pool, golf 3 km, garage, parking, restaurant. ᕁ
Pleasant hotel with rooms overlooking garden and swimming pool. Special rates for families. From Toulon, exit 5 from A57 towards Niice..
TARIFF: Double 250, Bk 34. Set menu 65–105.
CC: Amex, Diners, Euro/Access, Visa.

TOULOUSE Haute-Garonne 4D

Hôtel Albion ★★ 28 rue Bachelier, 31000 Toulouse.
☎ 61 63 60 36, Fax 61 62 66 95.
English spoken.
Open all year. 27 bedrooms (all en suite with telephone). Garage. ᕁ
Modern hotel with breakfast service in the rooms. 5 minutes from the station and near to the airport shuttle.
TARIFF: Single 240, Double 260, Bk 30.
CC: Amex, Diners, Euro/Access, Visa.

Hôtel Le Barry ★★ rue du Barry, 31150 Gratentour.
☎ 61 82 22 10, Fax 61 82 22 38.
Open all year. 22 bedrooms (all en suite with telephone). Outdoor swimming pool, golf 8 km, parking. ᕁ
RESTAURANT: Closed 15/08 to 31/08.
From Toulouse take the A62 north, exit at St-Jory. A pleasant hotel in Gratentour.
TARIFF: Single 265–330, Double 295–330, Bk 30, Set menu 85–130.
CC: Amex, Diners, Euro/Access, Visa.

LE TOUQUET Pas-de-Calais 2B

Hôtel Manoir ★★★
62520 Le Touquet-Paris-Plage.
☎ 21 05 20 22, Fax 21 05 31 26.
English spoken.

Open 28/01 to 31/12. 42 bedrooms (all en suite with telephone). Outdoor swimming pool, tennis, golf on site, parking.
RESTAURANT: Closed 03/01 to 28/01.
The hotel is situated in the forest estate of Le Touquet, right opposite the golf courses. Special rates are available for low season. Green fees at preferential rates for hotel guests.
TARIFF: Single 540–1150, Double 600–1210.
CC: Amex, Euro/Access, Visa.

France

France

Westminster Hotel ★★★★ 5 ave du Verger, 62520 Le Touquet.
📞 21 05 48 48, Fax 21 05 45 45. English spoken. Open all year. 115 bedrooms (all en suite with telephone). Indoor swimming pool, golf 1 km, garage, parking, restaurant. &

A hotel of great tradition, situated between the town and forest, 500 m from the beach and 150 m from the Convention Centre. Large entrance hall, cosy lounges and American bar.

TARIFF: Single 500–885, Double 680–1020, Bk 65.
CC: Amex, Diners, Euro/Access, Visa.

TOURNUS Saône/Loire 5B

Hôtel Le Rempart ★★★★ 2 av Gambetta, 71700 Tournus.
📞 85 51 10 56, Fax 85 40 77 22. English spoken. Open all year. 37 bedrooms (all en suite with telephone). Golf 18 km, garage, parking, restaurant. &

This highly recommended hotel, formerly a 15th-century guardhouse on the ramparts of the town wall, has been renovated to a high standard and is fully air conditioned. Take Tournus exit from A6/N6 and head towards town centre.

TARIFF: Single 320–690, Double 380–980, Bk 50, Set menu 159–399.
CC: Amex, Diners, Euro/Access, Visa.

TOURS Indre/Loire 2C

Hôtel Moulin Fleuri ★★ route du Ripault, 37250 Montbazon.
📞 47 26 01 12. English spoken. Open 09/03 to 30/01. 12 bedrooms (8 en suite, 12 telephone). Golf 12 km, parking.
RESTAURANT: Closed Mon.

Delightfully situated converted mill on the Loire châteaux route. Take D87 off N10, towards Azay-le-Rideau and Chinon.

TARIFF: Single 180–270, Double 180–320, Bk 45, Set menu 160–235.
CC: Amex, Euro/Access, Visa.

Hôtel de l'Univers ★★★ 5 bd Heurteloup, 37000 Tours.
📞 47 05 37 12, Fax 47 61 51 80. English spoken. Open all year. 89 bedrooms (all en suite with telephone). Garage.
RESTAURANT: good. Closed Sat.

In the heart of the city, near the TGV railway station. Completely refurbished in 1992, offering superior décor and discrete luxury.

From the A10, just 200 m from the Tours-Centre exit.

TARIFF: Single 680, Double 780, Bk 65, Set menu 170–220.
CC: Amex, Diners, Euro/Access, Visa.

TROUVILLE-SUR-MER Calvados 2A

Hôtel Beach ★★★ 1 quai Albert, 14360 Trouville-sur-Mer.
📞 31 98 12 00, Fax 31 87 30 29. English spoken. Open 05/02 to 31/12. 110 bedrooms (all en suite with telephone). Outdoor swimming pool, golf 10 km, garage, restaurant. &

In the heart of Trouville, facing the sea and close to the town centre. Directly linked to the casino and health centre. 2-hour drive from Paris on A13, then N177 to Trouville.

TARIFF: Single 320–425, Double 440–550, Bk 45, Set menu 140–160.
CC: Amex, Diners, Euro/Access, Visa.

TROYES Aube 3C

Hôtel de la Poste ★★★★ 35 rue E Zola, 10000 Troyes.
📞 25 73 05 05, Fax 25 73 80 76. English spoken.

Open all year. 28 bedrooms (all en suite with telephone).
RESTAURANT: good. Closed Sun eve & Mon.

In the centre of this historic town, Hotel de la Poste offers modern-day comforts and excellent cuisine. Close to museums, churches and pedestrian streets.

TARIFF: (1993) Single 420–750, Double 450–900, Bk 50.
CC: Amex, Euro/Access, Visa.

Hôtel Mercure Holigolf ★★★ Golf de la Forêt d'Orient, Rouilly-Sacey, 10220 Piney.
📞 25 43 80 80, Fax 25 41 57 58. English spoken. Open all year. 85 bedrooms (all en suite with telephone). Outdoor swimming pool,

golf on site, parking, restaurant. &

Brand new hotel, on the links, surrounded by woodland. Family rooms available. From Troyes head north-east on D960 towards Brienne, to Rouilly-Sacey.

TARIFF: Single 390–490, Double 390–590, Bk 50, Set menu 95–130.
CC: Amex, Diners, Euro/Access, Visa.

Auberge de la Scierie ★★★ a la Vove S, 10160 Aix-en-Othe.
☎ 25 46 71 26, Fax 25 46 65 69. English spoken.
Open 01/03 to 31/01. 13 bedrooms (all en suite with telephone). Outdoor swimming pool, parking, restaurant. &

Old inn in the champagne country near a river. N60 west of Troyes for 23 km, then left onto D374.

TARIFF: Double 350, Bk 40, Set menu 130–220.
CC: Amex, Diners, Euro/Access, Visa.

USSEL Corrèze 5A

Hôtel Les Gravades ★★★ St-Dezery, 19200 Ussel.
☎ 55 72 21 53, Fax 55 72 72 49.
Open all year. 20 bedrooms (all en suite with telephone). Outdoor swimming pool, golf 20 km, parking.
RESTAURANT: Closed Fri eve & Sat lunch LS.

This chalet-style hotel combines relaxation and good food. Restaurant specialises in local dishes. Good facilities for conferences and seminars.

TARIFF: (1993) Double 270–370, Bk 35, Set menu 120–160.
CC: Euro/Access, Visa.

VAISON-LA-ROMAINE Vaucluse 5D

Le Logis du Château ★★ Les Hauts de Vaison, 84110 Vaison-la-Romaine.
☎ 90 36 09 98, Fax 90 36 10 95. English spoken.

Open 01/04 to 31/10. 45 bedrooms (all en suite with telephone). Outdoor swimming pool, tennis, golf 1 km, parking, restaurant. &

Get away from it all. Panoramic views, silence and tranquillity.

TARIFF: Single 235–330, Double 250–360, Bk 38, Set menu 95–158.
CC: Euro/Access, Visa.

VALENCE Drôme 5B

Château de Clavel ★★★ Domaine Les Pécolets, 26800 Etoile-sur-Rhône.
☎ 75 60 61 93, Fax 75 60 66 01. English spoken.
Open all year. 23 bedrooms (all en suite with telephone). Outdoor swimming pool, tennis, golf 10 km, garage, parking, restaurant.

Attractive château situated in a large park surrounded by forest, pond and springs. Located south of Valence, just off the N7, between La Pallasse and Fiancey.

TARIFF: (1993) Double 420–680, Bk 50, Set menu 140–250.
CC: Amex, Euro/Access, Visa.

VALENCIENNES Nord 2B

Grand Hôtel ★★★ 8 pl de la Gare, 59300 Valenciennes.
☎ 27 46 32 01, Fax 27 29 65 57. English spoken.
Open all year. 98 bedrooms (all en suite with telephone). Golf 15 km, restaurant.

You will receive a warm welcome at this large, classic hotel opposite the station. Modern, well-equipped rooms. Snacks, gastronomic restaurant. Lounges for meetings or business meals.

TARIFF: Single 350–540, Double 390–650, Bk 45, Set menu 97–210.
CC: Amex, Diners, Euro/Access, Visa.

VALLON-PONT-D'ARC Ardèche 5D

Hôtel du Tourisme ★★ bd Peschaire Alizon, 07150 Vallon-Pont-d'Arc.
☎ 75 88 02 12, Fax 75 88 12 90.
English spoken.
Open 01/02 to 15/12. 29 bedrooms (all en suite with telephone). Golf 4 km, parking, restaurant.

Family-owned and run hotel with friendly atmosphere in town centre but just 100 m from open countryside. Lift. Terrace restaurant.

TARIFF: Double 250–395, Bk 28.50, Set menu 80–140.
CC: Euro/Access, Visa.

VALOGNES Manche   1B

Hôtel de l'Agriculture ★ 16 rue Léopold Delisle, 50700 Valognes.
☎ 33 95 02 02, Fax 33 95 29 33.
Open all year. 36 bedrooms (17 en suite, 1 bath/shower only, 36 telephone).
Golf 15 km, garage, parking.
RESTAURANT: Closed 01/01 to 15/1 & 21/09 to 04/10.

A pretty, creeper-clad building with many fine features inside. From the Valognes central square, head towards the station (Carteret road), turn second left.
TARIFF: Single 105–206, Double 116–225, Bk 26, Set menu 70–155.
CC: Euro/Access, Visa.

Hôtel Haut Gallion ★★ rte Cherbourg, 50700 Valognes.
☎ 33 40 40 00, Fax 33 95 20 20. English spoken.
Open 09/01 to 19/12. 40 bedrooms (all en suite with telephone). Golf 15 km, parking. &

Very modern rooms (2 for disabled people). Valognes is 22 km from Cherbourg on the N13. The hotel is just before the town centre on the left-hand side of the main road.
TARIFF: Double 265, Bk 34.
CC: Amex, Diners, Euro/Access, Visa.

VANNES Morbihan   1D

Hôtel Bretagne ★★★★ 56230 Questembert.
☎ 97 26 11 12, Fax 97 26 12 37. English spoken.
Open 01/02 to 31/12. 14 bedrooms (all en suite with telephone). Golf 10 km, garage, parking, restaurant. &

Small hotel with excellent cuisine. Opposite 15th-century chapel and near post office. From Vannes, east on N166, right on to D775 to Questembert (16 km).
TARIFF: Single 450–780, Double 570–990, Bk 75, Set menu 150–480.
CC: Amex, Euro/Access, Visa.

LES VANS Ardèche   5D

Château Le Scipionnet ★★★ route de Joyeuse, Chambonas, 07140 Les Vans.
☎ 75 37 23 84, Fax 75 37 26 83. English spoken.
Open 01/04 to 30/11. 26 bedrooms (24 en suite, 2 bath/shower only, 26 telephone). Outdoor swimming pool, golf 25 km, parking, restaurant.

19th-century château surrounded by woodland, with peaceful, comfortable rooms and a swimming pool. Take motorway to
Loriol, then Privas, Aubenas and Les Vans.
TARIFF: (1993) Single 325–425, Double 450–600, Bk 45, Set menu 150–215.
CC: Amex, Diners, Euro/Access, Visa.

VARENNES-SUR-ALLIER Allier   5A

Auberge de l'Orisse ★★★
03150 Varennes-sur-Allier.
☎ 70 45 05 60, Fax 70 45 18 55. English spoken.

"Le Vert et l'Assiette"

Open all year. 23 bedrooms (all en suite with telephone). Outdoor swimming pool, tennis, golf 8 km, parking, restaurant.

Small hotel with good restaurant. On N7 south of Moulins towards Laplisse.
TARIFF: Double 250–300, Bk 30, Set menu 75–200.
CC: Amex, Diners, Euro/Access, Visa.

VENCE Alpes-Marit   6C

Hôtel Diana ★★★ av des Poilus, 06140 Vence.
☎ 93 58 28 56, Fax 93 24 64 06. English spoken.
Open all year. 25 bedrooms (all en suite with telephone). Garage.

A modern hotel, 15 rooms with kitchenettes. Vence is a centre for art exhibitions. Foundation Maeght and Chapel du Rosaire, decorated by Matisse, is close by. 10 minutes from mountains or sea.
TARIFF: Double 350–400, Bk 35.
CC: Amex, Diners, Euro/Access, Visa.

Hôtel Relais Cantemerle ★★★★ 258 chemin Cantemerle, 06140 Vence.
☎ 93 58 08 18, Fax 93 58 32 89. English spoken.
Open 15/03 to 15/11. 20 bedrooms (all en suite with telephone). Outdoor swimming pool, golf 10 km, parking, restaurant.

Wonderfully situated in the hills surrounding Vence. The hotel offers luxury accommodation in 70s décor, a wooded park and views of the

France

*sea and mountains. Horse riding nearby.
Situated halfway between Vence and St-Paul.*
TARIFF: Double 550–890, Bk 65.
CC: Amex, Diners, Euro/Access, Visa.

VENDEUIL Aisne   2B

Auberge de Vendeuil ★★ N 44,
02800 Vendeuil.
℡ 23 07 85 85, Fax 23 07 88 58. English spoken.

Open all year. 22 bedrooms (all en suite
with telephone). Golf 10 km, parking,
restaurant. ⴷ
*Bordering woodland and close to the Oise
Valley, this auberge is a quiet and charming
country hotel with creative cuisine in the
restaurant. On the N44 between St-Quentin
and La Fère.*
TARIFF: Single 285, Double 335, Bk 45,
Set menu 90–190.
CC: Amex, Diners, Euro/Access, Visa.

VERNEUIL-SUR-AVRE Eure   2C

Hostellerie Le Clos ★★★★ 98 rue Ferte
Vidame, 27130 Verneuil-sur-Avre.
℡ 32 32 21 81, Fax 32 32 21 36.
English spoken.

Open 01/02 to 31/12. 11 bedrooms
(all en suite with telephone). Tennis,
golf 7 km, parking. ⴷ
RESTAURANT: Closed Mon.
*English-style manor house, tastefully furnished
with terrace overlooking lovely gardens. Fine
regional cuisine. On N12, 110 km east of
Paris.*
TARIFF: Single 600–800, Double 600–950,
Bk 80, Set menu 170–320.
CC: Amex, Diners, Euro/Access, Visa.

VERNON Yvelines   2B

Château de la Corniche ★★★ 5 route de la
Corniche, 78270 Rolleboise.
℡ 1 30 93 21 24, Fax 1 30 42 27 44.
English spoken.
Open 06/01 to 20/12. 38 bedrooms
(all en suite with telephone). Outdoor
swimming pool, tennis, golf 18 km, parking.
RESTAURANT: good. Closed Sun eve.
*Hotel set on the banks of the Seine. Tennis
court, bicycles for hire. 8 km from Giverny,
Monet's gardens. Motorway A13, exit Veron.*
TARIFF: Single 250–350, Double 350–750,
Bk 60, Set menu 180–350.
CC: Amex, Diners, Euro/Access, Visa.

VERSAILLES Yvelines   2D

Hôtel Résidence du Berry ★★★ 14 rue
Anjou, 78000 Versailles.
℡ 1 39 49 07 07, Fax 1 39 50 59 40.
English spoken.
Open all year. 38 bedrooms (all en suite
with telephone). Golf 3 km.
*Located in the centre of Versailles, 5 minutes'
walk from the Château and the railway station
to Paris.*
TARIFF: Single 380–400, Double 380–430,
Bk 40.
CC: Amex, Diners, Euro/Access, Visa.

Château du Tremblay ★★★ place de l'Eglise,
78490 La Tremblay-sur-Mauldre.
℡ 1 34 87 92 92, Fax 1 34 87 86 27.
English spoken.
Open 31/12 to 31/07 & 01/09 to 20/12.
30 bedrooms (all en suite with telephone).
Golf on site, parking.
RESTAURANT: good. Closed Sun eve.
*270-year-old château with private golf course,
set in 50 acres of parkland, 32 km west of
Paris. From Versailles, N12 in the direction of
Dreux, exit Pontchartrain, then left on to D13
to Le Tremblay-sur-Mauldre.*

France

TARIFF: Single 550–1150, Double 600–1200, Set menu 190–290.
CC: Amex, Diners, Euro/Access, Visa.

VERVINS Aisne 3A

Hôtel Le Clos du Montvinage ★★ 8 rue Albert Le Dent, 02580 Etréaupont.
☎ 23 97 91 10, Fax 23 97 48 92. English spoken.
Open 28/12 to 08/08 & 25/08 to 22/12.
20 bedrooms (all en suite with telephone).
Tennis, golf 7 km, garage, parking. &
RESTAURANT: Closed Sun eve & Mon lunch.

Charm and tranquillity on the banks of the Oise. Excellent cuisine. Nearby rock-climbing, canoeing, horse-riding. From Vervins north on the N2 for 10 km to Etréaupont.

TARIFF: Single 260–375, Double 305–500, Bk 45, Set menu 75–210.
CC: Amex, Euro/Access, Visa.

Hôtel Tour du Roy ★★★ 45 rue du Gén Leclerc, 02140 Vervins.
☎ 23 98 00 11, Fax 23 98 00 72. English spoken.

Open all year. 15 bedrooms (all en suite with telephone). Tennis, golf 6 km, parking, restaurant. &

A splendid manor house, steeped in history, overlooking the old city of Vervins. Excellent cuisine. Interior features include hand-painted bathrooms and stained-glass windows. Rooms overlook terraces, park or landscaped square. On N2 in the centre of Vervins.

TARIFF: Single 300–600, Double 300–800, Bk 60, Set menu 160–400.
CC: Amex, Diners, Euro/Access, Visa.

VESOUL Haute-Saône 3D

Hôtel Relais ★★★ 70000 Vesoul.
☎ 84 76 42 42, Fax 84 76 81 94. English spoken.
Open 07/01 to 23/12. 22 bedrooms (all en suite with telephone). Garage, parking. &
RESTAURANT: Closed Sun lunch.

A modern hotel with a Grill Room and gourmet restaurant. There is a lounge bar and terrace in the garden. On the N19 from Vesoul towards Chaumont-Troyes.

TARIFF: (1993) Single 250–350, Double 280–390, Bk 39, Set menu 90–150.
CC: Euro/Access, Visa.

VICHY Puy-de-Dôme 5A

Château de Maulmont ★★★
St-Priest-Bramefant, 63310 Randan.
☎ 70 59 03 45, Fax 70 59 11 88.
English spoken.
Open all year. 29 bedrooms (25 en suite, 4 bath/shower only, 29 telephone). Indoor swimming pool, outdoor swimming pool, golf 13 km, parking, restaurant.

Built on the site of a 12th-century fortress by the sister of King Louis Philippe, this château now provides elegant accommodation. Randan is on the D1093 south of Vichy, then left turn onto D59 to hotel.

TARIFF: Single 275–800, Double 350–900, Bk 55, Set menu 130–240.
CC: Amex, Euro/Access, Visa.

VIEUX-MAREUIL Dordogne 4B

Hôtel L'Etang Bleu ★★★
24340 Vieux-Mareuil.
☎ 53 60 92 63, Fax 53 56 33 20.
English spoken.
Open 01/04 to 15/01. 11 bedrooms (all en suite with telephone). Parking, restaurant.

A lakeside hotel in extensive wooded grounds. Traditional French country furnishings and regional cuisine. On the D93, 2 km from Vieux-Mareuil.

TARIFF: Double 320–350, Bk 35, Set menu 85–300.
CC: Amex, Diners, Euro/Access, Visa.

VILLEFRANCHE-DE-ROUERGUE 5C

Hôtel Relais de Farrou ★★★ au Farrou, 12200 Villefranche-de-Rouergue.
☎ 65 45 18 11, Fax 65 45 32 59.
English spoken.
Open all year. 26 bedrooms (all en suite with telephone). Outdoor swimming pool, tennis, garage, parking. &
RESTAURANT: Closed Sun eve & Mon LS.

Modern comfort in a former coaching inn. Set in the countryside 3 minutes from

France

Villefranche-de-Rouergue. Sports facilities, children's playground. South of Figéac on D922.

TARIFF: Single 260–335, Double 310–515, Bk 40, Set menu 105–350.
CC: Euro/Access, Visa.

VILLEFRANCHE-SUR-MER Alpes-Marit 6C

Hôtel Provençal ★★ 4 av mar Joffre, 06230 Villefranche-sur-Mer.
☎ 93 01 71 42, Fax 93 76 96 00. English spoken.
Open all year. 45 bedrooms (all en suite with telephone). Golf 15 km, garage.
RESTAURANT: Closed 01/11 to 23/12.

Central position 150 m from harbour. Comfortable and peaceful with some rooms overlooking sea. Provençal-style dining-room with air conditioning.

TARIFF: Single 210–400, Double 210–440, Bk 40, Set menu 75–125.
CC: Amex, Diners, Euro/Access, Visa.

Hôtel Versailles ★★★ av Princesse Grace, 06230 Villefranche-sur-Mer.
☎ 93 01 89 56, Fax 93 01 97 48. English spoken.
Open 31/12 to 31/10. 49 bedrooms (all en suite with telephone). Outdoor swimming pool, parking, restaurant. &

Air-conditioed rooms with balconies overlooking the sea. Take coast road eastwards from Nice.

TARIFF: Single 570–590, Double 590–650.
CC: Amex, Diners, Euro/Access, Visa.

Hôtel Welcome ★★★ 1 quai Courbet, 06230 Villefranche-sur-Mer.
☎ 93 76 76 93, Fax 93 01 88 81. English spoken.
Open 20/12 to 22/11. 32 bedrooms (all en suite with telephone). Golf 15 km. &
RESTAURANT: Closed Mon.

Waterfront hotel in former 17th-century convent and a favourite spot for the famous

(artists Jean Cocteau and Graham Sutherland, and Somerset Maugham used to stay here). Seafood specialities and haute cuisine. On coast road to the east of Nice.

TARIFF: Single 500–820, Double 550–840, Bk 50.
CC: Amex, Diners, Euro/Access, Visa.

VILLEFRANCHE-SUR-SAONE Rhône 5B

Hôtel Climat de France ★★ rte de Riottier Le Péage Limas, 69400 Villefranche-sur-Saône.
☎ 74 62 99 55, Fax 74 62 39 22. English spoken.
Open all year. 43 bedrooms (all en suite with telephone). Golf 5 km, parking, restaurant. &

Rooms can cater for from one to three people. Special children's menus. Buffet breakfast. Five minutes from the motorway exit.

TARIFF: Double 270, Bk 32, Set menu 68–100.
CC: Amex, Euro/Access, Visa.

Hôtel Plaisance ★★★ 96 av Libération, 69652 Villefranche-sur-Saône.
☎ 74 65 33 52, Fax 74 62 02 89. English spoken.
Open 02/01 to 24/12. 68 bedrooms (all en suite with telephone). Golf 8 km, garage, parking, restaurant.

Situated in centre of town, on a square. Villefranche is the capital of Beaujolais area, ideal for excursions into Beaujolais vineyards.

TARIFF: Single 310–365, Double 310–395, Bk 47.
CC: Amex, Diners, Euro/Access, Visa.

VILLENEUVE-SUR-LOT Lot/Garonne 4D

Studios Le Midi ★★ 47110 Ste-Livrade-sur-Lot.
☎ 53 01 00 32, Fax 53 88 10 22. English spoken.
Open 03/05 to 25/10. 23 bedrooms (21 en suite, 2 bath/shower only, 23 telephone). Golf 18 km, garage. &

St-Livrade is 9 km west of Villeneuve-sur-Lot.

TARIFF: Single 140–230, Double 140–280, Bk 22.
CC: Amex, Diners, Euro/Access, Visa.

France

VILLEREAL Lot/Garonne 4D

Hôtel Lac ★★ rte de Bergerac, 47210 Villeréal.
☏ 53 36 01 39. English spoken.
Open 01/05 to 30/09. 27 bedrooms (25 en suite, 25 telephone). Outdoor swimming pool, golf 20 km, garage, parking. ♿
RESTAURANT: Closed May/June/Sept lunch.
On the edge of the Périgord, in the heart of Bastide country. Racecourse nearby and a lake which is popular with anglers and where one may swim. Take the D14, south of Bergerac to Villeréal.
TARIFF: (1993) Single 200, Double 200–220, Bk 30.
CC: Euro/Access, Visa.

VILLERS-COTTERETS Aisne 2B

Hôtel Le Regent ★★★ 26 rue du Général Mangin, 02600 Villers-Cotterêts.
☏ 23 96 01 46, Fax 23 96 37 57. English spoken.
Open all year. 17 bedrooms (all en suite with telephone). Garage, parking. ♿
Charming 18th-century post house in the centre of the town. Elegant, period atmosphere with modern comfort.
TARIFF: Single 155–310, Double 310–370, Bk 29.
CC: Amex, Diners, Euro/Access, Visa.

VITTEL Vosges 3C

Hôtel Bellevue ★★★ 503 av de Châtillon, 88800 Vittel.
☏ 29 08 07 98, Fax 29 08 41 89. English spoken.
Open 01/03 to 30/11. 39 bedrooms (all en suite with telephone). Golf 1 km, garage, parking, restaurant. ♿
Family hotel situated just 5 minutes from the Parc Thermal and casino, on the edge of the forest. All rooms have TV.
TARIFF: Single 265–295, Double 310–350, Bk 35, Set menu 100–180.
CC: Amex, Diners, Euro/Access, Visa.

VOVES Eure-et-Loir 2D

Hôtel Quai Fleuri ★★★ 15 rue Texier-Gallas, 28150 Voves.
☏ 37 99 15 15, Fax 37 99 11 20. English spoken.
Open all year. 17 bedrooms (all en suite with telephone). Golf 15 km, garage, parking. ♿
RESTAURANT: Closed Sun eve.
A renovated former mill, set in wooded parkland between Chartres and Orléans. Terrace overloking the park. Fitness centre.
TARIFF: Single 295–600, Double 315–600, Bk 34, Set menu 79–250.
CC: Amex, Euro/Access, Visa.

WISSANT Pas-de-Calais 2B

Hôtel Normandy ★ 2 pl de Verdun, 62179 Wissant.
☏ 21 35 90 11, Fax 21 82 19 08. English spoken.
Open 01/02 to 20/12. 30 bedrooms (11 en suite, 8 bath/shower only, 29 telephone). Golf 13 km, parking, restaurant.
This is a family hotel, built in the 18th century. Lounge, garden, restaurant and rooms with sea view. Between Boulogne and Calais on N40. Eurotunnel 9 km.
TARIFF: Single 190–270, Double 210–330, Set menu 90–165.
CC: Euro/Access, Visa.

GERMANY

The former West and East Germany were unified under the West German constitution on 3 October 1990, restoring a country with an area of 356,945 sq km (almost half as big again as the UK). Germany is bordered to the north by the North Sea, Denmark and the Baltic Sea, to the east by Poland and Czech Republic, to the south by Austria and Switzerland, and to the west by France, Luxembourg, Belgium and the Netherlands. The undulating lowlands of the north rise through central forested uplands to the Alps in the south, with Germany's highest peak, the Zugspitze, at 2,962 m. The Danube flows east to Austria, the Rhine goes north-west through Frankfurt, Cologne and Düsseldorf to the Netherlands, and the Elbe passes through Hamburg in the north.

The climate is temperate in the west, with colder winters and shorter, hotter summers towards the east. A quarter of the land is forested, mainly with conifers, where deer, wild boar and wildcat still survive.

Eighty per cent of Germany's 80 million people live in towns and cities. The capital and largest city is Berlin, with 3.5 million people. It will take about ten years to transfer authority here from the former West German capital, Bonn. Local currency is the German mark (deutschmark), made up of 100 pfennigs. There are 530,000 km of roads, giving a road density (km per sq km) of 1.5, the same as the UK's, and the extensive system of autobahns (motorways) is free. Note that resorts for German islands, such as Fehmarn, are listed under their island names in the A–Z directory.

Germany

AACHEN   16A

Hotel Buschhausen ★★★ Adenauer Allee 215, 5100 Aachen.
☎ 0241 63071, Fax 0241 602830.
English spoken.
Open all year. 80 bedrooms (all en suite with telephone). Indoor swimming pool, golf 8 km, garage, parking, restaurant.
A family hotel, 2 km from the centre of Aachen. Many leisure facilities. From the A44 take the Lichtenbusch exit and go towards Aachen-Centrum. At the traffic lights, turn right.
TARIFF: (1993) Single 88–145, Double 135–180, Set menu 20–60.
CC: Amex, Diners, Euro/Access, Visa.

Hotel Steigenberger Quellenhof ★★★★
Monheimsalle 52, 5100 Aachen.
☎ 0241 152081, Fax 0241 154504.
English spoken.
Open all year. 160 bedrooms (all en suite with telephone). Golf 8 km, garage. &
RESTAURANT: Closed 15/07 to 20/08.
Spacious hotel in the Kongresscentrum, immediately next to the casino. A 10-minute walk from the city centre and old town.

TARIFF: Single 185–260, Double 280–420, Set menu 48.
CC: Amex, Diners, Euro/Access, Visa.

AALEN-UNTERKOCHEN   16D

Hotel Kalber Behringstrasse 26, 7080 Aalen-Unterkochen.
☎ 07361 8444, Fax 07361 88264.
Open all year. 20 bedrooms (all en suite).
TARIFF: (1993) Single 75–95, Double 92–136.
CC: Amex, Diners, Euro/Access, Visa.

ACHERN   16C

Hotel Gotz Sonne-Eintracht ★★★
Hauptstrasse 112, 7590 Achern.
☎ 07841 6450, Fax 07841 645645.
English spoken.
Open all year. 55 bedrooms (all en suite with telephone). Indoor swimming pool, golf 20 km, garage, parking, restaurant. &
Situated in the centre of Achern. From the A5 Frankfurt to Basel, exit at Achern and take the B3 into the town.
TARIFF: Single 89–179, Double 160–260, Set menu 49–125.
CC: Amex, Diners, Euro/Access, Visa.

ALTÖTTING 17C

Hotel Bauernsepp Kiefering 42,
8261 Tüssling.
☏ 08633 1045, Fax 08633 7994. English spoken.
Open all year. 20 bedrooms (all en suite
with telephone). Tennis, golf 15 km, parking,
restaurant.
*Modern hotel with romantic summer garden.
Gourmet restaurant. Just 2 km south-west of
Altötting, off the B299.*
TARIFF: (1993) Single 78–68, Double 118.
CC: Amex, Euro/Access.

AMORBACH 16B

Hotel Der Schafhof ★★★★ Schafhof 1,
8762 Amorbach.
☏ 09373 8088, Fax 09373 4120.
English spoken.

Open 10/02 to 31/12. 14 bedrooms
(all en suite with telephone). Tennis,
golf 15 km, parking.
RESTAURANT: Closed 24 Dec.
*In the heart of the Bavarian Odenwald, this
charming hotel dates back to 1446. Now
lovingly restored, it offers comfort, fine food
and wines in tranquil surroundings. From
Amorbach take the B47 to Amorbach-West,
then first right past the Amorbach chapel to the
hotel.*
TARIFF: Single 155–190, Double 180–350,
Set menu 70–140.
CC: Amex, Diners, Euro/Access, Visa.

ANDERNACH 16A

Rhein Hotel Konrad Adenauer Allee 20,
5470 Andernach.
☏ 02632 42240, Fax 02632 494172.
Open all year. 25 bedrooms (all en suite).
TARIFF: (1993) Single 50–55, Double 90–100.
CC: Amex, Diners, Euro/Access, Visa.

ASCHAFFENBURG 16B

Hotel Zum Ochsen ★★ Karlstrasse 16,
8750 Aschaffenburg.
☏ 06021 23132, Fax 06021 25785. English spoken.
Open all year. 39 bedrooms (all en suite
with telephone). Parking.
RESTAURANT: Closed Mon lunch.
*Fine historic hotel run by the same family
since 1894. Centrally located in one of the
most beautiful parts of Aschaffenburg with
views over the Schloss gardens.*
TARIFF: Single 80–90, Double 120–140,
Set menu 18–26.
CC: Amex, Diners, Euro/Access, Visa.

ASENDORF 14D

Hotel Zur Heidschnucke Zum Auetal 14,
2116 Asendorf.
☏ 04183 2094.
Open all year. 50 bedrooms (all en suite).
TARIFF: (1993) Double 75–91.
CC: Amex, Diners, Euro/Access, Visa.

ASPERG 16D

Hotel Adler Stuttgarterstrasse 2, 7144 Asperg.
☏ 07141 63001.
Open all year. 64 bedrooms (all en suite).
TARIFF: (1993) Single 125–165,
Double 184–260.
CC: Amex, Diners, Euro/Access, Visa.

ATTENDORN 16A

Burghotel Schnellenberg 5952 Attendorn.
☏ 02722 6490, Fax 02722 69469.
Open all year. 42 bedrooms (all en suite).
TARIFF: (1993) Single 140–190,
Double 200–280.
CC: Amex, Diners, Euro/Access, Visa.

AUERBACH 17A

Hotel Goldner Löwe Unterer Markt 9,
8572 Auerbach.
☏ 09643 1765, Fax 09643 4670.
Open all year. 23 bedrooms (all en suite).
TARIFF: (1993) Single 74–116, Double 124–180.
CC: Amex, Diners, Euro/Access, Visa.

AUGSBURG 17C

Hotel Langer Gogginger Strasse 39,
8900 Augsburg.
☏ 0821 578077, Fax 0821 592600.
Open all year. 25 bedrooms (all en suite).
TARIFF: (1993) Single 85–98, Double 98–158.
CC: Amex, Diners, Euro/Access, Visa.

Germany

Hotel Steigenberger Drei Möhren ★★★★
Maximilianstr 40, 86150 Augsburg.
☎ 0821 50360, Fax 0821 157864.
English spoken.

Open all year. 107 bedrooms (all en suite
with telephone). Golf 20 km, garage, parking,
restaurant.

*On the famous Maximilianstrasse, in the
centre of the historic old town of Augsburg.
Very comfortable hotel offering traditional
service and almost every facility. Choice of
restaurants, pretty garden terrace.*
TARIFF: Single 185–225, Double 270–340.
CC: Amex, Diners, Euro/Access, Visa.

BAD AIBLING 17C

Hotel Lindner Marienplatz 5,
8202 Bad Aibling.
☎ 08061 4050, Fax 08061 30535.
Open all year. 32 bedrooms (all en suite).
TARIFF: (1993) Single 50–130, Double 100–260.
CC: Amex, Diners, Euro/Access, Visa.

BAD BENTHEIM 14C

Hotel Grossfield Schloss Strasse 6,
4444 Bad Bentheim.
☎ 05922 828, Fax 05922 4349.
Open all year. 100 bedrooms (all en suite).
TARIFF: (1993) Single 50–80, Double 100–160.
CC: Amex, Diners, Euro/Access, Visa.

BAD BERGZABERN 16C

Hotel Pfalzer Wald Kurtalstrasse 77,
6748 Bad Bergzabern.
☎ 06343 1056/7.
Open all year. 26 bedrooms (all en suite).
TARIFF: (1993) Single 45–60, Double 90–120.
CC: Amex, Diners, Euro/Access, Visa.

BAD BRAMSTEDT 14B

Hotel Zur Post Bleeck 29, 2357 Bad Bramstedt.
☎ 04192 50060, Fax 04192 50068.
Open all year. 34 bedrooms (all en suite).
TARIFF: (1993) Single 86–115, Double 130–170.
CC: Amex, Diners, Euro/Access, Visa.

BAD DÜRRHEIM 16D

Hotel Waldeck Schrenk Waldstrasse 18,
7737 Bad Dürrheim.
☎ 07726 663100, Fax 07726 8001.
Open all year. 43 bedrooms (all en suite).
TARIFF: (1993) Single 106–136,
Double 190–250.
CC: Amex, Diners, Euro/Access, Visa.

BAD EMS 16A

Hotel Bad Ems Römerstrasse 1-3, 5427 Bad Ems.
☎ 02603 7990, Fax 02603 799252.
Open all year. 107 bedrooms (all en suite).
TARIFF: (1993) Single 140, Double 170.
CC: Amex, Diners, Euro/Access, Visa.

BAD HARZBURG 14D

Hotel Braunschweiger Hof Herzogwilhelm
Strasse 54, 3388 Bad Harzburg.
☎ 05322 7880, Fax 05322 53349.
Open all year. 78 bedrooms (all en suite).
TARIFF: (1993) Double 199–124.
CC: Amex, Diners, Euro/Access, Visa.

BAD HERSFELD 16B

Hotel Romantik-Zum Stern ★★★
Lingg Platz 11, 6430 Bad Hersfeld.
☎ 06621 1890, Fax 06621 18926. English spoken.

Open all year. 53 bedrooms (all en suite with
telephone). Indoor swimming pool, garage. ♿
RESTAURANT: Closed 01/01 to 22/01.

*Traditional hotel with friendly atmosphere, in
the pedestrian area of Bad Hersfeld.*

Originally part of an old monastery but now completely modernised. High quality restaurant. Access: Follow the blue signs Parkhaus Neumarkt and go another 50 m to hotel car park.

TARIFF: Single 115–148, Double 195–230, Set menu 39–69.
CC: Amex, Diners, Euro/Access, Visa.

BAD HOMBURG 16B

Queens Hotel Friedrichsdorf ★★★★
Im Dammwald 1, 61381 Friedrichsdorf/Bad Homburg.
☎ 06172 7390, Fax 06172 739852.
English spoken.
Open all year. 125 bedrooms (all en suite with telephone). Indoor swimming pool, garage, parking, restaurant.

The hotel offers a peaceful setting, and is easy to reach. Bad Homburg is 5 minutes' by car and Frankfurt's exhibition halls are reached via A5 or S-Bahn 5 suburban railway. The first-class rooms combine elegance with comfort. Sauna. Take Freiberg/Freidrichsdorf exit from the A5.

TARIFF: Single 180–228, Double 230–278, Bk 21, Set menu 35–65.
CC: Amex, Diners, Euro/Access, Visa.

BAD HONNEF 16A

Hotel Ditscheid Luisenstrasse 27, 4350 Bad Honnef.
☎ 02224 18090.
Open all year. 50 bedrooms (all en suite).
CC: Amex, Diners, Euro/Access, Visa.

Hotel Haus Hindenburg Siebengebirgstr 12, 53604 Bad Honnef.
☎ 02224 80115, Fax 02224 89017.
English spoken.
Open 01/01 to 31/10 & 01/12 to 31/12.
8 bedrooms (all en suite with telephone).
Outdoor swimming pool, parking.
Small, comfortable family hotel.
TARIFF: Single 65, Double 120.
CC: Amex, Diners, Euro/Access, Visa.

BAD KREUZNACH 16A

Hotel Avance Kurhaus ★★★★ Kurhausstr 28, 55543 Bad Kreuznach.
☎ 06712 061, Fax 06713 5477. English spoken.
Open all year. 108 bedrooms (all en suite with telephone). Indoor swimming pool, golf 7 km, garage, parking, restaurant. &
Comfort and tradition combined in this

renovated hotel. Elegant restaurant, bar.
TARIFF: Single 159–189, Double 250–280, Set menu 43–98.
CC: Amex, Diners, Euro/Access, Visa.

BAD LAASPHE 16B

Landhotel Doerr ★★★ Sieg Lahn Str 8, 5928 Bad Laasphe.
☎ 02754 3081, Fax 02754 3084. English spoken.
Open all year. 34 bedrooms (all en suite with telephone). Indoor swimming pool, parking, restaurant.

Traditional décor in this very comfortable hotel. Restaurant offers varied cuisine.
TARIFF: (1993) Single 100, Double 200–280, Set menu 28–45.
CC: Amex, Diners, Euro/Access, Visa.

BAD MERGENTHEIM 16B

Hotel Laurentius Marktplatz 5, 6992 Weikersheim.
☎ 07934 7007, Fax 07934 7077. English spoken.
Open 01/03 to 15/01. 13 bedrooms (all en suite with telephone). Restaurant.

In the old market-place and said to be the ancestral home of Goëthe. Next door to the Palace of the Princes. Cellar restaurant and outdoor café. 12 km east of Bad Mergentheim.
TARIFF: (1993) Single 85–105, Double 125–155, Set menu 35–89.
CC: Diners, Euro/Access, Visa.

BAD NAUHEIM 16B

Parkhotel ★★★★ Nordlicher Park 16, 61231 Bad Nauheim.
☎ 06032 3030, Fax 06032 303419.
English spoken.
Open all year. 99 bedrooms (all en suite with telephone). Indoor swimming pool, golf 1 km, garage, parking, restaurant. &
Lovely hotel surrounded by landscaped gardens. Light, spacious rooms with a welcoming atmosphere. Good restaurant and excellent sports/fitness facilities.
TARIFF: Single 170, Double 310.
CC: Amex, Diners, Euro/Access, Visa.

BAD NEUENAHR 16A

Hotel Giffels Goldener Anker Mittelstrasse 14, 5483 Bad Neuenahr.
☎ 02641 8040, Fax 02641 804192.
Open all year. 80 bedrooms (all en suite).
TARIFF: (1993) Single 89–125, Double 150–190.
CC: Amex, Diners, Euro/Access, Visa.

Germany

BAD OEYNHAUSEN 14D

Romantik Hotel Hahnenkamp ★★★ Alte
Reichsstrasse 4, 4970 Bad Oeynhausen.
☎ 05731 5041, Fax 05731 5047.
English spoken.
Open all year. 27 bedrooms (all en suite
with telephone). Golf 7 km, parking,
restaurant.

*Charming 200-year-old half-timbered
building with two restaurants. One specialises
in German/African cuisine and has "guest"
African cooks. From A2 Hannover Airport to
Dortmund, take exit for Autobahnkreuz Bad
Oeynhausen for 1 mile. Turn right at traffic
lights on to B61 towards Minden. After approx
300 m, at next traffic lights, turn right again.*
TARIFF: Single 105–149, Double 149–189,
Set menu 20–60.
cc: Amex, Diners, Euro/Access, Visa.

BAD RAPPENHAU-HEIMSHEIM 16B

Hotel Schloss Heimsheim
6927 Bad Rappenhau-Heimsheim.
☎ 07264 1045, Fax 07264 4208.
Open all year. 40 bedrooms (all en suite).
TARIFF: (1993) Single 130–170,
Double 160–260.
cc: Amex, Diners, Euro/Access, Visa.

BAD REICHENHALL 17C

Hotel Axelmannstein ★★★★★
Salzburger Str 2-6, 83435 Bad Reichenhall.
☎ 08651 7770, Fax 08651 5932.
English spoken.
Open all year. 151 bedrooms (all en suite
with telephone). Indoor swimming pool,
tennis, golf 6 km, garage, parking, restaurant.

*Situated in a lovely park in pedestrian zone of
city centre, 500 m from railway station, 5 km
from Salzburg airport. Health/fitness centre;
downhill and cross-country skiing within easy
walking distance.*
TARIFF: Single 175–275, Double 255–490,
Bk 20, Set menu 55.
cc: Amex, Diners, Euro/Access, Visa.

BAD SODEN-AM-TAUNUS 16B

Hotel Best Western Park Konigsteiner
Strasse 88, 6232 Bad Soden-am-Taunus.
☎ 06196 2000, Fax 06196 200153.
Open all year. 130 bedrooms (all en suite).
TARIFF: (1993) Single 190–310,
Double 250–370.
cc: Amex, Diners, Euro/Access, Visa.

BAD SOODEN-ALLENDORF 14D

Kurparkhotel Brunnenplatz 5,
3437 Bad Sooden-Allendorf.
☎ 05652 3031, Fax 05652 4918.
Open all year. 40 bedrooms (all en suite).
TARIFF: (1993) Single 63–93, Double 126–186.
cc: Amex, Diners, Euro/Access, Visa.

BAD TÖLZ 17C

Hotel Jodquellenhof-Alpamare
Ludwigstrasse 13-15, 8170 Bad Tölz.
☎ 08041 5091, Fax 08041 509441.
Open all year. 81 bedrooms (all en suite).
TARIFF: (1993) Double 130–170.
cc: Amex, Diners, Euro/Access, Visa.

BAD ÜBERKINGEN 16D

Hotel Bad ★★★ Badstr 12,
7347 Bad Überkingen.
☎ 07331 3020, Fax 07331 30220.
English spoken.
Open all year. 20 bedrooms (all en suite with
telephone). Golf 7 km, parking, restaurant.

*In the centre of the village, the original part of
the building dating back 600 years. Thermal
spring. Leave A8 south of Stuttgart at
Wiesensteig and go 2 km to Bad Überkingen.*
TARIFF: (1993) Single 140–150,
Double 210–280, Set menu 30–90.
cc: Amex, Diners, Euro/Access, Visa.

BAD WIESSEE 17C

Gasthof Wiesseer Hof
Sankt-Johanser-Strasse 46, 8182 Bad Wiessee.
☎ 08022 8670, Fax 08022 867165.
Open all year. 58 bedrooms (33 en suite).
TARIFF: (1993) Single 35–80, Double 66–150.
cc: Amex, Diners, Euro/Access, Visa.

BADEN-BADEN 16A

Queens Hotel ★★★★ Falkenstrasse 2,
76530 Baden-Baden.
☎ 07221 2190, Fax 07221 219519.
English spoken.
Open all year. 121 bedrooms (all en suite
with telephone). Indoor swimming pool,
golf 3 km, garage, parking, restaurant. &

*Situated on the famous Lichtentaler Allee, the
hotel is surrounded by beautiful parks and
trees. The town centre and the Kurhaus, with
its world-famous casino, are only minutes away.*
TARIFF: Single 160–260, Double 190–330,
Set menu 32–89.
cc: Amex, Diners, Euro/Access, Visa.

Germany

Romantik-Hotel Der Kleine Prinz
Lichtentaler Strasse 36, 76530 Baden-Baden.
📞 07221 3464, Fax 07221 38264.
English spoken.

Open all year. 39 bedrooms (all en suite
with telephone). Golf 2 km, garage.
RESTAURANT: Closed Jan.

*In the town centre near Congress and public
gardens. Luxurious, immaculate hotel.*
TARIFF: Single 175–275, Double 250–375,
Set menu 78–108.
CC: Amex, Diners, Euro/Access, Visa.

BADENWEILER   16C

Hotel Romerbad ★★★★★ Schlosspl 1,
7847 Badenweiler.
📞 07632 700, Fax 07632 70200. English spoken.

Open all year. 84 bedrooms (all en suite
with telephone). Indoor swimming pool,
outdoor swimming pool, tennis, golf 15 km,
garage, parking, restaurant.

*Situated at the edge of the Black Forest and
close to the French and Swiss borders, this
elegant hotel has been family owned and
managed since 1825. Tastefully decorated,
comfortable rooms, very good restaurant and
excellent health, sports and beauty facilities.*

TARIFF: Single 260–330, Double 380–460,
Set menu 55–80.
CC: Amex, Diners, Euro/Access, Visa.

BAMBERG   17A

Hotel National Luitpoldstrasse 37,
8600 Bamberg.
📞 0951 24112, Fax 0951 22436.
Open all year. 41 bedrooms (all en suite).
TARIFF: (1993) Single 87–107, Double 128–148.
CC: Amex, Diners, Euro/Access, Visa.

Hotel Sankt Nepomuk ★★★★ Obere
Mühlbrücke 9, 96049 Bamberg.
📞 0951 25183, Fax 0951 26651. English spoken.
Open all year. 47 bedrooms (all en suite
with telephone). Garage, restaurant. &

*Beautifully restored and converted watermill.
In a stunning location, right on the river and
in the centre of this lovely old town which
ranks among the finest architectural settings
in Germany. Tastefully decorated, open fires
and a good restaurant.*
TARIFF: Single 110–140, Double 170–220,
Set menu 30–100.
CC: Diners, Euro/Access, Visa.

BAUNATAL   14D

Hotel Ambassador Friedrich-Ebert Allee 1,
3507 Baunatal.
📞 0561 49930, Fax 0561 4993500.
Open all year. 120 bedrooms (all en suite).
TARIFF: (1993) Single 150, Double 200.
CC: Amex, Diners, Euro/Access, Visa.

BAYREUTH   17A

Transmar Travel Hotel ★★★ Bühlstrasse 12,
95463 Bayreuth-Bindlach.
📞 09208 371, Fax 09208 371. English spoken.

Open all year. 148 bedrooms (all en suite with
telephone). Golf 5 km, parking, restaurant. &

Located close to the A9 Berlin to München motorway. Exit Bayreuth Nord.
TARIFF: Single 165–185, Double 205–265.
CC: Amex, Diners, Euro/Access, Visa.

BEDERKESA 14B

Hotel Waldschlosschen Bösehof ★★★
Hauptmann-Böse-Str 19, 2852 Bederkesa.
☎ 04745 9480, Fax 04745 948200.
English spoken.
Open all year. 30 bedrooms (all en suite with telephone). Indoor swimming pool, garage, parking, restaurant. &

Family-run hotel with sun-terrace restaurant in the summer, Wintergarten restaurant and Böse's restaurant. Situated next to woodland. Access from A27 north of Bremerhaven, exit at Debstedt and follow signs to Bederkesa (12 km).
TARIFF: (1993) Single 65–85, Double 145–165, Set menu 40–85.
CC: Amex, Diners, Euro/Access, Visa.

BEILNGRIES 17C

Hotel Gams ★★★ Haupstrasse 16,
8432 Beilngries.
☎ 08461 256, Fax 08461 7475. English spoken.
Open all year. 70 bedrooms (all en suite with telephone). Garage, parking, restaurant.

Attractive hotel in small town in heart of Bavaria. From A9 Berlin to München, take exit for Denkendorf or Altmühltal. From A3 Nürnberg to Regensberg, take exit for Neumarkt or Parsberg.
TARIFF: Single 85–115, Double 130–190, Set menu 18–38.
CC: Amex, Diners, Euro/Access, Visa.

BEILSTEIN 16B

Hotel Burgfrieden Im Mühlental 62,
5591 Beilstein.
☎ 02673 1432, Fax 02673 1577.
Open all year. 38 bedrooms (30 en suite).
TARIFF: (1993) Single 45–65, Double 80–95.
CC: Amex, Diners, Euro/Access, Visa.

BERLIN 15D

Alsterhof Ringhotel Berlin ★★★ Augsburger
Strasse 5, 10789 Berlin.
☎ 030 212420, Fax 030 2183949.
English spoken.
Open all year. 200 bedrooms (all en suite with telephone). Indoor swimming pool, garage, restaurant.

A first-class hotel in the city centre, two minutes' walk to Kurfürstendamm.
TARIFF: Single 195–315, Double 290–390.
CC: Amex, Diners, Euro/Access, Visa.

Hotel Ambassador ★★★★
Bayreuther Str 42-43, 10787 Berlin.
☎ 030 219020, Fax 030 21902380.
English spoken.

Open all year. 200 bedrooms (all en suite with telephone). Indoor swimming pool, golf 10 km, garage, parking, restaurant.

An elegant first-class hotel in the heart of Berlin. Spacious bedrooms, conference facilities, restaurant and sauna adjoining the superb rooftop swimming pool.
TARIFF: Single 250–290, Double 310–350, Set menu 33–98.
CC: Amex, Diners, Euro/Access, Visa.

Hotel Bristol-Kempinski ★★★★★
Kurfürstendamm 27, 1000 Berlin.
☎ 030 884340, Fax 030 8836075. English spoken.
Open all year. 315 bedrooms (all en suite with telephone). Indoor swimming pool, garage, parking, restaurant.

The hotel is situated directly in the centre of the city near buses, underground, train and taxis.
TARIFF: Double 470–530, Bk 30.
CC: Amex, Diners, Euro/Access, Visa.

Hotel Palace Berlin ★★★★ Im Europa-
Centre, 30 Budapester Str, 1000 Berlin.
☎ 030 254970, Fax 030 2626577.
Open all year. 252 bedrooms (all en suite).
TARIFF: (1993) Double 314.
CC: Amex, Diners, Euro/Access, Visa.

BERNKASTEL 16A

Hotel Behrens Schanzstrasse 9,
54470 Bernkastel-Kues.
☎ 06531 6088, Fax 06531 6089. English spoken.

Germany

Open all year. 27 bedrooms (all en suite with telephone). Garage, parking, restaurant. &

Located 5 mins from medieval market square in the centre of town, right on the banks of the Mosel.

TARIFF: Single 55–85, Double 96–150.
CC: Amex, Diners, Euro/Access, Visa.

Hotel Burg Landshut Gestade 11, 54470 Bernkastel.
C 06531 3019, Fax 06531 7387. English spoken.
Open 28/02 to 15/12 & 27/12 to 03/01.
38 bedrooms (25 en suite, 3 bath/shower only, 30 telephone). Garage, parking, restaurant.

Town centre hotel.

TARIFF: Single 50–110, Double 80–190.
CC: Amex, Diners, Euro/Access, Visa.

Hotel Landhaus Arnoth Auf Dem Puetz, 5551 Kleinich.
C 06536 286, Fax 06536 1217. English spoken.
Open 01/01 to 25/07 & 19/08 to 31/12.
15 bedrooms (all en suite with telephone). Parking.
RESTAURANT: Closed Mon & Tues.

From the centre of Bernkastel, take the road to Longkamp. In Longkamp follow the signs to Kleinich.

TARIFF: Single 80–110, Double 120–150, Set menu 45–75.
CC: Euro/Access.

BINZEN   16C

Hotel Mühle 7851 Binzen.
C 07621 6771.
Open all year. 14 bedrooms (all en suite with telephone).
CC: none.

BITBURG   16A

Hotel Eifelbrau Romermauer 36, 5520 Bitburg.
C 06561 7031/2, Fax 06561 7060.
Open all year. 29 bedrooms (all en suite).
TARIFF: (1993) Single 60–65, Double 100–110.
CC: Amex, Diners, Euro/Access, Visa.

BLOMBERG   14D

Burghotel Blomberg ★★★ Blomberg 1 Lippe, 4933 Blomberg.
C 05235 50010, Fax 05235 500145.
Open all year. 52 bedrooms (all en suite).
TARIFF: (1993) Single 105–135, Double 170–220.
CC: Amex, Diners, Euro/Access, Visa.

BOCHOLT-BARLO   14C

Hotel Schloss Diepenbrock Schlossallee 5, 4290 Bocholt-Barlo.
C 02871 3545, Fax 02871 39607.
Open all year. 22 bedrooms (all en suite).
TARIFF: (1993) Single 135, Double 220.
CC: Amex, Diners, Euro/Access, Visa.

BOCHUM   14C

Hotel Arcade Universitastrasse 3, 4630 Bochum.
C 0234 33311.
Open all year. 157 bedrooms (all en suite with telephone).
TARIFF: (1993) Single 105, Double 149.
CC: Amex, Diners, Euro/Access, Visa.

BOLLENDORF   16A

Hotel Ritschlay Auf der Ritschlay 3, 5526 Bollendorf.
C 06526 212.
Open all year. 20 bedrooms (17 en suite, 6 telephone).
TARIFF: (1993) Single 59, Double 94–117.
CC: Amex, Diners, Euro/Access, Visa.

BONN   16A

Hotel Consul ★★★ Oxfordstrasse 12-16, 5300 Bonn.
C 0228 72920, Fax 0228 7292250.
Open all year. 90 bedrooms (all en suite).
TARIFF: (1993) Single 120–160, Double 170–210.
CC: Amex, Diners, Euro/Access, Visa.

Hotel Konigshof Adenauer Allee 9, 53111 Bonn.
C 0228 26010, Fax 0228 2601529.
English spoken.
Open all year. 137 bedrooms (all en suite with telephone). Garage, parking, restaurant.

Medium-size hotel in convenient location.

TARIFF: Single 200–230, Double 220–250, Bk 20, Set menu 38–48.
CC: Amex, Diners, Euro/Access, Visa.

Hotel President ★★★ Clemens August Strasse 32-36, 53115 Bonn.
C 0228 694001, Fax 0228 694090.
English spoken.
Open all year. 98 bedrooms (all en suite with telephone). Garage, parking, restaurant.

Situated in the historic quarter of Poppelsdorf, a short distance from the castle and botanical gardens. Comfortable, sound-proofed rooms. Good restaurant with international and

Germany

regional cuisine. Non-smoking rooms available on request.
TARIFF: Single 169–289, Double 199–349.
CC: Amex, Diners, Euro/Access, Visa.

Rheinhotel Dreesen Theinstrasse 45-49, 5300 Bonn.
☎ 0228 82020, Fax 0228 8202153.
Open all year. 74 bedrooms (all en suite).
TARIFF: (1993) Single 168–398, Double 198–460.
CC: Amex, Diners, Euro/Access, Visa.

BOPPARD 16A

Bellevue Rheinhotel ★★★★
Rheinallee 41-42, 56154 Boppard.
☎ 06742 1020, Fax 06742 102602. English spoken.

Open all year. 95 bedrooms (all en suite with telephone). Indoor swimming pool, tennis, golf 1 km, garage, parking, restaurant.
One of the Best Western group. Hotel is situated on the banks of the River Rhein and offers good facilities including indoor heated swimming pool, sauna, steam-bath and the famous Pepper Mill restaurant. Central location in Boppard and well signposted.
TARIFF: Single 125–220, Double 180–320, Set menu 35–95.
CC: Amex, Diners, Euro/Access, Visa.

Hotel Am Ebertor ★★ Heerstrasse B9, 56154 Boppard.
☎ 06742 2081, Fax 06742 102602.
English spoken.
Open 01/04 to 31/10. 140 bedrooms (all en suite with telephone). Tennis, golf 12 km, garage, parking, restaurant. ♿
Comfortable rooms with TV. Good continental cuisine, medieval grill room (Klosterkellar), large garden restaurant with river views. Leave the A61 at Boppard exit and hotel is just off the main street (B9).

TARIFF: Single 75–90, Double 84–124, Bk 16.
CC: Amex, Diners, Euro/Access, Visa.

Hotel Günther Rheinallee 40, 56154 Boppard.
☎ 06742 2335, Fax 06742 1557. English spoken.

Open 15/01 to 15/12. 19 bedrooms (all en suite with telephone).
Enjoy the friendly atmosphere of this attractive, family-run hotel with modern rooms. Ideally located on the Rhein promenade.
TARIFF: Single 59–120, Double 79–148.
CC: none.

Hotel Weinhaus Patt Steinstrasse 30, 56154 Boppard.
☎ 06742 2366, Fax 06742 81280. English spoken.
Open all year. 17 bedrooms (all en suite).
Quietly situated in the city centre, hotel has been run by the same family for three generations. Ideal location for exploring the Rhein and Mosel valleys.
TARIFF: Single 40–65, Double 66–100.
CC: none.

BRAUNLAGE 14D

Hotel Romantik-Zur Tanne ★★★
Herzog-Wilhelmstrasse 8, 3389 Braunlage.
☎ 05520 1034, Fax 05520 3992. English spoken.

Germany

Open all year. 22 bedrooms (all en suite with telephone). Garage, parking, restaurant.

In the historic centre of Braunlage, a wood-panelled building with window-boxes of red geraniums in summer. Large garden opposite.
TARIFF: Single 75–125, Double 100–225, Set menu 39–85.
CC: Amex, Diners, Euro/Access, Visa.

BRAUNSCHWEIG (BRUNSWICK)　　14D

Hotel Frühlings Bankplatz 7,
3330 Braunschweig.
☎ 0531 49317, Fax 0531 13268.
Open all year. 60 bedrooms (all en suite with telephone).
TARIFF: (1993) Single 85–118, Double 125–210.
CC: Amex, Diners, Euro/Access, Visa.

BREISACH　　16C

Hotel Am Münster Münsterbergstrasse 23,
7814 Breisach.
☎ 07667 8380, Fax 07667 838100.
Open all year. 42 bedrooms (all en suite).
TARIFF: (1993) Single 85–150, Double 126–260.
CC: Amex, Diners, Euro/Access, Visa.

BREMEN　　14B

Hotel Bremen Marriott ★★★★ Hillmannplatz 1, 2800 Bremen.
☎ 0421 17670, Fax 0421 1767238.
English spoken.
Open all year. 228 bedrooms (all en suite with telephone). Golf 5 km, garage, restaurant.
Located between the main station and city centre with good access to autobahns.

Federal Germany

Germany is the only large country in the European Community with a federal style of administration. The eleven federal states of former West Germany were joined by the five former East German states at reunification.

Each German state has its own parliament and president, elected by voters. The state is responsible for its own police force, education system, and cultural activities, including radio and television.

TARIFF: Single 235–295, Double 285–345, Bk 26, Set menu 45–55.
CC: Amex, Diners, Euro/Access, Visa.

Hotel Landhaus Louisenthal Leher Heerstrasse 105, 2800 Bremen.
☎ 0421 232076, Fax 0421 236716.
Open all year. 60 bedrooms (all en suite).
TARIFF: (1993) Single 69–120, Double 99–195.
CC: Amex, Diners, Euro/Access, Visa.

Hotel Munte-am-Stadtwald Aparkallee 2999, 2800 Bremen.
☎ 0421 212063, Fax 0421 219876.
Open all year. 123 bedrooms (all en suite).
TARIFF: (1993) Single 105–180, Double 140–210.
CC: Amex, Diners, Euro/Access, Visa.

Queens Hotel ★★★★ August Bebel Allee 4, 28329 Bremen.
☎ 0421 23870, Fax 0421 234617.
English spoken.
Open all year. 147 bedrooms (all en suite, all bath/shower only with telephone).
Golf 1 km, parking, restaurant. &

Follow directions to Worpswede and Lilienthal. When arriving in Kurfürstenallee, follow signposts to the hotel.
TARIFF: Single 170–220, Double 180–260, Bk 22, Set menu 40–200.
CC: Amex, Diners, Euro/Access, Visa.

Hotel Zur Post Bahnhofsplatz 11, 2800 Bremen.
☎ 0421 30590.
Open all year. 205 bedrooms (all en suite with telephone).
TARIFF: (1993) Single 165–250, Double 210–290.
CC: Amex, Diners, Euro/Access, Visa.

BREMERHAVEN　　14B

Nordsee-Hotel Naber Theodor-Heuss-Platz, 2850 Bremerhaven.
☎ 0471 48770, Fax 0471 4877999.
Open all year. 99 bedrooms (all en suite).
TARIFF: (1993) Single 100–150, Double 170–210.
CC: Amex, Diners, Euro/Access, Visa.

BUCHEN-ODENWALD　　16B

Hotel Prinz Carl Hochstadtstrasse 1, 6967 Buchen-Odenwald.
☎ 06281 1877, Fax 06281 1879.
Open all year. 20 bedrooms (all en suite).
TARIFF: (1993) Single 95–150, Double 170–190.
CC: Amex, Diners, Euro/Access, Visa.

BÜSUM 14B

Hotel Der Rosenhof Towurth 12,
25761 Büsum Deichhausen.
☎ 04834 9800, Fax 04834 98080.
English spoken.

Open all year. 21 bedrooms (all en suite
with telephone). Golf 2 km, parking.
RESTAURANT: Closed Mon.
*North of Hamburg on A23; if travelling by
train go to Heide station, telephone the hotel
and they will arrange transport for you.*
TARIFF: Single 90–103, Double 138–188.
CC: Amex, Euro/Access, Visa.

CELLE 14D

Hotel Fürstenhof Celle Hannoversche
Strasse 55-56, 3100 Celle.
☎ 05141 2010, Fax 05141 201120.
Open all year. 76 bedrooms (all en suite).
TARIFF: (1993) Single 160–220,
Double 190–400.
CC: Amex, Diners, Euro/Access, Visa.

Hotel Gasthof Schaper Heese 6-7,
3100 Celle.
☎ 05141 42310, Fax 05141 46965.
English spoken.
Open all year. 26 bedrooms (all en suite
with telephone). Golf 8 km, parking.
RESTAURANT: Closed 15/07 to 30/07.
*Modern, family-run hotel in quiet location
close to city centre.*
TARIFF: Single 85–110, Double 130–160,
Set menu 20.
CC: Euro/Access, Visa.

Hotel Schifferkrug Speicherstrasse 9,
3100 Celle.
☎ 05141 7015, Fax 05141 6350.
Open all year. 14 bedrooms (all en suite).
TARIFF: (1993) Single 75–85, Double 110–160.
CC: Amex, Diners, Euro/Access, Visa.

CHIEMING 17C

Hotel Zum Goldenen Pflug ★★★★
Kirchberg 3, 8224 Chieming.
☎ 08667 790, Fax 08667 79432. English spoken.
Open all year. 125 bedrooms (all en suite
with telephone). Indoor swimming pool,
outdoor swimming pool, tennis, golf on site,
garage, parking, restaurant.
*Very comfortable hotel with excellent facilities
and golf on the doorstep.*
TARIFF: Single 148–158, Double 227–244,
Set menu 35–180.
CC: Amex, Diners, Euro/Access, Visa.

COBURG 17A

Hotel Goldener Anker Rosengasse 14,
8630 Coburg.
☎ 09561 95027, Fax 09561 92560.
Open all year. 60 bedrooms (all en suite).
TARIFF: (1993) Single 70–110, Double 125–190.
CC: Amex, Diners, Euro/Access, Visa.

COCHEM 16A

Hotel Panorama ★★★ Klostergartenstrasse
44, 56812 Cochem.
☎ 02671 8430, Fax 02671 3064. English spoken.

Open all year. 43 bedrooms (all en suite
with telephone). Indoor swimming pool,
garage, parking, restaurant.
*Each room has colour TV and telephone.
Sauna, solarium and garden. Situated just off
the B259 Panoramastrasse, the south-western
side of Cochem.*
TARIFF: Single 65–95, Double 120–190,
Set menu 20–30.
CC: Euro/Access, Visa.

Hotel Wilhelmshöhe Auderath,
56766 Ulmen.
☎ 02676 260, Fax 02676 1527.
English spoken.

Germany

Open all year. 30 bedrooms (13 en suite).
Garage, parking, restaurant.

19 km from Cochem, the hotel offers a friendly welcome and warm atmosphere. Situated on the B259 in Auderath near Ulmen.

TARIFF: Single 45–50, Double 80–90.
CC: none.

CUXHAVEN   14B

Hotel Seepavillon Donner ★★★ Bei der
Alten Liebe 5, 2190 Cuxhaven.
☎ 04721 38064, Fax 04721 38167.
English spoken.
Open all year. 45 bedrooms (all en suite
with telephone). Golf 15 km, garage, parking,
restaurant.

The hotel is directly on the coast with good views of the sea and marina from the restaurant. It is easy to find, just follow the signs Alten Liebe or Fahrhafen once in Cuxhaven.

TARIFF: (1993) Single 69–110, Double 163–194,
Set menu 30–75.
CC: Amex, Diners, Euro/Access, Visa.

DANNENFELS   16A

Hotel Kastanienhof Donnersberger Strasse,
6765 Dannenfels.
☎ 06357 815.
Open all year. 20 bedrooms (all en suite).
TARIFF: (1993) Double 80–120.
CC: Amex, Diners, Euro/Access, Visa.

DARMSTADT   16B

Hotel Weinmichel
Schleiermacherstrasse 10-12,
6100 Darmstadt.
☎ 06151 26822, Fax 06151 23592.
Open all year. 74 bedrooms (all en suite).
TARIFF: (1993) Single 96–146, Double 168–188.
CC: Amex, Diners, Euro/Access, Visa.

DAUN   16A

Hotel Hommes Wirichstrasse 9, 54542 Daun.
☎ 06592 538, Fax 06592 8126.
English spoken.
Open 08/02 to 06/01. 42 bedrooms
(all en suite with telephone). Indoor
swimming pool, golf 16 km, garage, parking,
restaurant.

In the centre of town overlooking own gardens, forest, and beautiful unspoilt countryside. International cuisine as well as local specialities.

TARIFF: Single 89–93, Double 158–166,
Set menu 24–63.
CC: Amex, Diners, Euro/Access, Visa.

DETMOLD   14D

Hotel Lippischer Hof Hornsche Strasse 1,
4930 Detmold.
☎ 05231 31041, Fax 05231 24470.
Open all year. 25 bedrooms (all en suite).
TARIFF: (1993) Single 89–110, Double 150–200.
CC: Amex, Diners, Euro/Access, Visa.

DINKELSBÜHL   16D

Hotel Blauer Hecht Schweinemarkt 1,
8804 Dinkelsbühl.
☎ 09851 811, Fax 09851 814.
Open all year. 42 bedrooms (all en suite).
CC: Amex, Diners, Euro/Access, Visa.

Hotel Goldene Kanne Segringer Strasse 8,
8804 Dinkelsbühl.
☎ 09851 6011, Fax 09851 61107.
Open all year. 26 bedrooms (all en suite).
TARIFF: (1993) Single 79–99,
Double 120–170.
CC: Amex, Diners, Euro/Access, Visa.

Hotel Weisses Ross Steingasse 12,
8804 Dinkelsbühl.
☎ 09851 2274, Fax 09851 6770.
English spoken.
Open all year. 25 bedrooms (17 en suite,
17 telephone). Restaurant.

Very pretty, beamed, large-roofed building, surrounded by the cobbled streets of this 1,000-year-old walled town. Run as a hotel since 1645. Just behind the town hall in the centre of town. Exit from the A7 at Crailsheim.

TARIFF: Single 75–95, Double 75–160,
Set menu 27–50.
CC: Amex, Diners, Euro/Access, Visa.

Germany

DONAUWÖRTH 17C

Hotel Traube ★★ Kapellstrasse 14,
86609 Donauwörth.
✆ 09066 096, Fax 09066 23390. English spoken.
Open all year. 43 bedrooms (41 en suite,
2 bath/shower only, 43 telephone). Outdoor
swimming pool, tennis, golf 3 km, garage,
parking, restaurant.

*In the centre of Donauwörth, the hotel has the
Café Mozart, garden and sauna.*

TARIFF: Single 80–115, Double 130–180,
Set menu 19–38.
CC: Amex, Diners, Euro/Access, Visa.

DORTMUND 14C

Hotel Rombergpark Am Rombergpark 67,
4600 Dortmund.
✆ 0231 714073.
Open all year. 32 bedrooms (all en suite).
TARIFF: (1993) Single 110–120, Double 220.
CC: Amex, Diners, Euro/Access, Visa.

DÜSSELDORF 14C

Hotel Arcade Ludwig-Erhard Allee 2,
4000 Düsseldorf.
✆ 0211 77010, Fax 0211 7701716.
Open all year. 148 bedrooms (all en suite).
TARIFF: (1993) Single 110–142, Double 154.
CC: Amex, Diners, Euro/Access, Visa.

Hotel Eden ★★★ Adersstrasse 29-31,
4000 Düsseldorf.
✆ 0211 38970, Fax 0211 3897777.
English spoken.
Open all year. 129 bedrooms (all en suite
with telephone). Garage, parking, restaurant.

*Hotel Eden is perfectly located in the very heart
of Düsseldorf. Only 2 minutes to the "KO" and
a 10-minute stroll takes you to the legendary
Altstadt.*

TARIFF: (1993) Single 188–359,
Double 240–424.
CC: Amex, Diners, Euro/Access, Visa.

Hotel Graf Adolf ★★★ Stresemannplatz 1,
4000 Düsseldorf.
✆ 0211 35540, Fax 0211 354120.
English spoken.
Open all year. 147 bedrooms (all en suite
with telephone). Golf 10 km, garage.
RESTAURANT: Closed Sat & Sun.

*The hotel is located in the city centre, 5
minutes' walk from the main station.*

TARIFF: Single 195–295, Double 265–395.
CC: Amex, Diners, Euro/Access, Visa.

Queens Hotel ★★★★ Ludwig Erhard Allee 3,
40227 Düsseldorf.
✆ 0211 77710, Fax 0211 7771777.
English spoken.
Open all year. 220 bedrooms (all en suite
with telephone). Golf 6 km, garage, parking,
restaurant.

*Well situated in the city centre, close to the
main station, Konigsallee and shopping and
banking area.*

TARIFF: Single 250–520, Double 300–1200,
Bk 25, Set menu 30–80.
CC: Amex, Diners, Euro/Access, Visa.

ECHING 17C

Hotel Olymp Wielandstrasse 3,
8057 Eching.
✆ 089 319 0910, Fax 089 319 09112.
Open all year. 62 bedrooms (all en suite).
CC: Amex, Diners, Euro/Access, Visa.

EDIGER-ELLER 16A

Hotel Oster Moselweinstrasse 61,
5591 Ediger-Eller.
✆ 02675 232/1303.
Open all year. 12 bedrooms (10 en suite,
1 telephone).
TARIFF: (1993) Single 29–60, Double 60–100.
CC: none.

EISENACH 16B

Hotel Kaiserhof Wartburgallee 2,
O-5900 Eisenach.
✆ 03691 3274, Fax 03691 3653.
English spoken.
Open all year. 64 bedrooms (all en suite
with telephone). Tennis, golf 1 km, parking,
restaurant.

*One of the best known and oldest hotels of the
region, the Kaiserhof is now fully restored but
has retained its individual character. Exit at
Eisenach-Ost from the A4 motorway and
follow the Stadtmitte signs.*

TARIFF: Single 140–160, Double 185–240.
CC: Amex, Euro/Access, Visa.

EMDEN 14A

Hotel Deutsches Haus Neuer Markt 7,
2970 Emden.
✆ 04921 22048, Fax 04921 31657.
Open all year. 28 bedrooms (all en suite).
TARIFF: (1993) Single 85–110,
Double 130–150.
CC: Amex, Diners, Euro/Access, Visa.

Germany

ERFURT 17A

Hotel Erfurter Hof ★★★★
Willy-Brandt-Platz 1, 99084 Erfurt.
☎ 0361 5310, Fax 0361 6461021. English spoken.
Open all year. 173 bedrooms (all en suite
with telephone). Garage, parking, restaurant.
*Charming, centrally situated hotel with a
choice of restaurants, pub, café and night-
club. Non-smoking rooms and special weekend
rates available. Opposite train station and
6 km from airport.*
TARIFF: Single 200–250, Double 250–380, Bk 25.
CC: Amex, Diners, Euro/Access, Visa.

ERLANGEN 17A

Hotel Grille Bunsenstrasse 35,
91058 Erlangen.
☎ 09131 65036, Fax 09131 65534.
English spoken.
Open all year. 62 bedrooms (all en suite
with telephone). Garage, parking.
RESTAURANT: Closed August.
*Warm hospitality and culinary pleasures make
the stay a pleasant one. A3 Nürnberg-
Würzburg, exit Tennenlole. In Erlangen turn
left at the third set of traffic lights.*
TARIFF: Single 110–155, Double 192.
CC: Amex, Diners, Euro/Access, Visa.

Hotel Transmar Motor Wetterkreuzstrasse 7,
8520 Erlangen.
☎ 09131 6080, Fax 09131 608100.
Open all year. 126 bedrooms (all en suite
with telephone).
TARIFF: (1993) Single 164–254,
Double 194–294.
CC: Amex, Diners, Euro/Access, Visa.

ESCHWEILER 16A

Hotel Zum Fasschen Am Markt 27,
5180 Eschweiler.
☎ 02403 21024, Fax 02403 24573.
English spoken.
Open all year. 22 bedrooms (9 en suite,
15 telephone). Tennis, golf 3 km, garage,
parking, restaurant.
*On the marketplace in centre of town, near the
Municipal Offices and church (St Peter/St Paul).*
TARIFF: (1993) Single 50–85, Double 90–140.
CC: Euro/Access.

ESSEN 14C

Hotel Arcade Hollestrasse 50, 4300 Essen.
☎ 0201 24280, Fax 0201 2428600.

Open all year. 144 bedrooms (all en suite
with telephone).
CC: Amex, Diners, Euro/Access, Visa.

EUTIN-FISSAU 15A

Hotel Weisenhof 2420 Eutin-Fissau.
☎ 04521 2776.
Open all year. 30 bedrooms (all en suite).
TARIFF: (1993) Single 60, Double 98–146.
CC: Amex, Diners, Euro/Access, Visa.

FEUCHTWANGEN 16D

Hotel Greifen-Post ★★★ Marktplatz 8,
8805 Feuchtwangen.
☎ 09852 2002, Fax 09852 4841. English spoken.
Open all year. 42 bedrooms (40 en suite,
2 bath/shower only, 42 telephone). Indoor
swimming pool, golf 15 km, garage. &
RESTAURANT: Closed Jan.
*Delightful hotel, elegantly and traditionally
furnished, comprising two connecting
buildings, one dating back to 1369 and the
other to 1588. Situated in the marketplace and
very easy to find.*
TARIFF: Single 125–155, Double 185–250.
CC: Amex, Diners, Euro/Access, Visa.

FLENSBURG 14B

Hotel Glensburger Hof Süderhofenden 38,
2390 Flensburg.
☎ 0461 17320, Fax 0461 17331.
Open all year. 28 bedrooms (27 en suite).
TARIFF: (1993) Single 94–130, Double 170–180.
CC: Amex, Diners, Euro/Access, Visa.

FRANKFURT-AM-MAIN 16B

Hotel Arcade ★★ Speicherstrasse 3-5,
60327 Frankfurt-am-Main.
☎ 069 273030, Fax 069 237024.
Open all year. 193 bedrooms (all en suite
with telephone). Garage. &
TARIFF: Single 145, Double 190.
CC: Amex, Diners, Euro/Access, Visa.

Hotel Excelsior Monopol ★★★
Mannheimerstrasse 7-13,
6000 Frankfurt-am-Main.
☎ 069 256080, Fax 069 25608141.
English spoken.
Open all year. 184 bedrooms (all en suite
with telephone). Garage, restaurant.
*In the heart of Frankfurt and recently
updated. Located opposite the main railway
station with direct access to the subway and a
5-minute ride to the main shopping area.*

Germany

TARIFF: Single 145–172, Double 209–239, Set menu 30–38.
CC: Amex, Diners, Euro/Access, Visa.

Hotel Frankfurter Hof ★★★★★
Am Kaiserplatz, 6000 Frankfurt-am-Main.
☎ 069 21502, Fax 069 215900. English spoken.
Open all year. 540 bedrooms (all en suite with telephone). Golf 10 km, garage, restaurant.

For over a century the luxurious Frankfurter Hof has been the leading grand hotel in the city. Located in the heart of Frankfurt on the River Main, it is 1 km from the main railway station.

TARIFF: (1993) Single 345–485, Double 410–550, Bk 29, Set menu 45–98.
CC: Amex, Diners, Euro/Access, Visa.

Hotel Imperial ★★★ Sophienstrasse 40, 6000 Frankfurt-am-Main.
☎ 069 7930030, Fax 069 79300388.
English spoken.
Open all year. 60 bedrooms (all en suite with telephone). Garage, parking, restaurant.

Newly-built hotel near the fairground, Palmengarten and commercial area and only a few minutes from the city centre. Hotel bar, grill-restaurant La Provence. All rooms air conditioned and soundproofed.

TARIFF: (1993) Single 160–410, Double 210–410.
CC: Amex, Diners, Euro/Access, Visa.

Motel Frankfurt ★★ Eschersheimer Landstrasse 204, 6000 Frankfurt-am-Main.
☎ 069 568011, Fax 069 568010. English spoken.
Open all year. 65 bedrooms (all en suite with telephone). Garage, parking. ♿

Near the city but very quiet. Located near the end of the A66, 2 minutes' drive away.

TARIFF: Single 92–122, Double 132–162.
CC: Visa.

Movenpick Parkhotel ★★★★★
Wiesenhuttenplatz 28/38, 6000 Frankfurt-am-Main.
☎ 069 26970, Fax 069 2697884.
English spoken.
Open all year. 299 bedrooms (all en suite with telephone). Golf 12 km, garage, parking, restaurant. ♿

Although in the city centre, the hotel is opposite the Wiesenhutten Park and is quiet and peaceful. All rooms individually decorated and children under 16 stay free in their parents' room. From the A5 take Frankfurt-Süd exit and follow signs to the Hauptbahnhof.

TARIFF: Single 298–488, Double 398–538, Bk 21.
CC: Amex, Diners, Euro/Access, Visa.

Hotel National ★★★★ Baseler Strasse 50, 6000 Frankfurt-am-Main.
☎ 069 2739400, Fax 069 79300388.
English spoken.
Open all year. 70 bedrooms (all en suite with telephone). Golf 15 km, garage, parking, restaurant.

Situated opposite main railway station, close to fairground and banking area. Easy walk to places of interest. Comfortable and quiet, with antique furniture.

TARIFF: Single 190–240, Double 245–290, Set menu 29–39.
CC: Amex, Diners, Euro/Access, Visa.

Hotel Palmenhof ★★★ Bockenheimer Landstr 89-91, 60325 Frankfurt-am-Main.
☎ 069 7530060, Fax 069 75300666.
English spoken.
Open 02/01 to 23/12. 46 bedrooms (all en suite with telephone). Garage, parking.
RESTAURANT: Closed 23/12 to 02/01.

An oasis of quiet and comfort in this busy city! Tastefully decorated and a successful blend of antique and modern furniture. Good restaurant offering a warm welcome.

TARIFF: Single 180–220, Double 280–310, Set menu 45–48.
CC: Amex, Diners, Euro/Access, Visa.

Queens Hotel ★★★★ Isenburger Schneise 40, 60528 Frankfurt-am-Main.
☎ 069 67840, Fax 069 674861. English spoken.
Open all year. 278 bedrooms (all en suite with telephone). Golf 2 km, garage, restaurant.

The hotel is in a splendid location between Sachsenhausen and the Rhein-Main airport, in Germany's largest stretch of urban woodland, 2 km from the motorway A3.

TARIFF: Single 270–340, Double 350–420, Bk 23.
CC: Amex, Diners, Euro/Access, Visa.

FREIBURG IM BREISGAU 16C

Hotel Rappen Münsterpl 13, 7800 Freiburg.
☎ 0761 31353, Fax 0761 382252.
English spoken.
Open all year. 20 bedrooms (13 en suite, 20 telephone). Restaurant.

Comfortable, cosy hotel in the pedestrian zone. Typical Black Forest hospitality, restaurant with regional specialities.

TARIFF: Single 65–140, Double 110–180.
CC: Amex, Diners, Euro/Access, Visa.

Silence Waldhotel ★★★ Badstr 67,
79295 Bad Sulzburg.
☏ 07634 8270, Fax 07634 8212.
English spoken.
Open 15/02 to 10/01. 35 bedrooms
(all en suite with telephone). Indoor
swimming pool, tennis, golf 20 km, garage,
parking, restaurant.

In a beautiful, quiet position surrounded by
trees in the Black Forest. French cuisine.
20 km from French and Swiss borders. Sauna
and solarium. 30 km south of Freiburg,
Sulzburg is a tiny place in Markgrafterland.
TARIFF: Single 88–98, Double 130–172,
Set menu 42–78.
cc: Diners, Euro/Access, Visa.

FREUDENSTADT   16D

Gasthof See Forstrasse 15-17,
72250 Freudenstadt.
☏ 07441 2688, Fax 07441 1527.
English spoken.
Open 05/05 to 20/10. 25 bedrooms
(10 en suite). Garage, parking.
RESTAURANT: Closed Wed.

Family-run hotel in pedestrian area between
market square and railway station
Stadtbahnhof, 100 m away. Sun terrace.
TARIFF: Single 43–55, Double 80–106,
Set menu 19.50–40.
cc: Amex, Diners, Euro/Access, Visa.

Hotel Sonne Am Kurpark - Ringhotel
★★★★ Turnhallestrasse 63,
72250 Freudenstadt.
☏ 07441 6044, Fax 07441 6300. English spoken.

Open all year. 37 bedrooms (all en suite
with telephone). Indoor swimming pool,
golf 1 km, garage, parking, restaurant.

Quietly situated in the centre of Freudenstadt
and connected with the Kurhaus (casino) and
Peacock Pub. Solarium, sauna, horse-riding.

TARIFF: Single 120–170, Double 200–290,
Set menu 25–65.
cc: Amex, Diners, Euro/Access, Visa.

FRIEDRICHSHAFEN   16D

Hotel Buchhorner Hof Friedrichstrasse 33,
7990 Friedrichshafen.
☏ 07541 2050, Fax 07541 32663.
Open all year. 65 bedrooms (all en suite).
TARIFF: (1993) Single 99–139, Double 150–190.
cc: Amex, Diners, Euro/Access, Visa.

FRIEDRICHSRUHE   15A

Hotel Schloss Waldhotel ★★★★
Schloss Waldhotel, 74639 Friedrichsruhe.
☏ 07941 60870, Fax 07941 61468.
English spoken.
Open all year. 49 bedrooms (all en suite).
Indoor swimming pool, outdoor swimming
pool, tennis, golf 1 km, garage, parking,
restaurant.

Built in 1712, this superb hotel was once a
hunting lodge. Excellent cuisine. Health, sports
and beauty centre.
TARIFF: Single 165–280, Double 290–520,
Bk 30, Set menu 130–200.
cc: Amex, Diners, Euro/Access, Visa.

GAMMERTINGEN   16D

Hotel Posthalterei ★★★
Sigmaringer Strasse 4, 7487 Gammertingen.
☏ 07574 876, Fax 07574 878. English spoken.
Open 26/12 to 23/12. 30 bedrooms
(all en suite with telephone). Golf 17 km,
parking, restaurant.

In the middle of the small town of
Gammertingen. Traditional building and very
cosy atmosphere. Beautiful countryside. On
the B32, 5 km north of Sigmaringen.
TARIFF: (1993) Single 85–138, Double 130–195,
Set menu 25–85.
cc: Amex, Diners, Euro/Access, Visa.

GARMISCH-PARTENKIRCHEN   17C

Hotel Clausing's Post ★★★ Marienplatz 12,
82467 Garmisch-Partenkirchen.
☏ 08821 7090, Fax 08821 709205.
English spoken.
Open all year. 42 bedrooms (all en suite
with telephone). Golf 3 km, restaurant.

Located in the centre of Garmisch. Because of
its many cultural treasures the hotel is known
as the 'Little jewel box of the Werdenfell
district'.

TARIFF: Single 100–160, Double 180–250,
Set menu 25–60.
CC: Amex, Diners, Euro/Access, Visa.

Hotel Garmischer Hof Chamonixstrasse 10,
82467 Garmisch-Partenkirchen.
☎ 08821 51091, Fax 08821 51440.
English spoken.
Open all year. 43 bedrooms (all en suite
with telephone). Parking.

*Chalet-style hotel in centre of town. Quiet
rooms with lovely mountain views from
balcony. Pretty gardens. Close to railway
station and swimming pool.*

TARIFF: Single 75–100, Double 140–180.
CC: Amex, Diners, Euro/Access, Visa.

Grand Hotel Sonnenbichl ★★★★★
Burgstr 97, 8100 Garmisch-Partenkirchen.
☎ 08821 7020, Fax 08821 702131.
English spoken.

Open all year. 93 bedrooms (all en suite
with telephone). Indoor swimming pool,
golf 8 km, parking, restaurant.

*Quiet location on a sunny hillside overlooking
Garmisch-Partenkirchen, the Wetterstein
mountain range and the Zugspitze. 2 km from
centre of Garmisch.*

TARIFF: Single 100–200, Double 225–300.
CC: Amex, Diners, Euro/Access, Visa.

Hotel Obermühle ★★★★ Mühlstrasse 22,
8100 Garmisch-Partenkirchen.
☎ 08821 7040, Fax 08821 704112. English spoken.
Open all year. 97 bedrooms (all en suite
with telephone). Indoor swimming pool,
golf 10 km, garage, parking, restaurant.

*The hotel is in Garmisch-Partenkirchen, a
delightful town at the foot of the Alps near the
Swiss border.*

TARIFF: Single 195–240, Double 250–325,
Set menu 35–100.

Posthotel ★★★★ Ludwigstr 49,
82467 Garmisch-Partenkirchen.
☎ 08821 51067, Fax 08821 78568. English spoken.

Open all year. 60 bedrooms (all en suite with
telephone). Golf 2 km, parking, restaurant.

*Warm, inviting hotel with tastefully decorated,
wood-panelled rooms. Centrally situated and
ten minutes from the railway station.*

TARIFF: Single 125–185, Double 220–280,
Set menu 35–70.
CC: Amex, Diners, Euro/Access, Visa.

Queens Hotel ★★★★ Mittenwalder Str 2,
82467 Garmisch-Partenkirchen.
☎ 08821 7560, Fax 08821 74268.
English spoken.
Open all year. 117 bedrooms (all en suite
with telephone). Indoor swimming pool,
tennis, golf 5 km, parking, restaurant.

*At the foot of the Alps, offering first-class comfort,
tastefully decorated rooms and quality
restaurant. The hotel is in the centre of town.*

TARIFF: Single 160–226, Double 230–302,
Set menu 32–79.
CC: Amex, Diners, Euro/Access, Visa.

Hotel Reindl's Hof ★★★★ Bahnhofstrasse 15,
8100 Garmisch-Partenkirchen.
☎ 08821 58025, Fax 08821 73401.
English spoken.
Open 15/12 to 15/11. 65 bedrooms
(all en suite with telephone). Indoor
swimming pool, golf 4 km, garage, restaurant.

*In the middle of the town but with quiet, well-
appointed rooms, each having balcony or
terrace and facing the Bavarian Alps. 23
luxury apartments also available. Renowned
gourmet restaurant "Reindl's" offers typical
Bavarian dishes.*

TARIFF: Single 120–160, Double 140–200,
Bk 17, Set menu 45–118.
CC: Amex, Diners, Euro/Access, Visa.

Germany

GELSENKIRCHEN 14C

Hotel Maritim ★★★★ Am Stadtgarten 1,
4650 Gelsenkirchen.
☎ 02091 760, Fax 02092 07075. English spoken.
Open all year. 230 bedrooms (all en suite
with telephone). Indoor swimming pool,
parking, restaurant.

*Modern hotel in the centre of the town.
Cocktail bar, discotheque, jazz club, sauna,
steam-bath, solarium. Easily reached from
three motorways (A2, A42, A430). Three
minutes from main station.*
TARIFF: (1993) Single 179−263,
Double 248−328, Set menu 40.
CC: Amex, Diners, Euro/Access, Visa.

GERA 17A

Hotel Gera Heinrichstrasse 30, O-6500 Gera.
☎ 0365 6930, Fax 0365 23449. English spoken.
Open all year. 303 bedrooms (all en suite
with telephone). Tennis, golf 1 km, garage,
parking, restaurant.

*A modern building in a central situation near
the main shopping street.*
TARIFF: (1993) Single 135−195,
Double 225−280.
CC: Amex, Diners, Euro/Access, Visa.

GLOTTERTAL 16C

Hotel Zum Adler Talstr 11, 79286 Glottertal.
☎ 07684 1081, Fax 07684 1083. English spoken.

Open all year. 12 bedrooms (all en suite
with telephone). Parking.
RESTAURANT: Closed Tues.

*Well known for its famous gourmet restaurant,
wines and relaxing atmosphere. Located in a
romantic valley in the southern Black Forest
(8 miles to Freiburg). Old, typical Black Forest
'Gasthous' with local and seasonal specialities.
Home-made wines and brandies.*

TARIFF: Single 40−100, Double 70−160,
Set menu 18−40.
CC: Diners, Euro/Access, Visa.

GOPPINGEN 16D

Hotel Höhenstauffen Freihofstrasse 64-66,
7320 Goppingen.
☎ 07161 70077.
Open all year. 48 bedrooms (all en suite).
TARIFF: (1993) Single 85−130, Double 120−170.
CC: Amex, Diners, Euro/Access, Visa.

GOSLAR 14D

Hotel Landhaus Grauhof Am Grauhof-
Brunnen, Goslar-Grauhof, 3380 Goslar.
☎ 05321 84001, Fax 05321 50958.
Open 01/03 to 31/01. 46 bedrooms
(21 en suite, 26 telephone). Tennis, golf 6 km,
parking.
RESTAURANT: Closed Thurs.

*Situated in the small village of Grauhof and
close to the Harz Mountains. Renovated in
1991; German and international cuisine.
4 km from centre of Goslar.*
TARIFF: (1993) Single 60−120, Double 100−170,
Set menu 24−33.
CC: Amex, Euro/Access, Visa.

GRAFENAU 17D

Steigenberger Hotel ★★★★ Sonnenstr 12,
Sonnenhof, 8352 Grafenau.
☎ 08552 448, Fax 08552 4680. English spoken.

Open all year. 193 bedrooms (all en suite
with telephone). Indoor swimming pool,
outdoor swimming pool, tennis, garage,
parking, restaurant.

*Splendid location overlooking Grafenau and
close to city centre. Very comfortable hotel with
excellent facilities including health, fitness
and beauty centre. Good area for winter sports.*

TARIFF: Single 119–140, Double 208–248,
Set menu 30–50.
CC: Amex, Diners, Euro/Access, Visa.

GUTACH IM BREISGAU 16C

Hotel Stollen Elzacheistrasse 2,
7809 Gutach im Breisgau.
☎ 07685 207, Fax 07685 1550.
Open all year. 10 bedrooms (all en suite).
TARIFF: (1993) Single 80–105, Double 130–190.
CC: none.

HAGEN 14C

Queens Hotel ★★★ Wasserloses Tal 4,
58093 Hagen.
☎ 02331 3910, Fax 02331 391153.
English spoken.
Open all year. 147 bedrooms (all en suite
with telephone). Indoor swimming pool,
parking, restaurant.

*The dramatically-styled architecture of the
hotel dominates this part of Hagen. Close to the
A45 motorway, on the edge of the beautiful
Sauerland hills and offering the visitor an
ideal base for walks and nearby sporting
activities.*
TARIFF: Single 175–233, Double 236–293,
Set menu 40–90.
CC: Amex, Diners, Euro/Access, Visa.

HALVER-CARTHAUSEN 14C

Haus Frommann Halver Strasse,
5884 Halver-Carthausen.
☎ 02353 611, Fax 02353 5113.
Open all year. 22 bedrooms (all en suite).
TARIFF: (1993) Single 79–91,
Double 116–138.
CC: Amex, Diners, Euro/Access, Visa.

HAMBURG 14B

Hotel Graf Moltke Steindamm 1,
2000 Hamburg.
☎ 040 2801154, Fax 040 2802562.
English spoken.
Open all year. 97 bedrooms (all en suite
with telephone).
RESTAURANT: Closed Wed till 9 pm.

*Approaching the city by car, watch for signs to
Hauptbahnhof or Centrum. The hotel is
situated directly at the Hauptbahnhof, in the
city centre.*
TARIFF: Single 135, Double 175,
Set menu 18–29.
CC: Amex, Diners, Euro/Access, Visa.

Aussen Alster Hotel ★★★★
Schmilinskystr 11-13,
20099 Hamburg.
☎ 040 241557, Fax 040 2803231.
English spoken.
Open all year. 27 bedrooms (all en suite
with telephone). Golf 1 km, restaurant.

*Small, elegant and comfortable hotel with
pretty patio and garden in quiet, central
location. Italian-style restaurant.*

TARIFF: Single 180–210, Double 280–310,
Set menu 49–69.
CC: Amex, Diners, Euro/Access, Visa.

Travel Hotel Bellevue An der Alster 14,
20099 Hamburg.
☎ 040 248011, Fax 040 2803380.
English spoken.

Open all year. 80 bedrooms (all en suite
with telephone). Golf 12 km, garage, parking,
restaurant.

*Central location, 10 minutes' walk from
station. Overlooking beautiful Alster lake and
15 minutes' walk to two major shopping streets.*
TARIFF: Single 160–195, Double 230–260.
CC: Amex, Diners, Euro/Access, Visa.

Hotel Hamburg International ★★★
Hammer Landstrasse 200, 20537 Hamburg.
℡ 040 211401, Fax 040 211409. English spoken.
Open all year. 112 bedrooms (all en suite
with telephone). Garage, parking, restaurant.

*Comfortable, conveniently situated hotel with
modern facilities. Excellent buffet breakfast.
Conference facilities.*

TARIFF: Single 125–195, Double 170–275.
CC: Amex, Diners, Euro/Access, Visa.

Hotel Imperial Am Millerntorplatz 3-5,
2000 Hamburg.
℡ 040 3196021, Fax 040 315685.
English spoken.
Open all year. 65 bedrooms (40 en suite,
40 telephone). Parking.

*On the corner by the Reeperbahn, opposite the
theatre.*

TARIFF: (1993) Single 85–95, Double 130–150.
CC: Amex, Diners, Euro/Access, Visa.

Queens Hotel ★★★★ Mexikoring 1,
22297 Hamburg.
℡ 040 632940, Fax 040 6322472.
English spoken.
Open all year. 181 bedrooms (all en suite
with telephone). Golf 15 km, garage, parking,
restaurant.

*Close to the city centre and 10 minutes from
the beautiful Stadtpark. Roman steam-bath,
sauna, fitness equipment. Excellent cuisine
with seafood specialities. Follow signs to City
Nord and take motorway Ring 2. Special
weekend rates available.*

TARIFF: Single 235, Double 280, Bk 23,
Set menu 39.
CC: Amex, Diners, Euro/Access, Visa.

Hotel Ramada Renaissance ★★★★★
Grosse Bleichen, 2000 Hamburg.
℡ 040 349180, Fax 040 34918431. English spoken.
Open all year. 211 bedrooms (all en suite
with telephone). Tennis, golf 20 km, parking,
restaurant. &

*The hotel is located right in the city centre,
12 km from Hamburg International Airport,
1 km from bus and train stations and 10
minutes' drive from motorway (A1).*

TARIFF: (1993) Single 275–385,
Double 325–455, Bk 27, Set menu 49–125.
CC: Amex, Diners, Euro/Access, Visa.

HAMELN   14D

Hotel Zur Borse Osterstrasse 41a, 3250 Hameln.
℡ 05151 7080, Fax 05151 25485.

Open all year. 34 bedrooms (all en suite
with telephone).
TARIFF: (1993) Single 55–59, Double 110.
CC: Amex, Diners, Euro/Access, Visa.

Hotel Zur Krone Osterstr 30, 31785 Hameln.
℡ 05151 9070, Fax 05151 907217.
English spoken.
Open all year. 34 bedrooms (all en suite
with telephone). Golf 10 km, garage,
restaurant.

*In the centre of the historical part of town, this
timbered house/hotel has old, interesting
rooms together with modern-day comforts.*

TARIFF: Single 140–240, Double 190–420,
Bk 15, Set menu 19–49.
CC: Amex, Diners, Euro/Access, Visa.

HAMM   14C

Queens Hotel Hamm ★★★★ Neue
Bahnhofstr 3, 59065 Hamm.
℡ 02381 91920, Fax 02381 9192833.
English spoken.
Open all year. 273 bedrooms (all en suite
with telephone). Indoor swimming pool,
garage, restaurant. &

*In the city centre of Hamm, 500 m from the
station.*

TARIFF: Single 190–220, Double 245–265, Bk 22.
CC: Amex, Diners, Euro/Access, Visa.

HANNOVER   14D

Hotel Föhrenhof Kirchhorster Strasse 22,
3000 Hannover.
℡ 0511 61721, Fax 0511 619719.
Open all year. 78 bedrooms (all en suite).
TARIFF: (1993) Single 150–300,
Double 200–340.
CC: Amex, Diners, Euro/Access, Visa.

Queens Hotel ★★★★ Tiergartenstrasse 117,
30559 Hannover.
℡ 0511 51030, Fax 0511 526924.
English spoken.
Open all year. 176 bedrooms (all en suite with
telephone). Garage, parking, restaurant. &

*Located in a 250-acre deer park where guests
can relax among the greenery, and yet be only
a few minutes' from the city and the
motorway.*

TARIFF: Single 235–394, Double 315–500.
CC: Amex, Diners, Euro/Access, Visa.

Hotel Romantik-Georgenhof Herrenhäuser
Kirchweg 20, 3000 Hannover.
℡ 0511 702244, Fax 0511 708559.
English spoken.

Open all year. 20 bedrooms (14 en suite, 14 telephone). Indoor swimming pool, outdoor swimming pool, tennis, golf 2 km, parking, restaurant.

Situated in the suburbs of Hannover, but nevertheless only 5 minutes' drive from the city centre. Very quiet, standing in beautiful grounds and near the world-famous Herrenhäuser Gardens. Elegant furnishings and excellent restaurant.

TARIFF: (1993) Single 140–200, Double 200–300.
CC: Amex, Diners, Euro/Access, Visa.

HASELÜNNE 14C

Burghotel Steintorstrasse 7, 4473 Haselünne.
☎ 05961 1544.
Open all year. 17 bedrooms (16 en suite).
TARIFF: (1993) Single 50–65, Double 85–115.
CC: Amex, Diners, Euro/Access, Visa.

HASSMERSHEIM/HOCHHAUSEN 16B

Hotel Schloss Hochhausen
6954 Hassmersheim/Hochhausen.
☎ 06261 3142.
Open all year. 12 bedrooms (10 en suite).
TARIFF: (1993) Single 65–70, Double 120.
CC: none.

HEIDELBERG 16B

Hotel Alt Heidelberg ★★★
Röhrbacherstrasse 29, 6900 Heidelberg.
☎ 06221 9150, Fax 06221 164272.
English spoken.
Open all year. 80 bedrooms (all en suite with telephone). Garage, parking, restaurant.

One of the Best Western group. This is a comfortable, traditional hotel with modern management. Sophisticated furnishings, individual character. In Heidelberg, follow sign for Schloss. Turn right at traffic lights on Adenauer-Platz towards Röhrbach. Hotel is 200 m on left.

TARIFF: Single 195–210, Double 230–250.
CC: Amex, Diners, Euro/Access, Visa.

Der EuropÄisch Hof, Hotel Europa ★★★★★
Friedrich-Ebert-Anlage 1, 69117 Heidelberg.
☎ 06221 5150, Fax 06221 515555.
English spoken.
Open all year. 135 bedrooms (all en suite with telephone). Golf 20 km, garage.

Within walking distance of the castle, this hotel has the atmosphere of a traditional European grand hotel. Managed by the owner, with

exclusive service and international standards of efficiency.

TARIFF: Single 279–319, Double 360–420, Bk 27.
CC: Amex, Diners, Euro/Access, Visa.

Hotel Neckar ★★ Bismarkstrasse 19, 6900 Heidelberg.
☎ 06221 10814, Fax 06221 23260.
English spoken.
Open all year. 35 bedrooms (all en suite with telephone). Parking.

Modern hotel on the banks of the River Neckar and next to the Bismark Gardens.

TARIFF: Single 140–180, Double 170–240.
CC: Amex, Euro/Access, Visa.

Queens Hotel ★★★★ Pleikartförsterstrasse 101, 69124 Heidelberg.
☎ 06221 7880, Fax 06221 788499.
English spoken.
Open all year. 169 bedrooms (all en suite with telephone). Parking, restaurant. &

The hotel is only minutes away from the historic old town and not far from the A5. Executive rooms, suites and non-smoker rooms available on request. Sauna and fitness area.

TARIFF: Single 180–250, Double 220–290, Bk 23.
CC: Amex, Diners, Euro/Access, Visa.

Hotel Zum Ritter ★★ Neckarstrasse 40, 69151 Neckargemund.
☎ 06223 7035, Fax 06223 73339.
English spoken.

Open all year. 40 bedrooms (all en suite with telephone). Golf 15 km, garage, restaurant.

The hotel is 10 km from Heidelberg, on the River Neckar. Dating back to 1286, it was once a hunting lodge. From A6, exit at Sinsheim or A5, exit at Heidelberg.

TARIFF: Single 95–150, Double 120–210.
CC: Amex, Euro/Access, Visa.

Germany

HEILBRONN 16D

Hotel Arcade Weinsbergerstrasse 29, 7100 Heilbronn.
📞 069 108880.
Open all year. 51 bedrooms (all en suite with telephone).
TARIFF: (1993) Single 115–120, Double 145–150.
CC: Amex, Diners, Euro/Access, Visa.

HEITERSHEIM 16C

Landhotel Krone ★★ Haupstr 7, 79423 Heitersheim.
📞 07634 2811, Fax 07634 4588. English spoken.
Open all year. 15 bedrooms (all en suite with telephone). Garage, parking, restaurant.
Family-run hotel dating back to 1777. Warm, inviting interior with traditional furnishings; pretty terrace and good restaurant. About 20 km south of Freiburg.
TARIFF: Single 85–120, Double 118–180.
CC: Visa.

HINTERZARTEN 16C

Parkhotel Adler ★★★★★ Adlerplatz 3, 7824 Hinterzarten.
📞 07652 1270, Fax 07652 127717.
English spoken.
Open all year. 73 bedrooms (all en suite with telephone). Indoor swimming pool, tennis, golf 18 km, garage, parking, restaurant.
Beautiful hotel in Black Forest and set in parkland. Fitness centre, sauna, jacuzzi and massage. Varied cuisine. Hinterzarten is 1.5 km west of Titisee-Neustadt, off B31.
TARIFF: Single 160–350, Double 270–470.
CC: Amex, Diners, Euro/Access, Visa.

HOCHENSCHWAND 16C

Hotel Fernblick Im Grun 15, 7821 Hochenschwand.
📞 07672 766.
Open all year. 35 bedrooms (27 en suite).
TARIFF: (1993) Single 40–50, Double 50–90.
CC: Amex, Diners, Euro/Access, Visa.

INGOLSTADT 17C

Parkhotel Heidehof ★★★★ Ingoldstädter Strasse 121, Gamersheim, 85080 Ingolstädt.
📞 08458 640, Fax 08458 64230. English spoken.
Open all year. 104 bedrooms (all en suite with telephone). Indoor swimming pool, outdoor swimming pool, tennis, golf 7 km, garage, parking, restaurant. ♿

Modern, spacious, hotel. Facilities include superb health/fitness centre in a most attractive natural stone setting. Café, bistro, conference room.
TARIFF: Single 130–160, Double 180–236, Set menu 20–110.
CC: Amex, Diners, Euro/Access, Visa.

Queens Hotel-Ambassador ★★★
Goëthestrasse 153, 85055 Ingolstädt.
📞 08415 030, Fax 08415 037. English spoken.
Open all year. 119 bedrooms (all en suite with telephone). Indoor swimming pool, tennis, parking, restaurant.
Located near the old town and easily accessible from A9. 500 m from the Danube. Modern hotel with sauna, solarium and à la carte restaurant.
TARIFF: Single 168–188, Double 200–225, Bk 21, Set menu 35–85.
CC: Amex, Diners, Euro/Access, Visa.

IPHOFEN 16B

Hotel Zehntkeller Bahnhofstrasse 12, 8715 Iphofen.
📞 09323 3062, Fax 09323 1519.
Open all year. 43 bedrooms (all en suite).
TARIFF: (1993) Single 90–120, Double 140–190.
CC: Amex, Diners, Euro/Access, Visa.

ISSELBURG 14C

Parkhotel Wasserburg Anholt Klever Str 2, Anholt, 4294 Isselburg.
📞 02874 2044, Fax 03874 4035.
Open all year. 28 bedrooms (all en suite).
TARIFF: (1993) Single 135–155, Double 185–350.
CC: Amex, Diners, Euro/Access, Visa.

KAINSBACH 17A

Hotel Kainsbacher Mühle ★★★★ Hersbruck, 91230 Kainsbach.
📞 09151 7280, Fax 09151 728162.
English spoken.
Open all year. 34 bedrooms (all en suite with telephone). Indoor swimming pool, tennis, golf 12 km, garage, parking, restaurant.
Set in beautiful countryside and surrounded by lovely gardens and parkland. Very comfortable rooms with warm, relaxing colour schemes. Stylish restaurant offering good low-calorie menu. Health farm and good sports facilities; sailing and windsurfing nearby.
SEE ADJACENT ADVERTISEMENT

Germany

TARIFF: Single 110–140, Double 211–240, Set menu 55–75.
CC: none.

KAISERSBACH 16D

Hotel Schassbergers Hirsch Ebnisee ★★★★
Winnender Str 10, 73667 Kaisersbach.
☎ 07184 2920, Fax 07184 292204.
English spoken.
Open all year. 49 bedrooms (all en suite with telephone). Indoor swimming pool, outdoor swimming pool, tennis, golf 9 km, garage, parking, restaurant.

An exclusive country hotel directly on the Ebnisee. In the middle of the Forest, in a protected area - the upper Germanic Limes. Once a Roman outpost. With a spa, a health, beauty, fitness and sport centre. About 45 km north-east of Stuttgart.
TARIFF: Single 155–350, Double 200–490, Set menu 69–95.
CC: Amex, Euro/Access, Visa.

Hotel Wirtshaus Am Ebnisee ★★★
Ebnisee 2, 73667 Kaisersbach.
☎ 07184 292239, Fax 07184 292204.
English spoken.

Germany

Open all year. 18 bedrooms (all en suite).
Outdoor swimming pool, tennis, golf 1 km,
garage, parking.
RESTAURANT: Closed Mon.

*45 km north-east of Stuttgart, directly on the
banks of the Ebnisee. Very pretty countryside.*
TARIFF: Single 62.50–72.50, Double 100–135,
Set menu 22–45.
CC: none.

KAISERSLAUTERN 16A

Hotel Schweizer Stuben Konigstr 9,
6750 Kaiserslautern.
☎ 0631 13088.
Open all year. 11 bedrooms (all en suite).
TARIFF: (1993) Single 72–77, Double 107–111.
CC: Amex, Diners, Euro/Access, Visa.

KALTENKIRCHEN 14B

Hotel Kaltenkirchener Hof Alveslöher
Strasse 2, 2358 Kaltenkirchen.
☎ 04191 7861.
Open all year. 24 bedrooms (all en suite).
TARIFF: (1993) Single 75–90, Double 110–130.
CC: Amex, Diners, Euro/Access, Visa.

KARLSRUHE 16D

Hotel Eden Bahnhofstrasse 15-19,
7500 Karlsruhe.
☎ 0721 18180, Fax 0721 181822.
English spoken.
Open all year. 68 bedrooms (all en suite
with telephone). Garage, restaurant.

*Family owned and managed, this newly
renovated hotel is in a central but quiet
location with a large garden. Close to railway
station, Zoological Gardens and Congress and
shopping area.*
TARIFF: Single 140–150, Double 188–208,
Set menu 35–80.
CC: Amex, Diners, Euro/Access, Visa.

Hotel Kubler Bismarckstrasse 39-43,
7500 Karlsruhe.
☎ 0721 1440, Fax 0721 22639.
Open all year. 97 bedrooms (95 en suite).
TARIFF: (1993) Single 68–148, Double 120–220.
CC: Amex, Diners, Euro/Access, Visa.

Queens Hotel ★★★★ Kongresszentrum,
Ettlinger Strasse 23, 76137 Karlsruhe.
☎ 0721 37270, Fax 0721 3727170.
English spoken.
Open all year. 147 bedrooms (all en suite
with telephone). Parking, restaurant.

*By the conference and exhibition centre and
near the palace. Ideal for business travellers,
conference delegates and holidaymakers alike.
Rooms have cable TV, radio. Executive floor.
500 m to intercity station.*
TARIFF: Single 205–245, Double 245–285, Bk 21.
CC: Amex, Euro/Access, Visa.

Schlosshotel ★★★★ Bahnhofplatz 2,
7500 Karlsruhe.
☎ 0721 35040, Fax 0721 3504413.
English spoken.
Open all year. 96 bedrooms (all en suite with
telephone). Golf 10 km, parking, restaurant.

*Comfortable hotel with choice of restaurants
and good conference facilities. From
motorway, take exit for Karlsruhe-Mitte, then
go towards Hauptbahnhof. Close to railway
station.*
TARIFF: Single 155–185, Double 200–270,
Bk 18, Set menu 35.
CC: Amex, Euro/Access, Visa.

KASSEL 14D

Queens Hotel ★★★ Heiligenroder Strasse 61,
34123 Kassel.
☎ 05615 2050, Fax 05615 27400.
English spoken.
Open all year. 142 bedrooms (all en suite
with telephone). Indoor swimming pool,
parking, restaurant. &

*Close to A7, exit Kassel-Nord; from centre of
town go towards A7 (Hannover/Frankfurt).*
TARIFF: Single 195–235, Double 245–285, Bk 19.
CC: Amex, Diners, Euro/Access, Visa.

KELHEIM 17C

Hotel Ehrnthaller Donaustrasse 22,
8420 Kelheim.
☎ 09441 3333.
Open all year. 41 bedrooms (all en suite).
TARIFF: (1993) Single 55–75, Double 88–120.
CC: Amex, Diners, Euro/Access, Visa.

KEMPTEN 16D

Hotel Bahnhof Mozartstrasse, 8960 Kempten.
☎ 0831 22073, Fax 0831 10194.
Open all year. 40 bedrooms (37 en suite).
TARIFF: (1993) Single 48, Double 100.
CC: Amex, Diners, Euro/Access, Visa.

KERPEN 16A

Hotel Park ★★ Kerpenerstrasse 183,
5014 Kerpen-Sindorf.
☎ 02273 570094, Fax 02273 54985.
English spoken.

Open all year. 25 bedrooms (all en suite with telephone). Golf 10 km, garage, parking, restaurant.

Small, modern hotel. Leave A4 (Aachen to Köln) at Kerpen exit. Turn left for 500 m.

TARIFF: Single 75–95, Double 110–145, Set menu 18–45.

CC: Amex, Diners, Euro/Access, Visa.

KESTERT   16A

Hotel Goldener Stern Rheinstrasse 38, 56348 Kestert.

☎ 06773 7102, Fax 06773 7104.
English spoken.
Open all year. 10 bedrooms (all en suite with telephone). Parking.
RESTAURANT: Closed Mon.

Family run since 1779, the hotel stands on the banks of the Rhein. Completely renovated, it now provides comfortable accommodation with modern-day facilities. 8 km from Loreley. On the B42, 30 km south of Koblenz.

TARIFF: Single 45–65, Double 70–95, Set menu 14–50.

CC: Amex, Diners, Euro/Access, Visa.

KIEL   14B

Avance Conti-Hansa ★★★★ Schlossgarten 7, 24103 Kiel.

☎ 0431 51150, Fax 0431 5115444.
English spoken.
Open all year. 167 bedrooms (all en suite with telephone). Golf 10 km, garage, restaurant. ⚹

Modern and comfortable in downtown location. Opposite Oslo Kai and 5 minute drive from main station or Kiel to Hamburg motorway. Very good conference facilities.

TARIFF: Single 215–290, Double 260–340, Set menu 45–85.

CC: Amex, Diners, Euro/Access, Visa.

Parkhotel Kieler Kaufmann
Niemannsweg 102, 2300 Kiel.
☎ 0431 88110, Fax 0431 8811135.
English spoken.
Open all year. 47 bedrooms (all en suite with telephone). Indoor swimming pool, golf 10 km, parking, restaurant.

Most attractive hotel quietly situated in its own park-like grounds. Elegant but cosy restaurant specialising in regional and French cuisine.

TARIFF: Single 175–195, Double 220–300, Set menu 45–105.

CC: Amex, Diners, Euro/Access, Visa.

Hotel Wiking ★★ Schutzenwall 1-3, 2300 Kiel.
☎ 0431 673051, Fax 0431 673054.
English spoken.

Open all year. 42 bedrooms (all en suite with telephone). Garage, parking.
RESTAURANT: Closed Monday lunch.

In the centre of Kiel, close to motorway, railway station and ferries. Modern comfort and French restaurant. Sauna, solarium. From motorway exit at Kiel, follow the Schutzenwall 600 m to the hotel on the right.

TARIFF: Single 105–130, Double 160–195, Set menu 45–90.

CC: Amex, Diners, Euro/Access, Visa.

KOBLENZ   16A

Hotel Hamm St Josefstrasse 32, 56068 Koblenz.
☎ 0261 34546, Fax 0261 160972.
English spoken.
Open 15/01 to 15/12. 30 bedrooms (all en suite with telephone). Garage, parking.

City hotel, near main railway station. 1 km from arrival/departure point of Rhein and Mosel steamers.

TARIFF: Single 60–90, Double 130–160.

CC: Amex, Diners, Euro/Access, Visa.

Hotel Kleiner Riesen Jaiserin Augusta Anlagen 18, 56068 Koblenz.
☎ 0261 32077, Fax 0261 160725.
English spoken.
Open all year. 50 bedrooms (all en suite with telephone). Golf 15 km, garage, parking.

Situated on the banks of the Rhein in a pretty park.

TARIFF: Single 100–180, Double 150–220.

CC: Amex, Diners, Euro/Access, Visa.

Germany

City Hotel Metropol ★★★
Munzplatz/Altstadt, 56068 Koblenz.
📞 0261 35060, Fax 0261 160366.
English spoken.

Open all year. 50 bedrooms (47 en suite, 47 telephone). Garage, parking, restaurant. ♿
Historic setting in old town. Modern hotel, all rooms with TV. Bistro restaurant with traditional German fare, 50 m to swimming pool and fitness centre.
TARIFF: Single 90–170, Double 150–280.
CC: Amex, Diners, Euro/Access, Visa.

KÖLN (COLOGNE)   16A

Haus Lyskirchen Filzengraben 26-32, 5000 Köln.
📞 0221 20970, Fax 0221 2097718.
Open all year. 95 bedrooms (all en suite).
TARIFF: (1993) Single 150–250, Double 190–320.
CC: Amex, Diners, Euro/Access, Visa.

Hotel Merian Allerheiligenstr 1, 5000 Köln.
📞 0221 1665, Fax 0221 16650.
English spoken.
Open 06/01 to 20/12. 32 bedrooms (all en suite with telephone). Garage.
Modern hotel, quiet rooms with TV. In the centre of Köln behind the main station and near the cathedral, museum and shopping centre.
TARIFF: (1993) Single 120–185, Double 145–280.
CC: none.

Hotel Pullman Mondial ★★★ Kurt-Hackenber-Platz 1, 5000 Köln.
📞 0221 20630, Fax 0221 2063522.
English spoken.
Open all year. 204 bedrooms (all en suite with telephone). Parking, restaurant. ♿
In the centre of Köln, near the cathedral, the Rhein, the old town and the shopping area. Close to the main railway station.
TARIFF: Single 193–330, Double 214–355, Bk 22.
CC: Amex, Diners, Euro/Access, Visa.

Queens Hotel ★★★ Dürener Strasse 287, 50935 Köln.
📞 0221 46760, Fax 0221 433765. English spoken.
Open all year. 147 bedrooms (all en suite with telephone). Garage, parking, restaurant. ♿
Surrounded by trees and beautifully tended parkland, right on the Stadtwaldweiher. Well placed for access, within minutes of the motorway junction Köln-West and Köln city.
TARIFF: Single 261–435, Double 352–540, Set menu 35.
CC: Amex, Diners, Euro/Access, Visa.

Hotel Regent Melatengurtel 15, 5000 Köln.
📞 0221 54990, Fax 0221 5499998.
Open all year. 168 bedrooms (all en suite).
TARIFF: (1993) Single 203–333, Double 291–436.
CC: Amex, Diners, Euro/Access, Visa.

Hotel Im Wasserturm ★★★★★ Kaygasse 2, 50676 Köln.
📞 0221 20080, Fax 0221 2008888. English spoken.
Open all year. 90 bedrooms (all en suite with telephone). Golf 5 km, garage, parking, restaurant.
This extraordinary, circular building was formerly an historic water tower erected in 1872 and was converted into a luxury hotel in 1990. It stands in a city centre park with easy access to the road network. 500 m to Neumarkt, 1.5 km to the cathedral, 3 km to the exhibition halls. From A3, take A4 to Aachen. Exit at Köln-Deutz, then to Severinsbrücke. Over bridge, left at first traffic lights, first right into Poststrasse. Second right (Grosser Griechenmarkt) and first right into Kaygasse.
TARIFF: Single 370–480, Double 480–2400, Bk 29, Set menu 49–130.
CC: Amex, Diners, Euro/Access, Visa.

KONSTANTZ   16D

Seehotel Siber Seestrasse 25, 7750 Konstantz.
📞 07531 63044, Fax 07531 64813.
Open all year. 11 bedrooms (all en suite).
TARIFF: (1993) Double 320–380.
CC: Amex, Diners, Euro/Access, Visa.

KREFELD   14C

Parkhotel Krefelder Hof ★★★★
Uerdinger Strasse 245, 4150 Krefeld.
📞 02151 5840, Fax 02151 58435.
English spoken.

Germany

Open all year. 178 bedrooms (150 en suite,
150 telephone). Indoor swimming pool,
golf 5 km, garage, restaurant. &

*Set in a private park, this large, modern hotel
offers peace and quiet and easy access to all
major routes. 3 restaurants, sauna, solarium,
fitness and massage rooms. Open-air terraces.
25 km from Düsseldorf and its airport.*

TARIFF: Single 210–295, Double 300–400,
Set menu 40–150.
cc: Amex, Diners, Euro/Access, Visa.

KRONBERG   16B

Schlosshotel Kronberg Hainstrasse 25,
6242 Kronberg.
℡ 06173 70101.
Open all year. 57 bedrooms (all en suite).
TARIFF: (1993) Single 250–350,
Double 370–570.
cc: Amex, Diners, Euro/Access, Visa.

KRONENBURG   16A

Hotel Schloss Das Burghaus Burgbering 1-4,
5377 Kronenburg.
℡ 06557 1265, Fax 06557 11397.
English spoken.
Open all year. 13 bedrooms (all en suite).
Parking.
RESTAURANT: Closed Tues.

*Very quiet position. From A1, exit at
Blankenheim-Dahlem and take B51 towards
Trier, turning right to Kronenburg. The hotel is
at the end of village.*

TARIFF: Single 55–65, Double 75–160,
Set menu 25–45.
cc: Diners, Euro/Access, Visa.

LAMPERTHEIM   16B

Hotel Deutsches Haus ★★ Kaiserstrasse 47,
6840 Lampertheim.
℡ 06206 2022, Fax 06206 2024. English spoken.
Open 10/01 to 31/12. 31 bedrooms
(all en suite with telephone). Parking,
restaurant.

*Situated in the centre of town and 5 minutes
walk from the station.*

TARIFF: (1993) Single 75–80, Double 120–130,
Bk 80, Set menu 20–31.
cc: Amex, Diners, Euro/Access, Visa.

LANDSHUT   17C

Hotel Fürstenhof Stethaimerstrasse 6,
8300 Landshut.
℡ 0871 82025, Fax 0871 89042.

Open all year. 22 bedrooms (all en suite).
TARIFF: (1993) Single 165, Double 178.
cc: Amex, Diners, Euro/Access, Visa.

LANGENAU   16D

Hotel Weisses Ross Hindenburgstrasse 29-31,
7907 Langenau.
℡ 07345 8010, Fax 07345 80151.
Open all year. 72 bedrooms (all en suite).
cc: Amex, Diners, Euro/Access, Visa.

LEIPZIG   15C

Hotel Inter Continental Leipzig ★★★★★
Gerberstr 15, 04105 Leipzig.
℡ 0341 7990, Fax 0341 7991229.
English spoken.
Open all year. 447 bedrooms (all en suite
with telephone). Indoor swimming pool,
parking, restaurant. &

*Situated in the heart of the city, this is the
tallest building in Leipzig. Comfortable,
elegantly furnished rooms and new
restaurants. Excellent conference facilities.*

TARIFF: Single 290–350, Double 320–440,
Bk 29, Set menu 39–65.
cc: Amex, Diners, Euro/Access, Visa.

LIMBURG-AN-DER-LAHN   16A

Hotel Dom Grabenstrasse 57,
6250 Limburg-an-der-Lahn.
℡ 06431 24077, Fax 06431 6850.
Open all year. 59 bedrooms (51 en suite).
TARIFF: (1993) Single 86–145, Double 140–190.
cc: Amex, Diners, Euro/Access, Visa.

Hotel Zimmermann ★★★ Blumenroder
Strasse 1, 65549 Limburg-an-der-Lahn.
℡ 06431 4611, Fax 06431 41314. English spoken.
Open 05/01 to 20/12. 30 bedrooms
(25 en suite, 25 telephone). Golf 15 km,
garage, parking.
RESTAURANT: Closed Fri & Sun.

*An English-style hotel with a romantic
atmosphere. Furnished with antiques, original
paintings and Italian marble. Limburg is an
historic old town with an 800-year-old
cathedral. On the A3 between Frankfurt and
Köln.*

TARIFF: Single 135–205, Double 148–285.
cc: Amex, Diners, Euro/Access, Visa.

LINDAU IM BODENSEE   16D

Hotel Bayerischer Hof Seepromenade,
88131 Lindau im Bodensee.
℡ 08382 5055, Fax 08382 5054. English spoken.

Germany

Open 01/04 to 30/11. 106 bedrooms
(all en suite with telephone). Outdoor
swimming pool, golf 4 km, garage, parking,
restaurant.

*On the island's traffic-free promenade, with
magnificent south-facing view over the lake to
the Austrian and Swiss Alps. 1,300 feet above
sea level. Close to railway station, harbour and
landing stage.*

TARIFF: Single 139–242, Double 242–494,
Set menu 51–64.
CC: Diners, Euro/Access, Visa.

Hotel Reutemann Seepromenade,
88131 Lindau im Bodensee.
☎ 08382 5055, Fax 08382 5054. English spoken.
Open all year. 37 bedrooms (all en suite
with telephone). Outdoor swimming pool,
golf 4 km, garage, parking, restaurant.

*1,300 feet above sea level, this charming hotel
has spectacular south-facing views of the Alps
and lake and is quietly situated on traffic-free
promenade. 100 m from railway station,
harbour and landing stage.*

TARIFF: Single 118–200, Double 237–330,
Set menu 45.
CC: Diners, Euro/Access, Visa.

Hotel Seegarten Seepromenade,
88131 Lindau im Bodensee.
☎ 08382 5055, Fax 08382 5054. English spoken.
Open all year. 27 bedrooms (all en suite
with telephone). Outdoor swimming pool,
golf 4 km, garage, parking, restaurant.

*Small hotel on traffic-free promenade, 70 m
from the station, harbour and landing stage.
At 1,300 feet above sea level, has magnificent
south-facing views across the lake to the Swiss
and Austrian Alps.*

TARIFF: Single 118–170, Double 196–262,
Set menu 45.
CC: Diners, Euro/Access, Visa.

LOHMAR 16A

Hotel Schloss Auel Wahlscheid,
5204 Lohmar.
☎ 02206 2041, Fax 02206 2316.
Open all year. 23 bedrooms (all en suite).
TARIFF: (1993) Single 100–120,
Double 150–170.
CC: Amex, Diners, Euro/Access, Visa.

LÜBECK 15A

Hotel Jensen ★★★ Am Holstentor, An der
Obertrave 4-5, 23552 Lübeck-Travemünde.
☎ 04517 1646, Fax 04517 3386. English spoken.

Open all year. 42 bedrooms (all en suite
with telephone). Golf 20 km, garage, parking,
restaurant.

*A family-run hotel in the centre of Lübeck. An
historical building but with all modern
amenities.*

TARIFF: Single 110–130, Double 160–190,
Set menu 21–50.
CC: Amex, Diners, Euro/Access, Visa.

Movenpick Hotel ★★★★ Auf der
Wallhalbinsel 1-3, 23554 Lübeck.
☎ 04511 5040, Fax 04511 504111.
English spoken.
Open all year. 197 bedrooms (all en suite with
telephone). Garage, parking, restaurant. &

*Recently renovated, hotel is in the old town,
within sight of the Holstentor. Children under
16 sharing with their parents free of charge.
Non-smokers' floor.*

TARIFF: Single 130–250, Double 260–330,
Bk 21, Set menu 26–72.
CC: Amex, Diners, Euro/Access, Visa.

LÜDENSCHEID 16A

Queens Hotel LÜdenscheid ★★★ Parkstrasse
66, 58509 Lüdenscheid.
☎ 02351 1560, Fax 02351 39157.
English spoken.
Open all year. 165 bedrooms (all en suite
with telephone). Indoor swimming pool,
golf 5 km, garage, parking, restaurant.

*Situated only 3 km from Lüdenscheid in the
beautiful mountains of the Sauerland.
Extensive conference and leisure facilities,
complimented by good food in the
Wintergarten Restaurant and two bars.*

TARIFF: Single 190–210, Double 270–290,
Set menu 40–110.
CC: Amex, Diners, Euro/Access, Visa.

LUDWIGSHAFEN 16B

Hotel Excelsior Lorientallee 16,
6700 Ludwigshafen.
☎ 0621 59850, Fax 0621 5985500.
Open all year. 160 bedrooms (all en suite).
TARIFF: (1993) Single 170, Double 190–215.
CC: Amex, Diners, Euro/Access, Visa.

LÜNEBURG 14B

Hotel Bremer Hof Lüner Strasse 12-13,
21335 Lüneburg.
☎ 04131 36077, Fax 04131 38304.
English spoken.
Open all year. 56 bedrooms (all en suite with

Germany

telephone). Golf 10 km, parking, restaurant.
*Comfortable and interesting interior with lots
of exposed old brick and studwork. Follow the
red Hoteltouristikroute signs in Lüneburg.*
TARIFF: Single 78–160, Double 120–190,
Set menu 25–50.
CC: Amex, Diners, Euro/Access, Visa.

MAINZ 16B

Central Hotel Eden Bahnhofsplatz 8,
6500 Mainz.
📞 06131 674001, Fax 06161 672806.
Open all year. 61 bedrooms (all en suite).
CC: Amex, Diners, Euro/Access, Visa.

MANNHEIM 16B

Hotel Augusta Augusta-Anlage 43-45,
6800 Mannheim.
📞 0621 408001, Fax 0621 414624.
Open all year. 106 bedrooms (all en suite).
TARIFF: (1993) Single 190, Double 220–260.
CC: Amex, Diners, Euro/Access, Visa.

MARKTBREIT 16B

Hotel Löwen ★★ Marktstr 8, 97340 Marktbreit.
📞 09332 3085, Fax 09332 9438. English spoken.
Open all year. 50 bedrooms (all en suite
with telephone). Golf 15 km, garage, parking,
restaurant.
*Charming hotel dating from the 15th century,
located in the centre of town.*
TARIFF: Single 70–85, Double 105–125.
CC: Amex, Diners, Euro/Access, Visa.

MEERSBURG 16D

Hotel Erbguth's Landhaus ★★★
Neugartenstr 39, 7759 Hagnau.
📞 07532 6202, Fax 07532 6997. English spoken.
Open 01/03 to 04/01. 22 bedrooms
(20 en suite, 20 telephone). Outdoor
swimming pool, tennis, golf 18 km, garage,
parking, restaurant. ♿
*Beautiful, quiet situation close to the lake.
Separate accommodation available at Villa-
am-See, affiliated to hotel and 4 km east of
Meersburg, follow signs.*
TARIFF: (1993) Single 110–200,
Double 180–360, Set menu 35–120.
CC: Amex, Diners, Euro/Access, Visa.

MELDORF 14B

Hotel Dithmarscher Bucht
Helgolandstrasse 2, 2223 Meldorf.
📞 04832 7123. English spoken.

Open 01/03 to 01/01. 19 bedrooms
(9 en suite). Golf 15 km, parking.
RESTAURANT: Closed Mon.
*Small charming hotel with antique doll and
toy collection. Nouvelle cuisine. Between
Meldorf and Büsum.*
TARIFF: (1993) Single 70, Double 110.
CC: none.

MEMMINGEN 16D

Hotel Weisses Ross Kalchstrasse 16,
8940 Memmingen.
📞 08331 2020, Fax 08331 84057.
Open all year. 40 bedrooms (all en suite).
TARIFF: (1993) Single 60–85, Double 100–130.
CC: Amex, Diners, Euro/Access, Visa.

MINDEN 14D

Hotel Kruses Park Marienstrasse 108,
4950 Minden.
📞 0571 46033, Fax 0571 49022.
Open all year. 39 bedrooms (31 en suite).
CC: Amex, Diners, Euro/Access, Visa.

MITTENWALD 17C

Hotel Post Obermarkt 9, 8102 Mittenwald.
📞 08823 1094, Fax 08823 1096.
Open all year. 90 bedrooms (78 en suite).
TARIFF: (1993) Single 60–110, Double 100–190.
CC: Amex, Diners, Euro/Access, Visa.

MONSCHAU 16A

Hotel Burghotel Monschau Laufenstrasse 1,
52156 Monschau.
📞 02472 2332. English spoken.

Open 02/02 to 10/11 & 01/12 to 10/01.
14 bedrooms (9 en suite). Parking, restaurant.
*Town centre hotel, renovated throughout to the
highest standards.*
TARIFF: Double 84–110, Set menu 20–38.
CC: none.

MÜLLHEIM 16C

Euro-Hotel Alte Post An der Bundesstrasse 3, 7840 Müllheim.
☎ 07631 5522, Fax 07631 15524.
Open all year. 57 bedrooms (48 en suite).
TARIFF: (1993) Single 80−140, Double 120−240.
CC: Amex, Diners, Euro/Access, Visa.

MÜNCHEN (MUNICH) 17C

Austrotel München ★★★ Arnulfstrasse 2, 80335 München.
☎ 089 54530, Fax 089 54532255.
English spoken.
Open all year. 174 bedrooms (all en suite with telephone). Garage, parking, restaurant.

Opposite the station and airport with shuttle bus into city centre.
TARIFF: Single 205−270, Double 300−370, Set menu 38−78.
CC: Amex, Diners, Euro/Access, Visa.

Hotel Bayerischer Hof ★★★★★
Promenadeplatz 2-6, 80333 München.
☎ 089 2120900, Fax 089 2120906.
English spoken.
Open all year. 428 bedrooms (all en suite with telephone). Indoor swimming pool, garage, restaurant. &

Traditional hotel, privately owned since 1897 by the Volkhardt family. Opposite the cathedral and close to shops and boutiques. Guest rooms completely refurbished. Choice of restaurants.
TARIFF: Single 270−340, Double 380−510, Bk 29.50.
CC: Amex, Diners, Euro/Access, Visa.

Hotel Beiderstein Keferstrasse 18, 8000 München.
☎ 089 395072, Fax 089 348511.
Open all year. 45 bedrooms (all en suite).
TARIFF: (1993) Single 130−150, Double 150−180.
CC: Amex, Diners, Euro/Access, Visa.

Hotel Dreilöwen ★★★★ Schillerstrasse 8, 8000 München.
☎ 089 551040, Fax 089 55104905. English spoken.
Open all year. 130 bedrooms (all en suite with telephone). Garage, parking, restaurant.

Located in the centre, approximately 300 m from the main railway station, shopping area and pedestrian precinct. Other points of interest are within easy walking distance.
TARIFF: Single 182−190, Double 230−250.
CC: Amex, Diners, Euro/Access, Visa.

Hotel Germania ★★★★
Schwanthalerstrasse 28, 8000 München.
☎ 089 51680, Fax 089 598491.
Open all year. 99 bedrooms (all en suite).
TARIFF: (1993) Double 195−245.
CC: Amex, Diners, Euro/Access, Visa.

Queens Hotel ★★★★ Effnerstrasse 99, 81825 München.
☎ 089 927980, Fax 089 983813. English spoken.
Open all year. 152 bedrooms (all en suite with telephone). Garage, parking, restaurant.

15 minutes' drive from the city centre, and only 5 minutes from the English Garden.
TARIFF: Single 185−285, Double 235−335, Bk 27, Set menu 33−67.
CC: Amex, Diners, Euro/Access, Visa.

Hotel Rafael ★★★★ Neuturmstr 1, 8000 München 2.
☎ 089 290980, Fax 089 222539.
English spoken.
Open all year. 74 bedrooms (all en suite with telephone). Outdoor swimming pool, garage, restaurant.

Distinctive new luxury hotel in the heart of the city. Located between the Hofbrauhaus and Maximilianstrasse. The swimming pool is on the roof of the hotel and only open in the summer.
TARIFF: (1993) Single 420−560, Double 520−720, Set menu 45−98.
CC: Amex, Diners, Euro/Access, Visa.

Schlosshotel Grünwald Zeillerstr 1, 8022 Grünwald.
☎ 089 6417935, Fax 089 6414771.
English spoken.
Open all year. 16 bedrooms (all en suite with telephone). Tennis, golf 7 km, parking.
RESTAURANT: Closed Mon.

Once an old royal hunting lodge, the hotel has breathtaking views overlooking the river whilst still being close to the bustling city. Garden terrace, historic atmosphere with high ceilings and antique furniture. From motorway south of München take the Grünwald exit.
TARIFF: (1993) Single 145−190, Double 190−280.
CC: Amex, Diners, Euro/Access, Visa.

MÜNSTER 14C

Haus Eggert Zur Haskenau 81, 4400 Münster.
☎ 0251 32083, Fax 0251 327147.
Open all year. 33 bedrooms (all en suite).
TARIFF: (1993) Single 95−115, Double 140−180.
CC: Amex, Diners, Euro/Access, Visa.

Germany

Hotel Hof Zur Linde Handorfer-Werseufer 1,
4400 Münster.
☎ 0251 325002, Fax 0251 327147.
Open all year. 34 bedrooms (all en suite).
TARIFF: (1993) Single 95−115,
Double 140−180.
CC: Amex, Diners, Euro/Access, Visa.

MÜNSTERTAL   16C

Hotel Adler Stube Münster 59,
7816 Münstertal.
☎ 07636 234.
Open all year. 20 bedrooms (18 en suite).
TARIFF: (1993) Single 71−105,
Double 116−178.
CC: Amex, Diners, Euro/Access, Visa.

MURRHARDT   16D

Hotel Sonne-Post Karlstrasse 6-9,
7175 Murrhardt.
☎ 07192 8083, Fax 07192 1550.
Open all year. 37 bedrooms (all en suite).
TARIFF: (1993) Single 92,
Double 148.
CC: Amex, Diners, Euro/Access, Visa.

NAGOLD   16D

Hotel Post Gasthaus ★★ Bahnhofstrasse 3-4,
72202 Nagold.
☎ 07452 4048, Fax 07452 4040.
English spoken.
Open 06/01 to 23/12. 33 bedrooms
(all en suite with telephone). Golf 15 km,
parking.
RESTAURANT: Closed Fri.

*Small modern hotel in the heart of the historic
town of Nagold. The restaurant 'Alte Post' is
opposite the hotel. Nagold is approximately
halfway between Freudenstadt and Stuttgart.*
TARIFF: Single 86−102, Double 142−180,
Set menu 35−80.
CC: Amex, Diners, Euro/Access, Visa.

NECKARZIMMERN   16B

Hotel Burg-Castle Hornberg
Burg-Hornberg, 74865 Neckarzimmern.
☎ 06261 4064, Fax 06261 18864.
English spoken.
Open 01/03 to 15/12. 45 bedrooms
(23 en suite, 23 telephone). Golf 7 km,
parking.
RESTAURANT: Closed 15/12 to 28/02.

*Old medieval castle, high above the River
Neckar in the small village of Burg Hornberg,
just to the north of Neckarzimmern.*

TARIFF: Single 130−160, Double 180−220,
Set menu 50−98.
CC: Euro/Access, Visa.

NEUSTADT-AN-DER-AISCH   16B

Hotel Romerhof Richard Wagner Strasse 15,
8530 Neustadt-an-der-Aisch.
☎ 09161 3011, Fax 09161 2498. English spoken.
Open all year. 20 bedrooms (all en suite
with telephone). Garage, parking, restaurant.
*On route 8 halfway between Würzburg and
Nürnberg.*
TARIFF: Single 60−75, Double 115−150,
Set menu 15−35.
CC: Amex, Diners, Euro/Access, Visa.

NIDDA   16B

Hotel Jager OHG ★★★★ Kurstrasse 9-13,
Bad Salzhausen, 6478 Nidda.
☎ 06043 4020, Fax 06043 402100. English spoken.
Open all year. 29 bedrooms (all en suite with
telephone). Indoor swimming pool, tennis,
golf 10 km, garage, parking, restaurant. &
*Attractive hotel with an elegant restaurant.
50 km from Frankfurt-am-Main.*
TARIFF: (1993) Single 160−210,
Double 240−295, Set menu 39−100.
CC: Amex, Diners, Euro/Access, Visa.

NIEDERSTOTZINGEN   16D

Hotel Oberstotzingen Stettenerstrasse 35-37,
7908 Niederstotzingen.
☎ 07325 1030, Fax 07325 10370.
Open all year. 17 bedrooms (all en suite).
TARIFF: (1993) Single 193, Double 236−276.
CC: Amex, Diners, Euro/Access, Visa.

NIERSTEIN   16B

Rheinhotel Mainzer Strasse 16,
55283 Nierstein-am-Rhein.

Germany

☎ 06133 97970, Fax 06133 979797.
English spoken.
Open 10/01 to 15/12. 15 bedrooms
(all en suite with telephone). Golf 15 km,
garage, parking, restaurant.
*The hotel faces the river and has a terrace with
trees around. Drive along the B9 between
Mainz and Worms to Nierstein.*
TARIFF: Single 129–275, Double 159–375.
CC: Amex, Diners, Euro/Access, Visa.

NOHFELDEN   16A

Seehotel Weingartner Bostalstrasse 12,
6697 Nohfelden.
☎ 06852 1601, Fax 06852 81651.
Open all year. 67 bedrooms (all en suite).
TARIFF: (1993) Single 89–149, Double 136–226.
CC: Amex, Diners, Euro/Access, Visa.

NORTEN-HARDENBERG   14D

Hotel Menzhausen ★★★★ Lange Strasse 12,
37170 Uslar.
☎ 05571 2051, Fax 05571 5820. English spoken.

Open all year. 40 bedrooms (all en suite
with telephone). Indoor swimming pool,
garage, parking, restaurant. ♿
*Picturesque, family hotel, dating from 1565
when it served as an inn for travelling
merchants. Sympathetically restored, it now
provides very comfortable accommodation
with excellent facilities including heated
indoor pool, whirlpool and sauna. Pretty
gardens, terrace and grill restaurant. Uslar is
on the 241, south-west of Hannover via the A7,
and to the west of Norten-Hardenberg.*
TARIFF: Single 105–180, Double 165–310,
Set menu 28–65.
CC: Amex, Diners, Euro/Access, Visa.

NÜRNBERG   17A

Hotel Am Sterntor ★★★ Tafelhofstrasse 8-14,
90010 Nürnberg.
☎ 0911 23581, Fax 0911 203101.
English spoken.

Open all year. 100 bedrooms (all en suite
with telephone). Garage.
RESTAURANT: Closed lunch.
*Recently renovated, family-run hotel with bar,
restaurant and conference rooms. Quiet,
central area only 3 minutes' walk from the
main station.*
TARIFF: Single 60–140, Double 90–190,
Set menu 18–80.
CC: Amex, Diners, Euro/Access, Visa.

Hotel Arvena Park Gorlitzer Strasse 51,
8500 Nürnberg.
☎ 0911 89220, Fax 0911 8922115.
Open all year. 242 bedrooms (all en suite).
TARIFF: (1993) Single 198–315,
Double 248–390.
CC: Amex, Diners, Euro/Access, Visa.

Austrotel ★★★★ Kaulbachstrasse 1,
90408 Nürnberg.
☎ 0911 36570, Fax 0911 3657488.
English spoken.
Open all year. 121 bedrooms (all en suite
with telephone). Garage, restaurant. ♿
*Located in the city centre just behind the
Imperial Castle. By car, follow signs to the
airport.*
TARIFF: Single 195–270, Double 280–390,
Set menu 21–35.
CC: Amex, Diners, Euro/Access, Visa.

Hotel Bayerischer Hof Gleissbuhlstrasse 15,
90402 Nürnberg.
☎ 0911 23210, Fax 0911 2321511.
English spoken.
Open all year. 81 bedrooms (79 en suite,
81 telephone). Garage, parking.

Germany

Modern Bed and Breakfast hotel situated near town centre and station. Reservations are needed for parking places.
TARIFF: Single 119–125, Double 170–180.
CC: Amex, Diners, Euro/Access, Visa.

Hotel Drei Linden ★★★
Aubere Sulzbacher Strasse 1, 8500 Nürnberg.
☎ 0911 533233, Fax 0911 554047.
English spoken.
Open all year. 28 bedrooms (all en suite with telephone). Garage, parking, restaurant.

The hotel has been run as a family business since 1877. In addition to tradition it offers modern comfort and a large and varied menu in the restaurant. In a convenient location directly on the B41, only minutes away from the Berlin-München motorway.
TARIFF: (1993) Single 125–160, Double 190–250, Set menu 21–36.
CC: Amex, Euro/Access.

Queens Hotel ★★★★ Münchener Strasse 283, 90471 Nürnberg.
☎ 0911 94650, Fax 0911 468865.
English spoken.
Open all year. 141 bedrooms (all en suite with telephone). Indoor swimming pool, outdoor swimming pool, tennis, golf 2 km, parking, restaurant.

A modern hotel, located in a quiet park area which is surrounded by small lakes.
TARIFF: Single 198–246, Double 246–312, Bk 24, Set menu 39–49.
CC: Amex, Diners, Euro/Access, Visa.

OBERAMMERGAU 17C

Hotel Zur Rose Dedlerstr 9, 82487 Oberammergau.
☎ 08822 4706, Fax 08822 6753.
English spoken.

Open 15/12 to 31/10. 24 bedrooms (all en suite). Garage, parking, restaurant.
Cosy Bavarian inn with a very good kitchen. Also has 13 apartments.
TARIFF: Single 50–60, Double 90–100, Set menu 20–48.
CC: Amex, Diners, Euro/Access, Visa.

Hotel Alte Post Dorfstrasse 19, 8103 Oberammergau.
☎ 08822 1091.
Open all year. 32 bedrooms (29 en suite).
CC: Amex, Diners, Euro/Access, Visa.

OBERHAUSEN 14C

Parkhotel Zur Bockmühle Teutoburger Strasse 156, 4200 Oberhausen.
☎ 0208 69020, Fax 0208 690258.
Open all year. 85 bedrooms (all en suite).
TARIFF: (1993) Single 175, Double 140–240.
CC: Amex, Diners, Euro/Access, Visa.

OBERKIRCH 16C

Romantik Hotel Zur Obere Linde
Hauptstrasse 25, 7602 Oberkirch.
☎ 07802 8020, Fax 07802 3030.
Open all year. 39 bedrooms (all en suite with telephone).
TARIFF: (1993) Single 110–165, Double 160–240.
CC: Amex, Diners, Euro/Access, Visa.

OBERSTDORF 16D

Parkhotel Frank ★★★★ Sachensweg 11, 8980 Oberstdorf.
☎ 08322 7060, Fax 08322 706286.
English spoken.
Open 15/12 to 03/10. 123 bedrooms (all en suite with telephone). Indoor swimming pool, golf 4 km, garage, parking, restaurant.

Comfortable hotel with mountain views. Ideal for winter sports. Follow signs from centre of town.
TARIFF: Single 125–185, Double 260–430, Set menu 40–80.
CC: Amex, Euro/Access.

Hotel Wiese Stillachstr 4a, 8980 Oberstdorf.
☎ 08322 3030. English spoken.
Open all year. 13 bedrooms (all en suite with telephone). Indoor swimming pool, golf 4 km, parking.

Enjoys a good reputation. From Kempten go on A7 towards Oberstdorf, then towards Klein-

Walsertal and finally take B19 towards Fellhornbahn and you will be on Stillachstrasse.
TARIFF: Single 100–105, Double 170–190.
CC: none.

OBERSTHAUSEN 16B

Hotel Kroko Egerlander Platz 17, 6053 Obersthausen.
☎ 06104 79041, Fax 06104 79161.
Open all year. 28 bedrooms (all en suite).
TARIFF: (1993) Single 75–85, Double 110–130.
CC: none.

OBERWESEL 16A

Hotel Auf Schonburg 6532 Oberwesel.
☎ 06744 7027, Fax 06744 1613.
Open all year. 22 bedrooms (21 en suite).
TARIFF: (1993) Single 90–105, Double 145–270.
CC: Amex, Diners, Euro/Access, Visa.

OEVERSEE 14B

Hotel Historischer Krug An der Bundesstrasse 76, 2391 Oeversee.
☎ 04630 300, Fax 04630 780.
Open all year. 47 bedrooms (all en suite).
CC: none.

OFFENBURG 16C

Central Hotel Poststr 5, 7600 Offenburg.
☎ 0781 72004, Fax 0781 74003.
Open all year. 20 bedrooms (all en suite).
TARIFF: (1993) Single 98, Double 130.
CC: Amex, Diners, Euro/Access, Visa.

Hotel Sonne ★★ Haupstr 94, 7600 Offenburg.
☎ 0781 71039, Fax 0781 71033. English spoken.
Open all year. 35 bedrooms (20 en suite, 20 telephone). Garage, parking.
RESTAURANT: Closed Jan.

In the pedestrian zone and centre of Offenburg, next to the baroque town hall. One of the oldest hotels in Germany and has been in the same family since 1858.
TARIFF: Single 65–95, Double 90–135, Set menu 26–95.
CC: Amex, Euro/Access, Visa.

OLDENBURG 14B

Hotel Wieting Damm 29, 2900 Oldenburg.
☎ 0441 27214, Fax 0441 26149.
Open all year. 69 bedrooms (63 en suite, 69 telephone).
TARIFF: (1993) Single 55–95, Double 90–160.
CC: Amex, Diners, Euro/Access, Visa.

OPPENHEIM 16B

Hotel Kurpfalz Wormser Strasse 2, 6504 Oppenheim.
☎ 06133 94940, Fax 06133 949494.
English spoken.
Open 20/01 to 20/12. 17 bedrooms (all en suite with telephone). Garage, restaurant.

The hotel is in the old part of the city, near the marketplace and St Katherin church. Oppenheim lies between Mainz and Worms on the B9, exit Nierstein-Oppenheim.
TARIFF: Single 79–149, Double 99–199.
CC: Amex, Diners, Euro/Access, Visa.

OSNABRÜCK 14D

Hotel Hohenzollern ★★★★
Heinrich-Heine-Strasse 17, Postfach 24 04, 4500 Osnabrück.
☎ 05413 3170, Fax 05413 317351.
Open all year. 98 bedrooms (all en suite with telephone). Indoor swimming pool, parking, restaurant.

Modern hotel with a warm atmosphere and good restaurant. Suites also available. Situated near the station in Osnabrück.
TARIFF: Single 115–260, Double 160–310, Set menu 37–65.
CC: Amex, Diners, Euro/Access, Visa.

OYTEN 14B

Motel Hoper Haupstrasse 56-58, 2806 Oyten.
☎ 04207 5966.
Open all year. 26 bedrooms (all en suite with telephone).
TARIFF: (1993) Single 68, Double 95.
CC: Amex, Diners, Euro/Access, Visa.

PADERBORN 14D

Hotel Arosa Best Western ★★★★
Postfach 1127, 4790 Paderborn.
☎ 05251 1280, Fax 05251 128806.
English spoken.
Open all year. 112 bedrooms (all en suite with telephone). Indoor swimming pool, golf 12 km, garage, restaurant.

Modern high-rise city centre hotel. All rooms with cable TV; suites available. Garage and pool/sauna free of charge.
TARIFF: (1993) Single 150–260, Double 260–320, Set menu 35–65.
CC: Amex, Diners, Euro/Access, Visa.

Germany

PASSAU 17D

Hotel Weisser Hase Ludwigstrasse 23,
8390 Passau.
📞 0851 34066, Fax 0851 34069.
Open all year. 117 bedrooms (95 en suite).
CC: Amex, Diners, Euro/Access, Visa.

PEGNITZ 17A

Pflaums Posthotel ★★★★★
Nürnberger Str 12-16, 91257 Pegnitz.
📞 09241 7250, Fax 09241 80404.
English spoken.
Open all year. 50 bedrooms (all en suite with
telephone). Indoor swimming pool, tennis,
golf 12 km, garage, parking, restaurant. ♿
*Luxury, award-winning Bavarian country
inn, set in quiet, beautiful countryside and
run by the same family for 11 generations.
Excellent restaurant serving French and local
cuisine. Sauna and solarium. Fly-fishing.
Leave the Berlin to München motorway at
Pegnitz. 4 km to the hotel.*
TARIFF: Single 195–350, Double 255–690,
Bk 25, Set menu 115–175.
CC: Amex, Diners, Euro/Access, Visa.

PETERSHAGEN 14D

Hotel Schloss Petershagen
Schlossfreiheit 5-7, 4953 Petershagen.
📞 05707 346, Fax 05707 2373.
Open all year. 11 bedrooms (all en suite).
TARIFF: (1993) Single 110–120, Double 180–220.
CC: Amex, Diners, Euro/Access, Visa.

PFORZHEIM 16D

Queens Hotel Pforzheim/Niefern ★★★★
Pforzheimer Strasse 52, 75223 Niefern.
📞 07233 70990, Fax 07233 5365.
English spoken.
Open all year. 67 bedrooms (all en suite
with telephone). Golf 8 km, garage, parking,
restaurant.
*In an ideal location on the edge of the Black
Forest, between Karlsruhe and Stuttgart. Leave
the A8 at the Pforzheim-Ost exit and turn right
at the first light, towards Niefern.*
TARIFF: Single 125–210, Double 165–250.
CC: Amex, Euro/Access, Visa.

Hotel Ruf Bahnhofplatz 5, 7530 Pforzheim.
📞 07231 16011, Fax 07231 33139.
Open all year. 52 bedrooms (all en suite).
TARIFF: (1993) Single 122–130,
Double 150–175.
CC: Amex, Diners, Euro/Access, Visa.

PFRONTEN 16D

Hotel Bavaria ★★★★ Kienbergstr 62,
Pfronten Dorf, 8962 Pfronten.
📞 08363 15004, Fax 08363 16815.
English spoken.
Open all year. 100 bedrooms. Indoor
swimming pool, outdoor swimming pool,
garage, parking, restaurant. ♿
*The hotel is surrounded by woods and
mountains. Facilities include sauna, whirlpool
and massage. Village of Pfronten is nearby.
Take Nesselwang exit from motorway to
Pfronten following signs to the Tirol.*
TARIFF: (1993) Single 120–180,
Double 260–450.
CC: Amex.

PLÖN 15A

Kurhotel Plön ★★★ Olmühlenallee,
2320 Plön.
📞 04522 809, Fax 04522 809160.
Open all year. 53 bedrooms (all en suite
with telephone). Indoor swimming pool,
parking, restaurant.
*Overlooking the Plöner lake, a very
comfortable hotel plus apartments. Ideal for
discovering Holstein Switzerland. From A7,
exit Neumünster-Wittorf, then B340 to
Plön.*
CC: none.

POMMELSBRUNN 17A

Hotel Lindenhof Hubmersberg 2,
8561 Pommelsbrunn.
📞 09154 1021, Fax 09154 1288.
Open all year. 30 bedrooms (all en suite).
CC: Amex, Diners, Euro/Access, Visa.

POTSDAM 15C

Hotel Schloss Cecilienhof Neuer Garten,
0-1561 Potsdam.
📞 0331 37050, Fax 0331 22498.
English spoken.
Open all year. 42 bedrooms (all en suite
with telephone). Parking, restaurant.
*Site of the signing of the Potsdam Agreement in
1945; the conference rooms are now
commemorative and open to the public, whilst
the remainder of the palace is used as a hotel.
Sauna and massage. Beautiful surroundings
and situated to the north of Potsdam.*
TARIFF: (1993) Single 150–190,
Double 250–350, Set menu 35–130.
CC: Amex, Diners, Euro/Access, Visa.

Germany

PRIEN-AM-CHIEMSEE   17C

Hotel Bayerischer Hof ★★★ Bermauer
Strasse 3, 8210 Prien-am-Chiemsee.
☎ 08051 6030, Fax 08501 62917.
English spoken.
Open 01/12 to 30/10. 48 bedrooms
(all en suite with telephone). Golf 3 km,
garage, parking.
RESTAURANT: Closed Mon.

*Good medium-grade hotel in the centre of
Prien. Five minutes' walk from the station.
Well-appointed bedrooms, all with private
facilities and TV, most with balcony.
Attractively furnished restaurant offering very
good local cuisine.*

TARIFF: Single 85, Double 146–150,
Set menu 24–32.
CC: Euro/Access, Visa.

PRÜMZURLAY   16A

Hotel Haller Michelstrasse 1-3,
5521 Prümzurlay.
☎ 06523 656.
Open all year. 27 bedrooms (all en suite).
TARIFF: (1993) Single 37–60, Double 70–110.
CC: none.

RAVENSBURG   16D

Hotel Waldhorn Marienplatz 15,
7980 Ravensburg.
☎ 0751 16021, Fax 0751 17533.
Open all year. bedrooms.
TARIFF: (1993) Single 95–138, Double 135–240.
CC: Amex, Diners, Euro/Access, Visa.

REGEN   17D

Brauereigasthof Falter Am Sand 15,
8370 Regen.
☎ 09920 4313/4.
Open all year. 12 bedrooms (all en suite).
CC: Amex, Diners, Euro/Access, Visa.

REGENSBURG   17C

Hotel Münchner Hof Tandlergasse 9,
93047 Regensburg.
☎ 0941 58440, Fax 0941 561709. English spoken.
Open all year. 41 bedrooms (all en suite
with telephone). Parking, restaurant.

*The hotel is in the heart of the city's pedestrian
zone. You may load or unload your car at the
door.*

TARIFF: Single 90–120, Double 135–170,
Set menu 12–20.
CC: Amex, Diners, Euro/Access, Visa.

REICHSHOF   16A

Hotel Aggerberg Am Aggerberg,
Eckenhagen, 5226 Reichshof.
☎ 02265 9087, Fax 02265 8756.
Open all year. 21 bedrooms (11 en suite).
TARIFF: (1993) Single 80–95, Double 160–190.
CC: Amex, Diners, Euro/Access, Visa.

REMSCHEID   16A

Hotel Remscheider Hof ★★★★
Bismarckstrasse 38, 5630 Remscheid.
☎ 02191 432156, Fax 02191 432158.
Open all year. 106 bedrooms (all en suite).
CC: Amex, Diners, Euro/Access, Visa.

REUTLINGEN   16D

Hotel Ernst Am Leonhardsplatz,
7410 Reutlingen.
☎ 07121 4880, Fax 07121 488113.
Open all year. 62 bedrooms (all en suite).
TARIFF: (1993) Single 75–105, Double 112–146.
CC: Amex, Diners, Euro/Access, Visa.

RHEDA-WIEDENBRÜCK   14C

Hotel Ratskeller Wiedenbrück Langestrasse
am Marktplatz, 4840 Rheda-Wiedenbrück.
☎ 05242 7051, Fax 05242 7256.
Open all year. 37 bedrooms (all en suite).
TARIFF: (1993) Single 90–125, Double 150–200.
CC: Amex, Diners, Euro/Access, Visa.

ROSTOCK   15A

Hotel Neptun Seestr 19,
O-2530 Rostock-Warnemünde.
☎ 03815 460, Fax 03815 4023. English spoken.
Open all year. 350 bedrooms (all en suite
with telephone). Indoor swimming pool,
garage, parking, restaurant.

*Situated on the wide, sandy beach of
Warnemünde. Fitness centre with solarium
and sauna. Fresh seafood specialities in the
restaurant. Go north from Rostock to
Warnemünde.*

TARIFF: (1993) Single 254–324,
Double 338–398.
CC: Amex, Diners, Euro/Access, Visa.

ROTHENBURG-OB-DER-TAUBER   16B

Hotel Eisenhut Herrngasse 3-7,
91541 Rothenburg-ob-der-Tauber.
☎ 09861 7050, Fax 09861 70545.
English spoken.
Open all year. 79 bedrooms (all en suite
with telephone). Garage, parking.

Germany

Four patrician houses transformed into an hotel. In the centre of the old town and near the marketplace.

TARIFF: Single 150–195, Double 285–380.
CC: Amex, Diners, Euro/Access, Visa.

Hotel Goldener Hirsch Untere Schmiedgasse 16/25, 91534 Rothenburg-ob-der-Tauber.
☎ 09861 7080, Fax 09861 708100.
English spoken.
Open 11/01 to 20/12. 145 bedrooms (60 en suite, 72 telephone). Garage, parking.
RESTAURANT: Closed 21/12-10/01.

A first-class hotel in this famous medieval town. Quiet location overlooking the Tauber valley. Renowned restaurant "The Blue Terrace".

TARIFF: Single 140–210, Double 190–320.
CC: Amex, Diners, Euro/Access, Visa.

Hotel Kloster Stuble ★★
Heringsbronnengasse 5, 91541 Rothenburg-ob-der-Tauber.
☎ 09861 6774, Fax 09861 6474. English spoken.

Open all year. 13 bedrooms (all en suite).
Garage, parking.
RESTAURANT: Closed Jan & Feb.

Comfortable guest-house with excellent food. Situated behind the church only 200 m from the market square, in a beautiful, quiet setting above the Tauber valley. Open sun terrace.

TARIFF: Single 78, Double 118–158.
CC: Euro/Access, Visa.

ROTTWEIL   16D

Hotel Haus Zum Sternen ★★★ Haupstr 60, 7210 Rottweil.
☎ 0741 7006, Fax 0741 7008. English spoken.
Open all year. 13 bedrooms (all en suite with telephone). Tennis, garage, restaurant.

The hotel, a patrician house dating from 1278, is situated in the historic town centre and has

survived the centuries relatively intact. Atmospheric bar in the cellar vaults, historic wine tavern, garden terrace. Comfortably furnished in antique style.

TARIFF: Single 95–145, Double 185–250,
Set menu 38–80.
CC: Amex, Euro/Access, Visa.

RÜDESHEIM   16A

Hotel Cafe Post Rheinuferstrasse 2, 65382 Assmannshausen-am-Rhein.
☎ 06722 2326, Fax 06722 48249.
English spoken.

Open 01/03 to 15/11. 15 bedrooms (9 en suite). Garage, parking, restaurant.

Right on the banks of the Rhein with a wonderful view over the river and its castles. On the B42 in Assmannshausen, near Rüdesheim.

TARIFF: Single 80–100, Double 110–175.
CC: Amex, Diners, Euro/Access, Visa.

Hotel Jagdschloss Niederwald ★★★★
6220 Rüdesheim.
☎ 06722 1004, Fax 06722 47970. English spoken.

Open 15/02 to 31/12. 52 bedrooms
(all en suite with telephone). Indoor
swimming pool, tennis, garage, parking,
restaurant.

*Historic building in a peaceful location and
former hunting lodge of the Duke of Nassau.*

TARIFF: Single 145–185, Double 240–280.
cc: Amex, Diners, Euro/Access, Visa.

Hotel Krone ★★★★★ Rheinuferstrasse 10,
6220 Assmannshausen.
☎ 06722 4030, Fax 06722 3049.
English spoken.

Open 26/02 to 31/12. 65 bedrooms
(all en suite with telephone). Outdoor
swimming pool, garage, parking, restaurant.

*Beautiful old castle on the banks of the Rhein.
The rooms and suites are sumptuously
furnished offering the highest standard of
comfort and luxury. Gourmet restaurant and
excellent wine cellar. Located east of
Rüdesheim on the B42. German 'Hotel of the
Year' 1993.*

TARIFF: Single 140–280, Double 220–320,
Bk 22, Set menu 48–135.
cc: Amex, Diners, Euro/Access, Visa.

Hotel Rüdesheimer Hof ★★
Geisenheimerstr 1, 65385 Rüdesheim.
☎ 06722 2011, Fax 06722 48194.
English spoken.
Open 15/02 to 15/11. 42 bedrooms
(all en suite with telephone). Golf 20 km,
parking.
RESTAURANT: Closed 15/11 to 15/02.

*The hotel is located in the centre of town. All
tourist attractions and sightseeing places are
within walking distance. On the main road as
you approach the town centre.*

TARIFF: Single 85–95,
Double 120–160.
cc: Amex, Diners, Euro/Access, Visa.

SAARBRÜCKEN 16A

Hotel Alfa ★★ Ensheimer Gelosch 2,
St Ingbert-Sengscheid, 66386 St Ingbert.
☎ 06894 7090, Fax 06894 870146.
English spoken.
Open 02/01 to 22/12. 42 bedrooms
(all en suite with telephone). Golf 15 km,
garage, parking.
RESTAURANT: Closed Sun eve & Mon.

*On the A6 from Saarbrücken or Mannheim,
exit St Ingbert-West and then take next three
left turns. From St Ingbert city: towards Airport
Saarbrücken-Ensheim over the
Ensheimerstrasse.*

TARIFF: Single 99–139, Double 145–169,
Set menu 49–110.
cc: Amex, Diners, Euro/Access, Visa.

Hotel Bliesbruck Rubenheimer Strasse,
6657 Gersheim-Herbitzheim.
☎ 06843 1881, Fax 06843 8731. English spoken.

Open all year. 29 bedrooms (all en suite
with telephone). Golf 3 km, garage, parking,
restaurant.

*Modern, chalet-style hotel in a peaceful
situation in the village of Herbitzheim near the
French border. Take the Homburg/Einod exit
from the motorway and go southwards for
13 km to Gersheim-Herbitzheim.*

TARIFF: Single 58–80, Double 100–138,
Set menu 20–47.
cc: Amex, Diners, Euro/Access, Visa.

SAARLOUIS 16A

Hotel Altes Pfarrhaus Beaumaris
Hauptstrasse 2-4, 6630 Saarlouis.
☎ 06831 6383, Fax 06831 62898.
Open all year. 35 bedrooms (all en suite).
TARIFF: (1993) Single 130–170,
Double 160–250.
cc: Amex, Diners, Euro/Access, Visa.

SALEM   16D

Hotel Schwanen Am Salemer Schloss,
88682 Salem.
☏ 07553 283, Fax 07533 6418. English spoken.
Open 19/03 to 01/01. 16 bedrooms
(all en suite with telephone). Parking,
restaurant.

*Small, traditional-style hotel with garden
terrace restaurant.*

TARIFF: Single 89–105, Double 119–148, Bk .
CC: none.

SALZGITTER-BAD   14D

Hotel Ratskeller Marktplatz 10,
3320 Salzgitter-Bad.
☏ 05341 37025/7, Fax 05341 35020.
Open all year. 52 bedrooms (all en suite).
TARIFF: (1993) Single 60–85, Double 108–138.
CC: Amex, Diners, Euro/Access, Visa.

SAULGAU   16D

Hotel Kleber-Post Hauptstrasse 100,
7968 Saulgau.
☏ 07581 3051, Fax 07581 4437.
Open all year. 43 bedrooms (all en suite).
TARIFF: (1993) Single 75,
Double 130–176.
CC: Amex, Diners, Euro/Access, Visa.

SCHLESWIG   14B

Hotel Strandhalle Strandweg 2,
Am Jeachthafen, 2380 Schleswig.
☏ 04621 22021, Fax 04621 28933.
Open all year. 26 bedrooms (all en suite).
TARIFF: (1993) Single 85,
Double 130–155.
CC: Amex, Diners, Euro/Access, Visa.

SCHLIERSEE   17C

Hotel Schlierseerhof Am See Seestrasse 21,
8162 Schliersee.
☏ 08026 4071, Fax 08026 4953.
Open all year. 46 bedrooms (all en suite).
TARIFF: (1993) Single 120–170,
Double 160–230.
CC: Amex, Diners, Euro/Access, Visa.

SCHMALLENBERG   16B

Berghotel Hoher Knochen
5948 Schmallenberg.
☏ 02975 496, Fax 02975 421.
Open all year. 58 bedrooms (all en suite).
TARIFF: (1993) Single 75–130, Double 150–260.
CC: Amex, Diners, Euro/Access, Visa.

SCHÖNWALD   16C

Hotel Zum Ochsen ★★★★
Ludwig-Uhland-Strasse 18, 7741 Schönwald.
☏ 07722 1045, Fax 07722 3018. English spoken.
Open all year. 40 bedrooms (all en suite
with telephone). Indoor swimming pool,
tennis, golf 18 km, garage, parking.
RESTAURANT: Closed Tues & Wed.

*From A5 Frankfurt to Basel, take B33 to
Triberg, then go towards Schönwald.*

TARIFF: Single 91–121, Double 168–196,
Set menu 42.
CC: Amex, Diners, Euro/Access, Visa.

SCHOPFHEIM   16C

Hotel Löwen Gundenhausen 16,
7860 Schopfheim.
☏ 07622 2538, Fax 07622 5796.
Open all year. 25 bedrooms (14 en suite).
TARIFF: (1993) Single 38–65, Double 68–105.
CC: Amex, Diners, Euro/Access, Visa.

SCHWÄBISCH GMÜND   16D

Hotel Das Pelikan Turlensteg 9,
7070 Schwäbisch Gmünd.
☏ 07171 3590.
Open all year. 75 bedrooms (all en suite).
TARIFF: (1993) Single 130–150,
Double 165–225.
CC: Amex, Diners, Euro/Access, Visa.

SCHWALENBERG   14D

Hotel Schwalenberger Malkasten ★★ Neue
Torstr 1-3, 32816 Schieder-Schwalenberg 2.
☏ 05284 5278, Fax 05284 5108.
Open 01/02 to 31/12. 45 bedrooms
(all en suite with telephone). Golf 12 km,
garage, parking.
RESTAURANT: Closed Jan.

*Traditional hotel with exposed beams. Sauna
and solarium. From the Hannover to Rinteln
motorway, take Bad Eilsen exit. Through
Rinteln, Barntrup and Blomberg to Schieder-
Schwalenberg.*

TARIFF: Single 47–62, Double 94–144,
Set menu 20–45.
CC: Diners, Euro/Access, Visa.

SCHWANGAU   17C

Schlosshotel Lisl Neuschwansteinstr 1,
8959 Schwangau.
☏ 08362 81006/8, Fax 08362 81107.
Open all year. 56 bedrooms (45 en suite,
56 telephone).

TARIFF: (1993) Single 35–120, Double 70–240.
cc: Amex, Diners, Euro/Access, Visa.

SCHWETZINGEN   16B

Hotel Adler-Post Schloss Strasse 3,
6830 Schwetzingen.
☎ 06202 10036/7, Fax 06202 21442.
Open all year. 29 bedrooms (all en suite).
TARIFF: (1993) Single 99–133, Double 190.
cc: Amex, Diners, Euro/Access, Visa.

SEEG   16D

Pension Heim Aufmberg 8, 8959 Seeg.
☎ 08364 258.
Open all year. 18 bedrooms (all en suite).
TARIFF: (1993) Single 45, Double 86–96.
cc: Amex, Diners, Euro/Access, Visa.

SEESEN   14D

Hotel Goldener Löwe Jacobsonstrasse 20,
3370 Seesen.
☎ 05381 1201/2/3, Fax 05381 3840.
Open all year. 37 bedrooms (28 en suite).
TARIFF: (1993) Double 106–220.
cc: Amex, Diners, Euro/Access, Visa.

SIEGEN   16A

Hotel Johanneshöhe ★★★ Wallhausenstr 1,
5900 Siegen.
☎ 02713 10008, Fax 02713 15039.
English spoken.
Open all year. 25 bedrooms (all en suite with
telephone). Golf 12 km, garage, parking. &
RESTAURANT: very good. Closed Sun lunch.

*Situated about 2 km from the railway station
and town centre in a quiet position with a
panoramic view of Siegen. Good restaurant
with regional specialities.*

TARIFF: Single 75–120, Double 115–175,
Set menu 20–28.
cc: Amex, Diners, Euro/Access, Visa.

Queens Hotel ★★★★ Kampenstr 83,
57072 Siegen.
☎ 02715 0110, Fax 02715 011150.
English spoken.
Open all year. 94 bedrooms (all en suite
with telephone). Indoor swimming pool,
garage, parking, restaurant.

*First-class business hotel with a friendly,
family atmosphere. Rooms with every possible
amenity.*

TARIFF: Single 189–205, Double 230–260,
Bk 20, Set menu 30–80.
cc: Amex, Diners, Euro/Access, Visa.

SPANGENBERG   16B

Schlosshotel Spangenberg
3509 Spangenberg.
☎ 05663 866, Fax 05663 7567.
Open all year. 26 bedrooms (all en suite).
TARIFF: (1993) Single 90–120, Double 140–170.
cc: Amex, Diners, Euro/Access, Visa.

SPEYER   16B

Hotel Goldener Engel Mühlturmstrasse 1a,
6720 Speyer.
☎ 06232 13260, Fax 06232 132695.
Open all year. 42 bedrooms (all en suite).
TARIFF: (1993) Single 90–140, Double 140–190.
cc: Amex, Diners, Euro/Access, Visa.

ST-GOAR   16A

Hotel Hauser Heerstrasse 77,
56329 St-Goar-am-Rhein.
☎ 06741 333, Fax 06741 1464. English spoken.
Open 01/03 to 31/10. 39 bedrooms
(12 en suite). Golf 10 km, restaurant.

*Newly renovated hotel with views over the
Rhein and hills beyond. Close to swimming
pool. Good for walking, boat trips. On the west
bank, south of Koblenz.*

TARIFF: Single 65–95, Double 98–130.
cc: Amex, Diners, Euro/Access, Visa.

Hotel Landsknecht ★★★ An der Rheinuferstr,
5401 St-Goar.
☎ 0674 112011, Fax 0674 117499.
English spoken.
Open 01/03 to 01/12. 14 bedrooms
(all en suite with telephone). Garage, parking.
RESTAURANT: Closed 01/12 to 28/02.

*Standing by the river's edge on a castle-strewn
stretch of the Rhein almost opposite the Lorelei.
The restaurant, terrace and most of the very
comfortable bedrooms have panoramic river
views. 2 km north of St-Goar and one hour
from Frankfurt airport.*

TARIFF: Single 95–150, Double 115–360,
Set menu 35–110.
cc: Amex, Diners, Euro/Access, Visa.

ST-GOARSHAUSEN   16A

Hotel Erholung Nastaetter Strasse 15,
5422 St-Goarshausen.
☎ 06771 2684, Fax 06771 2502. English spoken.
Open 15/03 to 15/11. 57 bedrooms
(all en suite with telephone). Golf 10 km,
garage, parking. &
RESTAURANT: Closed 15/11 to 14/03.

Traditional hotel on banks of the Rhein by

*Lorelei Rock and opposite Rheinfeld castle.
Rhein specialities in restaurant. Wine bar. On
the B42, south of Boppard exit from A61.*
TARIFF: Single 45–52, Double 90–100,
Set menu 10–33.
CC: none.

ST-PETER-ORDING 14B

Hotel Ambassador International Im Bad 26,
2252 St-Peter-Ording.
📞 04863 7090, Fax 04863 2666.
Open all year. 90 bedrooms (all en suite).
TARIFF: (1993) Single 110–130,
Double 220–260.
CC: Amex, Diners, Euro/Access, Visa.

STADTALLENDORF 16B

Parkhotel Schillerstrasse 1,
3570 Stadtallendorf.
📞 06428 7080.
Open all year. 50 bedrooms (all en suite).
TARIFF: (1993) Single 55–119, Double 85–168.
CC: Amex, Diners, Euro/Access, Visa.

STADTKYLL 16A

Hotel Haus Am See Wirfstrasse,
5536 Stadtkyll.
📞 06597 2326.
Open all year. 19 bedrooms (all en suite).
CC: Amex, Diners, Euro/Access, Visa.

STROMBERG 16A

Park Village Golfhotel ★★★★
55442 Stromberg/Bingen.
📞 06724 6000, Fax 06724 600433.
English spoken.

Open all year. 125 bedrooms (all en suite
with telephone). Outdoor swimming pool,
tennis, golf, parking, restaurant.
Hotel and apartment complex set in large

*grounds with excellent sports facilities (indoor
pool opens 1995 season).*
TARIFF: Single 136–156, Double 156–216,
Set menu 30–90.
CC: Amex, Euro/Access, Visa.

STUTTGART 16D

Queens Hotel ★★★★ Wilhelm-Haspel Str 101,
71065 Sindelfingen.
📞 07031 6150, Fax 07031 874981.
English spoken.
Open all year. 137 bedrooms (all en suite
with telephone). Golf 12 km, parking,
restaurant. ⑂

*First-class business hotel. From Stuttgart, A81
south, exit Sindelfingen-Ost. Hotel is on the
right at first set of lights.*
TARIFF: Single 243–268, Double 334–366.
CC: Amex, Diners, Euro/Access, Visa.

TECKLENBURG 14C

Parkhotel Burggraf Meesenhof 7,
4542 Tecklenburg.
📞 05482 425, Fax 05482 6125.
Open all year. 43 bedrooms (all en suite).
TARIFF: (1993) Single 115–129,
Double 130–180.
CC: Amex, Diners, Euro/Access, Visa.

TITISEE-NEUSTADT 16A

Romantik Hotel Adler Post Haupstrasse 16,
Ortsteil Neustadt, 7820 Titisee-Neustadt.
📞 07651 5066, Fax 07651 3729.
Open all year. 30 bedrooms (all en suite
with telephone).

*Dating back to 1516 and once a mail staging
post, this very comfortable family-run hotel is
located 5 km east of Lake Titisee.*
TARIFF: Single 78–108, Double 138–178.
CC: Amex, Diners, Euro/Access, Visa.

TODTMOOS WEG 16C

Hotel Romantisches Schwarzwald
Alte Dorfstrasse 29, 7867 Todtmoos Weg.
📞 07674 273.
Open all year. 16 bedrooms (all en suite
with telephone).
TARIFF: (1993) Single 50–55, Double 85–110.
CC: Amex, Diners, Euro/Access, Visa.

TRABEN-TRARBACH 16A

Hotel Moseltor ★★★ Moselstrasse 1,
56841 Traben-Trarbach.
📞 06541 6551, Fax 06541 4922. English spoken.

Germany

Open all year. 11 bedrooms (all en suite with telephone). Garage.
RESTAURANT: Closed Tues.
On the right bank of the Mosel in Trarbach. Take B53 from Trier or B49 from Koblenz.
TARIFF: Single 85–105, Double 115–165, Set menu 53–110.
CC: Diners, Euro/Access, Visa.

TRIBERG   16C

Hotel Parkhotel Wehrle Gartenstrasse 24, 78094 Triberg-im-Schwarzwald.
☎ 07722 86020, Fax 07722 860290.
English spoken.
Open all year. 54 bedrooms (all en suite with telephone). Indoor swimming pool, outdoor swimming pool, garage, parking, restaurant.
Traditional, comfortable hotel consisting of main building plus three annexes, set in parkland but close to town square. Good local cuisine.
TARIFF: Single 98–140, Double 140–280, Bk 19, Set menu 52–136.
CC: Amex, Diners, Euro/Access, Visa.

TRIER   16A

Hotel Deutscher Hof Sudallee 25, 5500 Trier.
☎ 0651 46020, Fax 0651 4602412.
Open all year. 95 bedrooms (all en suite).
TARIFF: (1993) Single 95–110, Double 145–165.
CC: Amex, Diners, Euro/Access, Visa.

TÜBINGEN   16D

Hotel Am Bad ★★ Europastrasse 2, 7400 Tübingen.
☎ 07071 73071, Fax 07071 75336.
English spoken.
Open 07/01 to 21/12. 35 bedrooms (all en suite with telephone). Outdoor

swimming pool, tennis, garage, parking, restaurant. &
Very quiet location in the middle of a park. Autobahn Stuttgart-Singen, exit Herrenberg.
TARIFF: Single 76–108, Double 134–162, Bk 15.
CC: Amex, Euro/Access, Visa.

ÜBERLINGEN   16D

Hotel Zum Johanniter-Kreuz
Johanninterweg 11, Andelshofen, 7770 Überlingen.
☎ 07551 61091, Fax 07551 67336.
English spoken.
Open all year. 26 bedrooms (all en suite with telephone). Golf 1 km, garage, parking, restaurant.
300-year-old house with comfortable rooms in the small village of Andelshofen. Family atmosphere, good restaurant. 3 km to the lake.
TARIFF: Single 83–150, Double 150–230, Set menu 45–88.
CC: Amex, Diners, Euro/Access, Visa.

ULM   16D

Hotel Gasthof Zum Ritter Bertholdstr 8, Gogglingen, 7900 Ulm.
☎ 07305 7365.
Open all year. 17 bedrooms (12 en suite, 7 telephone).
TARIFF: (1993) Single 32–50, Double 66–85.
CC: Amex, Diners, Euro/Access, Visa.

Hotel Neuthor ★★★ Neuer-Graben 23, Postfach 31 45, 7900 Ulm.
☎ 07311 6160, Fax 07311 516513.
English spoken.
Open 10/01 to 22/12. 92 bedrooms (87 en suite, 92 telephone). Garage, parking, restaurant.
In the centre of Ulm (windows sound-insulated). The old quarters of Ulm are within walking distance. High quality restaurant, imposing entrance hall. 500 m from railway station.
TARIFF: (1993) Single 135–180, Double 170–220, Set menu 34–79.
CC: Amex, Diners, Euro/Access, Visa.

UNTERREICHENBACH   16D

Waldhotel Kappenhardter Muhle
7267 Unterreichenbach.
☎ 07235 7900, Fax 07235 790190.
Open all year. 65 bedrooms (all en suite).
TARIFF: (1993) Single 95–135, Double 170–240.
CC: Amex, Diners, Euro/Access, Visa.

VELLBERG 16D

Hotel Schloss Vellberg Postfach 50,
7175 Vellberg.
☎ 07907 8760, Fax 07907 87658.
Open all year. 35 bedrooms (all en suite).
TARIFF: (1993) Single 90–110,
Double 130–180.
CC: Amex, Diners, Euro/Access, Visa.

VIECHTACH 17C

Hotel Schmaus Stadtplatz 5, 8374 Viechtach.
☎ 09942 1627.
Open all year. 42 bedrooms (all en suite).
TARIFF: (1993) Single 55, Double 104–108.
CC: Amex, Diners, Euro/Access, Visa.

WALSRODE 14D

Hotel Heide-Kröpke ★★★★
Ostenholzer Moor, 29690 Essel.
☎ 05167 288, Fax 05167 291.
English spoken.
Open all year. 128 bedrooms (all en suite with
telephone). Indoor swimming pool, tennis,
golf 15 km, garage, parking, restaurant. &
*Traditional, family-run hotel, fitness room,
sauna with whirlpool, massage. From Hanover
to Hamburg motorway take Westenholz exit
and go 8 km to Ostenholz, then Ostenholzer
Moor.*
TARIFF: Double 195, Set menu 25–65.
CC: Diners, Euro/Access, Visa.

WARENDORF 14D

Hotel Im Engel ★★★★ Brünebrede 37,
48231 Warendorf.
☎ 02581 93020, Fax 02581 62726.
English spoken.
Open all year. 22 bedrooms (all en suite
with telephone). Golf 5 km, garage, parking,
restaurant. &
*Family-run hotel, steeped in history. Elegantly
furnished in traditional style. Good
restaurant.*
TARIFF: Single 90–95, Double 145–155,
Set menu 35–95.
CC: Amex, Diners, Euro/Access, Visa.

WASSENBERG 16A

Hotel Burg Wassenberg Kirchstrasse 17,
5143 Wassenberg.
☎ 02432 4044, Fax 02432 20191.
Open all year. 22 bedrooms (all en suite).
TARIFF: (1993) Single 95–160, Double 170–260.
CC: Amex, Diners, Euro/Access, Visa.

WEILBURG 16B

Schlosshotel Weilburg Langgasse 25,
6290 Weilburg.
☎ 06471 39096, Fax 06471 39199.
Open all year. 43 bedrooms (all en suite).
TARIFF: (1993) Single 115–145,
Double 165–220.
CC: Amex, Diners, Euro/Access, Visa.

WEILHEIM 17C

Doorm Hotel Brauwastl ★★★ Lohgasse 9,
82362 Weilheim.
☎ 0881 4547, Fax 0881 69485. English spoken.
Open all year. 48 bedrooms (all en suite
with telephone). Golf 10 km, garage, parking,
restaurant. &
Small, comfortable hotel in central location.
TARIFF: Single 99–128, Double 148–168,
Set menu 21.
CC: Amex, Euro/Access, Visa.

WEISSENBURG 17C

Hotel Rose Rosenstrasse 6, 8832 Weissenburg.
☎ 09141 2096, Fax 09141 70752.
Open all year. 29 bedrooms (28 en suite).
TARIFF: (1993) Single 70–140, Double 100–180.
CC: Amex, Diners, Euro/Access, Visa.

WERTHEIM 16B

Hotel Schwan 97877 Wertheim-am-Main.
☎ 09342 1278/9, Fax 09342 21182.
English spoken.
Open 24/01 to 22/12. 30 bedrooms
(all en suite with telephone). Garage, parking,
restaurant.
*Small, traditional hotel, tastefully and
comfortably furnished. Lovely surrounding
countryside. Conference facilities.*
TARIFF: Single 85–120, Double 120–240.
CC: Amex, Diners, Euro/Access, Visa.

Hotel Schweizer Stuben ★★★★
Geiselbrunnweg 11,
97877 Wertheim-Bettingen.
☎ 09342 3070, Fax 09342 307155.
English spoken.
Open all year. 33 bedrooms (all en suite with
telephone). Indoor swimming pool. outdoor
swimming pool, tennis, golf 12 km, parking.
RESTAURANT: excellent. Closed Mon and Tue
lunch.
*Set in the peaceful countryside of the Main
valley, this small, charming hotel has three
excellent restaurants (French, Italian and
Swiss). Apartments are also available. From*

Germany

*Würzburg and Frankfurt take Wertheim exit
and go left on the L2310. Turn right after
900 m and follow signs to hotel.*
TARIFF: Single 225–345, Double 275–395,
Set menu 135–198.
CC: Amex, Diners, Euro/Access, Visa.

WIESBADEN   16B

Hotel Arcade Maritiusstrasse, 6200 Wiesbaden.
☎ 069 1670, Fax 069 167750.
Open all year. 154 bedrooms (all en suite
with telephone).
CC: Amex, Diners, Euro/Access, Visa.

Hotel Schwarzer Bock ★★★★ Kranzplatz 12,
65183 Wiesbaden.
☎ 06111 550, Fax 06111 55111. English spoken.
Open all year. 150 bedrooms (all en suite
with telephone). Indoor swimming pool,
golf 8 km, garage, parking, restaurant. &
*Privately owned hotel in town centre. Old
European grandeur.*
TARIFF: Single 275–325, Double 325–375,
Bk 25, Set menu 45–130.
CC: Amex, Euro/Access, Visa.

WIESMOOR   14A

Hotel Friesengeist Am Rathaus 1,
2964 Wiesmoor.
☎ 04944 1044, Fax 04944 5369.
Open all year. 34 bedrooms (all en suite).
TARIFF: (1993) Single 67–94, Double 146–166.
CC: Amex, Diners, Euro/Access, Visa.

WILDESHAUSEN   14B

Hotel Landhaus Muller Wildeshausen Nord,
2878 Wildeshausen.
☎ 04431 3031/2.
Open all year. 9 bedrooms (all en suite).
CC: Amex, Diners, Euro/Access, Visa.

WILLINGEN   14D

Hotel Stryckhaus Mulenkopfstrasse,
3542 Willingen.
☎ 05632 6033, Fax 05632 69961.
Open all year. 63 bedrooms (all en suite).
TARIFF: (1993) Single 90–110, Double 180–252.
CC: Amex, Diners, Euro/Access, Visa.

WILLSTATT-SAND   16C

Aka Motel Europastrasse, 7608 Willstatt-Sand.
☎ 07852 2320.
Open all year. bedrooms.
TARIFF: (1993) Double 75.
CC: Amex, Diners, Euro/Access, Visa.

WINTERBERG   16B

Hotel Dorint U Ferienpark ★★★
Winterberg 7, Postwiese, 59955 Winterberg-
Neuastenberg.
☎ 02981 8970, Fax 02981 897700.
English spoken.

Open all year. 140 bedrooms (all en suite
with telephone). Indoor swimming pool,
tennis, golf 8 km, garage, parking, restaurant.
*Chalet-style hotel with self-catering apartments
also offered. Well known for winter sports.
Bowling alleys, sauna and solarium. Horse-
riding close by. Evening entertainment.
Regional cuisine. On B480.*
TARIFF: Single 145–165, Double 235–280,
Set menu 37–62.
CC: Amex, Diners, Euro/Access, Visa.

WIRSBERG   17A

Posthotel Marktplatz 11, 8655 Wirsberg.
☎ 09227 861, Fax 09227 5860.
Open all year. 43 bedrooms (all en suite).
TARIFF: (1993) Double 88–178.
CC: Amex, Diners, Euro/Access, Visa.

WITTLICH   16A

Hotel Molitors Muhle 5561 Eisenschmitt.
☎ 06567 581, Fax 06567 580.
English spoken.
Open 01/03 to 08/01. 30 bedrooms
(all en suite with telephone). Indoor
swimming pool, tennis, garage, parking,
restaurant. &
*Situated in the small village of Eisenschmitt,
40 km north of Trier and between Wittlich and
Kyllburg. Lying in a beautiful valley and
surrounded by fishing lakes.*
TARIFF: (1993) Single 75–110,
Double 125–200.
CC: Amex, Euro/Access, Visa.

Germany

WORMS   16B

Hotel Dom Obermarkt 10, 6520 Worms.
✆ 06241 6913.
Open all year. 60 bedrooms (all en suite).
TARIFF: (1993) Single 94–103, Double 125–140.
CC: Amex, Diners, Euro/Access, Visa.

WUPPERTAL   16A

Golfhotel Juliana ★★★★ Mollencotten 195,
42279 Wuppertal.
✆ 0202 64750, Fax 0202 6475777.
English spoken.
Open all year. 139 bedrooms (all en suite
with telephone). Indoor swimming pool,
tennis, golf on site, garage, parking, restaurant.
Attractive hotel in lovely surroundings.
Located on outskirts of town with easy access
to commercial centres. Good conference
facilities. Golf course next door.
TARIFF: Single 175–295, Double 225–345, Bk 25.
CC: Amex, Diners, Euro/Access, Visa.

Hotel Imperial Heckinshauser Strasse 10,
5600 Wuppertal.
✆ 0202 255440, Fax 0202 255441.
Open all year. 27 bedrooms (all en suite
with telephone).
TARIFF: (1993) Single 75–105, Double 115–125.
CC: Amex, Diners, Euro/Access, Visa.

Queens Hotel Velbert ★★★★ Günter Strasse
7, Weisenborn, 42549 Velbert.
✆ 02051 4920, Fax 02051 492175.
English spoken.
Open all year. 81 bedrooms (all en suite
with telephone). Golf 15 km, parking,
restaurant. &
In a quiet park area, ideal for business or
relaxation. Wuppertal (15 km), Düsseldorf
(30 km) and Essen (15 km).
TARIFF: Single 120–211, Double 141–277.
CC: Amex, Diners, Euro/Access, Visa.

Hotel Rubin Paradestrasse 59,
5600 Wuppertal.
✆ 0202 450077, Fax 0202 456489.
Open all year. 16 bedrooms (all en suite
with telephone). Garage, parking.
Small modern hotel, centrally located, but quiet.
TARIFF: Single 80–95, Double 110–130.
CC: none.

WÜRZBURG   16B

Hotel Zur Stadt Mainz Semmelstr 39,
8700 Würzburg.
✆ 0931 53155, Fax 0931 58510. English spoken.

Open 20/01 to 20/12. 15 bedrooms
(all en suite with telephone). Garage.
RESTAURANT: Closed Sun & Mon eve.
Acclaimed restaurant with regional cuisine.
Cosy atmosphere with rustic and antique
furniture. Würzburg is an artistic and historic
city with an 11th-century Romanesque
cathedral.
TARIFF: (1993) Single 120–150,
Double 180–200, Set menu 20–70.
CC: Amex, Euro/Access, Visa.

Hotel Walfisch ★★★ Am Pleidenturm 5,
8700 Würzburg.
✆ 0931 50055, Fax 0931 51690. English spoken.
Open all year. 40 bedrooms (all en suite
with telephone). Golf 2 km, garage, restaurant.
A good family-run hotel on riverside in town.
Pleasant atmosphere, friendly service, fine
views of Marienburg fortress, vineyards and
the river. Conference facilities.
TARIFF: Single 150–180, Double 200–280.
CC: Amex, Diners, Euro/Access, Visa.

Hotel Wittelsbacher Hoh Hexenbruchweg
10, 8700 Würzburg.
✆ 0931 42085, Fax 0931 415458.
Open all year. 75 bedrooms (all en suite).
TARIFF: (1993) Single 99–139, Double 165–235.
CC: Amex, Diners, Euro/Access, Visa.

ZWEIBRÜCKEN   16A

Hotel Romantik-Fasanerie Fasaneriestrasse
1, 6660 Zweibrücken.
✆ 06332 44074, Fax 06332 45176. English
spoken.
Open all year. 50 bedrooms (all en suite
with telephone). Indoor swimming pool,
garage, parking. &
RESTAURANT: Closed Sun.
From A8 motorway towards Karlsruhe, exit at
Zweibrücken-Niederauerbach then B10. Turn
right at the first lights, over bridge to wooded
hotel site.
TARIFF: (1993) Single 140–160,
Double 180–260, Set menu 55–100.
CC: Amex, Diners, Euro/Access, Visa.

Germany

GREECE

Sun and sea – Greece, or *Ellàs* in the modern Greek language, has them in abundance. This historic country has seas on three sides: Ionian to the west, Mediterranean to the south and Aegean in the east. There are borders in the north with Albania, states of the former Yugoslavia, Bulgaria and Turkey. Greece's land area of 131,944 sq km (roughly half that of the UK) has three main regions. These are the mainland peninsula, which is the southern extremity of the Balkans; the Peloponnesus, almost an island, connected to the mainland by the Isthmus of Corinth; and hundreds of islands dotted in the sparkling seas, of which Crete, in the far south, is the largest.

The Grecian landscape is generally rocky, the highest point being legendary Mount Olympus, at 2,917 m. There are long, hot summers, mild winters and little rain. Conifer forests cloak the mountains of the north-west. Farther south, the countryside is dry scrub and bare rock. Agriculture is the main industry, but less than a third of the land is cultivated, mainly on the coastal plains.

The population is about 10 million, and just over half of the people live in urban areas, Greek cities being small by European standards. Athens is the capital, with some 900,000 inhabitants. The local currency is the drachma, made up of 100 leptae. Greece has 35,000 km of variable-quality roads, giving a road density (km per sq km) of 0.26, compared to the UK's 1.5. Note that resorts for Greek islands, such as Andros and Crete, are listed under their island names in the A-Z directory.

ATHINA (ATHENS) 24C

Hotel Grande Bretagne Platia Syntagma, Athina.
☎ 01 323 0251. English spoken.
Open all year. 384 bedrooms (all en suite). Parking, restaurant.

First-class hotel in Athina's main square.

TARIFF: (1993) Single 9,000–14,000, Double 13,000–17,000.
CC: Amex, Diners, Euro/Access, Visa.

Hotel Herodion 4 Rovertou Galli St, 11742 Athina.
☎ 01 923 6832, Fax 01 923 5851.
English spoken.
Open all year. 90 bedrooms (all en suite). Parking, restaurant.

Comfortable hotel ten minutes from city centre and within walking distance of the Acropolis.

TARIFF: (1993) Single 9,000–14,000, Double 13,000–17,000.
CC: Amex, Diners, Euro/Access, Visa.

Hotel Lydia Loission 121, 10445 Athina.
☎ 01 821 9980. English spoken.
Open all year. 38 bedrooms (all en suite). Parking.

TARIFF: (1993) Single 7,000–11,000, Double 10,000–14,000.
CC: Amex, Diners, Euro/Access, Visa.

Hotel Pan 11 Metropoleos Street, Syntagma Square, 10557 Athina.
☎ 01 323 7817, Fax 01 322 5449.
English spoken.
Open all year. 48 bedrooms (all en suite with telephone). Tennis, golf 12 km, garage.

Conveniently situated in the centre of town, fully air conditioned and offering 24-hour room service.

TARIFF: Single 6,300–9,800, Double 9,500–13,900.
CC: Amex, Diners, Euro/Access, Visa.

Hotel St George Lycabettus Kleomenous 2, Athina.
☎ 01 729 0710. English spoken.
Open all year. 150 bedrooms (all en suite). Outdoor swimming pool, parking, restaurant. &

TARIFF: (1993) Single 9,000–14,000, Double 13,000–17,000.
CC: Amex, Diners, Euro/Access, Visa.

CRETE

AGHIOS NIKOLAOS 24C

Hotel St Nicholas Bay ★★★★★ Aghios
Nikolaos, Lassithi, Crete.
📞 0841 25041, Fax 0841 24556. English spoken.
Open 01/04 to 31/10. 128 bedrooms
(all en suite with telephone). Outdoor
swimming pool, tennis, parking, restaurant.

*A superbly positioned bungalow hotel built on
the beach overlooking the Mirabello Gulf. Set
among flowers, trees and green lawns in a
very quiet location, 25 minutes' walk from the
town centre, on the road towards Elounda.*

TARIFF: Single 18,000–30,000,
Double 22,000–50,000.
CC: Amex, Diners, Euro/Access, Visa.

AGIA PELAGIA 24C

Hotel Capsis Beach ★★★★ Agia
Pelagia, Iraklio, Crete.
Open 01/04 to 31/10. 650 bedrooms
(all en suite with telephone). Restaurant.

*20 km from International Airport, towards
Rethymnon. The resort is extensive and
includes three private beaches.*

TARIFF: Single 18,000–26,000,
Double 21,600–34,000,
Set menu 5,500–17,000.
CC: Amex, Diners, Euro/Access, Visa.

HANIA 24C

Hotel Samaria ★★★ Hania, Crete.
📞 0821 71271/5, Fax 0821 71270.
English spoken.
Open all year. 62 bedrooms (all en suite
with telephone). Parking.

*Comfortable, air-conditioned hotel, renovated
in 1992. All rooms with balcony and sound
insulation. Roof garden with good views.
Located in town centre, opposite central bus
terminal. Conference facilities.*

TARIFF: Single 12,000–14,900,
Double 15,000–19,000.
CC: Amex, Diners, Euro/Access, Visa.

END OF CRETE HOTELS

GLIFADA 24C

Hotel Astir Bungalows Vas Gheorgiou B'58,
16674 Glifada.
📞 01 894 4273. English spoken.
Open 15/04 to 15/10. 128 bedrooms
(all en suite). Outdoor swimming pool, tennis,
golf, parking, restaurant. &
TARIFF: (1993) Double 14,000–17,000.
CC: Amex, Diners, Euro/Access, Visa.

Hotel Atrium A 10 Leoforos Vas Gheorgiou,
16675 Glifada.
📞 01 894 0971. English spoken.
Open all year. 56 bedrooms (all en suite).
Parking, restaurant.
TARIFF: (1993) Single 9,000–14,000,
Double 13,000–17,000.
CC: Amex, Diners, Euro/Access, Visa.

LAKOPETRA 24C

Hotel Lakopetra Beach Lakopetra.
📞 0693 51394. English spoken.
Open 01/04 to 31/10. 194 bedrooms
(all en suite). Indoor swimming pool, outdoor
swimming pool, tennis, parking, restaurant.
CC: Amex, Diners, Euro/Access, Visa.

LEMNOS

MYRINA 24A

Hotel Akti Myrina 81400 Myrina, Lemnos.
📞 0254 22681, Fax 0254 22352. English spoken.

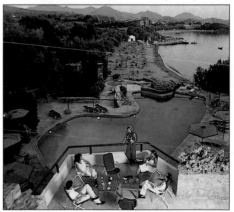

Open 18/05 to 02/10. 125 bedrooms
(all en suite with telephone). Outdoor
swimming pool, tennis, parking, restaurant.

*Beautiful self-contained Greek-style cottages
with private gardens and beach.*

TARIFF: Single 37,100–59,500,
Double 53,000–105,000.
CC: Amex, Diners, Euro/Access, Visa.

END OF LEMNOS HOTELS

Greece

METHONI 24C

Hotel Odysseas Methoni, Messinia.
☎ 0723 31600, Fax 0723 31646. English spoken.

Open all year. 9 bedrooms (all en suite
with telephone). Restaurant.

*A new (1988), family-run hotel, offering warm
hospitality and all modern comforts. Excellent
cuisine. 100 m from beautiful sandy beach, near
to the magnificent Venetian castle. Private yacht
charter can be arranged from the hotel.*

TARIFF: Single 8,000–12,000,
Double 10,000–15,000, Bk 1,200,
Set menu 2,800–2,800.
CC: Euro/Access.

METSOVO 24A

Hotel Egnatia 19 Tositsa, 44200 Metsovo.
☎ 0656 41263, Fax 0656 41485. English spoken.
Open all year. 36 bedrooms (all en suite
with telephone). Parking, restaurant.

*A traditional, friendly, family-owned hotel
near the museum, art gallery and town centre.*

TARIFF: Single 5,000–7,000,
Double 6,000–8,800, Bk 800,
Set menu 1,500–3,000.
CC: Amex, Diners, Euro/Access, Visa.

MYKONOS

MYKONOS 24C

Hotel Adonis PO Box 68, 84600 Mykonos.
☎ 0289 22434, Fax 0289 23449. English spoken.
Open 01/04 to 31/10. 32 bedrooms
(all en suite with telephone).

*A friendly hotel with balconies overlooking the
sea and only 5 minutes' walk to the beach.*

TARIFF: (1993) Single 7,140–12,636,
Double 9,720–16,920.
CC: Amex, Diners, Euro/Access, Visa.

END OF MYKONOS HOTELS

OLYMPIA 24C

Hotel Amalia Pyrgou Main Street Olympia.
☎ 0624 22190. English spoken.
Open all year. 147 bedrooms (all en suite).
Outdoor swimming pool, parking, restaurant.
CC: Amex, Diners, Euro/Access, Visa.

Hotel Kronion Tsoureka 1, Olympia.
☎ 0624 22188. English spoken.
Open all year. 39 bedrooms (all en suite).
Parking, restaurant.
TARIFF: (1993) Single 4,000–8,000,
Double 5,000–10,000.
CC: Amex, Diners, Euro/Access, Visa.

TOLON 24C

Hotel Minoa Aktis 56, 21056 Tolon.
☎ 0752 59207. English spoken.
Open 15/03 to 05/11. 44 bedrooms
(all en suite). Restaurant.
TARIFF: (1993) Single 4,000–8,000,
Double 5,000–10,000.
CC: Amex, Diners, Euro/Access, Visa.

VOULIAGMENI 24C

Astir Palace Hotel Vouliagmeni Beach,
16671 Vouliagmeni.
☎ 01 896 0211. English spoken.
Open all year. 580 bedrooms (all en suite).
Indoor swimming pool, outdoor swimming
pool, tennis, garage, parking, restaurant.
TARIFF: (1993) Single 14,000, Double 17,000.
CC: Amex, Diners, Euro/Access, Visa.

XILOKASTRON 24C

Hotel Chryssiavgi
Loutropoleos 9, Xilokastron.
☎ 0623 95224. English spoken.
Open 30/04 to 15/10. 10 bedrooms
(all en suite). Parking, restaurant.
CC: Amex, Diners, Euro/Access, Visa.

Greece

HUNGARY

In the heart of mainland Europe lies the former communist country of Hungary, which became a democratic republic in 1989. Its 93,030 sq km of land (less than a third the area of the UK) borders Austria to the west, Slovak Republic to the north, Ukraine and Romania in the east and the former Yugoslavia to the south. Within the 10 million inhabitants there are many ethnic groups, including gypsies, with their own language and traditions. Budapest, in the north, is the capital and by far the largest city – a fifth of Hungarians live here. Other large cities are Debrecen, Miskolc, Szeged, Pecs and Gyor. Local currency is the forint, made up of 100 filler.

Most of Hungary is rolling lowlands, with uplands to the west and mountains to the north. The highest peak is Kekes Mountain, at 1,015 m. The Danube and Tisza rivers flow south through central Hungary. The climate is variable, but generally moderate; most rain tends to fall in early summer, which can surprise tourists expecting a dry, central-continental summer season. Two-thirds of the land is farmed, though the vast Great Hungarian Plain in the south-east is used mainly for breeding horses and rearing cattle and pigs. A small proportion of the landscape is forested with mixed deciduous trees. Deer, wild boar and many species of wildfowl live in the nature reserves and extensive waterways.

The 30,000 km of roads are of generally high quality, and cities have efficient traffic systems. The road density (km per sq km) is 0.3, compared to 1.5 in the UK, so British tourists notice the wide open spaces and lack of vehicles.

BAJA 23C

Sugovica Hotel ★★★ Petofi-sziget, 6500 Baja.
☎ 79 321755, Fax 79 323155.
English spoken.
Open all year. 34 bedrooms (all en suite with telephone). Outdoor swimming pool, tennis, parking, restaurant.

Modern hotel with every facility and more - there's even a bowling alley! On a small island on the Danube, but only 500 m from the town centre. (Prices in DM.)

TARIFF: Single 68–86, Double 80–98.
CC: Amex, Diners, Euro/Access, Visa.

BALATONFÖLDVAR 23C

Pannonia Hotel Neptun ★★★
8623 Balatonföldvar.
☎ 844 0388, Fax 844 0212.
English spoken.
Open all year. 210 bedrooms (all en suite with telephone). Outdoor swimming pool, tennis, parking, restaurant.

Modern hotel on the southern shore of Lake Balaton, 300 m from the beach.

CC: none.

BALATONFÜRED 23C

Füred Hotel ★★★ Széchenyi u 20, 8230 Balatonfüred.
☎ 864 3033, Fax 864 3034. English spoken.
Open 01/04 to 01/11. 152 bedrooms (all en suite with telephone). Tennis, parking, restaurant.

This modern hotel is on the northern shore of Lake Balaton, the largest lake in central Europe. It has its own beach with good resort facilities.

TARIFF: (1993) Single 2450–4950, Double 3150–5600, Set menu 600–800.
CC: Amex, Diners, Euro/Access, Visa.

BUDAPEST 23A

Aero Hotel Ferde u 1-3, 1091 Budapest.
☎ 1 127 7690, Fax 1 127 5825. English spoken.
Open all year. 138 bedrooms (all en suite with telephone). Indoor swimming pool, golf 1 km, parking, restaurant.

Modern hotel with a garden and shaded terrace. Located halfway between the airport and the city centre, at the exit of the M4 and E15 highways. (Prices in DM.)

TARIFF: (1993) Single 70–82, Double 50–108.
CC: Amex, Diners, Euro/Access, Visa.

Buda Center Hotel ★★ Csalogany u 23, 1027 Budapest.
☎ 1 201 6333, Fax 1 201 7843. English spoken. Open all year. 37 bedrooms (all en suite with telephone). Parking, restaurant.
Modern, comfortable hotel situated in the heart of the city.
TARIFF: (1993) Single 3300–4500, Double 4000–5600.
CC: none.

Buda Penta Hotel Kirsztina körut 41-43, 1013 Budapest.
☎ 1 156 6333, Fax 1 155 6964. English spoken.

Open all year. 395 bedrooms (all en suite with telephone). Indoor swimming pool, garage, parking, restaurant.
Large, modern and well-equipped hotel, with easy access to the city centre. Located near the junctions of the M1 and M7, to the west of the city. (Prices in DM.)
TARIFF: Single 129–203, Double 170–247.
CC: Amex, Diners, Euro/Access, Visa.

Grand Hotel Corvinus Kempinski ★★★★ Erzsébet tér 7-9, 1051 Budapest.
☎ 1 266 1000, Fax 1 266 2000. English spoken. Open all year. 369 bedrooms (all en suite with telephone). Indoor swimming pool, garage, restaurant. ♿
A de luxe hotel opened in 1991 and situated in the city centre. Offers up-to-date conference facilities. (Prices in DM.)
TARIFF: Single 310–390, Double 390–470, Bk 27, Set menu 60–120.
CC: Amex, Diners, Euro/Access, Visa.

Eravis Hotel ★★ Bartok Béla u 152, 1113 Budapest.
☎ 1 166 7276, Fax 1 186 9320. English spoken. Open all year. 95 bedrooms (43 en suite). Tennis, parking, restaurant. ♿

Modern, well-equipped hotel situated in quiet surroundings, with easy access to the M1 and M7 motorways. Near the Kelenföldi railway station.
TARIFF: (1993) Single 1230–4000, Double 1660–5230.
CC: Amex, Diners, Euro/Access, Visa.

Hotel Flamenco Budapest ★★★★ Tas vezér u 7, 1113 Budapest.
☎ 1 161 2250, Fax 1 165 8007. English spoken.

Open all year. 358 bedrooms (all en suite with telephone). Indoor swimming pool, tennis, garage, parking, restaurant.
Modern hotel situated on the hilly Buda-side of Budapest overlooking a beautiful green park with a small lake. Fully air-conditioned rooms all with satellite TV, minibar, etc. Coffee shop, bar. 10 mins from city centre, with easy access to and from M1, M7, E6 highways. (Prices in DM.)
TARIFF: Single 130–200, Double 160–240, Set menu 20–35.
CC: Amex, Diners, Euro/Access, Visa.

Hotel Garden Budapest II, Ta'rogato u 2-4, 1021 Budapest.
☎ 1 115 8642, Fax 1 115 1235. English spoken.
Open all year. 100 bedrooms (all en suite with telephone). Tennis, garage, parking, restaurant.
This hotel is in an attractive district of Budapest, surrounded by parkland. It is ten minutes' drive from the city centre. Prices in DM.
TARIFF: Single 70–90, Double 80–120, Set menu 10–20.
CC: Amex, Diners, Euro/Access, Visa.

Gellert Hotel Szt Gellért tér 1, 1111 Budapest.
☎ 1 185 2200, Fax 1 166 6631. English spoken. Open all year. 239 bedrooms (239 telephone).

Hungary

Indoor swimming pool, outdoor swimming pool, parking, restaurant.

Traditional hotel located on the Danube embankment, close to the city centre and surrounded by the beautiful parks of Gellért Hill.

TARIFF: (1993) Single 7,000–12,000, Double 15,000–19,000, Set menu 800–4000.
CC: Amex, Diners, Euro/Access, Visa.

Ifjusag Hotel ★★★ Zivatar u 1-3,
1024 Budapest.
☏ 1 154 260, Fax 1 353 989. English spoken.
Open all year. 100 bedrooms (all en suite with telephone). Parking, restaurant. &

Situated in the green belt, in quiet surroundings, this hotel has fine views of the city. Panoramic restaurant. (Prices in DM.)

TARIFF: (1993) Single 75, Double 95, Bk 6.
CC: Amex, Diners, Euro/Access, Visa.

Korona Hotel Best Western
Kecskeméti u 14, 1053 Budapest.
☏ 1 117 4111, Fax 1 118 3867. English spoken.

Open all year. 433 bedrooms (all en suite with telephone). Indoor swimming pool, garage, restaurant. &

Newly built in downtown Budapest. It is a few minutes' walk from the Danube River and is opposite the National Museum. The underground and a bus stop are next to the hotel. (Prices in DM.)

TARIFF: Single 180–250, Double 220–310.
CC: Amex, Diners, Euro/Access, Visa.

Hotel Radisson Beke Budapest ★★★★
Teréz Korut 48, 1067 Budapest.
☏ 1 132 3300, Fax 1 533 380. English spoken.
Open all year. 246 bedrooms (all en suite with telephone). Indoor swimming pool, garage, parking, restaurant. &

Located in downtown Budapest, close to the

main business district and shopping area. Hungarian and international cuisine. (Prices in DM.)

TARIFF: Single 195–270, Double 245–320,
Set menu 35–55.
CC: Amex, Diners, Euro/Access, Visa.

Ramada Grand Hotel Margitsziget,
1138 Budapest.
☏ 1 131 7769, Fax 1 153 3029. English spoken.

Open all year. 162 bedrooms (all en suite with telephone). Indoor swimming pool, garage, parking, restaurant. &

Built in 1873, restored in 1987 to traditional style, set in picturesque surroundings on Margaret Island. Peaceful, yet in the heart of Budapest. (Prices in DM.)

TARIFF: Single 180–275, Double 230–325,
Set menu 30–50.
CC: Amex, Diners, Euro/Access, Visa.

Pannonia City Hotel Emke ★★★
Akacfa u 1-3, 1072 Budapest.
☏ 1 122 9230, Fax 1 122 9233. English spoken.
Open all year. 72 bedrooms (all en suite with telephone). Parking.

This seven-storey modern building is in the heart of Budapest, next to the city's business

Hungary

and shopping areas, with easy access to the cultural and tourist attractions. (Prices in £UK.)

TARIFF: (1993) Single 17–35, Double 24–48.
CC: Amex, Diners, Euro/Access, Visa.

Studium Hotel Harmat u 129, 1108 Budapest.
📞 1 147 4147, Fax 1 147 4147. English spoken.
Open all year. 73 bedrooms (all en suite).
Outdoor swimming pool, parking, restaurant.
TARIFF: Single 2200–2500, Double 2700–3300,
Set menu 270–500.
CC: Amex, Diners, Visa.

Thermal Hotel Helia Karpat u 62-64,
1133 Budapest.
📞 1 129 8650, Fax 1 120 1429.
English spoken.
Open all year. 262 bedrooms (all en suite
with telephone). Indoor swimming pool,
tennis, parking, restaurant. &

Modern, well-equipped hotel situated on banks of the River Danube. Includes conference and fitness facilities. (Prices in DM.)

TARIFF: Single 210–270, Double 250–320,
Set menu 38–55.
CC: Amex, Diners, Euro/Access, Visa.

Thermal Hotel Margitsziget ★★★★★
Margitsziget, 1138 Budapest.
📞 1 1323 373, Fax 1 1532 753.
English spoken.

Open all year. 206 bedrooms (all en suite
with telephone). Indoor swimming pool,
garage, parking, restaurant. &

The first ever metropolitan spa hotel in the world, in the picturesque surroundings of Margaret Island (drive in from the Arpad Bridge). Only 5 mins from the pedestrian area. (Prices in $US.)

TARIFF: Single 103–156, Double 132–185,
Set menu 21.
CC: Amex, Diners, Euro/Access, Visa.

Hotel Victoria ★★★★ Bem rakpart 11,
1011 Budapest.
📞 1 201 8644, Fax 1 201 5816. English spoken.

Open all year. 24 bedrooms (all en suite
with telephone). Garage, parking.

Small private hotel in the centre of Budapest with beautiful views of the Danube.

TARIFF: Single 7,000–10,000,
Double 7,500–10,500.
CC: Amex, Diners, Euro/Access, Visa.

DAVOD 23C

Fortuna Hotel ★★★ Rakoczi ut 55,
6524 Davod-Puspokpuszta.
📞 79 381181, Fax 79 361140.
English spoken.
Open all year. 22 bedrooms (all en suite
with telephone). Outdoor swimming pool,
tennis, parking, restaurant.

Hotel overlooks the River Ferenc, a tributary of the Danube. Davod is a spa town and is surrounded by the beautiful countryside of southern Hungary.

TARIFF: Single 1800, Double 2460–5500,
Bk 200, Set menu 125–565.
ÇC: Amex, Euro/Access.

EGER 23B

Hotel Korona ★★★ Tundérpart u 5,
3300 Eger.
📞 361 3670, Fax 361 0261.
English spoken.
Open all year. 21 bedrooms (18 en suite,
3 bath/shower only, 21 telephone). Garage,
parking, restaurant.

This hotel is quietly situated in the middle of the town, and is well signposted. (Prices in £UK.)

TARIFF: (1993) Single 16–22, Double 20–26.
CC: Amex, Diners, Euro/Access, Visa.

Hungary

FONYOD 23C

Kek To Hotel Kék to Udülöfalu,
8693 Lengyeltoti.
☎ 853 0422. English spoken.
Open 17/04 to 15/10. 37 bedrooms (all en suite
with telephone). Tennis, parking, restaurant.
*New hotel in a holiday village with many
amenities and by the side of a lake. Located
just off the road from Fonyod to Kaposvar, and
is well signposted.*
TARIFF: (1993) Single 2100–3800,
Double 2500–4500, Bk 260, Set menu 900.
CC: Amex.

GYOR 23A

Pax Hotel ★★★ Dozsa Gy u 2,
9090 Pannonhalma.
☎ 967 0006, Fax 967 0007.
English spoken.
Open all year. 25 bedrooms (all en suite
with telephone). Parking, restaurant.
*Country-style hotel situated in a town famous
for its Benedictine abbey. Pannonhalma is
20 km south of Gyor, on route 82.*
TARIFF: (1993) Single 850–3500,
Double 1000–5000, Bk 240,
Set menu 400–1400.
CC: Diners, Euro/Access, Visa.

Raba Hotel ★★★ Arpad ut 34, 9021 Gyor.
☎ 963 15533, Fax 963 11124.
English spoken.

Open all year. 167 bedrooms (all en suite
with telephone). Parking, restaurant.
*In the "town of four rivers", halfway between
Vienna and Budapest, near the Austrian and
Slovak borders. International cuisine and
Hungarian dishes. (Prices in DM.)*
TARIFF: Single 79, Double 99, Bk 7,
Set menu 12–16.
CC: Amex, Diners, Euro/Access, Visa.

HORTOBAGY 23B

Epona Hotel ★★★★ 4071 Hortobagy-Mata.
☎ 526 9092, Fax 526 9027. English spoken.
Open all year. 138 bedrooms
(all bath/shower only with telephone). Indoor
swimming pool, tennis, parking, restaurant.
*Attractive, well-equipped hotel specialising in
horse-riding holidays. Situated in the National
Park of Hortobagy, 35 km from Debrecen and
190 km east of Budapest. (Prices in DM.)*
TARIFF: (1993) Single 95–108, Double 120–148,
Set menu 20–40.
CC: Amex, Diners, Euro/Access, Visa.

MOSONMAGYAROVAR 23A

Hotel Saint Florian Fö u 43,
9200 Mosonmagyarovar.
☎ 981 3177, Fax 981 5064. English spoken.
Open all year. 24 bedrooms
(all bath/shower only with telephone).
Parking, restaurant. &
*Hotel is 10 km from the Austrian border. The
restaurant offers gipsy music in the evening,
with cocktail bar on a gallery. In summer the
garden has a pleasant atmosphere, with the
Lajta brook running between the two
buildings. (Prices in DM.)*
TARIFF: (1993) Single 72–75, Double 84–87,
Set menu 15–18.
CC: Amex.

SIOFOK 23C

Hotel Ezustpart ★★ Liszt Ference Sétany 3,
8609 Siofok.
☎ 841 3622, Fax 841 3358.
Open all year. 350 bedrooms
(all bath/shower only). Indoor swimming
pool, tennis, parking, restaurant.
*Large, modern hotel beside to Lake Balaton,
and the beach. Includes a fitness centre and
beauty parlour.*
TARIFF: (1993) Single 960–3900,
Double 1200–4800, Set menu 600.
CC: none.

SOPRON 23A

Solar Club Hotel Panorama St 16,
9400 Sopron.
☎ 991 1675, Fax 991 1675. English spoken.
Open all year. 104 bedrooms
(all bath/shower only with telephone).
Outdoor swimming pool, tennis, parking.
*Hotel consists of two or four-bedded self
catering apartments, all with well-equipped*

Hungary

kitchenette and dining area. Sopron is near the border with Austria and only about 70 km from Vienna.

TARIFF: Single 2200–2600, Double 3400–5400.
CC: Amex.

SZEGED 23D

Royal Hotel ★★★ Kölcsey u 1-3, 6721 Szeged.
☎ 621 2911, Fax 621 2123. English spoken.
Open all year. 110 bedrooms (74 bath/shower only, 110 telephone). Outdoor swimming pool, tennis, golf 1 km, garage, parking. ♿

This hotel is in the very centre of the town of Szeged, south-east of Budapest.

TARIFF: (1993) Single 2000–3500, Double 3600–6000.
CC: Amex, Diners, Euro/Access, Visa.

VELENCE 23A

Helios Hotel Topart u 34, 2481 Velence.
☎ 226 8159, Fax 226 8354. English spoken.
Open all year. 15 bedrooms (all en suite with telephone). Parking, restaurant. ♿

Quiet hotel, 50 m from Lake Velence. Located just north of Gardony, and 45 km from Budapest.

TARIFF: (1993) Single 2200–3000, Double 3000–4400, Set menu 250–350.
CC: none.

Juventus Hotel Topart u 25/A, 2481 Velence.
☎ 226 8159, Fax 226 8362. English spoken.
Open all year. 35 bedrooms (all bath/shower only with telephone). Tennis, parking, restaurant.

By the side of Lake Velence, with its facilities for water sports. Just north of Gardony, and 45 km from Budapest.

TARIFF: (1993) Single 2200–3000, Double 3200–4800, Set menu 550–750.
CC: none.

ITALY

Jutting into the warm Mediterranean, the "high-heeled boot" peninsula of Italy has land borders only along the Alps in the north, with France, Switzerland, Austria and the former Yugoslavia. The mainland is 1,100 km long and 150–200 km wide. Together with the islands, including Sardinia and Sicily, the land area is 301,287 sq km (a quarter as large again as the UK). Almost three-quarters of the 58 million Italians live in towns and cities. Local currency is the lire, made up of 100 centesimi (centimes).

The land sweeps down from the Alps to the northern lowland plain, with the Dolomites in the north-east. The rugged Apennines, forested on the lower slopes with deciduous and conifer trees, run along the central peninsula. Europe's only active volcano, Vesuvius, sits on the boot's southern "ankle", near Naples. Wolf, brown bear, boar, chamois, ibex and mouflon dwell in the forests and reserves. Italy's climate is warm and moist in the north, hot and dry in the south.

The capital, Rome, has a population of 2.7 million, and is one of the world's truly great and historic cities. Milan in the north is the main centre for commerce and industry and, along with Naples and Turin, has more than one million people. Venice and Florence are world centres for arts and architecture. The 305,000 km of roads, with more than 6,000 km of autostrada (motorway), give a road density (km per sq km) of 1, compared to the UK's 1.5. The main 1,250-km autostrada runs the length of Italy, linking Milan, Rome and Naples. Note that resorts for Italian islands are listed under their island names in the A–Z directory.

ABANO TERME 20C

Hotel Due Torri ★★★★
Via Pietro d'Abano 18, 35031 Abano Terme.
☎ 049 8669277, Fax 049 8669927.
English spoken.
Open 19/03 to 27/11. 80 bedrooms
(all en suite with telephone). Indoor
swimming pool, outdoor swimming pool,
tennis, golf 5 km, parking, restaurant.

In town centre, surrounded by own parklike setting. 50 km from Venezia. Fully air conditioned. Beauty parlour, 2 thermal swimming pools, Italian cuisine, own spa centre, ideal place for relaxation and the 'cure'.

TARIFF: Single 95,000, Double 145,000,
Bk 10,000, Set menu 40,000–45,000.
CC: Amex, Diners, Euro/Access, Visa.

Grand Hotel Trieste & Victoria Via Pietro
d'Abano 1, 35031 Abano Terme.
☎ 049 8669101, Fax 049 8669779.
English spoken.
Open 01/03 to 30/11. 113 bedrooms (all
en suite with telephone). Indoor swimming
pool, outdoor swimming pool, tennis,
golf 10 km, garage, parking, restaurant. &

First-class hotel, completely renovated to combine its tradional style and elegance with modern comfort. Thermal treatments, modern beauty and fitness centre, 4 swimming pools, one with fresh water, one with whirlpool and underwater-massage, one indoor and one outdoor with thermal, therapeutic water. 40 minutes' drive from Venezia, 15 minutes' drive from Padova.

TARIFF: Single 110,000–121,000,
Double 180,000–202,000.
CC: Amex, Diners, Euro/Access, Visa.

ALASSIO 20C

Hotel Diana Grand ★★★★ Via Garibaldi 110,
17021 Alassio.
☎ 0182 642701, Fax 0182 640304.
English spoken.
Open 01/01 to 20/11 & 24/12 to 31/12.
78 bedrooms (all en suite with telephone).
Indoor swimming pool, golf 15 km, garage,
parking, restaurant.

The hotel features large terrace restaurant overlooking a private, sandy beach. Inside is a fitness centre and pool. Situated in Alassio off the S1 south of Savonna. Air conditioning and inside pool with hydromassage.

TARIFF: Single 80,000–120,000,
Double 150,000–280,000,
Set menu 35,000–65,000.
CC: Amex, Diners, Euro/Access, Visa.

ANCONA   20D

Hotel Grand Palace 1 ★★★★ Lungomare
Vanvitelli 24, 60121 Ancona.
☎ 071 201813, Fax 071 2074832.
English spoken.
Open all year. 41 bedrooms (all en suite
with telephone). Golf 15 km, garage.

*First class hotel centrally located in a quiet
place facing the harbour. Every room with
bath and shower, telephone, air conditioning,
TV, comfortable suites. American bar, snack,
lounges. A pleasant place to stay for tourists
and businessmen.*
TARIFF: Single 120,000–130,000,
Double 210,000–230,000, Bk 20,000.
CC: Amex, Diners, Euro/Access, Visa.

ASSISI   21A

Hotel San Francesco ★★★
Via San Francesco 48, 06080 Assisi.
☎ 075 812281, Fax 075 816237. English spoken.
Open all year. 44 bedrooms (all en suite
with telephone). Outdoor swimming pool,
tennis, golf 1 km, parking, restaurant. &
*Recently modernised, opposite St Francis
Basilika. Rooms overlooking the church and
the plain of Umbria, with all comforts.*
TARIFF: Single 118,000, Double 178,000,
Set menu 40,000–50,000.
CC: Amex, Diners, Euro/Access, Visa.

Hotel Umbra Via Degli Archi 6, 06081 Assisi.
☎ 075 812240, Fax 075 813653. English spoken.
Open 15/03 to 31/12. 25 bedrooms
(all en suite with telephone). Restaurant. &
This small, family-run hotel is in a quiet back

*street just off the main square, Piazza del
Comune, in the heart of the town, with
panoramic views over the Umbrian plains
below.*
TARIFF: Single 75,000–95,000,
Double 95,000–125,000, Bk 15,000,
Set menu 30,000–45,000.
CC: Amex, Diners, Euro/Access, Visa.

BARBERINO MUGELLO   20C

Hotel Barberino ★★★ Viale don Minzoni 55,
Barberino Mugello, 50031 Firenze.
☎ 055 8420051. English spoken.
Open all year. 78 bedrooms (all en suite
with telephone). Outdoor swimming pool,
parking, restaurant.
Barberino is north of Firenze off the A1.
TARIFF: (1993) Single 70,000–95,000,
Double 110,000–140,000, Bk 15,000.
CC: Amex, Diners, Euro/Access, Visa.

BELGIRATE   20C

Hotel Milano ★★★★ Via Sempione 4-8,
28040 Belgirate.
☎ 0322 76525, Fax 0322 76295.
English spoken.

Open all year. 60 bedrooms (all en suite
with telephone). Outdoor swimming pool,
tennis, golf 9 km, garage, parking, restaurant.
*The hotel offers a private beach and terrace
restaurant with views over Lago Maggiore. On
the road to Simplon, 5 km south of Stresa.*
TARIFF: Single 75,000–98,000,
Double 136,000–158,000,
Set menu 45,000–58,000.
CC: Amex, Diners, Euro/Access, Visa.

Villa Carlotta 1 ★★★★ Via Sempione 117,
28040 Belgirate.
☎ 0322 76461, Fax 0322 76705. English spoken.

Open all year. 140 bedrooms (all en suite with telephone). Outdoor swimming pool, tennis, golf 9 km, parking, restaurant. &

The hotel is set in parkland with pool, tennis court and private beach. Situated in the basin of the Barromean Islands, 5 km south of Stresa.

TARIFF: Single 85,000–98,000, Double 140,000–198,000, Set menu 45,000–58,000.
CC: Amex, Diners, Euro/Access, Visa.

BOLOGNA   20C

Hotel San Donato ★★★★ Via Zamboni 16, 40100 Bologna.
☎ 051 235395, Fax 051 230547.
Open all year. 60 bedrooms (all en suite).
TARIFF: (1993) Single 90,000–180,000, Double 130,000–260,000.
CC: Euro/Access, Visa.

BOLZANO   20A

Hotel Grifone-Greif ★★★★ Piazza Walther 7, 39100 Bolzano.
☎ 0471 977056, Fax 0471 980613.
English spoken.
Open all year. 132 bedrooms (102 en suite, 132 telephone). Outdoor swimming pool, garage, parking, restaurant. &
Traditional hotel in the historic part of the town. Garden restaurant.

TARIFF: Single 80,000–170,000, Double 140,000–240,000, Set menu 25,000–95,000.
CC: Amex, Diners, Euro/Access, Visa.

BORDIGHERA   20C

Hotel Grand Cap Amelio ★★★★
Via Virgilio 5, 18012 Bordighera.
☎ 0184 264333, Fax 0184 264244. English spoken.

Open 23/12 to 15/11. 104 bedrooms (all en suite with telephone). Outdoor swimming pool, golf 12 km, garage, parking.
RESTAURANT: Closed Tues.

First-class hotel with good facilities and excellent restaurant.

TARIFF: Single 132,000–136,000, Double 228,000–236,000, Set menu 56,000–62,000.
CC: Amex, Diners, Euro/Access, Visa.

Italy

Grand Hotel del Mare ★★★★
Via Portico Della Punta 34, 18012 Bordighera.
☎ 0184 262201, Fax 0184 262394.
English spoken.

Open all year. 114 bedrooms (all en suite
with telephone). Outdoor swimming pool,
tennis, golf 8 km, garage, parking. ⅃
RESTAURANT: Closed Mon.

*Superior hotel with well-appointed rooms. Fax
(on request). Satellite TV, minibar, balcony
with sea view. Meeting facilities for 180,
outdoor salt-water pool, private beach, fitness
centre. 2 km from Bordighera, 55 km from
Nice airport, in France.*
TARIFF: Single 130,000–160,000,
Double 200,000–320,000, Bk 22,000,
Set menu 60,000–75,000.
CC: Amex, Diners, Euro/Access, Visa.

BRINDISI   21B

Hotel Majestic ★★★★ Corso Umberto 151,
72100 Brindisi.
☎ 0831 222941, Fax 0831 524071.
Open all year. 60 bedrooms (all en suite).
TARIFF: (1993) Single 77,000–80,000,
Double 115,000–123,000.
CC: none.

BRUNICO (BRUNECK)   20A

Hotel Post ★★★ Graben 9, 39031 Brunico.
☎ 0474 55527, Fax 0474 31603.
English spoken.
Open all year. 60 bedrooms (31 en suite,
10 bath/shower only, 60 telephone). Parking.
RESTAURANT: Closed Mon.

*A family-run hotel since 1850, situated in the
middle of the town.*
TARIFF: Single 64,000–76,000,
Double 112,000–136,000,
Set menu 20,000–25,000.
CC: Euro/Access, Visa.

CANNOBIO   20C

Hotel Pironi ★★★ Via Marconi, Cannobio,
28052 Novara.
☎ 0323 70624, Fax 0323 72398.
English spoken.
Open 01/03 to 31/10. 12 bedrooms
(all en suite with telephone). Parking.

*Fifteenth-century, newly restored house in the
historic centre of Cannobio, with very
comfortable accommodation.*
TARIFF: Single 60,000–80,000,
Double 90,000–120,000, Bk 15,000.
CC: Diners, Euro/Access, Visa.

CHATILLON   20C

Hotel Marisa ★★★ Via Pellissier 10,
11024 Chatillon.
☎ 0166 61845, Fax 0166 563110.
Open all year. 28 bedrooms (all en suite
with telephone). Garage, parking. ⅃
RESTAURANT: Closed Mon.

*Located 3 km from St-Vincent and 20 km east
of Aosta on the A5.*
TARIFF: Single 50,000–65,000,
Double 80,000–95,000, Bk 9,000,
Set menu 22,000–50,000.
CC: Amex, Diners, Euro/Access, Visa.

COMO   20C

Hotel Villa Flori ★★★★ Via per Cernobbio 12,
22019 Como.
☎ 031 573105, Fax 031 570379.
English spoken.
Open all year. 45 bedrooms (all en suite
with telephone). Garage, parking. ⅃
RESTAURANT: Closed Mon.

*Set in a beautiful private park, yet only a short
distance from the town centre with a splendid
view of Lake Como. The original portion of this
intimate hotel was constructed in 1860. Each
of the distinctly decorated guest rooms boasts a
lake-view terrace. Private mooring for sailing
and motor boats. Restaurant is very popular
with local people.*
TARIFF: Single 140,000–200,000,
Double 165,000–260,000, Bk 18,000,
Set menu 50,000–75,000.
CC: Amex, Diners, Euro/Access, Visa.

CORTINA D'AMPEZZO   20A

Hotel Menardi Via Majon 110/112,
32043 Cortina d'Ampezzo.
☎ 0436 2400, Fax 0436 862183.
English spoken.

Open 20/12 to 10/04 & 20/06 to 20/09.
53 bedrooms (all en suite with telephone).
Garage, parking.

A family-run hotel set in the scenic beauty of the Dolomites only 1.5 km from the town centre.

TARIFF: (1993) Single 80,000–180,000,
Double 140,000–220,000.
CC: none.

CREMONA 20C

Hotel Continental ★★★★
Piazza Liberta 27, 26100 Cremona.
✆ 0372 434141, Fax 0372 434141.
English spoken.
Open all year. 57 bedrooms (all en suite with telephone). Garage, parking, restaurant.

A first-class hotel centrally located near the station and motorways.

TARIFF: (1993) Single 110,000,
Double 160,000,
Set menu 35,000–45,000.
CC: Amex, Diners, Euro/Access, Visa.

DIANO MARINA 20C

Hotel Torino ★★★ Via Milano 42,
18013 Diano Marino.
✆ 018 3495105, Fax 018 3404602.
English spoken.
Open 09/01 to 31/10. 80 bedrooms
(all en suite with telephone). Outdoor swimming pool, garage, parking, restaurant.

Quietly situated in the town centre, with its own well-equipped private beach.

TARIFF: Single 60,000–80,000,
Double 70,000–130,000, Bk 10,000,
Set menu 25,000–45,000.
CC: none.

DOMODOSSOLA 20A

Hotel Eurossola ★★★ Piazza Matteotti 36,
28037 Domodossola.
✆ 0324 481326, Fax 0324 248748.
English spoken.
Open all year. 23 bedrooms (all en suite with telephone). Outdoor swimming pool, tennis, garage, parking, restaurant.

A first-class hotel of recent construction with all modern facilities. Restaurant with excellent cuisine.

TARIFF: Single 70,000, Double 100,000,
Set menu 22,000.
CC: Amex, Diners, Euro/Access, Visa.

ELBA

PROCCHIO 21A

Hotel Desiree Loc Spartaia,
57030 Procchio, Elba.
✆ 0565 907311. English spoken.
Open 01/04 to 31/10. 69 bedrooms
(all en suite with telephone). Outdoor swimming pool, tennis, golf 16 km, parking, restaurant. &

Well-equipped seaside hotel with its own private beach. Special rate for green fees at Acquabona Golf Club. Located in a green valley and 3 km from the airport.

TARIFF: (1993) Double 120,000–240,000.
CC: Amex, Diners, Euro/Access, Visa.

END OF ELBA RESORTS

FERRARA 20C

Hotel Ripagrande ★★★★ Via Ripagrande 21,
44100 Ferrara.
✆ 0537 965250, Fax 0532 764377.
English spoken.
Open all year. 40 bedrooms (all en suite with telephone). Garage, parking.
RESTAURANT: good. Closed Aug & Mon all year.

Exceptional hotel, in one of the many renaissance palaces in town. Stylish entrance hall made of the same brick used for most of the famous monuments in Ferrara, with marble columns reclaimed from Yugoslavian buildings. Restaurant offers typical local cuisine.

TARIFF: Single 180,000–210,000,
Double 240,000–290,000,
Set menu 35,000–55,000.
CC: Amex, Diners, Euro/Access, Visa.

FIESOLE 20C

Albergo Villa Bonelli ★★★ Via Poeti 1,
Fiesole, 50014 Firenze.
✆ 055 59513, Fax 055 598942. English spoken.
Open all year. 20 bedrooms (all en suite with telephone). Golf 7 km, garage, restaurant.

A family-run hotel in this old Etruscan village, surrounded by a magnificent landscape and has every modern convenience. Typical Tuscan cuisine served in the restaurant overlooking the Florentine valley. Only 15 minutes from Firenze.

TARIFF: Single 75,000–100,000,
Double 140,000–155,000, Set menu 40,000.
CC: Diners, Euro/Access, Visa.

Italy

FINALE LIGURE 20C

Hotel Punta Est ★★★★ Via Aurelia 1, 17024 Savona.
📞 0196 00611, Fax 0196 00611.
English spoken.

Open 01/05 to 30/09. 40 bedrooms (all en suite with telephone). Outdoor swimming pool, tennis, golf 25 km, parking, restaurant.

East of the historic town, converted from an 18th-century villa, overlooking the sea. The interior is cool and elegant. The terraces and pool have lovely views.

TARIFF: Single 100,000–180,000, Double 180,000–250,000, Bk 20,000, Set menu 40,000–70,000.
CC: Amex, Euro/Access, Visa.

FIRENZE (FLORENCE) 20C

Hotel Adriatico ★★★★ Via M Finiguerra 9, 50123 Firenze.
📞 055 2381781, Fax 055 2896611.
English spoken.
Open all year. 114 bedrooms (all en suite with telephone). Golf 1 km, parking, restaurant.
TARIFF: Single 110,000–180,000, Double 200,000–250,000.
CC: Amex, Diners, Euro/Access, Visa.

Hotel Azzi ★ Via Faenze 56, 50137 Firenze.
📞 055 213806, Fax 055 213806.
Open all year. 12 bedrooms (4 en suite, 3 bath/shower only). Garage. &

Popular with students and artists, this hotel offers attractive surroundings at a competitive price, only 200 m from the central station in the centre of Firenze.

TARIFF: (1993) Single 40,000–45,000, Double 65,000–74,000.
CC: Amex, Euro/Access, Visa.

Hotel Claridge ★★★ Piazza Piave 3, 50122 Firenze.
📞 055 2346736, Fax 055 2341199.
English spoken.
Open all year. 32 bedrooms (all en suite with telephone). Parking.

Close to the River Arno and within easy walking distance of the historic buildings, monuments and shopping centre of Firenze. Offers all the modern conveniences of a recently renovated hotel.

TARIFF: (1993) Single 90,000–120,000, Double 120,000–210,000.
CC: Amex, Diners, Euro/Access, Visa.

Hotel Consigli ★★★
Lungarno A Vespucci, 50, 50123 Firenze.
📞 055 214172, Fax 055 219367.
English spoken.
Open all year. 20 bedrooms (all en suite with telephone). Garage, parking. &

Comfortable hotel in a fine Renaissance building. Centrally located and overlooking the Arno River. Easy access and good parking facilities.

TARIFF: Single 80,000–100,000, Double 120,000–150,000.
CC: Euro/Access, Visa.

Albergo Croce di Malta ★★★★
Via della Scala 7, 50123 Firenze.
📞 055 218351, Fax 055 5287121.
English spoken.
Open all year. 98 bedrooms (all en suite with telephone). Outdoor swimming pool, golf 10 km. &
RESTAURANT: Closed Sun & Mon lunch.

A restored and converted convent, this hotel is in the historic and commercial centre.

TARIFF: (1993) Single 160,000–255,000, Double 200,000–340,000, Set menu 40,000–70,000.
CC: Amex, Diners, Euro/Access, Visa.

Grand Hotel ★★★★★ Piazza Ognissanti 1, 50123 Firenze.
📞 055 278781. English spoken.
Open all year. 107 bedrooms (all en suite). Golf 15 km, garage, parking, restaurant.

An historic hotel, situated beside the Arno within minutes of the Ponte Vecchio. The intimate restaurant serves Mediterranean cuisine.

TARIFF: (1993) Single 306,000–340,000, Double 450,000–500,000, Bk 25,000, Set menu 75,000.
CC: Amex, Diners, Euro/Access, Visa.

Hotel Loggiato dei Serviti ★★★
Piazza S S Annunziata 3, 50122 Firenze.
☎ 055 289592, Fax 055 289595. English spoken.
Open all year. 29 bedrooms (all en suite
with telephone). Restaurant.
Built in 1500, and situated in the centre of the
city. Rooms have period furnishings.
TARIFF: Single 110,000–155,000,
Double 170,000–225,000.
CC: Amex, Diners, Euro/Access, Visa.

Hotel Londra ★★★★ Via J Da Diacceto 16-20,
50123 Firenze.
☎ 055 2382791, Fax 055 210682.
English spoken.
Open all year. 158 bedrooms (all en suite
with telephone). Garage, restaurant.
Superior first-class hotel which has just been
renovated. Situated in the centre of the city it is
near the station, the most important museums
and buildings, Congress Centre and fair.
Comfortably furnished rooms. Restaurant,
American bar, piano bar, conference room for
up to 150 people, private garage.
TARIFF: Single 132,500–265,000,
Double 182,500–365,000.
CC: Amex, Diners, Euro/Access, Visa.

Hotel Select Via G Falliano 24, 50144 Firenze.
☎ 055 330342, Fax 055 351506. English spoken.
Open all year. 38 bedrooms (all en suite
with telephone). Parking.
A carefully renovated 19th-century villa near
the main thoroughfares of Firenze. Comfortable
and bright rooms with cherry-wood furniture.
Lots of antique furniture and marble.
TARIFF: Single 60,000–110,000,
Double 110,000–150,000, Bk 10,000.
CC: Amex, Diners, Euro/Access, Visa.

Hotel Vila Villoresi ★★★★ Via Ciampi, 2,
50019 Sesto Fiorentino.
☎ 055 4489032, Fax 055 442063. English spoken.

Open all year. 28 bedrooms (all en suite
with telephone). Outdoor swimming pool,
golf 20 km, parking, restaurant. &
The building dates from the 12th century and
was rebuilt during the Renaissance, complete
with frescos and vaulted ceilings. Now a stylish
and interesting hotel. Easy to reach from the
A1, Prato Calenzano exit, towards Sesto
Fiorentino. 8 km from Firenze.
TARIFF: Single 150,000,
Double 240,000–330,000,
Set menu 50,000–55,000.
CC: Amex, Diners, Euro/Access, Visa.

Hotel Ville sull'Arno ★★★★ Lungarno C
Colombo 3-5, 50136 Firenze.
☎ 055 670971, Fax 055 678244. English spoken.
Open all year. 47 bedrooms (all en suite
with telephone). Outdoor swimming pool,
golf 8 km, garage, parking. &
Air-conditioned hotel with garden, on the
banks of the River Arno. Only 5 minutes from
town centre.
TARIFF: (1993) Single 95,000–180,000,
Double 160,000–280,000.
CC: Amex, Diners, Euro/Access, Visa.

FOGGIA   20B

Hotel Cicolella ★★★★ Maggio 60,
71100 Foggia.
☎ 0881 3890, Fax 0881 78984.
Open all year. 125 bedrooms (all en suite
with telephone).
TARIFF: (1993) Single 83,000–116,000,
Double 143,000–225,000.
CC: none.

FORTE DEI MARMI   20C

Hotel Raffaelli Park ★★★★ Via Massini 37,
55042 Forte dei Marmi.
☎ 0584 787294, Fax 0584 787418.
English spoken.
Open all year. 28 bedrooms (all en suite
with telephone). Restaurant.
A Best Western hotel, surrounded by pretty
gardens and with its own private beach. Very
comfortable accommodation and good
restaurant. Ideal location for exploring the
surrounding countryside and taking
advantage of nearby sports facilities. West of
Lucca off the A11/A12.
TARIFF: Single 127,000–195,000,
Double 189,000–325,000,
Set menu 35,000–50,000.
CC: Amex, Diners, Euro/Access, Visa.

Italy

GARDA 20C

Hotel Regina Adelaide Via Settembre 32, 37016 Garda.
☎ 045 7255977, Fax 045 7256263.
English spoken.
Open all year. 60 bedrooms (all en suite with telephone). Golf 1 km, parking, restaurant.
Beside the lake, in a quiet shady park, the hotel offers all conveniences and comforts with good cuisine. Just off the A22, Affi exit.
TARIFF: (1993) Single 100,000–120,000, Double 130,000–270,000.
CC: Amex, Euro/Access, Visa.

GARDONE RIVIERA 20C

Hotel Grand ★★★★ Via Zanardelli 72, 25083 Gardone Riviera.
☎ 0365 20261, Fax 0365 22695.
Open 08/04 to 20/10. 180 bedrooms (all en suite with telephone). Outdoor swimming pool, golf 10 km.
Built at the end of the last century but has been fully modernised. There is a private lakeside promenade, heated swimming pool and motorboat jetty. It is situated north of Desenzano on the lakeside.
TARIFF: Single 126,000–185,000, Double 252,000–314,000.
CC: Amex, Diners, Euro/Access.

GEMONA DEL FRIULI 20B

Hotel Pittini ★★★ Udine-Piazza della Stazione, 33014 Gemona del Friuli.
☎ 0432 971195, Fax 0432 971380.
English spoken.
Open all year. 16 bedrooms (all en suite with telephone). Tennis, golf 2 km, garage, parking.
A new hotel opposite the railway station in Gemona, suitable for families. 20 km north of Udine.
TARIFF: Single 80,000, Double 120,000, Bk 10,000.
CC: Amex, Diners, Euro/Access, Visa.

GENOVA (GENOA) 20C

Hotel Agnello d'Oro ★★★
Vico Monachette 6, 16126 Genova.
☎ 010 262084, Fax 010 561124.
Open all year. 32 bedrooms (all en suite with telephone).
TARIFF: (1993) Single 50,000, Double 90,000.
CC: none.

Hotel Fado 78 ★★ Via Fado 82, 16010 Mele.
☎ 010 6971060. English spoken.
Open all year. 8 bedrooms (all en suite with telephone). Parking.
RESTAURANT: Closed Mon & Tues.
Small, family-run hotel, with secluded garden. From Voltri, west part of Genova, take 456 for 7 km (towards Ovada).
TARIFF: (1993) Single 50,000, Double 80,000, Bk 10,000, Set menu 30,000–40,000.
CC: none.

Hotel Savoia Majestic ★★★★ Via Arsenale di Terra 5, 16126 Genova.
☎ 010 261641, Fax 010 261883.
Open all year. 120 bedrooms (all en suite with telephone).
TARIFF: (1993) Single 120,000–160,000, Double 160,000–320,000.
CC: none.

GREVE 20C

Hotel Villa de Barone ★★★ Via S Leolino 49, 50020 Greve-Fi.
☎ 0558 52621, Fax 0558 52277. English spoken.
Open 01/04 to 21/11. 27 bedrooms (all en suite with telephone). Outdoor swimming pool, tennis, golf 20 km, parking, restaurant.
Only 30 minutes' drive from Firenze and Siena, this converted villa retains its original character with large gardens and pool among the vineyards and olive groves.
TARIFF: (1993) Double 160,000–185,000.
CC: Amex, Euro/Access, Visa.

IMPERIA-PORTO MAURIZIO 20C

Hotel Robinia ★★★ Via Pirinoli 14, 18100 Imperia.
☎ 0183 62720, Fax 0183 60635.
English spoken.

Open all year. 55 bedrooms (all en suite with telephone). Outdoor swimming pool, garage, parking, restaurant.

Centrally situated, about 100 m from the harbour and the sea. Fine views of the gulf. Private beach.

TARIFF: Single 45,000–58,000, Double 55,000–96,000, Bk 6,000, Set menu 27,000–32,000.
CC: Amex, Euro/Access, Visa.

LA SPEZIA 20C

Hotel Residence ★★★★ Via Rino 62, 19100 La Spezia.
℡ 0187 504141, Fax 0187 514959.
Open all year. 50 bedrooms (all en suite with telephone).
TARIFF: (1993) Single 110,000–125,000, Double 140,000–165,000.
CC: none.

LIDO DI JESOLO 20C

Park Hotel Brasilia ★★★★ Via Levantina 2, 30017 Lido di Jesolo.
℡ 0421 380851, Fax 0421 92244.
English spoken.
Open 01/04 to 30/09. 48 bedrooms (all en suite with telephone). Outdoor swimming pool, golf 10 km, garage, parking, restaurant.

Pleasant hotel with American bar and private beach.

TARIFF: (1993) Single 80,000–130,000, Double 120,000–216,000, Set menu 43,000–78,000.
CC: Amex, Diners, Euro/Access, Visa.

LIVORNO (LEGHORN) 20C

Hotel Giappone ★★★ Via Grande 65, 57123 Livorno.
℡ 0586 880241, Fax 0586 899955.
Open all year. 56 bedrooms (all en suite with telephone).
TARIFF: (1993) Single 68,000, Double 97,000.
CC: none.

LUCCA 20C

Hotel Country Club ★★ Via Pesciatina 874, 55010 Gragnano.
℡ 0983 434404, Fax 0583 974344.
English spoken.
Open all year. 88 bedrooms (all en suite with telephone). Outdoor swimming pool, parking, restaurant. ᕃ

Recently constructed holiday complex situated in the hills of Lucca. Lies 30 minutes away from Pisa and is 10 km north of Lucca.

TARIFF: (1993) Single 65,000–77,000, Double 95,000–109,000, Bk 12,000, Set menu 25,000–50,000.
CC: Amex, Diners, Euro/Access, Visa.

Hotel Villa Casanova ★★
55050 Nozzano.
℡ 0583 548449. English spoken.

Open all year. 40 bedrooms (all en suite). Outdoor swimming pool, tennis, parking, restaurant.

Set on a wooded hillside with good views down the valley.

TARIFF: Single 60,000, Double 95,000, Set menu 28,000.
CC: Amex.

MATTINATA 21B

Hotel Alba del Gargano ★★★★
Corso Matino 102,
71030 Mattinata del Gargano.
℡ 0884 4771, Fax 0884 4772.
English spoken.
Open all year. 40 bedrooms (all en suite with telephone). Garage, parking, restaurant. ᕃ

A family-run hotel in the centre of town and convenient for shopping and night life. The restaurant is known locally for being reliably good and plentiful. Motorboat hire available for exploring the spectacular coastline.

TARIFF: (1993) Single 43,500–90,000, Double 72,000–114,000, Bk 5,000, Set menu 35,000–114,000.
CC: Euro/Access, Visa.

Italy

MERANO 20A

Hotel Fragsburg ★★★★ Via Fragsburg 3, 39012 Merano.
☎ 0473 244071, Fax 0473 244493.
English spoken.

Open 15/04 to 05/11. 18 bedrooms (all en suite with telephone). Outdoor swimming pool, tennis, garage, parking. RESTAURANT: good. Closed Fri.

Once a hunting castle, this small hotel is perched on the hilltop with stunning views over valley and mountains, north of Bolzano. It stands in a very peaceful 22-acre park with tropical trees, and heated swimming pool.

TARIFF: Single 60,000–80,000, Double 90,000–150,000, Bk 10,000, Set menu 35,000–70,000.
CC: none.

Kurhotel Palace ★★★★★ Via Cavour 2-4, 39012 Merano/Meran.
☎ 0473 211300, Fax 0473 34181.
English spoken.
Open 01/03 to 30/11. 130 bedrooms (all en suite with telephone). Indoor swimming pool, outdoor swimming pool, parking, restaurant. &

Luxury hotel with excellent facilities.

TARIFF: Single 150,000–200,000, Double 260,000–360,000, Set menu 55,000–95,000.
CC: Amex, Diners, Euro/Access, Visa.

Schlosshotel Tscherms ★★★ Via Raffein 20, 39010 Tscherms.
☎ 0473 52352, Fax 0473 54559. English spoken.
Open 03/04 to 31/10. 27 bedrooms (all en suite with telephone). Indoor swimming pool, parking, restaurant. &

Tyrolean-style hotel with rustic ambience.
TARIFF: (1993) Single 29,000–46,000, Double 58,000–92,000, Bk 22,000, Set menu 20,000–27,000.
CC: Amex, Euro/Access, Visa.

MILANO (MILAN) 20C

Hotel Cavour ★★★★ Via Fatebenefratelli 21, 20121 Milano.
☎ 02 6572051, Fax 02 6592263.
Open all year. 130 bedrooms (all en suite with telephone).
TARIFF: (1993) Single 205,000, Double 230,000.
CC: none.

Hotel Duca di Milano ★★★★★ Piazza della Repubblica 13 Milano.
☎ 02 6284, Fax 02 6555966. English spoken.

Open all year. 99 bedrooms (all en suite with telephone). Golf 15 km, garage, restaurant. &

Situated in a quiet elegant corner of the business centre, the hotel is the ideal location for business and pleasure. Vacationing visitors will appreciate its convenience for historic monuments and fine shops. Businessmen will be pleased by the conference and business facilities. Comfortable accommodation at affordable prices.

TARIFF: Single 361,760–452,200, Double 504,560–630,700, Bk 30,940.
CC: Amex, Diners, Euro/Access, Visa.

Hotel Florida ★★★ Via Lepetit 33, 20121 Milano.
☎ 02 6705921, Fax 02 6692867.
Open all year. 52 bedrooms (all en suite with telephone).
CC: none.

Hotel Tiffany ★★★ Via L da Vinci 209, 20090 Trezzano s Naviglio.
☎ 02 48401178, Fax 02 4450944.
English spoken.

Italy

Open all year. 36 bedrooms (all en suite with telephone). Parking, restaurant.
Comfortable, modern hotel, 7 km from Milano.
TARIFF: Single 115,000, Double 170,000, Set menu 60,000.
CC: Amex, Diners, Euro/Access, Visa.

MOLVENO   20A

Hotel Du Lac ★★★ Via Nazionale 4, 38018 Molveno.
℡ 0461 586965. English spoken.
Open 01/06 to 30/09 & 20/12 to 06/01.
44 bedrooms (all en suite with telephone). Parking, restaurant.

A family-run hotel set in matchless surroundings of both lake and mountains, found near the lakeside in Molveno, north of Trento on the S421.
TARIFF: (1993) Single 40,000–80,000, Double 70,000–140,000, Set menu 20,000–30,000.
CC: Amex, Euro/Access, Visa.

MONTECATINI TERME   20C

Hotel Cappelli-Croce di Savoia ★★★ Viale Bicchieai 139, 51016 Montecatini Terme.
℡ 0572 71151, Fax 0527 71154. English spoken.

Open 31/03 to 15/11. 73 bedrooms (all en suite with telephone). Outdoor swimming pool, golf 10 km, garage, parking, restaurant.
Conveniently located in the spa area, this comfortable hotel has a lovely garden with terrace and heated pool. Rooms are air conditioned and tastefully furnished.
TARIFF: Single 80,000–90,000, Double 135,000–160,000, Set menu 30,000–40,000.
CC: Amex, Diners, Euro/Access, Visa.

Hotel Torretta II ★★★ Viale Bustichini 63, 51016 Montecatini Terme.
℡ 0572 70305, Fax 0572 70307. English spoken.
Open 20/03 to 31/10. 63 bedrooms (all en suite with telephone). Outdoor swimming pool, tennis, golf 10 km, parking, restaurant.
Carefully managed, well-appointed hotel with modern facilities. Guests enjoy 30% discount at the Montecatini Golf Club.
TARIFF: Single 82,000, Double 130,000, Bk 15,000, Set menu 35,000.
CC: Amex, Diners, Euro/Access, Visa.

MONTEFALCO   21A

Villa Pambuffetti ★★★★ Via della Vittoria 20, 06036 Montefalco.
℡ 0742 378823, Fax 0742 79245.
English spoken.
Open all year. 15 bedrooms (all en suite with telephone). Outdoor swimming pool, tennis, parking. &

Elegant, secluded, quiet and friendly hotel in the small hilltop town of Montefalco, south of Foligno and Assisi on the S616.
TARIFF: (1993) Single 100,000, Double 160,000–200,000.
CC: Amex, Diners, Euro/Access, Visa.

NAPOLI (NAPLES)   21B

Hotel Britannique ★★★★ Corso Vittorio Emanuele 133, 80121 Napoli.
℡ 081 7614145, Fax 081 669760.
English spoken.
Open all year. 90 bedrooms (all en suite with telephone). Garage, restaurant.
Panoramic views over the bay. Meeting and banquet halls.
TARIFF: (1993) Single 180,000, Double 240,000, Bk 11,000, Set menu 40,000–55,000.
CC: Amex, Diners, Euro/Access, Visa.

Hotel Miramare Via Nazario Sauro 24, 80132 Napoli.
℡ 081 7649298, Fax 081 7640775.
English spoken.
Open all year. 31 bedrooms (all en suite with telephone). Golf 10 km, garage, parking, restaurant.
Situated near the Royal Palace and Castle dell'Ovo and Maschio Angiono, close to the harbour. Rooms have all modern comforts.
TARIFF: (1993) Single 185,000–220,000, Double 240,000–300,000, Set menu 50,000–65,000.
CC: Amex, Diners, Euro/Access, Visa.

Italy

Hotel Cavour ★★★ Piazza Garibaldi 32, 80142 Napoli.
📞 081 283122, Fax 081 287488.
English spoken.

Open all year. 98 bedrooms (all en suite with telephone). Garage, parking, restaurant.

A comfortable, traditional hotel, elegantly renovated. Situated close to the historic centre of town about 500 m from the new Napoli 'Directional Centre', directly linked to the ring road, the central railway and the Napoli/Vesuvius/Sorrento railway.

TARIFF: Single 98,000–128,000,
Double 150,000–180,000,
Set menu 28,000–60,000.
CC: Amex, Diners, Euro/Access, Visa.

Hotel Nuovo Rebecchino ★★★
Corso Garibaldi 356, 80142 Napoli.
📞 081 5535327, Fax 081 268026.
English spoken.
Open all year. 58 bedrooms (all en suite with telephone). Garage, parking, restaurant. ♿

A completely renovated hotel near the main station with every modern comfort.

TARIFF: (1993) Single 105,000–115,000,
Double 145,000–180,000.
CC: Amex, Diners, Euro/Access, Visa.

ORTA SAN GIULIO 20C

Hotel San Rocco ★★★★ Via Gippini 11, 28016 Orta San Giulio.
📞 0322 905632. English spoken.
Open all year. 74 bedrooms (all en suite with telephone). Outdoor swimming pool, tennis, garage, restaurant. ♿

Stylish, well-equipped hotel situated on Lake Orta. Local and international cuisine. Hotel incorporates the 'Body Harmony Centre' for health and beauty treatment.

TARIFF: Single 160,000–220,000,
Double 240,000–340,000,
Set menu 60,000–80,000.
CC: Amex, Diners, Euro/Access, Visa.

PADOVA (PADUA) 20C

Hotel Le Calandre ★★★ Via Liguria 1, 35030 Sarmeola di Rubano.
📞 0496 35200, Fax 0496 33026. English spoken.
Open 06/01 to 24/12. 35 bedrooms (all en suite with telephone). Garage, parking.

The hotel was opened in July 1987. It is 5 km from the centre of Padova.

TARIFF: (1993) Single 90,000, Double 120,000,
Bk 10,000.
CC: Amex, Diners, Euro/Access, Visa.

PALERMO 21D

Hotel Esplanade ★★ Via Capo Gallo 22, Mondello, 90151 Palermo.
📞 0914 50003.
Open all year. 32 bedrooms (all en suite with telephone).
TARIFF: (1993) Single 28,000–40,000,
Double 45,000–62,000.
CC: Amex, Diners, Euro/Access.

PARMA 20C

Hotel Torino ★★★ Via A Mazza 7, 43100 Parma.
📞 0521 281046, Fax 0521 230725.
English spoken.
Open all year. 33 bedrooms (all en suite with telephone). Garage.

The hotel is situated right in the centre of Parma.

TARIFF: (1993) Single 95,000,
Double 145,000.
CC: Amex, Diners, Euro/Access, Visa.

PERUGIA 20C

Hotel La Rosetta ★★★★ Piazza Italia 19, 06121 Perugia.
📞 075 5720841, Fax 075 5720841.
English spoken.
Open all year. 96 bedrooms (all en suite with telephone). Garage, parking, restaurant. ♿

A hotel that believes in old-fashioned service and courtesy. The famous restaurant offers both regional and international dishes.

TARIFF: Single 90,000–115,000,
Double 190,000–235,000,
Set menu 36,000–75,000.
CC: Amex, Diners, Euro/Access, Visa.

PESARO 20D

Villa Serena ★★★ Via S Nicola 6/3,
61100 Pesaro.
☎ 0721 55211, Fax 0721 55927. English spoken.
Open all year. 10 bedrooms (all en suite
with telephone). Outdoor swimming pool,
parking, restaurant.

*This gorgeous 17th-century mansion is in a
large hillside park only 5 km from the sea.
Modern comfort plus rare antiques.*

TARIFF: Single 55,000–90,000,
Double 80,000–190,000, Bk 12,000,
Set menu 40,000–70,000.
CC: Amex.

PISA 20C

Hotel Granduca ★★★ Via Statale del
Brennero 13, 56017 San Giuliano Terme.
☎ 050 814111, Fax 050 818811. English spoken.
Open all year. 176 bedrooms (all en suite
with telephone). Outdoor swimming pool,
tennis, parking, restaurant. &

*On east side of Pisa, 5 km from Leaning
Tower, 8 km from Lucca, the new 'pearl of
Tuscany'. Air conditioned, rooms facing hills,
colour TV, direct dial phones. Specially
equipped for disabled.*

TARIFF: (1993) Single 90,000–100,000,
Double 110,000–130,000,
Set menu 25,000–40,000.
CC: Amex, Diners, Euro/Access, Visa.

Hotel Mediterraneo Via Turati 35, 56100 Pisa.
☎ 050 501133.
Open all year. 108 bedrooms (all en suite
with telephone). Restaurant.

*Very quiet hotel in business sector. Good
restaurant. Conference room.*

TARIFF: (1993) Single 90,000–100,000,
Double 110,000–130,000, Set menu 22,000.
CC: Amex, Diners, Euro/Access, Visa.

POSITANO 21B

Hotel Le Sirenuse Via Colombo 30,
84017 Positano.
☎ 0898 75066, Fax 0898 11798.
Open all year. 60 bedrooms (all en suite with
telephone). Outdoor swimming pool, restaurant.

*The hotel was originally the summer house of
the Marchese Sersale (still the owner). Recently
enlarged. 60 km to the south of Napoli.*

TARIFF: (1993) Single 230,000–410,000,
Double 360,000–560,000.
CC: Amex, Diners, Euro/Access, Visa.

RAPALLO 20C

Hotel Cuba and Milton ★★★
S Michele di Pagona 160, 16134 Rapallo.
☎ 0185 50610, Fax 0185 58422. English spoken.
Open all year. 34 bedrooms (29 en suite,
34 telephone). Golf 2 km, parking, restaurant.

*In the picturesque bay of S Michele, very close
to S Margherita and Portofino. All the sea-
facing rooms have balconies. There is a large
garden and sun terrace and private car park.*

TARIFF: (1993) Single 50,000–110,000,
Double 900,00–140,000,
Set menu 20,000–55,000.
CC: Amex, Euro/Access, Visa.

RAVELLO 21B

Hotel Giordano & Villa Maria II ★★★★
Via San Chiara 2, 84010 Ravello.
☎ 089 857255, Fax 089 857071. English spoken.

Open all year. 17 bedrooms (all en suite with
telephone). Outdoor swimming pool, parking.
RESTAURANT: Closed Mon.

*Luxury hotel with lovely gardens and
panoramic views over the sea. Superb location.*

TARIFF: Single 100,000–120,000,
Double 170,000–190,000,
Set menu 35,000–50,000.
CC: Amex, Euro/Access, Visa.

Hotel Palumbo ★★★★★ Via San Giovanni del
Toro 28, Ravello, 84010 Napoli.
☎ 089 857244, Fax 089 858133. English spoken.
Open all year. 20 bedrooms (all en suite
with telephone). Golf 1 km, garage, parking.
RESTAURANT: Closed Jan-Mar.

*A former 12th-century palace, this building is
typical of the varied architectural style which,
owing much to Arab and Oriental influences,
has developed in the Mediterranean,
particularly the area around Amalfi. From*

Naples city take the motorway A3 towards Salerno and exit Angri, follow signs for Chuinzi Pass and Ravello.

TARIFF: Set menu 75,000.
CC: Amex, Diners, Euro/Access, Visa.

RAVENNA 20C

Hotel Bisanzio I ★★★★ Via Salara 30, 48100 Ravenna.
☎ 0544 27111, Fax 0544 32539.
Open 16/01 to 16/12. 36 bedrooms (all en suite with telephone).
TARIFF: (1993) Single 98,000,
Double 126,000–166,000.
CC: none.

REGGIO DI CALABRIA 21D

Grand Hotel Excelsior 1 ★★★★ Via Vittorio Veneto 66, 89100 Reggio di Calabria.
☎ 0965 812211, Fax 0965 93084.
Open all year. 92 bedrooms (all en suite with telephone).
TARIFF: (1993) Single 120,000–210,000,
Double 160,000–250,000.
CC: none.

RESIA (RESCHEN) 20A

Hotel Etschquelle ★★ Val Ventosta, 39027 Resia.
☎ 0473 633125. English spoken.
Open 01/01 to 31/05 & 01/07 to 31/12.
23 bedrooms (21 en suite). Parking, restaurant.
Intimate and cordial atmosphere in a family-run hotel set in the mountains with both summer and winter activities.
TARIFF: Single 30,000–48,000,
Double 60,000–84,000, Set menu 15,000.
CC: Diners, Euro/Access, Visa.

RICCIONE 20C

Hotel Abner's ★★★★ Lungomare della Republica, 47036 Riccione.
☎ 0541 600601, Fax 0541 605400. English spoken.
Open all year. 60 bedrooms (all en suite with telephone). Outdoor swimming pool, tennis, golf 14 km, parking, restaurant.
Set on the promenade in the centre of town, this luxury hotel has every modern facility including rooms with balconies and sea views. Garden restaurant with orchestra or piano.
TARIFF: Single 80,000–130,000,
Double 115,000–190,000, Bk 20,000,
Set menu 39,000–65,000.
CC: Amex, Diners, Euro/Access, Visa.

Hotel Nevada 11 ★★★ Via Milano 54, 47036 Riccione.
☎ 0541 601245. English spoken.
Open 01/03 to 30/09. 48 bedrooms (all en suite with telephone). Golf 1 km, parking, restaurant.
Modern hotel, central position, near the sea. South of Rimini on S16.
TARIFF: (1993) Single 50,000–85,000,
Double 50,000–85,000,
Set menu 30,000–40,000.
CC: none.

Hotel Vienna & Touring ★★★★
Viale Milano 78C, 47036 Riccione.
☎ 0541 601700, Fax 0541 601762.
English spoken.
Open 01/05 to 30/09. 85 bedrooms (all en suite with telephone). Outdoor swimming pool, tennis, golf 14 km, parking, restaurant.
Set in private gardens and only 75 m from the beach, this hotel has a sauna and fitness centre. Italian and international cuisine, served in the garden if desired.
TARIFF: Single 77,000–110,000,
Double 110,000–175,000, Bk 20,000,
Set menu 35,000–60,000.
CC: Amex, Diners, Euro/Access, Visa.

RIMINI 20C

The Club House ★★★★ Viale Vespucci 52, 47037 Rimini.
☎ 0541 391460, Fax 0541 391442.
Open all year. 28 bedrooms (all en suite with telephone).
CC: none.

RIVA DEL GARDA 20C

Hotel Astoria ★★★ Viale Trento 9, 38066 Riva del Garda.
☎ 0464 552658, Fax 0464 521222.
English spoken.
Open 01/04 to 10/10. 96 bedrooms (all en suite with telephone). Outdoor swimming pool, tennis, golf on site, parking, restaurant.
Attractive hotel set in its own park. Golf course and sports complex adjacent.
TARIFF: Single 70,000–90,000,
Double 120,000–150,000,
Set menu 25,000–40,000.
CC: Amex, Diners, Euro/Access, Visa.

Hotel Europa ★★★ Piazza Catena 9, 38066 Riva del Garda.
☎ 0464 555433, Fax 0464 521777. English spoken.

Italy

Open 01/04 to 31/10. 63 bedrooms
(all en suite with telephone). Restaurant. &

*In the centre of the old town and facing the
port, this comfortable hotel is carefully and
lovingly managed by the owners. Pretty
terrace/restaurant with spectacular view of the
lake.*

TARIFF: Single 95,000–105,000,
Double 160,000–180,000,
Set menu 30,000–40,000.
cc: Amex, Diners, Euro/Access, Visa.

Hotel Mirage ★★★ Viale Rovereto 97-99,
38066 Riva del Garda.
✆ 0464 552671, Fax 0464 553211.
English spoken.

Open 02/04 to 21/10. 55 bedrooms
(all en suite with telephone). Outdoor
swimming pool, garage, parking, restaurant.

*Newly-built hotel 30 m from the lake and the
private moorings of Porto S Nicolo, and 90 m
from the beach. Enchanting views of the
northern part of Lake Garda. All rooms have
balcony and air conditioning.*

TARIFF: Single 70,000–95,000,
Double 120,000–160,000, Set menu 25,000.
cc: Amex, Diners, Euro/Access.

ROMA (ROME)   21A

Hotel Aldrovani Palace Via Aldrovani 15,
00197 Roma.
✆ 06 3223993, Fax 06 3221435. English spoken.
Open all year. 140 bedrooms (all en suite
with telephone). Parking.
RESTAURANT: Closed Sun.

*Located in one of the quietest and most
luxurious areas of town in a private park
facing the Borghese Gardens, close to the Via
Veneto and 'Spanish Steps'. All rooms are
richly decorated and suites have antique
furnishings.*

TARIFF: (1993) Single 300,000–385,000,
Double 385,000–470,000,
Set menu 80,000–120,000.
cc: Amex, Diners, Euro/Access, Visa.

Hotel Celio ★★★ Via dei SS Quattro 35C,
00184 Roma.
✆ 06 70495333, Fax 06 7096377.
English spoken.
Open all year. 10 bedrooms (all en suite
with telephone). Golf 3 km.

*This small hotel, more like a private house than
a grand hotel, is situated 100 m from the
Coliseum and roman forum in an elegant part
of Roma.*

TARIFF: Single 130,000–170,000,
Double 150,000–195,000.
cc: Amex, Euro/Access, Visa.

Hotel Lord Byron ★★★★★
Via G de Notaris 5, 00197 Roma.
✆ 06 3220404, Fax 06 3220405. English spoken.
Open all year. 37 bedrooms (all en suite
with telephone). Garage, parking, restaurant.

*Close to the Borghese Gardens, the hotel is
conveniently located near the Via Veneto for
shoppers and many of Roma's greatest cultural
attractions. Well-decorated rooms with fine
views. Award-winning gourmet restaurant
(Relais le Jardin).*

TARIFF: Single 300,000–350,000,
Double 350,000–540,000, Set menu 120,000.
cc: Amex, Diners, Euro/Access, Visa.

Hotel Milani ★★★ Via Magenta 12,
00185 Roma.
✆ 06 4457051, Fax 06 4462317. English spoken.
Open all year. 75 bedrooms (all en suite
with telephone).

*In the town centre, just a few minutes' walk
from main railway station and close to shops
and restaurants. Conference room.*

TARIFF: Single 135,000, Double 195,000.
cc: Amex, Diners, Euro/Access, Visa.

Hotel Mondial ★★★★ Via Torino 127,
00154 Roma.
✆ 06 472861, Fax 06 4824822. English spoken.
Open all year. 78 bedrooms (all en suite
with telephone). Garage, parking.

*Just 500 m from Roma's main railway station.
The hotel offers traditional hospitality with
modern interiors. Nearby are Via Veneto and
'Spanish Steps'.*

TARIFF: (1993) Single 130,000–210,000,
Double 240,000–280,000.
cc: Amex, Diners, Euro/Access, Visa.

Italy

Hotel New York ★★ Via Magenta 13,
00185 Roma.
☎ 06 4460456, Fax 06 4940714. English spoken.
Open all year. 50 bedrooms (45 en suite,
50 telephone). Golf 18 km, garage, parking.
*The hotel has been elegantly renovated. All
rooms have TV and video.*
TARIFF: (1993) Single 50,000–90,000,
Double 60,000–130,000.
CC: Amex, Diners, Euro/Access, Visa.

Hotel Pincio ★★★ Via di Capo le Case 50,
00187 Roma.
☎ 06 790758, Fax 06 791233. English spoken.
Open all year. 20 bedrooms (all en suite
with telephone).
*Conveniently situated near the 'Spanish Steps',
this bed-and-breakfast hotel has a roof garden
and air-conditioned rooms.*
TARIFF: Single 80,000–145,000,
Double 100,000–195,000.
CC: Amex, Diners, Euro/Access, Visa.

SALERNO   21B

Hotel Parsifal ★★★ Via G d'Anna 5,
84010 Salerno.
☎ 089 857144, Fax 089 857972.
Open 01/04 to 13/10. 19 bedrooms
(all en suite). Parking, restaurant.
*Hotel is within the ancient convent of the
Augustinian friars, founded in 1288 and the
cloisters of which still remain intact. Superbly
renovated, beautiful gardens and terraces and
spectacular views of the Amalfi coastline.*
TARIFF: Single 46,000–60,000,
Double 83,000–100,000, Bk 15,000,
Set menu 28,000–39,000.
CC: Amex, Diners, Euro/Access, Visa.

SAN GIMIGNANO   20C

Hotel Pescille ★★★ 53037 San Gimignano.
☎ 0577 940186, Fax 0577 940186.
English spoken.
Open 01/03 to 30/11. 40 bedrooms
(all en suite with telephone). Outdoor
swimming pool, tennis, parking.
RESTAURANT: Closed Wed.
*Set in wooded countryside, this former farm
has been converted into a comfortable hotel
with modern amenities. 3 km from San
Gimignano.*
TARIFF: Single 80,000, Double 110,000,
Bk 10,000, Set menu 45,000–60,000.
CC: Amex, Diners, Euro/Access, Visa.

Hotel Relais Santa Chiara ★★★★
Via Matteotti 15, 53037 San Gimignano.
☎ 0577 940701, Fax 0577 942096.
English spoken.
Open all year. 41 bedrooms (all en suite
with telephone). Outdoor swimming pool,
golf 15 km, parking. ♿
*Between Firenze and Siena, and just a
10-minute walk from the historical centre of
San Gimignano. The hotel looks over the
Tuscan countryside towards Volterra and is set
in its own elegant surroundings.*
TARIFF: Single 120,000–150,000,
Double 180,000–280,000.
CC: Amex, Diners, Euro/Access, Visa.

SAN MAMETE   20C

Hotel Stella D'Italia ★★★ Piazza Roma 1,
22010 San Mamete.
☎ 0344 68739, Fax 0344 68729. English spoken.
Open 01/04 to 06/10. 36 bedrooms
(all en suite with telephone). Outdoor
swimming pool, golf 15 km, garage, restaurant.
*From Lugano follow signs Gandria-St Moritz.
The hotel is situated directly on the shores of
Lake Lugano with an open air restaurant and
private lido.*
TARIFF: Single 77,000, Double 115,000–130,000,
Set menu 35,000–50,000.
CC: Amex, Euro/Access, Visa.

REP OF SAN MARINO   20C

Hotel Grand Via Onofri 31,
Republic of San Marino.
☎ 0541 992400. English spoken.
Open 01/03 to 31/01. 54 bedrooms
(all en suite). Outdoor swimming pool,
golf 15 km, garage, restaurant.
CC: Amex, Diners, Euro/Access, Visa.

SAN REMO   20C

Hotel Beau Rivage ★★★
Lungomare Trieste 49, 18038 San Remo.
☎ 0184 505026, Fax 0184 505026.
English spoken.
Open 15/12 to 31/10. 29 bedrooms
(all en suite with telephone). Golf 1 km,
restaurant.
*Town centre, beach-front hotel with garden
and balconies.*
TARIFF: Single 35,000–70,000,
Double 45,000–95,000, Bk 6,000,
Set menu 25,000–30,000.
CC: Diners, Euro/Access, Visa.

Hotel Paradiso ★★★ Via Roccasterone 12, 18038 San Remo.
☎ 0184 571211, Fax 0184 578176.
English spoken.

Open all year. 41 bedrooms (all en suite with telephone). Golf 3 km, garage, parking, restaurant.

Situated in a quiet and verdant area just 100 m from the sea and near to the town centre. Renovated in 1988. Restaurant with local specialities.

TARIFF: Single 70,000–110,000,
Double 90,000–150,000,
Set menu 23,000–46,000.
CC: Amex, Diners, Euro/Access, Visa.

Hotel Royal ★★★★★ Corso Imperatrice 80, 18038 San Remo.
☎ 0184 5391, Fax 0184 61445. English spoken.

Open 21/12 to 02/10. 147 bedrooms (all en suite with telephone). Outdoor swimming pool, tennis, golf 8 km, garage, parking, restaurant. &

A deluxe resort hotel, uniquely located on the charming Italian Riviera of Flowers, with a fine view of San Remo Bay. Close to the centre of the town in a quiet, spacious, subtropical garden. The hotel combines exclusive

atmosphere with comfort and good service. Penthouse floor with large terraces.

TARIFF: Single 150,000–265,000,
Double 270,000–430,000, Set menu 82,000.
CC: Amex, Diners, Euro/Access, Visa.

SAN VINCENZO 21A

Park Hotel I Lecci ★★★★ Via della Principessa, 57027 San Vincenzo.
☎ 0565 704111, Fax 0565 703224. English spoken.

Open all year. 74 bedrooms (all en suite with telephone). Outdoor swimming pool, tennis, parking, restaurant. &

Set in a large wooded park with its own beach. Very comfortable, spacious hotel, with relaxing atmosphere. Good restaurant with fish specialities.

TARIFF: Single 140,000–210,000,
Double 180,000–300,000,
Set menu 55,000–70,000.
CC: Amex, Diners, Euro/Access, Visa.

SANTA MARGHERITA LIGURE 20C

Hotel Continental ★★★ Via Pagana 8, 16038 Santa Margherita Ligure.
☎ 0185 286 512, Fax 0185 284 463.
English spoken.
Open all year. 76 bedrooms (all en suite with telephone). Tennis, golf 4 km, garage, parking, restaurant. &

Centrally placed, family-run hotel, lots to see and do both day and night.

TARIFF: Single 110,000–150,000,
Double 202,000–260,000,
Set menu 48,000–65,000.
CC: Amex, Diners, Euro/Access, Visa.

Hotel Laurin Lungomare G Marconi 3, 16038 Santa Margherita Ligure.
☎ 0185 289 971, Fax 0185 285 709.
English spoken.

Italy

Open all year. 45 bedrooms (all en suite with telephone). Golf 4 km. &

A modern hotel centrally located in this tourist port. Large terraces overlooking the sea. Fine views.

TARIFF: Single 98,000–135,000, Double 160,000–210,000.
CC: Amex, Diners, Euro/Access, Visa.

Hotel Eden ★★ Vico Dritto, 16034 Santa Margherita Ligure.
☎ 0185 269 091, Fax 0185 269 047.
English spoken.

Open all year. 12 bedrooms (all en suite with telephone). Golf 5 km, restaurant.

Charming hotel tucked away in a narrow street, but only a few minutes from the waterfront. Pretty, peaceful garden where meals are served in fine weather.

TARIFF: Single 100,000–150,000, Double 150,000–240,000.
CC: Amex, Diners, Euro/Access, Visa.

Hotel Grand Miramare I ★★★★
Via Milite Ignoto 30,
16038 Santa Margherita Ligure.
☎ 0185 287013, Fax 0185 284651.
English spoken.
Open all year. 84 bedrooms (all en suite with telephone). Outdoor swimming pool, golf 4 km, garage, parking, restaurant. &

The hotel boasts panoramic views of the Italian Riviera and a restful environment. Friendly service with 3 restaurants. On the road to Portofino (S1) from Genova.

TARIFF: Single 185,000–230,000, Double 310,000–370,000, Set menu 75,000.
CC: Amex, Euro/Access, Visa.

Hotel Metropole ★★★★ Via Pagana 2, 16038 Santa Margherita Ligure.
☎ 0185 286 134, Fax 0185 283 495.
English spoken.
Open all year. 50 bedrooms (all en suite with telephone). Garage, parking, restaurant.

In large garden with private beach and snack bar. Managed personally by the owner. 35 km from Genova-A12. Only 5 km from Portofino.

TARIFF: Single 100,000–130,000, Double 170,000–205,000,
Set menu 45,000–56,000.
CC: Amex, Diners, Euro/Access, Visa.

Hotel Regina Elena ★★★★ Lungomare Milite Ignoto 44, 16038 Santa Margherita Ligure.
☎ 0185 287 003, Fax 0185 284 473.
English spoken.
Open all year. 94 bedrooms (all en suite with telephone). Golf 4 km, parking, restaurant. &

A modern hotel on the picturesque coast road toward Portofino, with gardens, and private beach. Conference centre.

TARIFF: Single 110,000–204,000, Double 167,000–250,000,
Set menu 40,000–66,000.
CC: Amex, Diners, Euro/Access, Visa.

SARONNO 20C

Albergo della Rotonda ★★★★ Via Novara 53, 21047 Saronno.
☎ 0296 703232, Fax 0296 702770.
English spoken.
Open 01/01 to 04/08 & 22/08 to 31/12.
92 bedrooms (all en suite with telephone).
Tennis, golf 18 km, garage, parking, restaurant. &

Only one year old, this hotel is furnished in country-house style and is only 20 minutes from the centre of Milano and from the Monza motordrome. Ideal for business conferences. Near motorway Milano/Como/Lugano.

TARIFF: Single 170,000, Double 220,000, Set menu 40,000.
cc: Amex, Diners, Euro/Access, Visa.

SAVIGLIANO 20C

Hotel Granbaita ★★★ Via Cuneo, 25, 12038 Savigliano.
☎ 0172 711500, Fax 0172 711518.
English spoken.

Open all year. 46 bedrooms (all en suite with telephone). Outdoor swimming pool, tennis, golf 12 km, garage, parking. &
RESTAURANT: Closed May.

New hotel set in quiet grounds in centre of Piedmont region, only half an hour from Torino. Regional cuisine. Conference facilities.

TARIFF: Single 90,000, Double 115,000, Bk 14,000, Set menu 32,000.
cc: Amex, Diners, Euro/Access, Visa.

SICILIA (SICILY), MESSINA 21D

Hotel Royal Palace ★★★★
Via T Cannnizzaro 224, 98100 Messina, Sicilia.
☎ 0902 1161, Fax 0902 921075.
Open all year. 85 bedrooms (all en suite with telephone).
cc: Amex, Diners, Euro/Access, Visa.

SIENA 20C

Hotel Duomo Via Stalloreggi 38, 53100 Siena.
☎ 0577 289088, Fax 0577 43043.
English spoken.
Open all year. 23 bedrooms (all en suite with telephone).

Comfortable hotel in the heart of medieval

Siena. Five-minute walk from the Duomo and within easy reach of the shopping centre. Fine views of the hills surrounding Siena.

TARIFF: Single 61,000–110,000, Double 92,000–150,000.
cc: Amex, Euro/Access, Visa.

Hotel Villa Casalecchi ★★★★ Castellina in Chianti, 53100 Siena.
☎ 0577 740240, Fax 0577 741111.
English spoken.

Open 01/03 to 30/11. 19 bedrooms (all en suite with telephone). Outdoor swimming pool, tennis, parking, restaurant.

Once the home of the aristocracy, this elegant hotel is 12 miles north of Siena, set amongst oak trees in the heart of the Chianti Classico region. Lovely furnishings, renowned restaurant specialising in Tuscan cuisine, good sporting facilities.

TARIFF: Single 215,000–280,000, Double 235,000–300,000, Set menu 65,000–85,000.
cc: Amex, Diners, Euro/Access, Visa.

Hotel Podere Terreno Radda in Chianti, 53017 Siena.
☎ 0577 738312, Fax 0577 738312. English spoken.

Open all year. 7 bedrooms (all en suite).
Parking, restaurant.

*16th-century stone inn, an oasis among the
hills in true Chianti country. Guests join in to
make one big family. Prettily furnished rooms
and delightful living room with huge open
fireplace where meals are served at a long
wooden table.*

TARIFF: Single 130,000, Double 210,000.
CC: Euro/Access, Visa.

Hotel Relais La Suvera ★★★★ Pievescola,
Val d'Elsa, 53030 Siena.
📞 0577 960300, Fax 0577 960220. English spoken.
Open 15/03 to 15/11. 35 bedrooms
(all en suite with telephone). Outdoor
swimming pool, tennis, parking, restaurant. ♿

*Dating from the 12th century, this
Renaissance castle was once the home of Pope
Julius II. Superbly restored, the hotel has
antique furnishings and beautiful gardens.
Suites are also available.*

TARIFF: Single 220,000,
Double 270,000–370,000.
CC: Amex, Diners, Euro/Access, Visa.

SORRENTO   21B

Grand Hotel Excelsior Vittoria ★★★★
Piazza Tasso 34, 80067 Sorrento.
📞 0818 071044, Fax 0818 771206.
English spoken.
Open all year. 109 bedrooms (all en suite
with telephone). Outdoor swimming pool,
parking, restaurant.

*Built on the cliff overlooking the Golfo di
Napoli. Quiet position with private lift to the
harbour, nearest main town is Napoli.*

TARIFF: Single 251,000, Double 429,000,
Set menu 64,000.
CC: Amex, Diners, Euro/Access, Visa.

SPOLETO   21A

Hotel Dei Duchi ★★★★ Viale Giacomo
Matteotti 4, 06049 Spoleto.
📞 0743 44541, Fax 0743 44543. English spoken.
Open all year. 51 bedrooms (all en suite
with telephone). Parking, restaurant. ♿

*Peaceful atmosphere but in the centre of
Spoleto, surrounded by the Teatro Romano.
Restaurant with panoramic view of the valley.
Air conditioned.*

TARIFF: Single 115,000–135,000,
Double 140,000–175,000,
Set menu 35,000–48,000.
CC: Amex, Diners, Euro/Access, Visa.

Hotel Gattapone ★★★★ Via del Ponte 6,
06049 Spoleto.
📞 0743 223447, Fax 0743 223448.
English spoken.
Open all year. 13 bedrooms (all en suite).
Parking.

*The hotel is set below the castle (La Rocca
Albornoziana) which dominates the historic
town centre. It looks out over a green valley,
straddled by the medieval bridge (Ponte delle
Torri). Nearby are Perugia, Assisi and Roma.*

TARIFF: Single 125,000–130,000,
Double 160,000–240,000, Bk 15,000.
CC: Amex, Diners, Euro/Access, Visa.

STRESA   20C

Hotel Astoria ★★★★ Corso Umberto I, 31,
28049 Stresa.
📞 0323 32566, Fax 0323 933785.
English spoken.
Open 01/04 to 31/10. 101 bedrooms
(all en suite with telephone). Outdoor
swimming pool, tennis, golf 4 km, parking,
restaurant.

*Modern hotel on lakeside. Good restaurant
overlooking lake. Excellent views.*

TARIFF: Single 150,000, Double 230,000,
Set menu 45,000.
CC: Amex, Diners, Euro/Access, Visa.

Hotel Lido La Perla Nera ★★★ Viale Lido 15,
28049 Stresa.
📞 0323 33611, Fax 0323 933785.
English spoken.
Open 01/04 to 31/10. 27 bedrooms
(all en suite with telephone). Golf 4 km,
parking, restaurant. ♿

*A few metres from the lake, just opposite the
Borromee islands, the hotel is in a peaceful
area not far from the centre of the town.*

TARIFF: Single 100,000, Double 120,000,
Bk 10,000, Set menu 30,000.
CC: Euro/Access, Visa.

TODI   21A

Hotel Bramante ★★★★ Via Orvietana 48,
06059 Todi.
📞 0758 948381, Fax 0758 948074.
English spoken.
Open all year. 43 bedrooms (all en suite
with telephone). Outdoor swimming pool,
tennis, golf 25 km, parking, restaurant.

*A former convent, this hotel maintains the feel
of the 12th century with fine furnishings and
paintings. It is an ideal base to visit Umbria.*

TARIFF: (1993) Single 140,000, Double 190,000, Bk 15,000, Set menu 45,000–55,000.
CC: Amex, Diners, Euro/Access, Visa.

TORINO (TURIN) 20C

Hotel Turin Palace ★★★★★ Via Sacchi 8, 10128 Torino.
☎ 0115 15511, Fax 0115 612187.
Open all year. 125 bedrooms (all en suite with telephone).
TARIFF: (1993) Single 280,000, Double 350,000.
CC: Amex, Diners, Euro/Access, Visa.

TREMEZZO 20C

Hotel Rusall ★★★ Via S Martino 2, Frazione, Rogaro, 22019 Tremezzo.
☎ 0344 40408, Fax 0344 40447.

Open 18/03 to 31/12. 18 bedrooms (all en suite with telephone). Tennis, golf 6 km, parking.
RESTAURANT: Closed Wed.
Very quiet location with wonderful views and private gardens. All rooms have balconies.
TARIFF: Single 50,000–60.000, Double 85,000–90,000, Bk 12,000, Set menu 30,000–45,000.
CC: Diners, Euro/Access, Visa.

TRENTO 20C

Hotel Montana ★★★ 84 Vason di Monte Bondone, 38040 Trento.
☎ 0461 948200, Fax 0461 948177.
English spoken.
Open 01/12 to 15/04 & 01/06 to 30/09.
52 bedrooms (all en suite with telephone). Tennis, garage, parking, restaurant.
A traditional family-run hotel with views of the Dolomites. A panoramic mountain road connects Trento Valley (20 km) and Riva del Garda lake (38 km).

TARIFF: Single 60,000–75,000, Double 90,000–120,000, Set menu 20,000–35,000.
CC: Amex, Diners, Euro/Access, Visa.

TRIESTE 20D

Hotel Duchi d'Aosta ★★★★ Piazza Unita d'Italia 2, 34121 Trieste.
☎ 040 7351, Fax 040 366092.
Open all year. 52 bedrooms (all en suite with telephone).
TARIFF: (1993) Single 160,000–215,000, Double 220,000–290,000.
CC: Amex, Diners, Euro/Access, Visa.

UDINE 20D

Hotel Astoria ★★★★ Piazza XX Settembre 24, 33100 Udine.
☎ 0432 505091, Fax 0432 509010.
English spoken.
Open all year. 75 bedrooms (all en suite with telephone). Tennis, golf 10 km, garage, parking, restaurant.
Located in the heart of Udine's historical centre, the hotel has a warm atmosphere which has become the emblem of over a hundred years of tradition in service. Ideal meeting place for prestigious events and the perfect location for elegant entertaining.
TARIFF: Single 130,000–170,000, Double 170,000–225,000, Bk 18,000, Set menu 40,000–50,000.
CC: Amex, Diners, Euro/Access, Visa.

VARENNA 20C

Hotel du Lac ★★★★ Via del Prestino 4, Como, 22050 Varenna.
☎ 0341 830238, Fax 0341 831081.
English spoken.
Open 01/03 to 31/12. 18 bedrooms (all en suite with telephone). Garage, parking, restaurant. ♿
Imposing medieval building with terrace overlooking lake. Lovely views.
TARIFF: Single 125,000–165,000, Double 145,000–225,000, Bk 18,000, Set menu 52,000–80,000.
CC: Amex, Diners, Euro/Access, Visa.

VARESE 20C

Hotel Verese Lago ★★★ Via G Macchi 61, 21100 Varese.
☎ 0332 310022, Fax 0332 312697.
English spoken.

Open all year. 45 bedrooms (all en suite with telephone). Golf 10 km, parking. &

The hotel is set amongst the Lombardy lakes, tranquil, relaxing, modern, ideal for the motorist. Only 4 minutes from Varese town centre.

TARIFF: Single 90,000–100,000, .Double 110,000–145,000.

CC: Amex, Diners, Euro/Access, Visa.

VENEZIA (VENICE) 20C

Hotel Agli Arboretti Rio Terra Sant' Agnese, Dorsoduro 882/4, 30123 Venezia.
☎ 041 5230058, Fax 041 5210158.
English spoken.

Open all year. 20 bedrooms (19 en suite, 1 bath/shower only, 20 telephone).
RESTAURANT: Closed Wed.

This hotel, centrally located, has the ambiance of a homely, ancient, Venetian house.

TARIFF: Single 120,000, Double 180,000, Set menu 45,000–65,000.

CC: Amex, Euro/Access, Visa.

Hotel Carpaccio ★★★ San Polo 2765, 30125 Venezia.
☎ 041 5235946, Fax 041 5242134.
Open all year. 20 bedrooms (17 en suite).
TARIFF: (1993) Single 114,000, Double 163,000.
CC: Diners, Euro/Access, Visa.

Hotel Flora ★★★ S Marco 2283, 30124 Venezia.
☎ 041 5205844, Fax 041 5228217.
Open 01/02 to 20/11. 44 bedrooms (43 en suite).
TARIFF: (1993) Single 134,000, Double 168,000.
CC: Amex, Diners, Euro/Access, Visa.

Hotel Metropole ★★★★ Riva Schiavoni 4149, 30122 Venezia.
☎ 041 5205044, Fax 041 5223679.
English spoken.

Open all year. 74 bedrooms (all en suite with telephone). Golf 5 km, restaurant.

3 minutes' stroll along the waterfront from St Mark's Square with a fine collection of antiques.

TARIFF: Single 190,000–310,000, Double 280,000–440,000, Set menu 42,000.
CC: Amex, Diners, Euro/Access, Visa.

Albergo Quattro Fontane ★★★★ Via Quattro Fontane 16, 30126 Lido di Venezia.
☎ 0415 260227, Fax 0415 260726.
English spoken.
Open 20/04 to 20/10. 60 bedrooms (all en suite with telephone). Tennis, golf 6 km, parking, restaurant.

A very picturesque hotel set in its own garden.

TARIFF: (1993) Single 190,000–210,000, Double 240,000–280,000.
CC: Amex, Diners, Euro/Access, Visa.

Hotel La Residenza ★★ Campo Bandiera e Moro 3608, 30122 Venezia.
☎ 041 5285315, Fax 041 5238859.
Open 01/02 to 30/11 & 01/12 to 31/12.
15 bedrooms (14 en suite, 15 telephone).

A friendly hotel with the atmosphere of an old Venetian palace, a few steps from St Mark's Square, reached by boat from the Bacino S'Marco.

TARIFF: (1993) Single 95,000, Double 145,000.
CC: Amex, Diners, Euro/Access, Visa.

Hotel Sofitel Venezia ★★★★ S Croce 245, 30135 Venezia.
☎ 041 5285394, Fax 041 5230043.
English spoken.
Open all year. 100 bedrooms (all en suite with telephone). Golf 12 km, restaurant.

Decorated in 18th-century style, the hotel is in the Papadopoli gardens, in the historic centre of the city. Close to airport and station.

TARIFF: Single 160,000–220,000, Double 240,000–320,000, Set menu 65,000–120,000.
CC: Amex, Diners, Euro/Access, Visa.

Villa Mabapa ★★★★ San Nicolo 16 Lido, 30126 Venezia.
☎ 041 5260590, Fax 041 5269441.
English spoken.
Open all year. 60 bedrooms (all en suite with telephone). Outdoor swimming pool, tennis, golf 3 km, parking, restaurant. &

Liberty-style hotel, first opened in 1930, renovated in 1982 and 1992. Private park, beach facilities, private harbour, garden

restaurant 'Il Pitosforo'. Free entrance to the casino for all guests.
TARIFF: Single 105,000–190,000,
Double 145,000–290,000,
Set menu 35,000–70,000.
CC: Amex, Diners, Euro/Access, Visa.

VERBANIA   20C

Hotel Cannero ★★★ Lungo Lago 2,
28051 Cannero Riviera.
☏ 0323 788046, Fax 0323 788048. English spoken.

Open 01/03 to 02/11. 36 bedrooms (all en suite with telephone). Outdoor swimming pool, tennis, golf 14 km, garage, parking, restaurant. &
In one of the quietest resorts on the lake, lying right on the shore with fine views of the lake and mountains. The open-air pool is heated. Very good restaurant.
TARIFF: Single 65,000–75,000,
Double 100,000–130,000,
Set menu 35,000–65,000.
CC: Amex, Diners, Euro/Access, Visa.

VERONA   20C

Hotel Firenze ★★★★ Corso Porta Nuova 88,
37122 Verona.

☏ 045 8011510, Fax 045 8011510.
English spoken.
Open all year. 59 bedrooms (all en suite with telephone).
Modern and very comfortable hotel with every possible facility in the rooms and suites, including air conditioning. Well appointed conference rooms for up to 40 people. Close to the historic centre of Verona - Piazza Brà.
TARIFF: Single 125,000–170,000,
Double 174,000–240,000.
CC: Amex, Diners, Euro/Access, Visa.
SEE ADJACENT ADVERTISEMENT

Italy

Hotel Colomba d'Ora ★★★★
Via Cattaneo 10, 37121 Verona.
📞 045 595300, Fax 045 594974.
Open all year. 52 bedrooms (all en suite with telephone).
TARIFF: (1993) Single 114,000–150,000, Double 159,000–250,000.
CC: Amex, Diners, Euro/Access, Visa.

Hotel Due Torri Baglioni
Piazza S Anastasia 4, 37121 Verona.
📞 045 595044, Fax 045 58004130.
English spoken.
Open all year. 94 bedrooms (all en suite with telephone). Garage, restaurant. ᕫ
Luxury hotel decorated in various period styles. Valuable art treasures.
TARIFF: Single 250,000–310,000, Double 330,000–490,000, Set menu 65,000–90,000.
CC: Amex, Diners, Euro/Access, Visa.

Hotel Victoria ★★★★ Via Adua 8,
37121 Verona.
📞 045 590566, Fax 045 590155.
English spoken.

Open all year. 45 bedrooms (all en suite with telephone). Garage. ᕫ
Fully modernized hotel situated within the walls of the Palazzo Monga. Classically furnished and well equipped. Contains a small private museum of Roman antiquities. Apartments also available.
TARIFF: Single 160,000, Double 240,000, Bk 22,000.
CC: Amex, Diners, Euro/Access, Visa.

VICENZA 20C

Hotel Continental ★★★ Viale Trissino 89, 36100 Vicenza.
📞 0444 505476, Fax 0444 513319.
English spoken.
Open all year. 60 bedrooms (all en suite with telephone). Golf 20 km, parking. ᕫ
RESTAURANT: Closed Aug.
Air-conditioned modern hotel in quiet location near town centre. Follow signs for 'Stadio'.
TARIFF: Single 99,000, Double 130,000, Bk 13,000, Set menu 25,000–50,000.
CC: Amex, Diners, Euro/Access, Visa.

VITERBO 21A

Hotel Mini Palace ★★★★ 1 Via Santa Maria Della, Grotticella 2, 01100 Viterbo.
📞 0761 309743, Fax 0761 344715.
English spoken.
Open all year. 38 bedrooms (all en suite with telephone). Garage, parking.
Modern, comfortable, elegant hotel within easy walking distance of historical centre of this medieval town. One hour by car from Roma.
TARIFF: Single 100,000–120,000, Double 150,000–180,000.
CC: Amex, Diners, Euro/Access, Visa.

LIECHTENSTEIN

This tiny principality is one of the world's smallest states, with a land area of only 160 sq km, which is 0.06 per cent that of the UK. Liechtenstein is bordered to the east by Austria, and to the south and west by Switzerland, with the River Rhine forming most of the western border. The total population is about 30,000, with some 5,000 inhabitants living in the capital, Vaduz.

Liechtenstein shares much of its history, culture and traditions with Switzerland. Today, it also shares many economic activities with this neighbour, as well as the currency of the Swiss franc, and the postal system. This means the Liechtensteiners, like the Swiss, have a very high standard of living. The local language is Alemannish, a dialect of German.

The main agriculture is concerned with dairy farming, on the flat Rhine plains to the west. There are many diverse industries, from the manufacture of heavy machinery, to the precision production of medical drugs. Liechtenstein has favourable tax arrangements, which have attracted many banks and other financial institutions, and the headquarters of large international corporations. During winter, tourists flock to the mountains of the south-east, for skiing and other winter sports.

TRIESENBERG   19A

Hotel Kulm ★★★ Dortplatz, 9497 Triesenberg.
☎ 075 28777, Fax 075 82861. English spoken. Open all year. 20 bedrooms (all en suite with telephone). Garage, parking, restaurant. &
CC: Amex, Diners, Euro/Access, Visa.

VADUZ   19A

Park Hotel Sonnenhof ★★★★ Mareestrasse 29, 9490 Vaduz.
☎ 07523 21192, Fax 07523 20053.
English spoken.
Open 26/02 to 23/12 & 27/12 to 15/01.
50 bedrooms (29 en suite, 50 telephone). Indoor swimming pool, golf 15 km, garage, parking, restaurant.

Family-managed hotel, surrounded by a well-kept park in the quiet residential district above Vaduz, 10 minutes' walk from town centre. Magnificent panoramic views.

TARIFF: Single 190–250, Double 290–410.
CC: Amex, Diners, Euro/Access, Visa.

Liechtenstein

LUXEMBOURG

The Grand Duchy of Luxembourg is a tiny but fully independent country nestling between Belgium, Germany and France. It covers a land area of 2,586 sq km, and so is smaller than English counties such as Lancashire and Hampshire. More than three-quarters of the 380,000 people live in towns. The capital city, also called Luxembourg, is home to some 80,000 inhabitants, as well as the European Community's Court of Justice. Many people speak Letzeburgesch, of German origin; French and German are the two official languages. The currency is the Luxembourg franc, made up of 100 centimes.

The climate is generally cool, with no shortage of rain. To the north are the rolling, wooded hills of Oesling, extending from the Ardennes of Belgium, and bearing the country's highest point, the Burgplatz, at 559 m. The central-southern plateau is an extension of the Lorraine part of France, and has rich soils – it is called Bon Pays or Gutland, French and German respectively for "good earth". This plateau is the main farming region and is drained by numerous rivers that run east to the Moselle.

Southern Luxembourg has large deposits of iron, and the country has well developed industries, from iron and steel to chemicals and synthetics. In fact, up to a quarter of the population is composed of people from other countries, who have come for the employment opportunities. Another major industry is tourism, with many medieval castles and châteaux. There are about 5,000 km of roads, with a road density (km per sq km) of 2, compared to the UK's 1.5.

CLERVAUX 7D

Hôtel Le Claravallis ★★★★ 3 rue de la Gare, 9708 Clervaux.
☎ 90134, Fax 929089. English spoken.

Open 26/03 to 31/01. 28 bedrooms (all en suite with telephone). Golf 3 km, parking, restaurant. ⅙

Very comfortable hotel, set in lovely gardens and at the edge of the forest. 400 m from the centre of the picturesque town of Clervaux.

TARIFF: Single 1400–1800, Double 2200–2950.
CC: Amex, Diners, Euro/Access, Visa.

ECHTERNACH 7D

Hôtel Bel Air ★★★★ 1 route de Berdorf, 6409 Echternach.
☎ 729383, Fax 728694. English spoken.
Open 15/02 to 03/01. 33 bedrooms (all en suite with telephone). Tennis, golf 15 km, garage, parking.
RESTAURANT: very good. Closed 03/01 to 15/02.

Attractive hotel only 1 km from town in direction of Diekirch. Set in wooded parkland with views over River Sûre.

TARIFF: (1993) Single 2675–4100, Double 3500–5650.
CC: Amex, Diners, Euro/Access, Visa.

Hôtel La Bergerie ★★★★ 47 rue de Luxembourg, 6450 Echternach.
☎ 7285041, Fax 728508. English spoken.
Open 15/02 to 05/01. 15 bedrooms (all en suite with telephone). Golf 10 km, parking, restaurant.

Very comfortable hotel with garden grounds, located on the outskirts of Echternach. Excellent restaurant.

TARIFF: (1993) Single 2850–3250, Double 4300–4800.
CC: Amex, Diners, Euro/Access, Visa.

Luxembourg

ESCH-SUR-SURE — 7D

Hôtel du Moulin ★★★ 6 rue du Moulin, 9506 Esch-sur-Sûre.
☎ 89107, Fax 899137.
Open 01/02 to 15/12. 25 bedrooms (all en suite with telephone). Garage, parking, restaurant.

Comfortable hotel on the bank of the River Sûre in the centre of the village. Splendid view of the castle.

TARIFF: (1993) Single 1600, Double 2300–2550, Set menu 550–1400.
CC: Diners, Euro/Access, Visa.

ETTELBRÜCK — 7D

Hôtel Dahm ★★★★ 57 Porte des Ardennes, 9145 Erpeldange.
☎ 81622551, Fax 8162255210. English spoken.
Open all year. 25 bedrooms (all en suite with telephone). Tennis, golf 1 km, garage, parking. &
RESTAURANT: Closed Mon & Tues.

Traditional hotel in centre of village of Erpeldange, 1 km north of Ettelbrück.

TARIFF: Single 1800–2100, Double 2850–3100, Set menu 600–1800.
CC: Amex, Euro/Access, Visa.

GRUNDHOF — 7D

Hôtel Brimer ★★★★ 6360 Grundhof.
☎ 86251, Fax 86212. English spoken.

Open 25/02 to 15/11. 23 bedrooms (all en suite with telephone). Golf 15 km, parking.
RESTAURANT: Closed Tues.

Country hotel with lovely rooms and excellent restaurant. By the River Sûre on the German border, the village is 23 km east of Ettelbrück and south-east of Diekirch.

TARIFF: Single 2400–2700, Double 2850–3500, Set menu 900–1200.
CC: none.

LAROCHETTE — 7D

Hôtel du Château ★★★ 1 rue de Medernach, 7616 Larochette.
☎ 87009, Fax 879636. English spoken.

Open all year. 40 bedrooms (all en suite with telephone). Golf 4 km, parking, restaurant.

Comfortable hotel in the main square of this picturesque little town. Good restaurant specialising in fish and regional cuisine. Conference facilities.

TARIFF: Single 1900–2200, Double 2400–2700.
CC: Amex, Diners, Euro/Access, Visa.

LUXEMBOURG CITY — 7D

Hôtel Central Molitor ★★★★
28 av de la Liberté, 1930 Luxembourg City.
☎ 489911, Fax 483382. English spoken.
Open all year. 36 bedrooms (all en suite with telephone). Golf 6 km, parking.
RESTAURANT: Closed Sun eve & Mon.

Fine hotel well located halfway between financial centre and railway station, 3 blocks from air terminal. Old-style façade, new restaurant.

TARIFF: Single 3200, Double 4200, Set menu 650–1400.
CC: Amex, Diners, Euro/Access, Visa.

Hôtel Delta ★★★ 74-78 rue Adolphe Fischer, 1521 Luxembourg City.
☎ 493096, Fax 404320.
English spoken.
Open all year. 20 bedrooms (all en suite with telephone). Parking.
RESTAURANT: Closed Sun.

Hotel located in the heart of the city. Follow signs from La Place de Paris.

TARIFF: (1993) Single 2550–2900, Double 2750–3100.
CC: Amex, Diners, Euro/Access, Visa.

Luxembourg

Hôtel Grand Cravat ★★★★ 29 bd Roosevelt, 2430 Luxembourg City.
✆ 221975, Fax 226711. English spoken.
Open all year. 60 bedrooms (all en suite with telephone). Golf 5 km, restaurant.
Centrally located, elegant hotel in traditional style. Many rooms have lovely views.
TARIFF: Single 4900–5400, Double 5600–6500, Set menu 950–2000.
CC: Amex, Diners, Euro/Access, Visa.

Hôtel Président ★★★★ place de la Gare, 1930 Luxembourg City.
✆ 486161, Fax 486180. English spoken.
Open all year. 40 bedrooms (all en suite with telephone). Restaurant.
TARIFF: (1993) Single 5000, Double 6400.
CC: Amex, Diners, Euro/Access, Visa.

Hôtel Pullman ★★★★ European Center, 2015 Luxembourg City.
✆ 437761, Fax 438658. English spoken.
Open all year. 364 bedrooms (all en suite with telephone). Indoor swimming pool, golf 4 km, garage, parking. &
RESTAURANT: Closed Sat lunch.
Large modern hotel situated on Kirchberg plateau close to the EC institutions and motorway to city centre.
TARIFF: Single 5800–6300, Double 7200–7400, Set menu 700–2000.
CC: Amex, Diners, Euro/Access, Visa.

Hôtel Royal ★★★★★ 12 bd Royal, 2449 Luxembourg City.
✆ 41616, Fax 225948. English spoken.

Open all year. 180 bedrooms (all en suite with telephone). Indoor swimming pool, golf 6 km, garage, parking. &
RESTAURANT: very good. Closed Aug.
Attractive, modern hotel located in city centre, convenient for sightseeing, business and the international airport.

TARIFF: Single 7650–10950, Double 8700–11900.
CC: Amex, Diners, Euro/Access, Visa.

MONDORF-LES-BAINS 7D

Hôtel Grand Chef ★★★★ 36 av des Bains, 5610 Mondorf-les-Bains.
✆ 35268 012/122, Fax 352661510. English spoken.
Open 04/04 to 01/12. 38 bedrooms (all en suite with telephone). Golf 11 km, garage, parking, restaurant. &
A classically elegant Silence hotel in a private park near the spa, thermal park and sports facilities. 12 km from motorway E411/A4 and 17 km from Luxembourg City.
TARIFF: Single 2250–2550, Double 2880–3500.
CC: Amex, Diners, Euro/Access, Visa.

REMICH-SUR-MOSELLE 7D

Hôtel de l'Ecluse ★★ rte du Vin 29, 5450 Stadtbredimus.
✆ 69546, Fax 69546. English spoken.
Open all year. 16 bedrooms (all en suite with telephone). Golf 7 km, garage, restaurant. &
Modern family hotel in traditional style situated in the village of Stradbredimus, 2 km north of Remich, 23 km from Luxembourg City.
TARIFF: Single 1600, Double 2100, Set menu 380–1200.
CC: Amex, Euro/Access, Visa.

Hôtel St Nicolas ★★★★ 31 Esplanade, 5533 Remich-sur-Moselle.
✆ 698333, Fax 699069. English spoken.

Open all year. 43 bedrooms (all en suite with telephone). Golf 10 km.
RESTAURANT: Closed 15/11 to 15/12.
An elegant, Best Western hotel by Moselle in famous wine area. Beautiful tourist resort.
TARIFF: Single 2250, Double 2900, Set menu 750–1680.
CC: Amex, Diners, Euro/Access, Visa.

Luxembourg

NETHERLANDS

The Netherlands (Holland) is one of Europe's smallest , most densely populated, and most urbanised countries. Some 15 million inhabitants live in 41,863 sq km (about a sixth that of the UK). Ninety per cent are in towns and cities. The North Sea stretches along the west and north, and there are borders with Germany in the east and Belgium to the south. The currency is the gulden (guilder or florin), made up of 100 cents.

The Netherlands is aptly called one of Europe's "low countries" since more than half of the country is below or at sea level. The water held is held back from these lowlands, called polders, by dykes and pumps. The reclaimed areas are criss-crossed by canals and rivers, such as the Rhine and Meuse, and are very fertile. They produce the famous Dutch bulbs, and grazing livestock yield butter and cheese. The climate is mild in winter and cool to warm in summer. A twelfth of the land is planted with conifers, and the Waddenzee in the north is a valuable bird sanctuary.

Half of the Dutch dwell within the area bounded by the four largest cities – the capital Amsterdam with 700,000 people, the university centre of Utrecht, the world's largest port at Rotterdam, and the Hague, home of the International Court of Justice. There are some 120,000 km of roads forming an extensive modern network, with a road density (km per sq km) of 2.9, compared to the UK's 1.5. Note that resorts for Dutch islands, such as Schouwen and Texel, are listed under their island names in the A–Z directory.

AMSTERDAM 13A

Hotel Ambassade ★★★ Herengracht 341, 1016 Amsterdam.
☎ 020 6262333, Fax 020 6245321.
English spoken.
Open all year. 52 bedrooms (all en suite with telephone).
This hotel consists of nine 17th-century merchants' homes in the centre of Amsterdam, on one of the most beautiful canals.
TARIFF: Single 215–225, Double 265–275.
CC: Amex, Diners, Euro/Access, Visa.

Hotel Asterisk ★★ Den Texstraat 16, 1017 Amsterdam.
☎ 020 6241768, Fax 020 6382790.
English spoken.
Open all year. 29 bedrooms (23 en suite, 1 bath/shower only, 29 telephone).
A family-run hotel completely renovated and equipped with all modern conveniences. Tramline 16-24 or 25 from Central Station to the Weteringcircuit.
TARIFF: Single 65–90, Double 85–155, Bk 12.50.
CC: Euro/Access.

Hotel Canal House ★★★ Keizersgracht 148, 1015 Amsterdam.
☎ 020 6225182, Fax 020 6241317.
English spoken.
Open all year. 26 bedrooms (all en suite with telephone).
TARIFF: (1993) Single 150–170, Double 185–235.
CC: Amex, Diners, Euro/Access, Visa.

Hotel Caransa Karena ★★★★
Rembrandtplein 19, 1017 Amsterdam.
☎ 020 6229455, Fax 020 6222773. English spoken.
Open all year. 66 bedrooms (all en suite with telephone). Restaurant. &
TARIFF: (1993) Single 250, Double 320, Bk 25.
CC: Amex, Diners, Euro/Access, Visa.

Hotel Doelen Karena ★★★★ Nieuwe Doelenstraat 24, 1012 Amsterdam.
☎ 020 6235632, Fax 020 626831. English spoken.
Open all year. 86 bedrooms (all en suite with telephone). Restaurant.
TARIFF: (1993) Single 265, Double 335.
CC: Amex, Diners, Euro/Access, Visa.

Hotel de l'Europe ★★★★★ Nieuwe Doelenstraat 2, 1012 Amsterdam.
☎ 020 6234836, Fax 020 6242962. English spoken.

Open all year. bedrooms. Indoor swimming pool, garage, parking, restaurant. &
TARIFF: (1993) Single 408–508, Double 530–655.
CC: Amex, Diners, Euro/Access, Visa.

Hotel Estherea ★★★★ Singel 303, 1012 Amsterdam.
☎ 020 6245146, Fax 020 6239001. English spoken.

Open all year. 75 bedrooms (all en suite with telephone). Restaurant.

The hotel is ideally located on one of the most beautiful and quiet canals in the centre of the city, only 300 m from the Dam Square and the Royal Palace. Behind the 17th-century façade is a comfortable hotel with all rooms recently renovated.

TARIFF: Single 165–240, Double 190–340.
CC: Amex, Diners, Euro/Access, Visa.

Grand Hotel Krasnapolsky ★★★★★ Dam 9, 1012 Amsterdam.
☎ 020 5549111, Fax 020 6228607.
English spoken.
Open all year. 322 bedrooms (all en suite with telephone). Golf 15 km, garage, parking, restaurant. &

A late 19th-century hotel, in the heart of the city. Close to all the tourist attractions.

TARIFF: (1993) Double 355, Bk 27.50, Set menu 55.
CC: Amex, Diners, Euro/Access, Visa.

Hotel Memphis ★★★★ De Lairessestraat 87, 1071 Amsterdam.
☎ 020 6733141, Fax 020 6737312. English spoken.
Open all year. 74 bedrooms (all en suite with telephone).
TARIFF: (1993) Single 288, Double 365.
CC: Amex, Diners, Euro/Access, Visa.

Hotel King ★ Leidsekade 85, 1017 Amsterdam.
☎ 020 6249603, Fax 020 6207277.
English spoken.

Open all year. 25 bedrooms. Golf 2 km.

A Royal Budget hotel, formerly a 17th-century canal house. Located in the heart of Amsterdam, overlooking the Grand Canal, next to the Leidseplein and near the museums. Close to rail and trains.

TARIFF: Single 55–75, Double 75–125.
CC: Euro/Access, Visa.

Hotel Park ★★★★ Stadhouderskade 25, 1000 Amsterdam.
☎ 020 6717474, Fax 020 6649455.
English spoken.
Open all year. 186 bedrooms (all en suite with telephone). Garage, restaurant. &
TARIFF: (1993) Single 240, Double 332.
CC: Amex, Diners, Euro/Access, Visa.

Hotel Pullman Schiphol ★★★★
Oude Haagseweg 20, 1066 Amsterdam.
☎ 020 6179005, Fax 020 6159027.
English spoken.
Open all year. 151 bedrooms (all en suite with telephone). Parking, restaurant.
TARIFF: (1993) Single 205–225, Double 230–260.
CC: Amex, Diners, Euro/Access, Visa.

Hotel Rembrandt Karena ★★★★
Herengracht 255, 1016 Amsterdam.
☎ 020 6221727, Fax 020 6250630.
English spoken.
Open all year. 111 bedrooms (all en suite with telephone).
TARIFF: (1993) Single 230–375, Double 300–375.
CC: Amex, Diners, Euro/Access, Visa.

Netherlands

Hotel Victoria ★★★★ Damrak 1,
1012 Amsterdam.
☎ 020 6234255, Fax 020 6252997.
English spoken.
Open all year. 320 bedrooms (all en suite
with telephone). Parking, restaurant.
TARIFF: (1993) Single 295–325,
Double 370–395.
CC: Amex, Diners, Euro/Access, Visa.

ARNHEM 13D

Best Western Rijnhotel ★★★★
Onderlangs 10, 6812 Arnhem.
☎ 085 434642, Fax 085 454847.
English spoken.

Open all year. 57 bedrooms (all en suite
with telephone). Parking, restaurant.
*Standing on the banks of the Rhine, with well-
equipped rooms and suites. By car, follow
signs for Oosterbeek, or take bus from Arnhem
railway station.*
TARIFF: Single 195–280, Double 235–280,
Set menu 39.50.
CC: Amex, Diners, Euro/Access, Visa.

Hotel Postiljon Arnhem ★★★
Europaweg 25, 6816 Arnhem.
☎ 085 573333, Fax 085 573361.
English spoken.
Open all year. 90 bedrooms (all en suite).
Restaurant. ⚊
TARIFF: (1993) Single 120–146,
Double 154–180.
CC: Amex, Diners, Euro/Access, Visa.

BERGEN OP ZOOM 13C

Hotel de Draak ★★★★ Grote Markt 36,
4611 Bergen op Zoom.
☎ 01640 33661, Fax 01640 57001.
English spoken.

Open all year. 35 bedrooms (all en suite
with telephone). Parking, restaurant. ⚊
*Open since 1414, in a building dating from
1397, this is the oldest hotel in the Netherlands.*
TARIFF: Single 195–250, Double 250–300,
Set menu 65–100.
CC: Amex, Diners, Euro/Access, Visa.

BORN 13D

Hotel Born ★★★★ Langreweg 21, 6121 Born.
☎ 04498 51666, Fax 04498 51223.
English spoken.
Open all year. 49 bedrooms (all en suite).
Tennis, golf 15 km, parking, restaurant.
*Hotel is in the beautiful province of Limburg,
close to old and historic Maastricht and near
the Belgian and German borders. Hotel offers
a warm welcome combined with comfortable
accommodation. Excellent restaurant and
cosy bar.*
TARIFF: (1993) Single 145–172,
Double 170–222, Set menu 52.50.
CC: Amex, Diners, Euro/Access, Visa.

The 'White Horse' sign

This blue sign with a white horse emblem is
sometimes seen in built-up areas and is a
warning to drivers to take extra care and
can mean:

1 Drive at walking pace (children playing
   in the street);
2 Pedestrians have right of way;
3 Bicycles from the right have priority;
4 Park only in zones marked 'P'.

Netherlands

BOSCH EN DUIN 13C

Aub de Hoefslag ★★★★ Vossenlaan 28,
3735 Bosch en Duin.
℡ 030 251051, Fax 030 285821. English spoken.

Open all year. 38 bedrooms (all en suite with
telephone). Golf 2 km, garage, parking. &
RESTAURANT: good. Closed Sun.

*Elegant hotel/restaurant situated in wooded
residential area of Bosch en Duin, not far
from Utrecht. Excellent restaurant with
international cuisine.*
TARIFF: Single 300–500, Double 325–500,
Set menu 90–125.
CC: Amex, Diners, Euro/Access, Visa.

BREDA 13C

Hotel Brabant ★★★★ Heerbaan 4,
4817 Breda.
℡ 3176 224666, Fax 3176 219592.
English spoken.
Open all year. 72 bedrooms (all en suite
with telephone). Indoor swimming pool,
golf 15 km, parking, restaurant. &
*Modern hotel, completely renovated in 1992.
Near A27, exit Breda-Bavel. Only 5 mins from
historic town centre.*
TARIFF: Single 140–230, Double 155–230.
CC: Amex, Diners, Euro/Access, Visa.

DELFT 13C

Hotel de Ark ★★★★ Koornmarkt 65,
2611 Delft.
℡ 015 157999, Fax 015 144997.
English spoken.
Open 05/01 to 20/12. 24 bedrooms
(all en suite with telephone). Golf 5 km,
garage.
*Near the canal in the centre of Delft, this hotel
comprises three fully restored, 17th-century
houses. Five minutes' walk from the station.*

TARIFF: Single 140–175, Double 175–235.
CC: Amex, Diners, Euro/Access, Visa.

Hotel Juliana ★★★ Maerten Trompstraat 33,
2628 Delft.
℡ 015 567612, Fax 015 565707. English spoken.
Open all year. 25 bedrooms (20 en suite,
25 telephone).
*Business hotel, an 8-minute walk from the
centre of Delft. Near the 'Blue Delft' factory.*
TARIFF: Single 70–110, Double 105–145.
CC: Amex, Diners, Euro/Access, Visa.

Hotel Leeuwenbrug ★★★ Koornmarkt 16,
2611 Delft.
℡ 015 147741, Fax 015 159759.
English spoken.
Open all year. 38 bedrooms (all en suite
with telephone). Golf 3 km, parking.
*In the old part of town, ideal for sightseeing,
shops and restaurants. Comfortably furnished
and small enough to offer personal attention
and service.*
TARIFF: Single 80–125, Double 120–155, Bk 15.
CC: Amex, Diners, Euro/Access, Visa.

DEN HAAG (THE HAGUE) 13C

Hotel Bel Air ★★★★ Johan De Wittlaan 30,
2500 Den Haag.
℡ 07035 02021, Fax 07035 12682.
English spoken.
Open all year. 350 bedrooms (all en suite
with telephone). Indoor swimming pool,
parking, restaurant. &
TARIFF: (1993) Single 230–250,
Double 280–300.
CC: Amex, Diners, Euro/Access, Visa.

Hotel Corona ★★★★ Buitenhof 39,
2513 Den Haag.
℡ 070 3637930, Fax 070 3615785.
English spoken.
Open all year. 26 bedrooms (all en suite
with telephone). Parking, restaurant. &
TARIFF: (1993) Single 245–295,
Double 310–475.
CC: Amex, Diners, Euro/Access, Visa.

Hotel des Inter Lange Voorhout 56,
2514 Den Haag.
℡ 070 3632932, Fax 070 3451721.
English spoken.
Open all year. 76 bedrooms (all en suite
with telephone). Golf 7 km, parking,
restaurant.
*Stately palatial hotel set in a tree lined square
facing the Royal Palace. Nearby shopping and
entertainment. French cuisine.*

TARIFF: (1993) Single 355–380,
Double 455–480, Bk 35, Set menu 65–85.
CC: Amex, Diners, Euro/Access, Visa.

Hotel Europa Scheveningen ★★★★
Zwolsestraat 2, 2587 Den Haag.
☎ 070 3512651, Fax 070 3506473.
English spoken.

Open all year. 174 bedrooms (all en suite
with telephone). Indoor swimming pool,
golf 15 km, garage, restaurant.
*Part of the Queens Moat Houses group. Less
than 100 m from the beach and 5 km from
Den Haag shopping centre. Follow signs to
Den Haag/Scheveningen Bad.*
TARIFF: Single 180–275, Double 220–335,
Bk 21, Set menu 39.50–52.50.
CC: Amex, Diners, Euro/Access, Visa.

Parkhotel Den Haag ★★★★ 53 Molenstraat,
2513 Den Haag.
☎ 070 3624371, Fax 070 3614525.
English spoken.

Open all year. 114 bedrooms (all en suite
with telephone). Garage.
*Traditional hotel in the city centre on a
picturesque street bordering the gardens of the
Royal Palace. 2 km from the station.*

TARIFF: Single 144–172, Double 220–249.
CC: Amex, Diners, Euro/Access, Visa.

Hotel Petit ★★★ Groot Hertoginnelaan 42,
2517 Den Haag.
☎ 070 3465500, Fax 070 3463257.
English spoken.
Open all year. 18 bedrooms (all en suite
with telephone). &
TARIFF: (1993) Single 100–120,
Double 130–160.
CC: Amex, Diners, Euro/Access, Visa.

EINDHOVEN 13D

Dorint Hotel Cocagne ★★★★★ Vestdk 47,
5611 Eindhoven.
☎ 040 44 4755, Fax 040 440148.
English spoken.
Open all year. 203 bedrooms (all en suite
with telephone). Garage, restaurant. &
TARIFF: (1993) Single 210–260,
Double 260–300.
CC: Amex, Diners, Euro/Access, Visa.

Hotel Mandarin ★★★★ Geldropsweg 17,
5611 Eindhoven.
☎ 040 125055, Fax 040 121555. English spoken.
Open all year. 105 bedrooms (all en suite
with telephone). Indoor swimming pool,
parking, restaurant. &
TARIFF: (1993) Single 195–230,
Double 210–245.
CC: Amex, Diners, Euro/Access, Visa.

ERMELO 13D

Hotel Het Roode Koper Jhr Dr Sandbergweg
82, 3852 Ermelo.
☎ 05770 7393, Fax 05770 7561. English spoken.
Open all year. 26 bedrooms (all en suite
with telephone). Outdoor swimming pool,
tennis, golf 8 km, parking, restaurant.
*Attractive country house hotel with a large
garden, surrounded by woodland. From the
E35 motorway (Amersfoort to Zwolle) turn off
to Hardwerwyk and Lelystad in direction of
Apeldoorn/Elspeet. Hotel is 5 km, signposted
Leuvenum.*
TARIFF: (1993) Single 75–190, Double 150–250,
Set menu 57.50–95.
CC: Amex, Diners, Euro/Access, Visa.

GRONINGEN 13B

Hotel de Doelen ★★★ Grote Markt 36,
9711 Groningen.
☎ 050 127041, Fax 050 146112. English spoken.
Open all year. 49 bedrooms (45 en suite,

Netherlands

2 bath/shower only, 49 telephone). Golf 5 km, garage, parking, restaurant.

Dating from 1735, this hotel is situated in the centre of the town.

TARIFF: Single 95–150, Double 130–195.
CC: Amex, Diners, Euro/Access, Visa.

Hotel Mercure ★★★★ Expositielaan 7, 9727 Groningen.
☏ 050 258400, Fax 050 271828. English spoken.
Open all year. 156 bedrooms (all en suite with telephone). Indoor swimming pool, golf 5 km, parking, restaurant. &

A modern hotel on the ring road around Groningen, next to the Martinhal Congress Centre, and only a few minutes from the centre of town.

TARIFF: Single 140–180, Double 160–215, Set menu 37.50.
CC: Amex, Diners, Euro/Access, Visa.

HARDERWIJK 13B

Hotel Marktzicht Klomp ★★★ Markt 6-9, 3841 Harderwijk.
☏ 03410 13032, Fax 03410 13032. English spoken.

Open all year. 39 bedrooms (20 en suite, 7 bath/shower only, 39 telephone). Golf 2 km, garage, parking, restaurant.

Unusual hotel with historic links, situated in the marketplace in the middle of the town.

TARIFF: Single 42–118, Double 56–168, Bk 7.50, Set menu 18.50–35.
CC: Amex, Diners, Euro/Access, Visa.

LEEUWARDEN 13B

Hotel Oranje ★★★★ Stationsweg 4, 8911 Leeuwarden.
☏ 058 126241, Fax 058 121441. English spoken.
Open all year. 78 bedrooms (all en suite with telephone). Garage. &
RESTAURANT: Closed 25/12.

Modern hotel centrally located opposite the station in the ancient heart of Leeuwarden.

TARIFF: (1993) Single 140–225, Double 180–325, Set menu 40–95.
CC: Amex, Diners, Euro/Access, Visa.

MAASTRICHT 13D

Hotel Bergère ★★★ Stationstraat 40, 6221 Maastricht.
☏ 043 251651, Fax 043 255498. English spoken.
Open all year. 40 bedrooms (all en suite with telephone). Garage, parking, restaurant. &
TARIFF: (1993) Single 120, Double 140.
CC: Amex, Euro/Access, Visa.

Hotel du Casque ★★★ Helmstraat 14, 6211 Maastricht.
☏ 043 214343, Fax 043 255155. English spoken.
Open 02/01 to 31/12. 43 bedrooms (38 en suite, 38 telephone). Garage, restaurant.
TARIFF: (1993) Single 160–220, Double 190–250.
CC: Amex, Diners, Euro/Access, Visa.

NIJMEGEN 13D

Hotel Erica ★★★★ Molenbosweg 17, 6571 Nijmegen.
☏ 08895 43514, Fax 08895 43613. English spoken.
Open all year. 59 bedrooms (all en suite with telephone). Indoor swimming pool, tennis, golf 4 km, parking, restaurant. &

Well-equipped hotel located on the edge of woodlands, and only 3 km from the city of Nijmegen, at Berg en Dal.

TARIFF: Single 145, Double 200.
CC: Amex, Diners, Euro/Access, Visa.

Golden Tulip Val-Monte ★★★★
Oude Holleweg 5, 6572 Berg en Dal.
☏ 08895 41704, Fax 08895 43353. English spoken.
Open all year. 104 bedrooms (all en suite with telephone). Indoor swimming pool, tennis, golf 4 km, parking, restaurant. &

Comfortable hotel with friendly staff. Set in an area of outstanding natural beauty not far from German border and centre of Nijmegen.

TARIFF: Single 140–190, Double 195–245, Set menu 44.
CC: Amex, Diners, Euro/Access, Visa.

ROTTERDAM 13C

Hotel Atlanta ★★★★ Aert van Nesstraat 4, Cool Singel, 3012 Rotterdam.
☏ 010 4110420, Fax 010 4135320. English spoken.

Open all year. 170 bedrooms (all en suite with telephone). Golf 3 km, garage, restaurant.

In the heart of the city just off the Coolsingel, opposite World Trade Centre and Congress Hall. 6 km from airport.

TARIFF: Single 200–220, Double 260–280, Bk 22.50.
CC: Amex, Diners, Euro/Access, Visa.

Hotel Savoy ★★★ Hoogstraat 81,
3011 Rotterdam.
☏ 010 4139280, Fax 010 4045712.
English spoken.
Open all year. 94 bedrooms (all en suite with telephone). Restaurant.
TARIFF: (1993) Single 170, Double 205.
CC: Amex, Diners, Euro/Access, Visa.

Hotel Van Walsum ★★★
Mathenesserlaan 199, 3014 Rotterdam.
☏ 010 4363275, Fax 010 4364410.
English spoken.
Open all year. 27 bedrooms (all en suite with telephone). Parking, restaurant.

Small, friendly hotel in a tree-lined avenue in quiet surroundings, yet close to the city centre.

TARIFF: Single 100–145, Double 135–200.
CC: Amex, Diners, Euro/Access, Visa.

Hotel Wilgenhof ★★★
Heemraadssingel 92-94, Oldenzaal,
3000 Rotterdam.
☏ 010 4762526, Fax 010 4772611.
English spoken.
Open all year. 38 bedrooms (19 en suite).
Restaurant.
TARIFF: (1993) Single 95–105, Double 115–130.
CC: Amex, Diners, Euro/Access, Visa.

SLUIS 13C

Hotel Sanders de Paauw Kade 42, 4524 Sluis.
☏ 01178 1224, Fax 01178 2102. English spoken.
Open all year. 24 bedrooms (2 en suite,
19 bath/shower only, 24 telephone).
Golf 5 km, parking, restaurant.

On the edge of Sluis and a few kilometres from the North Sea beaches.

TARIFF: (1993) Single 45–80, Double 80–110,
Set menu 25–38.
CC: Amex, Euro/Access, Visa.

UTRECHT 13C

Hotel Malie ★★★★ Maliestraat 2-4,
3581 Utrecht.
☏ 030 316424, Fax 030 340661. English spoken.
Open all year. 30 bedrooms (all en suite

with telephone). Golf 10 km, parking.

This newly renovated hotel, takes pride in being small enough to offer a warm welcome and personal attention. Half an hour from Schiphol Airport, close to Rotterdam and Den Haag.

TARIFF: Single 140–160, Double 170–210.
CC: Amex, Diners, Euro/Access, Visa.

Hotel Mitland ★★★ Ariensplaan 1,
3573 Utrecht.
☏ 030 715824, Fax 030 719003. English spoken.
Open all year. 44 bedrooms (all en suite with telephone). Tennis, parking, restaurant. &
TARIFF: (1993) Single 108, Double 145.
CC: Amex, Diners, Euro/Access, Visa.

VALKENBURG 13D

Hotel Rooding ★★★★ Neerhem 68,
6301 Valkenburg.
☏ 04406 13241, Fax 04406 13240.
English spoken.

Open 01/04 to 29/10. 94 bedrooms
(all en suite with telephone). Indoor swimming pool, golf 7 km, garage, parking, restaurant. &

Attractive hotel in a unique garden setting within a small forest. Just on the edge of town. Run by the same family for 50 years. Valkenburg is 10 km from Maastricht.

TARIFF: Single 85–150, Double 150–240,
Set menu 35–65.
CC: Amex, Diners, Euro/Access, Visa.

Netherlands

NORWAY

The "Land of the Midnight Sun", on the roof of Europe, is almost 1,800 km long but little wider than 100 km except in the south. Norway shares borders with Sweden, Finland and Russia, and its heavily indented coast faces the north-eastern Atlantic Ocean. The spectacular coastline is almost 3,500 km long, with numerous islands and deep inlets, or fjords. The land area is 323,878 sq km (a third larger than the UK).

A third of Norway is inside the Arctic Circle. Here, the sun shines through the night during midsummer, but not at all in midwinter. The Norwegian coast can be surprisingly mild, due to the Gulf Stream flowing across the Atlantic from the Tropics, but inland it can be very cold and wet. There is little farmland as most of Norway is hilly or mountainous, and here reindeer, elk, wolf, and bear live in the pine and spruce forests. Many birds migrate from the south to breed in the long, light days of the Arctic summer. The discovery of oil off the coast has increased the already high standard of living.

Two-thirds of the 4.2 million Norwegians live in urban areas. The capital, Oslo, has a population of 460,000. Some 20,000 Lapps dwell in the north. The currency is the krone, made up of 100 öre. There are 90,000 km of roads, giving a road density (km per sq km) of 0.3 compared to the UK's 1.5. However a third of roads are unsurfaced and, in the north they may be closed in winter. Note that resorts for Norwegian islands, such as Stord, are listed under their island names in the A–Z directory.

BALESTRAND · 11A

Hotel Midtnes Pensjonat 5850 Balestrand.
☎ 57 69 11 33, Fax 57 69 15 84.
English spoken.

Open 01/02 to 20/12. 30 bedrooms (all en suite with telephone). Parking.

In the centre of Balestrand, close to the English church. Own jetty with rowing boats. Five minutes' walk from bus stop and express boat quay.

TARIFF: Single 420–450, Double 520–640.
CC: Visa.

BERGEN · 11A

Hotel Augustin C Sundtsgt 24, 5000 Bergen.
☎ 05 23 00 25, Fax 05 23 31 30. English spoken.
Open all year. 38 bedrooms (all en suite).
Parking, restaurant.
TARIFF: (1993) Single 595–680, Double 780–880.
CC: Amex, Diners, Euro/Access, Visa.

The Solstrand Fjord Hotel Os, 5200 Bergen.
☎ 56 30 00 99, Fax 56 30 20 80. English spoken.
Open all year. 132 bedrooms (all en suite with telephone). Indoor swimming pool, tennis, parking, restaurant. &

With a superb location right on the fjord, this 19th-century hotel has been run by the same family for three generations. Light and airy accommodation with wonderful views. Good restaurant. On the Os peninsula, about 30 km south of Bergen.

TARIFF: Single 875–1025, Double 990–1225.
CC: Amex, Diners, Euro/Access, Visa.

BREKKE · 11A

Hotel Brekkestranda Fjord 5950 Brekke.
☎ 05 78 55 00, Fax 05 78 56 00.
English spoken.
Open all year. 29 bedrooms (all en suite

Norway

with telephone). Parking, restaurant.

Family-run hotel, on the banks of Sognefjord and 2 hours from Bergen. 5 km from road 1, the hotel is signposted at Instefjord.

cc: Amex, Diners, Euro/Access, Visa.

GEILO   11A

Dr Holms Hotel 3580 Geilo.
☎ 32 09 06 22, Fax 32 09 16 20. English spoken.
Open all year. 124 bedrooms (all en suite with telephone). Indoor swimming pool, garage, parking, restaurant.

Unique location in Geilo, one of Norway's leading mountain resorts. Traditional in style and service, with a wide range of facilities, including saunas, sun beds, workout room and spa centre. On highway 7, 100 m from railway station.

TARIFF: Single 525–1030, Double 750–1410.
cc: Amex, Diners, Euro/Access, Visa.

HAMMERFEST   10B

Hotel Rica Soroygt 15, 9601 Hammerfest.
☎ 08 41 13 33, Fax 08 41 13 11. English spoken.
Open all year. 95 bedrooms (88 en suite). Parking, restaurant.
TARIFF: (1993) Single 950, Double 1025.
cc: Amex, Diners, Euro/Access, Visa.

KRISTIANSAND   11C

Hotel Christian Quart ★★★★ Markensgt 39, 4600 Kristiansand.
☎ 04 22 22 10, Fax 04 22 44 10. English spoken.
Open all year. 111 bedrooms (all en suite). Parking, restaurant. ᵫ
cc: Amex, Diners, Euro/Access, Visa.

LILLEHAMMER   11A

Hotel Lillehammer Turisthotellveien, PO Box 153, 2601 Lillehammer.
☎ 61 28 60 00, Fax 61 25 73 33. English spoken.
Open all year. 196 bedrooms (all en suite with telephone). Indoor swimming pool, outdoor swimming pool, parking, restaurant. ᵫ

Comfortable hotel with good facilities.

TARIFF: Single 895–995, Double 1095–1195.
cc: Amex, Diners, Euro/Access, Visa.

LOEN   11A

Hotel Alexandra Nordfjord, 6878 Loen.
☎ 05 77 76 60, Fax 05 77 77 70. English spoken.
Open all year. 212 bedrooms (all en suite

with telephone). Indoor swimming pool, tennis, parking, restaurant. ᵫ

In the midst of fjord country, surrounded by mountains and picturesque valleys. Close to Alexandra Park, which is ideal for outdoor activities and also the starting point for trips to Briksdal, Geiranger and Lodal.

TARIFF: Single 810–1450, Double 1180–2460, Set menu 275–498.
cc: Amex, Diners, Euro/Access, Visa.

OSLO   11A

Reso Hotel Oslo Plaza ★★★★★
Sonia Henies Plass 3, 0107 Oslo.
☎ 02 17 10 00, Fax 02 17 73 00. English spoken.
Open all year. 662 bedrooms (all en suite with telephone). Indoor swimming pool, garage, parking. ᵫ

Well-equipped, modern hotel in central Oslo. Scandinavia's tallest building, with 37 floors.

TARIFF: (1993) Single 1195–1445, Double 1395–1645.
cc: Amex, Diners, Euro/Access, Visa.

Reso Hotel Royal Christiania ★★★★
Biskop Gunnerusgate 3, 0109 Oslo.
☎ 02 42 94 10, Fax 02 42 46 22. English spoken.
Open 01/03 to 22/12. 451 bedrooms (all en suite with telephone). Indoor swimming pool, garage, parking, restaurant. ᵫ

Modern, Atrium hotel, in central Oslo, close to the main shopping area and financial district.

TARIFF: (1993) Single 1045–1245, Double 1245–1445.
cc: Amex, Diners, Euro/Access, Visa.

RINGEBU   11A

Hotel Venabu Fjellhotel 2632 Venabygd.
☎ 61 28 40 55, Fax 61 28 41 21. English spoken.
Open all year. 62 bedrooms (56 en suite, 36 telephone). Parking, restaurant. ᵫ

Family-run mountain hotel, south of Roudane National Park. Ideal for those who want to walk, ride or cross-country ski in winter, and really get away from it all. 18 km north of Ringebu on road 27, 78 km north of Lillehammer.

TARIFF: Single 400–500, Double 500–800.
cc: Amex, Diners, Euro/Access, Visa.

SANDNES   10A

Holiday Motel PB 310, 4300 Sandnes.
☎ 51 67 48 11, Fax 51 67 49 44. English spoken.
Open all year. 39 bedrooms (all en suite

Norway

with telephone). Parking, restaurant. ♿

Modern motel with good parking and large playground. Beside a Fina petrol station, 2 km from Sandnes on the rv44 and 600 m from the E18 to Stavanger.

TARIFF: Single 390–535, Double 390–650.
CC: Amex, Diners, Euro/Access, Visa.

SKEI I JØLSTER   11A

Hotel Skei 6850 Skei i Jøster.
☎ 57 72 81 01, Fax 57 72 84 23. English spoken.

Open 25/01 to 15/12. 72 bedrooms (all en suite with telephone). Outdoor swimming pool, tennis, parking, restaurant.

Friendly, comfortable, family-run hotel with traditions dating back to 1889. Situated in beautiful natural surroundings at the northern end of Lake Jølster. Ideal starting point for outings to fjords, lakes and glaciers.

TARIFF: Single 600–750, Double 830–910,
Set menu 210–325.
CC: Amex, Diners, Euro/Access, Visa.

SOLVORN   11A

Hotel Walaker Sognefjord, 5815 Solvorn.
☎ 05 68 42 07, Fax 05 68 45 44. English spoken.
Open 01/05 to 31/10. 24 bedrooms
(19 en suite, 19 telephone). Parking, restaurant.

Former inn and coach station owned and run by the same family since 1690. Situated on the north bank of the Sognefjord, 3 km off main road 55, 15 km east of Sogndal, 120 km west of Lom. Urnes stave church nearby. Art gallery on hotel premises, showing Norwegian contemporary art.

TARIFF: (1993) Single 380–550,
Double 520–840, Set menu 90–200.
CC: none.

STAVANGER   11A

Hotel Alstor Tjensvollveien 31,
4021 Stavanger.
☎ 04 87 08 00, Fax 04 87 09 75. English spoken.
Open all year. 79 bedrooms (all en suite).
Indoor swimming pool, parking, restaurant.
TARIFF: (1993) Single 525, Double 600.
CC: Amex, Diners, Euro/Access, Visa.

TRONDHEIM   10C

Hotel Nye Sentrum Lillstorvet,
7001 Trondheim.
☎ 07 52 05 24, Fax 07 53 21 43.
Open all year. 45 bedrooms (40 en suite).
TARIFF: (1993) Single 375, Double 525.
CC: Amex, Diners, Euro/Access, Visa.

UTNE   11A

Hotel Utne ★★★ 5797 Utne.
☎ 53 66 69 83, Fax 53 66 69 50. English spoken.

Open all year. 24 bedrooms (4 en suite, 16 bath/shower only). Parking, restaurant.

Established in 1722, this charming hotel is the oldest still operating in Norway. Comfortable, intimate lounges, traditional furnishings and a warm, welcoming atmosphere. Restaurant overlooks the fjord and has a 4-course set menu. Utne is about 120 km east of Bergen and the hotel is close to the ferry pier.

TARIFF: Single 415–535, Double 640–830,
Set menu 200.
CC: Amex, Diners, Euro/Access, Visa.

VOSS   10A

Hotel Jarl 5700 Voss.
☎ 05 51 19 33, Fax 05 51 37 69. English spoken.
Open all year. 80 bedrooms (all en suite).
Outdoor swimming pool, parking, restaurant.
TARIFF: (1993) Single 495, Double 740.
CC: Amex, Diners, Euro/Access, Visa.

Norway

POLAND

This eastern European country became a republic in 1989, after decades of communist rule. It covers 312,683 sq km (a quarter again as large as the UK), and has borders with Lithuania and CIS states to the east, the Czech and Slovak Republics to the south and Germany on the west – Berlin is only 70 km (50 miles) from the border. Poland's north coast is on the Baltic Sea, where Gdansk is the country's major port. Warsaw is the capital, with 1.6 million inhabitants; other large cities are Lodz, Krakow and Wroclaw. The population is 38 million, with sixty per cent in urban areas. The currency is the zloty, made up of 100 groszy.

Most of Poland consists of the flatlands of the North European Plain, farmed for crops such as barley, wheat, rye, oats, potatoes and sugar beet. To the south, the undulating hills rise to the Tatra Mountains on the Slovak border, where the highest peak is Rysy, at 2,499 m. A quarter of the country is covered by forests, both coniferous and deciduous. In the east, especially, the forests are very ancient and are the last stronghold of the European bison. Deer, wild boar, elk, mountain hare, lynx and brown bear also survive. Summers are warm and dry, but winters are cold and snowy.

Poland has some 340,000 km of roads, with a road density (km per sq km) of 1.1, compared to the UK's 1.5. However, more than 13,000 km of roads are unsurfaced, and access to villages and even smaller towns is sometimes awkward. In common with several other former communist states, most freight and passengers travel by rail.

KRAKOW 22D

Hotel Forum ★★★★ ul Marii Konopnickiej 28, 30302 Krakow.
☎ 12 66 95 00, Fax 12 66 58 27. English spoken.

Open all year. 277 bedrooms (all en suite with telephone). Indoor swimming pool, parking. &
RESTAURANT: Closed 25 Dec.

Modern hotel on the banks of the River Vistula overlooking the royal castle, and 1 km from the old town. Direct access from motorways 7 and 4. 15 km from Balice airport. (Prices in DMs.)

TARIFF: Single 205, Double 233, Set menu 30.
CC: Amex, Diners, Euro/Access, Visa.

Hotel Pollera ★★ ul Szpitalna 30, 31024 Krakow.
☎ 12 22 10 44, Fax 12 22 13 89. English spoken.

Open all year. 42 bedrooms (17 en suite, 12 bath/shower only, 42 telephone). Parking, restaurant. &

A family-run hotel with 150 years' tradition, offering large, light rooms and excellent restaurant. Near the station and a theatre.

TARIFF: Single 330,000–390,000,
Double 480,000–600,000,
Set menu 50,000–100,000.
CC: Amex, Diners, Euro/Access, Visa.

WARSZAWA (WARSAW)   22B

Novotel ★★★ ul Sierpnia 1, 02134 Warszawa.
☎ 22 46 40 51, Fax 22 46 36 86. English spoken.
Open all year. 150 bedrooms (all en suite).
Restaurant.
CC: Amex, Diners, Euro/Access, Visa.

Hotel Orbis Grand ★★★ ul Krucza 28,
522 Warszawa.
☎ 48 22 29 40 51, Fax 48 22 21 87 47.
English spoken.
Open all year. 395 bedrooms (all en suite
with telephone). Indoor swimming pool,
parking, restaurant.

*City centre hotel, ideally located for
sightseeing, museums etc. Small conference
room available. (Prices in $US.)*

TARIFF: Single 37–59, Double 50–77,
Set menu 10–30.
CC: Amex, Diners, Euro/Access, Visa.

Hotel Orbis Vera ★★★★ 16 Bitwy
Warszawskiej 1920r, 02366 Warszawa.
☎ 22 22 74 21, Fax 22 23 62 56. English spoken.
Open all year. 145 bedrooms (all en suite
with telephone). Parking, restaurant.

*Modern, comfortable hotel 5 km from centre of
Warszawa, 6 km from international airport.
Conference facilities. (Prices in $US.)*

TARIFF: Single 37–59, Double 50–77,
Set menu 10–30.
CC: Amex, Diners, Euro/Access, Visa.

Poland

PORTUGAL

The most westerly of European countries, Portugal has only one land border, with its large neighbour, Spain. The country is about 575 km by 200 km and, including the Portuguese Azores and Madeira Islands in the Atlantic, has a land area of 92,389 sq km (about 40 per cent that of the UK). The beautiful westerly beaches along the Atlantic Ocean are popular with tourists from all over Europe, although there are still many inaccessible, remote strips of coastline. About two-thirds of the population of 10 million live in small towns and villages, mostly in the north. The currency is the escudo, made up of 100 centavos.

Much of the north is mountainous, an extension of the Meseta Central plateau, with the Estrela peak rising to an altitude of 1,993 m. Forests of conifers and mixed deciduous trees are home to wolves and wild boar which are protected by law. There are some terraced farming areas in these uplands, but agriculture is concentrated in the south-western plains, the main crops being corn, wheat, beans, grapes and olives. The climate is warm and moist in the north, hot and dry farther south.

Portugal's capital is Lisbon, at the mouth of the River Tagus, with a population of 1.1 million. The second city is Porto (Oporto), at the mouth of the Douro river in the north, which has given its name to the fortified wines famous as port. There are 3,500 km of roads, with a road density (km per sq km) of 0.04 – the lowest in Europe – compared to the UK's 1.5. There are few motorways, and many local roads are steep, winding and variable in quality.

ABRANTES 8C

Hotel de Turismo ★★★ Largo de St-Antonio, 2200 Abrantes.
☏ 41 21 261, Fax 41 25 218. English spoken.
Open all year. 41 bedrooms (all en suite with telephone). Outdoor swimming pool, tennis, parking, restaurant.
Comfortable hotel with air-conditioned rooms and restaurant with panoramic views.
TARIFF: Single 9,500–10,500, Double 11,400–13,000, Bk 800, Set menu 3,200.
CC: Amex, Diners, Euro/Access, Visa.

ALBUFEIRA 8C

Cerro Alagoa ★★★★ Apt 2155, Via Rapida, 8200 Albufeira.
☏ 89 58 82 61, Fax 89 58 82 62. English spoken.
Open all year. 310 bedrooms (all en suite with telephone). Indoor swimming pool, outdoor swimming pool, golf 20 km, garage, parking, restaurant.
TARIFF: (1993) Single 8,000–35,000, Double 9,000–35,000, Set menu 900–3,000.
CC: Amex, Diners, Euro/Access, Visa.

ALMANSIL 8C

Hotel Dona Filipa Vale do Lobo, 8100 Loule.
☏ 89 94 141, Fax 89 39 42 88.
Open all year. 147 bedrooms (all en suite with telephone).
CC: Amex, Diners, Euro/Access, Visa.

AVEIRO 8A

Hotel Imperial ★★★
Rua Dr Nascimento Leitao, 3800 Aveiro.
☏ 34 22 141, Fax 34 24 148. English spoken.
Open all year. 107 bedrooms (all en suite with telephone). Restaurant. &
Comfortable, modern hotel in the city centre. Solarium with panoramic view of Aveiro and the sea.
TARIFF: (1993) Single 8,000–10,000, Double 10,500–12,500.
CC: Amex, Diners, Euro/Access, Visa.

BATALHA 8C

Hotel Dom Joao III ★★★ Av Dom Joao III, 2400 Leiria.
☏ 44 81 25 00, Fax 44 81 22 35. English spoken.
Open all year. 64 bedrooms (all en suite with

telephone). Garage, parking, restaurant. &

*Situated in a quiet location near the town
centre. 20 km from Fatima and one hour's
drive from Lisbon airport.*
TARIFF: Single 9,600, Double 11,800,
Set menu 2,500.
CC: Amex, Diners, Euro/Access, Visa.

Hotel Quinta do Fidalgo 2440 Batalha.
℡ 44 96 114, Fax 46 76 74 01. English spoken.
Open all year. 5 bedrooms (all en suite).
Garage, parking.

*An old manor house with its own private
chapel. In the town centre, opposite the
monastery, in extensive grounds.*
TARIFF: (1993) Single 6,000–10,500,
Double 9,000–16,000.
CC: none.

BRAGA 8A

Hotel Caranda Av da Liberdade 96,
4700 Braga.
℡ 53 61 45 00.
Open all year. 100 bedrooms (all en suite).
CC: Euro/Access, Visa.

CALDAS DA RAINHA 8C

Hotel Malhoa ★★★ Rua Antonio Sergio 31,
2500 Caldas da Rainha.
℡ 62 84 21 80, Fax 62 84 26 21. English spoken.
Open all year. 113 bedrooms (all en suite
with telephone). Outdoor swimming pool,
garage, parking, restaurant.

*Large, modern hotel. All rooms have air
conditioning, satellite television and mini-bar.
Located in town centre, 500 m from world's
oldest spa hospital.*
TARIFF: Single 7,900, Double 9,950,
Set menu 2,650.
CC: Amex, Diners, Euro/Access, Visa.

CALDELAS 8A

Grand Hotel da Bela Vista Termas de
Caldelas, Amares, 4720 Caldelas.
℡ 53 36 117.
Open all year. 69 bedrooms (all en suite).
CC: Euro/Access, Visa.

CARCAVELOS 8C

Hotel Praia-Mar Rua do Gurue 16,
2775 Parede.
℡ 1 24 73 131.
Open all year. 158 bedrooms (all en suite).
CC: Euro/Access, Visa.

CASCAIS 8C

Hotel Cidadela Av de 25 de Abril,
2750 Cascais.
℡ 1 74 83 29 21.
Open all year. 130 bedrooms (all en suite).
CC: Euro/Access, Visa.

Hotel Senhora da Guia ★★★★★ Estrada do
Guincho, 2750 Cascais.
℡ 1 48 69 155, Fax 1 48 69 227. English spoken.
Open all year. 28 bedrooms (all en suite
with telephone). Outdoor swimming pool,
golf 3 km, parking, restaurant.

*A manor house converted into small luxury
hotel with air-conditioned rooms. Motorway
A5 from Lisbon, take last exit and turn right to
Guincho.*
TARIFF: (1993) Single 11,200–28,800,
Double 13,200–30,800.
CC: Amex, Diners, Euro/Access, Visa.

COIMBRA 8A

Hotel Astoria Av Emidio Navarro 21,
3000 Coimbra.
℡ 39 22 055.
Open all year. 64 bedrooms (all en suite).
CC: Euro/Access, Visa.

ERICEIRA 8C

Hotel Morais ★★ Rua Dr Miguel Bombarda 3,
2655 Ericeira.
℡ 61 86 42 00, Fax 61 86 43 08. English spoken.
Open 01/12 to 31/10. 40 bedrooms
(all en suite with telephone). Outdoor
swimming pool, golf 25 km.

*Small family hotel only 300 m from shops and
cafés and 8 minutes' walk to beach.*
TARIFF: Single 3,500–7,500,
Double 4,000–12,500.
CC: Amex, Diners, Euro/Access, Visa.

ESTORIL 8C

Lennox Country Club Rua Eng Alvaro Pedro
Sousa 5, 2765 Estoril.
℡ 1 46 80 424, Fax 1 46 70 859. English spoken.
Open all year. 34 bedrooms (all en suite
with telephone). Outdoor swimming pool,
golf 5 km, parking, restaurant.

*Small, friendly yet elegant hotel set in private
gardens near the beach. Afternoon tea and
cake served at 4 pm! Convenient for the
casino.*
TARIFF: Single 7,500–15,500,
Double 10,000–23,500, Bk 600.
CC: Amex, Diners, Euro/Access, Visa.

Portugal

Hotel Palacio ★★★★★ Rua do Parque,
2765 Estoril.
☏ 1 46 80 400, Fax 1 46 84 867. English spoken.

Open all year. 162 bedrooms (all en suite
with telephone). Outdoor swimming pool,
tennis, golf 1 km, parking, restaurant.
*Large, traditional hotel in centre of Estoril,
elegantly decorated and furnished. Special
rates at Palacio Golf Club.*
TARIFF: Single 21,250–32,000,
Double 22,500–35,000, Set menu 3,500–3,500.
CC: Amex, Diners, Euro/Access, Visa.

EVORA   8C

Hotel Planicie ★★★
Rua Miguel Bombarda 40, 7000 Evora.
☏ 66 24 026, Fax 66 29 880.
English spoken.
Open all year. 33 bedrooms (all en suite
with telephone). Outdoor swimming pool,
golf 2 km, parking, restaurant. &
*Situated in the heart of the historical centre of
town. About 140 km from Lisbon.*
TARIFF: (1993) Single 9,000–10,500,
Double 11,300–13,000, Set menu 2,150–3,430.
CC: Amex, Diners, Euro/Access, Visa.

FARO   8C

Hotel Eva ★★★★ Av da Republica 1,
8000 Faro.
☏ 89 80 33 54, Fax 89 80 23 04.
English spoken.
Open all year. 150 bedrooms (138 en suite,
12 bath/shower only, 150 telephone). Outdoor
swimming pool, golf 18 km, parking,
restaurant. &
*Five-storey building overlooking the harbour,
lagoon, islands and sea. Large, air
conditioned, with roof-top terrace. 8 km to
airport and 9 km to beach.*

TARIFF: Single 8,500–13,300,
Double 13,200–18,000, Set menu 2,900.
CC: Amex, Diners, Euro/Access, Visa.

Hotel Faro ★★★ Praco D Francisco Fomes 2,
8000 Faro.
☏ 89 80 32 76/7/8, Fax 89 80 35 46.
English spoken.
Open all year. 52 bedrooms (all en suite
with telephone). Restaurant.
*Modern, air-conditioned hotel in town centre,
overlooking the harbour. Airport 7 km.*
TARIFF: Single 6,800–12,600,
Double 8,100–13,900, Set menu 2,350.
CC: Amex, Diners, Euro/Access, Visa.

FATIMA   8C

Hotel Dom Jose Av J Alves Correia da Silva,
2495 Fatima.
☏ 49 53 22 15.
Open all year. 63 bedrooms (all en suite).
CC: Euro/Access, Visa.

FIGUEIRA DA FOZ   8A

Grande Hotel da Figueira Av 25 de Abril,
3080 Figueira da Foz.
☏ 33 22 146.
Open all year. 91 bedrooms (all en suite).
CC: Euro/Access, Visa.

LAGOS   8C

Hotel de Lagos ★★★★ Rua Nova da Aldeia,
8600 Lagos.
☏ 82 76 99 67, Fax 82 76 99 20.
Open all year. 318 bedrooms (all en suite
with telephone). Indoor swimming pool,
outdoor swimming pool, tennis, golf 5 km,
garage, restaurant.
*A large, comfortable hotel in town, 2 km from
the magnificent Meia Praia beach and*

Portugal

5 km from the famous Palmares golf course.
TARIFF: (1993) Single 7,750–20,800,
Double 11,900–26,000.
CC: Amex, Diners, Euro/Access, Visa.

LAMEGO 8A

Hotel Villa Hostilina 5100 Lamego.
☎ 054 62 394. English spoken.

Open all year. 7 bedrooms (all en suite
with telephone). Outdoor swimming pool,
tennis, parking, restaurant.

*Small, comfortable 19th-century farmhouse
hotel on the edge of town, only a few hours by
car from Porto. Very peaceful.*
TARIFF: Single 9,000–11,000,
Double 12,000–14,500, Set menu 4,000–6,000.
CC: Visa.

LISBOA (LISBON) 8C

Hotel Altis ★★★★★ Rua Castilho II, 1200 Lisboa.
☎ 1 52 24 96, Fax 1 54 86 96. English spoken.
Open all year. 303 bedrooms (all en suite
with telephone). Indoor swimming pool,
golf 25 km, parking, restaurant. ⚹

*Luxury hotel, well-situated for exploring this
beautiful old city.*
TARIFF: Single 20,000–26,000,
Double 23,000–30,000.
CC: Amex, Diners, Euro/Access, Visa.

Hotel Borges ★★ Rua Garrett 108, 1200 Lisboa.
☎ 1 34 61 951, Fax 1 34 26 617. English spoken.
Open all year. 100 bedrooms (all en suite
with telephone). Restaurant.

*Located in the city centre in heart of good
shopping area. Convenient for airport and
railway station.*
TARIFF: (1993) Single 8,000, Double 9,000,
Set menu 2,000.
CC: Amex, Diners, Euro/Access, Visa.

Hotel Eduardo VII ★★★
Av Fontes P de Melo 5, 1000 Lisboa.
☎ 13 53 01 41, Fax 13 53 38 79. English spoken.
Open all year. 121 bedrooms (all en suite
with telephone). Golf 25 km, restaurant.

*Comfortable, air-conditioned hotel with roof-
top restaurant and panoramic view of Lisboa.
Centrally located, close to Eduardo V11 Park.*
TARIFF: Single 11,900–15,300,
Double 14,000–17,500, Bk 1,000,
Set menu 3,600.
CC: Amex, Diners, Euro/Access, Visa.

Hotel Flamingo ★★★ Rua Castilho 41,
1200 Lisboa.
☎ 1 38 62 191, Fax 1 38 61 216. English spoken.
Open all year. 39 bedrooms (all en suite
with telephone). Golf 22 km, restaurant.

*Situated near Praça Marquês de Pombal, with
an ideal central location. Air conditioning
and TV in all rooms.*
TARIFF: Single 13,200–13,500,
Double 15,700–16,500.
CC: Amex, Diners, Euro/Access, Visa.

Hotel Lisboa Plaza ★★★★
Travesso do Salitre, 1200 Lisboa.
☎ 1 34 63 922, Fax 1 34 71 630.
English spoken.

Open all year. 112 bedrooms (all en suite
with telephone). Golf 15 km, garage, parking,
restaurant.

*Charming, family-owned and operated hotel
in the heart of the city, just off Av Liberdade,
Lisbon's main street. Completely redecorated in
1991 by a famous Portuguese interior
designer, it is warm and inviting. Good
restaurant with Portuguese specialities.
Conference and banqueting facilities.*
TARIFF: Single 17,500–25,000,
Double 19,500–29,500, Set menu 2,750–4,950.
CC: Amex, Diners, Euro/Access, Visa.

Albergaria Senhora do Monte ★★★★

Calçada do Monte 39, 1100 Lisboa.
☎ 1 88 66 002, Fax 1 87 77 83. English spoken.
Open all year. 28 bedrooms (all en suite
with telephone).

*Small hotel on top of hill with panoramic views
of the city and River Tejo. Situated in older
part of the city in Graca district.*

TARIFF: (1993) Single 10,500–11,500,
Double 14,000–17,500.
CC: Amex, Diners, Euro/Access, Visa.

MONCHIQUE   8C

Hotel Abrigo da Montanha ★★★★

8550 Monchique.
☎ 82 92 131, Fax 82 93 660. English spoken.
Open all year. 10 bedrooms (all en suite
with telephone). Outdoor swimming pool,
parking, restaurant.

Small hotel 2 km outside town on road to Foia.

TARIFF: (1993) Double 6,000–12,000.
CC: Amex, Diners, Euro/Access, Visa.

NAZARE   8A

Hotel da Nazare ★★★ Largo Afonso Zuquete,

2450 Nazare.
☎ 62 56 13 11, Fax 62 56 12 38. English spoken.
Open all year. 52 bedrooms (all en suite
with telephone). Parking, restaurant.

*Comfortable hotel with modern facilities
including air conditioning and bar/solarium.
200 m from the beach.*

TARIFF: Single 5,250–12,020,
Double 6,850–12,500, Set menu 1,950–2,400.
CC: Amex, Diners, Euro/Access, Visa.

Hotel Praia ★★★ Av Vieira Guimaraes 39,

Leiria, 2450 Nazare.
☎ 62 56 14 23, Fax 62 56 14 36.
English spoken.
Open all year. 40 bedrooms (all en suite
with telephone). Garage, restaurant.

*A modern, comfortable hotel, completely
renovated in 1993. Conveniently situated only
50 m from the beach.*

TARIFF: Single 8,000–15,000,
Double 10,000–17,500.
CC: Amex, Diners, Euro/Access, Visa.

PONTE DE LIMA   8A

Hotel Quinta de Vermil Lugar de Vermil,

4990 Ardegao.
☎ 58 76 15 95, Fax 58 76 18 01.
English spoken.

Open all year. 10 bedrooms (all en suite).
Outdoor swimming pool, tennis, golf 15 km,
parking.
RESTAURANT: Closed winter.

*Small, 17th-century manor house surrounded
by lovely gardens, forests and vineyards from
which the owners produce their own wine,
completely renovated in 1988. Golf course
opens in 1994. Just over an hour from Porto.
From Ponte de Lima take the 201 towards
Brega. After 12 km, in Corvos take the 308 to
Freixo. 1 km after Freixo turn left to
Ardegao (1km).*

TARIFF: Single 9,500, Double 11,000,
Set menu 3,000–3,200.
CC: none.

PORTO (OPORTO)   8A

Hotel Boa Vista Esplanada do Castelo 58,

Foz do Douro, 4000 Porto.
☎ 26 80 083.
Open all year. 39 bedrooms (all en suite).
CC: none.

Hotel Estalagem do Brasao ★★★★

Av D Joao Canavarro, 4480 Vila Do Conde.
☎ 52 642016, Fax 52 642028.
English spoken.
Open all year. 30 bedrooms (all en suite
with telephone). Golf 2 km, parking,
restaurant.

*Renowned hotel, the property dating back to
1500. Now sympathetically restored, it still
retains its old classic style whilst offering all
modern comforts. Situated in the centre of the
old town within easy walking distance of the
beach and nearby river. North of Porto on
the E01.*

TARIFF: Single 4,850–7,300,
Double 7,300–10,500.
CC: Amex, Diners, Euro/Access, Visa.

Portugal

SERTA 8A

Hotel Vale da Ursa ★★★★ Vale da Ursa,
Cernache Bonjardin, 6100 Serta.
☎ 74 90 981, Fax 74 90 982. English spoken.

Open all year. 17 bedrooms (all en suite
with telephone). Outdoor swimming pool,
tennis, garage, parking, restaurant. &
*Small, comfortable family hotel with
wonderful views over lake. All rooms have
terrace, some with air conditioning. Special
winter rates. West of Serta on N238 for 17 km.
Regional and vegetarian cooking.*
TARIFF: Single 8,500–10,000,
Double 12,000–17,000, Set menu 2,500–3,000.
cc: Euro/Access, Visa.

SESIMBRA 8C

Hotel do Mar ★★★★
Rua General Humberto Delgado, 10,
2970 Sesimbra.
☎ 1 22 33 326, Fax 1 22 33 888. English spoken.
Open all year. 168 bedrooms (all en suite
with telephone). Indoor swimming pool,
outdoor swimming pool, tennis, parking,
restaurant.
*Very comfortable hotel facing sandy beach. All
rooms have air conditioning and sea view.
Panoramic restaurant. Excellent conference
and banqueting facilities. 30 km from Lisboa.*
TARIFF: Single 8,200–15,900,
Double 12,400–25,000, Set menu 3,600.
cc: Amex, Diners, Euro/Access, Visa.

SINTRA 8C

Hotel Central Largo Rainha D Amelia,
2710 Sintra.
☎ 1 92 30 963.
Open all year. 14 bedrooms (10 en suite).
cc: Euro/Access, Visa.

VIANA DO CASTELO 8A

Hotel do Parque ★★★★ Praca da Galiza,
Costa Verde, 4900 Viana do Castelo.
☎ 58 82 86 05, Fax 58 82 86 12. English spoken.
Open all year. 123 bedrooms (all en suite
with telephone). Outdoor swimming pool,
parking, restaurant.
*A large, modern hotel with up-to-date
amenities. Roof-top restaurant with
panoramic view. Solarium.*
TARIFF: Single 6,500–14,200,
Double 7,950–17,750, Set menu 2,750–3,250.
cc: Amex, Diners, Euro/Access, Visa.

Hotel Santa Luzia 4901 Viana do Castelo.
☎ 58 82 88 89, Fax 58 82 88 92. English spoken.
Open all year. 55 bedrooms (all en suite
with telephone). Outdoor swimming pool,
tennis, parking, restaurant.
*Situated on top of the hill of the same name,
this luxurious hotel is elegantly furnished in
30s' style. Good food, gardens and terrace.*
TARIFF: (1993) Single 7,700–16,000,
Double 9,700–18,000.
cc: Amex, Diners, Euro/Access, Visa.

VISEU 8A

Hotel Grao Vasco ★★★★ Rua Gaspar
Barreiros, 3500 Viseu.
☎ 32 423511, Fax 32 27047. English spoken.
Open all year. 110 bedrooms (all en suite
with telephone). Outdoor swimming pool,
garage, parking, restaurant.
*In the heart of this beautiful town, famous for
its historical past and artistic cultural trends.
The hotel offers modern, comfortable rooms
and a very good restaurant.*
TARIFF: Single 11,850–13,650,
Double 13,650–15,750, Set menu 900–1,900.
cc: Amex, Diners, Euro/Access, Visa.

Portugal

SPAIN

Spain is one of Europe's biggest, driest and most visited countries. It has only two land borders, with Portugal to the south-west and France to the north-east. The land area, including the Balearic and Canary Islands, is 504,782 sq km (more than twice that of the UK). Ninety per cent of the 40 million people live in towns and cities. The official language is Castilian Spanish, but there are several groups with their own language, such as Basques in the north and Catalans in the north-east. The currency is the peseta, made up of 100 centimos.

Holidaymakers familiar with the beaches and coastal plains are often surprised to find, on venturing inland, that Spain is very mountainous. From the Cantabrian range in the far north and the Pyrenees in the north-east, there are mountains across the centre, to the the highest mainland peak of Mulhacen, (3,478 m), in the southern Sierra Nevada. Deciduous and evergreen trees cloak some uplands; much of the lowlands is scrubby pasture. Wildlife abounds in remote areas, with boar, chamois, wolf, deer, eagle and vulture. The climate is mild and humid in the north, warm and dry in the south.

Spain's capital is Madrid, in the centre of the country, with more than 3.1 million inhabitants. Other major and historic cities are Barcelona and Valencia on the east coast, Bilbao and Zaragoza in the north-east, and Seville and Malaga to the south. The 320,000 km of roads give a road density (km per sq km) of 0.6, compared to the UK's 1.5. Note that the resorts for Spanish islands, such as Ibiza, are listed under their island names in the A–Z directory.

ALHAURIN EL GRANDE　　　　　　8D

Hotel Finca La Mota ★★ Ctra Mijas, Alhaurin El Grande, 29120 Malaga.
☎ 952 594120. English spoken.

Open all year. 10 bedrooms (7 en suite). Outdoor swimming pool, golf 4 km, parking, restaurant.

This country inn is a converted 16th-century farmhouse surrounded by beautiful mountainous countryside but only 15 km from beaches. Rustic, peaceful and informal. Some rooms have four-poster beds. Horse riding provided at the hotel. Take the Mijas road from Alhaurin el Grande and follow hotel signs 2 km from village.
TARIFF: Single 5,000, Double 7,000–9,000, Set menu 2,000.
CC: Amex, Diners, Euro/Access, Visa.

ALICANTE　　　　　　　　　　9C

Hotel Adoc ★★★★ Playa de la Albufereta, 03000 Alicante.
☎ 96 5265900. English spoken.
Open all year. 93 bedrooms (all en suite with telephone). Indoor swimming pool, outdoor swimming pool, parking.
TARIFF: (1993) Single 6,000, Double 7,200–8,000.
CC: Amex, Diners, Euro/Access, Visa.

Hotel Palas ★★★ Cervantes 5, 03002 Alicante.
☎ 96 5209211, Fax 96 5140120. English spoken.
Open 01/12 to 31/10. 49 bedrooms (all en suite with telephone). Golf, garage, restaurant.

Small hotel with restaurant in 19th-century mansion; former home of Count of Soto. Excellent food and occupying a central position near the sea.

TARIFF: (1993) Single 4,900–5,885,
Double 7,875–9,415, Bk 500, Set menu 1,850.
CC: Amex, Diners, Euro/Access, Visa.

ALMERIA　　　　　　　　　　　　　8D

Gran Hotel Almeria ★★★★
Avda Reina Regente 8, 04001 Almeria.
☎ 951 238011, Fax 951 270691. English spoken.
Open all year. 117 bedrooms (all en suite
with telephone). Indoor swimming pool,
garage.
TARIFF: (1993) Double 13,300–14,650.
CC: Amex, Diners, Euro/Access, Visa.

ARACENA　　　　　　　　　　　　8C

Finca Buenvino Los Marines, 21293 Huelva.
☎ 955 124034, Fax 955 124034. English spoken.
Open all year. 4 bedrooms (all en suite).
Outdoor swimming pool.

*Small guest house in the middle of the Sierra
de Aracena Nature Park, surrounded by cool
hills and woods. This is all about the other
Spain, horse-riding, walking, eating and
drinking with the family - no lager here! Prices
are for half-board. Los Marines is just west of
Aracena.*
TARIFF: Single 15,000, Double 24,000.
CC: Euro/Access, Visa.

ARENYS DE MAR　　　　　　　　9B

Hotel d'Arenys ★★ Avda Catalunya 8,
08350 Arenys de Mar.
☎ 937 920383, Fax 937 957553. English spoken.
Open all year. 100 bedrooms (all en suite).
Outdoor swimming pool, golf 5 km, parking,
restaurant. &
*On the coast and well situated for both
sightseeing and exploring the surrounding
area.*
TARIFF: Single 4,400–6,800,
Double 5,500–8,500, Bk 500,
Set menu 1,200–1,500.
CC: Amex, Diners, Euro/Access, Visa.

BADAJOZ　　　　　　　　　　　　8C

Gran Hotel Zurbaran ★★★★
Paseo Castelar 6, 06001 Badajoz.
☎ 924 223741, Fax 924 220142.
English spoken.
Open all year. 215 bedrooms (all en suite
with telephone). Outdoor swimming pool,
tennis, parking, restaurant.
TARIFF: (1993) Double 12,900–13,900.
CC: Amex, Diners, Euro/Access, Visa.

BARCELONA　　　　　　　　　　　9B

Hotel Gran Via ★★★
Gran Via Corts Catalanes 642,
08000 Barcelona.
☎ 93 3181900, Fax 93 3189997. English spoken.
Open all year. 53 bedrooms (all en suite with
telephone). Golf 5 km, garage, parking. &
*Elegant and grand hotel in centre of
Barcelona close to the Plaza Cataluña and so
in a good position for both business and
pleasure.*
TARIFF: Single 8,000, Double 11,500.
CC: Amex, Diners, Euro/Access, Visa.

Hotel Princesa Sofia ★★★★ Plaza Pio XII 4,
08028 Barcelona.
☎ 93 3307111, Fax 93 3307621. English spoken.

Open all year. 505 bedrooms (all en suite
with telephone). Indoor swimming pool,
outdoor swimming pool, golf 15 km, garage,
parking, restaurant.
*Luxury hotel located in the exclusive Avda
Diagonal in the new financial centre, and
conveniently situated for all business and
cultural points of interest. 20 minutes from
airport and 10 minutes to station.*
TARIFF: Single 17,000–20,000, Double 25,000,
Bk 1,800.
CC: Amex, Diners, Euro/Access, Visa.

Hotel Hesperia ★★★★ Los Vergos 20,
08017 Barcelona.
☎ 93 2045551, Fax 93 2044392. English spoken.
Open all year. 139 bedrooms (all en suite
with telephone). Golf 10 km, garage, parking,
restaurant.
Modern hotel in a quiet western suburb. Just

Spain

off the General Mitre ring road and close to the Vallvidrera Tunnel road.

TARIFF: Single 7,500–16,400, Double 10,000–30,500, Bk 1,250, Set menu 2,600.
CC: Amex, Diners, Euro/Access, Visa.

Hotel Metropol ★★★ Ample 31, 08002 Barcelona.
📞 93 3154011, Fax 93 3191276. English spoken.
Open all year. 68 bedrooms (all en suite with telephone). &

Small hotel in the Gothic quarter and near the main post office.

TARIFF: (1993) Single 8,500–13,200, Double 11,800–17,600, Bk 900.
CC: Amex, Diners, Euro/Access, Visa.

Hotel Ramblas ★★★ Ramblas 33, 08003 Barcelona.
📞 93 3015700, Fax 93 4122507. English spoken.
Open all year. 77 bedrooms (all en suite with telephone). Garage. &

In city centre, renovated throughout, very comfortable hotel.

TARIFF: (1993) Single 11,200–12,500, Double 14,700–16,500, Bk 1,125.
CC: Amex, Euro/Access, Visa.

Hotel Ritz ★★★★★
Gran Via Corts Catalanes 668, 08010 Barcelona.
📞 93 3185200, Fax 93 3180148. English spoken.
Open all year. 161 bedrooms (all en suite with telephone). Golf 20 km, garage, parking, restaurant. &

Luxury hotel with classical façade. Charming but elegant and incorporating modern features. Located in heart of city, convenient for airport.

TARIFF: (1993) Single 32,800–41,500, Double 43,000–52,000, Bk 2,150, Set menu 3,250.
CC: Amex, Diners, Euro/Access, Visa.

Hotel Suizo Pl del Angel 12, 08002 Barcelona.
📞 93 3154111, Fax 93 3153819. English spoken.
Open all year. 50 bedrooms. Parking, restaurant.

Completely modernised hotel situated in centre of the Gothic quarter. Close to cathedral, Las Ramblas, port and railway station.

TARIFF: (1993) Single 9,800, Double 13,500, Bk 675, Set menu 2,750.
CC: Amex, Diners, Euro/Access, Visa.

BEGUR 9B

Hotel Aigua Blava ★★★★ Platja de Fornells, 17255 Begur.
📞 972 622058, Fax 972 622112. English spoken.

Open 20/02 to 14/11. 85 bedrooms (all en suite with telephone). Outdoor swimming pool, tennis, golf 12 km, garage, parking, restaurant.

Very comfortable hotel in a superb location beside the sea and pine forests. Excellent restaurant. Special rates for hotel guests at nearby golf courses. Fornells is south-east of Begur.

TARIFF: Single 6,300–8,600, Double 10,000–16,000, Bk 1,300, Set menu 3,300–5,000.
CC: Amex, Euro/Access, Visa.

Hotel Begur ★★ Comas y Ros 8, 17255 Begur.
📞 972 622207. English spoken.
Open all year. 40 bedrooms (all en suite with telephone). Golf 6 km, garage, parking, restaurant.

Clean, whitewashed building in local style. Begur is a group of small old fishing villages within easy reach of rocky coves.

TARIFF: Single 5,500–7,000, Double 6,300–8,200, Bk 850, Set menu 1,400–1,900.
CC: Amex, Diners, Euro/Access, Visa.

Hotel Sa Riera ★★ Playa de Sa Riera, 17255 Begur.
📞 972 623000, Fax 972 623460. English spoken.
Open 01/05 to 31/10. 44 bedrooms (all en suite). Outdoor swimming pool, garage, parking, restaurant.
TARIFF: (1993) Double 4,100–6,800.
CC: Amex, Diners, Euro/Access, Visa.

BENAOJAN 8D

Hotel Molino del Santo ★★ Bda Estacion,
Benaojan, 29370 Malaga.
☎ 952 167151, Fax 952 167151. English spoken.

Open 01/03 to 01/12. 12 bedrooms
(all en suite). Outdoor swimming pool,
parking, restaurant.

*Charming, converted watermill alongside a
mountain stream in the national park, 15
minutes from Ronda. Friendly service and
good Spanish cooking.*
TARIFF: Single 4,000–6,500,
Double 6,000–9,000, Bk 750.
CC: Diners, Euro/Access, Visa.

BILBAO 8B

Hotel Conde-Duque ★★★ Campo de Volantin
22, 48007 Bilbao.
☎ 94 4456000, Fax 94 4456006. English spoken.
Open all year. 67 bedrooms (all en suite).
Garage, parking, restaurant.
TARIFF: (1993) Double 10,800–12,800.
CC: Amex, Diners, Euro/Access, Visa.

Hotel Grand Ercilla ★★★★ Ctra Ercilla 37-39,
48007 Bilbao.
☎ 94 4102000, Fax 94 4439335. English spoken.
Open all year. 346 bedrooms (all en suite
with telephone). Garage, restaurant.

*Completely renovated in 1990, hotel is in the
commercial area in the heart of Bilbao.
Comfortable accommodation with good
facilities. Disco, bar.*
TARIFF: Single 13,750–14,000,
Double 21,765–22,365, Bk 1,415,
Set menu 5,600.
CC: Amex, Diners, Euro/Access, Visa.

BLANES 9B

Hotel Horitzo ★★★ Paseo Maritimo S'Abanell
11, 17300 Blanes.

☎ 972 330400, Fax 972 337863. English spoken.
Open 01/04 to 31/10. 122 bedrooms
(all en suite with telephone). Golf 8 km,
garage, parking, restaurant.

*Family-run hotel with friendly atmosphere.
Faces the sea, some rooms with sea view
and TV.*
TARIFF: Single 3,550–5,450,
Double 5,700–9,550, Set menu 1,800.
CC: Amex, Euro/Access, Visa.

BURGOS 8B

Ciudad de Burgos ★★★ 09199 Rubena.
☎ 947 431041, Fax 947 431037. English spoken.
Open all year. 86 bedrooms (all en suite
with telephone). Parking, restaurant.

On the N1, 7 km from the centre of Burgos.
TARIFF: (1993) Single 4,200–4,850,
Double 6,450–7,400, Bk 500.
CC: Amex, Diners, Euro/Access, Visa.

Hotel Tres Coronas de Silos ★★★ Plaza
Mayor 6, Santo Domingo de Silos,
09610 Burgos.
☎ 947 380727.
Open all year. 16 bedrooms (all en suite).
Restaurant.

*An 18th-century hotel with many interesting
features including a fine staircase. The hotel
offers Castillian home cooking.*
TARIFF: (1993) Single 4,300–4,800,
Double 7,400–7,900, Bk 650.
CC: Amex, Euro/Access, Visa.

BURRIANA 9C

Hotel Aloha ★★ Avda Mediterraneo 74,
12530 Burriana.
☎ 964 585000, Fax 964 585000.
Open all year. 30 bedrooms (all en suite
with telephone). Outdoor swimming pool,
golf 12 km, parking, restaurant.

*Travellers in search of fine food, wines,
excellent bathing and a leisurely life will find
all they want at this hotel by the beach on the
Costa del Azahar (the Orange Blossom Coast).*
TARIFF: Single 4,150–4,850, ·
Double 6,200–7,250, Bk 475, Set menu 2,000.
CC: Euro/Access, Visa.

CADAQUES 9B

Hostal S'Aguarda ★★★ Ctra Port-Lligat 28,
17488 Cadaques.
☎ 972 258082, Fax 972 258756. English spoken.
Open 01/12 to 31/10. 28 bedrooms

Spain

(all en suite with telephone). Outdoor swimming pool, tennis, parking, restaurant.

Small comfortable family-run hotel with magnificent views of the sea. Situated in the highest part of the town.

TARIFF: (1993) Single 3,200–4,800, Double 4,200–6,800, Bk 475, Set menu 1,500. cc: Amex, Diners, Euro/Access, Visa.

CADIZ   8C

Hotel Capele ★★★ Corredera 58, Jerez de la Frontera, 11402 Cadiz.
✆ 956 346400, Fax 956 346242. English spoken.
Open all year. 55 bedrooms (all en suite with telephone). Golf 10 km, restaurant.

Centrally located hotel with modern facilities.

TARIFF: Single 4,000–6,000, Double 6,000–8,000, Bk 250. cc: Amex, Diners, Euro/Access, Visa.

SEE ADVERTISEMENT

CALPE   9C

Hotel Venta La Chata ★★ 03710 Calpe.
✆ 965 830308. English spoken.
Open all year. 17 bedrooms (all en suite with telephone). Tennis, golf 15 km, garage, parking.

Small hotel on the road between Calpe and Benisa, 4 km from Calpe.

TARIFF: Single 2,700, Double 5,000, Bk 360. cc: Diners, Euro/Access, Visa.

CHIPIONA   8C

Hotel Brasilia ★★★ Avda del Faro 12, 11550 Chipiona.
✆ 956 371054, Fax 956 371054. English spoken.

Open all year. 44 bedrooms (all en suite with telephone). Outdoor swimming pool, garage.
RESTAURANT: Closed 01/11 to 30/04.

Elegant, classical-styled hotel. Cool, clean and typically Spanish.

TARIFF: Single 4,100–6,100, Double 5,600–8,100, Bk 600, Set menu 1,500. cc: Amex, Diners, Euro/Access, Visa.

CORDOBA   8D

Parador de la Arruzafa ★★★★ Avda de la Arruzafa 33, 14012 Cordoba.
✆ 957 275900, Fax 957 280409. English spoken.
Open all year. 94 bedrooms (all en suite with telephone). Outdoor swimming pool, tennis, golf 5 km, parking, restaurant. ⅍

Spain

A modern building with magnificent views in the residential area known as El Brillante. Well signposted.

TARIFF: Single 11,600–12,000, Double 14,500–15,000, Bk 1,100, Set menu 3,000–4,200.
CC: Amex, Diners, Euro/Access, Visa.

Hotel Los Gallos ★★★ Avda Medina Azahara 7, 14005 Cordoba.
☎ 957 235500, Fax 957 231636. English spoken.
Open all year. 115 bedrooms (all en suite). Indoor swimming pool, restaurant.
TARIFF: (1993) Double 11,600–13,000.
CC: Amex, Diners, Euro/Access, Visa.

LA CORUÑA   8A

Hotel Finisterre Paseo del Parrote 2, 15001 La Coruña.
☎ 981 205400, Fax 981 2084621.
English spoken.
Open all year. 127 bedrooms (all en suite with telephone). Outdoor swimming pool, tennis, parking, restaurant.

Situated in the centre of the city, in the historic and artistic area. Excellent view of the bay. Sauna, gym, beauty parlour and park for children.

TARIFF: (1993) Single 10,000–12,000, Double 12,500–15,000, Bk 1,050.
CC: Amex, Diners, Euro/Access, Visa.

CUENCA   8D

Hotel La Cueva del Fraile ★★★ Ctra Buenache, 16001 Cuenca.
☎ 966 211571, Fax 966 256047. English spoken.
Open 10/01 to 28/11. 63 bedrooms (all en suite with telephone). Outdoor swimming pool, tennis, parking, restaurant.

This restored 16th-century building offers comfortable accommodation just outside the village of Cuenca.

TARIFF: Single 6,200–7,500, Double 9,500–11,500, Bk 675, Set menu 2,400.
CC: Amex, Diners, Euro/Access, Visa.

Posada de San Jose ★★
Calle Julian Romero 4, 16001 Cuenca.
☎ 966 211300, Fax 966 211300. English spoken.
Open all year. 30 bedrooms (21 en suite).
Golf 16 km.

In the heart of the old quarter, this 17th-century building overlooks the Huecar River. All rooms have magnificent views over the gorge. Terrace in summer. Comfortable bar area where light snack suppers are served:

home style tapas and "raciones", salads etc.
TARIFF: Single 1,800–4,000, Double 4,000–8,000, Bk 450.
CC: Amex, Diners, Euro/Access, Visa.

ESPOT   9A

Hotel Roya ★ Ctra de San Mauricio, 25597 Espot.
☎ 973 624040, Fax 973 624040.

Open 01/12 to 31/10. 34 bedrooms (all en suite with telephone). Parking, restaurant.

On the edge of a national park. Run by same family for more than a century. Regional cuisine. Particularly attractive for winter sports enthusiasts.

TARIFF: Single 2,600–3,500, Double 1,500–5,500, Bk 600, Set menu 1,100–1,500.
CC: Diners, Euro/Access, Visa.

Hotel Saurat ★★ Plaza San Martin Lerida, 25597 Espot.
☎ 973 624162, Fax 973 624037.
English spoken.
Open 15/01 to 17/10. 52 bedrooms (all en suite with telephone). Parking, restaurant. &

Quiet, traditional hotel in the heart of the Pyrénées. Near Aigües Tortes-Sant Maurici National Park and the Espot ski station.

TARIFF: Single 3,142–5,982, Double 6,284–11,964, Set menu 1,500–4,000.
CC: Diners, Euro/Access, Visa.

ESTEPONA   8D

Hotel Stakis Paraiso ★★★★ Ctra Cadiz-Malaga, Estepona.
☎ 952 883000/88431, Fax 952 882019.
English spoken.

Open all year. 200 bedrooms (all en suite with telephone). Indoor swimming pool, outdoor swimming pool, parking, restaurant. &

Located 10 km from centre of Marbella and Estepona. Panoramic views of mountains and towards the sea. Air-conditioned rooms. Spa clinic (alternative medicine) close by. 60 km from Malaga airport.

TARIFF: Single 9,900–13,100, Double 16,000–21,000, Bk 1,000, Set menu 4,000–7,000.
CC: Amex, Diners, Euro/Access, Visa.

FIGUERES   9B

Hotel Ampurdan ★★★ Antigua Carretera a Francia, 17600 Figueres.
☎ 972 500566, Fax 972 509358. English spoken. Open all year. 42 bedrooms (all en suite with telephone). Golf 10 km, garage, parking, restaurant. &

Famous for its cuisine, the hotel is just 1 km from the town centre. Small and comfortable with air conditioning.

TARIFF: Single 6,000–7,200, Double 9,100–10,500, Bk 910, Set menu 3,650–4,100.
CC: Amex, Diners, Euro/Access, Visa.

Hotel Duran ★★★ Calle Lasauca 5, 17600 Figueres.
☎ 972 501250, Fax 972 502609. English spoken. Open all year. 63 bedrooms (all en suite with telephone). Golf 6 km, garage, parking, restaurant. &

A small hotel/restaurant, built in 1842 but now refurbished and air conditioned. Comfortable and friendly atmosphere. Situated in town centre. Rooms with TV via satellite (Astra), the nearest hotel to the Dalí Museum. We have a garage for our clients.

TARIFF: Single 4,400–5,400,

Double 5,200–6,900, Bk 600, Set menu 1,600.
CC: Amex, Diners, Euro/Access, Visa.

FUENGIROLA   8D

Hotel Florida ★★★ Paseo Maritimo, 29640 Fuengirola.
☎ 952 476100, Fax 952 581529. English spoken. Open all year. 116 bedrooms (all en suite with telephone). Outdoor swimming pool, golf 4 km, restaurant. &

Comfortable hotel on seafront and opposite pleasure harbour. Sub-tropical garden and most rooms with sea view. 700 m from railway station.

TARIFF: Single 4,350–6,000, Double 6,500–9,000, Bk 600, Set menu 2,200.
CC: Amex, Diners, Euro/Access, Visa.

GRANADA   8D

Hotel America ★ Real de la Alhambra 53, 18009 Granada.
☎ 958 227471. English spoken. Open 01/03 to 31/10. 13 bedrooms (all en suite). Restaurant.
TARIFF: (1993) Double 8,000.
CC: none.

Hotel Atenas ★★ Grand Via Colon 38-1, 18010 Granada.
☎ 958 278750, Fax 958 292676. English spoken. Open all year. 78 bedrooms (70 en suite, 8 bath/shower only, 78 telephone). Golf 2 km, garage, parking, restaurant. &

Small comfortable hotel in a narrow city centre street. Renovated 1990. Large dining room. Special prices for group bookings.

TARIFF: Single 1,600–2,750, Double 3,000–3,900, Bk 225, Set menu 725–950.
CC: Diners, Euro/Access, Visa.

Hotel Condor ★★★ Avda de la Constitucion 6, 18000 Granada.
☎ 958 283711, Fax 958 285591. English spoken. Open all year. 101 bedrooms (all en suite with telephone). Garage, restaurant.
TARIFF: (1993) Double 9,000.
CC: Amex, Diners, Euro/Access, Visa.

Hotel Guadalupe Avda de los Alixares, 18009 Granada.
☎ 958 223424, Fax 958 223798. English spoken. Open all year. 58 bedrooms (all en suite with telephone). Parking, restaurant.

Set in the grounds of the Alhambra with views of Sierra Nevada. Furnished in elegant

Spain

Granadian style and air conditioned.
TARIFF: (1993) Single 4,500–5,800,
Double 7,000–9,850, Bk 600, Set menu 1,900.
CC: Amex, Diners, Euro/Access, Visa.

Hotel Kenia ★★★ Molinos 65, 18000 Granada.
☎ 958 227506. English spoken.
Open all year. 16 bedrooms (all en suite).
Parking, restaurant.
TARIFF: (1993) Double 7,200.
CC: Amex, Diners, Euro/Access, Visa.

Hotel Sierra Nevada ★★ Avda de Madrid 107,
18014 Granada.
☎ 958 150062, Fax 958 150954. English spoken.
Open 01/03 to 01/11. 23 bedrooms
(all en suite with telephone). Outdoor
swimming pool, tennis, golf 15 km, parking. &
RESTAURANT: Closed 01/11 to 01/03.

*A small hotel with centrally-heated double
rooms. On the north side of Granada.*
TARIFF: Single 3,400, Double 5,000, Bk 200,
Set menu 800–1,200.
CC: Amex, Diners, Euro/Access, Visa.

HARO   8B

Hotel Iturrimurri ★★★
Ctra Circunvalacion s/, 26200 Haro.
☎ 941 311213, Fax 941 311721. English spoken.

Open all year. 36 bedrooms (all en suite with
telephone). Indoor swimming pool, outdoor
swimming pool, parking, restaurant. &
*Small hotel in quiet situation with good views.
Restaurant specialises in regional dishes.*
TARIFF: Single 4,000–5,300, Double 7,100–8,100,
Bk 675, Set menu 1,900–3,500.
CC: Amex, Euro/Access, Visa.

HUELVA   8C

Hotel Tartessos Avda Martin Alonso
Pinzon 13, 21003 Huelva.
☎ 955 282711, Fax 955 250617. English spoken.

Open all year. 112 bedrooms (all en suite
with telephone). Golf 5 km, garage, parking,
restaurant.
*Completely updated in 1992, comfortable, air-
conditioned rooms. On main street in town
centre. New restaurant El Estero, piano bar.*
TARIFF: Single 6,000, Double 10,000, Bk 500,
Set menu 2,500.
CC: Amex, Diners, Euro/Access, Visa.

IRUN   9A

Apartments Jauregui ★★★ San Pedro 28,
20280 Fuenterrabia/Hondarribia.
☎ 943 641400, Fax 943 644404. English spoken.
Open all year. 53 bedrooms (all en suite
with telephone). Garage. &
*Small hotel surrounded by restaurants. 2 km
from Irun, follow signs to Hondarribia.*
TARIFF: Single 5,300–6,650,
Double 7,900–9,800, Bk 600.
CC: Amex, Diners, Euro/Access, Visa.

JAEN   8D

Hotel La Yuca ★ Apartado 117, 23080 Jaen.
☎ 953 221950, Fax 953 221659.

Open all year. 23 bedrooms (all en suite
with telephone). Parking, restaurant. &
*Set halfway between Madrid and the Costa del
Sol, this comfortable hotel makes an ideal
stopping place. Take the Jaen bypass and after
4 km the hotel is at Albarete/Granada junction.*
TARIFF: Single 3,975–4,982, Double 6,042–7,208,
Bk 318, Set menu 1,900–1,500.
CC: Amex, Diners, Euro/Access, Visa.

Parador de la Santa Catalina ★★★ 23001 Jaen.
☎ 953 264411, Fax 953 223930. English spoken.
Open all year. 43 bedrooms (all en suite
with telephone). Outdoor swimming pool,
parking, restaurant.
TARIFF: (1993) Double 11,000–12,500.
CC: none.

Spain

LA JUNQUERA   9B

Hotel Merce-Park ★★ 17700 La Junquera.
☎ 972 549038, Fax 972 549038. English spoken.
Open all year. 48 bedrooms (all en suite with
telephone). Golf 4 km, garage, restaurant. ♿

*Picturesque setting beside the river, just south
of La Junquera. 5 km from Spanish/French
border. A former spa, now completely
renovated with air-conditioned rooms.*

TARIFF: Single 3,500–3,600,
Double 3,500–5,600, Bk 600, Set menu 1,600.
CC: Amex, Diners, Euro/Access, Visa.

LA ALBERCA   8A

Hotel Las Batuecas ★★ Ctra Las Batuecas,
37624 Salamanca.
☎ 923 415188/94, Fax 923 415055.
English spoken.
Open all year. 24 bedrooms (all en suite
with telephone). Garage, parking, restaurant.

*Stone building in beautiful village, with
mountains covered in chestnut and walnut
trees. 75 km south-west of Salamanca and
54 km from Bejar.*

TARIFF: Single 3,260–4,000, Double 5,000–6,000,
Bk 425, Set menu 1,300–3,900.
CC: Visa.

LA BISBAL   9B

Mas de Torrent ★★★★★ 17123 Torrent.
☎ 972 303292, Fax 972 303293. English spoken.
Open all year. 30 bedrooms (all en suite
with telephone). Outdoor swimming pool,
tennis, golf 6 km, parking, restaurant. ♿

*A very comfortable former 18th-century
farmhouse, now converted to a 5-star hotel.
Between La Bisbal and Palafrugell.*

TARIFF: (1993) Single 17,000–20,400,
Double 20,000–28,000, Bk 1,500, Set menu 5,000.
CC: Amex, Diners, Euro/Access, Visa.

LLAFRANC DE PALAFRUGELL   9B

Hotel Llevant ★★ Francesc de Blanes 5,
17211 Llafranc de Palafrugell.
☎ 972 300366, Fax 972 300345. English spoken.
Open 15/12 to 30/10. 24 bedrooms
(all en suite with telephone). Golf 9 km.
RESTAURANT: Closed Sun eve 01/01 to 31/03.

*Small family-run hotel facing the sea. Good
restaurant, and rooms air-conditioned.*

TARIFF: (1993) Single 3,500–5,000,
Double 6,500–14,000, Bk 900,
Set menu 1,900–2,100.
CC: Amex, Euro/Access, Visa.

Hotel Terramar Paseo de Cypsele 1,
17211 Llafranc de Palafrugell.
☎ 972 300200, Fax 972 300626.
English spoken.

Open 14/04 to 06/10. 56 bedrooms
(all en suite with telephone). Golf 9 km,
garage, restaurant. ♿

*A pleasant family atmosphere at this well-
appointed hotel on the beach. Panoramic
views and terrace overlooking the beach.*

TARIFF: Single 5,000–7,000,
Double 6,500–9,500, Bk 850.
CC: Amex, Diners, Euro/Access, Visa.

LLANES   8B

Hotel Mirador de la Franca ★★★
33590 La Franca.
☎ 985 412145, Fax 985 412153.
English spoken.

Open 26/03 to 27/09. 56 bedrooms
(all en suite with telephone). Tennis,
golf 12 km, parking, restaurant.

*Comfortable hotel beside a lovely beach. Ideal
location for exploring the surrounding
countryside. On N634 east of Llanes, km 286.*

TARIFF: Single 3,500–6,500,
Double 5,900–9,900, Bk 600, Set menu 1,650.
CC: Amex, Diners, Euro/Access, Visa.

Spain

LLORET DE MAR 9B

Gran Hotel Monterrey ★★★★ Ctra de Tossa, 17310 Lloret de Mar.
✆ 972 364050, Fax 972 363512. English spoken.

Open 01/03 to 05/11. 224 bedrooms (all en suite with telephone). Indoor swimming pool, outdoor swimming pool, tennis, parking, restaurant. ♿

Large air-conditioned hotel situated in a quiet, wooded area. 10 minutes from town centre and beach, on road to Tossa de Mar. New beauty/health centre with pool, jacuzzi. Buffet service meals. Children very welcome.

TARIFF: Single 6,000–8,000,
Double 10,000–16,000.
CC: Amex, Diners, Euro/Access, Visa.

MADRID 8B

Hotel Husa Princesa ★★★★★ Princesa 40, 28008 Madrid.
✆ 91 5423500, Fax 91 5423501. English spoken.

Open all year. 406 bedrooms (all en suite with telephone). Indoor swimming pool, golf 2 km, garage, restaurant. ♿

Completely renovated in 1992, this town centre hotel offers facilities of the highest standards. Rooms are light, airy and tastefully furnished. Lovely dining room and pretty terrace. Health and beauty centre. Conference facilities.

TARIFF: Single 23,100–24,900,
Double 28,900–31,200, Set menu 2,800.
CC: Amex, Diners, Euro/Access, Visa.

Hotel Mindanao ★★★★★ Pas San Francisco de Sales 15, 28003 Madrid.
✆ 91 5495500, Fax 91 2445596. English spoken.

Open all year. 289 bedrooms (all en suite with telephone). Indoor swimming pool, outdoor swimming pool, garage, parking, restaurant.

Luxury-class hotel in exclusive area of Madrid. High comfort and service. Fully air conditioned.

TARIFF: Single 22,000, Double 27,500, Bk 1,750.
CC: Amex, Diners, Euro/Access, Visa.

Hotel Plaza ★★★★ Pl de Espana, 28013 Madrid.
✆ 91 2471200, Fax 91 2482389. English spoken.
Open all year. 306 bedrooms (all en suite with telephone). Parking, restaurant.

Ideally located with completely refurbished facilities, pleasant atmosphere and efficient service.

TARIFF: Single 15,200, Double 19,000–19,000, Bk 1,300, Set menu 3,000.
CC: Amex, Diners, Euro/Access, Visa.

Hotel Zurbano ★★★ Calle Zurbano 79/81, 28003 Madrid.
✆ 91 4415500, Fax 91 4413224. English spoken.
Open all year. 269 bedrooms (all en suite with telephone). Garage, parking, restaurant.
TARIFF: (1993) Double 20,000.
CC: Amex, Diners, Euro/Access, Visa.

Spain

MALLORCA (MAJORCA)

CALA RATJADA 9D

Hotel Ses Rotges ★★ Calle Rafael Blanes 21, 07500 Calla Ratjada, Mallorca.
☎ 971 563108, Fax 971 564345. English spoken.

Open 26/03 to 31/10. 24 bedrooms (all en suite with telephone). Tennis, golf 5 km.
RESTAURANT: very good. Closed Wed.

A converted old stone mansion of character in this small fishing resort. Pretty restaurant and terrace garden, excellent cuisine.

TARIFF: Single 7,135, Double 8,300, Bk 1,175, Set menu 3,100.
CC: Diners, Euro/Access, Visa.

DEYA 9D

Hotel La Residencia ★★★★ Finca son Canals, Deya.
☎ 971 639011, Fax 971 639370. English spoken.
Open all year. 66 bedrooms (all en suite with telephone). Outdoor swimming pool, tennis, parking, restaurant.

On the moutain side of the island. On the outskirts of Deya, between Valldemossa and Soller. 30 km from Palma. Comprises three 13th and 18th-century manor houses furnished with antiques and modern art. Air conditioning and central heating.

TARIFF: (1993) Single 16,000, Double 28,000, Set menu 5,200–9,800.
CC: none.

VALLDEMOSSA 9D

Vistamar de Valldemossa
07100 Valldemossa, Mallorca.
☎ 971 612300, Fax 971 612583. English spoken.
Open all year. 16 bedrooms (all en suite with telephone). Outdoor swimming pool, parking.
RESTAURANT: Closed Nov.

Very old house with antique furniture in Mallorcan style. 2 km from Andratx.

TARIFF: Double 20,000–26,000.
CC: Amex, Diners, Euro/Access, Visa.

END OF MALLORCA (MAJORCA) HOTELS

MALAGA 8D

Hotel Las Vegas ★★★ Paseo de Sancha 22, 29016 Malaga.
☎ 952 217712, Fax 952 224889. English spoken.
Open all year. 106 bedrooms (all en suite with telephone). Outdoor swimming pool, parking, restaurant.

Comfortable, with sea views and private garden. 2 km from town centre in residential area.

TARIFF: (1993) Single 7,525–9,545, Double 9,847–12,360, Set menu 2,100.
CC: Amex, Diners, Euro/Access, Visa.

MARBELLA 8D

Hotel Don Carlos ★★★★★ Ctra de Cadiz, 29600 Marbella.
☎ 952 831140, Fax 952 833429. English spoken.

Open all year. 238 bedrooms (all en suite with telephone). Outdoor swimming pool, tennis, golf 1 km, parking, restaurant.

East of Marbella (9 km) and in the heart of 130 acres of private estate with large exotic gardens, meandering to the finest beach in the area. Beach club offering watersports, disco (summer) and a bar with live music. Ideal place for a leisurely vacation.

TARIFF: Single 12,100–21,100, Double 14,900–26,000, Bk 1,200.
CC: Amex, Diners, Euro/Access, Visa.

Spain

MIAMI PLAYA 9A

Hotel Tropicana ★★ Ctra 340, km 1132,7, 43892 Miami Playa.
☎ 977 810340, Fax 977 810518. English spoken.

Open all year. 34 bedrooms (all en suite with telephone). Outdoor swimming pool, golf 2 km, garage, parking, restaurant.
350 m from the beach, just off the 340 route between Cambrils and Hospitalet del Infante. Good facilities, friendly atmosphere and efficient service.
TARIFF: Single 2,000–2,900, Double 3,100–4,800.
CC: Euro/Access, Visa.

MIRANDA DE EBRO 8B

Hostal El Desfiladero ★★ 09280 Pancorbo.
☎ 947 354027, Fax 947 354235. English spoken.
Open all year. 14 bedrooms (12 bath/shower only). Outdoor swimming pool, tennis, garage, parking, restaurant.
From motorway N1, via exit 4 (Km 305) to Pancorbo. Situated close to the famous Pancorbo Gorge.
TARIFF: (1993) Single 2,000, Double 3,700, Bk 500, Set menu 1,300.
CC: Euro/Access, Visa.

Hotel Tudanca ★★★ Ctra Madrid-Irun, km 318, 09200 Miranda de Ebro.
☎ 947 311843, Fax 947 311848. English spoken.
Open all year. 121 bedrooms (all en suite with telephone). Garage, parking. &
RESTAURANT: Closed Sun eve.

Modern hotel on outskirts of Miranda de Ebro, on N1. Restaurant serves regional food. Easily accessible.
TARIFF: (1993) Single 4,780–5,075, Double 6,995–7,395, Bk 550, Set menu 1,900–2,500.
CC: Amex, Diners, Euro/Access, Visa.

MONTBLANCH 9A

Hotel Coll de Lilla ★★★ Ctra Nacional 240, 43414 Tarragona.
☎ 977 860907, Fax 977 860423. English spoken.
Open all year. 26 bedrooms (all en suite with telephone). Tennis, garage, parking.
RESTAURANT: Closed Sun eve & Mon.

Situated on top of the hill between the Roman-walled village of Montblanc and Valls, on the N240, this comfortable hotel is elegantly furnished and air conditioned.
TARIFF: (1993) Single 5,000–6,000, Double 10,000–12,000.
CC: Amex, Diners, Euro/Access, Visa.

MURCIA 9C

Hotel Coronas Melia ★★★★ Paseo de Garay 5, 30003 Murcia.
☎ 968 217771, Fax 968 221294. English spoken.
Open all year. 122 bedrooms (all en suite with telephone). Parking, restaurant.
TARIFF: (1993) Double 14,700.
CC: Amex, Diners, Euro/Access, Visa.

NERJA 8D

Avalon Beach Hotel ★★ Punta Lara, 29780 Nerja.
☎ 952 520698, Fax 952 520698. English spoken.

Open 01/04 to 31/10. 8 bedrooms (all en suite). Parking.
RESTAURANT: Closed Mon.

Situated in lovely garden on hillside just above the beach. Magnificient view of mountains and town, which is 2 km away.
TARIFF: Single 2,500–4,500, Double 3,500–6,500, Bk 450, Set menu 1,700–3,000.
CC: none.

Hotel Fontainebleau ★★ Calle Alejandro Bueno 5, 29780 Nerja.
☎ 952 520939, Fax 952 521475. English spoken.

Spain

Open all year. 22 bedrooms (all en suite with telephone). Restaurant.

Hotel is just a few minutes from Nerja's five beaches, shops, market and the famous Balcony of Europe. Nerja Caves and the award-winning, beautiful white village of Frigiliana are nearby. All rooms are set around a patio with fountain.
TARIFF: Single 2,750–3,950, Double 3,500–4,900, Bk 550, Set menu 1,550.
CC: Euro/Access, Visa.

OROPESA   8B

Hotel Parador Nacional de Virrey Toledo
★★★★ Plaza del Palacio 1, 45560 Oropesa.
✆ 925 430000, Fax 925 430777. English spoken.
Open all year. 48 bedrooms (all en suite with telephone). Outdoor swimming pool, parking, restaurant. &

Former 16th-century palace, originally the ancestrial seat of the Count and Countess of Oropesa. Regional culinary specialities. On NV to Badajos and Lisboa, 149 km from Madrid.
TARIFF: Single 10,000, Double 12,000, Bk 1,100, Set menu 3,200.
CC: Amex, Diners, Euro/Access, Visa.

OVIEDO   8B

Hotel Ramiro 1 ★★★★ Avda Calvo Sotelo 13, 33000 Oviedo.
✆ 985 232850, Fax 985 236329. English spoken.
Open all year. 83 bedrooms (all en suite with telephone). Parking.
TARIFF: (1993) Double 10,100–11,725.
CC: Amex, Diners, Euro/Access, Visa.

Hotel de la Reconquista ★★★★★
Gil de Jaz 16, 33004 Oviedo.
✆ 985 241100, Fax 985 241166.
English spoken.
Open all year. 142 bedrooms (all en suite with telephone). Golf 15 km, garage, parking, restaurant.

This former 18th-century orphanage was converted into a luxurious hotel in 1973. First-class cuisine. Situated in the heart of the city.
TARIFF: Single 15,800–19,500, Double 19,900–24,400, Bk 1,700, Set menu 5,150.
CC: Amex, Diners, Euro/Access, Visa.

PALAMOS   9B

Hotel Rosamar ★★★ Paseo del Mar 33, 17252 San Antoni de Calonge.
✆ 972 650548, Fax 972 652161. English spoken.

Open 09/04 to 15/10. 52 bedrooms (all en suite with telephone). Golf 4 km, parking, restaurant. &

Small, modern hotel, beside beach and with views over bay. Family atmosphere. Between Palamos and Platja d'Aro.
TARIFF: Single 3,000–7,500, Double 5,000–10,000, Set menu 2,500–3,500.
CC: Amex, Diners, Euro/Access, Visa.

PALENCIA   8B

Hotel Castillo de Monzon ★★★
34410 Monzon de Campos.
✆ 988 808075, Fax 988 808076.
English spoken.
Open all year. 10 bedrooms (all bath/shower only with telephone). Outdoor swimming pool, tennis, garage, parking, restaurant.

A 10th-century castle set on the side of a mountain with wonderful views. 8 km north of Palencia on N611. Very peaceful.
TARIFF: Single 6,000–8,500, Double 7,000–13,000, Bk 800, Set menu 2,500.
CC: Amex, Diners, Euro/Access, Visa.

PAMPLONA   9A

Hotel Tres Reyes ★★★★
Jardines de la Traconera, 31001 Pamplona.
✆ 948 226600, Fax 948 222930.
English spoken.
Open all year. 168 bedrooms (all en suite with telephone). Outdoor swimming pool, garage, parking, restaurant.
TARIFF: (1993) Double 16,700–31,000.
CC: Amex, Diners, Euro/Access, Visa.

PANES   8B

La Tahona de Besnes Penamellera Alta, 33578 Besnes.
✆ 98 5414249, Fax 98 5414472.
English spoken.
Open all year. 20 bedrooms (all en suite with telephone). Parking, restaurant.

A rural touring centre set in the Picos de Europa, and close to Panes and Arenas de Cabrales. From Panes head towards Covadonga, then turn right after 10 km.
TARIFF: Single 4,160–5,760, Double 5,200–7,200, Bk 600, Set menu 1,500.
CC: Amex, Euro/Access, Visa.

Spain

PENISCOLA 9A

Hosteria del Mar ★★★★ Peniscola,
12598 Castellon.
☎ 964 480600, Fax 964 481363. English spoken.

Open all year. 86 bedrooms (all en suite
with telephone). Outdoor swimming pool,
tennis, garage, parking, restaurant.
*Castillian-styled luxury hotel, right on the
beach and promenade.*
TARIFF: Single 5,900–9,700,
Double 7,900–12,900, Bk 1,050,
Set menu 2,300.
CC: Amex, Diners, Euro/Access, Visa.

PLATJA D'ARO 9B

Hotel Columbus ★★★★ 17250 Platja d'Aro.
☎ 972 817166, Fax 972 817503. English spoken.
Open all year. 110 bedrooms (all en suite
with telephone). Outdoor swimming pool,
tennis, golf 2 km, parking, restaurant.
*Comfortable, air-conditioned hotel, next to the
beach and with terraces overlooking the sea.*
TARIFF: Single 6,100–12,500,
Double 9,200–21,000, Set menu 2,750.
CC: Amex, Diners, Euro/Access, Visa.

PORT DE LA SELVA 9B

Hotel Amberes ★★ Calle Selva de Mar 25,
17489 Port de la Selva.
☎ 972 387030. English spoken.
Open 01/04 to 30/09. 25 bedrooms
(20 en suite, 5 bath/shower only). Outdoor
swimming pool, parking, restaurant. &
*Family hotel 50 m from beach and 30 km from
Figueres. Excellent cooking and service. Piano
bar and garden restaurant.*
TARIFF: Double 4,000–7,000, Bk 525,
Set menu 1,500.
CC: Visa.

PUIGCERDA 9B

Hotel Can Borrell ★★
17539 La Cerdanya, Meranges.
☎ 972 880033. English spoken.
Open all year. 8 bedrooms (all en suite
with telephone). Golf 20 km, parking.
RESTAURANT: Closed Mon eve & Tues.
*Small alpine hotel in valley surrounded by
mountains. Very cosy. Meranges is west of
Puigcerda.*
TARIFF: Single 5,000, Double 7,000, Bk 500,
Set menu 3,000.
CC: Amex, Euro/Access, Visa.

RIBADEO 8A

Hotel Residencia Eo ★★★ Avda de Asturias 5,
27700 Ribadeo.
☎ 982 110750, Fax 982 110021. English spoken.
Open 12/04 to 12/10. 24 bedrooms
(all en suite). Outdoor swimming pool, garage,
parking. &
*Small hotel in the town and near the River Eo.
Sea-water swimming pool and lovely views
across the river.*
TARIFF: (1993) Single 6,500–7,000,
Double 7,000–7,500, Bk 400.
CC: Amex, Diners, Euro/Access, Visa.

PN de Ribadeo ★★★ Amador Fernandez,
Ribadeo, 27700 Lugo.
☎ 982 110825, Fax 982 110346. English spoken.
Open all year. 47 bedrooms (all en suite
with telephone). Garage, parking, restaurant.
*Hotel stands on high ground overlooking the
River Eo estuary and is close to many good
beaches and surrounding historic buildings.
Restaurant good for seafood.*
TARIFF: Single 7,200–8,800,
Double 9,000–11,000, Bk 1,100,
Set menu 3,200.
CC: Amex, Diners, Euro/Access, Visa.

RIBADESELLA 8B

Hotel Ribadesella Playa ★★★
33560 Ribadesella.
☎ 985 860715, Fax 985 860220.
Open all year. 17 bedrooms (all en suite
with telephone). Parking.
RESTAURANT: Closed 01/10 to 01/04.
*A small hotel in residential area and close to
the beach.*
TARIFF: Single 3,500–5,000,
Double 4,500–7,900, Bk 450, Set menu 1,800.
CC: Amex, Diners, Euro/Access, Visa.

RONDA 8D

Hotel Polo ★★★ Mariano Soubiron 8, 29400 Ronda.
☎ 952 872447/48, Fax 952 874378.
English spoken.
Open all year. 33 bedrooms
(all bath/shower only with telephone).
Small comfortable hotel with a friendly atmosphere. Central position and convenient for the Plaza de Toros.
TARIFF: (1993) Single 4,700–6,000,
Double 6,500–8,500, Bk 475.
CC: Amex, Diners, Euro/Access, Visa.

ROSES 9B

Hotel Almadraba Park ★★★★
Playa de la Almadraba, 17480 Roses.
☎ 972 256550, Fax 972 256750. English spoken.
Open 08/04 to 14/10. 66 bedrooms
(all en suite with telephone). Outdoor
swimming pool, tennis, golf 14 km, garage,
parking, restaurant. Ꮠ
A comfortable modern hotel with air conditioning and a delightful view across the bay. Regional cuisine. 5 km from Roses town centre.
TARIFF: Single 6,100–8,200,
Double 9,900–12,800, Bk 950, Set menu 3,800.
CC: Amex, Diners, Euro/Access, Visa.

RUGAT 9C

Hotel Casa Vieja ★★ Calle Horno 2, Rugat, 46842 Valencia.
☎ 9281 4013. English spoken.
Open all year. 5 bedrooms (all en suite).
RESTAURANT: Closed Mon.
400-year-old house, filled with antiques, on edge of small village. Set in mountains offering peace and tranquillity. English owned and run. Rugat is 2 km from Castellon de Rugat and 17 km from Gandia.
TARIFF: Single 2,500–3,500,
Double 3,500–5,000, Bk 200.
CC: none.

S'AGARO 9B

Hotel Caleta Park ★★★★ Platja de Sant Pol, 17248 S'Agaro.
☎ 972 320012, Fax 972 324096. English spoken.
Open 28/03 to 15/10. 100 bedrooms
(all en suite with telephone). Outdoor
swimming pool, tennis, golf 3 km, garage,
parking, restaurant.
Standing on a hill near the seafront, with
views over the bay from terraces and
swimming pool, this comfortable hotel is
decorated in traditional style.
TARIFF: Single 5,000–8,000,
Double 8,000–16,000, Bk 400, Set menu 2,200.
CC: Amex, Diners, Euro/Access, Visa.

Hostal de la Gavina ★★★★★ Plaza de la Rosaleda, 17248 S'Agaro.
☎ 972 321100, Fax 972 321573. English spoken.
Open 08/04 to 16/10. 74 bedrooms (all en suite
with telephone). Outdoor swimming pool,
tennis, golf 7 km, garage, parking.
RESTAURANT: Closed 17/10 to 07/04.
On a small hill and surrounded by gardens, this luxury hotel overlooks two of the most beautiful beaches on the Costa Brava. The architecture combines modern lines with the warm atmosphere of the classical traditional Catalan style.
TARIFF: Single 16,800–22,050,
Double 18,900–33,600, Bk 1,750,
Set menu 5,500.
CC: Amex, Diners, Euro/Access, Visa.

SAN PEDRO DE ALCANTARA 8D

Linda Vista Bungalows ★
29670 San Pedro de Alcantara.
☎ 952 781492, Fax 952 781492. English spoken.
Open all year. 56 bedrooms (all en suite).
Outdoor swimming pool, tennis, golf 1 km,
parking, restaurant. Ꮠ
1 and 2-bedroom bungalows with own parking and garden. Situated 1 km south of town by the sea.
TARIFF: Double 5,400–8,000, Bk 500.
CC: Amex, Euro/Access, Visa.

SANTANDER 8B

Hotel Romano ★ Cl Feredico Vial 8, 39009 Santander.
☎ 942 223071, Fax 942 223071. English spoken.
Open all year. 25 bedrooms (all en suite
with telephone). Golf 3 km.
Modern, town centre hotel, just five minutes' walk from the ferry terminal.
TARIFF: Single 2,900–4,500,
Double 4,750–8,000, Bk 375.
CC: Amex, Euro/Access, Visa.

Hotel Romano I ★★★ Bo la Picota, 39470 Renedo de Pielagos.
☎ 942 572060, Fax 942 223071. English spoken.
Open all year. 35 bedrooms (all en suite with
telephone). Garage, parking, restaurant. Ꮠ
Small hotel in peaceful setting. Situated on

main road N623 from Santander to Burgos, only 15 minutes from ferry by car.

TARIFF: Single 3,500–5,500,
Double 5,000–8,000, Bk 400.
CC: Euro/Access, Visa.

SANTIAGO DE COMPOSTELA   8A

Hotel Los Tilos ★★★★
15886 Santiago de Compostela.
📞 981 523797, Fax 981 801514. English spoken.
Open all year. 92 bedrooms (all en suite with telephone). Outdoor swimming pool, tennis, golf 10 km, parking, restaurant. ♿

A modern hotel only 2 km from the town centre, south, on road to La Estrada.

TARIFF: Single 9,500–10,500, Double 13,500,
Bk 750, Set menu 3,500–2,500.
CC: Amex, Diners, Euro/Access, Visa.

SANTILLANA DEL MAR   8B

Hotel Altamira ★★★ Canton No 1,
39330 Santillana del Mar.
📞 942 818025, Fax 942 840136. English spoken.
Open all year. 32 bedrooms (all en suite with telephone). Parking, restaurant.

Ancient 17th-century palace decorated in regional mountain style. Small and comfortable. Situated 100 m from the famous church of La Colegiata.

TARIFF: Single 4,200–5,000,
Double 5,500–9,875, Bk 500,
Set menu 1,500–2,500.
CC: Amex, Diners, Euro/Access, Visa.

SEGOVIA   8B

Posada de Don Mariano ★★ Calle Mayor 14,
40172 Pedraza de La Sierra.
📞 911 509886.
Open all year. 18 bedrooms (all en suite with telephone).

North-east of Segovia off N110, small hotel in picturesque surroundings.

TARIFF: (1993) Single 9,000, Double 11,000,
Bk 950.
CC: Amex, Diners, Euro/Access, Visa.

Hotel Los Linajes ★★★ Dr Velasco 9,
40003 Segovia.
📞 911 431712, Fax 911 431501. English spoken.
Open all year. 55 bedrooms (all en suite with telephone). Garage, parking. ♿

Small hotel located in old part of Segovia. 16th-century palace façade and terrace with views over the city's monuments.

TARIFF: Single 5,675–7,100,
Double 8,345–10,500, Bk 775.
CC: Amex, Diners, Euro/Access, Visa.

LA SEU D'URGELL   9B

Hotel El Castell ★★★★ Rte de Lerida,
25700 La Seu d'Urgell.
📞 973 350704, Fax 973 351574. English spoken.
Open all year. 38 bedrooms (all en suite with telephone). Outdoor swimming pool, parking, restaurant. ♿

Family-run hotel overlooking town and mountains. 10 km from Andorra.

CC: Diners, Euro/Access, Visa.

SEVILLA (SEVILLE)   8C

Hotel Becquer ★★★ Reyes Catolicos 4,
41001 Sevilla.
📞 95 4222172, Fax 95 4214400. English spoken.
Open all year. 120 bedrooms (all en suite with telephone). Golf 6 km, garage.

Elegant, air-conditioned hotel offering excellent service. Centrally positioned and very easy to locate. Convenient for Bull Ring and close to the river.

TARIFF: Single 7,500–10,600,
Double 10,600–15,000, Bk 750.
CC: Amex, Diners, Euro/Access, Visa.

Hotel Inglaterra ★★★★ Plaza Nueva 7,
41001 Sevilla.
📞 95 4224970, Fax 95 4561336. English spoken.

Open all year. 110 bedrooms (all en suite with telephone). Golf 5 km, garage. ♿
RESTAURANT: Closed Aug.

Situated in town centre, with terrace overlooking Plaza Nueva. Air-conditioned rooms and lounges.

TARIFF: Single 12,800–16,000,
Double 16,000–23,000, Bk 750, Set menu 3,000.
CC: Amex, Diners, Euro/Access, Visa.

Spain

SITGES 9B

Hotel Romantic Sant Isidre 33, Sitges, 08870 Barcelona.
✆ 93 8948375, Fax 93 8948167. English spoken. Open 01/04 to 31/10. 58 bedrooms (all en suite with telephone). Golf 3 km.

Three adjacent 19th-century villas, restored in the style of the period. Many rooms with terrace overlooking the gardens. Ideally located on a quiet street with ready access to transport, shops and entertainment. Beach short walk away.

TARIFF: Single 5,200–6,000, Double 7,500–8,500.
CC: Amex, Euro/Access, Visa.

Hotel La Santa Maria ★★★ Passeig de la Riberra 52, Sitges, 08870 Barcelona.
✆ 93 8940999, Fax 93 8947178. English spoken. Open 15/02 to 30/11. 45 bedrooms (all en suite with telephone). Golf 1 km, parking.
RESTAURANT: Closed 01/12 to 14/02.

Comfortable hotel in traditional local style with a privileged position close to sea and town centre. Terrace restaurant, buffet breakfast.

TARIFF: Single 4,800–6,000,
Double 6,000–8,000, Bk 1,000,
Set menu 1,300–2,800.
CC: Amex, Diners, Euro/Access, Visa.

TARRAGONA 9A

Hotel Astari ★★★ Via Augusta 97, 43003 Tarragona.
✆ 977 236911.
Open 01/05 to 30/10. 83 bedrooms (all en suite with telephone). Indoor swimming pool, garage, restaurant.
TARIFF: (1993) Double 5,000–6,500.
CC: Amex, Diners, Euro/Access, Visa.

Hotel Lauria ★★★ Rambla Nova 20, 43004 Tarragona.
✆ 977 236712, Fax 977 236700. English spoken. Open all year. 72 bedrooms (all en suite with telephone). Outdoor swimming pool, golf 5 km, garage. &

Modern, comfortable hotel in town centre and close to seafront. Air-conditioned rooms, satellite TV, safety deposit box.

TARIFF: Single 6,000, Double 9,000, Bk 550.
CC: Amex, Diners, Euro/Access, Visa.

TORREMOLINOS 8D

Hotel Don Pedro ★★★ Paseo Maritimo, 29620 Torremolinos.
✆ 952 386844, Fax 952 386935. English spoken.

Open all year. 289 bedrooms (all en suite with telephone). Outdoor swimming pool, tennis, golf 5 km, parking, restaurant. &

In a quiet location by the beach, hotel is built in Andalucian style, surrounded by attractive gardens. From Malaga, and just prior to entering Torremolinos, follow signs to the hotel and Bajondillo Beach.

TARIFF: Single 4,650–6,650,
Double 7,300–11,300.
CC: Amex, Diners, Euro/Access, Visa.

TOSSA DE MAR 9B

Hotel Diana ★★ Plaza d'Espana 6, Tossa de mar, 17320 Tossa De Mar.
✆ 972 341886, Fax 972 341103. English spoken. Open 01/05 to 31/10. 21 bedrooms (all en suite).

19th-century Art-Nouveau-style hotel built on edge of the sea. Comfortable with relaxing atmosphere and some sea views. 12 km from Lloret de Mar (north).

TARIFF: Single 3,600–5,100,
Double 6,700–9,200.
CC: Amex, Euro/Access, Visa.

TURRE 9C

Hotel Finca Listonero Cortijo Grande, 04639 Turre.
✆ 951 479094, Fax 951 468204. English spoken. Open all year. 5 bedrooms (all en suite). Outdoor swimming pool, golf 1 km, parking, restaurant.

Small hotel with restaurant menu changing daily. Turre is convenient for trips to Almeria and Murcia.

TARIFF: (1993) Single 5,000–6,000,
Double 7,500–9,000.
CC: Euro/Access, Visa.

VALENCIA 9C

Hotel Casino Monte Picayo ★★★★★ 46530 Puzol.
✆ 96 1420100, Fax 96 1422168. English spoken. Open all year. 82 bedrooms (all en suite with telephone). Indoor swimming pool, outdoor swimming pool, tennis, golf 10 km, garage, parking, restaurant.

Luxurious, peaceful hotel facing the sea with views over orange groves. A few minutes north of Valencia and convenient for the airport.

TARIFF: (1993) Single 15,950, Double 19,950, Bk 1,250, Set menu 2,500–3,000.
CC: Amex, Diners, Visa.

Spain

Hotel Expo ★★★ C/Pto XII 4, 46009 Valencia.
☎ 96 3470909, Fax 96 348318. English spoken.
Open all year. 396 bedrooms (all en suite
with telephone). Outdoor swimming pool,
restaurant.
TARIFF: (1993) Double 12,800–17,500.
CC: Amex, Diners, Euro/Access, Visa.

VALLADOLID   8B

Hotel Imperial ★★ Peso 4, 47001 Valladolid.
☎ 983 330300, Fax 983 330813. English spoken.
Open all year. 81 bedrooms (all en suite).
Parking, restaurant. &
TARIFF: (1993) Double 6,200–6,575.
CC: Amex, Diners, Euro/Access, Visa.

VIC   9B

Hostel de la Gloria ★★ Torreventosa 12,
08553 Viladrau.
☎ 938 849034, Fax 938 849465.
English spoken.
Open 01/11 to 30/09. 26 bedrooms
(all en suite with telephone). Golf 12 km,
garage, restaurant.
*25 km south-east of Vic. Small country lodge
set above the mountain village of Viladrau
and decorated in Catalan style. Food
interesting and recommended.*
TARIFF: (1993) Single 3,000, Double 6,000,
Bk 600, Set menu 1,700.
CC: Euro/Access, Visa.

Mas El Banus 08519 Tavernoles.
☎ 938 887012. English spoken.
Open all year. 8 bedrooms. Golf 20 km,
parking.
*Small family-run farmhouse, full of character.
Meals specially prepared by arrangement.
Located north of Vic.*
TARIFF: (1993) Single 1,500–2,000,
Double 3,000–3,500, Bk 450.
CC: Euro/Access, Visa.

Hotel NH Ciutat de Vic ★★★ Pje Can Mastrot,
s/n, 08500 Vic.
☎ 938 892551, Fax 938 891447.
English spoken.
Open all year. 36 bedrooms (all en suite
with telephone). Parking. &
RESTAURANT: Closed Sun eve.
*New, very comfortable hotel with air
conditioning. 67 km north of Barcelona, in
the centre of Vic.*
TARIFF: (1993) Single 6,100–7,300,
Double 7,800–9,800, Bk 650.
CC: Amex, Diners, Euro/Access, Visa.

VIELLA   9A

Hotel Aran ★★ Avda Castiero 5, 25530 Viella.
☎ 973 640050, Fax 973 640053. English spoken.
Open all year. 48 bedrooms (all en suite
with telephone). Parking, restaurant.
*Small and comfortable, in the centre of town.
Only 5 minutes from the ski resort of La Tuca.*
TARIFF: Single 2,750–5,050, Double 4,500–9,100,
Bk 450, Set menu 1,450–1,950.
CC: Amex, Diners, Euro/Access, Visa.

Hotel Tuca Ctra Baqueira, SIN, 25539 Betren.
☎ 973 640700, Fax 973 640754. English spoken.

Open 20/12 to 15/10. 118 bedrooms
(all en suite with telephone). Outdoor
swimming pool, garage, parking, restaurant. &
*A very comfortable, modern hotel in heart of
the Valle de Aran. Ten minutes by car to ski
resorts of Baqueira. From Viella, go east
towards La Tuca.*
TARIFF: Single 4,750–7,800,
Double 8,700–13,600.
CC: Amex, Diners, Euro/Access, Visa.

VILLAGARCIA DE AROSA   8A

Hotel Pazo O'Rial ★★★★ El Rial No 1,
36611 Villagarcia de Arosa.
☎ 986 507011, Fax 986 501676. English spoken.
Open all year. 60 bedrooms (all en suite
with telephone). Outdoor swimming pool,
parking, restaurant.
*A restored 17th-century building, in the heart
of the region.*
TARIFF: (1993) Single 6,000–8,000,
Double 7,500–10,000, Bk 600.
CC: Amex, Diners, Euro/Access, Visa.

VILLAJOYOSA   9C

Hotel Montiboli ★★★★ Apartado 8, Ctra
Alicante-Valencia, 03570 Villajoyosa.
☎ 96 5890250, Fax 96 5893857. English spoken.

Spain

Open all year. 53 bedrooms (all en suite with telephone). Outdoor swimming pool, tennis, golf 20 km, garage, parking, restaurant.

Overlooking the Mediterranean on the edge of Villajoyosa, the hotel stands between the sea, beaches and hills. Leave Villajoyosa on N332 towards Alicante. Well signposted.

TARIFF: Single 8,250–12,250, Double 13,500–20,500, Set menu 3,250.
CC: Amex, Diners, Euro/Access, Visa.

VINAROZ 9A

Hotel Roca ★★ 12500 Vinaroz.
✆ 964 401312. English spoken.
Open all year. 36 bedrooms (all en suite with telephone). Tennis, garage, parking, restaurant.

Comfortable hotel with family atmosphere. Beautiful gardens and only five minutes' walk to the beach.

TARIFF: Single 3,100–3,500, Double 4,300–5,000, Bk 450, Set menu 1,200.
CC: Euro/Access, Visa.

ZAMORA 8B

Hotel Il Infantas ★★★
Cortinas de San Miguel 3, 49002 Zamora.
✆ 988 532875, Fax 988 533548.
Open all year. 68 bedrooms (all en suite with telephone). Indoor swimming pool, outdoor swimming pool, tennis, golf 1 km, garage.

Small hotel in town centre, with air-conditioned rooms.

TARIFF: Single 5,725–6,150, Double 8,300–9,200, Bk 550.
CC: Amex, Diners, Euro/Access, Visa.

ZARAGOZA 9A

Hotel Casino de Zaragoza ★★★★
50172 Alfajarin.
✆ 976 100004, Fax 976 100087. English spoken.
Open all year. 37 bedrooms (all en suite with telephone). Outdoor swimming pool, tennis, golf 20 km, parking, restaurant.

A small hotel south-east of Zaragoza. Take N11 towards Barcelona and Exit 1 for Alfajarin.

TARIFF: Single 10,400, Double 13,000, Bk 800.
CC: Amex, Diners, Euro/Access, Visa.

Hotel El Cisne ★★★ 50012 Zaragoza.
✆ 976 332000, Fax 976 332000. English spoken.
Open all year. 51 bedrooms (4 en suite, 47 bath/shower only, 51 telephone). Outdoor swimming pool, golf 2 km, parking, restaurant. ⚹

Beautiful situation just outside the city, and 2 km from main road to Barcelona.

TARIFF: (1993) Single 4,500–5,000, Double 7,500–9,500, Bk 500, Set menu 1,250–2,250.
CC: Amex, Diners, Euro/Access, Visa.

Hotel Gran ★★★★★ Joaquin Costa 5, 50000 Zaragoza.
✆ 976 221901, Fax 976 236713. English spoken.
Open all year. 138 bedrooms (138 telephone). Garage, parking, restaurant.
TARIFF: (1993) Double 17,000.
CC: Amex, Diners, Euro/Access, Visa.

Spain

SWEDEN

Sweden is the largest of the five Nordic countries, about 1,600 km long and 500 km at its widest point. There are borders with Norway to the west and Finland to the north-east; the west and much of the south faces the Baltic Sea, with Denmark across the narrow waters of the Skagerrak. The land area is 449,964 sq km (almost twice that of the UK), and most of the 8.5 million inhabitants live in the south. The official language is Swedish, and groups such as the Lapps have their own language and customs. The capital of Stockholm has about 670,000 inhabitants. Local currency is the krona, made up of 100 öre.

An ancient mountain range runs along the west of the country, where Mount Kebne is the highest point, at 2,111 m. Owing to its northern latitude, Sweden has dark, cold winters and cool summers with long hours of daylight. Snow stays on the ground for much of the year in the north. The mountains give rise to many rivers that flow south-east, and Sweden is truly the land of lakes and forests. Trees are mainly deciduous in the south, mixed in the central regions and coniferous in the north. Much of the lowlands is peaty bog. Reindeer, elk, deer and wolves are found in the wilder regions. Farming concentrates on livestock and dairy products; where crops are grown, these are often as animal fodder. Timber and iron/steel products are major industries.

Sweden has 130,000 km of roads; half are surfaced. The road density (km per sq km) is 0.3, compared to the UK's 1.5. Note that the resorts for Swedish islands, such as Oland, are listed under their island names in the A–Z directory.

DALARÖ · 11B

Hotel Smådalarö Gård 13054 Dalarö.
℡ 08 571 40100, Fax 08 571 40171.
English spoken.
Open all year. 72 bedrooms (all en suite with telephone). Outdoor swimming pool, tennis, golf on site, parking, restaurant. &

A beautiful country house with golf hotel in lovely surroundings. 45 minutes by car from Stockholm city centre. From Stockholm, take the road 73, then 227 to Dalarö. Turn left at sign for Smådalarö for 5 km.

TARIFF: Single 550–850,
Double 700–970,
Set menu 250.
CC: Amex, Diners, Euro/Access, Visa.

GÖTEBORG · 11C

Hotel Ekoxen Norra Hamngatan 38, 41106 Göteborg.
℡ 031 805 080, Fax 031 153 370.
English spoken.
Open all year. 75 bedrooms (all en suite with telephone). Parking.
TARIFF: (1993) Double 1195.
CC: Amex, Diners, Euro/Access, Visa.

Hotel Scandic Backebolsvagen, Hisings-Backa, 42253 Göteborg.
℡ 031 520 060, Fax 031 528 333.
English spoken.
Open 27/12 to 24/12. 232 bedrooms (all en suite with telephone). Indoor swimming pool, garage, parking, restaurant. &
TARIFF: (1993) Single 835, Double 1035.
CC: Amex, Diners, Euro/Access, Visa.

Hotel Tidbloms Olskroksgatan 23, 41666 Göteborg.
℡ 031 192 070, Fax 031 197 835.
English spoken.
Open all year. 42 bedrooms (all en suite with telephone). Parking, restaurant.

Comfortable, peaceful hotel with good amenities including sauna, library and conference facilities.

TARIFF: Single 450–865, Double 660–995,
Set menu 100–300.
CC: Amex, Diners, Euro/Access, Visa.

HALMSTAD · 11C

Hotel Scandic Hallandia Radhusgatan 4, 30243 Halmstad.
℡ 035 118 800, Fax 035 148 956.

Open 27/12 to 23/12. 132 bedrooms
(all en suite). &
TARIFF: (1993) Single 940, Double 1140.
CC: Amex, Diners, Euro/Access, Visa.

HELSINGBORG   11C

Grand Hotel ★★★★ Stortoget 8-12,
25000 Helsingborg.
✆ 042 120 170, Fax 042 118 833.
English spoken.
Open all year. 130 bedrooms (all en suite
with telephone). Outdoor swimming pool,
tennis, golf 8 km, garage, parking, restaurant.
*This elegant hotel is privately owned and run
as a family business. Superbly furnished and
decorated, excellent restaurant. Just a few
minutes' walk from the ferry terminal.*
TARIFF: Single 825–925, Double 990–1500.
CC: Amex, Diners, Euro/Access, Visa.

HJO   11C

Hotel Bellevue ★★★ PO Box 66, 54400 Hjo.
✆ 0503 12000. English spoken.
Open all year. 88 bedrooms (66 en suite,
88 telephone). Outdoor swimming pool,
tennis, golf 5 km, parking, restaurant. &
*Beautiful location in a park, right on the edge
of Lake Vättern. A charming hotel in the centre
of town with turn-of-the-century atmosphere.*
TARIFF: Single 375–900, Double 450–990,
Set menu 60–180.
CC: Amex, Diners, Euro/Access, Visa.

JÖNKÖPING   11C

Hotel City Vastra Storgatan 25,
55113 Jönköping.
✆ 036 119 280, Fax 036 118 848.
English spoken.
Open all year. 70 bedrooms (all en suite).
Garage, parking, restaurant.
TARIFF: (1993) Single 725–920,
Double 990–1090.
CC: Amex, Diners, Euro/Access, Visa.

KARLSBORG   11A

Hotel Kanalhotellet ★★★ Storgatan 94,
54632 Karlsborg.
✆ 0505 12130, Fax 0505 12761. English spoken.
Open all year. 27 bedrooms (all en suite
with telephone). Golf 5 km, parking,
restaurant.
*About 2 hours' drive from Göteborg ferry.
Situated by Göta Canal and Lake Vättern.
Cable TV in all the rooms.*

TARIFF: (1993) Single 500–650,
Double 500–680.
CC: Amex, Diners, Euro/Access, Visa.

KARLSTAD   11A

Hotel Gosta Berling ★★★ Drottininggatan 1,
65224 Karlstad.
✆ 054 150 190. English spoken.
Open all year. 75 bedrooms (all en suite with
telephone). Golf 8 km, garage, parking. &
Situated in the centre of the town.
TARIFF: Single 400–750, Double 500–900.
CC: Amex, Diners, Euro/Access, Visa.

KRISTIANSTAD   11C

Hotel Grand Vastra Storgatan 15,
29121 Kristianstad.
✆ 044 103 600, Fax 044 125 782.
English spoken.
Open all year. 150 bedrooms (all en suite).
Garage, parking, restaurant. &
TARIFF: (1993) Single 825–1195, Double 1450.
CC: Amex, Diners, Euro/Access, Visa.

MALMÖ   11C

Hotel Continental Hospitalgat 2,
21133 Malmö.
✆ 040 121 977, Fax 040 122 766.
English spoken.
Open all year. 54 bedrooms (all en suite).
Parking, restaurant.
TARIFF: (1993) Single 650–750,
Double 790–890.
CC: Amex, Diners, Euro/Access, Visa.

MORA   11A

Hotel Mora Strandgatan 12, 79201 Mora.
✆ 0250 11750, Fax 0250 18981. English spoken.
Open all year. 148 bedrooms (all en suite
with telephone). Indoor swimming pool,
golf 2 km, garage, parking, restaurant. &
*Located in the town centre, and near Lake
Siljan.*
TARIFF: (1993) Double 800–1400.
CC: Amex, Diners, Euro/Access, Visa.

NORRKÖPING   11A

Hotel Grand Tyska Torget 2,
60041 Norrköping.
✆ 011 197 100, Fax 011 181 183. English spoken.
Open all year. 207 bedrooms (all en suite).
Parking, restaurant. &
TARIFF: (1993) Single 910–1085, Double 1250.
CC: Amex, Diners, Euro/Access, Visa.

Sweden

OLAND

FÄRJESTADEN   11C

Hotel Skansen ★★★ Tingshusgatan,
38600 Färjestaden.
☎ 048 530530, Fax 048 534804. English spoken.
Open all year. 24 bedrooms (15 en suite,
24 telephone). Golf 10 km, parking.

*Centrally located, surrounded by a park and
just 300 m to the beach. Newly renovated hotel
in the middle of the island and close to the
Öland bridge. Family owned with personal
atmosphere. Sauna, solarium.*

TARIFF: Single 400, Double 500.
cc: Amex, Diners, Euro/Access, Visa.

END OF OLAND HOTELS

SODERKÖPING   11C

Hotel Soderköpings Brunn Skonbergatan
35, 61430 Soderköping.
☎ 0121 10900, Fax 0121 13941. English spoken.
Open all year. 103 bedrooms (all en suite
with telephone). Indoor swimming pool,
tennis, golf 9 km, parking, restaurant. &

*Situated in a medieval town, this old spa hotel
was opened in 1774. The Göta Canal and
Lake Asplangen are nearby.*

TARIFF: (1993) Single 660–1050,
Double 850–1300.
cc: Amex, Diners, Euro/Access, Visa.

STOCKHOLM   11B

Hotel Diplomat ★★★★ Strandvagen 7c,
10440 Stockholm.
☎ 08 663 5800, Fax 08 783 6634.
English spoken.
Open all year. 133 bedrooms (all en suite
with telephone). Indoor swimming pool,
outdoor swimming pool, tennis, golf 2 km.
RESTAURANT: good. Closed Christmas.

*Very comfortable hotel with personal
atmosphere. In city centre, overlooking the
harbour and convenient for shopping and
cultural interests. Closed Christmas.*

TARIFF: Single 1095–1795, Double 1795–1995,
Set menu 175.
cc: Amex, Diners, Euro/Access, Visa.

Hotel Esplanade Strandvagen 7a,
11456 Stockholm.
☎ 08 663 0740, Fax 08 662 5992.
English spoken.
Open 03/01 to 22/12. 33 bedrooms

(29 en suite, 33 telephone).
TARIFF: (1993) Single 1175–1275,
Double 1400–1600.
cc: Amex, Diners, Euro/Access, Visa.

Hotel Kristineberg ★★★ Box 25052,
Hjalmar Soderbergsvag 10, 10023 Stockholm.
☎ 08 130 300, Fax 08 618 6686. English spoken.
Open all year. 98 bedrooms (all en suite
with telephone). Outdoor swimming pool,
parking. &
RESTAURANT: Closed Mon.

*This hotel promises a warm welcome and good
service. Situated 200 m away from the
underground. It takes 8 minutes to reach the
city centre.*

TARIFF: (1993) Single 420–895,
Double 550–1120.
cc: Amex, Diners, Euro/Access, Visa.

Hotel Lady Hamilton Storkyrkobrinken 5
Stockholm.
☎ 08 234680, Fax 08 111148. English spoken.
Open all year. 34 bedrooms (all en suite
with telephone). Tennis.

*Beautiful hotel with Swedish folk-art décor, in
the centre of the old town. 50 m from the Royal
Palace and close to all points of interest.*

TARIFF: Single 1150–1510, Double 1370–1860.
cc: Amex, Diners, Euro/Access, Visa.

Hotel Lord Nelson Vasterlanggatan 22,
10000 Stockholm.
☎ 08 232390, Fax 08 101089. English spoken.
Open all year. 31 bedrooms (all en suite
with telephone). Golf 22 km.

*Beautifully located on the old city island of
Stockholm. Near the Royal Palace and all
points of interest.*

TARIFF: Single 975–1220, Double 1100–1610.
cc: Amex, Diners, Euro/Access, Visa.

Hotel Mornington Nybrogatan 53,
10000 Stockholm.
☎ 08 663 1240, Fax 08 662 2179. English spoken.
Open 02/01 to 23/12. 140 bedrooms
(all en suite with telephone). Garage, parking,
restaurant.
TARIFF: (1993) Single 1150, Double 1400.
cc: Amex, Diners, Euro/Access, Visa.

Hotel Victory Lilla Nygatan 5, Old Town,
11128 Stockholm.
☎ 08 143 090, Fax 08 202 177. English spoken.
Open 07/01 to 23/12. 48 bedrooms
(all en suite with telephone). Golf 15 km.
RESTAURANT: Closed July.

Modern, comfortable hotel located in the old

Sweden

town, near the Royal Palace and other places of interest.
TARIFF: Single 690–1720, Double 1020–2020, Set menu 375–495.
CC: Amex, Diners, Euro/Access, Visa.

TÄLLBERG 11A

Hotel Siljansgården Gasthem Sjögattu 36, 79370 Tällberg.

✆ 0247 50040, Fax 0247 50013. English spoken.
Open 23/12 to 30/09. 27 bedrooms (15 en suite, 1 telephone). Tennis, golf 8 km, parking, restaurant.

A traditional old-style hotel with the personal touch situated on the shore of Lake Siljan, serving home-cooked meals at moderate prices. Centrally located for the area's many attractions. Also has self-catering cottages during the summer months.
TARIFF: Single 250–390, Double 410–670, Set menu 50–150.
CC: Diners, Euro/Access, Visa.

TANUMSHEDE 11A

Hotel Tanums Gastgifveri
45700 Tanumshede.
✆ 0525 29010, Fax 0525 29571.
English spoken.
Open 01/04 to 31/10. 29 bedrooms (all en suite with telephone). Tennis, golf 4 km, parking. &
RESTAURANT: Closed Nov to March.

A genuine atmosphere of over 300 years of innkeeping tradition. Near to idyllic fishing villages and beautiful countryside. It is situated on the west coast 150 km north of Göteborg, 50 m from the E6.
TARIFF: (1993) Single 425–690, Double 690–890, Set menu 225–410.
CC: Amex, Diners, Euro/Access, Visa.

TOFTAHOLM 11C

Manor Hotel Vittaryd, 34015 Toftaholm.
✆ 0370 44055, Fax 0370 44045. English spoken.
Open all year. 35 bedrooms (all en suite with telephone). Golf 10 km, parking, restaurant. &

600-year-old manor house situated in a large park on the shore of Lake Vidostern. Good regional cuisine.
TARIFF: (1993) Single 580–865, Double 860–1250, Set menu 235.
CC: Amex, Diners, Euro/Access, Visa.

UPPSALA 11A

Hotel Uplandia PO Box 1023, Dragarbrunnsgatan 32, 75140 Uppsala.
✆ 018 102 160, Fax 018 696 132.
English spoken.
Open all year. 133 bedrooms (all en suite with telephone). Garage, restaurant. &
TARIFF: (1993) Single 1190–1275, Double 1500–1605.
CC: Amex, Diners, Euro/Access, Visa.

VÄRMDÖ 11B

Hotel Fågelbrohus 13900 Värmdö.
✆ 08 501 53200, Fax 08 501 53383.
English spoken.
Open all year. 56 bedrooms (all en suite with telephone). Tennis, golf 20 km, parking. &
RESTAURANT: Closed Lunch.

An old manor house hotel in the heart of Stockholm archipelago, 30 min by car from Stockholm city centre. 3-hole golf course on site. Road 222 from Stockholm. After exit to Gustavsberg, turn right at roundabout towards Stavsnäs/Djurö. Cross Stromma channel. After 1 km, turn right at sign for Fågelbro Säkeri, go past sports centre to hotel.
TARIFF: Single 550–850, Double 700–970, Set menu 250.
CC: Amex, Diners, Euro/Access, Visa.

VISBY 11D

Hotel Villa Borgen Adelsgatan 11, 62157 Visby.
✆ 0498 79900, Fax 0498 49300. English spoken.
Open all year. 18 bedrooms (all en suite). Parking.
TARIFF: (1993) Single 790, Double 890.
CC: Amex, Diners, Euro/Access, Visa.

Sweden

SWITZERLAND

Sixty per cent of Switzerland consists of mountainous alpine scenery, where tourists flock for the skiing, climbing, walking and breathtaking views. This small, landlocked country has an area of 41,288 sq km (a sixth that of the UK), and shares borders with France to the west, Italy to the south, Austria to the east and Germany to the north. About two-thirds of the 6.5 million Swiss live in towns and cities. The main language depends on the nearest border; German, French or Italian are usually spoken. The currency is the famously stable Swiss franc, made up of 100 centimes.

The Alps are mainly in the south, with their foothills in the north. Dufourspitze is the highest peak at 4,634 m; the well-known point of the Matterhorn is 4,478 m high. The rivers Rhine and Rhone rise in the eastern Alps, and St Moritz in the far east is one of the many skiing centres. The highest mountains are topped with snow through the year, and the climate, though cool is often sunny. The lower altitudes are covered with deciduous forest, which merge with conifers higher up, and the alpine meadows above the treeline are famous for their wild flowers. Ibex, chamois, boar, marmot and eagle roam wild.

Switzerland's capital is Bern, in the east. The largest city is Zurich, with 350,000 inhabitants. Lausanne and Geneva in the west are on picturesque Lake Geneva. The network of 70,000 km of roads is being expanded during the 1990s by a system of motorways, linking to the tunnels through the mountains. The road density (km per sq km) is 1.7, compared to the UK's 1.5.

AIROLO   18D

Hotel Forni ★★★ Via Stazione, 6780 Airolo.
☎ 094 88 12 97, Fax 094 88 15 23. English spoken.
Open 04/12 to 08/11. 19 bedrooms (all en suite with telephone). Garage, parking, restaurant. ♿

Comfortable and elegant, traditional hotel in a mountain village in the Gotthard region. Pleasant gardens. 5 mins' walk from station, or take exit for Airolo.
TARIFF: Single 70–95, Double 130–150, Set menu 13–35.
CC: Amex, Diners, Euro/Access, Visa.

ALTDORF   18B

Hotel Goldener Schlussel ★★★
Schutzengasse 9, 6460 Altdorf.
☎ 044 21002, Fax 044 21167. English spoken.
Open all year. 50 bedrooms (20 en suite, 25 telephone). Garage, parking, restaurant.
Located in the centre of Altdorf, next to the theatre. Private parking is available behind the hotel. Take exit Altdorf-Flüelen. All rooms are equipped with modern comforts. Excellent food in the cosy restaurants.

TARIFF: Single 75–120, Double 120–195.
CC: Diners, Euro/Access, Visa.

ANDERMATT   18D

Hotel Krone ★★★ 6490 Andermatt.
☎ 044 67206.
Open all year. 50 bedrooms (all en suite).
TARIFF: (1993) Single 90–100, Double 160–180.
CC: Amex, Diners, Euro/Access, Visa.

Switzerland

APPENZELL   18B

Romantik Hotel Santis ★★★
Landsgemeindeplatz, 9050 Appenzell.
☎ 071 878722, Fax 071 874842. English spoken.
Open 01/03 to 15/01. 32 bedrooms
(all en suite with telephone). Parking,
restaurant. &

*Historic building. Comfortable and elegant,
traditionally-furnished rooms. Good food and
wine. Located in the centre of town, five
minutes' walk from station.*

TARIFF: Single 110–150, Double 160–240,
Set menu 32–55.
CC: Amex, Diners, Euro/Access, Visa.

ARBON   18B

Hotel Rotes Kreuz ★★ Hatenstr 3,
9320 Arbon.
☎ 071 46 19 14, Fax 071 46 24 85.
English spoken.
Open all year. 28 bedrooms (15 en suite,
28 telephone). Parking.
RESTAURANT: Closed Thurs.

*Comfortable hotel in pleasant location on the
edge of Lake Bodensee. Fish a speciality. North
of St-Gallen and north-east of Zurich.*

TARIFF: Single 55–60, Double 110–130,
Set menu 17.5.
CC: Euro/Access, Visa.

BASEL (BASLE)   18A

Hotel Admiral ★★★ Rosentalstrasse
5/Messeplatz, 4021 Basel.
☎ 061 691 7777, Fax 061 691 7789.
English spoken.
Open all year. 130 bedrooms (all en suite
with telephone). Outdoor swimming pool,
garage, parking, restaurant.

*Modern, comfortable hotel situated in central
location near the Trade Fair and Conference
Centre. Conference rooms, restaurant,
Wintergarden. 8 km from Basel airport.*

TARIFF: Single 110–165, Double 150–280.
CC: Amex, Diners, Euro/Access, Visa.

Hotel Europe ★★★★ Clarastrasse 43,
4005 Basel.
☎ 061 691 8080, Fax 061 691 8201.
English spoken.
Open all year. 170 bedrooms (all en suite
with telephone). Garage.
RESTAURANT: very good. Closed Sun.

*Completely renovated first-class hotel, with
non-smoking rooms available on request.
Underground garage with 130 parking spaces.*

*Motorway connections (Exit 3, Basel
Ost/Wettstein) for Berne/Lucerne/Zurich,
Germany and France only 450 m away.*

TARIFF: Single 180–250, Double 205–320,
Set menu 85–150.
CC: Amex, Diners, Euro/Access, Visa.

Hotel Krafft am Rhein ★★★ Rheingasse 12,
4058 Basel.
☎ 061 691 8877, Fax 061 691 0907.
English spoken.
Open all year. 52 bedrooms (45 en suite,
52 telephone). Garage, parking, restaurant.

*Classical-style hotel, sympathetically renovated
and situated right on the banks of the Rhein.
Family managed, two restaurants, pretty
terrace.*

TARIFF: Single 110–170, Double 180–270,
Set menu 14.50.
CC: Amex, Diners, Euro/Access, Visa.

Hotel Muenchnerhof ★★★ Riehenring 75,
4058 Basel.
☎ 061 691 77 80, Fax 061 691 14 90.
English spoken.
Open all year. 45 bedrooms (35 en suite,
3 bath/shower only, 45 telephone). Garage,
parking, restaurant. &

*Central position, close to the Swiss Trade Fair.
Restaurant specialises in French and Italian
cuisine.*

TARIFF: Single 75–190, Double 130–290.
CC: Amex, Diners, Euro/Access, Visa.

Hotel Les Trois Rois ★★★★★ Blumenrain,
4001 Basel.
☎ 061 261 52 52, Fax 061 261 21 53.
English spoken.
Open all year. 88 bedrooms (all en suite
with telephone). Golf 13 km, garage,
restaurant.

The oldest palace in Europe, now a luxury

hotel. Centrally located and on the banks of the Rhein. Good restaurants with river views. Member of The Leading Hotels of the World.
TARIFF: Single 240–330, Double 390–550, Bk 29.
CC: Amex, Diners, Euro/Access, Visa.

Hotel Victoria ★★★★ Centralbahnplatz 3-4, 4002 Basel.
☎ 061 271 5566, Fax 061 271 5501.
English spoken.
Open all year. 95 bedrooms (all en suite with telephone). Parking, restaurant.

Traditional first-class hotel. Situated next to the Swiss and French railway station and within 5 minutes' walking distance of the shopping and commercial centres of Basel. Ideal for both business and sightseeing.
TARIFF: Single 160–190, Double 210–270, Set menu 15–65.
CC: Amex, Diners, Euro/Access, Visa.

BELLINZONA   18D

Hotel Internazionale ★★★
Piazza Stazione 35, 6500 Bellinzona.
☎ 092 25 43 33, Fax 092 26 13 59.
English spoken.
Open all year. 20 bedrooms (19 en suite, 20 telephone). Golf 1 km, parking, restaurant. &
Situated in the centre of Bellinzona, opposite the station.
TARIFF: Single 90–110, Double 125–160.
CC: Amex, Diners, Euro/Access, Visa.

Hotel La Perla ★★ San Antonino, 6592 Bellinzona. •
☎ 092 62 15 38.
Open all year. 24 bedrooms (all en suite).
TARIFF: (1993) Single 98–105, Double 145–160.
CC: Amex, Diners, Euro/Access, Visa.

BERN   18A

Hotel Ambassador ★★★★ Seftigenstr 97, 3007 Bern.
☎ 031 3714111, Fax 031 3714117.
English spoken.
Open all year. 170 bedrooms (97 en suite, 97 telephone). Indoor swimming pool, golf 1 km, garage, parking, restaurant.
From the motorway, exit "Köniz" then follow Belp (airport) signs for approx 2 miles.
TARIFF: Single 130–190, Double 170–240.
CC: Amex, Diners, Euro/Access, Visa.

Hotel Bern ★★★★ Zeughausgasse 9, 3011 Bern.
☎ 031 211 021.
Open all year. 91 bedrooms (all en suite with telephone).
TARIFF: (1993) Single 130–175, Double 180–270.
CC: Amex, Diners, Euro/Access, Visa.

BIASCA   18D

Hotel Al Giardinetto ★★★
Via Aleardo Pini, 6710 Biasca.
☎ 092 72 17 71, Fax 092 72 23 59.
English spoken.
Open all year. 33 bedrooms (25 en suite, 8 bath/shower only, 27 telephone). Garage, parking, restaurant. &
Newly renovated hotel, centrally situated not far from N2. Large terrace. Restaurant serves specialities from Ticino. From N2 take Biasca exit and follow signs for Biasca Centro.
TARIFF: Single 80–100, Double 85–150, Set menu 21–38.
CC: Amex, Diners, Euro/Access, Visa.

BIEL/BIENNE   18A

Hotel Elite ★★★★ 14 rue de la Gare, 2501 Biel/Bienne.
☎ 032 22 54 41, Fax 032 22 13 83.
English spoken.
Open all year. 110 bedrooms (68 en suite, 68 telephone). Garage.
RESTAURANT: Closed 19/07 to 08/08.
Between rolling hills and the lake, a comfortable hotel, 3 minutes' walk from the main station. Traditional hospitality. Partly renovated in 1988, with good restaurant.
TARIFF: Single 140–170, Double 180–240.
CC: Amex, Diners, Euro/Access, Visa.

Hotel Plaza ★★★★ Neumarkstrasse 40, 2502 Biel/Bienne.
☎ 032 22 97 44, Fax 032 22 01 94. English spoken.
Open all year. 106 bedrooms (all en suite with telephone). Golf 20 km, garage, parking, restaurant. &
In the city centre, and 5 minutes from station.
TARIFF: (1993) Single 130–160, Double 190–220.
CC: Amex, Diners, Euro/Access, Visa.

BOURG-ST-PIERRE   18C

Hotel Bivouac Napoléon ★★★★
1931 Bourg-St-Pierre.
☎ 026 87 11 62, Fax 026 87 13 42.
English spoken.

Open all year. 37 bedrooms (all en suite with telephone). Indoor swimming pool, golf 5 km, parking, restaurant. &

Family hotel with modern amenities. Gourmet meals and Valais specialities. On ancient route used by the Romans and Napoléon and his army. Close to ski resort. On E27/N21 close to Italian border.

TARIFF: Single 45–69, Double 80–120.
CC: Amex, Diners, Euro/Access, Visa.

BRIGELS/BREIL 18B

Hotel Kistenpass ★★★ 7165 Brigels/Breil.
☎ 081 941 11 43, Fax 081 941 14 40.
English spoken.
Open 01/07 to 31/05. 65 bedrooms
(33 en suite, 33 telephone). Garage, parking.
RESTAURANT: Closed June.

Typical village on the borders of the Alpine Rhine with no through traffic. Quiet elevated setting, within 1 hour of Chur. Lovely scenery, panorama terrace. On route 19 between Chur and Andermatt, south-east of Zurich.

TARIFF: Single 63–82, Double 126–164.
CC: Amex, Diners, Euro/Access, Visa.

BULLE 18C

Hotel du Tonnelier ★★ Grand Rue 31,
1630 Bulle.
☎ 029 27745.
Open all year. 21 bedrooms (16 en suite).
TARIFF: (1993) Single 40–60, Double 85–95.
CC: Amex, Diners, Euro/Access, Visa.

CHEXBRES-LAVAUX 18C

Hotel du Signal ★★★★ Puidoux-Gare,
1604 Chexbres-Lavaux.
☎ 021 946 2525, Fax 021 946 2015.
English spoken.
Open 30/03 to 01/11. 80 bedrooms
(all en suite with telephone). Indoor swimming pool, tennis, golf 18 km, garage, parking, restaurant. &

Set in 50 acres overlooking Lac Léman. French restaurant, banqueting and meeting facilities. A few minutes from Vevey and Lausanne and 1 km from highway, exit Chexbres.

TARIFF: Single 87–144, Double 156–216.
CC: Euro/Access, Visa.

CHUR/COIRE 18B

Romantik Hotel Stern ★★★ Reichsgasse 11,
7000 Chur/Coire.
☎ 081 223555.

Open all year. 55 bedrooms (all en suite with telephone).
TARIFF: (1993) Single 100–115, Double 175–220.
CC: none.

DAVOS 18B

Hotel Schweizerhof ★★★★ Promenade 50,
7270 Davos.
☎ 081 44 11 51, Fax 081 43 49 66.
English spoken.

Open 04/12 to 18/04 & 26/05 to 30/09.
93 bedrooms (all en suite with telephone).
Indoor swimming pool, golf 1 km, garage, parking, restaurant. &

Modern, first-class hotel with a friendly atmosphere and offering personal attention. Several lounges, elegant dining room, bar with pianist mid-June to mid-September and winter season. Sun terrace and garden with children's playground. Situated in the centre near ski-lifts.

TARIFF: Single 104–242, Double 184–440.
CC: Amex, Diners, Euro/Access, Visa.

FAIDO 18D

Hotel Milano ★★★ 6762 Faido.
☎ 094 38 13 07. English spoken.
Open all year. 39 bedrooms (26 en suite, 13 bath/shower only, 39 telephone). Tennis, parking, restaurant.

Comfortable hotel just 100 m from the main road, and in a quiet location with excellent cuisine. On E35 between Airolo and Biasca.

TARIFF: Single 60–75, Double 95–140,
Set menu 15–38.
CC: Amex, Diners, Euro/Access, Visa.

Switzerland

GENEVE (GENEVA)   18C

Hotel Beau Rivage ★★★★★
13 quai du Mt Blanc, 1201 Genève.
☎ 022 731 0221.
Open all year. 104 bedrooms (all en suite
with telephone).
TARIFF: (1993) Single 353–403,
Double 506–706.
CC: Amex, Diners, Euro/Access, Visa.

Hotel Cornavin ★★★★ 33 bd James Fazy,
1208 Genève.
☎ 022 732 2100.
Open all year. 125 bedrooms (all en suite
with telephone).
TARIFF: (1993) Single 140–205, Double 200–290.
CC: Amex, Diners, Euro/Access, Visa.

Hotel Cristal ★★★★ 4 rue Pradier,
1201 Genève.
☎ 022 731 3400, Fax 022 731 7078.
English spoken.
Open all year. 79 bedrooms (all en suite
with telephone).

*Modern hotel in a quiet location but in easy
reach of parking, airport, station and shops.
Air conditioned, cable TV. Easy to find - 100 m
from the railway station.*
TARIFF: Single 135–165,
Double 190–220, Bk 7.5.
CC: Amex, Diners, Euro/Access, Visa.

Hotel Pax ★★ 68 rue du 31 décembre,
1207 Genève.
☎ 022 735 4440, Fax 022 786 4568.
English spoken.

Open all year. 32 bedrooms (13 en suite,
10 bath/shower only, 32 telephone). Parking.
*Family hotel in the centre of town. Colour TV,
mini-bar in rooms.*
TARIFF: Single 68–99, Double 80–115, Bk 9.
CC: Amex, Diners, Euro/Access, Visa.

Hotel Metropole ★★★★★
34 quai Gén Guisan, Rive gauche,
1204 Genève.
☎ 022 311 13 44, Fax 022 311 13 50.
English spoken.
Open all year. 127 bedrooms (104 en suite,
23 bath/shower only, 127 telephone).
Restaurant.

*Elegant, luxurious hotel dating from the 1850s
and now completely renovated. Town centre
position, facing the lake and the Jardin
Anglais.*
TARIFF: Single 260–325,
Double 330–435, Bk .
CC: Amex, Diners, Euro/Access, Visa.

Hotel Savoy ★★★★ 8 place Cornavin,
1201 Genève.
☎ 022 731 1255.
Open all year. 50 bedrooms (all en suite
with telephone).
TARIFF: (1993) Single 100–150,
Double 140–210.
CC: Amex, Diners, Euro/Access, Visa.

GLARUS   18B

Hotel Todiblick 8784 Braunwald.
☎ 058 84 12 36, Fax 058 84 20 95.
English spoken.

Open all year. 15 bedrooms (10 en suite,
15 telephone). Indoor swimming pool,
golf 1 km, restaurant.

*Simple chalet-hotel for family holidays. As
Braunwald is car-free, cars should be left at
Linthal. Take the funicular railway to
Braunwald where guests are met by the hotel
porter with a pony cart.*
TARIFF: Single 75–105,
Double 150–210.
CC: Amex, Diners, Euro/Access, Visa.

GOTTHARD 18D

Romantik Hotel Stern & Post ★★★
6474 Amsteg am Gotthard.
✆ 044 64440, Fax 044 63261.
English spoken.
Open all year. 40 bedrooms (30 en suite, 40 telephone). Garage, parking.
RESTAURANT: Closed Tue/Wed Nov to April.

This inn is the last coaching house along the St-Gotthard road; long established in the wonderful alpine landscape of the Maderaner valley. Traditional welcome and excellent cooking.

TARIFF: Single 55–100, Double 95–200, Set menu 45–70.
CC: Amex, Diners, Euro/Access, Visa.

GRINDELWALD 18C

Chalet Hotel Gletschergarten ★★★
3818 Grindelwald.
✆ 036 53 17 21, Fax 036 53 29 57.
English spoken.
Open 26/12 to 31/03 & 31/05 to 31/10.
26 bedrooms (all en suite with telephone).
Golf 20 km, parking.
RESTAURANT: Closed Mon.

Delightful chalet-hotel built in 1899, in the heart of the Bernese Oberland. Every comfort including sauna and solarium; all mountain sports available. 1 km from station.

TARIFF: Single 85–140, Double 150–250, Set menu 35–40.
CC: none.

Romantik Hotel Schweizerhof ★★★★
3818 Grindelwald.
✆ 036 53 22 02, Fax 036 53 20 04.
English spoken.
Open 19/12 to 12/04 & 29/05 to 10/10.
100 bedrooms (49 en suite, 3 bath/shower only, 100 telephone). Indoor swimming pool, golf 18 km, parking, restaurant.

In the centre of picturesque Grindelwald and two minutes' walk from the station. Prices quoted for half-board.

TARIFF: (1993) Single 152–213, Double 278–530, Set menu 18–20.
CC: Amex, Diners, Euro/Access, Visa.

GSTAAD 18C

Hotel Ermitage ★★★ Le Petit Pré, 1837 Château-d'Oex.
✆ 029 46003, Fax 029 45076.
English spoken.
Open 15/12 to 20/10. 20 bedrooms (all en suite with telephone). Golf 12 km, parking, restaurant.

Chalet-style hotel in magnificent surroundings, with family flats available all year. French restaurant; summer and winter sports. 10 minutes from Gstaad.

TARIFF: Single 80–100, Double 120–160, Set menu 12–54.
CC: Amex, Diners, Euro/Access, Visa.

Posthotel Rossli ★★★ 3780 Gstaad.
✆ 030 43412, Fax 030 46190. English spoken.
Open all year. 18 bedrooms (all en suite with telephone). Garage, restaurant.

Comfortable hotel in beautiful surroundings. Centre of town. Good Swiss food.

TARIFF: (1993) Single 85–135, Double 140–240.
CC: Diners, Euro/Access, Visa.

INTERLAKEN 18C

Hotel Bellevue-Garden ★★★★ Marktgasse 59, 3800 Interlaken.
✆ 036 224 431, Fax 036 229 250. English spoken.
Open all year. 60 bedrooms (50 en suite, 50 telephone). Parking, restaurant.

In the heart of the city, on the beautiful River Aare, close to shops, restaurants, attractions and railway station. Superbly furnished, good restaurant.

TARIFF: Single 79–137, Double 116–205, Bk 20.
CC: Amex, Diners, Euro/Access, Visa.

Hotel du Lac ★★★★ Höheweg 225, 3800 Interlaken.
✆ 036 222922, Fax 036 222915. English spoken.
Open 15/02 to 15/01. 40 bedrooms (all en suite with telephone). Golf 3 km, parking. ♿
RESTAURANT: Closed 15/01 to 15/02.

Picturesque location on River Aare with waterfront restaurant, public rooms and information desk. Ideal starting point for lake and mountain excursions in Junfrau region.

TARIFF: Single 100–150, Double 160–250, Set menu 19–21.
CC: Amex, Diners, Euro/Access, Visa.

Hotel Seiler au Lac ★★★★ Bonigen, 3806 Interlaken.
✆ 036 22 30 21, Fax 036 22 30 01.
English spoken.
Open 20/12 to 07/01 & 01/02 to 31/10.
45 bedrooms (all en suite with telephone).
Golf 5 km, garage, parking, restaurant. ♿

Completely refurbished family hotel in idyllic and peaceful location, overlooking Lake

Brienz. Good food, friendly atmosphere. 2 km from Interlaken. Bus/boat landing in front of hotel.
TARIFF: Single 95–165, Double 190–310, Set menu 40–50.
CC: none.

Hotel Splendid ★★★ Höheweg 33, 3800 Interlaken.
☎ 036 227612, Fax 036 227679. English spoken.
Open 25/12 to 31/10. 35 bedrooms (33 en suite, all bath/shower only with telephone). Golf 3 km, parking, restaurant.
TARIFF: Single 95–125, Double 145–190, Set menu 15–30.
CC: Amex, Euro/Access, Visa.

KANDERSTEG 18C

Hotel Adler ★★★ 3718 Kandersteg.
☎ 033 75 11 21, Fax 033 75 19 61. English spoken.

Open all year. 43 bedrooms (24 en suite, 24 telephone). Garage, parking, restaurant. &
Chalet-style, family-run hotel with mountain views. Some rooms with jacuzzi and fireplace.
TARIFF: Single 85–100, Double 150–180, Set menu 18–80.
CC: Amex, Diners, Euro/Access, Visa.

Hotel Alpenrose ★ 3718 Kandersteg.
☎ 033 751170. English spoken.
Open 01/01 to 30/04 & 01/05 to 30/09. 20 bedrooms (7 en suite). Parking, restaurant.
A pleasant family-run hotel in quiet mountain countryside. Comfortable bedrooms, spacious dining room.
TARIFF: (1993) Single 40–46, Double 80–112.
CC: Amex, Diners, Euro/Access, Visa.

KLOSTERS 18B

Hotel Alpina ★★★★ Bahnhofplatz, 7250 Klosters.
☎ 081 69 41 21, Fax 081 69 41 10.
Open all year. 80 bedrooms (all en suite with telephone).
TARIFF: (1993) Single 140–290, Double 260–460.
CC: Amex, Diners, Euro/Access, Visa.

LAUSANNE 18C

Hotel Agora ★★★★ av du Rond-Point 9, 1003 Lausanne.
☎ 021 617 1211, Fax 021 2626 05. English spoken.
Open all year. 83 bedrooms (all en suite with telephone). Golf 15 km, garage, parking.
RESTAURANT: Closed Sat & Sun.
Modern hotel within easy reach of all amenities. Only 5 mins from railway station on foot. Air-conditioned rooms.
TARIFF: Single 130–150, Double 170–190, Bk 7.5.
CC: Amex, Diners, Euro/Access, Visa.

Hotel Alpha ★★★★ rue du Petite-Chêne 34, 1000 Lausanne.
☎ 021 323 0131, Fax 021 230 145. English spoken.
Open all year. 133 bedrooms (all en suite with telephone). Golf 15 km, garage, parking, restaurant.
Modern hotel, completely renovated in 1987, within easy reach of all amenities. Individually air-conditioned. Regional specialities in restaurant. Quiet position between the station and the centre of St-Francois.
TARIFF: Single 130–150, Double 170–190, Bk 7.5.
CC: Amex, Diners, Euro/Access, Visa.

Hotel Carlton ★★★★ 4 av de Cour, 1000 Lausanne.
☎ 021 616 32 35, Fax 021 616 34 30. English spoken.
Open all year. 50 bedrooms (all en suite with telephone). Golf 8 km, parking, restaurant.
All rooms have television, radio and mini-bar. Coffee shop and summer garden restaurant.
TARIFF: Single 148–168, Double 186–248.
CC: Amex, Diners, Euro/Access, Visa.

Hotel City ★★★ rue Caroline 5, 1007 Lausanne.
☎ 021 202 141, Fax 021 202 149. English spoken.

Open all year. 51 bedrooms (all en suite with telephone). Golf 15 km.

Totally renovated in 1986, this hotel is central and next to the cathedral. All modern amenities.

TARIFF: Single 100–130, Double 140–170, Bk 7.5.
CC: Amex, Diners, Euro/Access, Visa.

Hotel Victoria ★★★★ 46 av de la Gare, 1003 Lausanne.
☎ 021 320 57 71, Fax 021 320 57 74.
English spoken.
Open all year. 60 bedrooms (all en suite with telephone). Golf 5 km, garage, parking.

Comfortable, quiet hotel near the station in town centre. Conference facilities for up to 50 people.

TARIFF: Single 140–160, Double 200–240.
CC: Amex, Diners, Euro/Access, Visa.

LOCARNO 18D

Hotel Belvedere ★★★ 44 Via ai Monti, 6601 Locarno.
☎ 093 310 363, Fax 093 315 239.
English spoken.

Open 20/02 to 03/01. 64 bedrooms (all en suite with telephone). Outdoor swimming pool, golf 3 km, garage, parking, restaurant. ﬔ

Lovely hotel with gardens and sports centre. 5 minutes' walk from town centre, served by funicular train. Two restaurants with fine Swiss-Italian cuisine. All rooms face south to lake.

TARIFF: Single 125–177, Double 190–254, Set menu 17–60.
CC: Amex, Diners, Euro/Access, Visa.

Hotel Esplanade ★★★★ Via delle Vigne, 6000 Locarno.
☎ 093 332 1212.

Open all year. 84 bedrooms (58 en suite).
TARIFF: (1993) Single 110–155, Double 200–260.
CC: Amex, Diners, Euro/Access, Visa.

LUGANO 18D

Hotel Continental-Beauregard ★★★
Via Basilea 28, 6903 Lugano.
☎ 091 561 112. English spoken.
Open 15/02 to 15/11. 100 bedrooms (all en suite with telephone). Parking, restaurant.

Central position near town centre, in large park with views of lake and mountains. Follow signs.

TARIFF: Single 85–130, Double 130–210, Set menu 20–30.
CC: Amex, Diners, Euro/Access, Visa.

Hotel International au Lac ★★★
Via Nassa 68, 6901 Lugano.
☎ 091 22 75 41, Fax 091 22 75 44.
English spoken.
Open 26/03 to 31/10. 80 bedrooms (all en suite with telephone). Outdoor swimming pool, golf 8 km, garage, parking, restaurant. ﬔ

Refined family hotel with traditional elegance. Located on the lake promenade. Parking garage in hotel. New swimming pool in garden.

TARIFF: Single 110–155, Double 180–260, Set menu 24–36.
CC: Amex, Diners, Euro/Access, Visa.

Motel Vezia ★★★ Via San Gottardo 32, 6943 Vezia.
☎ 091 56 36 31, Fax 091 56 70 22. English spoken.
Open 01/02 to 30/11. 60 bedrooms (50 en suite, 60 telephone). Outdoor swimming pool, golf 6 km, garage, parking, restaurant. ﬔ

Only 3 km from the centre of Lugano with buses every 12 minutes. Very modern hotel with quiet rooms, some of them sound-proofed. Gardens. Motorway exit Lugano-Nord.

TARIFF: Single 58–124, Double 78–162, Bk 9.50, Set menu 15–25.
CC: Amex, Diners, Euro/Access, Visa.

Hotel Queens Admiral ★★★★ Via Geretta 15, 6902 Lugano.
☎ 091 54 23 24.
Open all year. 92 bedrooms (all en suite with telephone).
TARIFF: (1993) Single 155–195, Double 240–310.
CC: Amex, Diners, Euro/Access, Visa.

Hotel Splendide Royal ★★★★★
7 Riva A Caccia, 6900 Lugano.
☎ 091 54 20 01, Fax 091 54 89 31.
English spoken.
Open all year. 105 bedrooms (all en suite
with telephone). Indoor swimming pool,
golf 12 km, garage, parking, restaurant.

*One of the most fashionable hotels in Lugano.
5 minutes from city centre, 1.5 km from
railway station and 8 km from local airport
Agno/Lugano. Member of Swiss Leading Hotels
and Leading Hotels of the World.*
TARIFF: Single 180–290, Double 340–540,
Set menu 38–68.
CC: Amex, Diners, Euro/Access, Visa.

LUZERN (LUCERNE)   18B

Hotel Belvedere ★★★ Seestrasse 16,
6052 Hergiswil.
☎ 041 95 01 01, Fax 041 95 28 00. English spoken.
Open all year. 100 bedrooms (all en suite
with telephone). Parking.

*The hotel is situated in a stunning position
beside the lake, with a mountain backdrop.
Just 300 m from the station for the 5-minute
journey to Lucerne.*
TARIFF: (1993) Single 90–110, Double 115–175.
CC: Amex, Diners, Euro/Access, Visa.

Hotel Hermitage ★★★ Seeburgstrasse 72,
6008 Luzern.
☎ 041 313 737.
Open all year. 33 bedrooms (28 en suite).
TARIFF: (1993) Double 260–370.
CC: Amex, Diners, Euro/Access, Visa.

Hotel Seeburg ★★★★ 6006 Luzern.
☎ 041 31 19 22, Fax 041 31 19 25.
English spoken.
Open all year. 89 bedrooms (87 en suite,
89 telephone). Golf 1 km, garage, parking,
restaurant.

*Set in extensive grounds bordering Lake
Luzern with beautiful mountain views. One
and a half miles from the town centre and
close to the Transport Museum and steamer
pier.*
TARIFF: Single 107–141,
Double 180–246,
Set menu 39–69.
CC: Amex, Diners, Euro/Access, Visa.

MARTIGNY   18C

Hotel Le Catogne ★★ La Douay,
1937 Orsières.
☎ 026 83 12 30, Fax 026 83 22 35.
English spoken.

Open 01/12 to 31/10. 25 bedrooms
(all en suite). Parking, restaurant. &

*Comfortable chalet-hotel. Good restaurant.
Extra beds available. 15 km from Martigny on
road to the Grand-St-Bernard tunnel.*
TARIFF: Single 40–60, Double 60–80.
CC: Euro/Access, Visa.

MONTREUX   18C

Hotel Eden au Lac ★★★★ 11 rue du Théâtre,
1820 Montreux.
☎ 021 635 551.
Open all year. 105 bedrooms (all en suite).
TARIFF: (1993) Single 180–220,
Double 230–300.
CC: Amex, Diners, Euro/Access, Visa.

MORGES   18C

Hotel du Mont-Blanc au Lac ★★★
quai du Mont-Blanc, 1110 Morges.
☎ 021 802 30 72, Fax 021 801 51 22.
English spoken.
Open all year. 46 bedrooms (all en suite
with telephone). Restaurant.

Situated on the lake promenade, next to charming old port of Morges, facing the Alps and Mont-Blanc. A few minutes' walk from shopping centre. Terrace restaurant offering French and regional specialities.

TARIFF: Single 100–145, Double 145–200.
CC: Amex, Diners, Euro/Access, Visa.

MORLON 18C

Hotel Gruyerien 1638 Morlon.
☎ 029 2 71 58, Fax 029 2 16 84. English spoken.
Open 11/01 to 24/12. 14 bedrooms
(9 en suite). Golf 10 km, parking, restaurant. &

Small hotel offering rest and relaxation. Located in a small rural village in the mountains of the Gruyère, by Lake Gruyère. Take N12/E27 to Bulle and follow the road for 3 km.

TARIFF: Single 50–75, Double 80–120.
CC: Amex, Diners, Euro/Access, Visa.

NEUCHATEL 18A

Novotel Neuchatel Thielle ★★★ Verger 1, 2075 Thielle.
☎ 038 33 57 57, Fax 038 33 28 84. English spoken.

Open all year. 60 bedrooms (all en suite with telephone). Outdoor swimming pool, golf 5 km, parking, restaurant.

8 km from Neuchâtel. From Neuchâtel go straight on to St-Blaise and follow signs to Thielle-Berne.

TARIFF: Single 95–115, Double 120–140, Bk 14.50, Set menu 14.
CC: Amex, Diners, Euro/Access, Visa.

ROUGEMONT 18C

Hotel Valrose ★★ 1838 Rougemont.
☎ 041 29 48146, Fax 041 29 48854.
English spoken.
Open 01/12 to 31/10. 16 bedrooms

(12 en suite, 4 bath/shower only). Tennis, golf 15 km, garage, parking.
RESTAURANT: Closed Nov.

Family owned for four generations, this small hotel in a pretty village, offers comfort with traditional cuisine in its restaurant. Local cheese specialities. 40 different sports on offer within 8 km.

TARIFF: Single 55–80, Double 100–145.
CC: Amex, Diners, Euro/Access, Visa.

RIGI-KALTBAD 18B

Hotel Bellevue ★★★★ Konigin der Aussicht, 6356 Rigi-Kaltbad.
☎ 041 83 13 51, Fax 041 83 13 54. English spoken.
Open 20/12 to 15/11. 80 bedrooms
(55 en suite, 55 telephone). Indoor swimming pool, tennis, restaurant. &

Spectacular situation and views; lovely comfortable rooms; 4 excellent restaurants. 1.5 km north of Vitznau.

TARIFF: (1993) Single 75–120, Double 70–130, Set menu 30–45.
CC: Amex, Diners, Euro/Access, Visa.

SAAS-FEE 18C

Alpenlandgasthof Höhnegg ★★★
3906 Saas-Fee.
☎ 028 57 22 68, Fax 028 57 12 49.
English spoken.

Open 20/06 to 20/10 & 20/12 to 05/05.
63 bedrooms (all en suite with telephone).
RESTAURANT: Closed Mon.

Very comfortable hotel in a magnificent situation amid mountains and forest. Traffic-free, but taxis available. Excellent cuisine. Cross-country and downhill skiing nearby. Suites and apartments also available.

TARIFF: Single 85–125, Double 150–210, Set menu 45–90.
CC: Euro/Access, Visa.

ST-MORITZ 18D

Hotel Crystal ★★★★ 7500 St-Moritz.
☎ 082 21165, Fax 082 36445. English spoken.
Open 07/12 to 10/04 & 01/06 to 15/10.
100 bedrooms (all en suite with telephone).
Golf 7 km, parking, restaurant.

*Comfortable hotel in town centre, 3 minutes'
walk from station, shops etc. Piano bar. Public
car park opposite. Italian restaurant.*
TARIFF: Single 130–200, Double 210–400.
CC: Amex, Diners, Euro/Access, Visa.

SCHAFFHAUSEN 18B

Hotel Park Villa ★★★ Parkstrasse 18,
8200 Schaffhausen.
☎ 053 25 27 37.
Open all year. 21 bedrooms (18 en suite).
TARIFF: (1993) Single 65–140, Double 100–190.
CC: none.

SION 18C

Hotel Castel ★★★ 38 rue du Scex, 1950 Sion.
☎ 027 229171, Fax 027 225724. English spoken.
Open all year. 30 bedrooms (all en suite
with telephone). Garage, parking. ♿
*In the heart of the Valais region with
spectacular views. Very comfortable Bed and
Breakfast hotel with adjoining restaurant.*
TARIFF: Single 80–93, Double 125–135.
CC: Amex, Diners, Euro/Access, Visa.

SOLOTHURN 18A

Hotel Krone ★★★★ Hauptgasse 64,
4500 Solothurn.
☎ 065 22 44 12.
Open all year. 42 bedrooms (all en suite).
TARIFF: (1993) Single 145–175,
Double 175–240.
CC: Amex, Diners, Euro/Access, Visa.

THUN 18A

Gasthof Rothorn 3657 Schwanden.
☎ 033 51 11 86, Fax 033 51 33 86.
English spoken.
Open all year. 20 bedrooms (10 en suite).
Indoor swimming pool, outdoor swimming
pool, tennis, golf 8 km, parking.
RESTAURANT: Closed Mon.
*Between Thun and Interlaken, above the lake
at Thun and near Sigriswil. Good sporting
area.*
TARIFF: (1993) Single 55–70, Double 90–120,
Set menu 15–30.
CC: none.

VALLORBE 18C

Motel Les Jurats ★★ 1337 Vallorbe.
☎ 021 843 19 91, Fax 021 843 18 83.
Open all year. 16 bedrooms (all en suite
with telephone). Indoor swimming pool,
tennis, golf 2 km, parking.
RESTAURANT: Closed 20/12 to 03/01.

*On the road through the valley (Vallée de
Joux). Comfortable and quiet, 30 km from
Pontarlier on E28/N57.*
TARIFF: Single 50–65, Double 70–80, Bk 7,
Set menu 35–55.
CC: Amex, Diners, Euro/Access, Visa.

VEVEY 18C

Hotel du Lac ★★★★ rue d'Italie 1,
1800 Vevey.
☎ 021 921 10 41, Fax 021 921 75 08.
English spoken.
Open all year. 56 bedrooms (all en suite
with telephone). Outdoor swimming pool,
golf 20 km, garage, parking, restaurant.
*Spacious, elegant hotel with 19th-century
charm and 20th-century comfort. Immediate
access to Lac Léman and its promenades. One
hour from Genève airport and easy access via
modern highways.*
TARIFF: Single 170–250, Double 240–320.
CC: Amex, Diners, Euro/Access, Visa.

VILLARS-SUR-OLLON 18C

Grand Hotel Du Parc ★★★★★
route du Col de la Croix, 1884 Villars.
☎ 025 35 21 21, Fax 025 35 33 63.
English spoken.
Open 19/12 to 17/04 & 01/06 to 30/10.
65 bedrooms (all en suite with telephone).
Indoor swimming pool, tennis, golf 7 km,
parking, restaurant.

*Luxurious hotel set in parkland and right on
the ski slopes. Two private ski-lifts. Three tennis
courts (summer), some horses for riding,
inside swimming pool with instructor.*
TARIFF: Single 155–260, Double 240–520,
Set menu 45.
CC: Amex, Euro/Access, Visa.

WEGGIS 18B

Hotel Beau-Rivage ★★★★ Lac Luzern,
6353 Weggis.
☎ 041 93 14 22, Fax 041 93 19 81.
English spoken.
Open 01/04 to 31/10. 45 bedrooms
(all en suite with telephone). Outdoor

Switzerland

swimming pool, golf 20 km, garage, parking, restaurant.

Situated right on the lake, just 3 minutes' walk from the boat station.

TARIFF: Single 100–1600, Double 180–280, Set menu 50–60.

CC: Amex, Diners, Euro/Access, Visa.

WENGEN 18C

Hotel Eiger ★★★ 3823 Wengen.
☎ 036 55 11 31, Fax 036 55 10 30.
English spoken.
Open 12/06 to 24/04. 33 bedrooms
(all en suite with telephone). Golf 13 km, parking, restaurant.

Centrally positioned modern, friendly hotel in car-free Wengen. Within sight of the Eiger and Jüngfrau. Children welcome; extra beds.

TARIFF: Single 80–120, Double 160–262, Set menu 35–50.

CC: Amex, Diners, Euro/Access, Visa.

WINTERTHUR 18B

Hotel Krone ★★★ Marktgasse 49,
8401 Winterthur.
☎ 052 213 2521. English spoken.
Open all year. 38 bedrooms (all en suite with telephone). Garage, restaurant.

Small, private hotel in the heart of old town of Winterthur, 15 mins by train from Zurich airport, 3 mins from main railway station.

TARIFF: Single 120–140, Double 180–200.

CC: Amex, Diners, Euro/Access, Visa.

ZERMATT 18C

Grand Hotel Zermatterhof ★★★★★
Bahnhofstrasse, 3920 Zermatt.
☎ 028 66 11 00, Fax 028 67 48 42.
English spoken.
Open 01/12 to 31/10. 146 bedrooms
(86 en suite, 146 telephone). Indoor swimming pool, tennis, restaurant.

Elegant accommodation and fine cuisine with excellent service. 5 minutes' walk from the station.

TARIFF: (1993) Single 190–310,
Double 360–1400, Set menu 70–90.

CC: Amex, Diners, Euro/Access, Visa.

ZUG 18B

Seehotel Rigi-Royal ★★★ 6405 Immensee.
☎ 041 813131, Fax 041 813137. English spoken.
Open 24/01 to 24/12. 44 bedrooms

(42 en suite, 2 bath/shower only,
44 telephone). Outdoor swimming pool,
golf 10 km, garage, parking, restaurant. ♿

Enchanting lakeside hotel with private beach and boat-house. Rooms have spectacular views of the surrounding countryside and pretty gardens. Good restaurant specialising in fish and regional delicacies. From Zug drive south around the west side of the lake towards Luzern and Immensee is half way around.

TARIFF: Single 90–105, Double 150–190.

CC: Amex, Diners, Visa.

ZÜRICH 18B

Hotel Glockenhof ★★★★ Sihlstr 31,
8000 Zürich.
☎ 01 211 5650.
Open all year. 108 bedrooms (all en suite with telephone).

TARIFF: (1993) Single 140–210, Double 210–310.

CC: Amex, Diners, Euro/Access, Visa.

Hotel Savoy Baur en Ville ★★★★★
Paradeplatz, 8022 Zürich.
☎ 01 211 53 60, Fax 01 221 14 67. English spoken.

Open all year. 146 bedrooms (112 en suite,
112 telephone). Golf 4 km, garage, restaurant. ♿

Situated in the heart of Zurich, hotel has elegant and spacious rooms. French and Italian cuisine; ideal for holidays or business.

TARIFF: Single 360, Double 540,
Set menu 49–95.

CC: Amex, Diners, Euro/Access, Visa.

Hotel Pullman Continental ★★★★
Stampfenbachstrasse 60-62,
8000 Zürich.
☎ 01 363 3363.
Open all year. 134 bedrooms (all en suite with telephone).

TARIFF: (1993) Single 200–300, Double 300–450.

CC: Amex, Diners, Euro/Access, Visa.

Switzerland

Hotel Tiefenau Zürich ★★★★
Steinwiesstrasse 8-10, 8032 Zürich.
☎ 01 251 24 09, Fax 01 251 24 76.
English spoken.
Open 03/01 to 17/12. 70 bedrooms
(all en suite with telephone). Golf 2 km,
parking, restaurant.

Right in the city centre near the Museum of
Fine Art, Conservatory, Playhouse and Opera.
Built in 1835 the hotel is furnished in Louis XV
style but has every modern comfort. The rooms
are especially comfortable and well-equipped.
Garden restaurant in summer. Private
parking. Sun terrace and bar.

TARIFF: Single 200–300, Double 280–400,
Set menu 20.50–28.80.
CC: Amex, Diners, Euro/Access, Visa.

Hotel Zurcherhof ★★★★ Zahringerstrasse 21,
8025 Zürich.
☎ 01 262 1040.
Open all year. 35 bedrooms (all en suite
with telephone).
TARIFF: (1993) Single 120–180,
Double 180–260.
CC: Amex, Diners, Euro/Access, Visa.

Sport Motel Zweisimmen ★★★
Saanenstrasse, 3770 Zweisimmen.
☎ 030 21431, Fax 030 21831. English spoken.

Open 01/06 to 30/04. 50 bedrooms
(20 en suite, 20 telephone). Parking,
restaurant.

Comfortable hotel with large grounds in quiet
location. Good restaurant supervised by the
owner. At the edge of the village on the road to
Gstaad/Montreux.

TARIFF: Single 60–85, Double 110–150.
CC: Euro/Access, Visa.

TURKEY

From the beginning of the 1980s, Turkey has enjoyed a rapid rise in popularity as an exotic holiday destination at the meeting of Europe and Asia – the "bridge" between West and East. This huge country covers 779,452 sq km, over three times the size of the UK. The currency is the lire, made up of 100 kurus.

Turkey is a mountainous land, its tallest peak is Mt Ararat in the east at 5,122 m, higher than any peak in the Alps. The Tigris and Euphrates rivers, cradle of ancient and historic cultures, rise in the east. The northern coasts are forested, while Mediterranean-type scrub covers much of the lowlands. Steppe grasses and stunted bushes are characteristic of the high central plateau.

Turkey's capital is Ankara, with 2.2 million people. The largest city, Istanbul, has almost 6 million people. There are 125,000 km of roads, giving a road density (km per sq km) of 0.16, compared to the UK's 1.5. About half the roads are unsurfaced, and the rough terrain means that it can be difficult to maintain the road system. Travel, too, may not be easy.

ANKARA 24B

Hotel Buyuk Ankara Oteli ★★★★★ Ataturk Bulvari no 183, Kavaklidere, 06680 Ankara.
☎ 4 125 66 55.
Open all year. 194 bedrooms (all en suite with telephone).
(Price in UK£s.)
TARIFF: (1993) Double 50–100.
CC: none.

Hotel Pullman Etap Mola ★★★ Ataturk Bulvari no 80, 0644 Ankara.
☎ 4 117 85 85.
Open all year. 57 bedrooms (all en suite with telephone).
(Price in UK£s.)
TARIFF: (1993) Double 20–45.
CC: none.

ANTALYA 24D

Hotel Turban Adalya Kaleici Yat Limani, 07100 Antalya.
☎ 31 118 066.
Open all year. 29 bedrooms (all en suite with telephone).
CC: none.

FETHIYE 24D

Hotel Meri Oludeniz Fethiye, Mugla, 48300 Fethiye.
☎ 615 66060, Fax 615 66456. English spoken.
Open all year. 75 bedrooms (all en suite with telephone). Tennis, parking, restaurant.

Beautifully situated in a totally unspoilt preservation area. In a private garden with steps down to the beach and children's playground. (Prices in US$).
TARIFF: (1993) Single 35.80–44.80, Double 44.80–56.00, Set menu 8.00–10.00.
CC: Amex, Diners, Euro/Access, Visa.

ISTANBUL 24B

Hotel Pera Palas ★★★★ Mesrutiyet Cad 98/100 Istanbul.
☎ 151 4560.
Open all year. 120 bedrooms (all en suite).
(Price in UK£s.)
TARIFF: (1993) Double 45–60.
CC: none.

Hotel Yesilev Cankurtaran Mahallesi, Kabasakal Sok, 534400 Sultanahmet, Istanbul.
☎ 151 5286764.
Open all year. 20 bedrooms (all en suite).
CC: none.

IZMIR 24D

Hotel Golden Dolphin Boyalik Mevrii, 35948 Izmir.
☎ 549 31250, Fax 549 32242. English spoken.
Open all year. 525 bedrooms (all en suite with telephone). Indoor swimming pool, outdoor swimming pool, tennis, parking, restaurant.
CC: Amex, Diners, Euro/Access, Visa.

Turkey

INDEX

This index covers the Hotel Directory. Places shown in **bold type** are headings used in the Hotel Directory under which towns are grouped.

KEY TO MAPS

Legend

• Tonnerre — town with one hotel

● Alençon — town with more than one hotel

═══════ motorway

─────── main road

•••••••••• international border

– – – – regional border

Cartography by RAC Publishing

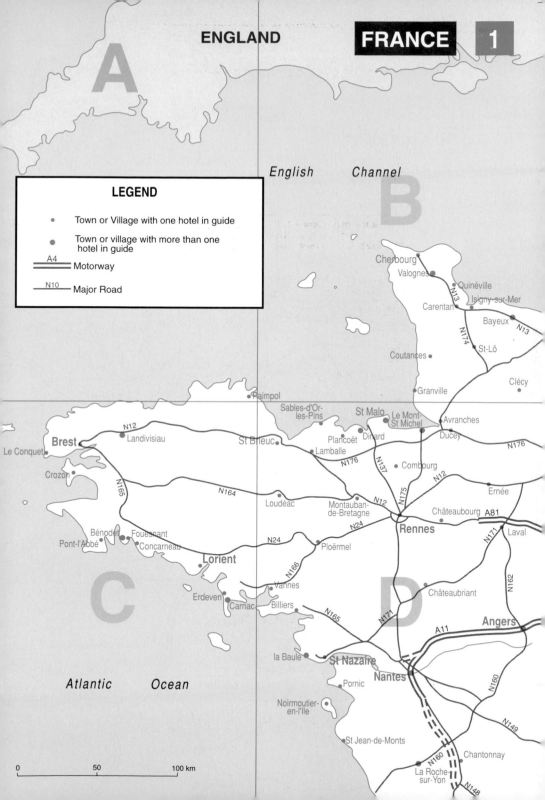

ENGLAND **FRANCE** `1`

A

B

English Channel

LEGEND

- Town or Village with one hotel in guide
- Town or village with more than one hotel in guide

A4 — Motorway

N10 — Major Road

Cherbourg
Valognes
Quinéville
Isigny-sur-Mer
Carentan
Bayeux
N13
St-Lô
N174
Coutances
Clécy
Granville
Paimpol
Sables-d'Or-les-Pins
St Malo
Le Mont-St Michel
Avranches
Brest
N12
Landivisiau
St Brieuc
Plancoët
Dinard
Ducey
N176
Le Conquet
Lamballe
Combourg
Crozon
N165
N137
N12
Ernée
N164
Loudéac
Montauban-de-Bretagne
N12
Châteaubourg
A81
N175
Rennes
Laval
N171
Bénodet
Fouesnant
N24
Ploërmel
N171
Pont-l'Abbé
Concarneau
N162
Lorient
N166
Vannes
Châteaubriant
Erdeven
Carnac
Billiers
N165
N171
A11
Angers
la Baule
St Nazaire
N160
Nantes
Atlantic Ocean
Pornic
Noirmoutier-en-l'Ile
N149
St Jean-de-Monts
Chantonnay
N160
La Roche-sur-Yon
N148

C

D

0   50   100 km

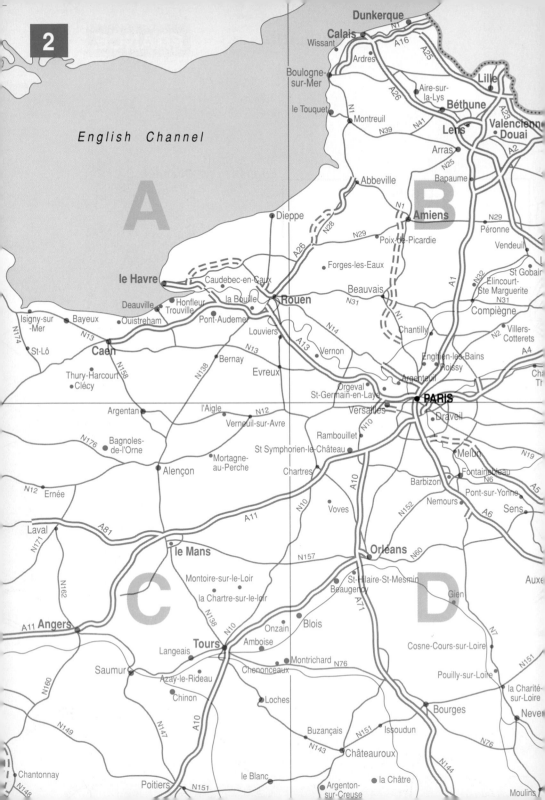

FRANCE 3

BELGIUM

GERMANY

SWITZERLAND

N2

N51

A

N43

Rocroi

Vervins

Charleville-
Mézières

N51

N43

N3

N31

Reims

A4

Epernay

Châlons-sur-Marne

N61

N4

N4

St-Dizier

N4

Nancy

Joinville

Troyes

N60

N19

Colombey-les-
-deux-Eglises

N74

Chaumont

A5

Vittel

Bar-sur-Seine

N77

Châtillon-sur-
Seine

Langres

C

N19

A31

Chablis

Combeaufontaine

Montbard

N71

Vesoul

allon

A6

A38

Dijon

A36

Besançon

Genlis

N57

Beaune

N83

Autun

Seurre

N81

N80

St Martin-en-Bresse

N73

N5

N70

A6

Lons-le-
Saunier

Dompierre-sur-Besbre

Tournus

Bonlieu

St Laurent-en-
Grandvaux

Metz

N74

A4

N63

A31

N57

Strasbourg

N420

Ribeauvillé

Kaysersberg

Colmar

Neuf-Brisach

N66

A35

Bussang

N57

N19

D

Mulhouse

Blotzheim

Altkirch

Montbeliard

St-Hippolyte

PARIS (inset)

le Bourget

le Blanc-Mesnil

Aulnay-
sous-Bois

Courbevoie

Rueil-
Malmaison

St
Cloud

Puteaux

Bagnolet

Noisy-
le-Grand

PARIS

B

**Boulogne-
Billancourt**

Charenton

St-Maurice

Créteil

Choisy-le-Roi

0   5   10   15 km

0   50   100 km

St Jean-de-Monts

La Roche-sur-Yon

Chantonnay

N160

N149

N147

Buzançais

le Blanc

Poitiers

N151

Argento
sur-Creus

Luçon

N148

N10

Niort

N11

N147

la Rochelle

Châtelaillon-Plage

A

B

N141

Limoges

Magnac-Bourg

Arvert

Royan

Cognac

N141

Angoulême

Vieux-Mareuil

Brantôme

N21

Pompadour

Atlantic

Ocean

Pauillac

A10

N10

Ribérac

Périgueux

Brive-la-Gailla

Salaunes

N89

les Eyzies-de-Tayac

Souill

Bergerac

Sarlat-la-Canéda

Bordeaux

Ste-Foy-
la-Grande

Beynac-
et-Cazenac

Payra

Gour

A63

N21

Villeréal

Laba
Mura

Caho

Casteljaloux

Villeneuve-
sur-Lot

Fumel

Labouheyre

Aiguillon

Agen

A62

N134

Mont-de-
Marsan

Barbotan-les-
Thermes

Montauban

N124

Manciet

Castéra-Verdazan

Auch

N10

N124

Aire-sur-L'Adour

Toulouse

Anglet/
Biarritz

C

D

N21

St Jean-de-Luz

A63

Salies-de-Béarn

A64

Ainhoa

Pau

St Jean-
Pied-de-Port

SPAIN

Lourdes

Cauterets

Barèges

0   50   100 km

FRANCE **5**

Issoudun
N151 N76 N81 N80 N73 N5
Châteauroux
la Châtre
N144 N145 Moulins Dompierre-sur-Besbre N79 N70 A6 Tournus Bonlieu St Laurent-en-Grandvaux
N145 Varennes-sur-Allier A40 Ferney-Voltaire
N71 Beaujeu Bourg-en-Bresse Natuna
Châteauneuf-les-Bains Vichy N144 Villefranche-sur-Saône N83 Annecy
Châtelguyon Roanne A72
Clermont-Ferrand Lyon A43 Aix-les-Bains
A71 Bourget-du-Lac
N89 Ussel Issoire St-Étienne A47 A48 Grenoble
Champagnac Brioude N122 N102 N88 A7 Chamrousse N91
N120 le Puy-en-Velay N86 La Chapelle-en-Vercors
Lamastre Valence
Aurillac Privas
madour Calvinet N102 Montélimar Gap
N140 St Geniez-d'Olt N86 N75 N85
Rodez les Vans Vallon-Pont-d'Arc Vaisons-la-Romaine
Villefranche-sur-Rouergue N88
Najac N106 Carpentras
Albi N9 Anduze Avignon
Gordes Apt
Lodève Noves N100 Gréoux-les-Bains
Avène-les-Bains Nîmes Cadenet
Castres Tarascon St Remy Cadenet
N126 C N110 Mus Fontvieille Salon-de-Provence
N112 Montpellier Arles A7 Aix-en-Provence
la Grande-Motte le Grau-du-Roi A8
Béziers A9 Agde Stes-Maries-de-la-Mer D Gémenos
Carcassonne Marseille le Cadiat d'Azur
A61 Narbonne la Ciotat
Sigean Port-la-Nouvelle Toulon
N30
Perpignan
N116 A9
Amélie Argelès-sur-Mer Calioure

Mediterranean Sea

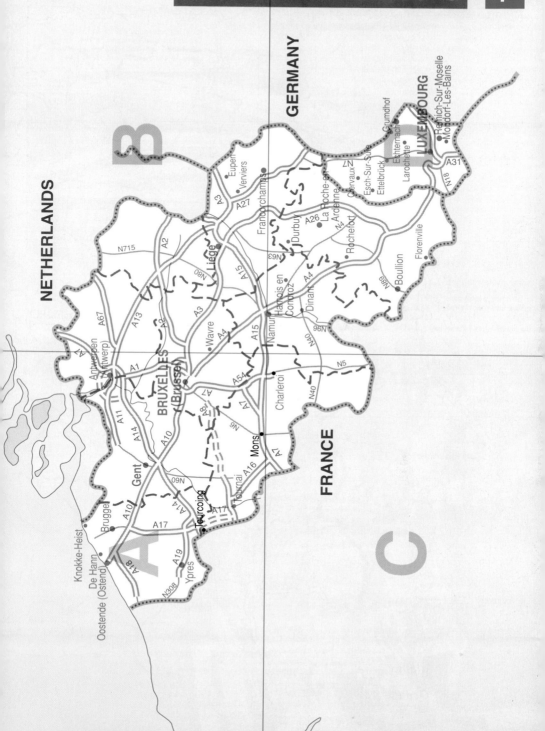

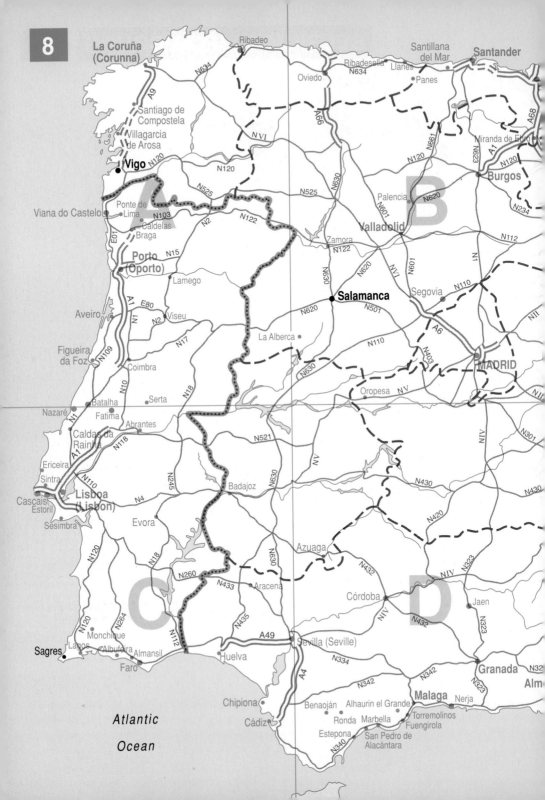

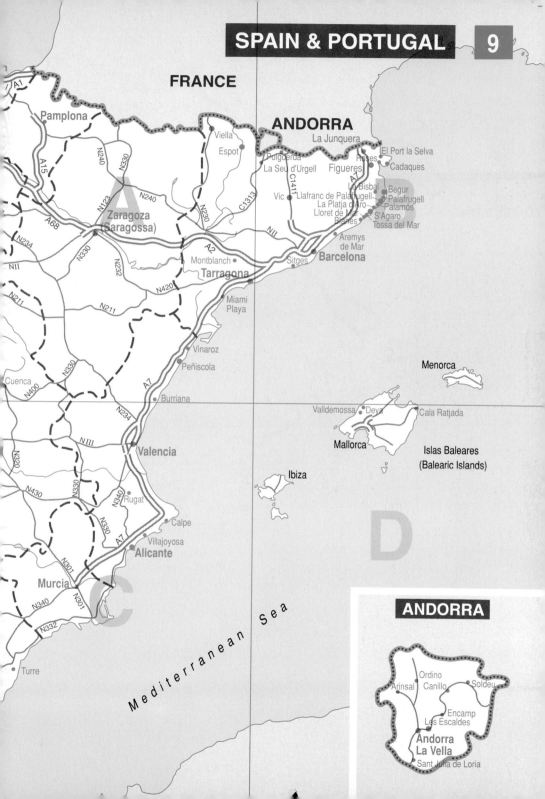

FRANCE

ANDORRA

Pamplona

Viella

Espot

La Junquera

El Port la Selva

Puigcerda

Roses

Cadaques

La Seu d'Urgell

Figueres

N240

N330

N123

N240

Zaragoza
(Saragossa)

Vic

La Bisbal

Begur
Palafrugell

Llafranc de Palafrugell

Palamós

La Platja d'Aro

S'Agaro

Lloret de Mar

Blanes

Tossa del Mar

A68

N230

N234

NII

NII

Montblanch

Aremys
de Mar

N332

Sitges

Barcelona

Tarragona

N420

N211

N211

Miami
Playa

N400

N330

Vinaroz

Cuenca

Peñiscola

A7

Burriana

N234

NIII

N320

Valencia

N430

N430

N340

Rugat

N330

N330

Calpe

A7

Villajoyosa

Alicante

Murcia

N301

N340

N301

C

N332

Turre

Menorca

Valldemossa

Deya

Cala Ratjada

Mallorca

**Islas Baleares
(Balearic Islands)**

Ibiza

D

Mediterranean Sea

ANDORRA

Ordino

Canillo

Soldeu

Arinsal

Encamp

Les Escaldes

**Andorra
La Vella**

Sant Julia de Loria

RUSSIA

Nordkinn

Hammerfest

Tromsø

Sandnes

Bodø

Oulo

Gulf of Bothnia

Strömsund

Norwegian
Sea

A

B

C

D

5

5

4

21

98

88

98

88

83

95

93

E79

E4

8

13

18

19

5

4

93

E75

88

B

Jyväskyla
14
23
4
9
6
23
8
Pori
7
9
8
Tampere
6
M5
Riihimäki
Turku
HELSINKI
(HELSINGFORS)
Espoo
M1

Gulf of Finland

D

Baltic Sea

Visby

Fårjestaden

STOCKHOLM
Värmdö
Dalarö
Uppsala
E4
E75
70
Mora
81
Tälberg
E18
Örebro
Norrköping
E4
Söderköping
E66
70
Karlstad
E18
E3
Karlsborg
Hjo
Jönköping
Toftaholm
30
Kristianstad
E62
40
Helsingborg
Malmö
OSLO
E6
Tanumshede
Halmstad
Ringebu
Lillehammer
Göteborg
(Gothenburg)
DENMARK
E68
Geilo
Sölvorn
E76
Kristiansand
Loen
Skei I Jolster
Utne
Voss
Balestrand
gen
anger

North Sea

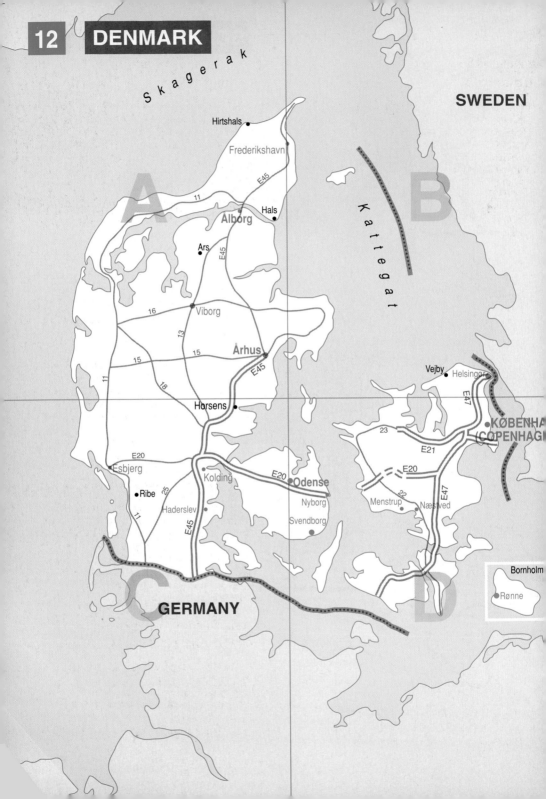

S k a g e r a k

SWEDEN

Hirtshals

Frederikshavn

E45

11

K a t t e g a t

Hals

Ålborg

Ars

E45

Vejby

Helsingør

Viborg

16

13

15

15

Århus

E47

E45

15

KØBENHA
(COPENHAG

11

18

23

Horsens

E21

E20

E20

Esbjerg

E20

Odense

Menstrup

22

E47

Kolding

Ribe

25

Nyborg

Næstved

Haderslev

Svendborg

11

E45

GERMANY

Bornholm

Rønne

A

Terschelling Ameland

Dokkum
A31 Leeuwarden N355 A7 Winschoten
Groningen

B

Waddenzee

Texel

N9

IJsselmeer

N32

N34

N802

N50

N35

A28

A50

A6

A1

AMSTERDAM Harderwijk Hengelo
Noordwijk Ermelo

A4 A2

S. Gravenhage Bos en Duin
(Den Haag) Utrecht A12 Arnhem

GERMANY

Hoek Van Holland Delft A13 A20
Rotterdam A15

A29 Nijmegen
Dordrecht

Oosterschelde N59 A16 A27 S' Hertogenbosch A73
Breda N65 N2 N271

Bergen op A58 A58 A67
Zoom Eindhoven

Veterschelde Sluis C A2 D

Westerschelde

BELGIUM

Born Valkenburg
Maastricht A76

N273

A2

DENMARK

North

Sea

Helgoländer

Bucht

Flensburg
Oeversee
Kiel
Bu

Schleswig

St-Peter-Ording

Büsum

A210

Kiel

A7

A215

A404

Bad Bramstedt

A21

Meldorf

Kaltenkirch

A404

Cuxhaven

A23

A27

Bederkesa

73

Hamburg

A

Bremerhaven

74

A25

Waldenzee

Emden

Wiesmoor

A31

A28

A1

Lüneburg

A31

70

A29

Bremen

Oyten

A27

A7

213

A1

Wildeshausen

Walsrode

Haselünne

51

Asendorf

3

Celle

6

A352

3

NETHERLANDS

Bad
Bentheim

Petershagen

Hannover

Osnabrück

Minden

Braunschwe
(Brunswick

Tecklenburg

Bad Oeynhausen

549

A30

A2

Blomberg

217

Hameln

A39

Salzgitter-Bad

Gosla

Münster

A43

64

Warendorf

A1

Detmold

1

Schwalenberg

3

Seesen

Bocholt-Barlo

A43

70

A31

Hamm

Rheda-
Wiedenbrück

Paderborn

D

Isselburg

A57

A2

Gelsenkirchen

Essen

Dortmund

A33

A7

27

Nörten-Harden

Oberhausen

Bochum

A44

A2

A430

A43

Hagen

Krefeld

Mülheim

Willingen

Kassel

80

Düsseldorf

A46

Wuppertal

Lüdenscheid

55

Winterberg

Baunatal

Bad Sooden
Allendorf

München-
gladbach

Remscheid

Halver-
Carthausen

Attendorn

Schmallenberg

7

Spangenberg

Wassenberg

A1

Köln (Cologne)

A4

Reichshof

A49

Bad
Hersfeld

Kerpen

A4

Bad Laasphe

3

A4

Eschweiler

Eisenach

Aachen

Stolberg

Bonn

Bad Honnef

A45

Stadt Allendorf

BELG.

A1

A61

A48

Bad Neuenahr

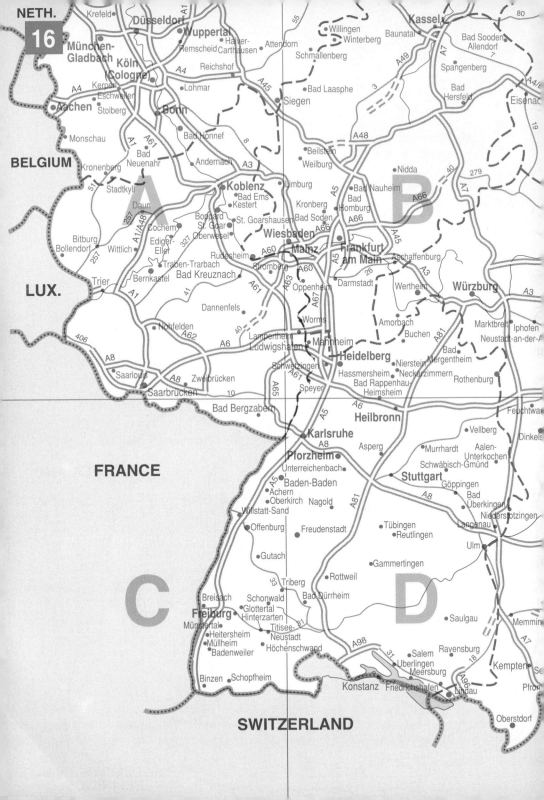

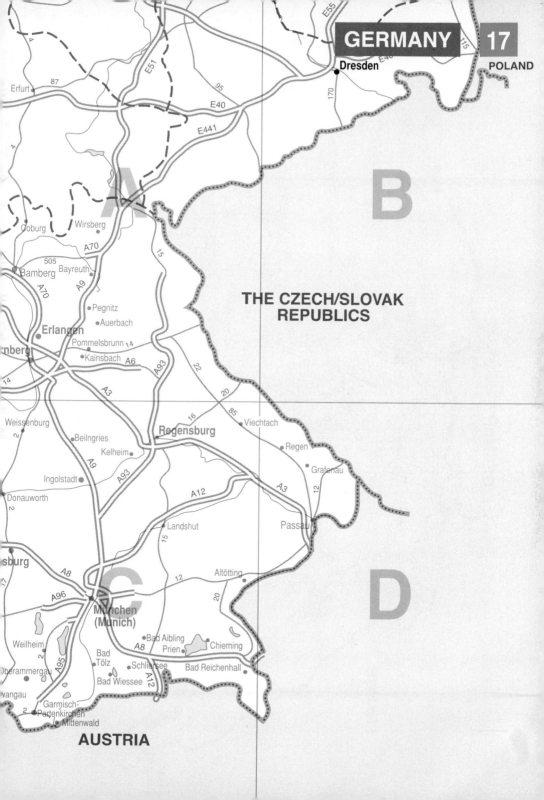

POLAND

Dresden

THE CZECH/SLOVAK
REPUBLICS

B

Erfurt

Coburg

Wirsberg

A70

505

Bamberg

Bayreuth

A70

A9

Pegnitz

Auerbach

Erlangen

Pommelsbrunn

Kainsbach

A6

A93

nberg

A3

Weissenburg

Beilngries

Kelheim

Regensburg

Viechtach

Regen

Grafenau

Ingolstadt

A9

A93

Donauworth

A12

Landshut

Passau

A

C

D

sburg

A8

A96

München
(Munich)

A8

Altötting

Weilheim

A95

Bad
Tölz

Bad Aibling

Prien

Schliersee

Chieming

Bad Reichenhall

Oberammergau

Bad Wiessee

A12

vangau

Garmisch-
Partenkirchen

Mittenwald

AUSTRIA

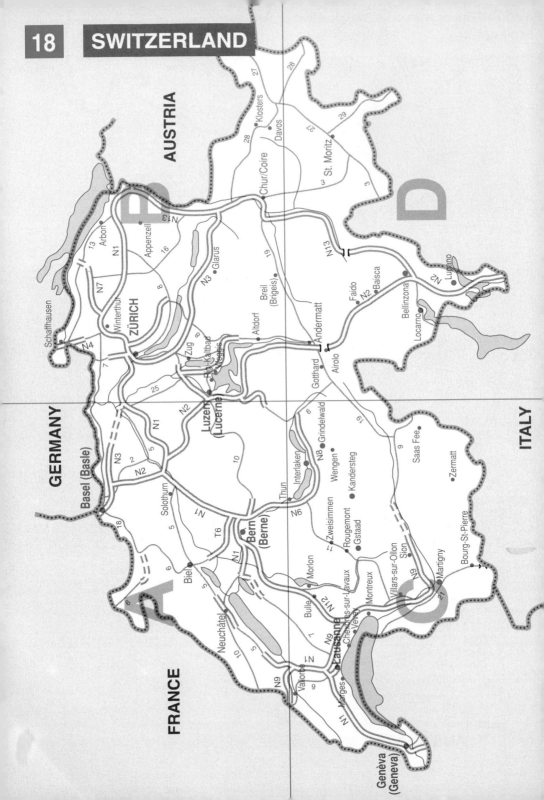

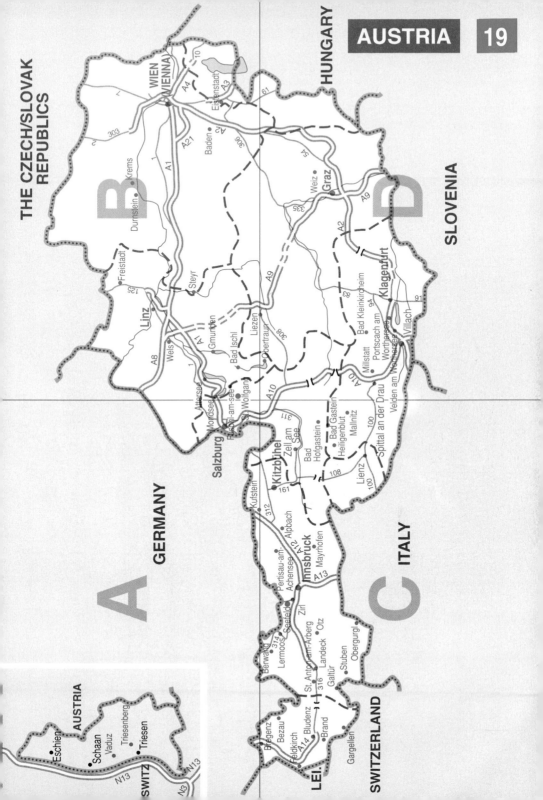

THE CZECH/SLOVAK REPUBLICS

HUNGARY

SLOVENIA

GERMANY

ITALY

SWITZERLAND

A **B** **C** **D**

WIEN VIENNA

Eisenstadt

A4
A3
61
A2
306
5A
Baden
A21
303
Krems
Dürnstein
1
A1
Weiz
Graz
335
A9
Freistadt
Steyr
A9
83
Bad Kleinkircheim
9A
Klagenfurt
91
125
Linz
Wels
A8
308
Millstatt
Pörtschach am
Wörthersee
Velden am Wörthersee
Villach
A1
1
Gmunden
Bad Ischl
Obertraun
Liezen
Attersee
Mondsee
Fuschl-am-see
St Wolfgang
Salzburg
A410
311
A410
A10
Spittal an der Drau
Zell am
See
Bad
Hofgastein
Bad Gastein
Heiligenblut
Mallnitz
100
Kitzbühel
161
Lienz
100
108
Kufstein
312
Alpbach
A12
Mayrhofen
Pertisau-am-
Achensee
Innsbruck
A13
Zirl
Seefeld
St Anton-am-Arberg
Ötz
Berwang
Lermoos
314
Landeck
Galtür
316
Obergurgl
Stuben

SWITZERLAND

LEI.

AUSTRIA
SWITZ
Eschen
Schaan
Vaduz
Triesenberg
Triesen
N13
N3

Bregenz
Bezau
Feldkirch
114
Bludenz
Brand
Gargellen

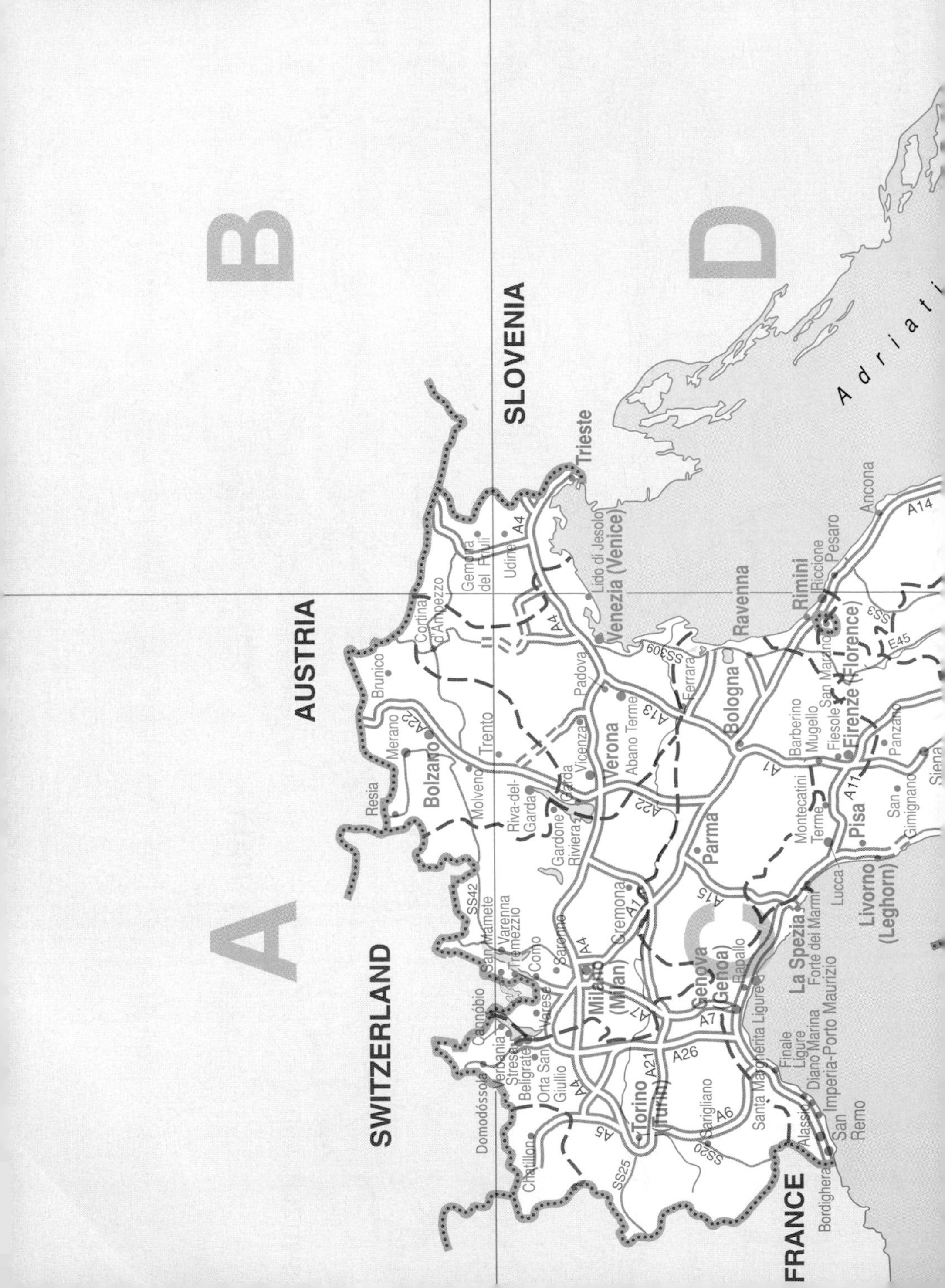

B

D

SLOVENIA

AUSTRIA

Adriati

A d r i a t i

Trieste

Udine A4

Gemona
del Friuli

Cortina
d'Ampezzo

Lido di Jesolo

Venezia (Venice)

Ancona

A14

Ravenna

Rimini

Riccione

Pesaro

Brunico

A4

Padova

Ferrara

SS309

Bologna

San Marino

A1

E45

SS3

Merano

Trento

Vicenza

Verona

A13

Fiesole

Firenze (Florence)

E45

Resia

Bolzano

A22

Molveno

Abano Terme

Barberino
Mugello

Panzano

Riva-del-
Garda

A22

Montecatini
Terme

San
Gimignano

Siena

AUSTRIA

SWITZERLAND

SS42

Gardone
Riviera

Lucca

Pisa

A11

Livorno
(Leghorn)

San
Miniato

Varenna
Tremezzo

Salòrne

A4

Cremona

A1

A15

Forte dei Marmi

Como

A1

La Spezia

Campóbio

Milano
(Milan)

Genova
(Genoa)

Banallo

Santa Margherita Ligure

Verbánia
Stresa

Orta San
Giulillo

A7

A7

Finale
Ligure

Diano Marina

Domodóssola

Varese

A4

Chátillon

A21

A26

Torino
(Turin)

A6

Sarigliano

Alassio

San Imperia-Porto Maurizio

Remo

SS25

A5

SS20

Bordighera

FRANCE

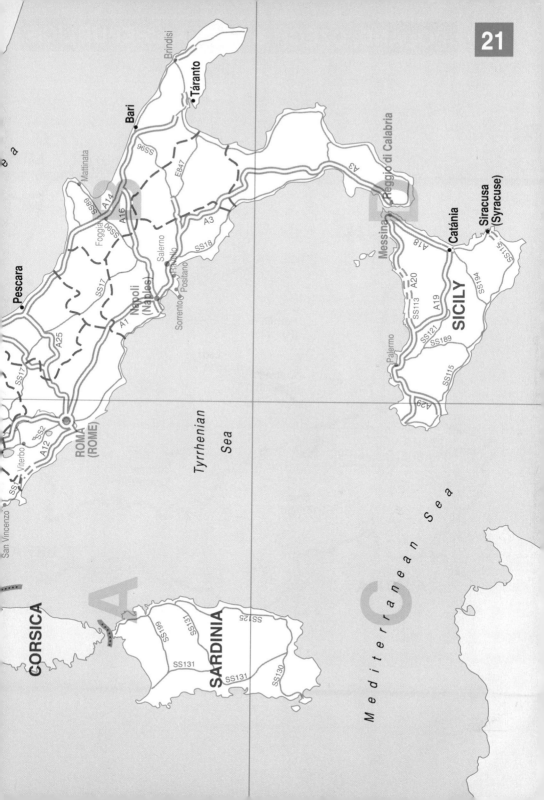

Brindisi

Táranto

Bari

Mattinata

96SS

E847

Reggio di Calabria

A3

Siracusa
(Syracuse)

Messina

Catánia

SICILY

SS114

A20

A18

SS113

A19

SS194

Palermo

SS121

SS189

A29

SS115

SS86

A14

A16

SS90

Foggia

Salerno

SS18

A3

Pescara

SS17

Napoli
(Naples)

Ravello

Positano

Sorrento

A1

A25

**ROMA
(ROME)**

A12

SS2

Viterbo

SS1

San Vincenzo

*Tyrrhenian
Sea*

M e d i t e r r a n e a n   S e a

CORSICA

SARDINIA

SS199

SS131

SS125

SS131

SS131

SS130

Baltic Sea

A

B RUSSIA LITH.

Szczecin

6

E28

GERMANY

10

E65

E261

E30

Poznan
(Posen)

E30

WARSZAWA
(WARSAW)

BEL.
RUS.

E30

Lodz

E67

E75

Lublin

E40

Wroclaw
(Breslau)

E77

E67

Karlovy
Vary

PRAHA
(PRAGUE)

D10

C

Kraków
(Cracow)

E40

E50

D5

26

D11

D1

Brno
(Brünn)

E77

D

UKRAIN

E55

D2

D61

66

AUSTRIA

HUNGARY

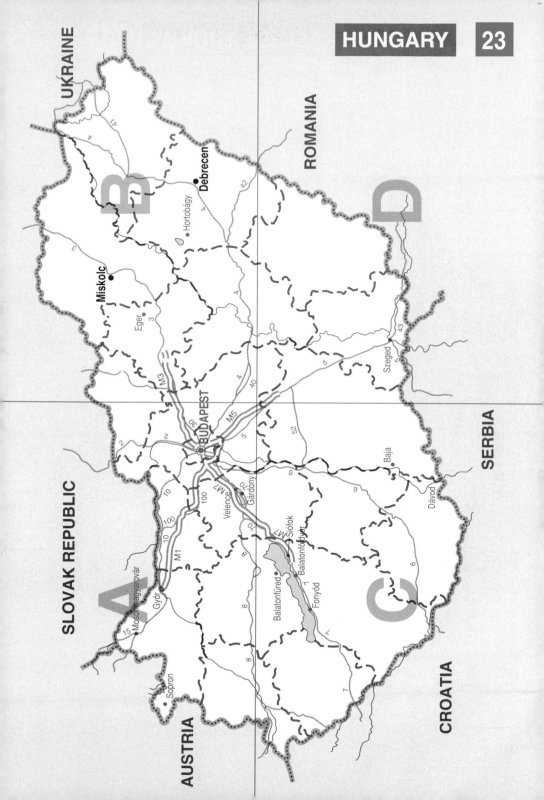

UKRAINE

ROMANIA

SERBIA

CROATIA

SLOVAK REPUBLIC

AUSTRIA

Debrecen

Hortobágy

Miskolc

Eger

BUDAPEST

Szeged

Baja

Dávod

Gárdony

Velence

Siófok

Balatonföldvár

Balatonfüred

Fonyód

Mosonmagyaróvár

Győr

Sopron

B

D

A

C

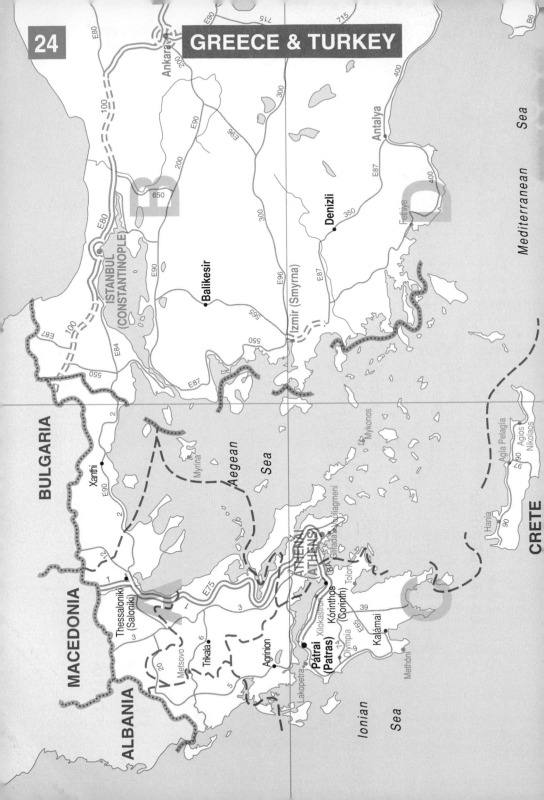

GREECE & TURKEY

Ankara

715

715

B6

E90

E80

E90

E96

400

Antalya

E87

200

100

200

300

E87

400

650

Fethiye

ISTANBUL (CONSTANTINOPLE)

E90

E87

350

Denizli

300

E96

Balıkesir

565

Izmir (Smyrna)

565

550

E84

E87

550

Mediterranean

Sea

100

E80

E87

100

2

BULGARIA

Xanthi

E90

2

Aegean

Sea

Myrina

Mykonos

Agia Pelagia

Agios Nikolaos

E90

E97

Hania

90

CRETE

1

2

Thessaloniki (Saloniki)

Metsovo

3

20

Trikala

6

Agrínion

E75

3

Vouliagmeni

ATHENS (ATHENS)

Tolon

1A

E65

39

Kalámai

Córinthos (Corinth)

Xilokastron

Pátrai (Patras)

Olympia

1A

9

Lakopetra

Methóni

MACEDONIA

ALBANIA

5

Ionian

Sea

RAC

YOUR CHANCE
TO BECOME AN
RAC/**Canon** RESORT REVIEWER

Every year people write to us telling us about holidays they have enjoyed in resorts they chose from RAC guides.

We enjoy reading the letters we receive and the comments people make on their holidays, and this year we've decided to make *reporting back* on your holiday more fun!

In association with Canon we're offering you the chance to have your Resort Review published in the 1995 RAC Hotels in Europe, Hotels in France or European Camping and Caravanning Guide and the chance to win a Canon E300 Camcorder or one of two runners-up prizes of Canon cameras – an EOS 500 camera or a Sureshot Mini.

HOW TO ENTER

To enter is quite simple – all you have to do is write a brief review (no more than 150 words) of a resort, camp site or hotel you stayed in that is featured in this guide.

When you've compiled your review, which must be legible, send it, either on or attached to the report form on the reverse of this page, to

RAC/CANON Europe Resort Review Competition
PO Box 100
South Croydon
Surrey
CR2 6XW

The closing date for receipt of entries is 31/10/94. An RAC/Canon panel of judges will select the winning entries no later than 14/11/94. Winners will be notified by post no later than 18/11/94.

Rules

1   Entries must be on or attached to an official entry form.
2   No correspondence can be entered into and there can be no cash alternative to prizes.
3   Not open to employees of the RAC or Canon UK Ltd.
4   Judges' decision is final.
5   Only open to entrants aged 18 and over.

We regret that we cannot return any entries. All entries become copyright of RAC Enterprises and we reserve the right to edit any published entries.

Please complete the following and return with your entry

Name

Address

Telephone number

RAC

HOTELS
IN EUROPE

HOTEL REPORT 1994

The publisher of this guide welcomes your comments about any hotels visited that appear in this guide. Whatever your experience good, indifferent or poor, do write to RAC Publishing expressing your views.

Hotel name
_____

Town
_____

Dates of your stay
_____

Please tick the appropriate box

	Yes	No
Did any of the hotel staff speak English?	☐	☐
Did the hotel have a restaurant?	☐	☐
Was the bed comfortable?	☐	☐
Was the hotel quiet?	☐	☐
Were the parking facilities adequate?	☐	☐

	Good	Poor		Good	Poor
Was the service	☐	☐	Was the food	☐	☐

Hotel report
_____

_____

_____

_____

_____

_____

_____

_____

_____

HOTELS
IN EUROPE
HOTEL RECOMMENDATION 1994

The publisher of this guide welcomes your suggestions for hotels which might be included in future editions of this guide.

Hotel name
_____

Address
_____
_____
_____

Telephone   Fax number
_____

Dates of your stay
_____

Reason for suggestion
_____
_____
_____
_____
_____
_____
_____
_____
_____
_____

Please return to: The Editor, RAC Hotels in Europe,
RAC Publishing, RAC House,
PO Box 100, South Croydon,
Surrey CR2 6XW

EUROPEAN MOTORING GUIDE 1994

EVERY MINUTE SAVED CROSSING THE CHANNEL IS A MINUTE LONGER IN FRANCE.

Next May Eurotunnel's Le Shuttle service will start to run between Folkestone and Calais. As the crossing will only take 35 minutes, you will be able to travel from motorway to autoroute in just 60 minutes.

Which means less time savouring the delights of the Channel and more time savouring the Loire, the Dordogne, the Beaujolais...

To find out more about Le Shuttle, please phone 0345 353535. Calls charged at local rate, lines open 24 hours, 7 days a week.

le Shuttle

EURO TUNNEL

Easy come. Easy go.

CONTENTS

THE INTERNATIONAL SIGN FOR OIL

Castrol

These signs are in general use in Europe

- Priority Road
- End of priority
- Intersection (priority rule applies)
- Intersection with tramway
- Approaches to level crossings
- Use of audible warning devices prohibited

AUSTRIA

 Diversion
 Tram turns at yellow or red
 Federal road with priority
 Federal road without priority
 Buses only
 U-turn compulsory

BELGIUM

 Turn right or left
 No parking from 1st to 15th of month
 No parking from 16th to end of month

BULGARIA

 U-turn allowed
 Road for private cars

DENMARK

 Sight-seeing
 Maximum weight of vehicle or trailer
 Compulsory slow lane
 Recommended speed in a bend
 Traffic merges
 Diversion due to road works

FINLAND

 8-18 Prohibition applies between 0800 and 1800 hrs Mon-Sat

FRANCE

 SERREZ A DROITE — Keep well over to the right
 Bus lane
 No parking from 1st to 15th of month
 No parking from 16th to end of month
 Fortnightly parking on alternate sides
 Relief route
 Holiday route

GERMANY

 Transit route
 Danger sudden fog patches

 Diversion
 Tram or bus stop
 U22 Emergency diversion for motorway traffic
 70-110 km Recommended speed range

HUNGARY

 Route for heavy vehicles
 Miskolc Diversion
 Lane reserved for buses from 0700 to 1900 hrs

ITALY

 Use chains or snow tyres from Km 174
 Traffic in parallel lanes

 Lane reserved for slow vehicles
 Restricted parking
 Overtaking by vehicles with trailers prohibited
 No entry for pedestrians
 Stop when meeting public transport bus on mountain road
 Easily inflammable forest

NETHERLANDS

 End of built-up area
 Crossing for cyclists and moped riders
 Compulsory route for vehicles with dangerous goods

NORWAY

 B 2,2m — B road (width and axle weight limits)
 Tunnel
 Parking 2 hrs from 0800-1700 hrs
 Sone Parking 2 hrs from 0800-1800 hrs (1600 hrs Sat.)
 Parking prohibited (upper panel) Allowed (lower)
 Sight-seeing
 Road merges (black lane priority)

PORTUGAL & SPAIN

 End of parking prohibition
 70 Recommended maximum speed

 Take care (yellow or white triangle)
 Tourist office — TURISMO
 Turning permitted
 No entry
 Compulsory lane for motorcycles
 Easily inflammable forest

SWEDEN

Maximum weight on double axle
Passing place (on narrow roads)
Tunnel

SWITZERLAND

Tunnel (lights compulsory)
Heavy coaches prohibited
Motorway
Semi-motorway
Flashing red light (level crossing)
Alternately flashing lights (level crossing)
Parking disc compulsory
Trailers prohibited
Postal vehicles have priority

PREPARING FOR THE JOURNEY

DOCUMENTS

Before a journey, allow plenty of time to arrange for the preparation of all necessary documents - passports, visas, driving licences, Green Cards, insurances and vaccinations.

The RAC will give advice on what documents are required for which countries; remember to ask about countries visited in transit as well as your destination country.

The following information applies only to British Subjects holding, or entitled to, a Foreign Office passport bearing the inscription "United Kingdom of Great Britain and Northern Ireland". Non-British citizens travelling in Europe should apply to their Embassy, Consulate or High Commission for information if in doubt.

PASSPORTS

A current passport should be held by each member of the family. Parents may have children registered on their passport if they are under 16 years old although youngsters will require their own passport when travelling on school excursions abroad.

A child cannot use its parent's passport and a wife may not travel without her husband on his passport if she is included on his passport.

The price of a full EC 'common format passport' is £15 for a 30-page, and £30 for a 94-page passport. Both last for ten years. Two photographs of not more than 63mm x 50mm (2^1/2in x 2in) are required and a doctor, lawyer, MP or someone of similar standing who has known you for not less than two years should sign the back of one of them. They should also countersign the form. The two photographs, the completed application form together with the applicable fee should then be sent to: Passport Office, Clive House, 70 Petty France, London SW1H 9HD, or to the appropriate Passport Office depending on where you live. Most main post offices stock passport application forms and have a list of Passport Office locations and addresses. The alternatives to a full passport are:

(1) A British Visitor's passport. It is obtainable from main post offices and is valid for Western Europe only. It is valid for one year only. Two passport-size photographs are required.

(2) A British Excursion Document for visits to France of not more than 60 hours at any one time. One passport-size photograph is required, countersigned as for a full passport. It costs £3. The document is valid for one month only and is available from main post offices.

VISAS

At the time of going to press, British nationals need a visa for **Bulgaria**, **the CIS**, **Latvia**, **Romania** and **Turkey**. Visa regulations are subject to change however, and it is advisable to contact the Consulate of the appropriate country well in advance of your departure date.

Non-UK passport holders should check the visa requirements with the appropriate Embassy/Consulate of the countries to be visited.

WORK PERMITS

Should the stay abroad exceed three months, or if repeated visits are made, or if employment is being sought (even on a temporary basis), a work permit may be required.

DRIVING LICENCES

A valid, full driving licence should be carried by all motorists in Europe. Most European countries recognise a UK driving licence, although reference should be made to the appropriate country in the *Europe by Country* section of this guide.

An International Driving Permit (IDP) is normally required in those countries where a UK licence is not recognised. Valid for one year, this is an internationally recognised document available for drivers holding a valid, full licence and aged 18 or over. The IDP currently costs £3 and application forms are available from the RAC Travel Service, ☎ 0800-550055. A passport-size photograph is required, in addition to a current driving licence.

If a locally registered vehicle is hired in the CIS, Algeria or Morocco, an IDP is required.

Holders of non-UK licences requiring an IDP must apply to the relevant licensing authority or motoring organisation in the country in which the licence was issued. In Europe people under 18 are not normally permitted to drive. Your driving licence should be carried with you at all times as it must be produced at once, on demand; there is no discretionary period as in the UK.

EC format 'pink/green' licences are issued to new drivers and when a 'green' licence is returned for amendment by the UK authorities. They cannot be issued purely for the purpose of European travel.

MOTOR INSURANCE

International Motor Insurance Certificate (Green Card)

Motor vehicle insurance for minimum Third Party risks is compulsory in Europe. This is provided by most UK and Eire policies covering all EC countries and certain other European countries. Unless your insurer is notified that you are travelling in Europe, your Comprehensive Insurance may be automatically reduced to Third Party Cover. You are strongly recommended to take out an International Motor Insurance through your motor insurer and to carry a 'Green Card'. This is not a legal requirement, but it provides effective comprehensive insurance. You should contact your insurers for advice and to ensure that you are adequately covered.

A Green Card is compulsory in **Andorra** and in certain eastern European countries. A Green Card is strongly recommended for travel in **Spain**, **Portugal**, **Italy** and **Greece**. Your Green Card should be valid for both the European and Asian sectors when travelling in **Turkey**. When taking a caravan abroad you should check with your insurance company that your policy covers towing

a caravan in Europe as you may have to pay an extra premium.

A bail bond is strongly recommended for **Spain** and this is available from your motor insurers, or by taking out the RAC's Eurocover Motoring Assistance which includes £1,500 bail bond cover.

VEHICLE REGISTRATION DOCUMENT

A vehicle registration document must be carried when driving a UK-registered vehicle abroad. If the document is in the process of being replaced at the time of travelling, a free Certificate of Registration (V379) can be applied for at your local Vehicle Registration Office. This is internationally recognised in lieu of the registration document and should be carried with you.

Should the vehicle not be registered in your name, eg a company car, written authority for you to use it should be obtained from its owner. A special form of authority should be used in this case when travelling in Portugal and this can be obtained from the RAC.

Taking a hired or leased vehicle abroad requires a Vehicle on Hire/Lease Certificate (VE 103) as the vehicle registration document is held by the leasing company. The VE 103 can be obtained from the RAC.

LOSS OF DOCUMENTS

Should any of the above documents be lost or stolen, immediately notify the nearest police station; inform the RAC and the National Club of the country concerned.

Foreign Customs can enforce payment of duty in lieu of evidence of export if your vehicle is stolen or destroyed by fire. Indemnity covering this is provided for under the RAC Eurocover Motoring Assistance providing that reasonable security measures have been taken.

MEDICAL REQUIREMENTS

No inoculations or vaccinations are required for travel to most European countries unless an infectious disease suddenly breaks out. For southern Mediterranean countries typhoid and paratyphoid vaccinations are recommended by British Health Authorities. Frequent travellers should keep up their inoculations, and a valid vaccination certificate should be produced when travelling into another country from one where there is, or has been, an outbreak of cholera.

When making travel arrangements, the Department of Health, Hannibal House, Elephant and Castle, London SE1 6TE, can assist with information about foreign health regulations should you be in doubt. As some inoculations require two doses with a time lapse in between, checks on requirements should be done well in advance. RAC Eurocover Personal Protection covers all medical expenses when travelling abroad and also offers a repatriation scheme.

If you have not taken out Eurocover Personal Protection cover, Form E111 covers at least some part of the cost of medical treatment in EC countries. The leaflet 'Health Advice for Travellers' (Ref. T4) gives information about the Form E111 and how to obtain medical treatment in the EC. It is obtainable from post offices. Form E111 is not required in Denmark, Portugal or Gibraltar, where a UK passport should be presented instead.

ESSENTIAL ACCESSORIES

RAC Travel Centres can supply most of the accessories which are useful or helpful when travelling in Europe.

FIRE EXTINGUISHERS

A fire extinguisher is an essential accessory for all vehicles travelling in **the CIS**, **Greece** or **Turkey**. It is strongly recommended that a fire extinguisher is carried at all times.

FIRST AID KIT

A First aid kit must be carried on all vehicles travelling in **Austria**, **Bulgaria**, **the CIS**, **Czech and Slovak Republics**, **Greece**, **Slovenia** and **Turkey**, but advisable in all countries at all times.

GB PLATE

A distinctive nationality plate must be displayed near the rear number plate as a legal requirement in all countries. It must have black letters on a white background and conform to a certain regulatory size as do those issued by the RAC.

HEADLAMPS

Headlamp beams should be adjusted before driving on the right. A headlamp conversion kit makes this an easy task as it contains specially shaped adhesive black plastic, which alters the direction of the beam when stuck to the glass. Don't forget to remove the beam converters on returning to the UK.

Carry spare bulbs of the correct wattage for your lights as they may be difficult to obtain abroad. In Spain and certain other countries it is compulsory to carry a spare set of bulbs.

WARNING TRIANGLES

You must carry a warning triangle in **Austria**, **Belgium**, **Bulgaria**, **the CIS**, **Czech and Slovak Republics**, **Denmark**, **France**, **Germany**, **Greece**, **Hungary**, **Italy**, **Luxembourg**, **Netherlands**, **Poland**, **Portugal**, **Romania**, **Slovenia** and **Switzerland**. It is advisable to carry one if visiting **Finland**, **Norway** or **Sweden**. Two are necessary if travelling through **Cyprus** or **Turkey**, and **Spain** (if the vehicle has 9 or more seats or weighs over 3,500kg).

Where to position the warning triangle
Warning triangles must be placed on the road at the rear of a vehicle (not a motorcycle) which has broken down on an open road at night, in poor visibility during the day, or on a bend in the road or on a hill. Different countries have different regulations as to how far away from the car the warning triangle should be placed if you need to use it. The table shows specific distances required.

	Distance behind vehicle	Minimum visible distance	Distance from kerb
Austria		100m	1m
Belgium	30m (road) 100m (m'way)	50m	
Greece	100m	110m	
Italy Finland Switzerland	50m (road) 150m (m'way)	110m	
France Luxembourg Netherlands Norway Portugal Spain Sweden	30m	100m	
Germany	100m (road) 200m (m'way)	100m	
(Former) Yugoslavia	50m	100m	1.5m

TACHOGRAPH

A tachograph is an essential fitment to all UK-registered vehicles travelling in the EC and constructed and equipped to carry ten or more people including the driver. Please refer to your local Department of Transport Traffic Area Office for further information.

PREPARING YOUR CAR

Even well-maintained cars can break down without any warning, but some simple preventive maintenance before you contemplate a long journey can minimise the chances of an unexpected road-side stop.

The main causes of breakdowns are the ignition/electrical system closely followed by the fuel and cooling systems. Preventive maintenance and inspection prior to your journey is quite a simple task and can help avoid the inconvenience and worry associated with a breakdown. Mechanical faults however are another matter, and when a major one occurs – either in the engine, gearbox or axle – a road-side repair is usually not practicable.

BATTERY

The main problems with the battery are usually associated with the two electrical connections to the battery terminals. When corrosion occurs the green or white powder fungus growing on the terminal can prevent power getting from the battery to the starter motor. Even though the connections may appear clean on the exterior, it is advisable to remove the terminal connector and clean the contact surfaces with a wire brush or emery paper. In order to prevent recurrence of corrosion, apply a smear of petroleum jelly to the connections before they are re-made and again afterwards to cover all outermost surfaces of the connector and battery terminal.

Another common cause for the starter motor not working, apart from the obvious flat battery, is the battery earth lead connection not making proper contact with the body or chassis of the vehicle. If this is the problem, remove the connector and clean as with the main battery terminals.

Check both battery cables and any earth straps for breakage or fraying (this usually occurs at the terminal ends) and replace if necessary. Finally, check the level of the battery electrolyte – that is the fluid inside the battery – which should be just above the battery plates. If the battery plates are exposed, top up using distilled water. Some batteries are sealed for life and topping up is not possible.

Safety tips

Never smoke whilst working in the vicinity of the battery as it could be giving off an explosive gas. Also, when disconnecting or reconnecting the live battery terminal, be very careful not to allow the spanner to contact any metalwork of the car. This could give you a bad burn or even worse the resulting spark could cause a battery to explode.

To be on the safe side, always remove the battery earth cable first – that is the one connected to the bodywork, chassis or engine – and reconnect it last.

IGNITION SYSTEM

Before attempting to carry out any checks or adjustments on any part of the ignition system, you must ensure that the ignition is switched off.

Contact points*

Remove the distributor cap and this will expose the contact points. The contact points are the most common cause of breakdown in the ignition system. If the contact point faces appear badly pitted or burnt then they will require replacing or cleaning.

The contact point *gap* is also critical, this can close up after a period of time. Contact point gaps vary from one model to another so consult your vehicle handbook. To check and adjust the contact point gap, it is necessary to rotate the engine until one of the lobes on the distributor cam has pushed the moving arm of the contact points to its fullest open position. Using a feeler gauge, make any adjustment to the gap by slackening the contact breaker retaining screw or screws and move the position of the contact points relative to the distributor base plate. This can usually be best achieved by placing a screwdriver between the adjustment notches and turning. Adjust the contact point gap until the feeler gauge will just fit between the contact points. Lock the adjusting screw and re-check the gap as sometimes the setting can alter when the retaining screw is tightened.

*not electronic ignition systems

Distributor cap

The distributor cap is another potential problem area. Carry out the following simple checks:
(1) Check the H. T. leads are secure in the cap.
(2) Make sure the distributor cap is free from any oil residue, dirt or moisture both inside and outside.
(3) Examine the rotor arm and distributor cap very closely both inside and outside for any hairline cracks or tracking caused by the H. T. current.

(4) Whilst the distributor cap is removed, check the centre connector. This should protrude far enough to contact the rotor arm when the cap is replaced. If the carbon brush is badly worn then a replacement cap will be needed.

H.T. leads

The H.T. leads are the thick cables coming out of the distributor cap. Any breakdown either in the conductive centre, the insulation or at the connections will cause faulty operation of the ignition system. First, wipe the outer insulation material clean and examine for cracking or deterioration. Check the connectors at both ends for security and cleanliness.

Remember that the H.T. leads to the spark plugs must be fitted in the correct positions; if the leads become mixed up, the car will not start. It is a good idea to number the leads to assist you in correct re-installation. Alternatively, only remove one H.T. lead at a time. Modern vehicles are fitted with carbon core type leads which can break down internally. This type of lead can be properly tested only by an auto electrician.

Coil connections

The coil is the source of power for the ignition system and it is vital that the connections for the two low-tension wires either side of the main H.T. lead are both secure and clean. Also, check the main H.T. lead to ensure this is secure. Examine the plastic top of the coil for any hairline cracks or tracking caused by the H.T. current short-circuiting and replace if need be. Finally ensure the coil top is clean of grease, dirt or damp.

FUEL SYSTEM

It is far more difficult to anticipate a breakdown in the fuel system although some simple checks can be carried out to minimise the risk.
(1) Examine any rubber fuel pipes for age cracking, softening, leakage and make sure they are secure at the connections.
(2) Most vehicle fuel systems will incorporate a fuel filter or dirt trap to prevent any debris being transmitted through the fuel lines to the carburettor. Ensure that the periodic checks detailed in the vehicle handbook are carried out – usually either cleaning or replacement.
(3) Check around the carburettor gasket joints, jet assemblies, and feed pipes for any evidence of fuel leakage. Rectification may

require the services of a specialist.
(4) The efficiency of the engine will greatly depend upon the correct mixture setting for the carburettor. With modern carburettors, this can be checked and reset only by a properly equipped workshop. Excessive exhaust emissions now constitute a legal offence.

COOLING SYSTEM

The efficiency of the engine cooling system is vital when contemplating a continental touring holiday as the climatic conditions and terrain may impose greater strains upon it.

Check the radiator to ensure it is free from external blockage or restrictions. Remove any debris such as leaves, paper or accumulated dirt. Inspect all the rubber coolant hoses for signs of age cracking, bulges (particularly adjacent to the securing clips) and check tightness of hose clips, although avoid overtightening as this will cut into the hose material.

When topping up the cooling system, it is advisable to do so with the recommended anti-freeze solution as anti-freeze contains a corrosion inhibitor to minimise corrosion build-up.

Check the fan belt for fraying, general deterioration or excessive glazing on the V-shape drive surfaces which may promote slip. If there is more than half an inch of free play on the belt's longest run, then some adjustment is required.

Safety tips

If the fan belt has not been replaced during the preceding 12 months then it is a good idea to replace it to avoid any possible inconvenience should it fail. Keep the old fan belt in the boot as a 'get you home' spare.

If your fan belt does break then this will be signalled by the generator/ignition warning light lighting up and an increased reading on the water temperature gauge if one is fitted. The car should be stopped immediately and the belt replaced, in order to minimise damage to the engine.

Finally, do not forget other parts of the vehicle that can break down and cause you considerable inconvenience. Tyres should be checked for condition, tread depth and pressure (see page 10 for notes on the care and use of tyres). Check the exhaust system for condition and security. Last, but certainly not least, check the braking system. If you do not feel competent to do so, call in the experts.

Firestone

TYRES

PRESSURE

Tyre pressures should be checked weekly, using a reliable gauge, and corrected as necessary. Pressure tests and correction of pressure should be made with the tyres cold and not after a period of running. It may be necessary to increase pressures because of loading or high speeds, particularly in hot countries (refer to the vehicle handbook). Both car and tyre manufacturers provide details of correct pressures for various types of driving condition. Under-inflation is a frequent cause of tyre failure.

TREAD DEPTH

By law, you must maintain a tread pattern of at least 1.6mm in one continuous band across three-quarters of the tread and around the entire circumference of each tyre. It is advisable to ensure that your spare tyre also complies with this regulation.

ALIGNMENT

Wheel alignment should be checked when abnormal front tyre wear is noted, and after even a minor front-end collision.

SHOCK ABSORBERS

Worn shock absorbers can affect the stability of a car and the life of the tyres. Shock absorbers should be checked visually for oil leaks, and by bouncing the appropriate corner of the car, and replaced when necessary.

WHEEL BALANCE

Wheels should be balanced whenever a tyre is changed or when vibration or wobble becomes apparent.

TYRE DAMAGE

Tyres can be damaged easily by nails, sharp stones, kerbs etc. Avoid brushing against kerbs – this can damage the sidewalls. If you have to drive up a kerb, do so slowly and at as near a right angle as possible to minimise any damage. Inspect tyres regularly; remove any stones or nails lodged in the tread.

It is illegal to drive on a tyre which has a break in its fabric, or a cut over 1 inch long and deep enough to reach the body cords.

TYRE LIFE

Maximum tyre life is largely in the driver's hands, although chassis design and maintenance also play a part. Prolonging tyre life usually means that the performance of the car cannot be exploited to its full extent; thus the driver can choose between obtaining maximum performance from the car or maximum life from the tyres.

Tyre life can be prolonged by: taking corners easily; avoiding high average speeds, especially on rough surfaces; avoiding rapid acceleration and/or violent braking; keeping brakes properly adjusted; avoiding damage by oil, grease, petrol, paraffin etc; maintaining correct pressures.

USEFUL INFORMATION

BOATS

It is a good idea to obtain a Certificate of Registration when temporarily importing a boat into Europe. The Small Ships Register, operated by DVLA, covers ships below 24 metres in length. Records include name, owner's details, description of the vessel, and details of make or class. The cost is £10 for a 5-year registration. Details may be obtained from: Small Ships Register, DVLA, Swansea, SA99 1BX, ☎ 0792-783355.

If you are considering taking a boat to the Continent it is advisable to contact the Royal Yachting Association, RYA House, Romsey Road, Eastleigh, Hants S05 4YA, ☎ 0703- 629962, for information on documentation and regulations.

BUSINESS TRAVEL

If your journey involves the carrying of samples, exhibition goods etc, further advice should be obtained from RAC Travel Information at Croydon, ☎ 0345-333222.

CAR TELEPHONES/CB RADIOS

The use of car telephones and CB radios is restricted in most European countries; contact the RAC or your supplier for further guidance.

FOREIGN CURRENCY

There is no limit on the amount of sterling or foreign currency that may be taken out of the country. It is obviously safer to carry the bulk of your money in travellers' cheques, but it is advisable to have a small amount of cash in the currency of the first country you will be visiting, especially if you are staying there overnight or travelling over a weekend. Major credit cards are widely accepted throughout Europe, and Eurocheques and Eurocheque cards provide a valuable facility for payment and cash withdrawal.

Large sums of currency should be declared to Customs when entering any country - including Britain.

PHRASE BOOKS

It can be very useful to have a phrase book when travelling on the Continent. Knowledge of the particular language is not necessary as most contain a guide to pronunciation and you can always point to a phrase in the book. You should expect it to cover all the situations you are likely to find yourself in, eg at Customs posts, shopping, using public transport. Concise pocket-sized phrase books are available from RAC Publishing, ☎ 0235-834885.

NATIONAL TOURIST OFFICES

ANDORRA

Andorran Delegation, 63 Westover Road, London SW18 2RF. ☎ 081-874 4806

AUSTRIA

Austrian National Tourist Office, 30 St George Street, London W1R 0AL. ☎ 071-629 0461

BELGIUM

Belgian National Tourist Office, Premier House, 2 Gayton Road, Harrow HA1 2XU. ☎ 081-861 3300

BULGARIA

Bulgarian National Tourist Office, 18 Princes Street, London W1R 7RE. ☎ 071-499 6988

CIS

Intourist Travel Ltd, Intourist House, 219 Marsh Wall, London E14 9FJ. ☎ 071-538 5965

CYPRUS

Cyprus Tourism Organisation, 213 Regent Street, London W1R 8DA. ☎ 071-734 9822

CZECH AND SLOVAK REPUBLICS

Czedok Tours & Holidays (London) Ltd, 49 Southwark Street, London SE1 1RU. ☎ 071-378 6009

DENMARK

Danish Tourist Board, 169-173 Regent Street, London W1R 8PY. ☎ 071-734 2637/8

FINLAND

Finnish Tourist Board, 66-68 Haymarket, London SW1Y 4RF. ☎ 071-839 4048

FRANCE

French Government Tourist Office, 178 Piccadilly, London W1V 0AL. (Personal or postal enquiries only.)

GERMANY

German National Tourist Office, Nightingale House, 65 Curzon Street, London W1Y 7PE. ☎ 071-495 3990

GIBRALTAR

Gibraltar Information Bureau, Arundel Great Court, 179 The Strand, London WC2R 1EH. ☎ 071-836 0777/8

GREECE

National Tourist Organisation of Greece, 4 Conduit Street, London W1R 0DJ. ☎ 071-734 5997

HUNGARY

Danube Travel Agency, 6 Conduit Street, London W1R 9TG. ☎ 071-493 0263

ITALY

Italian State Tourist Office, 1 Princes Street, London W1R 8AY. ☎ 071-408 1254

LUXEMBOURG

Luxembourg National Trade and Tourist Office, 122 Regent Street, London W1R 5FE. ☎ 071-434 2800

MONACO

Monaco Government Tourist and Convention Office, 3-18 Chelsea Garden Market, Chelsea Harbour, London SW10 0XE. ☎ 071-352 9962

NETHERLANDS

Netherlands Board of Tourism, 25-28 Buckingham Gate, London SW1E 6LD. ☎ 0891-200277 (calls charged 48p per minute peak period, 36p per minute off peak). Mailing address: PO Box 523, London SW1E 6NT

NORWAY

Norwegian National Tourist Office, Charles House, 5-11 Lower Regent Street, London SW1Y 4LR. ☎ 071-839 6255

POLAND

Polorbis Travel Ltd, 82 Mortimer Street, London W1N 7DE. ☎ 071-637 4971/2 or 071-636 8024

PORTUGAL

Portuguese National Tourist Office, 22-25a Sackville Street, London W1X 1DE. ☎ 071-494 1441

REPUBLIC OF IRELAND

Irish Tourist Board, 150 New Bond Street, London W1Y 0AQ. ☎ 071-493 3201

ROMANIA

Romanian National Tourist Office, 17 Nottingham Street, London W1M 3RD. ☎ 071-224 3692

SLOVENIA

Kompas International, Moghul House, 57 Grosvenor Street, London W1X 9DA. ☎ 071-499 7488

SPAIN

Spanish National Tourist Office, 57-58 St James's Street, London SW1A 1LD. ☎ 071-499 0901

SWEDEN

Swedish Travel and Tourism Council, 73 Welbeck Street, London W1M 8AN. ☎ 0891-200277 (calls charged 48p per minute peak period, 36p per minute off peak)

SWITZERLAND

Swiss National Tourist Office, Swiss Centre, New Coventry Street, London W1V 8EE. ☎ 071-734 1921

TURKEY

Turkish Embassy Information Counsellor's Office, 170 Piccadilly, London W1V 9DD. ☎ 071-734 8681

As a number of tourist offices now request a fee to cover postage, it is advisable to enclose a minimum of 50p or £1 with your written enquiries.

Over a million motorists can't be wrong

Over a million motorists
now insure their vehicles
with Eagle Star.

Talk to the RAC Insurance Service
to find out more about our
competitive rates, swift accident
repair and free foreign travel cover.

BRITISH DIPLOMATIC ADDRESSES

ALBANIA

(see Italy, Roma)

ANDORRA

(see Spain, Barcelona)

AUSTRIA

1030 Wien (Vienna)
EMBASSY
Jaurèsgasse 12
☎ (01) 7131575/9
CONSULATE
Jaurèsgasse 10
☎ (01) 756117/8

6923 Bregenz
CONSULATE (HON)
Bundesstrasse 110
☎ (05574) 38586 or 38611

8010 Graz
CONSULATE (HON)
Schmiedgasse 8-12
☎ (0316) 826105

6021 Innsbruck
CONSULATE (HON)
Matthias-Schmid Strasse 12
☎ (0512) 588320

5020 Salzburg
CONSULATE (HON)
Alter Markt 4
☎ (0662) 848133

BALTIC STATES

ESTONIA
Tallinn EE 0001
EMBASSY
Kentmanni 20
☎ (0142) 455328/9

LATVIA
226010 Riga
EMBASSY
Elizabetes Iela (3rd floor)
☎ (0132) 320737 or 325592

LITHUANIA
2055 Vilnius
EMBASSY
Antakalnio 2
☎ (0122) 222070

BELGIUM

1040 Bruxelles
EMBASSY
Rue d'Arlon 85
☎ (02) 2876211

2000 Antwerpen
CONSULATE-GENERAL
(HON)
Korte Klarenstraat 7
☎ (03) 2326940

4000 Liège
CONSULATE (HON)
rue Beeckmann 45
☎ (041) 235832

BULGARIA

Sofiya 1000
EMBASSY
Boulevard Vassil,
Levski 65-67
☎ (02) 885361/2

CIS

RUSSIA
Moskva (Moscow)
EMBASSY/CONSULATE
Sosiiskaya, Naberezhnaya
☎ 231-85-11 (8 lines)

St Petersburg
CONSULATE-GENERAL
c/o Astoria Hotel
☎ (0812) 210 5412

UKRAINE
252021 Kiev
EMBASSY/CONSULATE
Room 1008, Zhovtneva Hotel,
Ulitza Rozi Luxembourg
☎ (0044) 291 8907

CROATIA

50000 Dubrovnik
CONSULATE (HON)
Atlas, Pile 1
☎ (050) 27333

58000 Split
CONSULATE (HON)
Titova Obala 10/III
☎ (058) 41464

41000 Zagreb
EMBASSY
Ilica 12/II, PO Box 454
☎ (041) 424888 or 426200

CYPRUS

Nicosia
HIGH COMMISSION
Alexander Pallis Street,
PO Box 1978
☎ (2) 473131/7

CZECH AND SLOVAK REPUBLICS

12550 Praha (Prague)
EMBASSY
Thunovská 14
☎ (02) 533347-9

DENMARK

2100 København
EMBASSY
36-38-40 Kastelsvej
☎ 31 26 46 00

6200 Åbenrå
CONSULATE (HON)
Søndergade 24
☎ 74 62 30 85

9200 Ålborg
CONSULATE (HON)
Stationsmestervej 85
☎ 98 18 16 00

8100 Århus
CONSULATE (HON)
Havnegade 8
☎ 86 12 88 88

6700 Esbjerg
CONSULATE (HON)
Kanalen 1
☎ 75 13 05 11

7000 Fredericia
CONSULATE (HON)
Vesthavnen,
PO Box 235
☎ 75 92 20 00

7400 Herning
CONSULATE (HON)
Orebygaardvej 3-7
☎ 97 26 88 01

5000 Odense
CONSULATE (HON)
Albanitorv 4
☎ 66 14 47 14

3700 Rønne, Bornholm
CONSULATE (HON)
Fiskerivej 1
☎ 56 95 21 11

FR-110 Tórshavn, Faroe Islands
CONSULATE (HON)
Yviri vid Strond 19,
PO Box 49
☎ 13510

FINLAND

00140 Helsinki
EMBASSY
Itainen Puistotie 17
☎ (90) 661293

40101 Jyväskylä
CONSULATE (HON)
Valmet Paper Machinery Inc.,
PO Box 587
☎ (941) 295211

48100 Kotka
CONSULATE (HON)
Port Authority of Kotka,
Laivurinkatu 7
☎ (952) 274280

70100 Kuopio
CONSULATE (HON)
Chamber of Commerce,
Kasarmikatu 2
☎ (971) 220291

90101 Oulu
CONSULATE (HON)
Rautaruukki Oy,
Kiilakiventie 1,
PO Box 217
☎ (981) 327711

28101 Pori
CONSULATE (HON)
Repola Oy, Antinkatu 2,
PO Box 69
☎ (939) 823007

33101 Tampere
CONSULATE (HON)
Oy Finlayson AB,
PL 407
☎ (931) 35222

20101 Turku
CONSULATE (HON)
Turun Kauppakamari,
Puolalankatu 1
☎ (921) 501440

65100 Vaasa
CONSULATE (HON)
Royal Vaasa Hotel,
Hovioikeudenpuistikko 18
☎ (961) 278111

FRANCE

Paris
EMBASSY
35 rue du Faubourg St Honoré,
Cedex 08,
75383 Paris
☎ (1) 42 66 91 42
CONSULATE-GENERAL
9 av Hoche,
75008 Paris
☎ (1) 42 66 38 10

64202 Biarritz
CONSULATE (HON)
Barclays Bank SA,
7 av Edward VII,
BP 98
☎ 59 24 04 60

33073 Bordeaux
CONSULATE-GENERAL
353 blvd du Président Wilson
☎ 56 42 34 13

62201 Boulogne-sur-Mer
CONSULATE (HON)
c/o Cotrama,
Tour Administrative,
Hoverport
☎ 21 87 16 80

62100 Calais
CONSULATE (HON)
c/o P & O European Ferries,
41 place d'Armes
☎ 21 96 33 76

50104 Cherbourg
CONSULATE (HON)
c/o P & O European Ferries,
Gare Maritime Sud
☎ 33 44 20 13

59383 Dunkerque
CONSULATE (HON)
c/o L Dewulf, Cailleret & Fils,
11 rue des Arbres
☎ 28 66 11 98

76600 Le Havre
CONSULATE (HON)
c/o Lloyds Register of
Shipping,
7 rue Pierre Brossolette
☎ 35 42 42 15/27 47

59800 Lille
CONSULATE-GENERAL
11 sq Dutilleul
☎ 20 57 87 90

69002 Lyon
CONSULATE-GENERAL
24 rue Childebert
☎ 78 37 59 67 (4 lines)

13006 Marseille
CONSULATE-GENERAL
24 av du Prado
☎ 91 53 43 32
(also deals with MONACO)

Nantes
CONSULATE (HON)
L'Aumarière,
44220 Couëron
☎ 40 63 16 02

06000 Nice
CONSULATE (HON)
2 rue du Congres
☎ 93 82 32 04
(also deals with MONACO)

35800 St Malo/Dinard
CONSULATE (HON)
La Hulotte,
8 av de la Libération
☎ 99 46 26 64

31300 Toulouse
CONSULATE (HON)
c/o Lucas Aerospace
Victoria Centre, Bâtiment
Didier Daurat,
20 chemin de Laporte
☎ 61 15 02 02

GERMANY

1000 Berlin 19
EMBASSY
British Embassy Berlin Office,
Hans-Braun-Strasse
☎ (030) 3091

5300 Bonn 1
EMBASSY
Friedrich-Ebert-Allée 77
☎ (0228) 234061

2800 Bremen 1
CONSULATE (HON)
Herrlichkeiten 6,
Postfach 10 38 60
☎ (0421) 59090

4000 Düsseldorf 30
CONSULATE-GENERAL
Yorck Strasse 19
☎ (0211) 9448-1
☎ (0211) 9448 238 (passports)
☎ (0211) 9448 271 (visas)

6000 Frankfurt-am-Main
CONSULATE-GENERAL
Triton Haus,
Bockenheimer Landstrasse 42
☎ (069) 170002-0

7803 Freiburg im Breisgau
CONSULATE (HON)
Buchenstrasse 4,
Gundelfingen
☎ (0761) 583117

2000 Hamburg 13
CONSULATE-GENERAL
Harvestehuder Weg 8a
☎ (040) 446071

3000 Hannover 1
CONSULATE (HON)
Berliner Allee 5
☎ (0511) 9919 100

2300 Kiel 17
CONSULATE (HON)
c/o United Baltic Corporation
GmbH, Schleuse, PO Box 8080
☎ (0431) 30632

8000 München
CONSULATE-GENERAL
Bürkleinstrasse 10
☎ (089) 211090

8500 Nürnberg
CONSULATE (HON)
c/o Schwan-Stabilo
Schwanhausser GmbH & Co.,
Maxfeld Strasse 3,
PO Box 4553
☎ (0911) 3609 520-2

7000 Stuttgart 1
CONSULATE-GENERAL
Breite Strasse 2
☎ (0711) 16269-0

GREECE

106 75 Athína (Athens)
EMBASSY
1 Ploutarchou Street
☎ (01) 7236211

841 00 Hermoupolis, Síros
VICE-CONSULATE (HON)
8 Akti Petrou Ralli
☎ (0281) 22232 or 28922

712 02 Iráklion, Crete
VICE-CONSULATE
16 Papa Alexandrou Street
☎ (081) 224012

491 00 Kérkira, Corfu
CONSULATE
2 Alexandras Avenue
☎ (0661) 30055 or 37995

Pátrai (Patras)
(post temporarily closed)

851 00 Ródhos, Rhodes
CONSULATE (HON)
11 Amerikas Street,
PO Box 47
☎ (0241) 27247 or 27306

Sámos
(post temporarily closed)

541 10 Thessaloníki
CONSULATE (HON)
8 Venizelou Street,
Eleftheria Square,
PO Box 10332
☎ (031) 278006 or 269984

382 21 Vólos
VICE-CONSULATE (HON)
4 Iolkou Street
☎ (0421) 24642

HUNGARY

Budapest V
EMBASSY
Harmincad Utca 6
☎ (1) 118 2888

ITALY

00187 Roma
EMBASSY
Via XX Settembre 80A
☎ (06) 4825441 or 4825551
(also deals with ALBANIA)

70121 Bari
CONSULATE (HON)
c/o Anglo-Italian Shipping,
Via Montenegro 19
☎ (080) 5217859

72100 Brindisi
CONSULATE (HON)
The British School,
Via de Terribile 9
☎ (0831) 568340

50123 Firenze (Florence)
CONSULATE
Palazzo Castelbarco,
Lungarno Corsini 2
☎ (055) 212594 or 284133
(also deals with SAN MARINO)

16121 Genova
CONSULATE
Via XII Ottobre 2/132
☎ (010) 564833 (3 lines)

20121 Milano
CONSULATE-GENERAL
Via San Paolo 7
☎ (02) 723001

80122 Napoli
CONSULATE-GENERAL
Via Francesco Crispi 122
☎ (081) 663511 (3 lines)

10126 Torino
CONSULATE
Corso Massimo d'Azeglio 60
☎ (011) 687832 or 683921

34100 Trieste
CONSULATE (HON)
Vicolo Delle Ville 16
☎ (040) 302884

30123 Venezia
CONSULATE
Accademia,
Dorsoduro 1051
☎ (041) 5227207 or 5227408

LUXEMBOURG

2018 Luxembourg City
EMBASSY
14 Boulevard Roosevelt,
PO Box 874
☎ 229864 (3 lines)

MALTA

Valletta
HIGH COMMISSION
7 St Anne Street,
PO Box 506,
Floriana
☎ 233134-8

NETHERLANDS

Den Haag
EMBASSY
Lange Voorhout 10
☎ (070) 3645800

Amsterdam
CONSULATE-GENERAL
Koningslaan 44,
PO Box 75488
☎ (020) 6764343

NORWAY

0264 Oslo 2
EMBASSY
Thomas Heftyesgate 8
☎ (02) 552400

6001 Ålesund
CONSULATE (HON)
Farstadgarden,
St Olavs Place,
PO Box 130
☎ (071) 24460

Bergen
CONSULATE (HON)
A/S Bergens Rørhandel,
Carl Konowsgate 34,
PO Box 872
☎ (05) 348505

9401 Harstad
CONSULATE (HON)
Strandgate 7,
PO Box 322
☎ (082) 64631

5501 Haugesund
CONSULATE (HON)
Sørhauggt 139,
PO Box 128
☎ (04) 723033

4611 Kristiansand (S)
CONSULATE (HON)
Tollbodgaten 2,
PO Box 300
☎ (042) 22439

6501 Kristiansund (N)
CONSULATE (HON)
Vageveien 7,
PO Box 148
☎ (073) 75333

4001 Stavanger
CONSULATE (HON)
Mollegate 23,
PO Box 28
☎ (04) 526020

9001 Tromsø
CONSULATE (HON)
c/o L Macks Olbryggeri,
PO Box 1103
☎ (083) 84800

7003 Trondheim
CONSULATE (HON)
Sluppenveien 10,
PO Box 6004
☎ (07) 968211

POLAND

00556 Warszawa
EMBASSY
Aleje Roz 1
☎ (2) 6281001

PORTUGAL

1200 Lisboa
EMBASSY
Rua de San Domingos à Lapa
35-37
☎ (1) 3961191 or 3961147

9000 Funchal, Madeira
CONSULATE (HON)
Avenida de Zarco 2,
PO Box 417
☎ 21221

9500 Ponta Delgada, São Miguel, Azores
CONSULATE (HON)
Largo Vasco Bensaúde 13
☎ (096) 22201

8500 Portimão
CONSULATE (HON)
Rue de Santa Isabel 21
(1st Floor)
☎ (82) 27057

4100 Porto
CONSULATE
Avenida da Boavista 3072
☎ (2) 684789

ROMANIA

70154 Bucharest
EMBASSY
24 Strada Jules Michelet
☎ (0) 120303 (4 lines)

SERBIA

11000 Beograd (Belgrade)
EMBASSY/CONSULATE
Generala Zdanova 46
☎ (011) 645034/43/55/87

SLOVENIA

Ljubljana
EMBASSY

SPAIN

Madrid 4
EMBASSY
Calle de Fernando el Santo 16
☎ (91) 3190200 (12 lines)
CONSULATE-GENERAL
Centro Colon,
Marques de la Ensenada 16
(2nd floor)
☎ (91) 3085201

11202 Algeciras
VICE-CONSULATE
Avenida de las Fuerzas,
Armadas 11
☎ (956) 661600/04

03001 Alicante
CONSULATE
Plaza Calvo Sotelo 1/2-1,
Apartado de Correos 564
☎ (96) 5216190 or 5216022

Arrecife, Lanzarote
CONSULATE (HON)
Calle Rubicón No 7
☎ (28) 815928

08036 Barcelona
CONSULATE-GENERAL
Edificio 'Torre de Barcelona',
Avenida Diagonal 477
(13th floor)
☎ (93) 4199044 (8 lines)
(also deals with ANDORRA)

48008 Bilbao
CONSULATE-GENERAL
Alameda de Urquijo 2-8
☎ (94) 4157600 or 4157711

07800 Ibiza, Ibiza
VICE-CONSULATE
Avenida Isidoro Macabich 45,
Apartado 307 (1st floor)
☎ (71) 301818 or 303816

35007 Las Palmas, Gran Canaria
CONSULATE
Edificio Cataluna,
C/Luis Morote 6
(3rd floor)
☎ (28) 262508

29001 Málaga
CONSULATE
Edificio Duquesa,
Calle Duquesa de Parcent 8
☎ (952) 217571 or 212325

07002 Palma, Mallorca
CONSULATE
Plaza Mayor 3D
☎ (971) 712085 or 712445

San Luis, Menorca
VICE-CONSULATE (HON)
Torret 28
☎ (971) 151536

38003 Santa Cruz, Tenerife
CONSULATE
Plaza Weyler 8
(1st floor)
☎ (22) 286863 or 286653

39004 Santander
CONSULATE (HON)
Paseo de Pereda 27
☎ (942) 220000

41001 Sevilla
CONSULATE
Plaza Nueva 8-B
☎ (95) 4228875

43004 Tarragona
CONSULATE (HON)
Calle Real 33
(1st floor)
☎ (977) 220812

36201 Vigo
CONSULATE (HON)
Plaza de Compostela 23
(6th floor),
PO Box 49
☎ (986) 437133

SWEDEN

S-115 27 Stockholm
EMBASSY
Skarpögatan 6-8
☎ (08) 6670140

S-411 05 Göteborg
CONSULATE-GENERAL
(HON)
Götgatan 15
☎ (031) 151327

S-951 88 Luleå
CONSULATE (HON)
SCAB Tunnplåt AB
☎ (0920) 92000

S-211 39 Malmö
CONSULATE (HON)
Gustav Adolfs Torg 8C
☎ (040) 115525

S-851 88 Sundsvall
CONSULATE (HON)
SCA Timber AB
☎ (060) 193203

SWITZERLAND

3005 Bern 15
EMBASSY
Thunstrasse 50
☎ (031) 445021/6

1211 Genève 20
CONSULATE-GENERAL
37-39 rue de Vermont
(6th floor)
☎ (022) 7343800

6900 Lugano
CONSULATE (HON)
Via Motta 19, Via Nassa 32
☎ (091) 238606

Montreux
VICE-CONSULATE (HON)
La Chaumiére,
13 chemin de l'Aubousset,
1806 St Legier,
Vaud
☎ (021) 9433263

8008 Zürich
CONSULATE-GENERAL
and Directorate of British
Export Promotion
Dufourstrasse 56
☎ (01) 2611520-6
(also deals with LIECHTEN-STEIN)

TURKEY

Ankara
EMBASSY
Sehit Ersan Caddesi 461/A,
Cankaya
☎ (4) 1274310/15

Antalya
CONSULATE (HON)
Ucgen Mahallesi,
Dolaplidere Caddesi,
Pirilti Sitesi,
Kat 1 Kilit Sauna Karsisi
☎ (31) 177000/02

Bodrum
CONSULATE (HON)
Iren Sitesi (Turgutreis Road)
No. 13
☎ 4932 or 2343

Iskenderun
CONSULATE (HON)
c/o Catoni Maritime Agen-
cies, Maresal Cakmak
Caddesi 28
☎ 30361-3

Istanbul
CONSULATE-GENERAL
Mesrutiyet Caddesi No. 34,
Tepebasi, Beyoglu, PK 33
☎ 2447540 or 2447545

Izmir
VICE-CONSULATE
1442 Sokak No. 49,
Alsancak, PK 300
☎ 635151

48700 Marmaris
CONSULATE (HON)
c/o Yesil Marmaris Tourism
and Yacht Management Inc.,
Barbaros Caddesi No. 118
Marina, PO Box 8
☎ 16486-8

Mersin
VICE-CONSULATE (HON)
c/o Catoni Maritime Agen-
cies SA, Mersin Orta Okulu
Sokak 3/B,
Cakmak Caddesi
☎ 12728 or 34078

THE OLAU EXPERIENCE
BEYOND COMPARISON

- Luxury car ferry line • Sheerness, Kent to Vlissingen, Holland •
- Short breaks and mini-cruises to Holland • Direct access to European motorway network •
- Competitive prices • Ring Sheerness on (0795) 666666 for details •
- Olau Line (UK) Ltd., Sheerness, Kent ME12 1SN •

SHEERNESS (KENT) ⇌ VLISSINGEN (HOLLAND)

5% DISCOUNT ON ALL FARES FOR RAC MEMBERS

FERRY PORTS

GETTING THERE

FERRY ROUTES

BELGIUM

Ramsgate-Oostende 4 hr Sally Ferries (Ostend line) – up to 6 per day
Felixstowe-Zeebrugge (day) 5¾hr, (night) 8-9 hr P & O European Ferries – 2 per day
Hull-Zeebrugge 14 hr North Sea Ferries –1 per day

DENMARK

Harwich-Esbjerg 19½ hr Scandinavian Seaways – up to 3 per week
Newcastle-upon-Tyne-Esbjerg 19 hr Scandinavian Seaways – 2 per week (June-Sept only)

FRANCE

Dover-Calais 1½ hr Stena Sealink – up to 26 per day; 1¼ hr P & O European Ferries – up to 25 per day
Dover-Calais 35/50 min Hoverspeed Hovercraft/Seacat – up to 14 per day
Folkestone-Boulogne 55 mins Hoverspeed Seacat – up to 11 per day
Newhaven-Dieppe 4 hr Stena Sealink – up to 4 per day
Plymouth-Roscoff 6 hr Brittany Ferries – up to 3 per day
Poole-Cherbourg 4¼ hr Brittany Ferries (Truckline) – up to 4 per day
Portsmouth-Caen 6 hr Brittany Ferries – up to 3 per day
Portsmouth-Cherbourg (day) 4 hr, (night) 6½-7½ P & O European Ferries – up to 3 per day
Portsmouth-Le Havre (day) 5¾ hr, (night) 8¼ hr P & O European Ferries – up to 3 per day
Portsmouth-St Malo 9 hr Brittany Ferries – 1 per day
Ramsgate-Dunkerque 2½ hr Sally Ferries – 5 per day
Southampton-Cherbourg (day) 5 hr, (night) 8 hr Stena Sealink – up to 2 per day

Services from Ireland:
Cork-Cherbourg 17½ hr Irish Ferries – up to 1 per week
Cork-Le Havre 21½ hr Irish Ferries – up to 1 per week
Cork-Roscoff 13½ hr Brittany Ferries – up to 4 per week
Rosslare-Cherbourg 17-18½ hr Irish Ferries – up to 3 per week
Rosslare-Le Havre 21 hrs Irish Ferries – up to 3 per week

GERMANY

Harwich-Hamburg 20½ hr Scandinavian Seaways – 3-4 per week
Newcastle-upon-Tyne-Hamburg 23½ hr Scandinavian Seaways – 2 per week (summer only)

NORTHERN IRELAND

Cairnryan-Larne 2¼ hr P & O European Ferries – up to 6 per day
Stranraer-Larne 2 hr 20 min Stena Sealink – up to 9 per day

REPUBLIC OF IRELAND

Fishguard-Rosslare 3½ hr Stena Sealink – up to 2 per day
Holyhead-Dublin 3½ hr B & I Line – 2 per day
Holyhead-Dun Laoghaire 2 hr 50 min Stena Sealink – Sea Lynx/Ferry – up to 8 per day
Pembroke Dock-Rosslare 4¼ hr B & I Line – up to 2 per day
Swansea-Cork 10 hr Swansea Cork Ferries – up to 6 per week

NETHERLANDS

Harwich-Hoek van Holland (day) 6½ hr, (night) 10 hr Stena Sealink – 2 per day
Hull-Rotterdam (Europoort) 13-14 hr North Sea Ferries – 1 per day
Sheerness-Vlissingen (Flushing) 7-8½ hr Olau Line – 2 per day

NORWAY

Newcastle-upon-Tyne-Bergen 21¼-25½ hr Color Line – up to 3 per week
Newcastle-upon-Tyne-Stavanger 19-29½ hr Color Line – up to 3 per week

SPAIN

Plymouth-Santander 22-24 hr Brittany Ferries – up to 2 per week
Portsmouth-Santander (winter only) 30½ hr Brittany Ferries – 1 per week
Portsmouth-Bilbao 28½ -30 hr P & O European Ferries – 2 per week

SWEDEN

Harwich-Göteborg 24 hr Scandinavian Seaways – 2 per week
Newcastle-upon-Tyne-Göteborg 21-23 hr Scandinavian Seaways – 1 per week (June-Aug only)

THE CHANNEL TUNNEL AND FERRY PORTS

THE CHANNEL TUNNEL

The Channel Tunnel opens officially in 1994. Passenger shuttle services from the terminals near Folkestone and Calais are scheduled to begin on 5 May 1994.

Frequency and Fares

In the early years of operation, passenger vehicle shuttles will depart at approximately 15-minute intervals during peak periods and 20-minute intervals at other times during the day. At night the minimum frequency will be one shuttle per hour. Fares for the crossing were due to be announced in January 1994.

En Route

Payment will be made at toll booths, and both British and French Customs and Immigration formalities will be carried out prior to boarding.

The Journey

Vehicles will load from the rear of Le Shuttle, and drive forward until directed to park in one of the carriages. During the 35-minute journey, car passengers will be free either to stay in their cars or walk around the air-conditioned carriage. Motorcyclists will park their motorcycles in a special section of the shuttle and travel in separate passenger compartments. Progress information will be relayed throughout the journey.

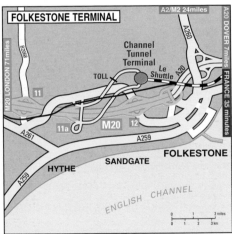

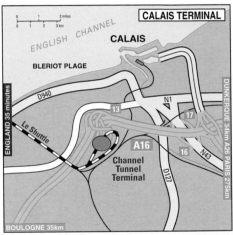

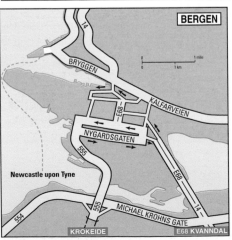

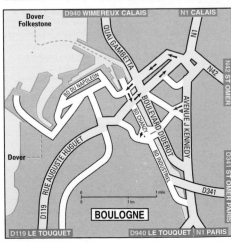

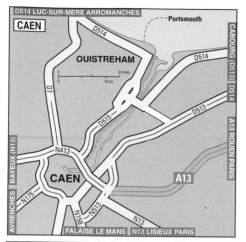

CAEN

D514 LUC-SUR-MERE ARROMANCHES — Portsmouth
OUISTREHAM
D514
D514
CABOURG (D513) D514
D515
D513
D7
A13 ROUEN PARIS
BAYEUX (N13)
N413
CAEN
A13
AVRENCHES
N175
N513
N158
N13
FALAISE LE MANS | N13 LISIEUX PARIS

CHERBOURG

NEZ DE JOBURG (D901)
Southampton
Weymouth
Portsmouth
Rosslare
R DE L'ABBAYE — AVE CESSART
RUE E LIAIS
RUE E ZOLA
Q DE CALIGNY
AVENUE BRIAND
RUE DU VAL DE SAIRE
ST PIERRE-EGLISE (D901)
BARNEVILLE-CARTERET (D940)
MAL LECLERC
D3
QUAI DE ALEX. III
AVENUE A LEMONNIER
PL JAURES
N13 BAYEUX ST LÔ

CAIRNRYAN

A77 BALLANTRAE GIRVAN
Larne
KIRKOLM
CAIRNRYAN
A718
A77
A751
A75
A75 DUMFRIES
STRANRAER
A77
GLENLUCE
A75
A77
A716
B7084
A747
Portpatrick
A716 DRUMMORE

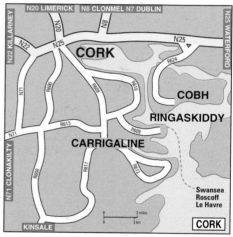

N20 LIMERICK | N8 CLONMEL N7 DUBLIN
N22 KILLARNEY
N20
N8
N25
N25
N25 WATERFORD
CORK
N22
R609
R624
N71
R610
COBH
R613
R609
RINGASKIDDY
N71 CLONAKILTY
N71
R600
CARRIGALINE
R611
R612
R610
Swansea
Roscoff
Le Havre
KINSALE
CORK

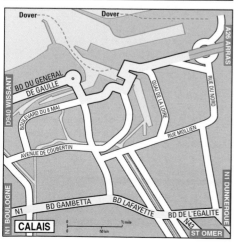

Dover — Dover
A26 ARRAS
BD DU GENERAL DE GAULLE
QUAI DE LA LOIRE
RUE DU NORD
D940 WISSANT
BOULEVARD DU 8 MAI
RUE MOLLIEN
AVENUE DE COUBERTIN
N1 BOULOGNE
N1
BD GAMBETTA
BD LAFAYETTE
BD DE L'EGALITE
N1 DUNKERQUE
N43
ST OMER
CALAIS

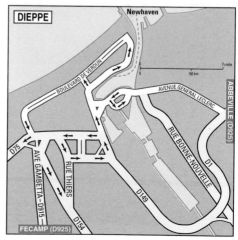

DIEPPE

Newhaven
BOULEVARD DE VERDUN
AVENUE GENERAL LECLERC
ABBEVILLE (D925)
RUE BONNE-NOUVELLE
D75
AVE GAMBETTA
RUE THIERS
D1
D149
AVE GAMBETTA - D915
D154
FECAMP (D925)

23

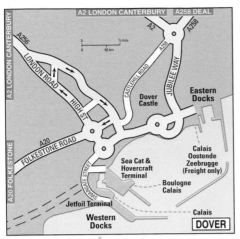

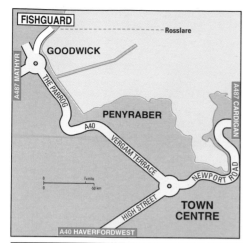

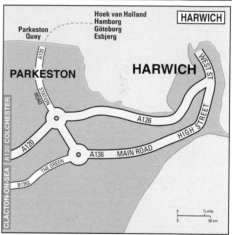

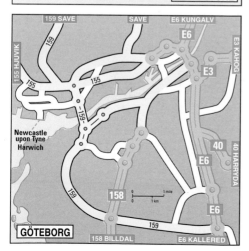

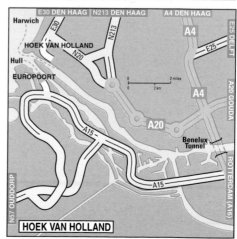

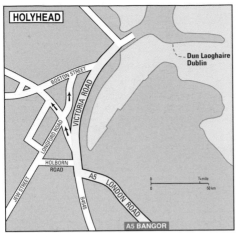

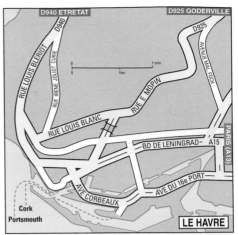

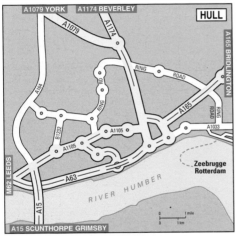

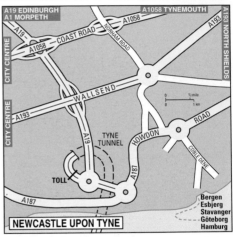

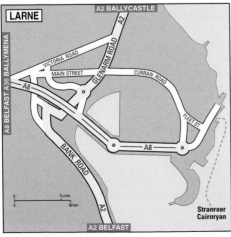

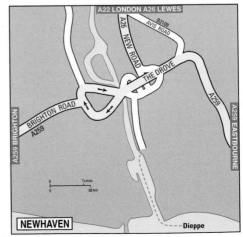

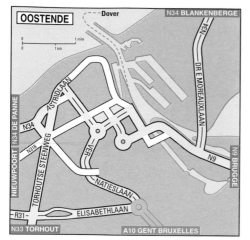

OOSTENDE

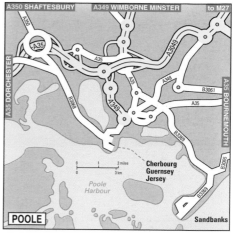

POOLE

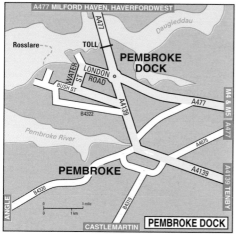

PEMBROKE DOCK

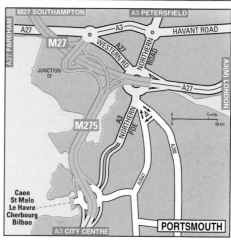

PORTSMOUTH

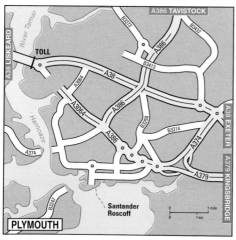

PLYMOUTH

RAMSGATE

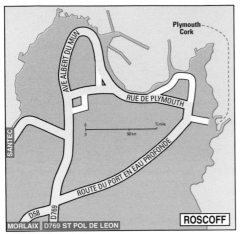

ROSCOFF

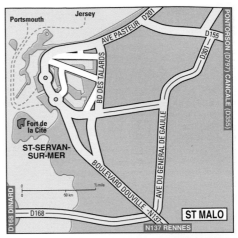

ST MALO

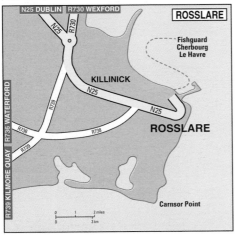

ROSSLARE

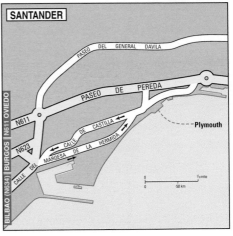

SANTANDER

ROTTERDAM

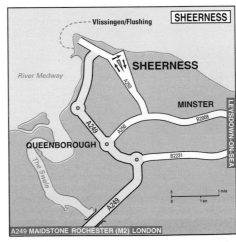

SHEERNESS

SOUTHAMPTON

SWANSEA

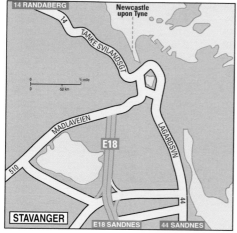

STAVANGER

VLISSINGEN/FLUSHING

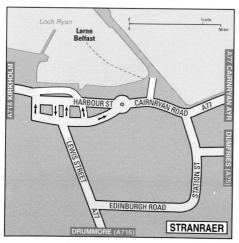

STRANRAER

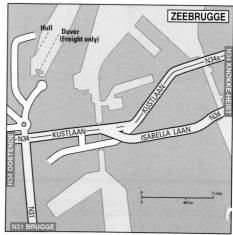

ZEEBRUGGE

DISTANCES FROM FERRY PORTS TO MAJOR EUROPEAN CITIES

	Santander	Roscoff	St Malo	Cherbourg	Caen	Le Havre	Dieppe
Amsterdam	945	609	502	472	403	361	299
Athína (Athens)	1590f	1621f	1521f	1520f	1448f	1420f	1446f
Avignon	536	695	593	648	577	548	544
Barcelona	435	767	682	750	669	745	741
Berlin	1282	999	842	814	742	701	645
Bern	843	667	563	567	462	470	460
Bilbao	65	615	529	597	580	612	630
Bordeaux	268	405	319	388	370	402	420
Brindisi	1440	1472	1391	1373	1304	1274	1266
Bruxelles	823	540	384	354	283	241	180
Den Haag	924	585	477	449	377	336	275
Dijon	665	515	415	414	342	314	310
Firenze (Florence)	946	1035	932	936	859	831	827
Genève	741	656	556	553	485	455	451
Genova	799	889	793	789	721	692	690
Gibraltar	648	1258	1172	1240	1216	1255	1273
København	1383f	1044f	937f	907f	832f	795f	734f
Köln (Cologne)	923	648	493	464	394	352	300
Lisboa	526	1153	1068	1135	1118	1151	1168
Luxembourg	857	574	474	454	383	355	291
Lyon	597	544	445	509	437	409	405
Madrid	237	847	761	829	811	844	862
Milano	876	857	757	756	682	652	651
München	1134	852	756	736	661	638	584
Nantes	475	197	117	197	184	247	270
Napoli	1232	1323	1223	1222	1150	1122	1118
Nice	680	846	746	797	726	698	693
Oslo	1746f	1406f	1299f	1268f	1201f	1158f	1095f
Paris	631	352	252	224	153	124	107
Porto	398	1033	948	1016	998	1031	1048
Praha (Prague)	1292	996	892	872	803	774	720
Roma	1111	1201	1104	1100	1028	1000	996
Stockholm	1770f	1430f	1323f	1293f	1224f	1181f	1119f
Strasbourg	928	645	545	525	454	426	372
Valencia	443	898	812	880	862	958	952
Venezia	1037	1013	910	914	846	817	815
Wien (Vienna)	1409	1135	1031	1010	943	913	859

f - includes a ferry crossing. These mileages are those by a good practicable route and are given as a guide only. It must not be expected that the mileage of a route provided by the RAC will necessarily coincide with the distance quoted here.

Calais*	Oostende	Rotterdam (Europoort)	Vlissingen (Flushing)	Hamburg	Esbjerg	Göteborg	Bergen	
229	176	66	128	289	451	616f	916f	Amsterdam
1482f	1403f	1428f	1403f	1493f	1660f	1844f	2125f	Athína (Athens)
609	622	691	638f	838	1000	1192f	1465f	Avignon
864	876	946	893f	1093	1255	1447f	1720f	Barcelona
581	523	450	495	180	347	411f	812f	Berlin
480	474	501	476	569	739	921f	1198f	Bern
751	763	863	780f	1129	1291	1486f	1760f	Bilbao
541	553	654	571f	921	1082	1273f	1547f	Bordeaux
1334	1255	1278	1339	1346	1510	1694f	1975f	Brindisi
128	70	106	89	370	531	723f	996f	Bruxelles
211	153	33	80	315	477	670f	942f	Den Haag
357	369	435	386f	582	744	935f	1209f	Dijon
897	826	849	914	913	1083	1265f	1592f	Firenze (Florence)
515	527	600	577	670	832	1022f	1297f	Genève
751	725	748	813	810	980	1162f	1445f	Genova
1394	1406	1506	1423f	1772	1934	2126f	2399f	Gibraltar
664f	611f	523f	568f	199f	166f	157f	702f	København
258	204	174	177f	263	425	615f	890f	Köln (Cologne)
1290	1301	1401	1318f	1668	1829	2021f	2294f	Lisboa
261	208	233	210	379	541	733f	1006f	Luxembourg
470	482	553	499f	700	862	1053f	1327f	Lyon
983	995	1095	1012f	1361	1523	1715f	1988f	Madrid
718	641	664	729	729	892	1074f	1361f	Milano
591	554	524	525	484	650	835f	1115f	München
420	432	531	449f	800	960	1152f	1425f	Nantes
1184	1116	1139	1209	1204	1371	1555f	1836f	Napoli
759	771	841	788f	988	1158	1385f	1712f	Nice
1031f	974f	888f	909f	551f	420f	199	312f	Oslo
180	193	294	212f	562	732	914f	1241f	Paris
1170	1181	1281	1199f	1548	1776	1067f	2294f	Porto
722	659	608	661	412	582	764f	1091f	Praha (Prague)
1062	995	1018	1078	1084	1254	1436f	1715f	Roma
1050f	997f	913f	933f	574f	511f	360	665f	Stockholm
384	344	368	346	441	611	476f	1120f	Strasbourg
1075	1087	1157	1104f	1304	1520	1702f	2029f	Valencia
876	818	786	817	805	975	1157f	1484f	Venezia
858	795	735	797	713	879	1065f	1392f	Wien (Vienna)

* Distances from Boulogne and Dunkerque are much the same as from Calais, except for those in a north-easterly direction; Dunkerque is approximately 25 miles from Calais.

MOTORAIL

There are a number of advantages to travelling by Motorail including savings on petrol and on autoroute tolls, plus avoiding wear and tear on your vehicle and the stress of an arduous drive.

Motorail services are available from Boulogne, Calais and Dieppe among Channel ports; Paris, Lille and Bruxelles are some of the other starting points. The following list shows some popular destinations and the approximate journey times.

AUSTRIA

Bruxelles-Salzburg, 12 hr.
Bruxelles-Villach, 15 hr.
Calais-Innsbruck, 13½-14 hr.

FRANCE

Calais-Avignon, 11½-13½ hr.
Calais-Biarritz, 13½ hr.
Calais-Bordeaux, 11½ hr.
Calais-Brive, 9-10 hr.
Calais-Fréjus, 15-15½ hr.
Calais-Narbonne, 13¼-14½ hr.
Calais-Nice, 14½-15 hr.
Calais-Toulouse, 12-12½ hr.
Dieppe-Avignon, 10½-11 hr.
Dieppe-Fréjus, 13¼-14½ hr.
Lille-Avignon, 11½ hr.
Lille-Biarritz, 10-12½ hr.
Lille-Bordeaux, 10½ hr.
Lille-Narbonne, 11¾-12½ hr.
Lille-Nice, 14½ hr.
Paris-Avignon, 7½ hr.
Paris-Biarritz, 8 hr.
Paris-Bordeaux, 6½-8 hr.
Paris-Briançon, 10½-12 hr.

Paris-Brive, 7 hr.
Paris-Evian, 7½ 10 hr.
Paris-Fréjus, 10½-11 hr.
Paris-Marseille, 9-10 hr.
Paris-Narbonne, 10¾ hr.
Paris-Nice, 12 hr.
Paris-St Gervais, 9-11 hr.
Paris-Tarbes, 9 hr.
Paris-Toulon, 9¾ hr.
Paris-Toulouse. 9 hr.

GERMANY

Paris-München, 10¼ -10¾ hr.

ITALY

Bruxelles-Milano, 14-14½ hr.
Calais-Bologna, 17½ hr.
Calais-Livorno, 16½ -17½ hr.
Calais-Milano, 12-15½ hr.
Calais-Roma, 20¼ -20¾ hr.
Paris-Milano, 10½ -11 hr.
Paris-Rimini, 15-15¼ hr.

PORTUGAL

Paris-Lisboa, 25¼ -28¼ hr. (car 48 hr.)

SPAIN

Paris-Madrid, 24½ -28½ hr.

SWITZERLAND

Bruxelles-Brig, 11-11½ hr.

TIME DIFFERENCES

In many European countries, local time is altered during the summer, as it is in the UK. Although most European countries are one hour ahead of the UK throughout the year, there is a period in October when European Summer Time has ended but British Summer Time has not. **Note:** Bulgaria, Cyprus, Finland, Greece, Romania and Turkey are two hours ahead of Greenwich Mean Time. In Portugal, the time is the same as in Great Britain.

EUROPE BY COUNTRY

In this section of the Guide, essential motoring information and valuable general information is given in detail for each individual country.

Driving in Europe can present the motorist with many unfamiliar problems, and advice on several of those likely to be encountered is presented here by way of an introduction.

'BISON FUTE'

In France you will see signs for exits off the autoroutes marked 'Bis' on an orange panel. This is short for Bison Futé, and indicates alternative routes which avoid areas prone to congestion at peak periods. A free map of 'Bis' routes is published in June each year by the French Government; contact RAC Travel Information ☎ 0345-333222 or the French Government Tourist Office (see page 12).

DRINKING AND DRIVING

Many motorists believe that they are safe with a blood alcohol level of 50 or 80mg: they are wrong. Even at a level of 20mg, symptoms of impaired concentration may be registered. It is worth remembering that factors like fatigue, illness or stress have additional adverse effects, and may cause severe concentration loss even when only small amounts of alcohol are consumed.

Blood alcohol limits are given for each country. (The limit in the UK is 80mg.) Penalties for exceeding these limits can be very severe.

FUEL

Information on the availability and octane rating of leaded and unleaded petrol, translations for unleaded petrol, and regulations concerning the carriage of spare fuel are detailed for each country.

The grades are shown as 'Regular' (the cheapest) and 'Super' (covering both 'Premium' and 'Super' grades in Europe, which correspond to the two British grades). The best guide to the grade is price. If you use 'Super' in the UK, then use the most expensive abroad. Where three grades are available, do not use the lowest unless you are sure that your car will run on it. Where only one grade is available, this is likely to be the equivalent of the cheaper UK grade. The current prices of petrol and diesel in European countries are available from RAC Travel Information, ☎ 0345-333222.

If in doubt, contact the car manufacturer prior to departure, or RAC Technical Advice, ☎ 0345-345500.

LEVEL CROSSINGS

A level crossing is indicated by three roadside signals, set at 80m intervals before the point where road and railway cross (see signs illustrated facing page 5). At the level crossing, approaching trains are often indicated by a beacon flashing red intermittently; this changes to white or amber when there are no trains approaching. Some level crossings do not have gates or barriers, and an approaching train is indicated by a flashing red light or continuous bell.

Headlights must be turned off when waiting at a level crossing after dark.

MOUNTAIN ROADS

Strong winds can affect steering, and a firm grip on the wheel is necessary.

Even in summer, mist is not uncommon at high altitudes. If you are unsure of your position on a mountain, draw well into your own side of the road, stop the car (keeping the lights on), and wait until visibility improves.

Traffic descending should give way to that ascending. Postal vans and coaches (usually marked with a bugle sign) have priority, and any instructions given by their drivers must be followed.

OVERHEATING

In hot weather generally, the level of water in the radiator needs to be checked frequently. If the radiator has lost water but the level is still above the bottom of the header tank, water may be added immediately, provided the engine is allowed to tick over and mix the cold water with the hot water in the engine. If the system has run dry, the engine must be allowed to cool before water is added, otherwise the cylinder block may be severely damaged.

If you suspect that the water in the radiator is overheating, do not attempt to open the radiator cap immediately. Allow the water to cool first.

High temperatures and prolonged ascents can cause petrol to vaporise in the fuel lines, pump or carburettor, and the engine will stop. If this happens, allow the engine to cool; a damp cloth placed over the engine will speed the cooling process.

OVERLOADING

Each passenger should have a fixed seat, and the luggage weight should not exceed that recommended in the manufacturer's handbook. Take care not to overload the roof rack; Switzerland, for example, normally applies a 50kg limit to roof rack loads.

In the case of an accident, the driver of an overloaded vehicle could be prosecuted and, in addition, might find himself inadequately covered by insurance. The French authorities, in particular, are concerned by the serious overloading of many British-registered cars touring France.

OVERTAKING

In Europe, one of the main problems for drivers of right-hand drive vehicles is overtaking, as vehicles in front block the view of the road ahead. It is necessary to keep well back from the vehicle in front in order to see whether it is safe to overtake. A mirror fitted on the left-hand side of the car will prove useful.

ROUNDABOUTS

These are often confusing for British drivers. In Germany and Sweden, if there is a 'Give Way' sign, traffic on a roundabout has priority, as in the UK. In France, it is now normal for traffic on a roundabout to have priority: a triangular sign with a red border showing a roundabout symbol with the legend *vous n'avez pas la priorité* indicates this. However, in a few areas the old ruling of priority given to traffic entering a roundabout still applies. So, where the above sign is not present, you should approach with care.

In all other countries, traffic on a roundabout should give way to traffic wishing to enter.

SAFETY

There have been a growing number of reports concerning a modern form of 'highway robbery' on some trunk routes through **France** and **Spain**. Although such incidents are minimal in relation to the thousands of journeys made to those countries, it could be well worth bearing in mind that the seemingly friendly stranger – only too keen to hear about your planned route and destination – may be making some plans of his own.

Many countries in Europe have undergone change recently, both peaceful and violent. At the time of going to press, the Foreign and Commonwealth Office offered the following advice to intending travellers.

Albania: touring on an individual basis is not recommended. **Bosnia:** because of continuing hostilities, travel to Bosnia is inadvisable. **CIS:** civil unrest and Nationalist tensions simmer in many areas; parts of Azerbaijan, Moldova and Tajikistan (as well as Armenia and Georgia) are not safe for tourists. **Croatia:** parts of northern Croatia are considered safe, but rapid deterioration of security is always a risk. **Slovenia:** the whole of Slovenia is considered safe for tourists. **Turkey:** terrorist activity renders travel hazardous in certain parts of the country. **(Former) Yugoslavia:** travellers should contact the FCO for advice.

Travel information for all countries may be obtained from the Foreign & Commonwealth Office Travel Advice Unit, ☎ 071-270 4129.

SWISS VIGNETTE

In order to drive on Swiss motorways, motorists must buy a vignette. These can be bought at Customs posts, post offices, garages, etc in Switzerland, or in this country from the Swiss National Tourist Office in London. The vignette is valid for one year, must be displayed on the windscreen and is non-transferable. A separate vignette must be bought and displayed on a trailer or caravan.

The Swiss advise travellers to buy them in advance to avoid delays and queues at border crossings; credit cards are not accepted for payment of a vignette. You will be fined 100 Swiss francs if you do not have one, plus the cost of the vignette.

ANDORRA

MOTORING INFORMATION

National motoring organisation
Automobil Club d'Andorra, FIA, Babet Camp 4, Andorra la Vieja. ☎ 20-8-90.
Emergencies
Police ☎ 17, Fire Brigade, Ambulance ☎ 18.
Fuel
Leaded petrol: Super (98 octane) available.
Speed limits
Built-up areas: 25mph (40kmh); *outside built-up areas:* 44mph (70kmh). The police are empowered to collect on-the-spot fines.

GENERAL INFORMATION

Banks
Open Mon-Fri 0900-1300 and 1500-1700, Sat 0900-1300.

Currency
French francs and Spanish pesetas are both used but telephone boxes and post offices take one currency only, not both.
Post Offices
Open Mon-Fri 0900-1300 and 1500-1700, Sat 0900-1300.
Public holidays
Canillo, third Sat in July; St Julia de Loria, last Sun in July and following Mon and Tue; Escaldos Engerdany, 25, 26 and 27 July; Andorra la Vieja, first Sat in Aug, and following Sun and Mon; La Massana, 15, 16 and 17 Aug; Meritxett Pilgrimage, 8 Sep; Ordino, 16, 17 Sep.
Shops
Open daily 0900-2000 (except 8 Sep).

AUSTRIA (A)

MOTORING INFORMATION

National motoring organisation
Osterreichischer Automobil, Motorrad-und Touring Club (OAMTC), FIA & AIT, Schubertring 1-3, 1010 **Wien (Vienna)** 1. ☎ (0222) 711 99. Office hours: weekdays 0800-1700. Closed Sat/Sun and public holidays, except the breakdown assistance service.
Breakdowns
Purchasers of Eurocover Motoring Assistance should consult their Assistance Document.
The OAMTC operate a Breakdown and Technical Assistance service on major roads throughout Austria, ☎ 120 (24-hr Breakdown service, Wien).
Children in front seats
Not permitted under the age of 12, unless a special seat or seat belt is fitted.
Crash helmets
Compulsory for motorcyclists and passengers.
Drinking and driving
The blood alcohol legal limit is 80mg.
Drivers
The minimum age for drivers is 18.
Driving licence
UK driving licence accepted.
Emergencies
Police ☎ 133, Fire Brigade ☎ 122, Ambulance ☎ 144. These numbers are standardised through-

out Austria but the local prefix number must also be used.
First aid kit
Compulsory.
Fuel
Most petrol stations are open from 0800 to 2000, and many operate 24 hours a day in large cities. *Leaded petrol:* **Super has been withdrawn from sale. Super Plus (98 octane), containing a special lead additive, should be used by vehicles unable to take unleaded petrol.** *Unleaded petrol:* Regular (91 octane) and Super (98 octane) available; pump legend *bleifrei normal* or *bleifrei super. Credit cards:* although rarely accepted as payment for fuel, the RAC has received information that the AVANTI chain accepts charge and credit cards. *Spare fuel:* 10 litres of petrol in a can may be imported duty free in addition to the fuel in the tank.
Hitchhiking
Prohibited on motorways and dual carriageways. In Styria, Upper Austria and the Vorarlberg hitchhiking is prohibited for young people under 16.
Lighting
Dipped headlights are compulsory in built-up areas. No parking lights are required if the vehicle can be seen from a distance of approximately 55 yards (50 metres). If visibility is bad, sidelights should be switched on. Mopeds and

motorcycles must use lights at all times.

Overtaking

Overtake vehicles on the left. Overtaking on the right is permitted only when overtaking trams, in one-way streets, or when overtaking vehicles which indicate they are turning left. **Do not** cross or straddle the continuous yellow line at the centre of the road.

Parking

Do not park in the following areas (except for a short wait of ten minutes):

(a) At places indicated by 'No parking' signs.

(b) Where there are crosses on the roadway, in front of houses, entrances, or petrol stations.

(c) On narrow roads, on the left in one-way streets, or on priority roads outside built-up areas at dusk, in darkness, fog or any road condition which reduces visibility.

In Wien, parking on roads with tramrails is prohibited between 2000 and 0500 from 15 December to 31 March to allow for snow clearing.

Do not park or wait where a sign says *Halten Verboten* (no waiting). In Baden, Bludenz, Bregenz, Feldkirch, Graz, Innsbruck, Klagenfurt, Krems, Linz, St Pölten, Salzburg, Schwaz, Wien, Villach and Wiener Neustadt, a fee is charged for motor vehicles parked in the Blue Zone. Motorists must buy parking tickets in advance from banks, tobacconists etc. The date and time of arrival must be indicated on the ticket and displayed on the windscreen. Unless otherwise indicated under the *Kurzparkzone* (short-term parking) road sign, parking is allowed for up to 3 hours.

In other towns free parking is allowed for up to 90 minutes in Blue Zones. Parking tickets are not required but a parking disc must be used for all vehicles including motorcycles. This disc can be obtained free of charge from tobacconists. Parking discs are not required when parking tickets are used.

It is prohibited to leave a caravan trailer without its towing vehicle in a public parking place (eg motorway service area). In the Tyrol, Upper Austria and Salzburg, it is prohibited to park caravans outside specially authorised parking places or within 500 metres of a lake. Caravans must not be parked within 200 metres of the Grossglockner High Alpine Road and the motorway in Salzburg. Heavy fines and possible forcible removal of a caravan can result if these regulations are not observed.

Pedestrian crossings

In most large towns where there are traffic light controlled junctions without pedestrian lights, pedestrians may cross only when the lights are green for travelling in the same direction. It is forbidden to wait at the edge of the kerb.

Priority

Priority is given to main roads or those roads bearing the 'Main Road' symbol. In the case of roads of equal importance, priority is given to traffic approaching from the right. **Do** give priority to trams coming from the left, also to police cars, ambulances, fire engines, and all emergency vehicles with a flashing blue light and multi-toned sirens. When passing traffic on mountain roads, ascending vehicles have priority.

Road signs

Most conform to the international pattern. Other road conditions may be indicated as follows:

Anhänger Verboten: trailers not allowed
Ausweiche: detour
Beschränkung für Halten oder Parken: stopping or parking restricted
Halten Verboten: no waiting
Hupverbot: use of horn prohibited
Lawinen Gefahr: avalanche danger
Querstrasse: crossroads
Steinschlag: falling rocks
Strasse Gesperrt: road closed

Seat belts

If fitted, compulsory use in front and rear seats.

Signalling

Give warning of approach by flashing head-lamps. Horns may not be used where their use is prohibited by a road sign. This applies in many large towns, mostly at night, and in Wien at all times.

Speed limits

Built-up areas: 31mph (50kmh); *outside built-up areas:* 62mph (100kmh); *motorways:* 81mph (130kmh). Speed limits are lowered to 68mph (110kmh) between 2200 and 0500 on the following motorways: A8 (Innkreis), A9 (Pyhrn), A10 (Tauern), A12 (Inntal), A13 (Brenner), A14 (Rheintal).

Cars towing a caravan or trailer under 750kg are restricted to 62mph (100kmh) on all roads outside built-up areas, including motorways. If the trailer is over 750kg contact RAC Travel Information (☎ 0345-333222) for guidance on speed limits. In the Vorarlberg and the Tyrol, the maximum speed limit is 50mph (80kmh) at all times.

Tolls

Payable on certain roads (see page 73).

Traffic offences

Police are empowered to impose and collect fines up to AS 500 on the spot for drivers who violate traffic regulations. The police officer collecting the fine is required to issue an official receipt. The motorist may pay the fine during the following two weeks, and with the original paying-in slip; the fine is payable in most European currencies. Motorists refusing to pay the fine may request that the case be brought before a police court; however, the police may ask for a security to be deposited.

Warning triangle
Compulsory.

GENERAL INFORMATION

Banks
Open Mon-Fri 0800-1230 and 1330-1500 (Thu 1330-1730).

Currency
Austrian schilling.

Post Offices
Open Mon-Fri 0800-1200 and 1400-1800. Main and station post offices are often open 24 hours a day.

Public holidays
New Year's Day; Epiphany; Easter Monday; Labour Day; Ascension; Whit Monday; Corpus Christi; Assumption, 15 Aug; National Day, 26 Oct; All Saints, 1 Nov; Immaculate Conception, 8 Dec; Christmas, 25, 26 Dec.

Shops
Open Mon-Fri 0700/0800-1800/1830, with a one- or two-hour break at midday. Sat 0800-1200, but this varies. In central Wien shops do not close for lunch.

BALTIC STATES   (EW)(LV)(LT)

MOTORING INFORMATION

National motoring organisations
Estonia: Estonian Auto-Moto Union (AUTOM), *FIA & AIT*, Pikk 41, 200 001 Tallinn. ☎ (70142) 601 215.
Latvia: Auto-Moto Society of Latvia (LR AMB), *FIA & AIT*, 16B Raunas, LV-1039 Riga. ☎ (3712) 56 83 39, 56 62 22. Fax: (3712) 33 19 20 (marked for the attention of Auto-Moto).
Lithuania: Association of Lithuanian Automobilists, *FIA & AIT*, Lvovo 9, 2005 Vilnius. ☎ (370-2) 35 12 73, 35 21 86. Fax: (370-2) 35 89 19.

Breakdowns
The Finnish oil company, Neste Oy, provides a 24-hr roadside breakdown service, operating from Vilnius and Riga, ☎ 372-2-296884 or 295980 (calls are answered in English). Minor repairs are undertaken on the spot, and there is a towing service to the nearest Neste station if required.

Drinking and driving
Do not drink and drive: the blood alcohol legal limit is 0mg.

Emergencies
Police ☎ 02, Fire Brigade ☎ 01, Ambulance ☎ 03. When an accident occurs, it is compulsory to contact the police.

Ferries
Estonian New Line and Tallink Line operate all-year car ferry services between Tallinn and Helsinki.

Fuel
Availability of fuel in the Baltic States has improved with the establishment of a chain of

11 service stations by Neste Oy along the M-12 ('Via Baltica') motorway. These are located every 150km (90 miles) and are open 24 hours. Service stations may be found in Tallinn (2), Parnu, Savikrasti (north of Riga), Riga (2), Kekava, Panevezys, Marijampole and Vilnius (2).

Leaded, unleaded (95 octane Euro-Super) and diesel fuel, imported from Finland, are available from Neste outlets. Away from the Via Baltica, fuel is likely to be scarce, of poor quality, and long queues are a probability. *Diesel:* central European diesel fuel congeals in winter, and motorists should purchase a special winter diesel with a high congealing point, from Neste and Kesoil stations. *Spare fuel:* cans of fuel may be imported.

Night driving
Visitors are not recommended to drive at night. Local drivers tend to use sidelights only, and additional hazards include slow-moving vehicles and obstructions caused by goods falling from vehicles.

Repairs
Spare parts for western makes of car are not available.

Speed limits
Built-up areas: 37mph (60kmh); *outside built-up areas:* 56mph (90kmh) – vehicles over 3.5 tonnes are limited to 44mph (70kmh).

Temporary importation of vehicles
On arrival in the Baltic States, the visitor must sign an undertaking to re-export his vehicle at the end of his stay. He must present this declaration when leaving the country.

Vehicle insurance
Car insurance (does not include motorcycles) can

be arranged in advance by Black Sea & Baltic General Insurance Co. Ltd, 65 Fenchurch Street, London EC3, ☎ 071-709 9202/9292.

GENERAL INFORMATION

Accommodation
A range of accommodation is available in the main towns of Vilnius, Kaunas, Tallinn, Riga and Pärnu. Accommodation may be booked through the Independent Travel Department, Intourist Travel Ltd, Intourist House, 219 Marsh Wall, London E14 9FJ, ☎ 071-538 5965.

Currency
Estonia: the Estonian crown (Kron) is the only currency accepted, and can be bought in advance or at Estonian banks. Credit cards are accepted by international hotels and shops.
Latvia: restaurants and international hotels only accept western currencies. Latvian or Russian roubles can be used in shops and purchased in hotels, shops and banks, subject to a fluctuating exchange rate. Latvia intended to adopt its own currency unit (the Lati) in late 1993.
Lithuania: the Talonas, a transition currency, was still in use in 1993. Introduction of a new currency unit (the Lit) is expected in 1993/94.

Customs
Formalities at the Latvian and Estonian border posts are reasonably smooth, but motorists should be prepared for long queues at the border between Poland and Lithuania (a new Customs post was due to open at the end of 1993).

Language
Each country has its national language. Russian is generally understood, but may not be welcome.

Public holidays
Estonia: New Year's Day; Independence Day, 24 Feb; Good Friday; Easter Monday; May Day, 1 May; Victory Day, 23 June; Christmas, 25, 26 Dec.
Latvia: New Year's Day; Good Friday; Easter Monday; May Day, 1 May; St John's Day, 23 June; National Day, 18 Nov; Christmas, 25, 26 Dec.
Lithuania: New Year's Day; Independence Day, 16 Feb; Good Friday; Easter Monday; May Day, 1 May; National Day, 6 July; Christmas, 25, 26 Dec.

Shops
Usually open weekdays 0900-1800, Sat 0900-1600 (often closed 1400-1500). Department stores open until 2000.

Telephone, telefax
Outgoing international and long-distance calls are routed via Moscow and must be pre-booked.

Visa
For Estonia and Lithuania, visas are no longer required for British citizens wishing to visit these countries for up to six months. Nationals from all countries require a visa for Latvia. This can be obtained at the border on arrival, but it is recommended that visitors obtain a visa in advance from the Latvian Embassy, 72 Queensborough Terrace, London W2 3SP, ☎ 071-727 1698. A visa costs £7 (or £10 by post). There is no fixed processing time.

BELGIUM   Ⓑ

MOTORING INFORMATION

National motoring organisations
Royal Automobile Club de Belgique (RACB), *FIA*, 53 rue d'Arlon, 1040 Bruxelles. ☎ (02) 2300810. Office hours: weekdays 0830-1700.
Touring Club Royal de Belgique (TCB), *AIT*, 44 rue de la Loi, 1040 Bruxelles. ☎ (02) 2332211. Office hours: weekdays 0900-1800, Sat 0900-1200.

Breakdowns
Purchasers of Eurocover Motoring Assistance should consult their Assistance Document.

Children in front seats
Not permitted under the age of 12, unless a child safety seat is fitted.

Crash helmets
Compulsory for motorcyclists and passengers.

Drinking and driving
The blood alcohol legal limit is 80mg.

Drivers
The minimum age for drivers is 18.

Driving licence
UK driving licence accepted.

Emergencies
Police ☎ 101, Fire Brigade, Ambulance ☎ 100.
When an accident occurs, especially if injuries are involved, Belgian police may insist that drivers undergo a blood alcohol content test. Although in law a driver can refuse, such refusal may result in his arrest. Belgian law also requires all parties involved in an accident to remain at the scene as long as required by police, and proof of identity may be requested.

Fuel
Most petrol stations are closed overnight from 2000 to 0800, and often all day on Sunday. Petrol stations on motorways and main roads are open 24 hours a day, including Sunday.

Leaded petrol: Super (98/99 octane) available.
Unleaded petrol: Regular (92 octane) and Super
(95 octane) available; pump legend *normale sans
plomb, normale onglood, normale unverbleit* or
bodvrije benzine. Credit cards: major cards
accepted at most petrol stations on motorways
and in large towns. *Spare fuel:* 10 litres of petrol
in a can may be imported duty free in addition
to the fuel in the tank.

Lighting
It is compulsory to use dipped headlights when
travelling between dusk and dawn, and during
the day if weather conditions are bad. **Do not**
use headlights as parking lights. It is compulsory for motorcyclists to use dipped headlights
during the day.

Overtaking
Do not overtake if there are vehicles approaching in the opposite direction; or at intersections,
unless the road used is marked as a main road
or if the traffic is controlled by a policeman or
traffic lights; at level crossings; where there is a
sign prohibiting overtaking, or if the motorist in
front is about to overtake another motorist.

Parking
Blue Zone parking areas exist in Bruxelles,
Oostende, Brugge, Liège, Antwerpen and Gent.
Parking discs follow the international pattern.
In Bruxelles, discs can be obtained from the
police station and offices of the RACB. **Do not**
park where parts of the road are crossed by
tram or rail lines which are in use. Wheel
clamps are used on illegally parked vehicles in
Antwerpen and Gent.

Priority
Priority must be given to traffic approaching
from the right, exceptions being indicated by
signs. **Do** give trams priority over other
vehicles.

Seat belts
If fitted, compulsory use in front and rear seats.

Signalling
Audible warnings may be used when necessary
to indicate your intention to overtake, but only
outside built-up areas.

Speed limits
Built-up areas: 31mph (50kmh); *outside built-up
areas:* 56mph (90kmh); *motorways:* 74mph
(120kmh).

Tolls
There are no motorway tolls in Belgium. A toll
is charged for the Liefenhoeks Tunnel in
Antwerpen.

Traffic offences
Police are empowered to impose and collect on-
the-spot fines. The amount of fine depends on
the severity of the offence (either 750 BF or 4,000
BF). If the offender refuses to pay, a deposit will
be requested. Further non-payment can result in
vehicle seizure. Payment is accepted in a
number of currencies including £ Sterling.

Warning triangle
Compulsory.

GENERAL INFORMATION

Banks
Open Mon-Fri 0900-1200 and 1400-1600. Some
banks remain open at midday.

Currency
Belgian franc.

Post Offices
Open Mon-Fri 0900-1800, Sat 0900-1200.

Public holidays
New Year's Day; Easter Monday; Labour Day;
Ascension; Whit Monday; Flemish National
Day, 21 July; Assumption, 15 Aug; All Saints, 1
Nov; Armistice Day, 11 Nov; Christmas, 25 Dec.

Shops
Open 0900-1800 (Fri usually 0900-2100). Some
shops close for two hours at midday, but stay
open until 2000.

BULGARIA   (BG)

MOTORING INFORMATION

National motoring organisation
Union of Bulgarian Motorists (SBA), *FIA &
AIT,* 3 Place Positano, 1090 Sofia. ☎ 2 86 151.
Office hours: Mon-Fri 0900-1800.

Breakdowns
Purchasers of Eurocover Motoring Assistance
should consult their Assistance Document.

Children in front seats
Not permitted under the age of 10.

Crash helmets
Compulsory for motorcyclists and passengers.

Drinking and driving
Do not drink and drive: the blood alcohol legal
limit is 0mg.

Drivers
The minimum age for drivers is 18.

Driving licence
UK driving licence accepted only with an
official Bulgarian translation, otherwise an
International Driving Permit is required.

Emergencies

Police ☎ 166, Fire Brigade ☎ 160, Ambulance ☎ 150.

In the case of accident, if there is only minor damage to the vehicles, drivers may agree on the procedure to adopt without calling the police. However, if one of the drivers is not insured, the other driver is advised to call the police to draw up a report of the damage which he can produce to his insurance company. If the vehicles are seriously damaged, or if anyone is injured, the police must be called.

First aid kit

Compulsory.

Fuel

Petrol stations are located in large towns and on main roads, at an average distance of 30-40km (18-25 miles). Some stations are open 24 hours but most open from 0600 to 2130 daily. Motorists should buy fuel from blue pumps. *Leaded petrol:* Regular (86 octane) and Super (96 octane) available. *Unleaded petrol:* Super (93 octane) available; pump legend *bes olovo bleifrei. Spare fuel:* up to 20 litres of petrol may be imported.

Lighting

In town, drivers must use dipped headlights if public lighting is insufficient. Sidelights may be used in well-lit streets. Foglights may be used **only** in case of fog, rain or snow, at the same time as sidelights. Dipped headlights should be used if the vehicle is not equipped with foglights.

Parking

In built-up areas there are no parking meters or discs. Stopping and parking are prohibited at places where they might obstruct traffic. These places are indicated by signs. In one-way streets, parking is on the right only. Outside built-up areas drivers should stop off the road on the hard shoulder and park at places indicated by the international 'P' sign.

Pedestrian crossings

Pedestrians have priority over all vehicles on 'zebra type' crossings, except trams. When crossing at an intersection, pedestrians who are already on the carriageway have priority over vehicles, again excepting trams.

Priority

At intersections without right of way, and 'T' junctions, drivers must give way to vehicles coming from the right. Trams have priority over other vehicles approaching from right or left.

Roads

Main roads are numbered, and display international road signs, with distances in kilometres. Town names appear in both Bulgarian and French.

There are over 530km (330 miles) of motorways in Bulgaria. The 'Trakia' motorway (156km/96 miles) links the towns of Sofia and Plovdiv.

Road tax

A road tax of 20 DM is payable on all cars entering Bulgaria.

Seat belts

If fitted, compulsory use in front seats.

Signalling

Audible warning devices (horns) may be used outside large towns to prevent an accident. Places where the use of horns is prohibited are indicated by the international sign.

Speed limits

Built-up areas: 37mph (60kmh); *outside built-up areas:* 50mph (80kmh); *motorways:* 74mph (120kmh).

Traffic offences

On-the-spot fines are imposed by police. A receipt is issued.

Warning triangle

Compulsory.

GENERAL INFORMATION

Banks

In Sofia and main towns, usually open Mon-Fri 0800-1230 and 1300-1500, Sat 0800-1400.

Currency

Lev.

Post Offices

Open Mon-Fri 0700-1900, Sat 0700-1300.

Public holidays

New Year's Day; National Day, 3 Mar; Easter Mon; Labour Day, 1 May; Education Day, 24 May; Christmas, 25 Dec.

Shops

In Sofia and main towns, usually open Mon-Fri 0800-1700, Sat 0800-1400. Some shops remain open all day.

Visa

A tourist entry visa (valid for 3 months) is required by British Nationals who arrange their own holiday and stay in Bulgaria for more than 30 hours. For visa application forms send an sae to: Visa Section, Bulgarian Embassy, 188 Queens Gate, London SW7 5HL or ☎ 071-584 9400/9433 (Visa section open Mon-Fri 0930-1230). Seven working days' notice is required. Motorists are recommended to obtain visas in advance of arrival at the border.

CIS

MOTORING INFORMATION

Drinking and driving
Do not drink and drive: the blood alcohol legal limit is 0mg.

Driving licence
An International Driving Permit is required by each driver.

Fire extinguisher
Compulsory.

First aid kit
Compulsory.

Fuel
Despite being subsidised, there is a severe shortage of fuel, particularly unleaded petrol. Check that your engine can run on 76 octane petrol, or the local diesel. Petrol coupons are issued at the border.

Seat belts
If fitted, compulsory use in front and rear seats.

Speed limits
Built-up areas 37mph (60kmh); *outside built-up areas* 68mph (110kmh).

Vehicle insurance
British insurance is not valid in the CIS, and insurance cover may be taken out through the insurance agency (Ingosstrakh) – there are offices in various European countries. Cover may also be obtained on arrival at the frontier posts at Brest (Polish border) and Uzhgorod (Czech border).

Alternatively, insurance (does not include motorcycles) can be arranged in advance by Black Sea & Baltic General Insurance Co. Ltd, 65 Fenchurch Street, London EC3, ☎ 071-709 9202/ 9292.

Warning triangle
Compulsory.

GENERAL INFORMATION

The Commonwealth of Independent States (CIS) comprises Armenia, Azerbaijan, Beloruss, Kazakhstan, Kirkghizia, Moldova, Russia, Tajikistan, Turkmenistan, Ukraine and Uzbekistan.

Currency
Soviet roubles are still the official currency throughout the CIS. Visitors should take US dollars, ideally in small denominations, and should remember that the fluctuating exchange rate can alter prices considerably. Travellers' cheques are not widely accepted.

Itinerary
Visitors must plan their route and book accommodation before departure (see Visa below). The visa should detail the visitor's full itinerary, and will not normally be issued directly to individual applicants unless booked through an accredited tour company.

Motorists require a special 'Autotourist' visa and an itinerary card. In addition, there is an official limit of 300 miles (500km) a day.

Itineraries may be arranged through the Independent Travel Department, Intourist Travel Ltd, Intourist House, 219 Marsh Wall, London E14 9FJ, ☎ 071-538 5965.

Language
Away from the main cities, a slight knowledge of the Russian language is beneficial. An ability to read Cyrillic is helpful in order to understand road signs.

Maps
As at the end of 1993, maps – especially small-scale maps – are difficult to obtain.

Visa
Visas are required by holders of British passports, and must be obtained in advance for Russia, the republics other than Ukraine, and for Georgia, from the Russian Embassy, 5 Kensington Palace Gardens, London W8, ☎ 071-229 8027. (The visa section is open from 1000 to 1230, except Wednesdays. Allow 14 working days.) For Ukraine, a visa (costing about £30) is issued at the border.

In order to obtain a visa, visitors must plan their route and book accommodation before departure (see Itinerary above).

CROATIA

see (Former) Yugoslavia

CYPRUS   (CY)

MOTORING INFORMATION

National motoring organisation
Cyprus Automobile Association, 12 Chr.
Mylonas Street, Nicosia 141. ☎ 02-313233. Office
hours: (June-Sep) Mon/Tue/Thu/Fri 0800-1300
and 1500-1900, Wed/Sat 0800-1300.
Children in front seats
Not permitted under the age of 5.
Crash helmets
Recommended.
Drinking and Driving
Persons suspected of driving under the influence
of alcohol may be subjected to a blood test. Fines
imposed.
Drivers
The minimum age for drivers is 18.
Driving
In Cyprus, drive on the left.
Driving licence
UK driving licence accepted.
Fuel
Leaded petrol: Regular (87 octane) and Super (98
octane) available. *Unleaded petrol:* available in
major towns. *Spare fuel:* it is prohibited to carry
spare fuel in cans.
Lighting
Lights must be used between half an hour after
sunset and half an hour before sunrise. Spotlights
are prohibited, but foglights may be used.
Priority
As a general rule give way to vehicles coming

from the right. However, traffic on main roads has
priority at intersections where a 'Stop' or 'Give
Way' sign is placed on the secondary road.
Seat belts
If fitted, compulsory use in front seats.
Signalling
Unnecessary use of the horn is prohibited,
particularly from 2200-0600 and near hospitals.
Speed limits
Built-up areas: 31mph (50kmh); *outside built-up
areas:* 37-62mph (60-100kmh).
Warning triangle
It is compulsory to carry two warning triangles.

GENERAL INFORMATION

Banks
Open Mon-Sat 0830-1200, and for tourists only
1530-1730.
Currency
Cypriot pound, which is divided into 100 cents.
Post Offices
Open Mon-Fri 0730-1330, Sat 0730-1200.
Public holidays
New Year; Epiphany, 6 Jan; Greek National
Day, 25 Mar; Easter according to Greek
Orthodox Calendar; National Holiday, 1 Apr;
OXI Day, 28 Oct; Christmas, 24, 25 and 26 Dec.
Shops
Open Mon-Fri 0800-1300 and 1600-1900 (winter
1430-1730), Sat 0800-1300. Shops close Wed
afternoons.

CZECH AND SLOVAK REPUBLICS   (CZ) (CS)

MOTORING INFORMATION

National motoring organisations
Ustřední Automotoklub CSFR (UAMK), *FIA &
AIT,* Cernomorska 9, 101 50 **Praha (Prague)** 10.
☎ 2-746 000 Tourist/Information Service for
motorists: Autoturist, Na Rybnicku 16, 120 76
Praha 2. ☎ 2-203 355. Office hours: Mon-Fri
0745-1645.
CSAK, *FIA,* Opletalova 29, 110 00 Praha 1.
☎ 2-264 753. Office hours: Mon-Fri 0730-1600.
Border crossing
All visitors must present their passports at an
official border crossing post. However, there are
currently no formalities for private cars.
Breakdowns
Purchasers of Eurocover Motoring Assistance
should consult their Assistance Document. The

Automotoklub CSFR has a breakdown service
which operates from fixed points. For assistance
in Praha, ☎ 773455. Breakdown service is
provided to members of affiliated foreign clubs
on a reciprocal basis.
Children in front seats
Children below the age of 12, and persons
under 4ft 9in (150cm), may not travel in front
seats.
Crash helmets
Compulsory for motorcyclists and passengers.
Drivers of motorcycles over 50cc must wear
goggles at all times.
Drinking and driving
Do not drink and drive: the blood alcohol legal
limit is 0mg.
Drivers
The minimum age for drivers is 18.

Driving licence
UK driving licence accepted.

Emergencies
Police ☎ 158, Fire Brigade ☎ 150, Ambulance ☎ 155. If an accident causes bodily injury or material damage exceeding 1,000 Kcs, it must be reported to the police immediately.

First aid kit
Compulsory.

Fuel
Petrol stations on international roads and in main towns are open 24 hours a day. *Leaded petrol:* Regular (90 octane) and Super (96 octane) available. *Unleaded petrol:* Super (95 octane) available; pump legend *Natural.* Maps showing outlets for unleaded petrol are issued at border crossings. *Diesel:* designated by the sign 'TT Diesel', and available at about 80 service stations. *Credit cards:* accepted in main towns and tourist areas. *Spare fuel:* 20 litres of petrol in a can may be imported duty free. It is prohibited to export fuel in cans.

Lighting
Foglights may be used in case of fog, snow or heavy rain. If the vehicle is not equipped with foglights, the driver must use dipped headlights in these conditions. Motorcyclists must use dipped headlights at all times.

Overtaking
Overtaking regulations conform with international usage. In built-up areas, when there are at least two lanes of traffic in each direction, drivers may use either lane. Trams are overtaken on the right. Only when there is no room on the right may the tram be overtaken on the left. In Praha it is prohibited to overtake trams on the left, the driver must follow the tram until he has enough room to pass on the right. Drivers must not overtake beside a tram refuge.

Parking
Vehicles may be parked only on the right of the road. If it is a one-way road, parking is also allowed on the left. Stopping and parking are prohibited in all places where visibility is poor or where the vehicle could cause an obstruction and, in particular, near an intersection, pedestrian crossing, bus or tram stop, level crossing and alongside a tram line unless there is still a 3.5m-wide lane free.

If visiting Praha, it is advisable to park outside the city centre and use public transport. It is forbidden to enter Wenceslas Square by car, unless you are staying at a hotel in the immediate vicinity. Vehicles illegally parked will be removed or clamped. For further information on parking in Praha, contact RAC Travel Information, ☎ 0345-333222.

Priority
At uncontrolled crossroads or road intersections not marked by a priority road sign, priority must be given to vehicles coming from the right. A driver approaching an intersection marked by priority road signs must give right of way to all vehicles approaching this intersection along the priority road.

Drivers may not enter crossroads unless their exit beyond the intersection is clear. A tram turning right and crossing the line of a vehicle on its right has priority once the driver has signalled his intention to turn.

Road signs
Most conform to the international pattern. Other road signs which may be seen are:
CHOĎTE VLEVO: pedestrians must walk on the left
DALKOVÝ PROVOZ: bypass
H NEMOCNICE: hospital
JEDNOSMERNY PROVOZ: one-way traffic
OBJÍZDĎKA: diversion
PRUJEZD ZAKÁZÁB: closed to all vehicles

Seat belts
If fitted, compulsory use in front and rear seats.

Signalling
Horns may be used only to warn other road users in case of danger or to signify that you are going to overtake. Warning may also be given by flashing the headlights. The use of horns is prohibited in central Praha between 2100 and 0500 from 15 March to 15 October and between 2000 and 0600 from 15 October to 15 March; and it is prohibited to give audible warning in Bratislava at all times.

Speed limits
Built-up areas: 0500-2300 37mph (60kmh), 2300-0500 56mph (90kmh); *outside built-up areas:* 56mph (90kmh); *motorways:* 68mph (110kmh). Cars towing a caravan or trailer are limited to 50mph (80kmh).

Traffic offences
On-the-spot fines not exceeding 500 Kcs may be imposed.

Warning triangle
Compulsory.

GENERAL INFORMATION

Banks
Open Mon-Fri 0830-1700. Closed Sat.

Currency
Koruna (Czech Kcs, Slovak Ks).

Museums
Open Tue-Sat 1000-1700, closed Mon.

Post Offices
Open Mon-Sat 0800-1600.

Public holidays

New Year's Day; Easter Monday; May Day; National Liberation Day (Slovak only), 8 May; St Cyril and St Method, 5 July; Johannes Hus Festival Day (Czech only), 6 July; Day of Reconciliation (Slovak only), 1 Nov; Christmas 24, 25, 26 Dec.

Shops

Food shops open Mon-Fri 0700-1800, Sat 0700-1200. Department stores open Mon-Fri 0800/0900-1900 (Thu 2000), Sat 0800-1500.

Visa

British Nationals no longer require a visa.

DENMARK (DK)

MOTORING INFORMATION

National motoring organisation

Forenede Danske Motorejere (FDM), *AIT,* FDM-Huset, Firskovvej 32, Lyngby, København. ☎ (02) 93 08 00. Head Office hours: Mon-Fri 0900-1700, Sat 0900-1200.

Breakdowns

Purchasers of Eurocover Motoring Assistance should consult their Assistance Document.

Children in cars

Children between the ages of 3 and 7 must be seated with a special child restraint, or in a seat which allows the use of normal seat belts.

Crash helmets

Compulsory for motorcyclists and passengers.

Drinking and driving

The blood alcohol legal limit is 80mg.

Drivers

The minimum age for drivers is 18.

Driving licence

UK driving licence accepted.

Emergencies

Police, Fire Brigade and Ambulance ☎ 112.

Fuel

Fuel availability is limited on motorways, and motorists are advised to fill their tank before joining a motorway. Petrol stations are often closed at night other than in large towns. There is an increasing number of self-service stations open 24 hours with pumps that require 20 Kr notes. *Leaded petrol:* Super (98 octane) available. *Unleaded petrol:* Regular (92 octane) and Super (95 octane) available; pump legend *blyfri benzin.* *Credit cards:* major cards accepted at larger petrol stations. *Spare fuel:* a full can may be imported if entering from an EC country.

Lighting

Dipped headlamps must be used at all times.

Parking

In central København, in addition to restrictions indicated by signs, parking discs are required where there are no parking meters. Disc parking is usually restricted to 1 hour. At meters, parking is allowed for up to 3 hours. They are in use weekdays 0900-1800 and on Saturdays 0900-1300. 1 Kr and 25 Ore coins are used. In other large towns kerbside parking is usually restricted to 1 hour. Discs are available from post offices, banks, petrol stations, tourist offices and FDM offices.

Do not park where there is a sign *Parkering forbudt,* or stop where signed *Stopforbudt.* Unlawful parking will result in the police towing the vehicle away. The vehicle will be released only upon payment of a fine.

Priority

Give way to traffic from the right except at roundabouts, where traffic already on the roundabout has priority. **Do** give way to traffic on a major road at a line of triangles painted across the carriageway or at a triangular 'Give Way' sign, and also to buses. Do not turn right at a red light, even if the road is clear, unless a green arrow indicates that you may. At junctions give way to cyclists and motorcyclists moving ahead when you are turning. When turning right, watch out for cyclists approaching from behind.

Road signs

Most conform to the international pattern. Other road signs are:

Ensrettet kørsel: one-way street
Fare: danger
Farligt sving: dangerous bend
Fodgaengerovergang: pedestrian crossing
Gennemkørsel forbudt: no through road
Hold til højre: keep to the right
Hold till venstre: keep to the left
Indkørsel forbudt: no entry
Korsvej: crossroads
Omkørsel: diversion
Parkering forbudt: no parking
Vejarbejde: road up
Vejen er spaerret: road closed

Seat belts

If fitted, compulsory use in front seats.

Signalling

Do not use your horn except in case of danger. Flash your lights instead.

Speed limits

Built-up areas: 31mph (50kmh); *outside built-up*

areas: 50mph (80kmh); motorways: 68mph (110kmh). Cars towing a caravan or trailer are limited to 44mph (70kmh).

Traffic offences
On-the-spot fines not exceeding 2000 Kr are imposed by police for each offence.

Warning triangle
Compulsory.

GENERAL INFORMATION

Banks
Open Mon-Wed, Fri 0930-1600, Thu 0930-1800. Closed Sat.

Currency
Kroner.

Medical treatment
Medical pharmacies are called *Apoteck* and in

the larger Danish towns a number of these operate a 24-hr service.

Post Offices
Open Mon-Fri 0900/1000-1700/1730, Sat 0900/1000-1200 (some post offices in København are closed all day).

Public holidays
New Year's Day; Maundy Thursday; Good Friday; Easter Monday; Constitution Day, 5 June; Ascension; Whit Monday; Christmas 24, 25, 26 and 31 Dec.

Shops
København: open Mon-Thu 0900-1730, Fri 0900-1900/2000, Sat 0900-1300/1400. Provinces: open Mon-Thu 0900-1730, Fri 0900-1730/1900, Sat 0900-1200/1300. Larger stores: open Mon-Fri 0900-1800/1900, Sat 0900-1200/1400.

FINLAND   (FIN)

MOTORING INFORMATION

National motoring organisation
Autoliitto Automobile and Touring-Club of Finland (ATCF), *FIA & AIT,* Hameentie 105, 00551 Helsinki. ☎ 0-694 0022 Office hours: (Sep-May) Mon-Fri 0830-1630; (June-Aug) Mon-Fri 0830-1530.

Breakdowns
Purchasers of Eurocover Motoring Assistance should consult their Assistance Document.

Carriage of children
Children must be restrained either with a seat belt or in a child seat.

Crash helmets
Compulsory for motorcyclists and passengers.

Drinking and driving
The blood alcohol legal limit is 50mg.

Drivers
The minimum age for drivers is 18.

Driving licence
UK driving licence accepted.

Emergencies
Police ☎ 10022, Fire Brigade and Ambulance ☎ 112. If you have an accident, report it to the Finnish Motor Insurance Bureau: Liikennevakuutusyhdistys, Bulevardi 28, 00120 Helsinki 12, ☎ (9) 019251.

Fuel
Petrol stations are usually open from 0700 to 2100 weekdays, shorter hours at weekends. Some petrol stations are open 24 hours. There are automatic pumps which operate upon insertion of bank notes. *Leaded petrol:* Regular

(92 octane) and Super (99 octane) available. *Unleaded petrol:* Regular (95 octane) and Super (98 octane) available; pump legend *lyijyton polttaine. Credit cards:* accepted at most petrol stations. *Spare fuel:* petrol imported in cans must be declared to Customs.

Lighting
Outside built-up areas all motor vehicles must use their headlights at all times.

Overtaking
Overtake on the left, unless the vehicle to be overtaken is signalling to turn left. In parallel lines of traffic, vehicles may be overtaken on the right. Vehicles being overtaken should not cross the white line which indicates the lane for cyclists and pedestrians.

Parking
Stopping and parking prohibitions follow international practice. Parking meters are usually grey and operate for between 15 minutes and 4 hours. Parking lights must be used if the parking place is not sufficiently lit. Although wheel clamps are not in use, illegally parked vehicles can be removed by the police, and a fine payable.

Priority
At intersections, vehicles coming from the right have priority except on main roads. The approach to these main roads is indicated by a sign with a red triangle on a yellow background. When this sign is supplemented by a red octagon with 'STOP' in the centre of the sign, vehicles **must** stop before entering the intersection. Trams and emergency vehicles,

even when coming from the left, always have priority over other vehicles.

Seat belts

If fitted, compulsory use in front seats.

Signalling

It is prohibited to sound a horn in towns and villages except in cases of immediate danger. Outside built-up areas horns and headlights should be used when and wherever visibility is not perfect.

Speed limits

Built-up areas: 31mph (50kmh); *outside built-up areas:* 50-62mph (80-100kmh); *motorways:* 74mph (120kmh). Cars towing a caravan or trailer are limited to 50mph (80kmh).

Traffic offences

The police are empowered to impose on-the-spot fines but are not authorised to collect them. Fines should be paid at banks and post offices. The minimum fine is 150 FIM.

Warning triangle

Advisable.

GENERAL INFORMATION

Banks

Open Mon-Fri 0915-1615. Exchange offices are

open longer hours, especially at Helsinki airport and at ports.

Currency

Markka (FIM or Finnish mark).

Post Offices

Open Mon-Fri 0900-1700. Closed Sat.

Public holidays

New Year's Day; Epiphany; Good Friday; Easter Monday; May Day; first Sat after Ascension; Whit Saturday; All Saints, first Sat in Nov; Independence Day, 6 Dec; Christmas Day; St Stephen's Day. Other days are Vappu night, 30 Apr, (a student and spring festival). Midsummer, 24 June, is celebrated throughout Finland on the Saturday nearest to 24 June with bonfires and dancing.

Shops

Open Mon-Fri 0900-1700, Sat 0900-1400/1600 according to season, and there are local variations. Shops at Helsinki railway and Metro stations are open Mon-Sat 1000-2200, Sun 1200-2200.

FRANCE (F)

MOTORING INFORMATION

National motoring organisations

Automobile Club de France, FIA, 6-8 Place de la Concorde, 75008 Paris. ☎ 42 65 34 70. Office hours: Mon-Fri 0900-1800.

Automobile Club National (ACN), FIA & AIT, 9 rue Anatole de la Forge, 75017 Paris. ☎ 42 27 82 00. Office hours: Mon-Fri 0830-1300 and 1345-1745 (Fri until 1645).

Breakdowns

Purchasers of Eurocover Motoring Assistance should consult their Assistance Document. Orange emergency telephones are situated every 2km along autoroutes and main roads.

Carriage of children

Children under 10 occupying any seat must travel in an approved child seat adapted to their size. If a foreign-registered vehicle is not fitted with front-seat child restraints, children under 10 must occupy a rear seat.

Crash helmets

Compulsory for motorcyclists and passengers.

Drinking and driving

The blood alcohol legal limit is 80mg.

Drivers

The minimum age for drivers is 18.

Driving licence

UK driving licence accepted.

Emergencies

Police ☎ 17, Fire Brigade ☎ 18. For Ambulance, if no number given in telephone box, call Police. In the case of an accident you should inform the Bureau Central Français des Sociétés d'Assurances contre les Accidents Automobiles, 36 ave du Général de Gaulle, 93171 Bagnolet cedex, ☎ (1) 49 93 65 50.

Fuel

Leaded petrol: Regular (90 octane) and Super (98 octane) available. *Unleaded petrol:* Super (95/98 octane) available; pump legend *essence sans plomb. Diesel:* sold at pumps marked 'gas-oil' or 'gaz-oil'. *Credit cards:* major credit cards accepted. *Spare fuel:* up to 10 litres of spare fuel may be imported in cans.

Internal ferries

Car ferry services operate across the Gironde estuary between Royan and Le Verdon, and in the south between Blaye and Lamasque. Crossing time is 30 minutes and 25 minutes respectively. Services operate during daylight hours throughout the year.

Lighting

Headlight beams must be adjusted for right-hand drive vehicles. Beam converter sets, which can be fitted quickly and easily, are obtainable from the RAC. There is now no legal requirement for vehicles to emit a yellow beam.

It is compulsory to use headlights at night in all areas, but these must be dipped in built-up areas. Motorcycle headlights are compulsory, day and night.

Do use headlights in poor visibility. Parking lights are obligatory, unless public lighting is sufficient for the vehicle to be seen distinctly from an adequate distance. A single offside parking light is permissible, provided that the light is illuminated on the side nearest the traffic. In Paris and some other large towns illegally parked vehicles will be clamped or towed away. The vehicle will be released only upon payment of a fine.

If a driver 'flashes' you he **does not** mean 'you go first'. He expects you to pull to one side and let him pass.

Visiting motorists are recommended to carry a set of spare bulbs for the front lights, rear lights, stop lights and direction indicator lights.

Overloading

The French authorities are concerned by the serious overloading of many British-registered cars touring in France. Apart from the possible danger to himself and passengers, if involved in an accident the driver could well find himself prosecuted or held responsible for the accident by carrying more passengers and/or excessive weight than the vehicle manufacturer recommends.

Overtaking

Do not overtake where the road is marked with one or two continuous unbroken lines or when a vehicle is already being overtaken, or when a tram is stationary with passengers alighting or boarding. Processions, funerals or troops must not be overtaken at over 18mph. You may overtake, giving the correct signal, where the road is marked by broken lines, although the line may only be crossed for the time taken to pass. A tram in motion may be overtaken on the right only, but on the left in a one-way street if there is sufficient space.

Parking

The usual restrictions on parking operate as in the UK with the following additions:

(a) **Do not** park where the kerbs are marked with yellow paint or where you will cause an obstruction.

(b) On roads outside town limits you must pull off the highway. Unilateral parking on alternate days is indicated by signs *Coté du Stationnement, jours pairs* – even (or *impairs* - odd).

In narrow streets in Paris, where parking both sides would obstruct the passage of double line traffic, this regulation applies automatically. Fines for towing away are very heavy.

Parking is prohibited in Paris along two main access routes designated *axes rouges* (red routes). The east-west route includes the left banks of the Seine and the Quai de la Mégisserie; the north-south route includes the Ave du Général Leclerc, part of the Blvd St Michel, the rue de Rivoli, blvds Sébastofol, Strasbourg, Barbès, Ornano, rue Lafayette and Ave Jean Jaurès.

Do not leave a parked vehicle in the same place in Paris for more than 24 consecutive hours. This restriction also applies in Hauts-de-Seine, Seine-St Denis and Val de Marne. Parking on the left-hand side of the road is permitted in one-way streets only.

In Paris and the larger cities, there are Blue Zones, where parking discs must be used. They may be obtained from police stations, tourist offices and some shops. When a kerbside space has been found, the disc must be displayed on the windscreen and the clock set showing both the time of arrival and when the parking space will be free. The time limits are: between 0900 and 1230 – 1 hour; between 1430 and 1900 – 1 hour except Sundays and public holidays. In other places, parking is shown by the international parking signs on which particular regulations are shown in black letters on a white background.

Priority

The *priorité à droite* for all roads no longer holds. Traffic on major roads now has priority. Where two major roads cross, the sign *Danger Priorité à Droite* is used, indicating that traffic coming from the right has priority. *Passage protégé* (priority road) signs indicate those major roads where traffic has priority. In the absence of signs, give way to traffic coming from the right. Since 1984 traffic already on a roundabout has priority, and a triangular sign with a red border showing a roundabout symbol with the legend *vous n'avez pas la priorité* indicates this. However, in a few areas the old ruling of priority given to traffic entering the roundabout still applies. So, where the signs are not present, you should approach with care.

Road signs

Conform to the international pattern but other road signs are:

Allumez vos lanternes: switch on your lights

Attention au feu: fire hazard
Attention travaux: beware roadworks
Barrière de dégel: applies to lorries when ice
is thawing and roads are closed to lorries
to prevent deterioration of road surface
Chaussée déformée: uneven road surface
Fin d'interdiction de stationner: end of
prohibited parking
Gravillons: loose chippings
Haute tension: electrified line
Interdit aux piétons: forbidden to pedestrians
Nids de poules: potholes
Rappel: remember (displayed on speed limit
signs)
Route barrée: road closed

Seat belts

If fitted, compulsory use in front and rear seats.

Signalling

Do not use horns except when it is absolutely
necessary in an emergency.

Speed limits

*Motorcycles over 80cc, private cars, vehicles towing
a caravan or trailer with total weight under 3.5
tonnes:* in built-up areas the speed limit is
31mph (50kmh), but this can be raised to 44mph
(70kmh) on important through roads as
indicated by signs; outside built-up areas on
normal roads 56mph (90kmh); priority roads
and toll free urban motorways 68mph
(110kmh); toll motorways 81mph (130kmh).

*Cars towing a caravan or trailer with total
weight exceeding 3.5 tonnes:* outside built-up
areas the speed limit is 50mph (80kmh) on
normal roads; priority roads 50mph (80kmh),
but increased to 62mph (100kmh) on dual
carriageways and to 68mph (110kmh) on
motorways. Special speed limits apply if the
weight of the trailer exceeds that of the towing
vehicle – the RAC can supply further information.

On the Paris *Périphérique* ring road the
speed limit is 49mph (80kmh). A minimum
speed of 49mph (80kmh) applies in the left lane
of level sections of motorways in good visibility.

In rain and bad weather, speed limits are
lowered to: motorways 68mph (110kmh); dual
carriageways 62mph (100kmh); other roads
outside built-up areas 50mph (80kmh).

Visitors who have held a licence for less
than one year are limited to 56mph (90kmh),
but are not required to display this speed limit
on their vehicle.

Tolls

Payable on the autoroute network (see page 73).
Tolls are also payable on the following bridges:
from the mainland (west coast) onto Ile de Ré
and Ile de Noirmoutier; Pont de Martrou,
Rochefort (Charente Maritime); Pont de St
Nazaire (Loire Atlantique); Pont de Brotonne
(Seine Maritime).

Traffic lights

As in Britain except there is no amber light after
the red light. Flashing amber means proceed
with caution. Flashing red means no entry.
Flashing yellow arrows mean the drivers may
proceed in direction indicated, but must give
way to pedestrians and the traffic flow they are
joining.

Traffic offences

Some French police are authorised to impose
and collect fines of up to 2,500F on the spot
from drivers who violate traffic regulations. An
official receipt should be requested.

If a minor offence is committed, a reduced
fine is payable within 30 days. A court hearing
must be arranged if the fine is to be contested. A
serious offence can result in a heavy fine,
suspension of driving licence or a prison
sentence.

Warning triangle

Compulsory.

GENERAL INFORMATION

Banks

Open weekdays 0900-1200 and 1400-1600. Some
provincial banks are open Tue-Sat 0900-1200
and 1400-1600.

Currency

French franc.

Museums

Most museums closed Mon.

Post Offices

Open Mon-Fri 0800-1900, Sat 0800-1200.

Public holidays

New Year's Day; Easter Monday; Labour Day;
VE Day, 8 May; Ascension; Whit Monday;
Bastille Day, 14 July; Assumption, 15 Aug; All
Saints, 1 Nov; Armistice Day, 11 Nov; Christ-
mas, 25 Dec.

Shops

Often closed Mon, all or half day, and for lunch
two hours daily. Food shops are open Sun
morning.

GERMANY

MOTORING INFORMATION

National motoring organisations
Allgemeiner Deutscher Automobil-Club (ADAC), *FIA & AIT*, Am Westpark 8, 81373 München. ☎ (089) 76760. 24-hr information service, ☎ (089) 22222. Office hours: weekdays 0800-1700, Sat ADAC District Offices in main towns open 0800-1200.
Automobil-Club von Deutschland (AVD), *FIA*, Lyonerstrasse 16, 60528 Frankfurt-am-Main. ☎ (069) 6606-0. Office hrs: weekdays 0800-1700.

Breakdowns
Purchasers of Eurocover Motoring Assistance should consult their Assistance Document. Both the motoring clubs (see above) maintain emergency patrol services on motorways and main routes.

Carriage of children
Children under the age of 12 are not permitted in front seats unless a seat equipped with a child restraint is fitted. In the rear of a vehicle, children under 12 must use a child seat, if fitted (a fine of 40 DM can be imposed if this regulation is not observed).

Crash helmets
Compulsory for motorcyclists and passengers.

Drinking and driving
The blood alcohol legal limit is 80mg.

Drivers
The minimum age for drivers is 17.

Driving licence
UK driving licence accepted.

Emergencies
Police ☎ 110, Fire Brigade ☎ 112, Ambulance ☎ 110 (115 in former East German states).

Fuel
Leaded petrol: Super (98 octane) available. *Unleaded petrol:* Regular (91 octane) and Super (95/98 octane) available; pump legend *bleifrei normal* or *bleifrei super*. *Credit cards:* accepted at most petrol stations. *Spare fuel:* a full can of fuel may be imported duty free for use by vehicles registered in an EC country.

Lighting
When visibility is reduced by rain, fog or snow, use dipped headlights – driving with sidelights only is prohibited. Auxiliary/foglights should be used only with dipped headlights, even in daylight.

Motorways
There are no tolls payable on autobahns. Fuel, restaurant and accommodation facilities, usually open 24 hours, are widely available on the network.

Overtaking
Do not overtake when passengers are boarding or alighting from a bus or tram. **Do not** overtake a tram if there is insufficient room on the right. In one-way streets trams can be overtaken on either side, but normally on the right when in motion. You must indicate your intention when overtaking or changing lanes. In urban areas there is free choice of traffic lane if several lanes are available. It is prohibited to overtake or pass a school bus, which has stopped outside a built-up area, when red lights are flashing.

Parking
Except for one-way streets, parking is only permitted on the right side unless loading, boarding, or unloading. **Do not** park on roads with 'Priority Road' signs, or where it would be dangerous to other traffic or pedestrians, outside built-up areas. Both meters and parking disc zones are in use.

Pedestrian crossings
Do give a pedestrian absolute priority on all pedestrian crossings, which are indicated on the road by white bands 50cm wide.

Priority
At the junction of two main roads or two minor roads, traffic from the right has priority, unless the contrary is indicated. Main road traffic has priority and that travelling on motorways has priority over vehicles entering or leaving.

Vehicles turning left at an intersection must give way to all oncoming vehicles. Trams do not have priority; buses do have priority when leaving bus stops. You must give way to a bus driver who has signalled his intention to leave the kerb.

Road signs
Most conform to the international pattern. Other road signs which may be seen are:
Autobahn kreuz: motorway junction
Baustofflagerung: roadworks material
Einbahnstrasse: one-way street
Fahrbahnwechsel: change traffic lane
Frostschäden: frost damage
Glatteisgefahr: ice on the road
Radweg kreuzt: cycle track crossing
Rollsplitt: loose grit
Seitenstreifen nicht bafahrbar: use of verge not advised
STAU: slow-moving traffic - drive with care
Strassenschäden: road damage
Umleitung: diversion

Seat belts

If fitted, compulsory use in front and rear seats.

Signalling

Do not sound your horn unnecessarily; this is forbidden. Outside built-up areas audible warning may be given if the driver intends to overtake another vehicle. At night, drivers must give warning of their approach by flashing their headlights.

Speed limits

Built-up areas: 31mph (50kmh); *outside built-up areas:* 62-81mph (100-130kmh); on *motorways,* the recommended maximum is 81mph (130kmh).

In the five new Federal states (formerly East Germany), the speed limit *outside built-up areas* is 50mph (80kmh), and on *motorways* 62mph (100kmh). On the A24 motorway the limit is increased to 75-80mph (120-130kmh) as indicated. Cars towing a caravan or trailer are limited to 50mph (80kmh) on all roads outside built-up areas.

There is a minimum speed of 37mph (60kmh) on motorways and expressways. When visibility is below 50 metres, the maximum speed limit is 31mph (50kmh) on all roads.

Traffic lights

In west Germany, the international three colour system is in use. In the new Federal states, the sequence is green-amber (simultaneously), amber, red, red-amber (simultaneously). In addition, drivers will see a red light with a green arrow pointing to the right, which means a right turn is permitted, but drivers must give way to other road users and pedestrians.

Traffic offences

The German police are empowered to impose and collect on-the-spot fines of up to 75 DM. Motorists may pay the fine during the course of the following week.

In cases of speed limit violations, a sliding scale of fines operates. A visitor can be asked to deposit a sum of money, and if he refuses or cannot pay, the vehicle may be impounded.

Warning triangle

Compulsory.

GENERAL INFORMATION

Banks

Open Mon-Fri 0830-1230 and 1400-1600 (Thu 1400-1730). Closed Sat.

Currency

Deutschmark.

Post Offices

Open Mon-Fri 0800-1800, Sat 0800-1200.

Public holidays

New Year's Day; Good Friday; Easter Monday; Labour Day; Ascension; Whit Monday; Day of Unity, 17 June; Unification Day, 3 Oct; Christmas, 25, 26 Dec. In addition, some areas observe Epiphany, Corpus Christi, Assumption, All Saints and Repentance days.

Shops

Open Mon-Fri 0830/0900-1800/1830. Closed Sat at 1400.

GIBRALTAR   (GBZ)

MOTORING INFORMATION

RAC Agent A M Capurro and Sons Ltd, 20 Line Wall Road, Gibraltar. ☎ 74813/75149.

Caravans and camping

The temporary importation of trailer caravans and motor caravans is prohibited, although Customs may grant an exception provided the owner is a bona fide visitor and does not intend to use the vehicle for camping purposes.

Crash helmets

Compulsory for motorcyclists and passengers on machines over 50cc.

Driving licence

UK driving licence accepted.

Emergencies

Police ☎ 190, Fire Brigade and Ambulance ☎ 199.

Fuel

Leaded petrol: Super (98 octane) available. *Unleaded petrol:* Super (95 octane) available. *Credit cards:* not accepted. *Spare fuel:* 20 gallons may be imported in a sealed steel container. It must be declared to Customs, and duty is payable.

Lighting

It is compulsory to drive with dipped headlights at night.

Parking

Car parks are located at Grand Parade (near lower cable car station), at Eastern Beach, Catalan Bay and at Casemates Square. Street parking is allowed in Queensway, Line Wall Road, Devils Tower Road and Rosia Road. Much of the town centre is pedestrianised, so motoring visitors should park outside the city walls. Vehicles parked in restricted areas will be towed away or immobilised. If this occurs the driver should go to the Central Police Station in

Irish Town. Parking areas are clearly marked.

Priority

Vehicles already on a roundabout have priority.

Roads

On the Upper Rock, roads are narrow, winding and steep. Signposts indicate those roads not open to civilian traffic. Visitors are therefore recommended to take a Rock Tour by taxi or minicoach.

Seat belts

Recommended.

Speed limits

Maximum 25mph (40kmh). Lower limits are signposted.

GENERAL INFORMATION

Banks

Open Mon-Thu 0900-1530 (Fri some banks open 0900-1800).

Border crossing

Motorists should beware of civilians illegally selling tickets for the border crossing.

Public holidays

New Year's Day; Commonwealth Day, 13 Mar; Easter; May Day; Spring Bank Holiday; Queen's Birthday; Late Summer Bank Holiday; Christmas.

Shops

Open Mon-Fri 0900-1700, Sat 0900-1300.

GREECE   GR

MOTORING INFORMATION

National motoring organisations

The Automobile and Touring Club of Greece (ELPA), *FIA & AIT,* 2-4 Messogion Street, 115 27 **Athína (Athens).** ☎ 779 1615. Office hours: Mon-Fri 0830-1930, Sat 0830-1330.
Hellenic Touring Club, *AIT,* 12 Politechniou Street, Athína 104 33. ☎ 52 40 854 and 52 48 600. Office hours: Mon-Fri 0800-1500 and 1730-2100, Sat 0800-1500.

Breakdowns

Purchasers of Eurocover Motoring Assistance should consult their Assistance Document. ELPA's road assistance service (OVELPA) operates on a 24-hr basis and covers all main roads, as well as the islands of Crete and Corfu. Motorists requiring assistance should dial 104.

Children in front seats

Not permitted under the age of 10.

Crash helmets

Compulsory for motorcyclists and passengers.

Drinking and driving

The blood alcohol legal limit is 50mg.

Drivers

The minimum age for drivers is 18.

Driving licence

UK driving licence accepted.

Emergencies

Police ☎ 100 (Athína, Pireás, Thessaloníki, Pátrai, Corfu), 109 (suburbs of Athína); Fire Brigade ☎ 199, Ambulance ☎ 166 (Athína) - for other towns see local directory.

Fire extinguisher

Compulsory.

First aid kit

Compulsory.

Fuel

Leaded petrol: Regular (91/92 octane) and Super (96/98 octane) available. *Unleaded petrol:* Super (95 octane) available; pump legend *amoliwdi wensina. Credit cards:* accepted at some petrol stations. *Spare fuel:* it is prohibited to import fuel in cans.

Lighting

Do not use undipped headlights in towns. A motor vehicle parked at night on a public road must have the rear red light clearly illuminated.

Overtaking

Overtaking is prohibited when approaching an unguarded level crossing.

Parking

The usual restrictions apply. Some streets have unilateral parking only, or impose a 30-minute limit. In Athína you may park only at meters although special parking sites are available to visitors. Caravans are also admitted for parking. The police will remove your registration plates if you stop or park in a no-parking zone. This practice applies also in some areas outside Athína. Greek-registered vehicles have been banned from a zone in the centre of Athína on certain days. Visiting motorists are exempted if their stay in Greece does not exceed 40 days.

Priority

In towns priority must be accorded to traffic entering from the right. In the open country, main road traffic has priority.

Road signs

International road signs are in use.

Seat belts

If fitted, compulsory use in front seats.

Signalling

Your warning device must be of low-pitched

regular tone. Multitone sirens, klaxons, whistles and hooters are forbidden. The horn may be used in open country, but in towns it is allowed only in an emergency.

Speed limits

Built-up areas: motorcycles 25mph (40kmh), car with or without caravan/trailer 31mph (50kmh). *Outside built-up areas:* motorcycles 44mph (70kmh), car with or without caravan/trailer 56mph (90kmh). *Motorways and national roads:* motorcycles 44mph (70kmh), car with or without caravan/trailer 75mph (120kmh) on motorways, 68mph (110kmh) on dual carriageways.

Temporary importation of vehicles

Vehicle details will be entered into a visitor's passport on entry into Greece. A foreign-registered vehicle may be temporarily imported for a maximum period of 6 months.

Tolls

Payable on certain roads (see page 75).

Traffic offences

Fines imposed by the Greek police are payable to the Public Treasury, not to a police officer.

Warning triangle

Compulsory.

GENERAL INFORMATION

Banks

Open Mon-Fri 0800-1400. Foreign exchange counters often open again in the afternoon and evening.

Currency

Drachma.

Post Offices

Open Mon-Fri 0800-1500, although some offices open longer hours. In Athína, many post offices open Sat mornings during the summer.

Public holidays

New Year's Day; Epiphany; Shrove Monday; Independence Day, 25 Mar; Good Friday; Easter Monday; Labour Day; Whit Monday; Assumption, 15 Aug; Ohi Day (National Day), 28 Oct; Christmas, 25, 26 Dec

Shops

Usually open Mon 0930-1900, Tue-Fri 0900-1900, Sat 0900-1530.

HUNGARY

MOTORING INFORMATION

National motoring organisation

Magyar Autóklub (MAK), *FIA & AIT,* Rómer Flóris utca 4/a, Budapest II. ☎ 1-115 2040. Office hours: Mon-Thu 0730-1600, Fri 0730-1500. Closed Sat.

Breakdowns

Purchasers of Eurocover Motoring Assistance should consult their Assistance Document. For MAK breakdown service, ☎ 1-115 1220.

Children in front seats

Not permitted under the age of 12.

Crash helmets

Compulsory for motorcyclists and passengers on machines over 50cc which can exceed 50kmh.

Drinking and driving

The blood alcohol legal limit is 80mg.

Drivers

The minimum age for drivers is 18.

Driving licence

EC format 'pink/green' licence accepted; old-style 'green' licence accepted only if accompanied by an International Driving Permit.

Emergencies

Police ☎ 07, Fire Brigade ☎ 05, Ambulance ☎ 04. An '0' prefix should be added when calling emergency services from outside Budapest. Accidents causing damage or injury to persons must be reported to the nearest policeman or police station (☎ Budapest 07) and to the Hungarian State Insurance Company within 24 hours. The police will issue a statement, which the motorist must show when leaving Hungary, in order to avoid lengthy delays at the frontier.

Fuel

On motorways and in large towns, petrol stations are open 24 hours. Otherwise, hours are 0600-2000. *Leaded petrol:* Regular (86 octane) and Super (92 octane) available. *Unleaded petrol:* Regular (91 octane) and Super (95 octane) available; pump legend *olommentes uzemanyag.* Availability is indicated by a white sign with blue border and an illustration of two pumps – black (leaded) and green (unleaded). *Diesel:* visiting motorists are recommended to fill their tanks at SHELL or AFOR stations to avoid inferior fuel on sale at some filling stations. *Credit cards:* Eurocard accepted at some petrol stations. *Spare fuel:* it is prohibited to import or export fuel in cans. *Coupons:* the coupon scheme has been discontinued.

Lighting

Outside built-up areas, dipped headlights must

be used day and night. In built-up areas at night, the use of full headlights is prohibited, and dipped headlights must be used. Motorcyclists must use dipped headlights day and night. Additional stop lights are prohibited. A spare set of bulbs must be carried by residents only.

Motorways
Emergency telephones are located at 2km intervals on motorways. Catering facilities are usually located near petrol stations. Motel accommodation is rarely available on motorways.

Overtaking
Vehicles must overtake on the left. On roads where tram-rails are placed in the middle of the road, a moving tram or vehicle signalling its intention to turn left must be overtaken on the right.

Parking
To reduce traffic congestion and pollution, the centre of Budapest is closed to private traffic. On two-way roads vehicles must be parked on the right-hand side of the road, facing in the direction of the traffic. They may be parked on either side of one-way roads. **Do not** park in places where you would not park in Britain.

Pedestrian crossings
Pedestrians have right of way at pedestrian crossings and priority at intersections over turning traffic. They do not have priority on the roadway between tramloading islands and the kerb. Drivers must show special care on these sections.

Priority
Major roads are indicated by a 'Priority Road Ahead' sign. At the intersection of two roads of equal importance, where there is no such sign, vehicles coming from the right have priority. However, emergency vehicles, with a blue light or siren, and trams and buses have absolute priority at any intersection and, indeed, on any road.

Buses also have right of way when leaving bus stops after the driver has signalled his intention to pull out.

Seat belts
If fitted, compulsory use in front and rear seats.

Signalling
The use of horns in built-up areas is not permitted between 2200 and 0600. During these hours, warning signals must be given by means of headlights. Motorists are also prohibited to use a horn at any time in Budapest and in certain other towns and villages on main roads, except in an emergency.

Speed limits
Built-up areas: motorcycles, cars with or without caravan/trailer 31mph (50kmh). *Outside built-up areas:* motorcycles, cars 50mph (80kmh), dual carriageways 62mph (100kmh), motorways 75mph (120kmh). Car with caravan/trailer on normal roads and dual carriageways 44mph (70kmh), on motorways 50mph (80kmh).

Traffic offences
On-the-spot fines are imposed and collected by the police. Alternatively, fines may be paid by post within 15 days.

Warning triangle
Compulsory.

GENERAL INFORMATION

Banks
Open Mon-Fri 0700-1300.
Currency
Forint.
Museums
Open Tue-Sat 1000-1800.
Post Offices
Usually open Mon-Fri 0800-1800. At Budapest main railway station, open Mon-Sat 0700-2100.
Public holidays
New Year; National Day, 15 Mar; Easter Monday; Whitsun; Labour Day; Constitution Day, 20 Aug; Proclamation of the Republic, 23 Oct; Christmas, 25, 26 Dec.
Shops
Open Mon-Fri 1000-1800, Sat 1000-1300.
Visa
British Nationals no longer require a visa.

REPUBLIC OF IRELAND   (IRL)

MOTORING INFORMATION

Children in front seats
Not permitted under the age of 12, unless the seat is equipped with a child restraint.
Crash helmets
Compulsory for motorcyclists and passengers.

Drinking and driving
A person convicted of driving or attempting to drive with a blood alcohol level exceeding 100mg per 100ml will be liable to a severe penalty.
Drivers
The minimum age for drivers is 17.

Driving licence
UK driving licence accepted.
Emergencies
Police, Fire, Ambulance ☎ 999.
Fuel
Petrol stations are usually open from 0730 to 2200, and some are open 24 hours. *Leaded petrol:* Super (98 octane) available. *Unleaded petrol:* widely available. *Credit cards:* accepted. *Spare fuel:* although up to 10 litres may be imported duty free in containers, do remember that it is illegal to carry spare fuel on ferries.
Internal ferries
A car ferry operates across the River Shannon from Tarbert (Co. Kerry) to Killimer (Co. Clare). The ferry leaves Killimer hourly on the hour, and Tarbert hourly on the half-hour. Crossing time is 30 minutes.

A 10-minute car ferry service operates between Ballyhack (Co. Wexford) and Passage East (Co. Waterford). First sailing 0720 week-days, 0930 Sunday. Last sailing 2200 in summer, 2000 in winter.
Lighting
Foglights may only be used in fog or falling snow.
Parking
The usual restrictions apply to parking as in Great Britain. Parking meters are in use. They operate from Monday to Saturday from 0800 to 1830 and the maximum authorised parking time is 2 hours. Free use of unexpired time on meters is authorised. On-the-spot fines may be levied for parking offences.
Road signs
The 'Give Way' sign consists of a red triangle with the point downwards, and the words 'Yield Right of Way' or 'Geill sli'.
Seat belts
If fitted, compulsory use in front and rear seats.
Signalling
Horns must not be used between 2330 and 0700 on any road where a permanent speed limit is in force.

Speed limits
Built-up areas: 30mph (48kmh); *outside built-up areas:* 60mph (96kmh); *motorways:* 70mph (112kmh). On certain roads, and clearly marked, the speed limits are 40mph (65kmh) or 50mph (80kmh). These limits also apply to a car and caravan/trailer.
Temporary importation of vehicles
Drivers of motor caravans, caravans and trailers will be issued with a temporary importation permit by Irish Customs at the port of arrival. A temporarily imported vehicle must not be driven by an Irish resident.
Traffic offences
If a motorist has committed an offence the Garda Siochana (Civic Guard) may issue the person with a notice instructing the offender to pay a fine within 21 days at a Garda Station. The offender has an alternative choice of letting the case go to court.

GENERAL INFORMATION

Banks
Open Mon-Fri 1000-1230 and 1330-1500 (in Dublin, until 1700 on Thursdays).
Currency
Irish pound.
Museums
Generally open 1000-1700 daily except public holidays.
Passport
British citizens born in the United Kingdom do not require a passport to visit Ireland.
Post Offices
Open Mon-Fri 0900-1730, Sat 0900-1300.
Public holidays
New Year's Day; St Patrick's Day, 17 Mar; Easter; first Mon in June and Aug; last Mon in Oct; Christmas.
Shops
Open Mon-Sat 0900-1730/1800.

ITALY

MOTORING INFORMATION

National motoring organisations
Automobile Club d'Italia (ACI), *FIA & AIT,* Via Marsala 8, 00185 Roma. ☎ (06) 49981. Office hours: Mon-Sat 0800-1400. There are offices in most large towns.
Touring Club Italiano (TCI), *AIT,* Corso Italia

10, 20122 Milano. ☎ (02) 85261. Telex: 321160. Head Office hours: Mon-Fri 0900-1800, Sat 0830-1230. For breakdown service information, ☎ 8526263.
Breakdowns
Purchasers of Eurocover Motoring Assistance should consult their Assistance Document. In the case of breakdown on any Italian road,

☎ 116. This puts the traveller in touch with the ACI breakdown service.

Carriage of children
Children aged between 4 and 12 must occupy a front or rear seat which is equipped with a special restraint.

Crash helmets
Compulsory for motorcyclists and passengers.

Drinking and driving
The blood alcohol legal limit is 80mg.

Drivers
The minimum age for drivers is 18.

Driving licence
EC format 'pink/green' licence accepted; old-style 'green' licence accepted only with an official Italian translation.

Emergencies
Police, Fire Brigade and Ambulance ☎ 113.

Fuel
On motorways, petrol stations are open 24 hours. On other roads, fuel is available (May to September) from 0700 to 1230, and 1530 to 1930. From October to April, petrol stations close at 1900. Only 25% of petrol stations on these roads are open on Sundays and public holidays, and are subsequently closed on Mondays. Opening hours are displayed, along with the address of the nearest garage open. *Leaded petrol:* Regular (85/88 octane) and Super (98/100 octane) available. *Unleaded petrol:* Super (95 octane) available; pump legend *benzina sensa piombo*. *Credit cards:* accepted. *Spare fuel:* it is prohibited to import and carry fuel in cans. *Coupons:* the coupon scheme has been discontinued.

Lighting
It is compulsory to use vehicle lights half an hour after sunset until half an hour before sunrise. Main beam headlights can only be used outside towns, and when no other vehicle is approaching. At all other times only low beam headlights can be used. Lights must be used under bridges and dipped lights must be used in tunnels. Foglights should only be used in bad visibility.

Overtaking
You may overtake on the right when the other driver has signalled he is turning left and has moved to the centre of the road, or when travel is in parallel rows.

Parking
This is allowed on the right side of the road, except on motorways (*autostrada*) and in places where you would not park in Britain.

There are Blue Zones in all major towns, indicated by road signs. Within these zones a parking disc must be displayed from Monday to Saturday (except holidays) 0900 to 1430 and 1600 to 2000. The maximum period is 1 hour. Discs

can be obtained from the tourist and automobile organisations and also from petrol stations. In addition there are Green Zones where parking is strictly prohibited on weekdays 0800 to 0930 and 1430 to 1600.

VENEZIA Owing to the limited parking facilities at the Venezia end of the causeway, especially in the Piazzale Roma, it is advisable to park at one of the special car parks on the mainland. The car parks are linked by ferry and bus services to destinations in Venezia.

ROMA Parking is strictly prohibited in the central area on weekdays, indicated by a sign reading *zona tutelato*. Illegal parking will result in a fine and a prison sentence.

FIRENZE (FLORENCE) All vehicles are banned from the centre on weekdays between 0730 and 1830. Visitors staying within the area may stop to offload luggage, but then must park outside the restricted area.

Priority
On three-lane roads the middle lane is reserved for overtaking. At crossroads give way to traffic from the right.

Outside built-up areas priority must be given to vehicles travelling on national roads (*strade stratali*). On certain mountain roads, a red circular sign bearing a black post horn on a white triangle indicates that vehicles are required to stop at the approach of buses belonging to the postal services.

Road signs
Most conform to the international pattern. Other road signs which may be encountered are:
Entrata: entrance
Incrocio: crossroads
Lavori in corso: roadworks ahead
Passaggio a livello: level crossing
Rallentare: slow down
Senso Vietato: no entry
Sosta Autorizzata: parking permitted (fol-
   lowed by indication of times)
Sosta Vietata: no parking
Svolta: bend
Uscita: exit
Vietato Ingresso Veicoli: no entry for vehicles
Vietato Transito Autocarri: closed to heavy
   vehicles

Seat belts
If fitted, compulsory use in front and rear seats.

Signalling
In built-up areas use of the horn is prohibited except in cases of immediate danger. At night, flashing headlights may be used instead of a horn. Outside built-up areas, when it is required that warning of approach be given, the use of the horn is compulsory.

Speed limits

Motorcycles over 150cc and cars: in built-up areas 30mph (50kmh); outside built-up areas, on secondary roads 55mph (90kmh), main roads 68mph (110kmh), motorways 80mph (130kmh). Visitors should watch for signs indicating variations in limits. Cars towing a caravan or trailer are limited to 44mph (70kmh) outside built-up areas and 50mph (80kmh) on motorways.

Tolls

Payable on the autostrada network (see page 75).

Traffic lights

These are often suspended over the centre of crossroads.

Traffic offences

Italian traffic police are authorised to impose and collect fines on the spot for violation of traffic regulations. These are no longer regarded as criminal offences, but fines have been increased considerably.

A new Italian Highway Code introduced in 1993 stipulates that visiting motorists will be treated in the same way as Italian residents. The Italian police can therefore withdraw a visiting motorist's driving licence for serious offences or for non-payment of an on-the-spot fine.

Warning triangle

Compulsory.

GENERAL INFORMATION

Banks
Open Mon-Fri 0830-1330 and 1500-1600.
Currency
Lire.
Post Offices
Open Mon-Sat 0800-1700.
Public holidays
New Year's Day; Easter Monday; Liberation Day, 25 Apr; Labour Day; Assumption, 15 Aug; All Saints Day, 1 Nov; Immaculate Conception, 8 Dec; Christmas, 25, 26 Dec. It is wise to check locally for shop and bank closing times on special Feast days.
Purchase of meals
Visitors to Italy should obtain a specially numbered receipt (a *Ricevuta fiscale*) when paying for a meal in restaurants, hotels, etc. This fiscal receipt must show the amount paid for each part of the meal and the VAT paid. Visitors must ensure that this receipt is issued, as a fine may be imposed for non-compliance.
Shops
Open Mon-Sat 0830/0900-1300 and 1530/1600-1930/2000 with some variations in the north, where the lunch break is shorter and shops close earlier.

LUXEMBOURG

MOTORING INFORMATION

National motoring organisation
Automobile Club du Grand Duché de Luxembourg (ACL), *FIA & AIT,* 13 route de Longwy, Helfenterbruck, Bertrange. ☎ 450045. Office hours: Mon-Fri 0830-1200 and 1330-1800.
Breakdowns
Purchasers of Eurocover Motoring Assistance should consult their Assistance Document.
Children in front seats
A child under 12, or below 1.5 metres in height, may occupy a front seat if seated in a special safety-approved seat. In the rear of a vehicle, a child should be seated in a child seat, otherwise a seat belt should be used.
Crash helmets
Recommended.
Drinking and driving
The blood alcohol legal limit is 80mg.
Drivers
The minimum age for drivers is 18.

Driving licence
UK driving licence accepted.
Emergencies
Police, Fire Brigade and Ambulance ☎ 012.
Fuel
Leaded petrol: Super (98 octane) available. *Unleaded petrol:* Regular (91 octane) and Super (95 octane) available; pump legend *essence sans plomb. Credit cards:* Visa and Eurocard accepted. *Spare fuel:* it is prohibited to purchase and carry spare fuel in cans.
Lighting
Use dipped headlights when following another vehicle, and in case of fog, heavy rain or snow during daylight hours. **Do** use sidelights, even in places lit by public lighting systems. In other places vehicles must have dipped or undipped headlights. Motorcyclists must use dipped headlights day and night.
Overtaking
Do not overtake when this might endanger or obstruct traffic.

Parking

A Blue Zone parking area exists in Luxembourg City, Esch-sur-Alzette, Dudelange and Wiltz. Parking discs follow the usual pattern and are obtainable from the ACL, police stations, local tourist office, shops, etc. In addition, Luxembourg City has coin parking meters and ticket parking with tickets obtainable at dispensing boxes. Illegally parked vehicles will be clamped by the police.

Priority

The rule of the road is keep to the right, overtake on the left. At a crossing of two roads in the same category, traffic from the right has priority. In towns, **do** give priority to traffic coming from the right, unless the crossing is marked with a triangular sign.

Seat belts

If fitted, compulsory use in front and rear seats.

Signalling

Unnecessary use of the horn is prohibited. **Do not** use it between nightfall and dawn, or in built-up areas, except in an emergency. During the day, warning of approach should be given before overtaking another vehicle, or at places where visibility is restricted or whenever road safety requires it. At night, in these circumstances, it is compulsory to flash headlights.

Speed limits

Built-up areas: 30mph (50kmh); *outside built-up areas:* 56mph (90kmh); *motorways:* 74mph (120kmh). Cars towing a caravan or trailer are limited to 46mph (75kmh) outside built-up areas, and 56mph (90kmh) on motorways.

Traffic offences

On-the-spot fines are imposed by police in cases of traffic offences.

Warning triangle

Compulsory.

GENERAL INFORMATION

Banks

Open Mon-Fri 0830-1200 and 1330-1630.

Currency

Luxembourg and Belgian francs.

Post Offices

Open Mon-Fri 0800-1200 and 1400-1700. The post office at Luxembourg Central Station is open 24 hours.

Public holidays

New Year's Day; Easter Monday; May Day; Ascension; Whit Monday; National Day, 23 June; Assumption, 15 Aug; All Saints; All Souls; Christmas, 25, 26 Dec.

Shops

Open Mon 1400-1830, Tue-Sat 0830-1200 and 1400-1830.

NETHERLANDS (NL)

MOTORING INFORMATION

National motoring organisations

Koninklijke Nederlandsche Automobiel Club (KNAC), *FIA,* Westvlietweg 118, Leidschendam. ☎ (070) 399 7451. Office hours: Mon-Fri 0900-1700.

Koninklijke Nederlandsche Toeristenbond (ANWB), *AIT,* Wassenaarsweg 220, Den Haag. ☎ (070) 314 7147. Office hrs: Mon-Fri 0800-1730.

Breakdowns

Purchasers of Eurocover Motoring Assistance should consult their Assistance Document. Road patrol assistance can be obtained by telephoning ANWB Head Office.

Children in front seats

Children under 3 must travel in a rear seat with a suitable safety system adapted to their size. Children aged 3 to 12 may occupy a front seat if seated in a special safety seat.

Crash helmets

Compulsory for motorcyclists and passengers.

Drinking and driving

The blood alcohol legal limit is 50mg.

Drivers

The minimum age for drivers is 18.

Driving licence

UK driving licence accepted.

Emergencies

For Police, Fire Brigade and Ambulance, refer to local telephone directory.

Fuel

Leaded petrol: Super (98 octane) available. *Unleaded petrol:* Regular (91 octane) and Super (95 octane) available; pump legend *loodvrije benzine. Credit cards:* accepted. *Spare fuel:* 10 litres of petrol in a can may be imported duty free.

Internal ferries

A frequent car ferry service operates across the Westerschelde estuary between Breskens and Vlissingen, and further east between Perkpolder and Kruiningen. Journey time is 20 minutes and 15 minutes respectively.

Lighting

Parked vehicles do not have to be illuminated at night, provided they are parked in a built-up area, within 30 metres of a street lighting point, or in an official car park. Inside built-up areas only dipped headlights (low beam) are permitted. Dipped or full headlights must be used in fog.

Overtaking

Do not cross a continuous white line on the road, even to make a left turn. You may overtake stationary trams on the right at moderate speed, provided no inconvenience is caused to persons entering or leaving the tram. The overtaking of moving trams is normally permitted only on the right, although if there is insufficient room and no danger to oncoming traffic, vehicles may overtake on the left. The 'Overtaking Prohibited' sign does not apply to scooters or solo motorcycles. Do follow correct lanes, these are well marked with arrows.

Parking

Do not park on roads signposted 'No Parking', in front of driveways or where you may obscure road, street or traffic signs; on priority roads outside built-up areas. Do not halt a vehicle on roads signposted *Stop-verbod* – a blue disc with a red border and red diagonals; on access roads to and from main highways; cycling paths or footpaths, or along a yellow line or black and white line painted on road or pavement alongside a bus stop; in the middle of a three-carriageway road, or on a road with more than three carriageways (this does not stop passengers getting in or out of a car); on level crossings. Blue Zones have been introduced in most towns and free parking discs are obtainable from police stations. A parking fee is charged at guarded car parks. There are also parking meters. Wheel clamps will be used on illegally parked vehicles.

Priority

Priority roads are indicated by diamond-shaped orange signs with white borders. At junctions where the sign 'Major Road Ahead' or 'Stop, Major Road Ahead' is displayed, priority must be given to all traffic on that road. At the intersection of two roads of the same class where there are no signs, traffic from the right has preference. Motor vehicles have right of way over slow traffic, such as bicycles. Ambulances, fire engines, police cars and emergency rescue vehicles always have right of way. Trams have priority at intersections of equal importance but they must yield right of way to traffic on priority roads. At intersections, cyclists proceeding straight ahead have priority over all traffic. At pedestrian crossings do give a pedestrian absolute priority if he is on the zebra crossing first.

Road signs

Most conform to the international pattern but other road signs which may be seen are :

Doorgaand verkeer gestremd: no throughway

Langzaam rijden: slow down

Opspattend Grind: loose grit

Pas op: filevorming: attention: single or double lane traffic ahead

Rechtsaf toegeslaan: right turn allowed

Tegenliggers: traffic from the opposite direction

Wegomlegging: detour

Werk in uitvoering: road building in progress

Do watch for a blue sign with a white house emblem (*Woonerf*): built-up areas. This can mean:

1. Drive at walking pace (children playing in street);
2. Pedestrians have right of way;
3. Bicycles from the right have priority;
4. Park only in zones marked 'P'.

Seat belts

If fitted, compulsory use in front seats.

Signalling

Do sound your horn where there is any risk to other road users. At night you should give warning by flashing headlights instead, unless this might cause interference to other traffic, in which case the horn may be used.

Speed limits

Built-up areas: 31mph (50kmh); *outside built-up areas:* 50mph (80kmh); *motorways:* 62-74mph (100-120kmh). The minimum speed on motorways is 44mph (70kmh). Cars towing a caravan or trailer with one axle are limited to 50mph (80kmh) outside built-up areas.

Traffic offences

In some districts, on-the-spot fines are imposed and collected by the police in cases of traffic offences.

Warning triangle

Compulsory.

GENERAL INFORMATION

Banks

Open Mon-Fri 0900-1600. At border towns, exchange offices (GWK) are open Mon-Sat, also often Sun and in the evenings.

Currency

Guilder (florin).

Museums

Open Tue-Fri 1000-1700, Sat/Sun 1100-1700 or 1300-1700.

Post Offices
Open Mon-Fri 0830-1700. Some offices open Sat 0830-1200.

Public holidays
New Year's Day; Good Friday; Easter Monday; Queen's Birthday, 30 Apr; Liberation Day, 5 May; Ascension; Whit Monday; Christmas, 25, 26 Dec.

Shops
Department stores open Mon-Fri 0830/0900-1730/1800, Sat 0830/0900-1600/1700. Food shops open Mon-Sat 0800-1800.

All traders are required by law to close their shops for one half day per week. Local regulations stipulate when all shops will be closed either until 1300, or from 1300 onwards.

NORWAY (N)

MOTORING INFORMATION

National motoring organisations
Kongelig Norsk Automobilklub (KNA), *FIA,* Drammensveien 20-C, 0255 Oslo. ☎ (47) 22-56 19 00. Office hours: Mon-Fri 0830-1600 (1500 in summer).
Norges Automobil-Forbund (NAF), *AIT,* Storgt. 2, 0155 Oslo 1. ☎ (47) 22-34 15 00. Telex: 71671. Office hours: Mon-Fri 0830-1600, Sat 0830-1300.

Breakdowns
Purchasers of Eurocover Motoring Assistance should consult their Assistance Document. During the summer season road patrols are maintained on most mountain passes and on certain main roads.

Crash helmets
Compulsory for motorcyclists and passengers.

Drinking and driving
The blood alcohol legal limit is 50mg.

Drivers
The minimum age for drivers is 17, or 18 to hire or borrow a locally registered vehicle.

Driving licence
UK driving licence accepted.

Emergencies
In Oslo, Police ☎ 002, Ambulance ☎ 003. In other areas refer to the telephone directory.

Fuel
On weekdays, petrol stations are closed between 1900 and 0500. At weekends, they are open only in densely populated areas. *Leaded petrol:* Super (98 octane) available. *Unleaded petrol:* Super (95 octane) available; pump legend *blyfritt kraftstoff. Credit cards:* major cards accepted at larger petrol stations. *Spare fuel:* it is recommended that no more than 15 litres is carried in approved storage cans, which may be imported duty free.

Lighting
It is compulsory to use dipped headlights at all times. Foglights are not compulsory, but if used must be in conjunction with other lights. They may be used in fog or falling snow and during clear weather on winding roads.

Mountain passes
Many of the high mountain roads are closed during the winter, duration of closure depending on weather conditions. However, some mountain passes are kept open all year, eg Road No. 11 (Oslo-Bergen/Stavanger) across Haukelifjell mountain, the E6 (Oslo-Trondheim) across Dovrefjell mountain, and Road No. 7 (Oslo-Bergen) over the Hardangervidda plateau.

Overtaking
In Oslo, normally overtake trams on the right: they may be overtaken on the left if in motion in a one-way street, or where there is no room on the right.

Parking
Do not park on main roads; where visibility is restricted; where there is a sign *All Stans Forbudt* (No stopping allowed), or you may have your car towed away. Parking regulations in Norwegian towns are very strict, and parking offences are invariably subject to fines. Parking meters are in use in the main towns. Free use of unexpired time on meters is authorised. There are three types of parking meter: Yellow – 1 hour parking, Grey – 2 hours and Brown – 3 hours.

Priority
Give way to traffic from the right, except on some main roads which are given permanent priority. Intersecting junctions will bear the international priority symbol. Vehicles climbing uphill **must** be given priority, and down-hill drivers must reverse into a parking bay if necessary. Trams always have right of way.

Road signs
International road signs, but other road signs which may be seen are:
Arbeide pa Vegen: roadworks ahead
Bakketopp: hill top
Enveiskjøring: one-way traffic
Ferist: cattle grid

Gammel Veg: old road
Grøfterens: ditching work
Ikke Møte: no passing, single line traffic
Kjør Sakte: drive slowly
Løs Grus: loose gravel
Møteplass: passing bay
Omkjøring: diversion
Rasteplass: lay-by
Svake Kanter: soft verges
Veg under Anlegg: road under construction
Veiarbeide: roadworks

Seat belts
If fitted, compulsory use in front and rear seats. On-the-spot fines are imposed for non-compliance.

Signalling
Use horns, traffic indicators and lights **only** when necessary to avoid accidents.

Speed limits
Built-up areas: 31mph (50kmh); *outside built-up areas and on motorways:* 50-56mph (80-90kmh). Outside built-up areas, cars towing a caravan or trailer (with brakes) 50mph (80kmh); (without brakes) 37mph (60kmh).

Tolls
All vehicles entering Bergen by road on a weekday must pay a toll of 5 Kr. No charge at weekends or on public holidays. Cars or vehicles up to 3.5 tonnes entering Oslo pay a toll of 10 Kr.

Traffic offences
Police are empowered to impose and collect fines on the spot in cases of traffic offences.

Warning triangle
Advisable.

GENERAL INFORMATION

Banks
Open Mon-Fri 0815-1500 (1530 in winter). Some banks open until 1700 on Thursdays.

Currency
Krone (plural kroner).

Post Offices
Generally open Mon-Fri 0800/0830-1600/1700, Sat 0800-1300.

Public holidays
New Year's Day; Maundy Thursday; Good Friday; Easter Monday; Labour Day; Constitution Day, 17 May; Whit Monday; Ascension Day; Christmas, 24 (part), 25 and 26 Dec.

Shops
Open Mon/Wed/Fri 0900-1700, Thu 0900-1800, Sat 0900-1300. In July some shops close at 1500.

POLAND

MOTORING INFORMATION

National motoring organisations
Polski Zwiazek Motorowy (PZM), *FIA & AIT,* 66 Kazimierzowska Street, PL-02-518 Warszawa. ☎ (48) 22 499 361, 22 499 212. Touring office: Autotour s.r.l., 85 Solec Street, 00-950 Warszawa. ☎ (48) 22 498 449. Head Office hours: Mon-Fri 0745-1545; PZM Touring office hours: Mon-Fri 0800-1600.
Auto Assistance, 19 Sandomierska Street, 00-950 Warszawa. ☎ (48) 22-290 374.

Breakdowns
Purchasers of Eurocover Motoring Assistance should consult their Assistance Document. The Polski Zwiazek Motorowy operates a road patrol service within a 25km radius of towns in which there is a PZM office. Details may be obtained from PZM frontier offices and provincial touring offices. In most towns, the telephone number for breakdown assistance is 981. Technical help is free to motorists belonging to AIT and FIA Clubs for repairs within the 25km area, which can be effected in a period of one hour. For more serious breakdowns the vehicle will be towed to a garage.

Children in front seats
Not permitted under the age of 10.

Crash helmets
Compulsory for motorcyclists and passengers.

Drinking and driving
The blood alcohol legal limit is 20mg.

Drivers
The minimum age for drivers is 18.

Driving licence
EC format 'pink/green' licence accepted; old-style 'green' licence accepted only if accompanied by an International Driving Permit.

Emergencies
Police ☎ 997, Fire Brigade ☎ 998, Ambulance ☎ 999.
If you are involved in an accident you must report it to the nearest police station and to the nearest Polish Insurance Association. It is an offence not to render first aid to accident victims or to leave the scene of an accident.

Fuel
Petrol stations generally open from 0800 to 1900. In large towns, some stations are open 24 hours. *Leaded petrol:* Regular (86 octane) and

Super (94/98 octane) available. *Unleaded petrol:* Regular (82.5 octane) and Super (91 octane) available; pump legend *benzyna bezolowiu. Spare fuel:* up to 10 litres of fuel may be imported and exported.

Lighting
At night in built-up areas, where street lighting is insufficient, drivers must use dipped headlights. During bad visibility, drivers must use passing lights and/or foglights. Use of front foglights is permitted on winding roads at night. Motorcyclists must use headlights at all times outside built-up areas. Between 1 November and 1 March, it is compulsory for all vehicles to use dipped headlights at all times.

Overtaking
The usual restrictions apply. Trams may be overtaken on the right. At tram stops where there are no pedestrian islands, motorists should stop to let passengers walk between tram and pavement. During bad visibility drivers must give short audible warning signals before overtaking.

Parking
Parking is prohibited on certain streets signposted to that effect. On unlit streets, parking lights are obligatory during the hours of darkness.

Priority
In general, priority is given to vehicles coming from the right, but vehicles on major roads have right of way. Trams may be overtaken on the right. Vehicles on roundabouts have right of way over approaching traffic.

Road signs
International road signs.

Seat belts
If fitted, compulsory use in front seats.

Signalling
Do not sound your horn in built-up areas. Some localities display signs prohibiting the use of horns in particular areas. Warning of approach should be given by flashing headlights and by short horn signals when driving in fog.

Speed limits
Built-up areas: 37mph (60kmh); *outside built-up areas:* 56mph (90kmh); *motorways:* 68mph (110kmh). The minimum speed on motorways is 24mph (40kmh). Cars towing a caravan or trailer are limited to 44mph (70kmh) outside built-up areas, including motorways.

In addition to built-up areas there are 'residential zones', indicated by 'entry/exit' signs, where the maximum speed permitted is 12mph (20kmh).

Traffic offences
Motorists who infringe traffic regulations may receive a verbal or written warning, or an on-the-spot fine of between 25,000 and 500,000 zlotys. A receipt must be provided by the police officer.

Warning triangle
Compulsory.

GENERAL INFORMATION

Banks
Usually open Mon-Fri 0800-1800, Sat (variable) 0800-1300/1700.

Currency
Zloty. Currency control regulations have been lifted and as a result the compulsory daily exchange procedure has been abolished, as have accommodation vouchers. Import and export of zlotys is prohibited. Foreign currency can be exchanged at frontier posts; branches of the Narodowy Bank Polski; the Bank of Commerce in Warszawa; hotel exchange offices, travel agencies and PZM frontier offices. It is essential to keep the conversion slips issued when currency is exchanged.

Post Offices
Open Mon-Fri 0800-2000, Sat 0800-1400.

Public holidays
New Year's Day; Easter Monday; Labour Day; Constitution Day, 3 May; Corpus Christi; National Day, 22 July; Feast of the Assumption, 15 Aug; All Saints, 1 Nov; Independence Day, 11 Nov; Christmas, 25, 26 Dec.

Shops
Food shops open Mon-Fri 0600-1900, Sat 0700-1300. Other shops open Mon-Fri 1100-2000, Sat 0900-1600.

Visa
No longer required by British nationals.

PORTUGAL $\quad$ (P)

MOTORING INFORMATION

National motoring organisation
Automóvel Club de Portugal (ACP), *FIA &*

AIT, Rua Rosa Araújo 24, 1200 Lisboa. ☎ 1-356 39 81. Office hours: Mon-Fri 0900-1300 and 1400-1645. Touring reception: (Apr-Sep) Mon-Fri 0900-1730; (Oct-Mar) 0900-1645.

Breakdowns

Purchasers of Eurocover Motoring Assistance should consult their Assistance Document. For ACP breakdown service south of Pombal, ☎ Lisboa 942 50 95 and to the north, ☎ Porto 830 11 27.

Children in front seats

Not permitted under the age of 12, unless a child safety seat is fitted.

Crash helmets

Compulsory for motorcyclists.

Drinking and driving

The blood alcohol legal limit is 50mg.

Drivers

The minimum age for drivers is 17.

Driving licence

UK driving licence accepted.

Emergencies

Police, Fire Brigade and Ambulance ☎ 115.

Fuel

Petrol stations are open from 0700 to 2200, from 0700-2400, or 24 hours. *Leaded petrol:* Regular (85 octane) and Super (98 octane) available. *Unleaded petrol:* Super (95 octane) available; pump legend *gasolina sin plomo. Credit cards:* accepted. Purchase of fuel with a credit card incurs a surcharge of 100 Esc. *Spare fuel:* it is permitted to carry spare fuel.

Internal ferries

A car ferry service, operated by the Transado company, crosses the Sado estuary between Setúbal and Troia. There are 10 crossings per day between midnight and 2300, journey time 30 minutes. Services also operate from Lisboa across the Tagus (Tejo) estuary to Cacilhas, Barreiro, Montijo and Porto Brandão.

Lighting

Headlights must be dipped in built-up areas.

Overtaking

The overtaking of stationary trams is permitted only if there is an island for passengers wishing to embark or disembark.

Parking

Parked vehicles must face in the same direction as moving traffic, except where parking is officially allowed on one side of the road only. In some towns there are Blue Zones. Parking is permitted within these zones with a parking disc obtainable free from the ACP or the police. Illegally parked vehicles will be immobilised and released only upon payment of a fine.

Priority

Do allow priority to traffic coming from the right.

Registration document

A special certificate, *Autorizacao*, will be required if the vehicle is not registered in your name – available from RAC Travel Information, ☎ 0345–333222.

Roads

Roads are classified as follows: motorways (AE), principal roads (IP), national roads (EN), municipal roads (EM), other municipal roads (CM).

Seat belts

Outside built-up areas, compulsory use in front seats.

Signalling

Do not use the horn except to signal danger. Use flashing headlights at night and hand or mechanical indicators during the day.

Spare parts or touring kits

Should be temporarily imported under cover of a 'spare parts' triptyque issued by the RAC.

Speed limits

Built-up areas: 37mph (60kmh); *outside built-up areas:* 56mph (90kmh); *motorways:* 74mph (120kmh). Cars towing a caravan or trailer are limited to 31mph (50kmh) in built-up areas, 43mph (70kmh) outside built-up areas, and 56mph (90kmh) on motorways. Minimum speed on motorways is 24mph (40kmh) unless otherwise indicated.

On the 25 de Abril Bridge, Lisboa, drivers must maintain a speed of 18-31mph (30-50kmh).

Visiting motorists who have held a full licence for under a year are limited to 56mph (90kmh), and a yellow disc showing the figure '90' must be displayed. Discs are available from ACP border offices.

Temporary importation of caravans

An inventory of the contents of a caravan must be provided on plain paper or by filling in a form available at the frontier.

Tolls

Payable on certain roads (see page 76).

Traffic offences

The police are authorised to impose on-the-spot fines. A receipt is issued to show that the fine has been paid. Fines are imposed for unauthorised parking, speeding, excess blood alcohol level, and failure to wear seat belts, if fitted.

Warning triangle

Compulsory.

GENERAL INFORMATION

Banks

Open Mon-Fri 0830-1500. Some large city banks operate a currency exchange service for tourists 1830-2300.

Currency

Escudos.

Museums

Open Tue-Sun 1000-1230 and 1400-1700.

Post Offices

Open Mon-Fri 0830-1800 in main towns, 0900-1300 and 1400-1800 in other towns.

Public holidays

New Year's Day; Carnival (Shrove Tuesday); Good Friday; Liberty Day, 25 Apr; Labour Day; Corpus Christi; National Day, 10 June; St António, 13 June (Lisboa); São João, 24 June (Porto); Corpus Christi; Assumption, 15 Aug;

Republic Day, 5 Oct; All Saints, 1 Nov; Independence Day, 1 Dec; Immaculate Conception, 8 Dec; Christmas, 24, 25 or 25, 26 Dec.

Shops

Open Mon-Fri 0900-1300 and 1500-1900, Sat 0900-1300. Shopping centres are open every day from 1000-2400.

ROMANIA   RO

MOTORING INFORMATION

National motoring organisation

Automobil Clubul Român (ACR), *FIA & AIT,* Str. Tache Ionescu 27, 70154 Bucureşti 22. ☎ 1-615 5510, 659 3910. Office hours: Mon-Fri 0800-1630, Sat 0800-1330. Touring services are operated by the National Tourist Office 'Carpati-Bucaresti', 7 Bulvardul Magheru, Bucureşti 1. ☎ 14 51 60. Office hours: Mon-Fri 0800-1630, Sat 0800-1330.

Breakdowns

Purchasers of Eurocover Motoring Assistance should consult their Assistance Document. The ACR has contracted local motor repairers to attend motorists in need of breakdown assistance; ☎ 927 in Bucureşti, or ☎ 12345 in most areas. A reciprocal breakdown service is available to members of affiliated foreign clubs.

Children in front seats

Not permitted under the age of 12.

Crash helmets

Compulsory for motorcyclists and passengers.

Drinking and driving

Do not drink and drive: the blood alcohol legal limit is 0mg.

Drivers

The minimum age for drivers is 18.

Driving licence

UK driving licence accepted.

Emergencies

For Police and Ambulance, ☎ 061 in Bucureşti, ☎ 06 in other towns. In the event of an accident, a visitor in possession of a foreign insurance policy valid in Romania will receive all necessary assistance by 'ADAS' (State Insurance Administration).

Fuel

Leaded petrol: Regular (88/90 octane) and Super (96/98 octane) available. *Unleaded petrol:* Super (98 octane) available; pump legend *benzina fara plumb.* About 25 PECO petrol stations sell unleaded petrol; for further details contact RAC

Travel Information, ☎ 0345-333222. *Spare fuel:* up to 5 litres of spare fuel in cans may be imported duty free. 10 litres may be exported when leaving the country. *Coupons:* no longer required.

Lighting

In built-up areas, where roads are not lit, undipped headlights may be used for passing and at intersections. Where roads are lit, drivers must use dipped headlights only.

Overtaking

With the exception of trams, which are overtaken on the right, all other vehicles must be overtaken on the left.

Parking

Drivers must stop or park their vehicles on the right-hand side of the road in the direction of the traffic. Parking is prohibited on the carriageway of national highways.

Priority

At roundabouts, priority must be given to vehicles coming from the right. Vehicles already in the roundabout traffic must give way to vehicles entering the roundabout, as the latter come from the right.

Seat belts

Recommended.

Signalling

Use of the horn is prohibited in towns between 2200 and 0600. At night, warning must be given by the use of lights. In Bucureşti and other towns, use of the horn is prohibited, and signs to this effect – *claxonarea interzisa* – warn motorists of this regulation.

Speed limits

Cars with or without caravan/trailer: built-up areas 37mph (60kmh); outside built-up areas and on motorways: (under 1000cc) 44mph (70kmh), (1100-1800cc) 50mph (80kmh), (over 1800cc) 56mph (90kmh). *Motorcycles:* built-up areas 25mph (40kmh), outside built-up areas 37mph (60kmh).

Tolls

Tolls are charged for crossing the River Danube

from Giurgiu to Ruse (Bulgaria), and from Giurgeni to Vadu Oii.

Traffic offences

Members of the Militia (police) have the right to impose fines on the spot for violation of traffic regulations.

Warning triangle

Compulsory.

GENERAL INFORMATION

Banks

Open Mon-Fri 0900-1200 and 1300-1500, Sat 0900-1230.

Currency

Leu (plural lei).

Post Offices

Open Mon-Sat 0700-2000, Sun 0700-1200.

Public holidays

New Year, 1, 2 Jan; International Labour Day, 1, 2 May; National Holiday, 23, 24 Aug.

Shops

Open Mon-Fri 0800-2000, Sat 0800-2100, Sun 0800-1200.

Visa

British nationals must hold a valid passport and visa, available from: Romanian Consulate, 8 Palace Green, London W8, ☎ 071-937 9667; or at the border and airports.

SLOVENIA

MOTORING INFORMATION

National motoring organisation

Auto-Moto Zveza Slovenije, Dunajska 128, 61113 Ljubljana. ☎ 61-181 111.

Children in front seats

Not permitted under the age of 12.

Drinking and driving

The blood alcohol legal limit is 50mg.

Drivers

The minimum age for drivers is 18.

Driving licence

UK driving licence accepted.

Emergencies

Police ☎ 92, Fire Brigade ☎ 93, Ambulance ☎ 94. In the event of an accident, the police must be called. A visitor must obtain a certificate from the police, detailing damage to the vehicle, in order to facilitate export from the country.

First aid kit

Compulsory.

Fuel

Service stations at entry points and on motorways are open 24 hours, otherwise from 0700 to 2000 Monday to Saturday. *Leaded petrol:* 86 and 98 octane available. *Unleaded petrol:* 91 and 95 octane available from most service stations. *Credit cards:* not accepted. *Spare fuel:* importation of spare fuel is prohibited.

Lighting

Spare bulbs must be carried. Motorcyclists must use headlights day and night.

Seat belts

If fitted, compulsory use in front and rear seats.

Speed limits

Motorcycle, car, car and caravan: in built-up areas the limit is 37mph (60kmh); outside built-up areas 50mph (80kmh). On motorways, motorcycles and cars are limited to 75mph (120kmh), cars and caravans to 50mph (80kmh).

Traffic offences

Police are empowered to impose on-the-spot fines which must be paid in the national currency.

Vehicle insurance

Croatia Insurance Company has appointed Dalmatian and Istrian Travel Ltd* to provide insurance and compulsory Green Card cover to all motorists travelling to Slovenia and Croatia. *Dalmatian and Istrian Travel Ltd, 3rd floor, 37 New Bond Street, London W1Y 9HB, ☎ 071-493 6612.

Warning triangle

Compulsory.

GENERAL INFORMATION

Banks

Open Mon-Fri 0800-1800, Sat 0800-1200.

Currency

The currency is the Tolar. Foreign currency may be exchanged at all international border crossings, and in all major towns at tourist agencies, hotels and banks.

Photography

It is prohibited to take photographs in sensitive areas, eg railways, airports, bridges etc.

Post Offices

Open Mon-Fri 0800-1800, Sat 0800-1200.

Public holidays

1, 2 Jan; Easter Monday; 27 Apr; 1, 2 May; 26 June; 1 Nov; Christmas.

Shops

Open Mon-Fri 0730-1900, Sat 0730-1300.

SPAIN

MOTORING INFORMATION

National motoring organisation
Real Automóvil Club de España (RACE), *FIA & AIT,* José Abascal 10, 28003 Madrid. ☎ 447 3200. Office hours: Mon-Fri 0900-1400.

Breakdowns
Purchasers of Eurocover Motoring Assistance should consult their Assistance Document.

Carriage of children
Children under 12 travelling in the front of a vehicle must be seated in an approved child seat, otherwise they must be seated in the rear of a vehicle.

Crash helmets
Compulsory for motorcyclists and passengers on machines over 125cc.

Drinking and driving
The blood alcohol legal limit is 80mg.

Drivers
The minimum age for drivers is 18.

Driving licence
EC format 'pink/green' licence accepted; old-style 'green' licence accepted only if accompanied by an International Driving Permit.

Emergencies
In the case of an emergency in Madrid, Barcelona or other main town, Police ☎ 091, medical assistance ☎ 092, Fire Brigade ☎ 080. Elsewhere consult the telephone directory. The Traffic Control Department operates an assistance service for road accidents, which includes a telephone network on motorways and some other roads. Drivers in need of assistance should ask the operator for *auxilio en carretera.*

Fuel
Leaded petrol: Regular (92 octane) and Super (97 octane) available. *Unleaded petrol:* Regular (95 octane) available; pump legend *gasolina sin plomo.* Most readily found at the popular tourist resorts between Costa del Sol and Costa Brava, at Autopista service areas, and in the Burgos-Bilbao area. *Credit cards:* accepted at some petrol stations. *Spare fuel:* 10 litres of petrol in a can may be imported duty free.

Glasses
Motorists who wear glasses for driving should ensure that a spare pair is carried in the vehicle.

Internal ferries
Compania Transmediterranea SA operate all-year car ferry services to the Balearic and Canary Islands on the following routes.
Balearic Islands: Barcelona/Valencia to Palma (Mallorca), Mahón (Menorca) and Ibiza. There is an inter-island service from Palma to Mahón and Ibiza.
Canary Islands: Cádiz to Las Palmas (Gran Canaria) and Santa Cruz (Tenerife). Inter-island services operate to Fuerteventura, Lanzarote, Gomera, Hierro and La Palma.

The UK agent for reservations and tickets is Southern Ferries, 179 Piccadilly, London W1V 9DB, ☎ 071-491 4968.

Lighting
The use of dipped headlights is compulsory at night on motorways and fast roads, even if well lit. It is compulsory for motorcycles to use lights at all times. Motor vehicles must have their lights on in tunnels. A spare set of light bulbs must be carried.

Mirrors
Temporarily imported vehicles should be equipped with a minimum of two rear-view mirrors. Drivers must have a clear rear view of at least 50 metres, and caravans should therefore be equipped with extension mirrors.

Overtaking
Outside built-up areas, signal your intention to overtake by sounding your horn in the daytime, or by flashing headlights at night. The overtaking motorist **must** use his indicators when doing so.

The driver of a commercial vehicle will switch on his nearside flashing indicator when he thinks it is safe for you to overtake (this is the one next to the right-hand verge). While this light is flashing, it is safe to pass, but if there is danger ahead he will switch off, and he will flash his offside light until the road is clear to pass.

Stationary trams may not be overtaken when passengers are boarding or alighting.

Parking
Follow the usual restrictions on parking. On uneven dates in one-way streets in towns, vehicles should be parked on the side of the road where the houses bear uneven numbers. On the side where houses bear even numbers, parking is allowed on even dates. **Do** park facing the same direction as the traffic flow on that side. Parking meters and traffic wardens operate in Madrid and Barcelona.

Blue Zones, *zona azul,* are indicated by signs. Maximum period of parking between 0800 and 2100 is $1^1/_2$ hours. Discs are available from hotels, town halls and travel agencies. In the centre of some large towns there is a *zona*

ORA where parking is allowed only against tickets bought in tobacconists; tickets are valid for 30, 60 or 90 minutes. Vehicles parked against regulations may be removed.

Pedestrian crossings
Jay walking is **not** permitted. In main towns pedestrians may not cross a road unless a traffic light is at red against the traffic, or a policeman gives permission. Offenders can be fined on the spot.

Priority
Traffic coming from the right has priority. When entering a major road from a minor one, where there is normally a sign *Stop* or *Ceda el Paso* (give way), traffic from both directions on the major road has priority. Trams always have priority.

Road signs
Most conform to the international pattern. Other signs are:
    Ceda el Paso: give way
    Cuidado: take care
    Obras: roadworks
    Peligro: danger

Seat belts
If fitted, compulsory use in front and rear seats.

Signalling
Do warn road users of your whereabouts by horn or light signals. **Do not** make unnecessary use of loud horns. In urban areas horns may only be used in an emergency.

Speed limits
Built-up areas: 31mph (50kmh); *outside built-up areas:* 56-62mph (90-100kmh); *motorways:* 74mph (120kmh). In residential areas the maximum speed is 12mph (20kmh). Outside built-up areas, and for the purpose of overtaking, speed limits are increased by 12mph (20kmh). Cars towing a caravan or trailer are limited to 50mph (80kmh) on dual carriageways and motorways, 44mph (70kmh) on other roads.

Tolls
Payable on certain roads (see page 76).

Traffic lights
As in the UK, but two red lights mean 'No Entry'.

Traffic offences
Police can impose on-the-spot fines of up to 50,000 Ptas. Visiting motorists must pay immediately unless they can give the name of a person or company in Spain who will guarantee payment of the fine, otherwise the vehicle will be impounded until the fine is paid. However, except in certain cases, there is a standard reduction in the fine of 20% for immediate settlement. A *Boletin de Denuncia* is issued specifying the offence and the amount of the fine. You should check carefully that the amount written tallies with the amount paid. There are instructions in English on the back of the form for an appeal. This must be made within ten days and you should not delay until your return home. You may write in English. If the police take no action about your protest, that is the end of the matter.

Warning triangle
For vehicles with 9 or more seats, or over 3,500kg weight, it is compulsory to carry two warning triangles.

GENERAL INFORMATION

Banks
Open Mon-Fri 0900-1400, Sat 0900-1300 in some towns.

Currency
Peseta.

Post Offices
Open Mon-Sat 0800-1500.

Public holidays
New Year's Day; Epiphany; St Joseph's Day, 19 Mar; Maundy Thursday; Good Friday; Labour Day; Ascension; Corpus Christi; St James Day, 25 July; Assumption 15 Aug; National Day, 12 Oct; All Saints Day, 1 Nov; Constitution Day, 6 Dec; Immaculate Conception, 8 Dec; Christmas Day. There are many local variations.

Shops
Open Mon-Sat 0900/1000-1300/1330 and 1500/1530-1930/2000.

SWEDEN   Ⓢ

MOTORING INFORMATION

National motoring organisations
Motormännens Riksförbund (M), *AIT,* Sturegatan 32, Stockholm. ☎ (08) 7 82 38 00. Office hours: Mon-Thu 0900-1800, Fri 0830-1700.
Kungl Automobil Klubben (KAK), *FIA,*

Gyllenstiernsgatan 4, S-11526, Stockholm. ☎ 0860 0055.

Breakdowns
Purchasers of Eurocover Motoring Assistance should consult their Assistance Document. In the case of breakdown on any Swedish road, motorists may contact the alarm service

(Larmtjänst), ☎ (020) 910 040.

Carriage of children

Children aged 7 or under should be seated in a special child restraint, or in a seat which allows them to use normal seat belts.

Climbing lanes

A climbing lane in Sweden is an extra lane sometimes provided on steep hills to the right of the regular lane. The lane allows easy overtaking of slow-moving vehicles, and it merges with the regular lane a short way past the end of the climb. It should not be confused with slow lanes in other countries.

Crash helmets

Compulsory for motorcyclists and passengers.

Drinking and driving

The blood alcohol legal limit is 20mg.

Drivers

The minimum age for drivers is 18.

Driving licence

UK driving licence accepted.

Emergencies

Police, Fire Brigade and Ambulance ☎ 90000. Do not leave the scene of an accident if you are involved.

Fuel

Away from large towns, petrol stations are rarely open 24 hours. *Leaded petrol:* Super (95/98 octane) available. The 95 octane petrol is a low-leaded mixture of unleaded 95 and leaded 98 octane. *Unleaded petrol:* Super (95 octane) available; pump legend *blyfri 95. Diesel:* rarely available at self service pumps. Ideally, diesel should be purchased during normal working hours. *Credit cards:* generally accepted, but at 24-hr service stations on main roads and in major towns, payment must be made with 10 or 100 Kr notes. *Spare fuel:* motorists are allowed to carry up to 30 litres in cans.

Lighting

All motor vehicles must use dipped headlights day and night all year round.

Overtaking

Many roads in Sweden have wide shoulders – if you are driving slower than other traffic, or if you are driving a very wide vehicle, you are allowed to move out onto the shoulder to make it easier for other people to overtake you, but do not use the shoulder as another traffic lane. If you drive onto the shoulder, give way to vehicles behind you before driving back onto the road again, as you will be held responsible for any accident. Do not force another vehicle onto the shoulder if you wish to overtake it – no vehicle is obliged to move onto the shoulder.

On some narrow roads there are warning lines – elongated markings at short intervals, instead of unbroken lines. These mean that visibility is limited in one or both directions. You may cross a warning line, so long as you can cross safely and do not break the rules for overtaking. For instance, you may cross a warning line to pass a pedestrian, a cyclist, or a stationary or slow-moving vehicle.

Trams should be overtaken on the right if the position of the tracks so permit. If there is no refuge at a tram stop, motorists should stop and give way to passengers boarding and alighting from the tram.

Parking

Vehicles parked on the carriageway must be on the right-hand side of the road. If in doubt about local regulations ask the police. Do not park or stop on motorways or arterial roads other than in the parking areas provided. Do observe local parking restrictions. Maps showing parking regulations in Stockholm and some other towns may be obtained from the motoring organisations or through the local authority concerned. Parking meters are in use in several larger towns, usually from 0800 to 1800. The permitted parking time varies, but is generally 2 hours and is always indicated on the meter. Parking fees vary according to locality, between 1 and 3 Kr per hour. Fines are imposed for illegal parking.

Pedestrian crossings

Do give pedestrians the right of way on a pedestrian crossing. Pedestrians must use official crossings. It is an offence for them to cross the road against a red light.

Priority

Give way to vehicles already on a priority road before you enter it, also when you leave a petrol station, car park, camping site, or similar area. At other road junctions give way to traffic coming from the right, unless there is a road sign to the contrary. When turning left give way to oncoming traffic. When you see a 'Stop' sign, you must stop at a point where you can see up and down the other road (usually at the stop line), and you must give way to any traffic approaching along it. At most roundabouts traffic already on the roundabout has priority and this is clearly indicated by signposting. Do give trams priority.

Seat belts

If fitted, compulsory use in front and rear seats.

Signalling

Do give warning of your approach by using the horn, or by light signals, where this is necessary to prevent an accident. In built-up areas do not give audible warning, unless it is essential to prevent an accident.

Speed limits

Built-up areas: 31mph (50kmh); *outside built-up areas:* 44-56mph (70-90kmh); *motorways:* 68mph (110kmh), reduced to 56mph (90kmh) on certain stretches around major towns: these limits are always signposted. Lower limits apply to vehicles towing a caravan or trailer. Further guidance is available from RAC Travel Information, ☎ 0345-333222.

Traffic offences

The Swedish police are authorised to impose, but not collect, fines on the spot in cases of violation of traffic regulations. Fines range from 300 to 1,200 Kr, but if two or more offences are committed and the total fines exceed 2,500 Kr, the offender will be taken to court. Some fineable offences are: driving without lights in daylight; exceeding the speed limit; not having a warning triangle or GB plate; registration plate dirty or missing.

Warning triangle

Advisable.

GENERAL INFORMATION

Banks

Open 0930-1500. City centres have a bank open until 1800.

Currency

Krona (plural kronor).

Post Offices

Open Mon-Fri 0900-1800, Sat 0900-1300.

Public holidays

New Year's Day; Epiphany; Good Friday; Easter Monday; Labour Day; Ascension; Whit Sunday; Whit Monday; Midsummer, Sat between 20 and 26 June; All Saints, Sat between 31 Oct and 6 Nov; Christmas, 25, 26 Dec.

Shops

Open Mon-Fri 0900-1800, Sat 0900-1300/1600, although hours vary throughout the week. In some large towns, department stores remain open until 2000/2200.

SWITZERLAND   (CH)

MOTORING INFORMATION

National motoring organisations

Automobile Club de Suisse (ACS), *FIA,* 39 Wasserwerkgasse, 3000 Bern 13. ☎ (031) 311 77 22. Office hours: Mon-Fri 0800-1200 and 1400-1730.

Touring Club Suisse (TCS), *AIT,* 9 rue Pierre Fatio, 1211 Genève 3. ☎ (022) 737 12 12. Road & Touring Information, ☎ (022) 735 80 00. Office hours: Mon-Fri 0800/0900-1145/1230 and 1300/1400-1700/1830, according to office and season. Sat 0800/0900-1130/1200 and 1330-1600, according to office and season. Head Office closed Sat.

Breakdowns

Purchasers of Eurocover Motoring Assistance should consult their Assistance Document.

Children in front seats

Not permitted under the age of 7, unless an approved child restraint is fitted.

Crash helmets

Compulsory for motorcyclists and passengers.

Drinking and driving

The blood alcohol legal limit is 80mg.

Drivers

The minimum age for drivers is 18.

Driving licence

UK driving licence accepted.

Emergencies

Police ☎ 117, Fire Brigade ☎ 118, Ambulance ☎ 114 or 117 in Genève, Zürich, Bern, Basel, Interlaken, Winterthur and other major towns.

Fuel

On motorways, service stations are usually open from 0600 to 2200/2400, with the exception of Basel North, Pratteln North/South, Coldrerio North/South (N2) which are open 24 hours. On normal roads, usual opening hours are 0600/0700 to 2000; smaller stations are open from 0700/0800 to 1800. A few service stations open 24 hours during the summer. Outside these hours, petrol is widely available from 24-hr automatic pumps, which accept 10 or 20 SF notes.

Leaded petrol: Super (98 octane) available. *Unleaded petrol:* Super (95 octane) available; pump legend *bleifrei, essence sans plomb* or *benzina sensa piomba. Credit cards:* accepted by automatic pumps at about 10 service stations on motorways, and more widely on other roads. *Spare fuel:* 25 litres of petrol in a can may be imported duty free.

Internal ferries

A car ferry operates across Lake Lucerne between Beckenreid and Gersau (April-October), and across Lake Zürich between Horgen and Meilen (all year). There are also international ferry services to Germany across Lake Constance

(Bodensee) from Romanshorn to Frederichshafen and from Constance to Meersburg.

Lighting

Do use sidelights after nightfall or in thick fog if the vehicle is stationary, except if parked where there is sufficient street lighting, or in an authorised car park. Dipped headlights are compulsory in tunnels. Motorcyclists should use lights at all times.

Motorways

Signposted in green. All vehicles using the motorway network must display a vignette (see page 34). Motel accommodation is available at a number of locations on the network.

Mountain roads

Do show extra care when travelling on mountain roads. You must be able to pull up within half the distance of clear vision, especially when negotiating a blind bend. When two vehicles meet on a narrow mountain road, the descending car must keep to the extreme right-hand side of the road and even stop or go into reverse if necessary.

Mountain postal roads are indicated by a sign with the traditional post-horn in yellow on a blue rectangle. On these roads, postal vehicles have priority. The same sign with the addition of a red diagonal stripe indicates the end of the postal road. Drivers of private cars **must** pull up if signalled to do so by postal motor coach drivers.

A sign showing a disc with a wheel and chains in the centre indicates that snow chains are necessary for the mountain road ahead.

Some mountain postal roads are one-way only. This is indicated by a white rectangle beneath the blue rectangle with the yellow horn. On others during certain hours, one-way single file traffic is in operation. Circulation hours in both directions are posted at each end of the road.

Overtaking

Do overtake on the left and leave sufficient space between your vehicle and the one to be overtaken. When overtaking it is compulsory to signal right before returning to the right-hand lane. A moving tram must be overtaken on the right if there is sufficient room; if not, the vehicle may be overtaken on the left. **Do** overtake a stationary tram or train only on the right if there is a refuge. If not, only overtake on the left if there is no danger to traffic. Motorcyclists must not overtake a column of vehicles or weave between vehicles.

Parking

Do not park where there is a notice *Stationierungsverbot* or *Interdiction de Stationner* (no parking) or where parking might hinder traffic. Motorists with parking discs may park in Blue Zones without payment. Parking discs can be obtained free of charge from ACS and TCS offices, and in some towns with Blue Zones (Basel, Bern, Genève), discs can be obtained from most petrol stations, garages, kiosks, restaurants and police stations.

Do ensure that your vehicle is really immobilised by leaving it in bottom or reverse gear, according to the way the vehicle is facing, by use of a chock, or by turning the front wheels towards the kerb. Wheel clamps may be used on illegally parked vehicles. Parking on pavements is forbidden unless authorised by specific signs.

The resorts of Murren, Wengen, Zermatt, Braunwald and Rigi are inaccessible by car. Parking facilities are located at railway stations, and journeys may be completed by public transport.

Priority

All main roads are marked in the centre by a white line. When the road is clear, a broken white line may be crossed when overtaking or turning left. **Do not** cross a double white line. In open country, main road traffic has right of way over that entering from secondary roads. In built-up areas, traffic entering from the right has priority. **Do** give trams right of way on all roads.

The international priority sign is placed on most secondary highways where they intersect with main roads having priority. Blue posts will frequently be seen, which indicate a main road.

In built-up areas, buses have priority when leaving a bus-stop.

Seat belts

If fitted, compulsory use in front seats.

Signalling

Do not use a horn unnecessarily, and only with consideration in residential areas. After dark, **do** use your headlamp flasher instead of the horn unless there is an emergency.

Speed limits

Built-up areas: 31mph (50kmh); *outside built-up areas:* 50mph (80kmh); *motorways:* 62-74mph (100-120kmh). Cars towing a caravan or trailer (up to 1000kg) are limited to 50mph (80kmh) outside built-up areas; those over 1000kg are limited to 37mph (60kmh) outside built-up areas, and 50mph (80kmh) on motorways.

Temporary importation of caravans

Caravans and trailers not exceeding 2.30 metres in width and 8 metres in length may be imported without formality. Caravans up to

2.50 metres in width may enter Switzerland if they are towed by a 4-wheel drive vehicle or by a vehicle exceeding 3.5 tonnes: the total length of the combination must not exceed 18 metres. No authorisation is required. A number of roads are closed to touring caravans and light trailers – RAC Travel Information can provide details.

Touring information

For general information on touring in Switzerland, ☎ 111; weather reports, ☎ 162; mountain pass conditions, ☎ 163.

Traffic offences

Police are empowered to impose and collect on-the-spot fines for traffic offences.

Warning triangle

Compulsory.

GENERAL INFORMATION

Banks

Generally open Mon-Fri 0800/0830-1630/1800.

In Lausanne, banks close between 1230 and 1330.

Currency

Swiss franc.

Post Offices

Open Mon-Fri 0730-1200 and 1345-1800, Sat 0730-1100 except for a few main offices which close later.

Public holidays

New Year's Day; Good Friday; Easter Monday; Ascension; Whit Monday; Christmas Day. In addition, other days are observed in some Cantons.

Shops

Open Mon-Fri 0800/0900-1830 (1845 in Genève), Sat 0800-1600/1700. Hours vary between towns. In Bern and Genève shops are closed Mon mornings.

TURKEY $\quad$ (TR)

MOTORING INFORMATION

National motoring organisation

Türkiye Turing Ve Otomobil Kurumu (TTOK), *FIA & AIT,* Halaskargazi Cad. 364 Sisli, 80222 Istanbul. ☎ 2314631. Office hours: Mon-Fri 0830-1200 and 1230-1700.

Children in front seats

Not recommended.

Crash helmets

Compulsory for motorcyclists.

Drinking and driving

The blood alcohol legal limit is 50mg.

Drivers

Normally, only those 18 and over may drive in Turkey but visitors holding a valid full driving licence in their country of residence may do so even if they are under 18, although they may only drive foreign-registered vehicles.

Driving licence

UK driving licences are accepted for visitors driving a vehicle temporarily imported into Turkey, for visits up to 3 months.

Emergencies

Police ☎ 155, Fire Brigade ☎ 110, Ambulance ☎ 112. Tourist police: Istanbul ☎ 527 45 03, Ankara ☎ 434 17 56, Izmir ☎ 218 652. **All** accidents (whether there are injuries caused or not) must be reported to the police, as a report

has to be prepared by them for the Turkish Insurance Bureau.

Fire extinguisher

Compulsory.

First aid kit

Compulsory.

Fuel

Motorists are advised to 'top-up' their tanks at every opportunity. *Leaded petrol:* Regular (91 octane) and Super (96 octane) available. *Unleaded petrol:* Super (95 octane) available; pump legend *kursunsuz benzin. Credit cards:* not accepted. *Spare fuel:* a maximum of 25 litres in cans may be imported duty free.

Lighting

Dipped headlights must be used after sunset in built-up areas. A vehicle parked at the roadside after dark must display sidelights, whether or not the road is lit. However, this does not apply in built-up areas if the vehicle is visible from a distance of 150 metres.

Overtaking

Do not overtake at intersections, level crossings, curves, on bridges, in tunnels or where road signs indicate that it is forbidden.

Parking

The sign *Park Yapilmaz* indicates that parking is forbidden. Parking is not permitted on pedestrian crossings, outside garage/car park entrances, on tramways, near intersections or bends, on level crossings, underpasses, overpasses or within 25 metres of danger signs.

Priority
Except where otherwise indicated, priority must be given to vehicles coming from the right. Vehicles on a main road have priority over those entering from a secondary road.

Road signs
Most signs conform to the international pattern, but other road signs which may be seen are:
Dikkat: attention
Dur: stop
Gümrük: Customs
Hastahane: hospital
Park Yapilmaz: no parking
Tamirat: roadworks
Yavas: slow
The word 'Nufus' (inhabitants) often appears on signs at the entrance into towns to indicate the population. 'Rakim' indicates the altitude.

Seat belts
If fitted, compulsory use in front seats, and recommended in rear seats.

Signalling
Use of the horn is forbidden except in case of absolute necessity.

Speed limits
Built-up areas: 31mph (50kmh); *outside built-up areas and motorways:* 56mph (90kmh). Cars towing a caravan or trailer are limited to 25mph (40kmh) in built-up areas and 44mph (70kmh) on all other roads.

Temporary importation of vehicles
Vehicle details will be entered in the visitor's passport, and the vehicle must be exported by the same person. If a vehicle is imported by a person other than the owner, a letter of authorisation from the owner must be held by the driver and certified either by a lawyer or the RAC.

Traffic offences
Police are empowered to impose on-the-spot fines for violations of traffic regulations.

Warning triangle
It is compulsory to carry two warning triangles.

GENERAL INFORMATION

Banks
Open Mon-Fri 0830-1200 and 1330-1700.

Currency
Turkish lira.

Museums
Open Tue-Sun 0830-1200 and 1330-1700 (winter), 0830-1730 (summer).

Photography
Photography is forbidden in certain areas as indicated by signs *Yasak Bolge* or *Yabancilara Yasaktir.*

Post Offices
Open Mon-Fri 0830-1230 and 1330-1730. In Istanbul and Ankara, the central post office is open 24 hours.

Public holidays
New Year's Day; Seker Bayrami religious festival (moveable in March); Independence and Children's Day, 23 Apr; Youth, Sports and Atatürk Commemoration Day, 19 May; Kurban Bayrami religious festival (moveable in June); Victory Day, 30 Aug; Republic Day, 29 Oct.

Shops
Open Mon-Sat 0930-1300 and 1400-1900. Tourist shops operate similar hours.

Visa
British nationals visiting Turkey for less than 3 months must purchase a visa (costing £5), on arrival at the airport or frontier.

(FORMER) YUGOSLAVIA   (YU)

MOTORING INFORMATION

National motoring organisation
Auto-Moto Savez Jugoslavije (AMSJ), *FIA & AIT,* Ruzveltova 18, 1101 **Beograd (Belgrade).** ☎ (011) 401699. Office hours: (summer) Mon-Sat 0730-1730, Sun 0730-1530; (winter) Mon-Fri 0730-1530 (Wed 0730-1730).

Breakdowns
Purchasers of Eurocover Motoring Assistance should consult their Assistance Document. For AMSJ 24-hr service, ☎ Beograd 987.

Children in front seats
Not permitted under the age of 12.

Crash helmets
Compulsory for motorcyclists and passengers.

Drinking and driving
The blood alcohol legal limit is 50mg.

Drivers
The minimum age for drivers is 18.

Driving licence
UK driving licence accepted.

Emergencies
Police ☎ 92, Ambulance ☎ 94. In the event of

fire, contact the Police. It is compulsory to report to the police any accident which causes serious damage, injury or death. You **must** also give assistance in the event of an accident whether you are involved or not.

The driver of a vehicle registered abroad, which is damaged in an accident, receives a certificate on the spot from an authorised official. If the driver of a damaged vehicle cannot produce a certificate on leaving the country (eg if the vehicle was removed from the accident site before the official arrived), the driver and the vehicle will be held until the circumstances of the damage can be ascertained. If entering Yugoslavia with a damaged car, notify the authorities at the time of entry.

Fuel
Unleaded petrol: bezolovini benzin 95 octane. *Credit cards:* not accepted. *Spare fuel:* a quantity of fuel in a can may be imported on payment of Customs duty. *Coupons:* concessionary coupons are available at frontiers in denominations of 120 dinars. Unused coupons are refundable.

Lighting
International rules apply, and lights should be used for parking at night where street lighting is insufficient. Motorcyclists must use dipped headlights outside built-up areas, even during daylight. A spare set of bulbs must be carried.

Overtaking
Regulations correspond to international practice. When overtaking a stationary tram or other public service vehicle reduce speed to ensure the safety of passengers. Drivers must stop behind such vehicles if the passengers have to cross the carriageway when there is no pedestrian island. Stationary school buses **must not** be overtaken or passed.

Parking
In some larger towns there are Blue Zone areas. International parking signs operate, and there are meters in some towns which can be used Monday to Saturday 0800 to 1900.

Priority
At intersections, drivers must give way to traffic from the right unless a priority road is indicated by signs. Trams have priority over all vehicles. Vehicles entering a roundabout have priority over those already on it.

Registration document
If the vehicle is not registered in your name it is advisable to carry a letter of authorisation from its owner.

Signalling
Do not sound your horn in built-up areas at night, and only sound it in an emergency during the day.

Speed limits
Built-up areas: 37mph (60kmh); *outside built-up areas:* 50-62mph (80-100kmh); *motorways:* 74mph (120kmh). Cars towing a caravan or trailer are limited to 37mph (60kmh) in built-up areas, 50mph (80kmh) outside built-up areas.

Tolls
Payable on certain roads (see page 77).

Traffic offences
Police are empowered to impose on-the-spot fines for traffic offences.

GENERAL INFORMATION

Banks
Open Mon-Fri 0800-1900 (large towns), 0800-1300 (small towns), Sat 0800-1300 (all towns).

Currency
Dinar.

Post Offices
(Winter) Mon-Sat 0800-1200 and 1700-1900.
(Summer) Mon-Sat 0700-1300 and 1700-2000.

Public holidays
New Year, 1, 2 Jan; Labour Days, 1, 2 May; Veteran's Day, 4 July; Republic Days, 29, 30 Nov. **Croatia:** New Year, 1, 2 Jan; 1, 30 May; 22 June; 15 Aug; 1 Nov; 25, 26 Dec.

Shops
General and self-service stores open Mon-Fri 0800-2000, Sat 0800-1500.

FROM COUNTRY TO COUNTRY

TOLL ROADS

Toll charges are correct at the time of going to press, and details for certain countries are selective. An up-to-date, comprehensive leaflet is available from RAC Travel Information at Croydon, ☎ 0345-333222.

AUSTRIA

The major Austrian toll road companies issue multiple journey cards which allow an appreciable reduction in the price charged for a single journey. An additional charge may be made per person for over two or three people in cars or minibuses but children travel at reduced prices, sometimes free. Tolls are given in Austrian schillings.

Brenner motorway (A13) Tyrol – Italy
motorcycle	100
car, motor caravan, minibus (up to 9 seats)	130
car with caravan or trailer	170

Felber Tauern road Kitzbuhel – East Tyrol
motorcycle	100
car, summer/winter	180/110
caravan or trailer	40

Gerlos road Salzburg – Tyrol
motorcycle	50
car with or without trailer	80

Grossglockner Pass
motorcycle	200
car with or without trailer	280

Silvretta Pass Bludenz – Landeck
per person	single	30
	return (same day)	10
	child 6–16	10
	under 6	free
(no caravans permitted)		

Tauern motorway (A10) Salzburg – Carinthia
motorcycle	100
car, minibus (up to 9 seats) May – October	190
November – April	120
caravan or trailer	40

Timmelsjoch Pass Austria – Italy
motorcycle	single	50
	return	70
car	single	80
	return	120
(no trailers or caravans permitted)		

FRANCE

Tolls are payable on most routes, usually by taking a ticket at the point of entry and paying at the exit, although some toll barriers are operated automatically by depositing the exact toll in coins. On numerous sections of autoroute, particularly around cities and large towns, no tolls are levied. Visa and Access (Mastercard) are accepted for payment. Tolls are given in French francs.

Tolls are applied as follows:
(1) Light motor vehicle with 2 axles with a height less than 1.30 metres measured at right angles to the front axle, with or without a luggage trailer; family minibus with up to 9 seats. (**Motorcyclists** pay a lower rate than this category.)
(2) Vehicle, or vehicle combination (car and trailer/caravan), with more than 2 axles and with a height of not more than 1.30 metres measured at right angles to the front axle.
(3) Commercial vehicle with 2 axles with a height of more than 1.30 metres measured at right angles to the front axle; coach with 2 axles; motorhome; minibus, unless it has a maximum of 9 seats and is for private use only, when it is charged as category (1).

	(1)	(2)	(3)
A1 PARIS – LILLE (214 km)			
Autoroute du Nord			
Paris - Roye (Amiens)	30.00	45.00	49.00
Paris - Lille	58.00	87.00	94.00
A2 COMBLES (Jct A1) – BELGIAN FRONTIER			
(78 km)			
Bapaume - Hordain	23.00	36.00	38.00

A4 PARIS – STRASBOURG (470 km)
Autoroute de l'Est

Paris - Metz	108.00	165.00	174.00
Paris - Strasbourg	162.00	245.00	259.00
Calais - Strasbourg* (617km)	202.00	306.00	322.00

A5 PARIS (MELUN) – LANGRES (247 km)

Troyes - Langres	32.00	42.00	62.00

A6 PARIS – LYON (456 km)
Autoroute du Soleil

Paris - Beaune	79.00	103.00	149.00
Paris - Lyon (Villefranche)	124.00	161.00	232.00
Calais - Lyon* (765 km)	244.00	336.00	443.00

A7 LYON – MARSEILLE (313 km)
Autoroute du Soleil

Lyon - Aix - Marseille	100.00	155.00	160.00
Calais - Marseille* (1068 km)	344.00	491.00	603.00

A8 AIX-EN-PROVENCE (Coudoux, A7) – NICE – MENTON (200 km)
La Provençale

Aix-en-Provence - Cannes	59.00	88.50	95.00
Calais - Cannes* (1197 km)	403.00	579.50	698.00

A9 ORANGE (A7) – LE PERTHUS (280 km)
La Languedocienne-Catalane

Orange - Narbonne sud	67.00	104.00	108.00
Orange - Le Perthus	101.00	157.00	165.00
Calais - Le Perthus* (1230 km)	413.00	598.00	717.00

A10 PARIS – BORDEAUX (585 km)
L'Aquitaine

Paris - Tours centre	85.00	128.00	136.00
Paris - Bordeaux (Virsac)	209.00	319.00	338.00
Calais - Bordeaux (870 km)	301.00	456.00	483.00

A11 PARIS – NANTES (383 km)
L'Océane

Paris - Le Mans nord	71.00	105.00	111.00
Paris - Nantes	141.00	209.00	218.00

A13 PARIS – CAEN (225 km)
Autoroute de Normandie

Paris - Tancarville (Le Havre)	27.00	38.50	41.50
Paris - Caen	54.00	82.50	85.50

A26 CALAIS – TROYES (400km)
Autoroute des Anglais

Calais - Reims	86.00	131.00	138.00
Reims-Troyes	46.00	59.00	93.00

A31 BEAUNE – LUXEMBOURG (364 km)

Beaune - Dijon	11.00	14.00	20.00
Dijon - Langres nord	27.00	35.00	52.00
Langres nord - Toul (Gye)	33.00	43.00	64.00

A36 BEAUNE – MULHOUSE (232 km)
La Comtoise

Beaune - Besançon centre	24.00	32.00	47.00
Paris - Mulhouse (535 km)	152.00	198.00	288.00

A40 MACON – LE FAYET (212 km)

Calais - Genève* (828 km)	289.00	392.50	529.00
Calais - Le Fayet* (880 km)	314.00	435.00	572.00
(for Mt Blanc Tunnel)			

A41 GRENOBLE – SCENTRIER (130 km)

Grenoble - Chambéry	22.00	33.00	33.00
Chambéry - Scentrier (A41)	34.00	51.00	51.00

A42 LYON – PONT D'AIN (A40) (64 km)

	17.00	22.00	33.00

A43/A431 LYON – ALBERTVILLE (150 km)

Lyon - Les Abrets	28.00	44.00	44.00
Lyon - Albertville	75.00	117.00	117.00

A48 BOURGOIN (A43) – GRENOBLE (49 km)

	26.00	39.00	39.00
Calais - Grenoble* (860 km)	289.00	405.00	512.00

A49 GRENOBLE – VALENCE

Voreppe - Bourg de péage	40.00	61.00	61.00

A50 MARSEILLE – TOULON (62 km)

	18.50	28.00	29.50

A51 AIX-EN-PROVENCE – SISTERON (103 km)
Autoroute du Val de Durance

Aix-en-Provence - Aubignosc	37.50	56.00	60.00
Aubignosc - Sisteron nord	5.00	8.00	8.50

A52 CHATEAUNEUF-LE-ROUGE (A8) – AUBAGNE (A50) (15km)

Aix-en-Provence - Aubagne	14.50	22.00	23.50

A54 ARLES – NIMES OUEST (24 km)

	9.00	14.00	14.00

A61 TOULOUSE – NARBONNE SUD (150 km)
Autoroute des Deux-Mers

	56.00	91.00	98.00

A62 BORDEAUX – TOULOUSE (244 km)
Autoroute des Deux-Mers

	83.00	129.00	137.00

A63 BORDEAUX – SPANISH FRONTIER (192 km)
Autoroute de la Côte Basque

St Geours de Maremne - Hendaye	40.00	62.00	62.00

A64 BAYONNE – TARBES (149 km)
La Pyrénéenne

Ste Suzanne - Tarbes est	32.00	50.00	54.00

A71 ORLEANS – CLERMONT FERRAND (293 km)

Orléans centre - Bourges	44.00	66.00	67.00
Bourges - Clermont Ferrand	61.00	80.00	117.00
Calais - C. Ferrand (687 km)	236.00	341.00	388.00

A72 CLERMONT FERRAND – ST ETIENNE (140 km)

	48.00	74.00	81.00

* via Reims/A26

A81 LE MANS (Joué-en-Charnie) – LAVAL (La Gravelle) (84 km)

	26.00	37.00	38.00
Paris - La Gravelle (278 km)	111.00	166.00	176.00
Nantes - Montaigu (A83) (25km)	9.00	14.00	15.00

Tolls are charged for crossing the following bridges:

Tancarville Bridge

motorcycle	1.00
car (according to horsepower)	min 11.50
car and trailer	11.50

St Nazaire Bridge

motorcycle	2.00-5.00
car (according to horsepower)	22.00-30.00
car and trailer	28.00

GREECE

Tolls are levied on several routes, and are given in Drachmas. Tolls are applied as follows:

(1) Motorcycle, scooter.
(2) Passenger car; minibus with up to 10 seats.
(3) Motor caravan.
(4) Car and caravan.

	(1)	(2)	(3)	(4)
Athína - Kórinthos	200	400	600	800
Kórinthos - Pátrai	200	500	800	1000
Kórinthos - Trípolis	400	700	1000	1400
Athína - Lamía	550	900	1450	1800
Lamía - Lárisa	200	400	600	800
Lárisa - Kateríni	200	400	600	800
Kateríni - Evzoni	200	400	800	800

ITALY

Toll tickets are collected on entry to the motorway system and paid on exit. Motorists may pay tolls with a Viacard on the majority of motorways (except A18 and A20). The card can be used for any vehicle and is available in two amounts: 50,000 lire and 90,000 lire. Motorists may obtain it from motorway toll booths and service areas, certain banks, tourist offices and tobacconists. When leaving a motorway on which the Viacard is accepted, the motorist gives his card and entry ticket to the attendant who will deduct the amount due. At motorway exits with automatic barriers the Viacard should be inserted into the machine. The card is valid until the credit expires. Full details are available from RAC Travel Information, ☎ 0345-333222. Tolls are given in Lire.

Tolls are applied as follows:
(1) Motorcycle; car with a height measured at the front axle of less than 1.30 metres.

(2) Three-wheeled vehicle; vehicle with a height at the front axle exceeding 1.30 metres.
(3) Motor vehicle (with or without trailer) with 3 axles.
(4) Motor vehicle (with or without trailer) with 4 axles.
(5) Motor vehicle (with or without trailer) with 5 axles.

	(1)	(2)	(3)	(4)	(5)
A1 MILANO – ROMA					
Milano - Bologna	12900	13500	17200	26600	31300
Milano - Roma (ring road)	41000	42000	52200	82100	98300
Milano - Napoli	56000	57000	71200	111600	133800
A3 NAPOLI – REGGIO					
Napoli - Salerno	1100	1400	2500	3000	3500
A4 TORINO – TRIESTE					
Torino - Milano	10300	10300	13100	20500	24500
Milano - Mestre (Venezia)	17500	18200	21300	34600	41700
A5 TORINO – AOSTA					
Torino - Aosta	11300	11800	16300	25500	29500
Aosta - Santhià	9200	9700	13200	20400	23900
A6 TORINO – SAVONA (A10)	12000	12500	17000	26500	31000
A7 MILANO – GENOVA	10500	11500	14200	22100	25800
A8 MILANO – VARESE/SESTO CALENDE	3000	3200	3800	6000	7000
A9 MILANO – COMO/BROGEDA CH	3500	4100	4900	7500	9000
A10 GENOVA – FRENCH BORDER					
Genova - Savona Vado	4100	4100	4900	8000	9500
Savona Vado - French Border	16100	18900	30100	39600	45600
A11 FIRENZE – PISA	6000	6000	7500	11500	14000
A12 GENOVA – CIVITAVECCHIA					
Genova - Livorno	18600	19200	25000	39600	45700
A13 BOLOGNA – PADOVA (A4)	8000	8000	10000	16000	19000

A14 BOLOGNA – TARANTO
Bologna - Pescara (A25)

25500	25500	32000	49500	78500

Bologna - Taranto

52500	54000	67000	105500	126000

A15 PARMA – LA SPEZIA (S. STEFANO M.)

12000	12000	16300	25500	30000

A16 NAPOLI – CANOSA

14500	15000	18500	29000	35000

A18 MESSINA – CATANIA

4500	5300	8300	11100	13000

A20 MESSINA – PALERMO
Messina - Sant Agata di Militello

8000	8500	9500	16000	19000

Cefalù - Buonfornello (A19)

1200	1200	1400	2500	3000

A21 TORINO – BRESCIA
Torino - Piacenza (A1)

6500	7800	15100	17200	20100

Piacenza - Bréscia (A4)

6200	6200	7900	12300	14600

A22 BRENNERO – MODENA
Brénnero - Verona (A4)

19000	19500	23500	37500	45000

Brénnero - Módena

25500	26000	32000	51000	61000

A23 PALMANOVA – TARVISIO
Palmanova (A4) - Udine N.

2100	2100	2600	4100	4900

Udine N. - Tarvísio

7500	7500	9500	15000	18000

A24 ROMA – L'AQUILA – VILLA VOMANO

21000	10500	12000	20000	24500

A25 ROMA – PESCARA

12500	13000	15000	24500	29500

A26 VOLTRI – SANTHIA
Voltri - Tortona

6000	6000	7600	12000	14200

A27 MESTRE – VITTORIA VENETO

4600	4600	5800	9300	11000

A30 CASERTA – NOLA – SALERNO

4500	4500	5500	9000	10500

A31 VICENZA – PIOVENE ROCCHETTE

2000	2000	2500	4000	5000

THE NETHERLANDS

Tolls are payable on the following, and are given in Florins.

Zeelandbridge

motorcycle	1.00
car	4.00
car and caravan	6.00

Kiltunnel (Dordecht – Hoekse)

motorcycle, car	3.50

Waalbridge (Prins Willem Alexander Bridge)

car (up to 800kg)	2.90
car (over 800kg)	3.50

NORWAY

On the E6 west of Oslo, there is a toll charge of 10 Kroner near Drammen.

PORTUGAL

On the 25 de Abril Bridge, which links Lisboa with the south bank of the River Tagus at the Lisboa end of the Vila Franca de Xira motorway, toll charges are levied on southbound traffic only.

Tolls are levied on the following auto-estradas out of Lisbon, and are given in Escudos.

Tolls are applied as follows:
(1) Motorcycles and vehicles with an axle height less than 1.10 metres (with or without trailer).
(2) Vehicles with 2 axles, with an axle height exceeding 1.10 metres.
(3) Vehicles with 3 axles, with an axle height exceeding 1.10 metres.

		(1)	(2)	(3)
A1	Lisboa - Santarém (64 km)	480	840	1080
	Santarém - Fatima (49 km)	450	790	1030
	Fatima - Coimbra (76 km)	700	1220	1700
	Coimbra - Aveiro (44 km)	350	600	770
	Aveiro - Porto (71 km)	530	910	1170
A2	Almada - Setúbal (36 km)	170	300	380
A3	Porto - Cruz (34 km)	300	520	670
A4	Porto - Penafiel (32 km)	330	590	780
A5	Lisboa - Cascais (25 km)	190	190	370
A8	Lisboa - Malveira (18 km)	100	190	240

SPAIN

The following tolls apply to motorcycles, and private cars (with or without a caravan), and are given in Pesetas.

A1	Burgos (Castañares) – Miranda de Ebro (A68)	975
A2	Junction A7 – Zaragoza (Alfajarin)	1890
A4	Sevilla (Dos Hermanas) – Cadiz (Puerto Real)	1085
A6	Madrid (Villalba) – Adanero	870
A7	La Jonquera – Barcelona N.	1745
	Barcelona S. – Salou	1560
	Salou – Valencia (Puzol)	2740
	Valencia (Silla) – Alicante (San Juan)	1810
A8	Bilbao (Basauri) – Irun	1415
A9	La Coruña – Santiago de Compostela	490
	Pontevedra – Vigo	340
A15	Pamplona (Noain) – Tudela	1245
A18	Barcelona – Manresa	565
A19	Barcelona – Mataró	220
A66	Oveido (Campomanes) – Leon	1105
A68	Bilbao – Zaragoza	3180
C1411	Cadi Tunnel	935
	Tunnel de Garraf (A16)	
	Castelldefels – Sitges	445

(FORMER) YUGOSLAVIA

Tolls were payable on the following motorway sections. Current details are available from the RAC.

E63 & E70	Razdrto (Trieste) – Ljubljana
E57	Maribor (Hoce) – Arja Vas
E57	Ljubljana – Naklo
E70	Zagreb – Prvca
E59-E65	Zagreb – Kralovac
E75	Belgrade – Nis
E75	Belgrade – Novi Sad
E75	Novi Sad – Feketic (north only)
E75	Kumanovo – Titov Veles
E70	Ruma – Simanovci
	Tito Bridge
	Ucka Tunnel (near Ryeka)

TUNNELS

In many countries it is an offence to drive through a tunnel without headlights. At the exit, police may impose an on-the-spot fine.

ARLBERG

The 14km-long road tunnel is parallel to and south of the Arlberg Pass. It is usually open all through the year but when it is closed vehicle/trailer combinations may be transported through the Arlberg rail tunnel between Langen and St Anton. Reservations should be made at least 3 hours before departure of the train, ☎ Langen 05582 201 or ☎ St Anton 05446 2242

Rates

motorcycle	AS	100
car, motor caravan, minibus (up to 9 seats)	AS	150
car with caravan or trailer	AS	210

BOSRUCK (A9 PYRHN M/WAY)

This road tunnel is 5.5km long and runs between Spital am Pyhrn and Selzthal, to the east of the Pyhrn Pass. It forms part of the Pyhrn Autobahn between Linz and Graz.

Rates

motorcycle	AS	60
car, minibus (up to 9 seats)	AS	70
caravan or trailer	AS	30

GLEINALM (A9 PYRHN M/WAY)

The road tunnel between St Michael and Friesach, near Graz, is 8.3km long and forms part of the A9 road from Linz to Slovenia.

Rates

motorcycle	AS	100
car, minibus (up to 9 seats)	AS	130
caravan or trailer	AS	30

KATSCHBERG

A two-lane carriageway 5.4km long forming part of the motorway between Salzburg and Carinthia (Tauern autobahn).

Rates

motorcycle	AS	50
car, summer	AS	95
winter	AS	60
caravan or trailer	AS	20

RADSTADTER TAUERN

The road tunnel is 6.5km long and runs parallel to the Tauern railway tunnel, on the Salzburg-Carinthia route. Tolls are the same as for the Katschberg tunnel.

TAUERN

Rail tunnel: Up to 47 trains a day convey vehicles between Bockstein and Mallnitz. Passengers may travel in closed cars, but only drivers in lorries and coaches. Vehicles must be loaded at least 30 minutes before departure. The journey takes 10 minutes. The Austrian Federal

Railways issue a leaflet with full details and timetable.

Rates

motorcycle	AS 100
car, summer (1/5-31/10)	AS 180
winter (1/11-30/4)	AS 110
caravan or trailer	AS 40

MONT BLANC

The road tunnel between Chamonix and Entrèves is 11.6km long, and at an altitude of 1370m. The Customs are at the Italian end. Sidelights and rear lights must be used.

Rates

motorcycle	85 FF
car (according to wheelbase)	85-170 FF
car with caravan or trailer	170 FF

FREJUS

The road tunnel between Modane and Bardonecchia is 12.8km long and is open all year. Tolls are similar to the Mont Blanc tunnel. Sidelights must be used.
Speed limits: min 60kph - max 80kph.

BIELSA

The 3km-long road tunnel through the Pyrénées between Aragnouet and Bielsa is open 0800-2200 from Easter Saturday to mid-November, usually closed in winter. It is on the C138 secondary road from Toulouse to Zaragoza, west of the N230.

VIELLA

The road tunnel between Viella and Vilaller on the N230 is 6km long. It is not recommended however, as the approach roads are narrow and twisting, with only minimum provision of safety barriers.

CADI

The 5km-long tunnel between Bellver de Cerdanya and Bagá on the C1411, to the west of the Tosas Pass.

Rates

car with or without caravan	935 Ptas

ST GOTTHARD

The two-lane road tunnel is 16.3km long running under the Gotthard Pass from Göschenen to Airolo. The tunnel is part of the national motorway network and vehicles using the road are required to display the special vignette.

SAN BERNARDINO

The 6.6km road tunnel runs parallel to the Pass on the N13. It is part of the national motorway network and the special vignette must be displayed.

SIMPLON & LOTSCHBERG

Motor vehicles are transported through the Lotschberg Tunnel between Kandersteg and Goppenstein; journey time is 15 minutes. Further details are available from the RAC or the Swiss National Tourist Office. For details of the service through the Simplon Tunnel contact the Swiss National Tourist Office or RAC Travel Information, ☎ 0345-333222.

ALBULA

Thusis – Tiefencastel – Samedan. There are at least five services daily in each direction.

Rates

car	85 Sw F
car with caravan	140 Sw F
	plus 10–50 Sw F per passenger

GREAT ST BERNARD

The road tunnel between Bourg St Pierre and Aosta (Etroubles) is 6km long. From both sides there are modern approach roads with wide curves, gradual inclines and permanent protection against snow, ensuring easy access all year. Swiss and Italian frontier posts are on the Swiss side and there is a money exchange office, restaurant, snack bar, petrol station and parking at each entrance to the tunnel.

Rates

motorcycle	27 Sw F
car (according to wheelbase)	27 Sw F
car with caravan or trailer	27 Sw F
motor caravan	56.50 Sw F

KARAWANKEN

This road tunnel links Austria with Slovenia between St Jakob and Jesenice.

Rates

motorcycle	AS	90
car (not exceeding 1.3 metres height)	AS	90
car with caravan or trailer	AS	135
motor caravan	AS	135

MOUNTAIN PASSES

Mountain passes are listed by country, and by road classification within each country.

The major passes are tinted blue on the following tables. Dates of availability during the winter months are approximate only. The term 'intermittent closure' refers to regular snow clearance which may take two or three days.

On all Swiss passes listed, there are emergency telephones at 2-mile intervals. These may be used without charge to summon mechanical, police or medical aid. Emergency

water supplies are usually available.

The Automobile Club de Suisse and the Touring Club de Suisse organise a Road Assistance Service in the Alpine regions. Foreign visitors may take advantage of this service against payment.

The RAC strongly recommend not driving over mountain passes at night and would advise inexperienced drivers either to avoid mountain passes or to drive with extreme care.

Key to abbreviations

Altr	alternative	NR	not recommended
Ch	winter snow chains	Oc	occasionally
Min rad	minimum radius	Pic	picturesque
Mod	moderate/ly	S	South
N	North	Tr	treacherous
nec	necessary	u/c	unclassified road
No	prohibited by law	( )	partly, in places, eg (narrow) = narrow in places

Road number and road, (borders), Name of Pass and height (in metres)	Min width (ft)	Max grad	Condition of Pass in winter	Recom. for caravans	Remarks
ANDORRA					
N2 L'Hospitalet to Andorra ENVALIRA 2407	20	1:8	Oc closed Nov-April	Yes*	*Extra care req'd. Good snow clearance, but can be closed after a heavy fall. Max height of vehicles 11'6". Highest pass in Pyrénées.
AUSTRIA					
B20 St Pölten to Mariazell ANNABERG 976	13	1:8	Usually open	Yes	Pic. Light traffic.
B82 Völkermarkt to Ljubljana (Austria-Slovenia) SEEBERG 1218	16	1:8	Usually open	No	Good altr to Loibl & Wurzen passes.
B95 Predlitz to Feldkirchen TURRACHER HOHE 1763	13	1:4½	Usually open	No	Care req'd although no hairpins and little traffic. Road is much improved.
B99 Spittal to Radstadt KATSCHBERG 1641	20	1:5	Usually open	No*	Fairly difficult. Light traffic. *Altr motorway tunnel (toll).
B99 Radstadt to Spittal RADSTADTER-TAUERN 1739	16	1:6	Oc closed Jan-Mar	No*	Easy pass. Mod to heavy traffic. *Use altr motorway tunnel (toll).
B107 Bruck to Lienz GROSSGLOCKNER 2505	16	1:8	Closed late Oct-early May	No*	Toll. *Only powerful caravan units, preferably S-N. Hairpin bends, exceptional views. Seasonal traffic. Tunnel at summit.
B109 Villach to Kranjska Gora (Austria-Slovenia) WURZEN 1073	13	1:5½	Usually open	No*	Steep road, fairly difficult. Heavy traffic summer weekends. *Caravans prohibited. NR for other vehicles.
B110/SS52B Kötschach-Mauthen to Tolmezzo (Austria-Italy) PLOCKEN 1362	16	1:7	Oc closed Dec-April	No*	Heavy traffic summer weekends – delays likely at frontier. *Some sections reconstructed so pass just negotiable for caravans. Extra care req'd.

Road number and road, (borders), Name of Pass and height (in metres)	Min width (ft)	Max grad	Condition of Pass in winter	Recom. for caravans	Remarks

AUSTRIA CONT'D

Road number and road, (borders), Name of Pass and height (in metres)	Min width (ft)	Max grad	Condition of Pass in winter	Recom. for caravans	Remarks
B138 Windischgarsten to Liezen PYHRN 945	13	1:10	Usually open	Yes	Several hairpins. Altr road tunnel (toll).
B145 Bad Ischl to Bad Aussee POTSCHEN 972	23	1:11	Usually open	Yes	Views of the Dachstein. Mod to heavy traffic.
B161 Kitzbühel to Mittersill THURN 1274	16	1:12	Usually open	Yes	Scenic. Mod to heavy traffic.
B165 Zell am Ziller to Mittersill GERLOS PLATTE 1628	13	1:12	Usually open	No*	Mod to heavy traffic. Toll road. *Caravans prohibited.
B181/B307 Jenbach to Tegernsee (Austria-Germany) AACHEN 941	19	1:7	Usually open*	No	Pic. Mod to heavy traffic. *Closed in winter to lorries with trailers, and truck tractors.
B182/SS12 Innsbruck to Bolzano (Austria-Italy) BRENNER 1374	20	1:7	Usually open	No*	Pic. Lowest, busiest transalpine pass. Ch sometimes. *Use altr route via autobahn (toll). Pass is closed to vehicles towing, except luggage trailers.
B186/SS44B Otz to Merano (Austria-Italy) TIMMELSJOCH 2509	12	1:7	Closed early Oct- late June	No*	Toll. No minibuses. NR. *The pass is **only** open to private cars without trailers.
B188 Bludenz to Landeck SILVRETTA/BIELERHOHE 2032	16	1:9	Closed late Oct- early June	No*	Toll. Light traffic. *Caravans prohibited. 32 hairpin bends.
B197 Feldkirch to Innsbruck ARLBERG 1793	20	1:7½	Oc closed Dec-April	No*	Pic. Fairly easy, heavy traffic. *Closed to vehicles towing. Altr road tunnel (toll).
B198 Stuben to Reutte FLEXEN 1773	18	1:10	Usually open*	No	Fine views, light traffic. *The road N of the pass from Lech-Warth is usually closed Nov-April through danger of avalanches.
B200 Egg to Warth HOCHTANNBERG 1679	13	1:7	Oc closed late Dec-Mar	No	Road has been reconstructed.
B306 Gloggnitz to Mürzzuschlag SEMMERING 985	20	1:16	Usually open	Yes	Fine views. Heavy traffic. Several hairpin bends.
B314 Imst to Reutte FERN 1210	20	1:10	Usually open	Yes	Easy pass. Heavy traffic. Extra care req'd after rain.
B315/SS40 Landeck to Malles (Austria-Italy) RESIA 1504	20	1:10	Usually open	Yes	Mod to heavy traffic. Pic altr to the Brenner Pass.

FRANCE

Road number and road, (borders), Name of Pass and height (in metres)	Min width (ft)	Max grad	Condition of Pass in winter	Recom. for caravans	Remarks
N5 Morez to Genève FAUCILLE 1323	16	1:10	Usually open	No*	*Experience necessary. Altr via Nyon-Genève. View of Mt Blanc.
N6 Chambéry to Torino MT CENIS 2083	16	1:8	Closed early Nov-mid May	Yes	Heavy summer traffic, easy to drive. Poor surface. Altr road tunnel (toll).
N20 Toulouse to Bourg-Madame PUYMORENS 1915	18	1:10	Oc closed Nov-April	Yes	Altr rail tunnel. Not suitable for night driving. Max height of vehicles 11'6".
N75 Grenoble to Sisteron CROIX-HAUTE 1176	18	1:14	Usually open	Yes	Hairpin bends. Open to all vehicles.
N85 Grenoble to Gap (Route des Alpes) BAYARD 1248	20	1:7	Usually open	No*	Fairly easy, but steep S side and several hairpins. *Just negotiable for caravans N-S. Altr route via N75.
N90/SS26 Bourg-St-Maurice to Aosta (France-Italy) PETIT ST BERNARD 2188	16	1:12	Closed mid Oct-mid June	No	Light traffic. Pic. **No** vehicles over 15 tons. Unguarded edges at summit.

Road number and road, (borders), Name of Pass and height (in metres)	Min width (ft)	Max grad	Condition of Pass in winter	Recom. for caravans	Remarks
N91 Briançon to Vizille LAUTARET/ALTARETO 2058	14	1:8	Oc closed Dec-Mar	Yes	Unguarded edges. **NR** buses. Heavy summer traffic. Magnificent scenery.
N94/SS24 Briançon to Torino (France-Italy) MONTGENEVRE 1850	16	1:11	Usually open	Yes	Open all year. Altr Mt Cenis. Heavy traffic. Pic. Ch.
N204/SS20 La Giandola to Borgo San Dalmazzo (France-Italy) COL DE TENDE 1321	18	1:11	Usually open	Yes*	Heavy summer traffic. Tunnel at summit. Many well-engineered hairpin bends. *Caravans prohibited in winter. Tunnel closed 2100-0600 hrs.
N506 Chamonix to Martigny COL DES MONTETS 1461	10	1:8	Oc closed Dec-early April	Yes*	*Small caravans only. Narrow and rough surface in places.
D64 Jausiers to St Etienne-de-Tinée RESTEFOND 2802	10	1:9	Closed Oct-June	No	The highest pass in the Alps. Narrow, rough unguarded ascent. Many hairpin bends. Extra care req'd.
D118 Carcassonne to Mont-Louis QUILLANNE 1714	16	1:12	Oc closed Nov-Mar	Yes	Easy drive.
D465 St Maurice-sur-Moselle to Belfort BALLON D'ALSACE 1178	13	1:9	Oc closed Dec-end Mar	Yes*	Fairly easy, but many bends. *Care req'd.
D618 Arreau to Bagnères-de-Luchon PEYRESOURDE 1563	13	1:10	Usually open	No	Fairly easy to drive, but several hairpins. (Narrow).
D618 St-Girons to Tarascon-sur-Ariège PORT 1249	14	1:10	Oc closed Nov-Mar	Yes*	Pic, narrow road. *NR large caravans.
D900/SS21 Barcelonnette to Cúneo (France-Italy) LARCHE/ARGENTERA 1994	10	1:12	Oc closed Dec-Mar	Yes	Light traffic, easy to drive. Narrow/rough on descent.
D902 St Michel-de-Maurienne to Lautaret Saddle GALIBIER 2645	10	1:8	Closed Oct-June	No	Weekend heavy traffic. Numerous hairpin bends, unguarded edges. Tunnel under summit is closed.
D902 Lanslebourg to Bourg-St-Maurice ISERAN 2770	13	1:9	Closed mid Oct-late June	No	Care req'd on northern approach – unlit tunnels.
D902 Briançon to Guillestre IZOARD 2361	16	1:8	Closed late Oct-mid June	No	Winter avalanches. Narrow/winding road. Care req'd near Guillestre – unlit tunnels.
D902 Barcelonnette to Guillestre VARS 2111	16	1:10	Oc closed Dec-Mar	No	Many hairpins and steep sections. **NR** buses.
D908 Barcelonnette to Entrevaux ALLOS 2250	13	1:10	Closed early Nov-early June	No	Pic, narrow road mostly unguarded. NR inexperienced drivers. Max width 5'11".
D909 Annecy to Chamonix ARAVIS 1498	13	1:11	Oc closed Dec-Mar	No	Pic. Fairly easy. NR buses.
D918 Arreau to Luz-St-Sauveur ASPIN 1489	13	1:8	Closed Dec-April	Yes	Pic.
D918 Laruns to Argelès-Gazost AUBISQUE 1710	11	1:10	Closed mid Oct-June	No	Pic but Tr. Rough and narrow in parts. Unguarded edges with a steep drop.
D918 Luz-St-Sauveur to Arreau TOURMALET 2115	14	1:8	Closed Oct-mid June	No	Highest pass in French Pyrénées. NR buses: sufficiently guarded.
D934/C136 Pau to Huesca (France-Spain) POURTALET 1792	11	1:10	Closed late Oct-early June	No	Fairly easy, unguarded road. Narrow in places.
D2202 Barcelonnette to Nice CAYOLLE 2327	13	1:10	Closed early Nov-early June	No	Fairly difficult. Sharp hairpin bends, unfenced in places with steep drops. Much single-track road.

Road number and road, (borders), Name of Pass and height (in metres)	Min width (ft)	Max grad	Condition of Pass in winter	Recom. for caravans	Remarks
GERMANY					
B307/B181 Tegernsee to Jenbach (Germany-Austria) AACHEN 941	19	1:7	Usually open*	No	Pic. Mod to heavy traffic. *Closed in winter to lorries with trailers, and truck tractors.
ITALY					
SS12/B182 Bolzano to Innsbruck (Italy-Austria) BRENNER 1374	20	1:7	Usually open	No*	Pic. Lowest, busiest transalpine pass. Ch sometimes. *Use altr route via autobahn (toll). Pass is closed to vehicles towing, except luggage trailers.
SS20/N204 Borgo San Dalmazzo to La Giandola (Italy-France) COL DE TENDE 1321	18	1:11	Usually open	Yes*	Heavy summer traffic. Tunnel at summit. Many well-engineered hairpin bends. *Caravans prohibited in winter. Tunnel closed 2100-0600 hrs.
SS21/D900 Cúneo to Barcelonnette (Italy-France) ARGENTERA/LARCHE 1994	10	1:12	Oc closed Dec-Mar	Yes	Light traffic, easy to drive. Narrow/rough on ascent, better surface on descent.
SS23 Cesana Torinese to Torino SESTRIERE 2033	16	1:10	Usually open	Yes*	Access to winter sports resort. Fine scenery. Fairly easy pass. *Care req'd.
SS24/N94 Torino to Briançon (Italy-France) MONTGENEVRE 1850	16	1:11	Usually open	Yes	Open all year. Altr Mt Cenis. Heavy traffic. Pic. Ch.
SS26/N90 Aosta to Bourg-St-Maurice (Italy-France) PETIT ST BERNARD 2188	16	1:12	Closed mid Oct-mid June	No	Light traffic. Pic. **No** vehicles over 15 tons. Unguarded edges at summit.
SS27/A21 Aosta to Martigny (Italy-Switzerland) GREAT ST BERNARD 2473	16	1:10	Closed Oct-June	No*	*Pass closed to vehicles towing – use altr toll tunnel. Fairly easy – care req'd over summit. Ch sometimes req'd on approach roads, but not permitted through tunnel.
SS36 Chiavenna to Splügen (Italy-Switzerland) SPLUGEN 2113	10	1:7½	Closed early Nov-June	No	Pic. Many hairpin bends, not well guarded. Max height of vehicles 9'2". Max width of vehicles 7'6".
SS38 Bormio to Spondigna STELVIO 2757	13	1:8	Closed Oct-late June	No	Many hairpins, very scenic. **No** vehicles over 30ft in length.
SS38 Bormio to Santa Maria (Italy-Switzerland) UMBRAIL 2501	14	1:11	Closed early Nov-early June	No	Mod difficult. **No** trailers. **No** vehicles over 7'6" wide.
SS39 Edolo to Tresenda APRICA 1176	13	1:11	Usually open	Yes	Pic. Ch nec at times.
SS40/B315 Malles to Landeck (Italy-Austria) RESIA 1504	20	1:10	Usually open	Yes	Mod to heavy traffic. Pic altr to the Brenner Pass.
SS42 Bolzano to Fondo MENDOLA 1363	16	1:8	Usually open	Yes	Light traffic. Superb views.
SS42 Edolo to Bolzano TONALE 1883	16	1:8	Usually open	Yes	Easy drive.
SS44 Merano to Vipiteno MONTE GIOVO 2094	13	1:8	Closed Nov-May	No*	Scenic. Hairpin bends. *Caravans prohibited.
SS44B/B186 Merano to Otz (Italy-Austria) TIMMELSJOCH 2509	12	1:7	Closed early Oct-late June	No*	Toll. **No** minibuses. **NR**. *The pass is **only** open to private cars without trailers.
SS46 Rovereto to Vicenza FUGAZZE 1159	10	1:7	Usually open	No	Hairpin bends. Narrow on N side; extra care req'd.
SS48 Ora to Cortina FALZAREGO 2117	16	1:12	Oc closed Dec-April	No*	Many hairpins. *Only just suitable for powerful cars.

Road number and road, (borders), Name of Pass and height (in metres)	Min width (ft)	Max grad	Condition of Pass in winter	Recom. for caravans	Remarks
SS48 Arabba to Canazei PORDOI 2239	16	1:10	Oc closed Dec-April	No	Excellent views of the Dolomites. Hairpin bends.
SS48 Cortina to Auronzo TRE CROCI 1809	16	1:9	Oc closed Dec-Mar	Yes	Very easy drive. Pic.
SS50 Predazzo to Primiero ROLLE 1970	16	1:11	Oc closed Dec-Mar	Yes*	Beautiful scenery. *Not easy.
SS52 Pieve di Cadore to Piani MAURIA 1298	16	1:14	Usually open	Yes	Winding road.
SS52B/B110 Tolmezzo to Kötschach-Mauthen (Italy-Austria) PLOCKEN 1362	16	1:7	Oc closed Dec-April	No*	Heavy traffic summer weekends – delays likely at frontier. *Some sections reconstructed so pass just negotiable for caravans. Extra care req'd.
SS239 Tione di Trento to Dimaro CAMPIGLIO 1682	-	1:8½	Oc closed Dec-Mar	Yes	Easy pass. Pic.
SS241 Cortina to Bolzano COSTALUNGA 1753	16	1:7	Oc closed Dec-April	No*	Many blind bends (difficult). * **No** caravans.
SS242 Ortisei to Canazei SELLA 2240	16	1:9	Oc closed late Nov-early June	No	Pic. Winding roads. Good views of the Dolomites.
SS243 Selva to Corvara GARDENA 2121	16	1:8	Oc closed Dec-June	No	Pic. Very winding on descent.
SS244 Corvara to Arabba CAMPOLONGO 1875	16	1:8	Oc closed Dec-Mar	Yes	Pic. Winding, but easy.
SS300 Bormio to Ponte di Legno GAVIA 2621	14	1:5½	Closed Oct-July	No	Beautiful rocky scenery. Experienced drivers only. Max width 5'11".

SPAIN

Road number and road, (borders), Name of Pass and height (in metres)	Min width (ft)	Max grad	Condition of Pass in winter	Recom. for caravans	Remarks
NIII Tarancon to Requena CONTRERAS 890	22	1:14	Open	Yes	Min rad bends 32'. Well protected. Using NIII avoids the pass.
NVI Madrid to La Coruña GUADARRAMA 1511	26	1:8	Intermittent closure	Yes	Min rad turning 82'. Altr road tunnel on A6 motorway.
N111 Logroño to Donostia/San Sebastián LIZARRAGA 1031	17½	1:14	Open	Yes	Min rad turning 32'.
N152 Barcelona to Puigcerdà TOSAS 1800	16	1:10	Usually open	Yes*	Fairly straightforward but some sharp bends and a few unguarded edges. *Negotiable for caravans with extra care.
N240 Pamplona to Donostia/San Sebastián AZPIROZ 616	19	1:10	Usually open	Yes	Double bends. Min rad bends 42'.
N240 Gasteiz/Vitoria to Bilbao BARAZAR 604	21	1:11	Open	Yes*	Min rad bends 39'. *Approach roads require care when towing.
N330/N134 Huesca to Pau SOMPORT 1632	12	1:10	Usually open	Yes	Easy drive. Usual route across Pyrénées. Narrow and unguarded in parts.
N400 Tarancon to Cuenca CABREJAS 1166	16	1:7	Usually open	Yes	
N525 Zamora to Orense CANDA 1260	23	1:8	Intermittent closure	Yes	Min rad turning 49'. Easy road.
N601 Madrid to Segovia NAVACERRADA 1860	19½	1:11	Usually open	No	Some tricky hairpin bends.

Road number and road, (borders), Name of Pass and height (in metres)	Min width (ft)	Max grad	Condition of Pass in winter	Recom. for caravans	Remarks
SPAIN CONT'D					
N623 Burgos to Santander CARRALES 1020	22	1:16½	Open*	No*	*Other passes on this road NR for caravans & closed in winter.
C135 Pamplona to St-Jean-Pied-de-Port IBANETA 1057	13	1:10	Usually open	Yes*	Pic. *Drive with care.
C136/D934 Huesca to Pau (Spain-France) POURTALET 1792	11	1:10	Closed late Oct-early June	No	Fairly easy, unguarded road. Narrow in places.
C142 Esterri d'Aneu to Viella BONAIGUA 2072	14	1:12	Closed Nov-April	No	Narrow road, hairpin bends. Dangerous. Altr Viella road tunnel is open in winter.

SWITZERLAND

Road number and road, (borders), Name of Pass and height (in metres)	Min width (ft)	Max grad	Condition of Pass in winter	Recom. for caravans	Remarks
N2 Andermatt to Bellinzona ST GOTTHARD 2108	20	1:10	Closed mid Oct-early June	Yes*	**No** vehicles over 8'2½" wide or 11'9" high. Many hairpins and heavy summer traffic. *Altr motorway tunnel is better – Swiss tax charged.
N8 (N4) Meiringen to Lucerne BRUNIG 1007	20	1:12	Usually open	Yes	**No** vehicles over 8'2½" wide. Ch sometimes. Heavy traffic at weekends.
N9 Brig to Domodossola SIMPLON 2005	23	1:9	Oc closed Nov-April	Yes	Max width 8'2". Hairpins. **No** trailers over 2 tons. Altr rail tunnel (toll).
N13 Chur to Bellinzona SAN BERNARDINO 2006	13	1:10	Closed Oct-late June	No*	Easy approach roads, but narrow, winding summit. *Use motorway tunnel altr – Swiss tax charged. Max width 7'6".
A3 Tiefencastel to Silvaplana JULIER 2284	13	1:7½	Usually open	Yes*	*Easier N-S. Max width 8'2½". Altr rail tunnel Tiefencastelsamedan.
A3 Chiavenna to Silvaplana MALOJA 1815	13	1:11	Usually open	Yes*	Many hairpin bends on descent. **No** trailers. *Easier on descent than ascent. Just negotiable. Max width 8'2½" on all vehicles.
A6 Gletsch to Innertkirchen GRIMSEL 2165	16	1:10	Closed mid Oct-late June	No	No vehicles over 7'6" wide. Many hairpins, seasonal traffic. Max weight trailers 2½ tons.
A11 Aigle to Saanen COL DES MOSSES 1445	13	1:12	Usually open	Yes	Pic. **No** coaches. Ch req'd in winter. Max width 7'6".
A11 Innertkirchen to Wassen SUSTEN 2224	20	1:11	Closed late Oct-early June	Yes*	Well engineered, scenic, heavy traffic. Long delays at 3ml single-track section. **No** vehicles over 8'2½" wide. *Extra care req'd.
A17 Altdorf to Glarus KLAUSEN 1948	16	1:11	Usually closed late Oct-early June	No*	**No** vehicles over 7'6" wide. Caravans prohibited.
A19 Andermatt to Brig FURKA 2431	13	1:10	Closed Oct-June	No	Seasonal traffic. **No** vehicles over 7'6" wide. Many hairpin bends. Altr rail tunnel.
A19 Andermatt to Disentis OBERALP 2044	16	1:10	Closed early Nov-late May	No*	Max width 7'6". Road improved but still many hairpins. *Pass just negotiable for caravans, extra care req'd. Altr rail tunnel available in winter.
A21/SS27 Martigny to Aosta (Switzerland-Italy) GREAT ST BERNARD 2473	16	1:10	Closed Oct-June	No*	*Pass closed to vehicles towing – use altr toll tunnel. Fairly easy – care req'd over summit. Ch sometimes req'd on approach roads, but not permitted through tunnel.
A28 Landquart to Susch FLUELA 2383	16	1:8	Oc closed Nov-May	Yes*	Toll. Light traffic, easy drive. No vehicles over 7'6" wide, 11'2" high. *Extra care req'd. **Closed** at night.

Road number and road, (borders), Name of Pass and height (in metres)	Min width (ft)	Max grad	Condition of Pass in winter	Recom. for caravans	Remarks
A28 Zernez to Santa Maria OFEN 2149	12	1:8	Usually open	Yes	No vehicles over 7'6" wide. Ch sometimes req'd.
A29 Celerina to Tirano BERNINA 2330	16	1:8	Oc closed late Dec-Mar*	No	Pic, narrow and winding on S side. Care needed. Max width 7'6". **Closed** at night.
A189 Bulle to Spiez JAUN 1509	13	1:10	Usually open	No	Very attractive scenery. **No** vehicles over 7'6" wide.
A203 Martigny to Chamonix FORCLAZ 1527	16	1:12	Usually open	Yes*	**No** vehicles over 8'2½" wide. **No** trailers over 5 tons. *Just negotiable.
A461 Disentis to Biasca LUKMANIER 1916	16	1:11	Closed early Nov-late May	No*	*Caravans prohibited on part of road. Max width 7'6".
(SS36) Splügen to Chiavenna (Switzerland-Italy) SPLUGEN 2113	10	1:7½	Closed early Nov-June	No	Pic. Many hairpin bends, not well guarded. Max height of vehicles 9'2". Max width of vehicles 7'6".
(SS38) Santa Maria to Bormio (Switzerland-Italy) UMBRAIL 2501	14	1:11	Closed early Nov-early June	No	Mod difficult. **No** trailers. **No** vehicles over 7'6" wide.
u/c Tiefencastel to La Punt (via Bergün) ALBULA 2315	12	1:10	Closed early Nov-early June	No	Light traffic, sharp bends. No lorries and trailers. Altr rail tunnel. Max width 7'6".
u/c Aigle to Saanen (via Gstaad) COL DU PILLON 1546	13	1:11	Oc closed Jan-Feb	Yes	**No** vehicles over 7'6" wide. Ch sometimes req'd.
u/c Brig to Airolo (via Bedretto) NUFENEN 2478	13	1:10	Closed mid Oct-mid June	No*	Approach roads narrow, but road over pass good. *Just negotiable to light caravans (less than 1½ tons). Max width 7'6".

EMERGENCIES

WHAT TO DO IF YOU ARE INVOLVED IN AN ACCIDENT

The following represents the procedure that should be adopted if you are involved in an accident while abroad.

1. Immediately report the accident to the police. This action is compulsory in the event of personal injuries.
2. Give your name and address, and that of your insurance company, to the other party and produce your International Motor Insurance Certificate (Green Card) if required.
3. Accidents involving a third party must be reported at once to the appropriate insurance bureau of the country concerned, the details of which appear on the Green Card. Also immediately notify your own insurance company.
4. In no circumstances should you make any statement or sign any document without the advice of a lawyer or competent official of the local automobile club.
5. Should a camera be available, take photographs of the post-accident positions of the vehicles, marks on the road, etc, from as many different angles as possible.
6. If it is essential to move the vehicles, first mark the positions of their wheels with chalk on the roadway.
7. Make a rough sketch showing position of the vehicles both before and at the time of the accident and indicate the direction in which you were travelling.
8. Be sure that you take the following particulars:
   a. Make and registration number of the other vehicle and whether right- or left-hand drive.
   b. Full name, address and occupation of the driver of the other vehicle and number, etc, of his driving licence, as well as full name, address and occupation of the owner if not the driver.
   c. Name and address of the other party's insurance company, policy number and Green Card number.
   d. Full names, addresses and occupations of independent witnesses.
   e. Date, time and exact place of accident.
   f. Speeds of your own and other vehicle.
   g. Signals given by yourself and other driver.
   h. Condition of brakes, tyres, lights (front and rear) of both vehicles.
   i. Weather and road conditions.
   j. Names and addresses of persons injured and nature of injuries.
   k. Damage to your own and other vehicle.
   l. Address of police to whom accident reported.
9. RAC members should seek advice from the local FIA or AIT Club, or from RAC European Support, ☎ 081-686 0088. Addresses and telephone numbers of the FIA and AIT clubs are given for each country in the *Europe by Country* section of this guide.
10. Purchasers of RAC Eurocover Vehicle Protection should also consult their Assistance Document.

In **Belgium**, unless people have been injured, you must, if possible, move your vehicle to the side and off the road so that traffic is not obstructed.

In **France**, if an accident involving personal injury or substantial damage occurs in a town, get a policeman (*agent de police*) to make a report. On country roads send for a *gendarme*. In accidents involving damage only, ask for the services of a *huissier* from a neighbouring town or village. A *huissier* is a court official who acts partly as an assessor and partly as a bailiff. The party requesting his services is responsible for the fee for drawing up a report of the accident.

WHAT TO DO IF YOU BREAK DOWN

We strongly advise you to take out either RAC Eurocover Motoring Assistance, or Eurocover Premier Protection before setting out on your journey. If in need of help refer to your Assistance Document, which provides clear detailed instructions on the action to be taken in the section 'Breakdown Procedure Abroad'.

Members who have not taken out Eurocover Protection should contact the national motoring association of the country they are in. These organisations are members of either Alliance Internationale de Tourisme, AIT, or the Fédération Internationale de l'Automobile, FIA, to which the RAC is affiliated. Their symbols are shown on the RAC membership card. Many clubs offer assistance to members of fellow clubs in the AIT and FIA on a reciprocal basis. To obtain this it is essential to produce your membership card.

Non-members who have not taken out Eurocover Protection and who require breakdown assistance should contact the nearest garage, or the nearest agent for their make of car. If you drive one of the rarer makes of car it may be worth your while to obtain a list of European dealers before you begin your journey.

If you cannot find a local garage which is open, try contacting the Police who often have lists of garages open 24 hours a day and at weekends.

An emergency telephone system is in operation on most European motorways, which will connect you to the police, or the company operating the motorway.

WHAT TO DO IN THE EVENT OF AN ENGINE FIRE

Should you find yourself in the unfortunate position where you suspect your vehicle may have an underbonnet fire, you should take the following precautions.

1. Bring the vehicle to a standstill (assuming vehicle is being driven), switch off the engine and all electrics and remove all passengers to a place of safety.
2. If carrying a fire extinguisher on board your vehicle, follow the instructions on the extinguisher with regard to its use. This is usually:
   a. Remove safety pin.
   b. Direct nozzle at fire.
   c. Squeeze handle to commence operation. It is important you are aware of the method of operation of your own fire extinguisher.
3. Having identified an underbonnet fire it is permissible to release the bonnet catch, allowing the bonnet to pop up as far as the safety catch. **Under no circumstances lift the bonnet to identify the seat of the fire. Once the bonnet is lifted, the fire is likely to intensify, and the angle of the bonnet will direct the flames straight at you.** The fire extinguisher can then be activated and discharged into the underbonnet cavity around the bonnet edge.
4. If you are carrying passengers, they should attempt to gain additional assistance whilst you are tackling the fire, ie. telephone fire brigade or gain assistance from other motorists.
5. Should the fire continue to grow in intensity and the extinguisher is ineffective, everyone should retire to a safe distance and await the arrival of the fire brigade.
6. The same rules apply to car fires as building fires. Do not attempt to retrieve anything from the vehicle.

KEEPING IN CONTACT

EMERGENCY RADIO MESSAGES

Members touring abroad can be informed of serious illness in the family through the courtesy of the BBC. In an emergency contact RAC Travel Information at Croydon, ☎ 0345-333222, and if the following information is provided, arrangements will be made for a message to be transmitted in the relevant country.

1. Full name and home address of person for whom message is intended.
2. Their possible whereabouts.
3. Registration number and description of vehicle.
4. Full name and address of the person ill and relationship.

5. Name, home address and telephone number of the doctor attending or of hospital.
6. Reason for message (eg mother seriously ill).
7. Full name, address and telephone number of person sending the message.

If the use of this service is foreseen, a member should leave details of the day to day itinerary.

These emergency messages can be broadcast in most European countries.

The BBC cannot broadcast a notification of death in the family and only very important messages will be accepted.

RADIO FREQUENCIES

BBC WORLD SERVICE

The BBC World Service broadcasts in English 24 hrs each day. World News is broadcast on the hour.

Radio frequencies in kHz

	0500 - 0730 hrs	0730 - 1600 hrs	1600 - 2230 hrs
Albania	15070, 12095, 9410	17640, 15070, 9660	15070, 12095, 9410
Austria	15575, 9410, 6195	15070, 12095	12095, 9410, 6195
Belgium	15575, 9410, 648	12095, 9750, 648	12095, 9410, 6195
Bulgaria	15070, 12095, 9410	17640, 15070, 9660	15070, 12095, 9410
CIS/ Baltic States	12095, 9410	15070, 12095	15070, 12095, 6180
Czech and Slovak Republics	15575, 9410, 6195	15070, 12095	12095, 9410, 6195
Denmark	9410, 6195	12095, 9410	12095, 9410, 6195
Finland	12095, 9410	15070, 12095	15070, 12095, 9410
France (North)	6195, 3955, 648	12095, 9760, 648	12095, 9410, 6195
France (South)	9410, 6195, 3955	15070, 12095, 9760	12095, 9410, 6195
Germany (North East)	15575, 9410, 6195	15070, 12095	12095, 9410, 6195
Germany (North West)	15575, 9410, 648	12095, 9750, 648	12095, 9410, 6195

Germany (South)	15575, 9410, 6195	15070, 12095	12095, 9410, 6195
Gibraltar	9410, 6195	17705, 15070, 12095	12095, 9410, 6195
Greece	15070, 12095, 9410	17640, 15070, 9660	15070, 12095, 9410
Hungary	15575, 12095, 9410	15070, 12095	15070, 12095, 9410
Irish Republic	15575, 9410, 648	12095, 9750, 648	12095, 9410, 6195
Italy (North)	15575, 9410, 6195	15070, 12095	12095, 9410, 6195
Italy (South)	15575, 12095, 9410	17640, 15070, 12095	15070, 12095, 9410
Luxembourg	15575, 9410, 648	12095, 9750, 648	12095, 9410, 6195
Malta	15575, 12095, 9410	17640, 15070, 12095	15070, 12095, 9410
Netherlands	15575, 9410, 648	12095, 9750, 648	12095, 9410, 6195
Norway (North)	12095, 9410	15070, 12095	15070, 12095, 9410
Norway (South)	9410, 6195	12095, 9410	12095, 9410, 6195
Poland	15575, 9410, 6195	15070, 12095	12095, 9410, 6195
Portugal	9410, 6195	17705, 15070, 12095	12095, 9410, 6195
Serbia	15070, 6180, 1323	17640, 15070, 9660	15070, 12095, 6180
Slovenia	15575, 12095, 9410	15070, 12095	15070, 12095, 9410
Romania	15070, 12095, 9410	17640, 15070, 9660	15070, 12095, 9410
Spain	9410, 6195	17705, 15070, 12095	12095, 9410, 6195
Sweden	12095, 9410	15070, 12095	15070, 12095, 9410
Switzerland	15575, 9410, 6195	15070, 12095	12095, 9410, 6195
Turkey	15070, 6180, 1323	17640, 15070, 9660	15070, 12095, 6180
(Former) Yugoslavia	15070, 12095, 9410	17640, 15070, 9660	15070, 12095, 9410

All times quoted are Greenwich Mean Time. Full programme and frequency details can be obtained from BBC World Service Publicity, PO Box 76, Bush House, Strand, London, WC2B 4PH.

Of the BBC's domestic services, Radio 1 on 275/285m (1089/1053kHz) medium wave, Radio 4 on 1515m (198kHz) long wave, and Radio 5 on 433/330m (693/909kHz) medium wave are widely audible in north-west Europe.

TELEPHONING HOME

To call the UK from a European country, the complete number you will need to dial comprises: **Access code + Country code + UK area (STD) code (leaving out the initial 0) + local number**.

In Europe, dialling tones may differ from those in Britain. Dial steadily without pauses, unless it is necessary to wait for a second dialling tone (where indicated by an asterisk in the following pages).

Connection can take up to one minute; a persistent tone or recorded announcement means that your call has not gone through, and you should try again.

INTERNATIONAL TELEPHONE CODES

The following dialling codes are used for direct dialling from one European country to another. The Access code is used for the country from which the call is being made, and the Country code for the country to which the call is going. For example, to call Spain from Finland, dial 990 34 followed by the internal area code and local number.

	Access code	Country code
Austria	00	43
Belgium	00 or 00*	32
Bulgaria	00	359
Cyprus	00	357
Czech and Slovak Republics	00	42
Denmark	009	45
Finland	990	358
France	19*	33
Germany	00	49
Gibraltar	00	350
Great Britain	010	44
Greece	00	30
Hungary	00*	36
Italy	00	39
Luxembourg	00	352
Netherlands	09*	31
Norway	095	47
Poland	0*0	48
Portugal	00	351
Spain	07*	34
Sweden	009	46
Switzerland	00	41
Turkey	9*9	90
(Former) Yugoslavia	99	38
* Await a second tone at this stage		

HOW TO SET UP A CALL

from	Procedure	Additional information
Austria	Lift receiver, check for dial tone. Insert at least 15 Schillings or phonecard, dial. A signal indicates when to insert more money. Fully unused coins refunded.	**Coins accepted:** 1, 5, 10, 20 Sch. **Phonecards:** 50, 100 Sch. **Local international operator:** 09. **UK Direct operator:** 022 903 044. Reverse charge calls available.
Belgium	Lift receiver, check for dial tone. Insert money or 'Telecard', dial. A signal indicates when to insert more money or 'Telecard'. Fully unused coins refunded.	**Coins accepted:** 20 BF. **Phonecards:** 200, 1,000 BF 'Telecards' (available from railway stations, post offices, newsagents and tobacconists). **UK Direct operator:** 078 11 00 44. Reverse charge calls available. **Cheap rate:** Mon-Sat 2000-0800, all day Sunday.
Cyprus	Lift receiver, check for dial tone. Insert at least 10 cents or 'Telecard', dial. A signal indicates when to insert more money. Fully unused coins refunded.	**Coins accepted:** 2, 5, 10, 20c. **Phonecards:** 2, 5, 10 Cyprus pound 'Telecards' (available from banks, post offices and some kiosks). **Local international operator:** 198. **UK Direct operator:** 080 900 44. Reverse charge calls available.
Denmark	Lift receiver, check for dial tone. Insert at least 1 Krona or phonecard, dial. A signal indicates when to insert more money. Fully unused coins refunded.	**Coins accepted:** 1, 5, 10, 20 Kr. **Phonecards:** available from Telecom shops ('Telebutik'). **Local international operator:** 115. **UK Direct operator:** 8001 0444. Reverse charge calls available.
Finland	Lift receiver, check for dial tone. Insert 1 Markka coin, dial.	**Coins accepted:** 1, 5 Mk. **Phonecards:** accepted at some phones. **UK Direct operator:** 9800 1 0440.
France	Lift receiver, check for dial tone. Insert money or 'Télécarte', dial. A signal indicates when to insert more money. Fully unused coins refunded.	**Coins accepted:** 1, 5, 10F. **Phonecards:** 40, 96F 'Télécartes' (available from post offices, SNCF counters, tobacconists and France Telecom commercial agencies). **Local international operator:** 19*33 44. **UK Direct operator:** 19*00 44. Reverse charge calls available. **Cheap rate:** Mon-Fri 2130-0800, Sat 1400-2400, all day Sunday.
Germany	Lift receiver, check for dial tone. Insert at least 2 DM or phonecard, dial. A signal indicates when to insert more money.	**Coins accepted:** 10pf; 1, 5 DM. **Phonecards:** available from post offices and tobacconists. **Local international operator:** 01114 (available only from former East Germany). **UK Direct operator:** 0130 80 0044 (available only from former West Germany). Reverse charge calls available. **Cheap rate:** Mon-Fri 1800-0800, all weekend.
Greece	Lift receiver, check for dial tone. Insert at least 10 Drachmas, dial. A red light indicates when to insert more money. Fully unused coins refunded.	**Coins accepted:** 10 Dr. **Local international operator:** 161. Reverse charge calls only via local international operator. **Cheap rate:** Mon-Fri 1500-1700 & 2200-0900, Sat after 1500, all day Sunday.
Irish Republic	Lift receiver, check for dial tone. Insert at least 50p or phonecard, dial. A signal indicates when to insert more money. Fully unused coins refunded.	**Coins accepted:** 5, 10, 20, 50p. **Phonecards:** IR £2, £3.50, £8, £16. **Local international operator:** 114 Dublin; 10 elsewhere. **UK Direct operator:** 1 800 55 0044. Reverse charge calls only via local international operator. **Cheap rate:** Mon-Fri 1800-0800, all weekend.
Italy	Lift receiver, check for dial tone. Insert at least 2,000 Lira, tokens or phonecard, dial. A signal indicates when to insert more money, tokens or phonecard. Press button to recover fully unused coins or tokens.	**Coins accepted:** 100, 200, 500L coins or tokens ('gettoni'). **Phonecards:** 5,000, 10,000L (available from newsagents, post offices and some railway stations). **Local international operator:** 15. **UK Direct operator:** 172 0044. Reverse charge calls available. **Cheap rate:** Mon-Sat 2200-0800, all day Sunday.

from	Procedure	Additional information
Luxembourg	Lift receiver, insert 5 Francs. Check for dial tone, dial.	**Coins accepted:** 1, 5, 20F (Lux/Belgian). **Local international operator:** 0010. **UK Direct operator:** 0800 0044. Reverse charge calls available.
Netherlands	Lift receiver, insert at least 2 x 25c coins or phonecard. Check for dial tone, dial. A signal indicates when to insert more money or phonecard. Fully unused coins refunded.	**Coins accepted:** 25c; 1, 2.5G. **Phonecards:** 5, 10, 25, 40 DF (available from railway stations, post offices, tourist offices and outlets displaying the cardphone sign). **Local international operator:** 06*0410. **UK Direct operator:** 06*022 9944. Reverse charge calls available. **Cheap rate:** Mon-Fri 2000-0600, all weekend.
Norway	Lift receiver, check for dial tone. Insert at least 5 Kroner or phonecard, dial. A signal indicates when to insert more money or phonecard. Fully unused coins refunded.	**Phonecards:** 24, 100 Kr. **Local international operator:** 0115. **UK Direct operator:** 050 11 044. Reverse charge calls available. **Cheap rate:** Daily 2200-0800.
Portugal	Lift receiver, check for dial tone. Insert at least 4 x 50 Escudos or phonecard, dial. A signal indicates when to insert more money or phonecard. Fully unused coins refunded.	**Phonecards:** 500, 1,200 Esc. (available from post offices, tobacconists and telephone bureaux). **Local international operator:** 098 or 099. **UK Direct operator:** 0505 00 44. Reverse charge calls available.
Spain	Insert at least 150 Pesetas in sloping groove at top of payphone (do not press button to left of dial). Lift receiver, check for dial tone, dial. A signal indicates when to insert more money. Fully unused coins refunded.	**Coins accepted:** 5, 25, 50, 100 Ptas (newer payphones also accept 200, 500, 1,000 Ptas). **Phonecards:** 1,000, 2,000, 5,000 Ptas (available from post offices, tobacconists and some banks). **Local international operator:** 008 Barcelona, Madrid; 9198 or 9398 elsewhere. **UK Direct operator:** 900 99 00 44. Reverse charge calls available. **Cheap rate:** Daily 2200-0800.
Sweden	Lift receiver, check for dial tone. Insert at least 2 Kronor or phonecard, dial. A signal of two tones indicates when to insert more money. Fully unused coins refunded.	**Coins accepted:** 50 Ore; 1, 5 Kr. **Phonecards:** 25, 50, 100 Kr. **Local international operator:** 0018. **UK Direct operator:** 020 795 144. Reverse charge calls available.
Switzerland	Lift receiver, check for dial tone. Insert at least 40c or phonecard, dial. A signal indicates when to insert more money. Fully unused coins refunded.	**Coins accepted:** 10, 20, 50c; 1, 2, 5F. **Phonecards:** 10, 20F (available from post offices and newsagents). **Local international operator:** 114. **UK Direct operator:** 155 2444. Reverse charge calls available. **Cheap rate:** Mon-Fri 2100-0800, all weekend.
Turkey	Lift receiver, check for dial tone. Insert token or phonecard, dial. A signal indicates when to insert more tokens or phonecard. Fully unused tokens refunded.	**Coins accepted:** Tokens only – minimum value 750TL (from post offices). **Phonecards:** 4,300, 8,600, 17,100TL (from post offices). **Local international operator:** 032 Ankara, Istanbul, Izmir; 062 other cities. **UK Direct operator:** 99800 441177. Reverse charge calls available.

COMING HOME

CUSTOMS ALLOWANCES

	DUTY FREE Goods obtained anywhere outside the EC or duty and tax free within the EC, including purchases from a UK duty free shop	DUTY PAID Goods obtained duty and tax paid in the EC
Cigarettes, **or** Cigarillos, **or** Cigars, **or** Tobacco	200 100 50 250g	800 400 200 1kg
Still table wine	2 litres	* see below
Spirits, strong liqueurs over 22% volume, **or**	1 litre	10 litres
Fortified or sparkling wines, other liqueurs, **or**	2 litres	* 20 litres of fortified wine, **or** 90 litres of wine (of which no more than 60 litres of sparkling wine)
An additional still table wine allowance	2 litres	
Perfume	50g/60cc (2 fl oz)	no limit
Toilet water	250cc (9 fl oz)	no limit
All other goods including gifts and souvenirs	£72 worth, but no more than 50 litres of beer, 25 mechanical lighters	no limit except for the beer allowance, which is increased to 110 litres

DUTY-FREE SALES

The EC has reprieved duty-free sales until 1999. Under an agreed Community system for each journey to another member state of the EC, you are entitled to buy the quantities of duty-free goods shown above.

DUTY-PAID GOODS

Provided they are for your personal use, there is no further tax to be paid on goods you have obtained duty and tax paid in the European Community. Personal use includes gifts. Member states still reserve the right to check

that products are for personal use only, and not for resale purposes. For this reason, the EC has set guide levels, as shown above, and if you bring more than the amounts in the guide levels you are required to show that the goods are for your personal use.

TRAVELLING WITHIN THE EC

If you are travelling to the UK directly from another EC country, you do not need to go through a red or green channel, and you do not need to make any declaration to Customs. However, selective checks will still be carried out by Customs to detect prohibited goods.

ENTERING THE UK

You may have valuable items such as cameras, radios or watches which were bought in the UK, or which have been brought through Customs before and any Customs charges paid. It is a good idea to carry receipts for these items where possible, so that they can be checked by a Customs officer if necessary.

If you are entering the UK in a vehicle, it is important that everyone travelling with you knows what goods are prohibited or restricted. If goods are smuggled in a car, the car may be confiscated.

Never carry anything into the UK for someone else.

No-one under the age of 17 is entitled to tobacco or drink allowances.

PROHIBITED AND RESTRICTED GOODS

In order to protect health and the environment, certain goods cannot be freely imported. The main items are as follows:

Animals, birds and reptiles The importation of most species, whether alive or dead (eg stuffed), and many items derived from protected species, eg fur skins, ivory, reptile leather and goods made from them, is restricted. Such items can be imported only if you have prior authority (eg a licence) to import them.

Counterfeit or 'Copy' Goods Goods bearing a false indication of their origin and goods in breach of UK copyright are prohibited and must not be brought into the UK.

Drugs Do not import controlled drugs, eg heroin, cocaine, cannabis, amphetamines and LSD. If you require drugs for medical reasons, further information can be obtained from: The Home Office Drugs Branch, 50 Queen Anne's Gate, London SW1H 9AT.

Endangered Species The Department of the Environment operates controls on the import of endangered species. Enquiries should be made to: DoE, Endangered Species Branch, Tollgate House, Houlton Street, Bristol BS2 9DJ. ☎ 0272-218202.

Firearms and Ammunition Firearms and ammunition (including gas pistols, gas canisters, electric shock batons and similar weapons) are restricted and can be imported only if you have prior authority (eg a licence) to import them. Explosives (including fireworks) are banned completely.

Foodstuffs The importation of meat, poultry and their products including ham, bacon, sausage, paté, eggs, milk and cream is restricted.

Pets Cats, dogs and other mammals must not be brought into the UK unless a British import licence (rabies) has previously been issued. A period of six months quarantine is required. All live birds also require an import licence.

Plants There is currently an exception to the requirements for a health certificate for plants and plant produce imported as passenger baggage from any country within the European-Mediterranean area, provided the consignment does not exceed:

up to 2 kg of tubers, bulbs and corms free of soil
up to 5 plants or cuttings
a small bouquet of cut flowers
up to 2 kg of fruit and vegetables together (BUT NOT POTATOES – because of the danger of importing Colorado beetle)
up to 5 retail packets of seeds

This concessional arrangement does not apply to: plants & seeds of the genus 'beta'; forest trees; fruit tree material (including Bonsai); Chrysanthemums; vine plants; cut Gladioli; Fodder Pea seeds; plants of the grass family (Graminae).

There are no restrictions on flower seeds from any country. Should you wish to import more than these quantities you will have to obtain a phytosanitary certificate from the Plant Protection Service in the country of origin.

Further details can be obtained from: Plant Health Division, Ministry of Agriculture, Fisheries and Food, Room 504, Ergon House, c/o Nobel House, Smith Square, London SW1P 3JR. ☎ 071-238 6477/6479.

Other prohibited goods include offensive weapons such as flick knives, butterfly knives, knuckledusters, swordsticks, and some martial arts weapons; counterfeit currency; radio transmitters and cordless telephones not approved for use in the UK; obscene books, videos etc; horror comics; anglers' lead weights.

CONVERSION TABLES

MILES	KILOMETRES
1	1.60
2	3.21
3	4.82
4	6.43
5	8.04
6	9.65
7	11.26
8	12.87
9	14.48
10	16.09
15	24.13
20	32.18
25	40.23
30	48.27
35	56.32
40	64.37
45	72.41
50	80.46
100	160.93

KILOMETRES	MILES
1	0.62
2	1.24
3	1.86
4	2.48
5	3.10
6	3.72
7	4.34
8	4.97
9	5.59
10	6.21
15	9.32
20	12.32
25	15.53
30	18.64
35	21.74
40	24.85
45	27.96
50	31.07
100	62.14

IMP. GALLONS	LITRES
1	4.54
2	9.09
3	13.63
4	18.18
5	22.73
6	27.27
7	31.82
8	36.36
10	45.46
15	68.19

LITRES	IMP. GALLONS
1	0.22
5	1.10
10	2.20
20	4.40
25	5.50
30	6.60
40	8.80
50	11.00
75	16.50
100	22.00

POUNDS PER SQUARE INCH	KILOGRAMS PER SQUARE CENTIMETRE
18	1.27
20	1.41
22	1.55
24	1.69
26	1.83
28	1.97
30	2.11
32	2.25
34	2.39
36	2.53
38	2.67
40	2.81

GRADIENT	PERCENTAGE
1 in 4	25.0
1 in 5	20.0
1 in 6	16.4
1 in 7	14.2
1 in 8	12.4
1 in 9	11.1
1 in 10	10.0
1 in 11	9.1
1 in 12	8.4
1 in 13	7.9
1 in 14	7.2
1 in 15	6.6

VOLTAGES

In most European countries the voltage is 220 AC although in Greece and Spain it may occasionally be 110 AC, and the 2-pin plug is in general use. If you are taking any electrical equipment to Europe you should buy either a special adaptor in Britain or some 2-pin plugs on your arrival.